Carolyn Meggitt

Tina Bruce

Julia Manning-Morton

Chi
& E

6th Edit

HODDER
EDUCATION
AN HACHETTE UK COMPANY

Orders: please contact Bookpoint Ltd, 130 Milton Park, Abingdon, Oxon OX14 4SB. Telephone: (44) 01235 827720. Fax: (44) 01235 400454. Email education@bookpoint.co.uk Lines are open from 9 a.m. to 5 p.m., Monday to Saturday, with a 24-hour message answering service. You can also order through our website: www. hoddereducation.co.uk

ISBN: 978 14718 6363 9

© Carolyn Meggitt, Julia Manning-Morton and Tina Bruce 2016

First published in 2016 by
Hodder Education,
An Hachette UK Company
Carmelite House
50 Victoria Embankment
London EC4Y 0DZ
www.hoddereducation.co.uk
Impression number 10 9 8 7 6 5 4 3 2 1
Year 2020 2019 2018 2017 2016

Cover photo by©Getty Images/iStockphoto/Thinkstock/naumoid
Illustrations by Aptara
Typeset in India
Printed in Dubai
A catalogue record for this title is available from the British Library.

Contents

Acknowledgements

From the authors

We would like to thank the following people for their contributions: Chris Rice for her help with the section on operant conditioning: Ruth Forbes and the parents for the case studies of babies; Michelle Samson and Judith Stevens for their help on special needs and inclusion; Cathal Ryan for invaluable insights into safeguarding; Anne-Louise de Buriane and the staff and families of Langford Extended Primary School; everyone on the staff team at Kate Greenaway Nursery School and Children's Centre.

For the quiet but solid support, the feeling of belonging with people who help and empower, and the team spirit between us – thank you Ian, Hannah and Tom, from Tina.

This book is dedicated with love and thanks to Dave, Jonathan, Leo and Laura, from Carolyn. I would also like to thank Stephen Halder, Sundus Pasha and Sebastian Rydberg at Hodder Education and copyeditor Llinos Edwards for all their work on the new edition.

From Julia: Thank you to Tina Bruce for having faith in me and once again, generously handing the baton on. Thanks also to Mary Dickens for her invaluable expertise on children with special needs and disabilities in the revising of Chapter 2. Most of all though, thank you to my son Levi, for 'troubling' all my ideas about how children play, grow, develop and learn; you have taught me so much.

Publisher acknowledgements

The book uses intellectual property/material from books previously co-authored with Julian Grenier, who agreed to its inclusion in this book in order to share what is important for high-quality childhood practice.

The publisher would like to thank all the staff, children and families at Vanessa Nursery School, Ark Alpha Nursery, Godinton Day Nursery, Bilston Nursery School, Kate Greenaway Nursery School and Children's Centre for their help with many of the photographs. A special thanks to Michele Barrett, Julie Breading, Jenni Hare, Michael Winch, Joanne Winch and Wendy Binder for all their assistance with the organisation of the photoshoots.

Picture credits

The authors and publishers would like to thanks the following for use of photographs in this volume:

P160 © *t* © Bubbles Photolibrary / Alamy Stock Photo, *m* ©Tobias Küttner / Alamy Stock Photo, *b* © Picture Partners / Alamy Stock Photo; p161 *t* ©Catchlight Visual Services / Alamy Stock Photo, *b* ©Robert Dant / Alamy Stock Photo; p233 © ASTIER /SCIENCE PHOTO LIBRARY; p257 © Stockbyte -Thinkstock/Getty Images; p285 © Lullaby Trust; p309 © GUSTOIMAGES/ SCIENCE PHOTO LIBRARY; p312 /© IAN HOOTON/ SCIENCE PHOTO LIBRARY, m © CAROLYN A. MCKEONE/SCIENCE PHOTO LIBRARY, r ©Amawasri - Thinkstock/Getty Images; p320 /© PHOTOTAKE Inc. / Alamy Stock Photo, r©Mediscan / Alamy Stock Photo; p333 © Jens Molin - Thinkstock/Getty Images; p335 © Andy Crawford and Steve Gorton / Getty Images; p348 © Covered by the Open Government Licence; p354 © Flashon Studio - 123RF; p361 © Covered by the Open Government Licence; p369 © CX1DKC.

All other photographs in this volume taken by Jules Selmes.

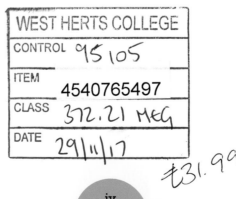

How to use this book

Written by an expert team of childcare authors, the sixth edition of this classic textbook offers an in-depth approach to Childcare and Early Years study unmatched by any course specific texts.

Key features

KEY TERM

Understand important terms.

Reflecting on practice

Learn to reflect on your own skills, experiences with numerous Reflecting on practice boxes, and see how concepts are applied in settings with scenarios.

Look, listen and note

Focus on the practicalities of working within a real-life setting using case studies and observation tasks.

Think about ideas

Short tasks prompt you to think about a topic in detail and help to enhance your understanding.

Analyse and explore theories and theorists key to the understanding of the topics.

Guidelines for good practice

Helpful tips and guidelines to develop your professional skills in the setting.

Moving on

Take your learning and understanding to the next level with post level 3 activities and content.

Weblinks and resources

Includes references to books, websites and other various sources for further reading and research.

Equality, diversity, rights

This chapter focuses on the importance of equality in children's care and education. Every child and family has certain human rights which are enshrined in law and which serve to promote equality of opportunity and to prevent discrimination. All early years settings should provide an environment which is inclusive. This means that the focus is not on moulding the individual child to fit the setting, but instead ensuring that the setting responds in its practice to the needs of every child.

KEY TERM

Anti-discriminatory practice – This is an approach to working with young children that promotes diversity, valuing difference and that actively challenges prejudice and discrimination. Anti-discriminatory practice means understanding the connections between all aspects of our social identity such as our gender, ethnicity, class, ability, our sexuality, religion and language/s, and so operates in all aspects of early years practice.

Defining equality, diversity, inclusion and discrimination

There can be no quality in early years services unless there is equality. Being equal means having equal rights and status so equality consists of equality of access, equality of opportunity and anti-discriminatory practices, policies and procedures. In early years practice there is sometimes the misunderstanding that equality means treating children all the same, which of course does not ensure that each child's individual needs are addressed.

Equality of opportunity means opening up access for every child and family to have full participation in early years settings. Lack of access causes:

- lack of respect
- misunderstandings
- lack of inclusion.

These behaviours can arise from prejudice and stereotyping, and lead to discrimination and potentially, low levels of confidence and self-esteem in an individual experiencing them.

Equality of opportunity has the intention of creating a level playing field for all to gain access and achieve but does not account for the unequal starting points of different children and families. A more active approach is to develop **anti-discriminatory practices** to promote equality of outcome for children and equal representation for families.

Diversity

Diversity refers to the differences in values, attitudes, cultures, beliefs, skills and life experience of each individual in any group of people. In the UK, early years

curriculum frameworks emphasise the importance of developing every child's sense of identity and promoting a positive sense of pride in each child's family origins.

Inclusion

Inclusion is a term used within education to describe the process of ensuring the equality of learning opportunities for all children, whatever their disabilities or disadvantages. This means that all children have the right to have their needs met in the best way for them.

What do we mean by stereotypes and prejudice?

Stereotypes

When applied to people, stereotyping refers to forming an instant or fixed picture of a person or group of people, usually based on false or incomplete information. **Stereotypes** are often negative as we unfairly believe that people who share certain characteristics are the same.

Prejudice

Prejudice means to hold beliefs, opinions or attitudes which are based on ignorance or incorrect information. In this way everyone has prejudices until they have the experiences and knowledge to give them a better understanding. Prejudice results in prejudging people based on assumptions – for example, racial prejudice would include assumptions about a person's abilities, behaviours and background based on their skin colour and other physical features.

Discrimination

At an institutional level, discrimination is the way the systems in society deny certain groups equal access to resources. So in different societies,

Reflecting on practice

Prejudice

Sade (4 years) is British-born Nigerian, but she has never been to Nigeria. Both Sade's parents were born in the UK and grew up there. Sade only eats Nigerian food at family gatherings that happen a few times a year when relatives visit. She finds it rather hot and spicy compared with the European food that she usually eats at home and at nursery. Her key person has set up a 'tasting table' which includes black pepper and ginger root, and says, 'I expect Sade knows what these are; does Mummy use them at home?' Sade is confused and embarrassed and does not respond.

- How would you evaluate this practitioner's practice?
- How could it be improved?
- What might Sade and the other children be learning in this scenario?

KEY TERMS

Prejudice – A preconceived opinion that is not based on reason or actual experience.
Stereotype – A set idea that people have about what someone or something is like, especially an idea that is wrong. These ideas are usually based on certain characteristics.
Sociocultural – The combination or interaction of social and cultural elements that influence outcomes.
Homosexuality – Emotional and sexual relationships between members of the same sex.
Bisexuality – Emotional and sexual relationships with members of both sexes.

different groups may be discriminated against more than others, according to which group holds the structural power. As a result of **sociocultural** history in the UK and Europe, this power is traditionally held by upper-class, white, able-bodied, heterosexual men. So some of the groups usually discriminated against tend to include women, homosexual people (lesbian women, gay men), **bisexual** people, people with disabilities, the lower or working classes and people from minority ethnic backgrounds.

Denial of equality also takes place on a group and individual level and is usually based on **prejudice** and **stereotypes**. Although prejudice and stereotyping happens between all groups, some groups of people hold more 'structural power' in society than others. This, for example, may mean that a working class woman may be prejudiced against an upper class man and make assumptions about him; however, if she does not hold institutional or official power, she is not in a position to create laws and systems that would disadvantage him in society.

We need to be aware of different forms of discrimination so that we can act to promote equality.

Racism and racial discrimination

The word 'race' is controversial because it comes from historical attempts to categorise people according to their skin colour and physical characteristics. There is no scientific basis for divisions into biologically determined groups (Lane 1999) as there is as much variation within 'races' as between them, and as many similarities between races as within them (Rose 1985, cited in Brown 1998).

The term 'ethnicity' is, perhaps, more helpful. This refers to an individual's identity with a group sharing some or all of the same language, religion, history culture and lifestyle. However, the term 'race' rather than ethnicity is still used in legislation.

Racism is the belief that some 'races' are superior, based on the false idea that skin colour, for example, makes some people better than others. Examples are: failing to address the needs of children from a minority religious or cultural group, such as children from traveller families; and only acknowledging festivals from the mainstream culture, such as Christmas and Easter.

Institutional racism is defined by the Macpherson Inquiry (1999) into the murder of Stephen Lawrence, as:

> *the collective failure of an organisation to provide an appropriate and professional service to people because of their colour, culture or ethnic origin. It can be seen or detected in processes, attitudes and behaviour which amount to discrimination through unwitting prejudice, ignorance, thoughtlessness and racist stereotyping which disadvantage minority ethnic people.*

It can be difficult to detect and combat institutional racism as it tends to be integrated into an organisation's culture and practices as a result of its past history. For this reason, it is vital that all early years settings adhere to an up-to-date policy of equality, and that the policy is monitored regularly.

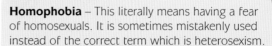

Disability discrimination

Children with disabilities or impairments may be denied equality of opportunity with their non-disabled peers. Examples are:

- failing to provide children with special needs with appropriate facilities and services
- organising activities in a nursery setting in a way that ignores the special physical, intellectual and emotional needs of certain children.

Sexism and sex discrimination

Sex is the biological differences between females and males. Gender is a term used to describe those aspects of being male or female which are not attributable or due to biological differences. It takes account of psychological and cultural expectations of differences in behaviour, abilities, qualities and attitudes between men and women, that is: femininity and masculinity. The expression of femininity and masculinity will vary historically and from culture to culture.

Sexism occurs when people of one gender are discriminated against and seen as inferior to the other. It is more usual for women and girls to experience sexism as the majority of people in positions of power are men. In early years practice, gender stereotypes can lead to discriminatory practices; for example, boys may be expected and allowed to engage in rough-and-tumble play more than girls, and practitioners encourage girls to help tidy up more.

Transgender people are those whose gender identity or expression does not conform to the sex they were assigned at birth. Those who decide to live their lives as the gender which they feel is right often face a lot of prejudice and discrimination. Transgender people (or transsexuals in the legislation) are now also protected against harassment or discrimination in the workplace under the Equality Act 2010.

Heterosexism and homophobia

Heterosexism is a set of ideas and practices which assume that heterosexuality (emotional and sexual relationships between men and women) is the 'natural' and therefore superior form of relationship. It exists where societies are organised in a way that discriminates against lesbian women and gay men. It also exists in the kind of harassment and abuse that lesbian women and gay men often face. This is sometimes called **homophobia**; literally a 'fear' of same sex relationships. In early years settings heterosexism may be revealed in the absence of any mention, acknowledgement or recognition of same-sex relationships. In primary schools homophobic bullying is commonplace, with almost half of primary

> **KEY TERM**
>
> **Homophobia** – This literally means having a fear of homosexuals. It is sometimes mistakenly used instead of the correct term which is heterosexism.

school teachers claiming that pupils in their school have experienced this, and seven in ten primary school teachers having heard children use the phrases, 'that's so gay' or 'you're so gay' as a term of abuse (Guasp 2012).

Social class, poverty and discrimination

When we talk about social class we are usually referring to a group of people with similar levels of influence, wealth and status. Typically, social class is subdivided into working class, middle class and upper class.

Defining someone's social class usually includes their education, their accent and dress, the social background of their parents, their level of wealth, home ownership and value, their social connections and their power and influence in society. However, the boundaries and levels of each of these and which class it relates to is defined very differently by individuals and academics.

Although class and wealth/poverty are separate, they are also interrelated. Anyone can experience poverty whichever class or social background they are from. However, class is often an indicator of life chances and future wealth. Poverty can lead to deprivation and social exclusion where individuals are excluded from the benefits of mainstream society.

Class discrimination is evident when assumptions are made about a person's intelligence or education because of their accent or the way they speak. This can occur in early years settings between practitioners and parents in both directions as well as between practitioners and children.

Legislation relating to equality and discrimination

UK laws deal with overt discrimination which results from prejudice, especially when combined with power. If a prejudiced person has power, they may discriminate against the people towards whom they are prejudiced. This might be in the form of **racism** or **sexism**, or being disablist, ageist or homophobic. There are laws that try to deal with all these kinds of discrimination. In the past, legal restraints against **disablism**, **ageism** and heterosexism were less well developed than on racism and sexism, but more recent legislation has improved this balance.

KEY TERMS

Racism – Prejudice, discrimination, or antagonism directed against someone of a different race based on the belief that one's own race is superior.
Sexism – Prejudice, stereotyping, or discrimination, typically against women, on the basis of sex.
Disablism – Discriminating or prejudice against people who are disabled.
Ageism – Prejudice or discrimination on the grounds of a person's age.

The Equality Act 2010

The Equality Act came into force on 1 October 2010. It provides a legal framework to protect the rights of individuals and to advance equality of opportunity for all (Equality and Human Rights Commission). The Equality Act brings together over 116 separate pieces of legislation into one single Act, including the Equal Pay Act 1970, the Sex Discrimination Act 1975, the Race Relations Act 1976 and the Disability Discrimination Act 1995.

All early years settings, whether in the statutory, voluntary, independent or private sectors, including childminders, must comply with the Act.

The Act uses the term 'protected characteristics' to identify the groups that are to be protected from discrimination, as follows:

- age
- disability
- gender reassignment
- marriage and civil partnership
- pregnancy and maternity
- race (includes colour; nationality; ethnic or national origins)
- religion or belief
- sex
- sexual orientation.

The Act identifies four different types of discrimination. They are:

1 Direct discrimination: this happens when someone is treated less favourably than another person in relation to a 'protected characteristic'. For example, it would be unlawful to refuse a child a place in an early years setting because of their 'race', nationality, religion or sex.

2 Direct discrimination by association: this happens when there is a direct discrimination against a person because they are associated with another person who has a 'protected characteristic'. For example, a parent not being allowed into her local community centre with her son because he is disabled.

3 Direct discrimination by perception: this happens when there is direct discrimination against a person because they are perceived to have a 'protected characteristic'.

4 Indirect discrimination: this happens when there is a rule, a policy or even a practice that applies to everyone but which particularly disadvantages people who share a particular 'protected characteristic'. For example, having staff or parent meetings on a Friday afternoon will disadvantage staff and families whose religious practices take place at that time.

The Children and Families Act 2014

From September 2014, Government reforms mean that everyone aged from birth to 25 years with Special Educational Needs (SEN) will have a *single plan* setting out all the support they will receive from education, health and social care and who is responsible for each part of the plan. Also two-year-olds for whom Disability Living Allowance is paid will be entitled to free early education.

The Special Educational Needs and Disabilities (SEND) Code of Practice 2014

This applies to England only. The code tells local authorities, schools and others how they must carry out their duties under the new law. It includes changes to the way in which services are planned and provided, through the new EHC plan (see below).

The Education, Health and Care (EHC) Plan

The EHC plan replaces the statement of SEN. All agencies will jointly plan and commission the services that are needed and will be responsible for monitoring whether these are improving outcomes. The EHC plan will have more parts to it than the statement. In early years provision, it will describe:

- the child's views and future goals
- the outcomes the child is expected to achieve
- health needs linked to the child's SEN
- health provision the child needs because of their SEN. If health provision is included in a plan, it must be provided
- social care needs and provision linked to the child's SEN. There is a separate law covering social care assessments and provision, but details must be included in the EHC plan.

Each local authority must publish a 'local offer'. This is information about all the support the local authority expects to be available for the children with SEN and disabilities who live in their area.

Local authorities must ensure that there is a source of independent information and advice available to parent carers and children with SEN and disabilities.

The Race Relations (Amendment) Act 2000

The general duty of the Act, says you must have 'due regard to the need':

- to eliminate unlawful racial discrimination; and
- to promote equality of opportunity and good relations between persons of different racial groups.

This has been superceded by the Equality Act 2010 covered earlier in this section.

See Moving on, p. 15 for information on the United Nations Convention on the Rights of the Child.

There is also some useful information in Chapter 2 on p. 20 in relation to SEN, inclusive practice and the Early Years Foundation Stage (EYFS) 2014, which may also be useful to the understanding of this chapter.

The effects of prejudice and discrimination in child care and education

Children can experience discrimination in a number of ways. Discrimination can be direct or indirect: this may be very obvious in the case of a child whose self-esteem is seriously damaged by other people's behaviour towards them. For example, **ablism** closes off educational possibilities and may inhibit the development of a proud self-concept for children with disabilities, while racism may undermine black children's self-esteem and self-confidence and thereby their academic performance (Purkey 1970).

However, it is also the case that the development of the child who does not experience discrimination may also be adversely affected. If children learn that one group of people are better than another, the children who are identified as part of the 'superior' group will develop a false sense of who they are and a distorted perception of the world. This affects their ability to reason effectively and to make balanced judgements (Derman-Sparks 1991).

So, it is important to consider that the development of all young children can be harmed by the effects of stereotyping, prejudice and discrimination. For example, gender stereotyping and **bias** (see page 8 for definition) closes off whole areas of experience for both girls and boys, and may limit their ability to deal with the emotional and intellectual realities of adult life. For example, in the past, stories of elderly widowers who could not cook for themselves or elderly widows who did not know how to deal with financial matters, were common because their gender roles had been very strictly defined.

There can also be more subtle, less personal effects of discrimination on children, such as the perpetuation or spread of general misunderstandings and stereotypes. When this happens, different groups in society tend not to treat each other with respect.

The restricting effect of stereotypes

Young children are affected most strongly by the attitudes and beliefs of their close adults and practitioners in the setting. The expectations parents and practitioners have of children will impact on their self-esteem, behaviours and achievements. From an early age, young children are developing an understanding of themselves as part of a particular social category, and receive messages from the people around them about how a child in this particular category is expected to be. The degree to which these expectations match the child's inner sense of self will impact on their self-esteem. So, for example, expectations which are too high may lead to a sense of failure in a child who cannot live up to them, while expectations which are too low may result in very able children becoming uninterested and possibly being disruptive (Brown 1998).

Where expectations arise from stereotyped ideas of how a child of a certain gender/ethnicity/ability/class will behave or will typically achieve, then whole groups of children will be disadvantaged. Ideas, such as Asian girls are quiet and compliant, Chinese children are studious, black boys are physically rather than academically able, are outdated and incorrect but still subtly pervade and influence the expectations of early years practitioners and teachers.

If practitioners describe a child as 'the one with glasses', or comment, 'what a pretty dress', or talk about 'the Afro-Caribbean child', they are stereotyping these children and seeing them narrowly rather than as whole people. The most important thing about working with 'the child with glasses' might be the fact that he loves music. The most important thing about

KEY TERM

Ablism – Discrimination in favour of able-bodied people.

'the Afro-Caribbean child' might be that she loves mathematics, and can remember all the sequences and measurements of cooking, even at three years of age. The most important thing about the girl 'in the pretty dress' might be that she is worried about getting it dirty, so never plays with clay. Gender stereotypes are also restricting because behaviour is seen as 'what boys do' and 'what girls do'. By encouraging boys and girls alike to be active and to explore, to be gentle and nurturing, all children are enabled to lead fuller lives with broader roles. It equips them much better for their future lives.

Early years practitioners need to empower children rather than to narrowly stereotype them. To focus on one feature of the child is much too narrow. It is important not to stereotype children through labels. Children are people, and they have names, not **labels**!

Stereotyping, prejudice and discrimination in children's development

In the past many adults have put forward the view that very young children are too young to notice differences between people. Yet learning about groups of objects that have things in common and also have different properties is a significant area of interest for babies, toddlers and young children.

Therefore children are learning that they have similarities and differences that connect them to and distinguish them from other people. In this process young children will classify groups of people; men, women, children, adults, black or white. But the things that identify people as belonging to a particular group vary so much (for example, women have short hair as well as men, and skin colour comes in a wide range of tones) that they need to find a way of simplifying such complex information. So in the same way as they may at first call all fruit 'apple', they may call all men 'Daddy'. They will also over-emphasise the common characteristics of people and rely on stereotypes to help them order information, so they may be adamant that the boy next door is a girl because his hair is long, for example.

Even when children have developed a more mature understanding of categories of people, they are likely to use stereotypes to manage large amounts of information, such as when they meet even more people when they start at an early years setting. One strategy they use is to gravitate towards the children with whom they feel they have something in common. Gender is an obvious similarity and is therefore something that children quickly identify with. Play may take place more with children of the same sex, and children may start to want to conform to gender stereotypes where previously they did not; suddenly wanting a 'Barbie' doll as a present, for example. It is as if they need to emphasise their 'maleness' or 'femaleness' to reinforce their sense of self and to gain a sense of belonging. However, although we may understand a child resorting to stereotypes because of their stage of cognitive understanding, practitioners need also to gently challenge them in order to model different ways of thinking. If we allow children to conform to stereotypes they will be cut off from important strategies for learning.

▲ **Figure 1.1** Gender stereotyping and bias may subtly put girls and boys off from some forms of play which otherwise would provide them with opportunities to explore all aspects of their experience

Reflecting on practice

Exploring stereotypes

You could arrange to carry out this activity with a group of children in a reception class. The aim is to develop children's understanding of stereotyping.

1   Present children with a choice of two DVDs: one is in its own colourful cover; the other is a very popular film inside a plain box.

2   Ask children which video they wish to watch. After viewing the selected DVD for five minutes, show the children some of the other DVD.

3   Repeat with two books, one of which is covered in plain brown paper. Talk to the children about what these examples tell us; that you should not judge a book by its cover!

The development of prejudice

There is a popular poster depicting a row of very young babies with the inscription: 'One place where racism does not exist'. But of course, children are absorbing information, attitudes, beliefs and behaviours from their close adults from the beginning of life, including prejudiced ideas. They look to their caring adults for how to respond to others with different languages, skin tones, abilities and gender.

As well as classifying groups of people as discussed above, children also construct evaluative categories very early on, i.e. which things or people are good/bad/important/better/best (Derman-Sparks 1991). Research reveals that young children ascribe different values to groups of people according to the influence and responses of the adults and children around them (Siraj-Blatchford 1994). They will notice who is listened to, who is ignored, who is acknowledged, who is interrupted, and so on. From this they will come to understand who is valued more than others. In this way stereotyping and bias from practitioners and adults generally will influence their attitudes towards differences between people.

Derman-Sparks (1991) identifies that very young children may display the influence of adults' attitudes through what she calls 'pre-prejudice' towards others in their play. Pre-prejudice takes the form of less noticeable behaviours than overt comments or statements, for example not wanting to sit next to a black child, hold hands with a child with a disability or refusing to let a girl play on a bike.

 Theory & Theorists: Prejudice

F. E. Aboud (2003) writes about prejudice:

1 Prejudice as a reflection of society:
- Prejudice reflects the different values given to different groups in society based on the status of the groups. This is known by all members of the society so the positive and negative values attached to different groups will be the same for all children regardless of their own group membership.
- Prejudice reflects parents' values, including a preference for their own group and a rejection of out-groups (an in-group is the group of people you identify with or are brought up with, and an out-group is the group of people that you are not part of or do not identify with). So attitudes are tied to one's cultural group membership.

2 Prejudice as an inner state:
- Anger and the use of defence mechanisms to deal with the anger are the sources of prejudice. This is where children deal with difficult feelings by projecting them on to others, particularly to enable them to feel more powerful when they feel powerless; they make their problems someone else's fault.

3 Prejudice as part of social-cognitive development (based on Piagetian theory):
- Prejudice is inevitable in young children because of their immature cognitive understanding of the world. As their cognitive understanding of the world, self and others grows, prejudice is less influenced by emotion and so becomes less intense. Babies' survival needs means they recognise and need to be with those they recognise as meeting their needs (who may be of any ethnicity or gender), and they develop a fear of strangers who might threaten that. But as young children come to cognitively understand how and why people are different to each other, they have less need to hang on to stereotypes or to discriminate.

Developing cultural identities

What is culture?

Culture is the way that society expresses itself; through its social institutions (such as the law for example), through creative arts and through its education and rearing of children. It therefore includes ideas about what is important in life and the way that those beliefs are expressed and passed on from one generation to the next; in this view culture is something that everybody has, not just a few. People not only learn the culture of which they are part, they also test out and develop that culture further; so culture develops and changes over time and place (Williams 2000).

The term 'culture' is also applied to distinct groups of people. In this context culture can be used as shorthand for differences; differences of ethnicity, language and religion are often described as cultural (Cole 1998) but it is usually the culture of the minority group that is identified as 'different' as the culture of the majority is seen to be the norm.

Think about ideas

Observe children's responses and attitudes to adults or other children who are similar or different to them. Can you relate what you have observed to any of these theoretical perspectives?

This view can be seen in early years practices such as 'cultural evenings', when there is dancing, singing and food from countries other than the host nation, or where anti-bias practice is limited to celebrating festivals and having multicultural resources. This kind of tokenism is sometimes called 'cultural tourism', where an often stereotypical view of a group culture is 'visited' for a day or a week rather than the actual home cultural experiences of children being integrated into everyday practice and provision (Brown 1998). 'Culture' or 'cultural' can then have a negative meaning as it is used to emphasise a group of people as being outside mainstream or acceptable culture.

Cultural identity

It is important to recognise the complexity of children and families' cultural contexts.

All of the following play their part in children's developing cultural identity and therefore their self-concept:

- nationality
- language (spoken or sign)
- religion
- gender
- disability
- sexual orientation
- social class
- skin colour.

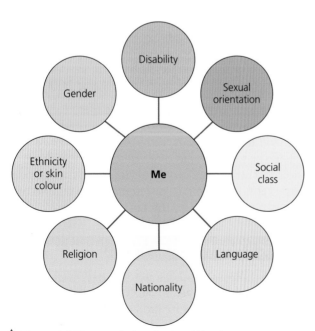

▲ **Figure 1.2** The complexity of cultural identity

Each of these will be expressed differently in individual families through:

- food and dress
- stories, music and songs
- heritage, myths and legends
- home objects (artefacts)
- family relationships and occupations
- the values and beliefs of the family and community.

Promoting equality through anti-discriminatory and anti-bias practice

As early years practitioners, we are responsible for promoting equality within our settings. We can do this firstly by ensuring that practice in settings is of a high quality and promotes a sense of belonging and inclusion for all the children in our care. Secondly, promoting equality means implementing anti-discriminatory and anti-bias practice. This starts with examining our own bias and prejudices, followed by directly addressing any inequalities, prejudices or bias that we encounter in practice and then by ensuring that the curriculum reflects the backgrounds of the children in the setting and also promotes interest, acceptance and respect for differences between people.

High-quality practice and provision promotes a sense of belonging and inclusion.

Promoting a sense of belonging

As children grow up they need to feel that they belong to the group, whether that group is their family, the community they live in and experience, or their early years setting.

Belonging to a group is the result of either:

- being allocated to a group defined by someone else – for example, being British-born
- deciding to join a group – for example, choosing to be a vegetarian or joining a football club.

The early years setting is often the first group outside the family and its friendship network that the child joins. It is important when welcoming families to a setting that they feel a sense of belonging.

KEY TERM

Bias – An inclination or prejudice for or against a person or group, especially in a way considered to be unfair.

Children need to feel a sense of their own worth. This comes from feeling:

- that they matter to other people
- able to take an active part in things
- competent and skilled enough to do so.

A feeling of belonging obviously contributes to a sense of worth, and language is of deep importance to both. If a child's first language is not reflected in settings beyond the home, a large part of the child's previous experiences are being ignored or even actively rejected. Some linguistic experts argue that 'language is power': the dominant language of the culture gives those who speak it the power to discriminate against and exclude those who do not.

Encouraging children to use what they know

Children gain by using their own cultural experience and knowledge in their play. This is most effective where there are open-ended materials. For example, the advantage of play dough, rather than pre-structured plastic food, is that children can bring their own experiences to it. They can make it into roti, pancakes, pasties or pies, depending on their own experiences. Similarly, lengths of material can be made into whatever type of dress the child wants. Children love to construct their own play props; allowing them to do so makes for a much more culturally diverse selection, because they can create what they need in order to make a play setting like their homes. All experiences can then be valued, not just those that a toy manufacturer has set in plastic or in a dressing-up outfit.

Inclusivity

Inclusivity is usually used in relation to including children with disabilities into mainstream education services. But other groups of people also experience exclusion (for example, historically on the grounds of race under **apartheid**). So inclusion is about how we remove exclusionary practices and increase participation by all users of our settings (Nutbrown 2006).

KEY TERM

Apartheid – This is when groups of people are segregated from others, in education, housing and employment. This almost inevitably means that groups of people become ignorant about each other. The practice of apartheid was taken to an extreme in South Africa before 1990, when black South African people were segregated by law from white South Africans. This situation was repeated in the southern states of North America and in Australia.

Guidelines for good practice

Belonging and inclusion

✔ All children and their families, especially if they belong to a minority group, need to feel valued and respected.

✔ Children and their families need to feel part of things, and to develop a sense of belonging.

✔ Accompany all children's actions with language by describing what is happening. For example, talk with the child and describe what they are doing when they cook or use clay.

✔ Think how you can make yourself understood using body language, gestures and facial expression, by pointing, using pictures and using actions with your words. Try asking children if they would like a drink using one of these strategies. You could use objects as props.

✔ When you meet children, whether they are in a mainstream school, a special school or an early years setting, make sure that your expectations of what each child can do are high enough.

✔ Set children tasks that help them to make decisions and to exercise choice. It is important to let all children make choices and decisions so that they feel a sense of control in their lives. When people feel they have some control over what they do, they learn better. It gives them greater equality of opportunity.

✔ Encourage children to speak to other children and adults within the early years setting. Remember that children might feel powerless if they cannot speak to other people.

✔ It is important to be warm towards children. Remember to smile and to show that you enjoy interacting with them. Make sure that you are giving comprehensible language input.

In early years practice, instances of segregation on a smaller scale can be seen in instances such as:

- children learning English as a second language being taken out of the classroom and taught separately
- children who are vegetarian being made to sit at a separate table during school lunchtimes.

Examining our own bias and prejudices

Practitioners who are genuinely committed to providing equally for all children will be willing to examine their own behaviours, attitudes and values, as they will understand that both their conscious and unconscious ways of responding to children will impact on their identity and self-esteem.

Sometimes we are not aware of the ways in which we have internalised stereotypes and how this affects our expectations; such as being surprised by an Afro-Caribbean boy who is academically gifted or a child with a disability who is interested in sport. We need to be aware of any internalised layers of expectation based on our upbringing and experiences that are limited and limiting of children's potential and ability. We then also need to be reflective of our practice in order to avoid reinforcing stereotyping.

The process of inspecting our basic thinking needs to be done on three levels:

1 within the legal framework
2 in the work setting as part of a team
3 as individuals.

From time to time you will make mistakes. Each of us has to work at this all the time, throughout our lives. It is not useful to feel guilty and dislike yourself if you find you are discriminating against someone. It is useful to do something about it.

▲ **Figure 1.3** Practitioners must be aware of the ways in which they have internalised stereotypes and how this affects their expectations

Examining our attitudes to strangers

Some people are not very good at dealing with new situations or meeting new people. They feel more comfortable with the people they know and situations they are very familiar with. Meeting people who are in some way different can sometimes cause a reaction called 'stranger fear'. Rather than deal with our feelings, we might ignore or avoid the person or situation, but we must confront our own feelings before we can help children with theirs.

Having an awareness of gender roles

Creating an environment where girls and boys are respected and cared for equally in early years is the first step towards breaking cycles of discrimination and disadvantage, and promoting a child's sense of self-worth as it relates to their gender.

It is important to remember that some children will have learned narrow gender roles, such as their mothers always doing the cooking, cleaning and caring. Children need to see practitioners and adults generally taking on broader gender roles, and to learn about alternative ways for men and women to behave.

Sometimes staff think there should be 'girls only' sessions on bicycles or with block play and 'boys only' sessions in the home area when cooking, or with the dolls. This introduces children to experiences that broaden ideas of gender roles away from traditional stereotypes. It helps to dispel the idea that 'boys will be boys' or that girls are born to be mothers. However, such single-sex sessions do not support friendships between boys and girls nor help them to learn about negotiating with each other.

The way that fathers and mothers work together in bringing up children is an area of great interest for researchers. Children often see their fathers at times when children and parents relax and have fun together, but spend more time with their mothers doing the chores and tasks of daily life. Research is showing that fathers and mothers want to redefine the roles they play in the family, so that both parents are involved in daily life tasks and both have leisure time to enjoy with their children (Dowd 2000). This is the case whether family members live apart from or with their children. In countries like Sweden, where there is paternity and maternity leave after children are born, these issues are being actively explored.

Understanding religions

Children do not choose their religion; they are born into it. As they grow up they will either accept the belief structure or not. This is also true for children who are born into families who are atheist, agnostic or humanist. Atheists do not believe in a god or gods.

Guidelines for good practice

Individuals matter

Individuals matter because each of us can influence a group's efforts towards more equality.

✔ Be willing to find out about different religions and to respect them. Every religion has variety within it – for example, there are Orthodox and Reformed Jews, and many different forms of Christianity and Islam. Ask religious leaders and parents for information.

✔ Find out about different disabilities. Ask parents and voluntary organisations (e.g. SCOPE, RNIB, Action on Hearing Loss formerly RNID, NAS) to help you.

✔ Do not be afraid to say that you do not know and that you want to find out and learn.

✔ Remember that the important thing about a child is not how they look or the extent of their learning difficulty or impairment, but that they are a person. The way you behave and talk will give messages about your mental image of each child.

✔ You cannot be trained to know everything. You cannot be an expert in every area, but you can be a good networker. This means linking people together who might be useful to each other. Get in touch with people who know about:

✔ welfare rights and social services

✔ health services

✔ voluntary organisations and self-help groups.

✔ Remember that you are part of a multi-professional team and that each member has something different to bring to an early years setting.

✔ Respect yourself and others alike. Try to think why people have different views and customs from your own. Keep thinking about what you do. Think about issues of race, gender, sexual orientation, age, economics, background, disability, assertiveness, culture and SEN. Keep changing what you do not like about what you do.

✔ Value the things you keep learning about equality of opportunity so that you can look forward with positive images about yourself and other people.

✔ Most discriminating behaviour is not intended. We need to look at what we do and what we take for granted, so that we do not discriminate.

✔ Do not forget that you need to have a sense of your own worth too. What did you do today that made you feel that you had a worthwhile day?

Agnostics think that we cannot know whether a god or gods exists. Humanists believe that people can be good without believing in a god or gods. They think that the world can be understood through science and research.

Some children are taught monotheistic revelatory religious beliefs (one god, i.e. Judaism, Islam and Christianity). Others learn polytheistic revelatory beliefs (more than one god, i.e. Hinduism). A revelatory god is a supernatural being who is believed to have created the world and who intervenes. Buddhists believe in a god, or gods, who created the world but who does not intervene.

In order that every child feels accepted beyond their home, those working with young children and their families need to learn about belief structures other than their own. It is also important to remember that morality and moral development, that is, being a good person and leading a good life does not necessarily have anything to do with belief in any god or gods; people may be humanists, agnostics or atheists and still lead good lives.

Moreover, some children are brought up in families which follow more than one religion – for example, there might be a Roman Catholic Christian father and a Jewish mother, or an atheist father and a Quaker Christian mother, and it is also important to keep this in mind.

Look, listen and note

- Observe the practice in your setting. Notice how you and your colleagues behave in the workplace.
- Do you and others respond differently to boisterous behaviour in girls and boys, black or white children?
- Would you or they look closely at the four-year-old boy who often ignores the boisterous activities and spends time in the home corner?

Working as a team

It is important to pause at regular intervals and examine what happens in every work setting. Does what the team members say they believe in match what they actually do? Identifying problems in the way practitioners work with children and in the way children and practitioners relate to each other is essential before positive action can be taken by the whole team. It helps to work as a team when doing this because it is hard for individual team members to inspect their own thinking in isolation from other people. It helps to share and discuss things with colleagues.

The team should devise a policy of equality of opportunity and a code of practice and then, as a team, review them regularly.

- The policy states the values of the team and the aims of its work.
- The code of practice sets out how the team will put the policy into practice.
- The review process covers all aspects of the team's work in relation to its policy and code of practice.

Using the age range of the team

It is ideal if every team of staff has a good spread of ages among its members. This means that there are some people who have many years of life experience to bring to the team, and others who are at the beginning of their work with children and families; those who have done other things before training to work with children, and those who will go on to other kinds of work. It is important that young children and their families are with people who:

- value each other and learn from one another
- are trained and informed about children
- are sensitive to the needs and concerns of others, especially parents.

It is important that staff learn to make constructive criticisms of each other, to trust each other, respect each other and to build on each other's strengths.

The role of the individual member of staff

Each practitioner needs to be committed and empowered to carry out the team's policy using the code of practice. Individual staff members can play a very important part in promoting the aims and values of the team in their work. You can make a difference to the lives of the children and families you work with. You can make a difference in your work setting.

Addressing inequalities, prejudices or bias

Challenging discriminatory behaviour

When you encounter prejudice or discrimination, it is important to be assertive and not aggressive. Being assertive means expressing your views clearly but with respect for the other person as an equal human being. This is very different from being rude and angry. For example, you might say: 'I felt very uncomfortable when you asked me to give a drink to the girl with a hearing aid. I felt I needed to know her name, because I am worried that I might stop seeing her as a person if I just think of her as "the girl with a hearing aid".'

Being assertive is also vital for children. You should make sure that the setting's policies and procedures

▲ **Figure 1.4** Implementing an anti-bias approach may include focusing on encouraging girls or boys to play with resources that they might otherwise not access

refer to promoting children's assertiveness to combat aggression through bullying. Children need to feel protected from aggression and to be able to assert themselves sufficiently to partake fully in the activities provided. In some early years settings children are helped to learn to be assertive – even very young children can be helped to tell each other, 'No thank you, no more tickling/pushing/snatching', for example.

Both the bully and the victim need help to be assertive: one needs help with aggression, and the other with timidity or fearfulness. Visualisation techniques can help children to use positive images (i.e. seeing themselves as assertive) rather than negative images (i.e. being the bully or victim).

If you see a child hurting or insulting someone, explain to him or her that such behaviour is not acceptable. Criticise the behaviour rather than the child.

Reflecting on practice

Challenging stereotypes

On an outing to a live music event, a class of 28 children was seated in the front rows. They all thoroughly enjoyed the jazz-style pieces and many of them were standing up and swaying or moving in time with the music. Chantelle was the only mixed-heritage child present, being part Afro-Caribbean and part white English. After the concert, when the children had all gone home, an adult helper (who had watched the children with pleasure) said to you, 'I suppose it's because she's black that Chantelle has such a good sense of rhythm.'

- How would you reply to her comment?
- After you have thought about what you might say, discuss your ideas with another learner or in a group.
- Can you think of three or more ways in which stereotyping might get in the way of making an accurate observation of Chantelle and the other children?

Being aware of discrimination in children's resources

Books that are discriminatory can be discussed with other early years practitioners, removed and replaced with others containing positive images of people with disabilities, with different kinds of families, and of people with different ethnicities, cultures and genders.

Having an impact on the bigger picture

There are some issues regarding equality that seem too big for one person to tackle alone. But there are other things that are easier for each and every one of us to do something about. One individual person can have a great impact on the lives of young children and their families.

Action on children's rights

Working towards children's rights through international cooperation is an important way to make progress towards better quality early years services. It might seem that an individual cannot do very much in this respect. However, in every country there are organisations with which you can link up. In the UK these include the National Children's Bureau, Save the Children, UNICEF and the *Organisation Mondiale pour l'Éducation Préscolaire* (OMEP; in English, the World Organisation for Early Childhood Education). It is also important to remember that you can get in touch with your MP and your MEP via their local surgeries or by writing to them directly.

Action on poverty

Many children in the world live in poverty. Reports by voluntary organisations estimate that around one in three children in the UK are living in poverty. There are absolute limits that humans can bear in terms of a lack of food, shelter and clothing. These result in starvation, disease and slow death. However, in the developed world poverty is more often relative. The reports on poverty in the UK show that, in relation to most people living in the UK, an increasing number of families are living below an acceptable minimum level. This creates stress as families struggle to make ends meet, especially when most other people appear to be financially comfortable.

In the early years setting it is important not to have expensive outings or activities, and to be sure to invite all parents to take part in the life of the group. No parent or child should be left out because of their economic background. This is an important equality of opportunity issue.

Promoting interest, acceptance and respect for differences between people

In early years settings it is a core purpose to promote an attitude of interest, acceptance and respect for others, therefore the whole environment (both physical and psychological) needs to reflect this approach.

This will include ensuring that the physical environment and resources in the setting reflect a multicultural and multilingual approach. For example, every area of the environment should include objects that are familiar to children and link with their homes and culture. This must be based on real information from parents: there is no point having a fan and pair of castanets on a display table because there are Spanish children in the group, when these items are not significant to the child; it is far better to make sure that you know how to sing 'Happy Birthday' in Spanish. Also, the activities of daily life should be familiar to the children. For example, ways of preparing food and cooking, types of foods, implements and ways of eating should reflect all the children's backgrounds as a matter of course, not just once a week or on special occasions.

Integrating certain childcare practices that originate in different cultural traditions can contribute both to continuity of experience for children and also to the repertoire of practices of all the practitioners. For example, traditions of massaging babies are now widely used in British clinics and family centres, and carrying babies in a sling is now widely used by European as well as African parents and practitioners.

These practices are straightforward in settings where children, parents and practitioners are from diverse backgrounds. Where a setting's cultural experiences are less diverse, practitioners can still use the differences that do exist to promote interest, acceptance and respect but they need to think carefully about how to introduce different cultural experiences in a way that avoids 'cultural tourism' or tokenism. This means that practitioners must first ensure that their knowledge and understanding of traditional Polish food, for example, is well grounded.

Sharing books, stories, poems, songs, action songs and games

These are useful in linking children with their previous experiences. For example, stories are available about children with disabilities and about children from different cultures. There are stories which look at gender issues. In the last 20 years authors have been recognising the need for children's books to link with the huge range of experiences that different children have.

With older children books can also be used to encourage discussion about fairness, stereotyping and prejudice.

Guidelines for good practice

Anti-discrimination and anti-bias

✔ Every early years setting needs:

  ✔ a policy on equality of opportunity and inclusivity

  ✔ a code of practice which puts the policy into action

  ✔ regular meetings to review policy and practice.

✔ An adult can choose whether to be described as deaf, hearing impaired or aurally challenged. Give children as much choice as possible about these aspects of their lives.

✔ It is very important to try to pronounce and spell names correctly, and to try to understand the different systems that different cultures use when choosing names for people. It is also very important to learn about the different clothes people wear in different cultures, and to try to learn what these garments are called.

✔ Provide familiar objects for every child in the different areas of the room. These artefacts of their home culture might be cooking utensils, clothes or fabrics but they must be meaningful to the child not based on a stereotype.

✔ Respect and value the child's home language.

✔ Create opportunities for children to talk with other children and adults who speak their home language as well as those who are already fluent in English.

✔ Make sure you tell stories and display positive images of children with disabilities and children from different backgrounds. These stories should also be in the book area.

✔ Make sure that children meet adults with broad gender roles, to show them that men and women respectively are not restricted to a narrow range of activities.

✔ Introduce older children to myths, legends and folk tales from a range of cultures. The same themes crop up over and over again in different stories across the world. Find some of these universal themes in the stories you look at from different cultures.

✔ Make sure the indoor and outdoor areas offer full access to activities for children with disabilities.

✔ When telling stories you could:

  ✔ use puppets and props, flannel boards, magnet boards, and so on

  ✔ invite children to act out pictures as you go through the story

  ✔ use facial expressions, eye contact and body language to 'tell' a story and make it meaningful for the children.

✔ Storytelling: asking storytellers (e.g. parents) to tell stories in their own languages, as well as in English. This helps children to hear different languages, so that the idea becomes familiar that there are many languages in the world.

✔ Music: use a wide range of music types that children hear at home and from other cultures too. Being introduced to different cultures in this way helps children not to reject unfamiliar music – for example, Chinese music has a pentatonic scale (five notes); African music sometimes has five beats in a bar; European music has two, three or four beats, but not usually five.

✔ Dance: children love to move to music and to stand at the edge while people perform. They often 'echo-dance' (i.e. observing and imitating how the adults dance). Look out for this the next time you go to an event. Introduce different forms of dancing to the children; Morris or folk dancing, ballet, Hip-Hop or Indian dance will be new or familiar to different children.

✔ Cookery: borrow or make multi-language, picture-based cookery books – for example, there could be a copy of a recipe for roti in English, Urdu and French, or for bread in English, Greek and Swahili; the choice of languages would depend on which are used in the early years setting.

✔ Plan the menu carefully: make sure that the menu includes food that children will enjoy and that is in some way familiar. One of the things young children worry about when they are away from home is whether they will like the food. Food and eating with others is a very emotional experience.

Look, listen and note

Activities to promote diversity and inclusivity

The following suggested activities can often be done as a group exercise. Each provides good opportunities for you to develop these important skills:

● observing children

● planning to meet each child's needs

● implementing and evaluating the activities.

1 **Plan a multicultural cooking library**: make six cookery cards, each with a simple recipe from a different country or culture, preferably those that are familiar to at least one child in the group. Find or draw pictures to illustrate the books. Write the text in English and the language of the place of origin of the recipe. If you write in Urdu or Chinese, remember that text in these languages runs from right to left. Use the cards with groups of children and run a series of cookery sessions. **Observe** the way the children use and respond to the recipes and ingredients. **Evaluate** the aim of your plan, the reason for the activity, how the activities were carried out and what you observed in the children's cooking activities.

2 **Storytelling**: plan a story that you can tell (rather than read from a book). Choose a story you enjoy and make or find suitable props. You could make puppets out of stuffed socks, finger puppets out of gloves, stick puppets or shadow puppets; or use dolls and dressing-up clothes and various other artefacts. Observe the children listening as you tell the story. Focus on their understanding and their language, especially children whose first language is not English. Evaluate your activity.

3 **Religious festivals**: review how you celebrate different festivals in your setting. How much emphasis is given to each? How can you introduce the children to less familiar festivals in a way that is not tokenistic? How can you offer children meaningful first-hand experiences? **Observe** the children while a festival is being celebrated and assess how much they understand. Look particularly at the reactions of children who are familiar with the festival you choose, and compare their behaviour to that of children for whom this is a new experience. **Evaluate** your practice and observations.

4 **Inclusion**: observe one aspect of provision, for example, the home area, outside, wheeled toys, music etc. Note which children use this provision most or least. Are any children particularly encouraged into the area by other children or adults? Are any children overtly or unconsciously excluded from this provision?

5 **Music**: review your musical resources. Do they include recorded music and songs of different types and from a range of cultures and places across the world? Plan a series of activities that introduce children to the music of a variety of cultures. You will need to help children to listen to music and make music.

Learn a lullaby or nursery rhyme in another language, preferably one that is known by at least one of the children in your care.

6 **Equality policy**: read your setting's policy on equality and look at actual practices in the daily routine – for example, mealtimes and books. Does what happens match the policy? Evaluate your observations.

Moving on

The rights of children and their families

What are children's rights?

Children are entitled to basic human rights such as food, health care, a safe home and protection from abuse. However, children are a special case because they cannot always stand up for themselves. They need a *special* set of rights that take account of their vulnerability and ensure that adults take responsibility for their protection and development.

The UN Convention on the Rights of the Child

This is an international treaty. These rights are for children and young people (up to the age of 18 years). The only two countries in the world that have not signed the Convention are the USA and Somalia. As an early years practitioner you must know and understand the basic requirements of the United Nations Convention on the Rights of the Child. The rights embodied by the UN Convention which particularly relate to childcare and education are these:

All children – without discrimination – have the right to:

- survive
- develop to their fullest potential
- be protected from harmful influences, abuse and exploitation
- participate fully in family, cultural and social life
- express and have their views taken into account on all matters that affect them
- play, rest and enjoy leisure.

The rights embodied by the UN Convention which particularly relate to childcare and education are these:

- Children have the right to be with their family or with those who will care best for them.
- Children have the right to enough food and clean water for their needs.
- Children have the right to an adequate standard of living.
- Children have the right to health care.
- Children have the right to play.
- Children have the right to be kept safe and not hurt or neglected.
- Children with disabilities have the right to special care and training.
- Children must not be used as cheap workers or as soldiers.
- Children have the right to free education.

The balance of rights and responsibilities

Children and young people have responsibilities as well as rights. Many have jobs; some care for relatives; a large proportion are school or college students; and they all must respect other people's rights and act within the law. However, these responsibilities do not detract from their human rights, which everybody has from the moment they are born.

A parent is responsible for the care and upbringing of their child. The Children and Young Persons Act 1933 (modified by the Children and Young Persons Act 1963, the Children and Young Persons Act 1969 and the Children and Young Persons Act 2008) imposes criminal liability for abandonment, neglect or ill-treatment of any person over the age of 16 years who is responsible for a child under 16 years. Because parental responsibility cannot be surrendered or transferred, parents are liable for neglecting their child if they choose an inadequate babysitter.

Think about ideas

Children as an oppressed group?

In her discussions about liberation theory and oppression, Sherover-Marcuse defines oppression as 'the systematic mistreatment of one group of people by another group or by society as a whole' (Sherover-Marcuse 2000).

Oppression consists of any or all of the following list. Consider to what degree children, as a group, experience:

1. Being treated without respect as a human being.
   - Think about how it is often seen as acceptable to behave towards children in a way that would not be allowed were they an adult.

2. Being treated as less capable, less intelligent and less than the 'norm'.
   - Children are often treated as if their relative immaturity and limited knowledge and experience of the world is a failing rather than to do with their stage of development.

3. Being stereotyped into limited restricted roles.
   - As well as being stereotyped according to other social groups they belong to, children are also stereotyped as children, for example, babies just being seen as cute or boring, toddlers as like wild animals on the rampage (Manning-Morton and Thorp 2003, 2015) and children generally are often seen as a messy, chaotic nuisance.

4. The use of oppressive language.
   - Make a list of all the different words and terms used for children that you have heard, like 'kids' or 'little monkeys'. Identify which of them are terms of endearment and which are labels and stereotypes. Is it the case that the terminology could be both affectionate and stereotyping?

5. Jokes and verbal abuse that insult and humiliate the target person and reinforce the stereotypes.
   - Think about the videos that adults post to the internet showing children being laughed at when they make mistakes, cry or are scared.

6. Denial of access to education, jobs, housing, money, power and political influence.
   - Although children experience these issues more indirectly through their family situation, it is important to consider how they are empowered in the early years setting to influence what happens and how things are done. Identify how you listen to children and involve them in the organisation of the day and the decisions about the curriculum.

7. Harassment.
   - Children are regularly bullied and harassed by people who are bigger, stronger and more powerful than they are. Reflect on your own childhood experience or on the current experience of a child you know. Can you identify instances of bullying and coercion?

8. Physical violence and murder.
   - Children are frequently attacked and killed. Review the research and statistics produced by the NSPCC and Ofsted. How many children under five die every year in the UK? How does that compare to other developed countries?

Do you think children are oppressed as a group or not? What would be your arguments for and against this idea?

Further reading, weblinks and resources

Baldock, P., 2010, *Understanding Cultural Diversity in the Early Years*, London: Sage.

Lane, J., 2008, *Young Children and Racial Justice*, London: NCB.

Yelland, N. (ed.), 1998, *Gender in Early Childhood*, London: Routledge.

Robinson, K. and Jones Diaz, C., 2006, *Diversity and Difference in Early Childhood Education: Issues for Theory and Practice*, Maidenhead: Open University Press.

Siraj-Blatchford, I. and Clarke, P., 2000, *Supporting Identity, Diversity and Language in the Early Years*, Maidenhead: Open University Press

National Children's Bureau

A charitable organisation dedicated to advancing the health and well-being of all children and young people across every aspect of their lives, and providing them with a powerful and authoritative voice
www.ncb.org.uk

Save the Children

Works to save lives in emergencies, campaigning for children's rights, and improving their futures through long-term development work.
www.savethechildren.org.uk

UNICEF

Helps children receive the support, health care and education they need to survive the threats of child poverty, such as preventable disease or malnutrition, and grow up to become healthy adults.
www.unicef.org.uk

Stonewall

Stonewall is a national organisation that campaigns for lesbian, gay and bisexual equality. They have recently gained additional funding to widen their educational work to include the early years.
www.stonewall.org.uk

Books for Keeps

Includes guidelines and selected titles: 100 Picture Books chosen by The Working Group Against Racism in Children's Resources.
http://booksforkeeps.co.uk

Equality, diversity and inclusion

Website guidance for preschool playgroups.
www.pre-school.org.uk/providers/inclusion

Equality Advisory Support Service

The Equality Advisory Support Service (EASS) is an advice service aimed at individuals who need expert information, advice and support on discrimination and human rights issues and the applicable law.
www.equalityadvisoryservice.com

ACE Education Advice

National charity that provides advice and information to parents and carers on a wide range of school-based issues including exclusion, admissions, special education needs, bullying and attendance.
www.ace-ed.org.uk

Race and Equality Centre

Charity that aims to eliminate discrimination and promote equality.
www.discriminationhelp.org.uk

Equality and Human Rights Commission (EHRC)

EHRC has a statutory remit to promote and monitor human rights; and to protect, enforce and promote equality across the seven 'protected' grounds – age, disability, gender, race, religion and belief, sexual orientation and gender reassignment.
www.equalityhumanrights.com

Early Education

The leading national voluntary organisation for early years practitioners and parents, Early Education promotes the right of all children to education of the highest quality.
www.early-education.org.uk

Organisation Mondiale Education Pre-Scholaire (OMEP World Organisation for Early Childhood Education)

OMEP is an international, non-governmental organisation founded in 1948 to benefit children under the age of eight years throughout the world. OMEP's aim is to promote the optimum conditions for all children, in order to ensure their well-being, development and happiness, both within their family unit and the wider communities in which they live.
http://www.omepuk.org.uk/

Relevant Acts of Parliament

http://www.nidirect.gov.uk/government-citizens-and-rights

References

Aboud, F. E. 'The Formation of In-group Favoritism and Out-group Prejudice in Young Children: Are they Distinct Attitudes?' *Developmental Psychology*, 39: 1, Jan 2003, 48–60.

Brown, B., 1998, *Unlearning Discrimination in the Early Years*, Staffs: Trentham Books

Cole, M., 1998, 'Culture in Development' in Woodhead, M. et al., *Cultural Worlds of Early Childhood*, London: Routledge and Open University.

Derman-Sparks, L. and the ABC Task Force, 1991, *Anti-Bias Curriculum: Tools for Empowering Young Children*, Washington DC: NAEYC.

Dowd, N., 2000, *Redefining Fatherhood*, New York: New York University Press.

Equality and Human Rights Commission, *What is the Equality Act?* Available at: http://www.equalityhumanrights.com/legal-and-policy/legislation/equality-act-2010/what-equality-act.

Guasp, A., 2012, *The School Report: The Experiences of Gay Young People in Britain's Schools in 2012*, London: Stonewall

Lane, J., 1999, *Action for Racial Equality in the Early Years: Understanding the Past, Thinking About the Present, Planning for the Future*, London: National Early Years Network.

Manning-Morton, J. and Thorp, M., 2003, *Key Times for Play, The First Three Years*, Maidenhead: Open University Press.

Manning-Morton, J and Thorp, M., 2015, *Two Year Olds in Early Years Settings; Journeys of Discovery*, Maidenhead: Open University Press.

Macpherson, W (1999) *The Stephen Lawrence Inquiry, Report Of An Inquiry By Sir William Macpherson Of Cluny*. Available at: www.gov.uk/government/publications/the-stephen-lawrence-inquiry.

Nutbrown, C., 2006, *Inclusion in the Early Years: Critical Analysis and Enabling Narratives*, London: Sage.

Purkey, W., 1970, *Self-concept and School Achievement*, London: Paul Chapman.

Sherover-Marcuse, R., 2000, *Liberation Theory: A Working Framework*. Available at: http://www.unlearningracism.org/writings/lib_theory.htm.

Siraj-Blatchford, I., 1994, *The Early Years. Laying the Foundations for Racial Equality*. London: Trentham Books.

Williams, R., 2000, 'Culture is Ordinary' in Levinson, B. et al. (eds.), *Schooling the Symbolic Animal*, Lanham, Maryland: Rowman and Littlefield.

Early years practitioners have an important role in identifying any special needs a child might have, supporting that child and their family and liaising with other professionals, and being an advocate for the child. This chapter discusses the issues that practitioners need to consider in terms of the legal requirements and their own attitudes to disability. It suggests that settings should consider the model of working with children with disabilities that they use and how they develop inclusive practice and provision. An overview of some specific disabilities and learning difficulties is given with useful resources for practitioners to access to develop their understanding further.

What are special needs, disabilities and impairments?

Children with special needs and disabilities are not an easily defined group. Some have a disability such as Down's syndrome that also means that they have special educational needs (SEN); other children may be defined as having a disability under the Equality Act (2010) due to a health condition such as diabetes but not be considered to have SEN. However, children with more significant SEN, including those who have a statement, or an Education Health and Care plan (EHCP), are more likely to meet the definition of disability in the Equality Act (Stobbs 2015).

The Equality Act (2010) says that a person has a disability if they have:

> *a physical or mental impairment and the impairment has a substantial and long-term adverse effect on their ability to carry out normal day-to-day activities.*

- 'Long-term' means that the condition has lasted for 12 months, is likely to last for at least a further 12 months, or is lifelong.
- A 'physical or mental impairment' includes learning difficulties, mental health conditions, medical conditions and hidden impairments such as specific learning difficulties, autism, and speech, language and communication impairments.

The Special Educational Needs and Disability Code of Practice: 0–25 years (SENCoP) (DfE 2015) states that a child or young person has SEN if they have a learning difficulty or disability which calls for special educational provision to be made for him or her.

A child of compulsory school age or a young person has a learning difficulty or disability if he or she:

- has a significantly greater difficulty in learning than the majority of others of the same age, or
- has a disability which prevents or hinders him or her from making use of facilities of a kind generally provided for others of the same age in mainstream schools or mainstream post-16 institutions.

So a child may have a specific learning need such as dyslexia, giftedness or a lifelong learning disability such as an **autistic spectrum disorder** (see page 20 for definition). On the other hand, a child might have a special need for a short period of time – for example, a child who has periods of hearing loss caused by glue ear, when fluid builds up in the middle ear.

This means that the definition of what is considered a disability is wider than is often thought, and that there is often an overlap between having a disability and a special educational need but not always. This puts considerable responsibility on early years practitioners to observe children carefully and to be in good communication with parents and other professionals to ensure that they identify, understand and provide appropriately for each child's needs.

Despite some improvement in social attitudes to disability, people with disabilities still experience a great deal of discrimination and prejudice. It is therefore very important to reflect on how we think about people with disabilities, starting with the terms and labels we use.

Three terms have already been used in this chapter that need to be clarified:

Impairment

Impairment is the loss or limitation of physical, mental or **sensory function** (see page 20 for definition) on a long-term or permanent basis. Often children are described as having a hearing impairment rather than a hearing disability. A criticism of this term, though, is that it focuses attention on the child's disability as a set of problems rather than seeing the whole child (Dickins with Denziloe 2004).

Learning disability

People who have a learning disability have difficulties with learning and find it particularly hard to understand new and complex information, and to develop new skills. A learning disability is a lifelong condition that is usually present from birth, although it may not become apparent until a child fails to reach particular developmental milestones. Examples of learning disabilities include delayed speech or a major difficulty with social interaction.

Learning difficulty

Learning difficulty is a term used to describe any one of a number of barriers to learning that a child may experience. It is a broad term that covers a wide range of needs and problems – including dyslexia and behavioural problems – and the full range of ability. Children with learning difficulties may find activities that involve some kinds of thinking and understanding particularly difficult, and many need support in their everyday lives as well as at school.

 ## Theory and theorists: models of disability

Dickins (2014, pp. 44–5) describes three main ways of understanding disability:

1. The moral or religious model: not all individuals who hold religious beliefs will think like this but it is a view that still influences negative attitudes to people with disabilities today.

    This is the idea that disability is a punishment for evil behaviour. Societies in which this model is prevalent are much more likely to feel that people with disabilities and their families should be stigmatised and avoided.

2. The medical model: the medical model of disability sees disability as a 'problem' which we must 'treat'. It focuses on the impairment or condition; seeing the child as deficient or lacking, and the role of the professional as curing, alleviating or reducing the condition to fit into society. Obviously, alleviating pain, discomfort or difficulty is important but only focusing on treating the disability means that the child is not celebrated as a whole person, and the child may be seen as 'faulty' or a 'failure', particularly where a disability is lifelong so cannot be 'cured'.

3. The social model: in this model there is a distinction between impairment and disability; it emphasises that people are 'disabled' by the social context in which they live. It is the physical and social barriers that society creates that are regarded as the disabling factors, so the 'problem' is located outside the sphere of children with disabilities and their families. This

KEY TERMS

Disability – Under the Equality Act 2010, a person has a disability if they have a physical or mental impairment, and if the impairment has a substantial and long-term negative effect on their ability to perform normal day-to-day activities.

Autism spectrum disorder (ASD) and **autism** are both general terms for a group of complex disorders of brain development. These disorders are characterised, in varying degrees, by difficulties in social interaction, verbal and non-verbal communication and repetitive behaviours. See p. 32 for more information on ASD.

Sensory function – The extent to which an individual correctly senses skin stimulation, sounds, proprioception, taste and smell, and visual images.

Giftedness: The National Association for Gifted Children (NAGC) defines giftedness as the following:

> *Gifted individuals are those who demonstrate outstanding levels of aptitude (defined as an exceptional ability to reason and learn) or competence (documented performance or achievement in top 10% or rarer) in one or more domains.*

model of disability is intrinsic to the inclusive approach as it is the only model that encourages us to accept and value children whatever their differences. The social model has been adopted by the World Health Organisation and now underpins much of current thinking and developments.

Think about ideas

Models of disability

It is important to think of each child as an individual, rather than making an assumption based on a label. Children are more alike than they are different. Every child needs to:

- feel welcome
- feel safe, both physically and emotionally
- have friends and to feel as if he or she belongs
- be encouraged to reach his or her potential
- be celebrated for his or her uniqueness.

In other words, children are always children first – the disability or special need is secondary.

Think about a child you know with a disability or special educational need. How do you ensure that the needs listed here are met?

▲ **Figure 2.1** Children are always children first – the disability or special need is secondary.

Causes of disability

There are three main causes of disability:

1 **Congenital** causes – a gene anomaly leads to a disabling condition such as Down's Syndrome or Cystic Fibrosis.

    Genetic counselling is available for anyone with a child or other member of the family with a chromosomal anomaly, and chromosome analysis is offered in early pregnancy. Genetic counselling advises family members about the consequences and nature of the disorder, the probability of developing or transmitting it, and the options open to them in management and family planning.

2 **Developmental** causes – something goes wrong when the baby is growing in the womb; the first three months (the first trimester) of a pregnancy are when the foetus is particularly vulnerable.

    At this time, disabilities can be caused by infections such as **Rubella** potentially causing deafness, blindness and learning disability, or through ingesting substances that can harm foetal development such as the drug Thalidomide (which led to babies being born with limb deformities in the 1960s) or illegal drugs or excessive alcohol intake (which can lead to **Foetal Alcohol Syndrome (FAS))**.

Alternatively, something may go wrong during birth, leading to conditions such as **Cerebral Palsy** or Erb's Palsy.

3 **Environmental** causes – severe neglect and abuse can lead to learning difficulties in children, and dangerous or toxic environments can lead to illness and injury that might be long-term. Illness and accidents can affect anyone throughout life, whether it is through the aging process and losing our sight or hearing abilities or through an accident or illness that causes disability; almost all of us will have some life experience of disability at some point.

KEY TERMS

Rubella – Also called German measles or three-day measles, this is a contagious viral infection best known by its distinctive red rash.

Foetal Alcohol Syndrome (FASD) – This is a group of conditions that can occur in a person whose mother drank alcohol excessively during pregnancy. Problems may include an abnormal appearance, short height, low body weight, small head, poor coordination, low intelligence, behaviour problems, and problems with hearing or seeing.

Cerebral Palsy – The general term for a number of neurological conditions that affect movement and coordination.

Disability and discrimination

Anyone with a disability forms part of a group whose particular needs may not be adequately recognised or taken into account. Having a different appearance, way of communicating or behaving can lead to people with disabilities being treated differently and unequally.

The following attitudes are commonly encountered by people with disabilities:

- **Stereotyping** – a term used when certain characteristics of any given group are applied to all the individuals within that group; for example, a common stereotype of children with Down's syndrome is that they are always cheerful, placid and affectionate.
- **Hostility** – this may take the form of loud comments being made about the person with disabilities or aggression towards them. It is often a result of people's fear of the unknown.
- **Invasion of privacy** – certain physical characteristics evoke such strong feelings that people often have to express them in some way. Physical differences can make the bodies of people who have disabilities objects for public comment.
- **Dependency** – the assumption of dependency can lead people to try to be helpful without being asked. This invades the privacy of the disabled person's life – for example, helping a blind person across a road that he or she did not want to cross.
- **Being patronised** – this means people talking or directing questions to the disabled person's able-bodied companions, rather than to the person with the disability, as if the person with the disability would not be able to understand what was being said; this attitude is summed up by the famous patronising phrase, 'Does he take sugar?'

Early years settings and schools must not discriminate against children with disabilities, the families of children with disabilities, or against parents or carers with disabilities. They must not treat children with disabilities less favourably, and they must make reasonable adjustments for them. They must supply adapted equipment – for example, large-print books – where appropriate and must not charge extra for any such adaptation. Prejudice towards people with disabilities is not innate but learned, so the early years practitioner's role in modelling and promoting positive attitudes towards disability is crucial.

Special educational needs

With reference to inclusive practice, the EYFS framework makes it clear that all providers have a responsibility:

> *to ensure that diversity of individuals and communities is valued and respected and that no child or family is discriminated against. Settings need to provide individualised opportunities based on each child's needs, particularly those related to ethnicity, language and disability.*

Current legislation in relation to inclusive practice is discussed in Chapter 1, including new legislation introduced in 2014 relating to children with SEN and disabilities.

Provision and support for children with disabilities and their families

The legislation and procedures in relation to disability and SEN are frequently updated and changed, so reference should always be made to the most recent legislation and policy documents.

The Special Educational Needs and Disability Regulations 2014 specify the requirements that all local authorities must meet in developing, publishing and reviewing their 'local offer' to children and families. The purpose of the local offer is to enable parents and young people to see more clearly what services are available in their area and how to access them. The offer will include provision from birth to 25 years, across education, health and social care.

SENCoP (DfE 2015) is the statutory guidance for organisations who work with and support children and young people who have SEN or disabilities. It sets out all the terminology, processes and procedure that must be followed.

About 7 per cent of children in schools and early years settings have a disability, and about 20 per cent will have a special educational need of some kind at some time during their education. The SENCoP (DfE 2015 p.142) assumes that 'the majority of children and young people with SEN or disabilities will have their needs met within local mainstream early years settings' but that where the child might need special provision in relation to their educational, health and/or social care needs, the local authority, in partnership with the child, parents and setting, will assess the child's needs and put an EHCP in place. This EHCP replaces the previous 'statement of special needs'. (See p. 28 for more information).

Professionals involved in the care of children with disabilities

The Special Educational Needs Co-ordinator (SENCO) in a setting has responsibility for coordinating SEN provision. Early years settings in group provision arrangements are expected to identify an individual to perform the role of SENCO, and childminders are encouraged to do so, possibly sharing the role between them where they are registered with an agency.

The SENCO is responsible for:

- ensuring that all practitioners in the setting understand their responsibilities to children with SEN and the setting's approach to identifying and meeting SEN
- advising and supporting colleagues
- ensuring that parents are closely involved throughout and that their insights inform action taken by the setting
- liaising with professionals or agencies beyond the setting.

(SENCoP, DfE 2015)

An Education, Health and Care Plan (EHCP) may mean that there are potentially many professionals involved with the child and the family. This may include:

- family doctors (GPs)
- health visitors
- dieticians
- physiotherapists
- occupational therapists (OTs)
- community nurses
- speech therapists
- play specialists
- play therapists
- clinical psychologists
- educational psychologists
- Portage outreach workers (advisers specially trained in understanding child development)
- special needs teachers
- special needs support assistants
- social workers.

In practice, while the involvement of a range of professionals can provide families with a great deal of expertise, it can also be overwhelming. Families can sometimes find that they are offered lots of different advice by different people. They may also find themselves having to repeatedly tell the same story about their child's birth, early difficulties, tests and their findings, for example.

The lead professional or SENCO has a crucial role in coordinating the team of professionals to avoid this happening. However, working across professional disciplines of education, health and social care is often a major challenge.

The main place for families to access support, advice and early intervention for a child up to five years old with a special need or disability will be the local children's centre. Children's centres offer parents access to a multi-professional team. This includes easy access to specialist services, such as speech and language therapy and child psychology, who are experts in speech and language development or in the mental states and functioning of children. The centre's Family Support Service can also help parents with issues such as applying for benefits to support them in caring for their child with the disability, finding suitable housing, and linking up with voluntary and statutory agencies that offer support. The children's centre will have links with the local Children's Services team and with the specialist health teams to support children with disabilities.

Parent partnership services

The Parent Partnership Scheme (PPS) is a statutory service that offers the following support:

- information, advice and support for parents of children and young people with SEN
- putting parents in touch with other local organisations
- making sure that parents' views are heard and understood – and that these views inform local policy and practice.

Some parent partnerships are based in the voluntary sector, although the majority of them remain based in their LEA (Local Education Authority) or Children's Trust. All parent partnerships, wherever they are based, work separately and independently from the LEA; this means that they are able to provide impartial advice and support to parents. For more information, visit the IASS Network (Information, Advice and Support Services Network) website at http://www.iassnetwork.org.uk/.

Every Disabled Child Matters (EDCM)

Every Disabled Child Matters is a campaign to make sure that children with disabilities and their families get the same rights as everyone else. The aims of the campaign are for children with disabilities and their families to:

- have the same rights as everyone else so that they are fully included in society

- get the services and support they need to live their lives in the way they want
- stop living in poverty
- receive education that meets their needs
- have their say about services for disabled children.

The Early Support Programme

Early Support is an integral part of the delivery of the EYFS for babies and young children under five with disabilities or emerging SEN. It helps staff in early years settings to identify impairments early and to work in partnership with families and other services to provide the best possible care and support for young children with disabilities. An important part of the Early Support programme is the Family File, which the family holds. The Family File:

- is used by the professionals and the family together, to plan appropriate support to be provided for the child
- informs the family about the different professionals they may meet and what their role is
- explains how the different health, education and social services can provide support
- allows parents and carers to share information about their child with the professionals they meet, without having to say the same things to every new person
- provides information about sources of financial support and childcare.

Under the provisions of the Children and Families Act 2014, there is a new graduated approach to supporting children with SEN, called SEN support. Information on SEN support is available in the SENCoP, starting at paragraphs 5.36: this is available at https://www.gov.uk/government/publications/send-code-of-practice-0-to-25.

Including children with disabilities: mainstream or specialist provision?

There are views both for and against inclusion of children with disabilities and special needs in mainstream education. Some people believe that:

> *inclusion has the potential to become our most powerful tool in changing society's attitudes towards disability and combating the injustices and inequalities that result.*

(Dickins 2003:19)

Others, including parents, argue that mainstream provision cannot meet their children's needs. So a dual system is being maintained, which may become a two-tier system which segregates those children with more

severe and complex needs and those whose behaviour is perceived as challenging.

Comparing mainstream schools and schools for children with special needs

In a school for SEN:

- Staff need to be careful to concentrate on the child as a whole person and not on their disability only. When the latter happens, it narrows the child's experiences. Concentrating on disability means concentrating on what children find difficult to do, rather than being positive and thinking about all the things that the child can do.
- The curriculum might become rather rigid and be based on exercises, instead of equipping the children to make choices and decisions, and to become autonomous or independent learners. For example, schools for hearing-impaired children used to concentrate on language teaching in a narrow curriculum, with little art, play, dance, science, and so on. All the effort went into getting the children to talk, read and write. In spite of this emphasis on language and literacy, few children reached a reading age of above nine years (the reading age required to read tabloid newspapers).

Reflecting on practice

Inclusion or specialist provision?

Winnie (six years) had a range of disabilities, including severe learning difficulties, visual and hearing impairment, and difficulty in sitting. Her parents valued joining a parents' group run by the staff of the special school. All the parents had children with similar disabilities. This gave them support. The equipment in the special school was geared to Winnie's needs, and the staff were specialists trained to work with children like Winnie.

The children were visited regularly by children from the local primary school, and they would go on outings together. Winnie lived at home and went to school daily.

- What do you think are the advantages and disadvantages for Winnie in going to a school for SEN?
- Think about a mainstream setting you know well. What do you think it might be like to be a child with a disability in this service?
- What would the setting need to provide well for child with either a physical disability like a sight or hearing impairment or a learning difficulty like Down's syndrome or an ASD?

- It may be difficult to arrange for the children to meet children who do not have a disability. This can mean that children begin to imitate mannerisms from each other, leading to added difficulties.

In a mainstream school:

- Staff need to consider different problems – for example, a child might be very lonely if he or she is the only child in the school with a hearing impairment. It is very important to help children to make friends in this setting.
- It is also very easy to underestimate what the child can do. It is essential for practitioners to have high enough expectations of children with SEN in mainstream settings.
- There might not be any expert teachers who know about the particular disability that the child has. Even if expert teachers do visit, their visits may be irregular and infrequent, which makes it hard to get the information that is needed in order to help the child.
- It is very important to be up to date with current legislation and policy guidance and to bear in mind generally expected levels of achievement for children. Practitioners should find ways of helping children with SEN to move towards this, or to do as much as they can.
- Sometimes children with disabilities are overprotected and are not expected to manage things that they could do with a little encouragement.
- It is very important to establish links with voluntary organisations that may be able to put children with similar disabilities in touch with each other. For example, there are summer camps where children who attend mainstream schools can come together and enjoy each other's company.

Providing well for children with disabilities and SEN in early years settings

Over the years, a significant amount of research has shown how good early years education and care can be particularly beneficial for children with SEN and their families. An example of this is the Effective Provision of Pre-School Education (EPPE) project, which found that high-quality early years education and care reduced levels of SEN (Sylva et al. 2004). Some of the reasons for this are:

- support for the child and family
- early assessment and support
- planning ahead.

Support for the child and family
Support for the family
Having a baby who has a disability in any way will have social, psychological and financial implications for the family and affect the way the family functions. Each family is unique in the way that it reacts initially and adjusts in the long term, but when a mother gives birth to a baby who has a disability or an additional need, she may experience feelings of guilt – 'It must be because of something I did wrong during pregnancy' – or even of rejection, although this is usually temporary. This is sometimes not helped by the reactions of medical staff, family and friends who may emphasise the difficulties rather than celebrate the child's birth.

Common reactions of parents to having a child with disabilities include:

- A sense of tragedy – parents who give birth to a child with a disability experience complex emotions. They may grieve for the loss of a 'normal' child, but they have not actually been bereaved. They still have a child with a unique personality and identity of his or her own. Relatives and friends can be embarrassed if they do not know how to react to the event, and their awkward response can leave parents feeling very isolated at a time that is normally spent celebrating.
- A fear of making mistakes – sometimes there is an over-reliance on professional help. If the disability seems like the most important aspect of the child's personality, parents may believe that only a medical expert can advise on the care of their child. The reality is that the parent almost always knows what is required for their child. A great deal of what the child needs is not related to his or her disability in any case.
- Being overprotective – a desire to cocoon the child can be counterproductive (have the opposite or desired effect). The child needs to be equipped for life and can only learn by making mistakes. In addition, siblings may resent the child with disabilities who may be seen as spoilt or never punished.
- Exercising control – parents may take freedom of choice away from the child, so disempowering him or her. Parents and carers often dictate where and with whom the child plays, thus depriving him or her of an opportunity for valuable social learning.

It can be very stressful to look after a child with SEN. Part of that stress can be caused by isolation – a fear of taking a child to group activities, or even out to the shops or the park, perhaps because of the reactions of other people. An early years setting or a school can provide a welcoming, friendly community where the parents can feel confident that their child is safe, and can enjoy the company of other children and appropriate stimulation.

Early years settings can also provide considerable help through early identification of SEN. Sometimes parents are unaware that their child's development is delayed compared to other children of the same age, especially in the case of their first or oldest child. On other occasions, parents may have felt that 'something is not right', but have either been anxious about sharing their worries, or have talked to other professionals but not been fully understood. Sometimes a child can present as developing well during a check-up, but have difficulties in less structured environments or when in the company of other children. Early identification means that the child can be helped while still very young; in many cases, prompt help early on can prevent or minimise later difficulties.

When working with a child who has special needs and disabilities, it is important to respect the child's family and the ways they have developed to manage the difficulties that will certainly have arisen in their lives. With sensitivity, you can often help families to feel more confident about their child being with other children. You may need to use a great deal of tact and diplomacy to encourage parents to allow their children to take some risks, and to be exposed to the usual daily life in an early years setting or school.

Support for the child

In an inclusive setting, children with disabling conditions will be celebrated and accepted as they are, and practitioners will encourage self-acceptance and a positive self-image and identity in them. The notion of inclusion is based on the idea that we will ultimately benefit as a society when people with disabilities are enabled to fully participate and contribute (Dickins 2014). This is different to integration, which emphasises the ways in which a child can be brought into the community. Inclusion sees the child already as part of the community, but needing additional help within it.

Inclusion is about access for people with disabilities in its widest sense – not just about physical access to buildings, vehicles, education, health care, leisure facilities and employment, but to be part of the community as a whole. To develop their own self-worth, people with disabilities need to have the same opportunities, services and facilities that are available to other people. Excluding children with disabilities from everyday experiences that are the norm for most children can lead to a lifetime of segregation. In addition, if children lack contact with people with

Look, listen and note

Observe a child with a disability or special educational need in a setting. Note down:

- How is the child's positive sense of self supported?
- How are their friendships nurtured?
- Are they enabled to access all aspects of the curriculum and the environment, including visits?
- How do practitioners talk to all the children about this child's disability and other disabilities?
- How are issues of dis/ability woven into the curriculum?

disabilities it can lead to fear and ignorance of those who seem 'different'.

The SENCoP (DfE 2015) stipulates that all children should have access to a broad and balanced curriculum and that practitioners should have ambitious expectations of children whatever their previous attainment.

Ensuring the setting meets the needs of children with disabilities

It is necessary to make sure that both indoor and outdoor areas of the early years setting are arranged so that children with disabilities can take full part in activities. This might involve:

- providing ramps for wheelchairs
- making sure the light falls on the practitioner or adult's face, so that a child wearing a hearing aid is able to lip-read and a child with a visual impairment can use any remaining eyesight to see facial expressions
- having a tray on the table so that objects stay on the table and a child with a visual impairment or difficulties with motor control does not 'lose' objects that fall off
- having the opportunity to learn sign languages (e.g. British Sign Language and Makaton). See Moving on section for more detail on these.

To help children with a special need or disability to feel included, you should consider the following:

- Your displays – do these include images of children and adults with disabilities? If you are making a display about transport, for example, you could include an image of an adult with a disability getting onto an accessible bus.
- Your layout and organisation – is there enough space for a child to negotiate or move around the tables and equipment, if they have a difficulty

▲ **Figure 2.2** In an inclusive setting, children with disabling conditions will be enabled to access all aspects of a broad curriculum

with their mobility? Are displays low-glare, so they can be seen by people with a visual impairment? (Laminated sheets, for example, can be very hard to read.)

● Your organisational culture – do you use Makaton and visual symbols as a matter of course? Do you think carefully about where you position children at group time, taking account of needs like hearing impairment, visual impairment and language delay? Do leaflets and other forms of information make it clear you are welcoming to children with special needs and disabilities?

● Your resources – do you have dolls and small-world play equipment which represent different disabilities, for example, people with hearing aids, people in wheelchairs? Do your books have stories that include children with disabilities, or do you only have books about a particular disability?

Advocacy, empowerment and listening

Advocacy is when another individual takes on the responsibility of speaking out on behalf of a person to ensure that their views are heard and that they receive all the rights that they are entitled to. In the UK, the Children Act 1989 Act (later updated in 2004, see Chapter 4, p. 76 for more information) makes social services departments responsible for providing for children with special needs, according to the definition given above. The concept of advocacy is

enshrined in the Act. It recognises that children in the category 'disabled' are the least likely to grow up to be able to speak for themselves – that is, to recognise their own needs and to know how to achieve their potential. Therefore, they need an advocate. Usually the advocate is an adult care worker who acts as a spokesperson for the person 'in need'.

The concept of empowerment is closely linked to advocacy. In the case of children with special needs, the adult advocate should undertake activities with the child that will empower (or enable) the child to make his or her own wishes known. This includes helping with communication, giving the child choices and developing the child's decision-making skills.

These strategies are part of the Young Children's Voices Network project at the National Children's Bureau. This project promotes listening to children in the early years. The network supports local authorities in developing good practice so that young children's views may inform policy and improve early years services. They define listening as:

● an active process of receiving (hearing and observing), interpreting and responding to communication; it includes all the senses and emotions and is not limited to the spoken word

● a necessary stage in ensuring the participation of all young children, as well as parents and staff, in matters that affect them

- an ongoing part of tuning in to all young children as individuals in their everyday lives
- sometimes part of a specific consultation about a particular entitlement, choice, event or opportunity.

(Clark 2011)

The project emphasises that the reasons for listening to young children with disabilities are the same as the reasons for listening to all children, but that there are issues for children with disabilities that make listening particularly important.

For example, children with disabilities:

- are subject to a much higher degree of adult intervention, and their scope for making day-to-day choices and decisions is often severely limited
- are more likely to be subject to various kinds of assessment procedures and less likely to be involved in the process
- are more likely to be excluded from consultation processes because these are often based on written and spoken language
- are supported by parents and staff who are more likely to see their roles as advocates rather than listeners
- are more likely than other children to have contact with multiple carers who lack the skills to understand their communication system.

(Dickins 2011)

Dickins (2011) emphasises that, although some new skills and techniques might be useful, it is most often practitioner's attitudes and fears that get in the way of listening to young children with disabilities. She gives the following advice to practitioners:

- Show interest in everything the child has to say, using your judgement later on to draw out the information you actually need for future planning.
- Give children time and try not to interrupt or finish sentences.
- Do not attempt to fill every silence.
- When the child has finished talking, sum up what he or she has said and reflect it back, for example, 'It sounds like you felt very angry when Tommy took your ball away.'
- Do not feel that you have to have an answer or a solution for everything.
- Acknowledge the feelings that are being expressed and give them validity.
- Avoid closed questions that leave you open to a yes/no answer ('Are there things you like at nursery?'); use open-ended questions instead ('Tell me some of the things you like about nursery.').

- Make eye contact and get down to the child's level (but bear in mind that some children, for example those with autism, find eye contact very difficult).
- Remember that 'why?' questions can sound like an accusation.
- Talk respectfully to children; they know when they are being patronised.
- Be honest if you do not know something.
- If you make a mistake, apologise.

(Dickins 2011)

Early assessment and support

Early years settings and schools provide a place for children's development to be assessed and monitored, and for specialist programmes to be developed. Assessment processes for children with disabilities and their families can be a difficult experience and should be approached with sensitivity and respect and in close partnership with parents.

Education, Health and Care Plans, and Individual Education Plans

Where an early years setting wants to offer additional support for a child as a result of identifying a special educational need, this must be discussed and agreed

Guidelines for good practice

Creating an effective EHCP

Individuals matter because each of us can influence a group's efforts towards more equality.

✔ It is important to remember that, first and foremost, each child is entitled to a broad, balanced and stimulating curriculum. In the early years, this means a curriculum planned around the EYFS, with the commitments to play, learning outdoors and relationships. For this reason, you would not plan in a way that was so focused on the child's targets that there was no time for play.

✔ Plans exist to give extra help, not to take children away from the main opportunities to learn and socialise with their peers. You would not plan for the child to be so frequently removed from the main group that it was impossible to form relationships and friendships.

✔ Plans should build on the child's strengths as well as addressing difficulties. If all the focus is on what the child finds hard, life might soon become a struggle and the child might become rather demoralised. A careful balance of enjoyment and challenge is called for.

✔ Plans should be clearly written and not too long. No one can remember eight different targets in the middle of a busy day with the children.

Guidelines for good practice

Children with disabilities and their families

Provision and the setting

- Make reasonable adjustments to ensure that children (and practitioners/adults) with special needs and disabilities can participate in all activities and aspects of life.

- If a child is coming into your setting who has difficulty walking and uses a standing frame, you would need to:
  - think about whether there is enough space between the tables and equipment
  - consider where you will store the frame when it is not being used
  - consider how you will help the child to access any activities that are normally at floor-level, such as block play or a train set.

- Good early years practice includes offering children a broad and balanced curriculum, with both indoor and outdoor play opportunities. You need to think about how you can help all children to access this broad curriculum.

- If a child's parent uses a wheelchair and wants to come on a trip, you should check the accessibility of the venue and the transport you are using to get there, and make plans to ensure the parent can come in the same way as any other parent.

- It is unlawful to say that 'you cannot meet a child's needs' without any investigation of the necessary adaptations.

- Ensure that you have checked with parents/carers about any allergies or reactions that the child may have to resources/equipment in the setting, for example playdough or shaving foam.

Supporting the child

- Always encourage independence. Ask how the child wants to do things – let him or her make as many choices as possible.

- Try to imagine yourself in the child's situation. How would you like to be helped?

- Always be patient with children, particularly if communication is difficult or time-consuming.

- Try to anticipate the child's feelings. Having one's most intimate needs attended to by a stranger can be embarrassing.

- Show awareness of a child's personal rights, dignity and privacy; never allow other children to poke fun at a child with a disability.

- Develop good listening skills. Non-verbal communication is just as important as what you say.

- An open-minded and non-judgemental attitude is important, as is a warm, friendly manner.

- Praise effort rather than achievement. Provide activities that are appropriate to the child's ability, so that he or she has a chance of achieving.

- Make an effort to involve the child with other children. For example, teach all the children Makaton so that they can communicate with each other. If you are using a visual timetable, use it with all the children. Explain special needs to children: 'If you want to ask Jamal to play, use this Makaton sign because he finds it hard to understand words.' See Moving on section for more information on Makaton.

- Guidelines for behaviour should be the same for all children but with understanding of (not excuses for) a child's disability.

Supporting the family

- Support the child's parents or carers to enable them to provide a lifestyle that is as fulfilling as possible.

- Know what sort of difficulties might be experienced by the family of a child with a special need or disability. Work in a team to support the whole family; for example, by helping the child and taking time to listen to the parents and respond to their ideas.

- Understand that offering families choices and helping children with disabilities to participate fully is more helpful than showing sympathy or feeling pity.

KEY TERM

Transition – Times of change; they are part of everyday life and take place from the earliest years. Children make transitions from home to setting, within settings and from early years setting to school.

with the child's parents first. Then an EHCP needs assessment will be arranged.

This is a process for identifying and putting into place additional support for children who need, or are likely to need, more support than is available through SEN support. An EHCP identifies educational, health and social needs and sets out the additional support to meet those needs including specified outcomes for the child. The plan should enable the child to progress in their learning and, as they get older, prepare them for adult life.

Individual Education Plans (IEPs), although no longer required (as there will be an EHCP), can be a good way to promote discussion between parents and professionals, for the benefit of the child. An IEP can help parents feel that something is being done to help their child, and ensure that support is offered in a consistent way at home and in the early years setting or school. In inclusive early years settings and schools, supporting children with SEN is a team approach, not the responsibility of just one person. Although one member of staff may take the lead in supporting the child, having sole responsibility can soon become overwhelming and can also limit the child, who may feel tethered or bound to that person. A team approach balances individual and intensive support, with opportunities for the child to enjoy free-flow play (see Chapter 17) and move autonomously around the setting.

A good EHCP or IEP:

- builds on the specialist knowledge that parents have about their own children

- promotes a consistent, team approach in the early years setting or school

- has a small number of targets or goals for the child to work towards

- has targets that are specific enough to be reviewed.

Planning ahead

By seeing the child's strengths as well as difficulties in a group setting, possible future needs in school can be anticipated and planned for. If a child can start nursery or reception with appropriate additional support, equipment and plans, school will start off on a sound footing. It is at times of **transition** (see page 29 for definition) that practitioners will be in a position to act as an advocate for the child and their family.

Approaches to supporting different kinds of disability and special educational need

It is not possible to list all possible types of SEN, so here we look at those that practitioners may encounter more frequently in settings. However, as the information we can discuss here is limited, practitioners will always need to research the disability of a child in their care, finding out information from parents, other professionals and from specific reading.

It is also not always possible to put a child clearly into a single category. Many children will have needs that cross over one or more of the categories described below. Children will also have specific areas of strength in addition to their special needs.

▲ **Figure 2.3** Use of technology can help children to access learning in different ways.

Areas of development affected by disability

Communication and interaction

Most children with SEN have difficulties in one or more of the areas of communication, interaction and speech. A child might show a delay in his or her speech and language. Other children might have a speech difficulty – for example, a stammer or unclear speech – but understand language perfectly well. They might, therefore, understand what you say to them, but have difficulties in replying to you. Children who have difficulties with communication and social interaction might have features from the autistic spectrum. Hearing difficulties and specific learning difficulties like dyslexia and dyspraxia (see p. 36 for more information) also fall into this category. Children with severe or complex difficulties in this area of development may have only a small number of words they can use. They may use a system of communication to help their spoken language such as Picture Exchange Communication System (PECS), discussed below (augmentative communication), or they may use a system of communication instead of spoken language (alternative communication).

Cognition and learning

Children with difficulties in this area will find it difficult to understand new concepts, solve problems and learn skills. Children with moderate difficulties in this area will need additional support to develop their learning, possibly including additional time, repetition and practical experiences. Children with a specific difficulty include those with dyslexia (see p. 36 for more information), who have a specific difficulty learning to read, write and process some types of information, and those with dyspraxia, who have difficulties planning and coordinating sequences of actions. Children with severe or complex difficulties in their cognition and learning will need considerable help to develop early concepts like full and empty, over and under. Their play may stay at the level of sensory exploration, without moving into pretend or role play. Their communication is likely to be functional – for example, making a need known, like hunger – without the use of language for thinking.

Behaviour, emotional and social difficulties

Children with these difficulties may present as withdrawn, anxious and isolated; disruptive, aggressive and behaving in disturbing ways; lacking in concentration and hyperactive; and having difficulties in their social development – for example, around sharing attention, regulating their emotional state when in a group or cooperating with others.

Sensory and/or physical needs

Sensory difficulties can range from the profound and long-term – for example, being deaf or registered blind – to lower levels of visual and hearing impairment, which are sometimes temporary – for example, glue ear. Physical impairments can arise from physical causes – for example, lung disease might lead to a child being oxygen-dependent. They can also arise from neurological causes like cerebral palsy, which is usually caused by the failure of part of the brain to develop, leading to a loss of control over certain muscles, posture or balance.

Some children with sensory or physical needs can access most or all of their learning with appropriate support – for example, a deaf child might go to a school where BSL is used, and develop language and learning differently, but just as well as a child who can hear. Children who are blind or have visual impairments might use some or all of Braille, equipment to magnify print and pictures, and computer software that reads text out loud. Other children may have a combination of profound sensory and physical needs, with significant effects on their development.

Medical conditions

Some medical conditions can affect children's learning. The child's condition may cause him or her to become quickly tired, or may lead to frequent absences for treatment. Examples include childhood leukaemia or chronic lung disease. Other medical conditions, such as asthma or diabetes, may be adequately managed by taking medication and do not need to cause significant interference in the child's development and learning.

Different types of disability and SEN

Cerebral palsy

There is no cure for cerebral palsy (see page 21 for definition). It is a non-progressive condition, which means that it does not become more severe as the child gets older, but some difficulties may become more noticeable.

Therapy can help children with cerebral palsy. Physiotherapists, occupational therapists (individuals who support individuals to engage in daily activities) and speech therapists often work very closely together to devise a treatment programme that will meet the needs of both the child and the family. As the nature of cerebral palsy varies immensely, the therapy is adapted to the needs of the individual child.

Find out more about cerebral palsy at www.scope.org. uk or search online for 'SCOPE'.

Visual impairment

The picture of total darkness conjured up by the word 'blindness' is inaccurate: only about 18 per cent of blind people in the UK are affected to this degree; the other 82 per cent all have some remaining sight. In the UK there are just over one million blind and partially sighted people, of whom 40 per cent are blind and 60 per cent are partially sighted (or have a visual impairment).

More than 55 per cent of children who have visual impairments in education attend mainstream schools alongside sighted children. About 5 per cent attend schools for children with a visual impairment. The other 40 per cent are children who have special needs in addition to their visual impairment, and attend schools that are resourced for these additional needs – for example, schools for children with profound and multiple learning difficulties.

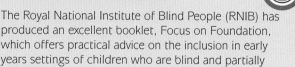

Think about ideas

The Royal National Institute of Blind People (RNIB) has produced an excellent booklet, Focus on Foundation, which offers practical advice on the inclusion in early years settings of children who are blind and partially sighted.

Find out more about people who are blind or have visual impairments at www.rnib.org.uk or search online for 'RNIB'.

Guidelines for good practice

Working with children with a visual impairment

✔ Help the child to develop all the senses – encourage exploration of materials by touch, smell and taste, allowing for plenty of time. Listening is especially important for a child with a visual impairment as a way of finding out what is going on. Babies and toddlers may seem still and uninterested; when in reality they are listening out for every sound. Remember to communicate the warmth that you would convey with a smile, with a warm tone of voice; and when the child smiles, show your warmth through words or touch.

✔ Help language development – much language development ordinarily depends on being able to see. Children see objects and hear the names of objects in daily life. You can help a baby or child with a visual impairment by naming items every time the child uses or explores them. This might include clothes, bottles, cups, cutlery and toys. But remember that all children need uninterrupted time to play and explore – do not overwhelm the child with words. Finger and other action rhymes are a fun way to associate movements and body parts with words. Audio books with interesting sound effects can be a good way into stories.

✔ Encourage exploratory play – touching and feeling objects can be scary. Encourage and soothe the child. You can introduce messy play with tiny dabs of substances, first on fingertips, and slowly building up until you judge the child is ready to dip a finger into the wet sand or shaving foam.

✔ Encourage movement – it is important to create good open spaces for babies to crawl and toddle in. Older children need opportunities to move freely inside and outside.

✔ Encourage looking – nearly all babies and young children with a visual impairment have some sight. Shiny and sparkly objects and light toys can be used to stimulate the child's vision. Hold things close to the child in good light and give plenty of time. Children's eyes will not be damaged by sitting close up to computers and televisions.

✔ Help develop independence – starting to eat solid foods is an important part of every child's development, but it is frustrating too, and all the more so for a child with a visual impairment. It is good to allow plenty of time for the child to feel food and not to worry too much about mess. A bowl or plate resting on a non-slip mat is helpful, as it is difficult to manage when things keep moving around. You will need to judge the balance between allowing for experimentation and exploration and the need for the child to eat something without becoming too frustrated.

✔ In early years settings, good natural lighting, without too much glaring artificial light, makes for the best possible environment. Well-ordered and uncluttered storage systems, and plenty of space in areas for play, will help the child with a visual impairment to get used to where things are and operate more independently. These approaches will help all children to find the setting or school an ordered and relaxing environment.

Hearing impairment

Deafness is often called 'the hidden disability', as it may not be outwardly apparent that a person has a hearing impairment. As with total blindness, total deafness is rare and is usually congenital (present from birth).

About 900 babies are born in the UK every year with a permanent hearing loss. New technology has transformed the process of early identification and treatment of babies with a hearing loss. A special computerised system called the otoacoustic test detects the sounds that the healthy ear itself makes in response to sounds.

The Newborn Hearing Screening Programme means that all babies are now screened in hospital. Following the introduction of this programme, the average age when a child is identified as being deaf is now three months. Before the universal screening of newborn children, the average age for identification was 20 months. This is a significant advance, because

an important part of the sensitive period for the development of communication and language is in the first two years of life.

Recent research has shown that many children who do not have any kind of hearing impairment have difficulties in tuning in to language and picking out words from other background noises. These children will also be helped a great deal if you follow the advice given above. This is a typical example of how inclusive practice is good for many children, not just those with a special need or disability.

You can find out more about people who are deaf or have a hearing impairment at www.actiononhearingloss.org.uk formerly RNID.

Autistic spectrum disorders

Autism is a disability that disrupts the development of social interaction and communication. Children are affected in many different ways by autism, which is why we use the term 'autistic spectrum'. The most

Guidelines for good practice

Working with children with a hearing impairment

✔ A baby with a hearing impairment may not show the 'startle' reaction or reflex to a loud noise; this is evident shortly after birth.

✔ A baby of about four months will visibly relax and smile at the sound of his or her mother's voice, even before he or she can see her; if the baby does not show this response, there may be some hearing loss.

✔ If babbling starts and then stops after a few weeks, this is often an indication of hearing loss.

✔ A child with hearing loss will be much more observant and visually aware than a hearing child – be aware that the child may respond to the ringing of doorbells and telephones by reading the body language of those around them and reacting appropriately.

✔ Toys that make a lot of noise are still popular, because children can feel the vibration, even if they cannot hear the sound; children may also dance to music for the same reason.

✔ A child with a profound hearing loss may still react quite normally, even turning round in response to someone's approach, since they may be using their other senses to compensate for the loss of hearing – for example, they may notice a smell of perfume or see the reflection of the person in a window or other reflective surface.

✔ Use your well-developed observational skills to detect hearing loss. If you do think there is a problem, refer it to the parent if you are a nanny, or to your line manager or teacher in a nursery or school.

✔ During activities, cut down on background noise – for example, from the radio or dishwasher. Use carpets, rugs and pillows to absorb excess sound.

✔ Make eye contact before you start to speak. A gentle tap on the shoulder will usually get a child's attention.

✔ Talk in a normal voice – do not shout. Use gestures and facial expressions to clarify your message.

✔ Provide headphones for music recorders or set up a special area where a music recorder can be played at a higher volume.

✔ Teach children to use gestures and sign language – for example, Sign along, Makaton or BSL.

✔ Encourage children to talk about what they are doing. Ask open-ended questions (questions that require a detailed answer), which will encourage children to practise using language.

✔ Use stories, songs and finger-play to enhance language development.

✔ Encourage dancing to music; children will feel the vibrations and enjoy the chance to express themselves.

✔ Provide children with visual cues – for example, label shelves with a picture of toys to make tidying away easier. Use pictures to illustrate the steps of a recipe during cooking activities.

✔ Find out how to look after hearing aids and how to protect them from loss or damage within the school or nursery – for example, sand and dirt can damage them.

✔ Be aware that early diagnosis and treatment can make a significant difference to the language development and learning potential of a child with a hearing impairment.

✔ Special training for staff – for example, in language acquisition, and in using BSL is recommended.

✔ If a child wears a hearing aid, it is important to remember that the aim of all hearing aids is to amplify or intensify sounds but in amplifying sounds, distortion also increases. Children wearing hearing aids in early years settings and schools may hear a loud din of background noises, which can be very stressful.

seriously affected children have profound learning disabilities and delayed language, and will need intensive support and care. At the other end of the spectrum, children with **Asperger's syndrome** may manage the intellectual demands of schooling very well, although they will still find aspects of social interaction and communication difficult.

Early years settings and schools can be difficult places for children with an ASD. A lot of early learning is based on language and play, two areas of great difficulty for a child with an ASD. The noise and amount of visual stimulation from displays and boxes of equipment can quickly become overwhelming. In this context, a child with an ASD might gain some feeling of security by rigidly following the same

sequences of activity, or repeating the same action over again. While it is important not to deprive a child under stress of actions that provide some comfort, constant repetition is not the basis for successful development and learning, and the child will need

KEY TERM

Asperger's syndrome – People with Asperger's syndrome have difficulties with social communication, social interaction and social imagination. There are diagnostic differences between conditions on the autism spectrum. Sometimes people may receive a diagnosis of autism or ASD, high-functioning autism (HFA) or atypical autism instead of Asperger syndrome.

Displays indifference

Joins in only if adult insists and assists

One-sided interaction

Indicates needs by using an adult's hand

Does not play with other children

Talks incessantly about only one topic

- Difficulty with social relationships
- Difficulty with verbal communication
- Difficulty with non-verbal communication
- Difficulty in the development of play and imagination
- Resistance to change in routine

Bizarre behaviour

Echolalic-copies words like parrot

Inappropriate laughing or giggling

Handles or spins objects

No eye contact

Variety is not the spice of life

Lack of creative, pretend play

But some can do some things very well, very quickly; but *not* tasks involving social understanding

◀ **Figure 2.4** Some characteristics of a child with autism

Guidelines for good practice

Working with children with an autistic spectrum disorder

✔ **Visual learning is stronger than language-based learning or learning through exploratory play** – putting things into symbols really helps children with an ASD. A visual timetable, showing the main sequence of events and routines in the day, can help the child to understand what is going to happen next. Symbols that the child can pick up or point to, in order to make choices and express preferences, will aid early communication.

✔ **Reduce visual stimulation** – keep displays and labels orderly: pictures all over the windows and labels at jaunty angles can be visually overwhelming. Have some places with blank walls, which can be calming.

✔ **Keep everything as clear and consistent as you can** – while for most children a sudden announcement of a trip or a special activity is fun, for many children with an ASD such changes in routine are very scary.

As far as possible, keep routines consistent and alert the child when something is about to happen by using symbols or the visual timetable. When something new is coming up, try to prepare the child as much as you can. You might have a symbol that means 'a change', or be able to use a photograph to signal what is going to happen. Use as few words and as few symbols as possible: communicate clearly and briefly.

✔ **Show how things work** – a child with an ASD can be helped when adults show, step by step, how to put Lego bricks together, or model pretending to eat in the home corner. Allow plenty of time and encourage the child to copy you.

✔ **Introduce new things slowly** – sensory play can be very difficult. Start with just a very brief attempt, and introduce materials in small amounts in areas of low distraction. To encourage sand play, for example, start in a quiet zone, without any children, and encourage the child to touch a small amount of sand on a tabletop or on the floor.

skilled and sensitive support to interact with others and to extend his or her interests.

Read the Early Support guides at www.education.gov. uk and search for 'Early Support'.

Find out more about people with autistic spectrum disorders at www.nas.org.uk or search online for 'NAS'.

Speech and language difficulties

Children with a speech and language impairment have difficulties with:

- talking (expressive language)
- understanding (receptive language)
- both of the above.

More than one million schoolchildren in the UK have a speech and language difficulty of some sort. For some, this is a delay – their language is developing, but more slowly than usual. In some cases, this may be connected with a hearing impairment, such as glue ear, in early childhood. For others, with a language disorder, the difficulty may be more complex. They may know lots of words, but may get words in the wrong order and have difficulties understanding and taking part in conversations. Often, speech and language disorders are associated with other special needs, like autism.

Yet another group of children has a specific difficulty with language, sometimes called dysphasia. These children do not stammer or lisp, and are not autistic. Their general intelligence is often average or above. Their language impairment is specific or primary – not the result of any other disability.

The cause of delayed speech and language may be environmental – to do with the amount of opportunities the child has had to communicate and talk with others from an early age.

Speech and language difficulties can also be caused by a health problem or by delayed physical development. This can be due to dyspraxia (difficulty in planning and making the movements which produce speech; see below) or delayed muscle development in the mouth, lips, tongue and palate.

The Every Child a Talker (ECAT) programme sought to support language development for all children, with an emphasis on those who may be at risk of language delay. As learning becomes increasingly language-based

---

Guidelines for good practice

Working with children with delayed speech, language and communication

✔ Evaluate your early years setting – find out where the most communication takes place. Which are the areas of least communication? Think about how you could act on your findings – for example, if there is almost no talk in the computer area, you might need to think about programmes and activities that require children to collaborate and talk together. If it is too noisy to talk in the block area because it is right by the door, you could move it or make it quieter by using curtains or other sound-absorbing barriers. ECAT can help you here, with the section on assessing the environment to identify what they call 'talking hotspots (places where adults and children engage in conversation or where children talk to each other). Remember that some children communicate best when outdoors, or when you take them out to the shop or on the bus – it does not all happen indoors.

✔ Careful consideration and assessment – regularly record children's language and include what they say in your observations, or use audio or video recordings. Compare what they are saying with the expected levels

of development (see Chapter 5). Identify which children need extra help with communication from you and the other staff.

✔ Work closely with your local speech and language therapy service and early years advisory team – often they are only too pleased to come and offer training and development.

✔ Observe each other – what strategies encourage children to talk? How can the whole team build on the good practice you observe? If there is a high level of trust among staff, you could video each other listening to and talking with children. There is more guidance on this in the ECAT programme, together with some helpful case studies.

✔ If you are concerned about a child's development in this area, talk to the parent about your worries – sometimes children are very quiet and uncommunicative in nursery or school, but good communicators at home with family and friends. Think about how you can make the child feel more confident. If the difficulties are similar, recommend a referral to speech and language therapy for further checking.

when children move through primary school, it is important to offer this help early.

But remember that the following are not signs of a language delay or communication difficulty:

- Speaking little in nursery, because the child may be learning English as an additional language, for example.
- Speaking in a different accent or using a different dialect to most other children or adults in the early years setting or school.
- Having a different pattern of communication to that which is expected or usually valued by staff and other professionals. Remember that some children are not good at answering direct questions, for example, because the pattern of communication in their home may be more about discussing things together.

To find out more about speech and language difficulties, search for 'Every Child a Talker' and you will find a range of useful documents.

Developmental dyspraxia

Dyspraxia is developmental disorder of the brain resulting in messages not being properly transmitted to the body. It affects at least 2 per cent of the population in varying degrees, and 70 per cent of those affected are male. Dyspraxia is a specific learning difficulty; this means that it does not affect a person's overall intelligence or ability in general, only specific aspects. Children with dyspraxia can be of average or above intelligence, but are often behaviourally immature. They try hard to fit in with the range of socially accepted behaviour when at school, but often throw tantrums when at home. They may find it difficult to understand logic and reason. Dyspraxia is a disability, but, as with autism, those affected do not 'look' disabled. This is both an advantage and a disadvantage. Sometimes children with dyspraxia are labelled as 'clumsy' children. Such labelling is very unhelpful.

The Dyspraxia Foundation has further information: http://www.dyspraxiafoundation.org.uk/about-dyspraxia/

Dyslexia

Dyslexia is another specific learning difficulty, with particular impact on the child's language.

There are many children who will fit into some, or most of the categories that define dyslexia. It is important to offer children continued support, to observe closely, to work with parents and to involve a specialist – for example, an educational psychologist – if necessary. Early years practitioners should avoid

jumping to conclusions or applying a label to a child prematurely.

The British Dyslexia Association (BDA) describes the indicators of dyslexia in the young child: www.bdadyslexia.org.uk

Attention deficit hyperactivity disorder

Attention deficit hyperactivity disorder (ADD/ADHD) is another specific learning difficulty. Children with ADHD show problems with focusing their attention and, at the same time, hyperactivity. If the difficulties generally present on their own, the child probably does not have ADHD. Some children may appear hyperactive in early years settings and schools because they need to move around to learn: in response to long carpet times and circle times, they may become fidgety and frustrated. Others may have poor capacity to direct their attention because they have experienced neglect in early childhood – for example, no one has interacted with them regularly, so they have not become used to focusing their attention.

The cause of ADHD is not known, but there is some evidence to suggest that a pattern of hyperactivity is inherited. There may also be a biological cause, perhaps due to a slower metabolism of glucose by the brain. Treatment may be by a stimulant medication (usually Ritalin), which often has an immediate improving effect on the child's behaviour but is a controversial treatment. Arriving at the correct dosage for the individual takes time and a high degree of cooperation between the parents and other professionals. It is generally agreed that medical treatment on its own is not an appropriate response to ADHD, and should be combined with therapeutic input:

For example:

- art therapy
- occupational therapy or counselling for older children
- a programme to help with managing behaviour, setting clear limits, helping children anticipate difficulties and find their own ways of coping – for example, taking a moment or two out, or engaging in something calming
- sometimes lifestyle changes – for example, watching less television, spending less time on computers and electronic games, taking more exercise, and eating more healthily.

Behavioural, emotional and social difficulties

Behavioural, emotional and social difficulty (BESD) is classed as a special educational need; in many cases, a child with a BESD will also be considered to fall within the remit of the Equality Act 2010. This means that the child must not be treated less favourably than others, and that reasonable adaptations must be made to support the child's inclusion in an early years setting or school.

BESD covers a very wide range of special needs, including:

- conduct disorders – where a child has difficulties following instructions and keeping to rules
- hyperkinetic disorders – for example, attention deficit disorder or ADD/ADHD
- other syndromes – for example, Tourette's, which can cause a child to have vocal tics (repeating the same words, echoing words or compulsive swearing) and physical tics (continual eye-blinking and throat-clearing, for example)
- other disorders – for example, anxiety, school phobia (being afraid to go to school), self-harming or depression.

Some children will have a medical diagnosis, but this is not necessarily the case.

As with many special needs, BESD can be prompted by a difficulty that is within a child or, equally, by environmental, cultural or family factors. For example, a child who has been shouted at and physically hurt by his or her parents may respond by behaving in an aggressive way towards others, and may have little self-control and resort swiftly to violence. A child may present with a severe conduct disorder in an early years setting where there is a degree of structure that the child is not developmentally ready for. The difficulties might then recede in a setting where there is a clear and firm management of behaviour, together with opportunities for children to play, make choices, and to move freely inside and outside.

There are more children diagnosed with BESD in socially deprived areas, and there are many more boys diagnosed with BESD than girls. BESD which results in difficult or aggressive behaviour is the most likely to be noticed, so it is important for practitioners also to consider the needs of anxious and withdrawn children, and those who are nervous or phobic about coming into early years settings and schools.

Guidelines for good practice

Working with a child with BESD

✔ Develop a positive relationship with the child, following the principles of the key person approach.

✔ Ensure that your policy and practice in managing children's behaviour combines an approach which takes account of children's different rates of development, while setting clear boundaries for all children and helping them to learn self-discipline.

✔ Think about how you can reduce the number of people who intervene when the child's behaviour is difficult. If a child is constantly told off by a range of staff, behaviour is unlikely to improve. The child is likely to respond with further negativity and difficult behaviour. Behaviour management should be coordinated by the key person, in the context of a positive relationship.

✔ As a team, decide together what behaviour you can ignore, and what behaviour is unsafe or unacceptable in all cases. Work consistently and remember that improvement is likely to be in small steps.

✔ Help other children to be assertive in the face of aggressive or bullying behaviour, but remember that it is ultimately the adult's responsibility to ensure that children feel safe and secure.

✔ Develop a positive relationship with the child's parents. By working together, you can help the child effectively. Parents will have valuable information and ideas to share with you, regarding the triggers and causes of their child's difficult behaviour and emotional outbursts. But if they feel that they are being 'told off' for the child's behaviour, the relationship will quickly deteriorate. If you are giving the parent feedback on the child's day, carefully consider time and place. No parent wants to be told of their child's difficult behaviour in the corridor or in public; and remember that you are giving feedback and seeking the parent's cooperation, not offloading the stresses of a difficult day.

✔ Work closely with specialist services – educational psychology and Child and Adolescent Mental Health Services (CAMHS). You cannot meet the child's needs on your own.

✔ If the child's difficulties arise in part, or mainly, from family or environmental circumstances, you will need to work collaboratively with a range of professionals using the Common Assessment Framework (CAF), and you may need to make a referral to Children's Social Care if you think the child is in immediate danger. CAF is an early help inter-agency assessment. It offers a basis for early identification of children's additional needs, the sharing of this information between organisations and the coordination of service provision.

✔ All staff need time to talk about the difficulties the child presents, and the child's key person will need particular support.

Legislation relating to children with special needs and disabilities

For legislation relating to children with special needs and disabilities, see Chapter 1, pages 3–5.

For legislation relating to children with special needs and disabilities, see Chapter 1, pages 3–5.

Think about ideas

Find out more about helping children in the EYFS with behavioural, emotional and social difficulties: search online for 'Inclusion Development Programme: Supporting children with Behavioural, Emotional and Social Difficulties' or http://www.sebda.org. SEBDA have produced a Well-being Toolkit in partnership with the Nurture group Network: www.nurturegroups.org

Moving on

Techniques that support all children

To create inclusive environments and to support listening to young children with disabilities together with all children, it is useful to enhance the ways in which you communicate with children in your setting.

Makaton

Makaton is a set of signs that are used to support spoken language. Unlike BSL, Makaton is not a language in itself. The Makaton vocabulary is a list of over 400 items with corresponding signs and symbols, with an additional resource vocabulary for the UK national curriculum. The Makaton Charity publishes a book of illustrations of the Makaton vocabulary. Most signs rely on movement as well as position, so you cannot really learn the signs from the illustrations. Also, in many signs, facial expression is important. If a child at a school or nursery is learning Makaton, the parents should be invited to learn too. The Makaton Charity will support schools and parents in this, as they know that everyone involved with the child must use the same signs.

See http://www.makaton.org.

Picture Exchange Communication System (PECS)

The PECS begins with teaching children to exchange a picture of a desired item with a teacher, who immediately honours the request – for example, if the child wants a drink, he or she will give a picture of 'drink' to an adult, who directly hands the child a drink. Verbal prompts are not used, thus encouraging spontaneity and avoiding prompt dependency. The system goes on to teach discrimination of symbols and how to construct simple 'sentences'. Ideas for teaching commenting and other language structures, such as asking and answering questions, are also incorporated. It has been reported that both pre-school and older children have begun to develop speech when using PECS. The system is often used as a communication aid for children and adults who have an autistic spectrum disorder.

See http://pecs-unitedkingdom.com.

Objects of reference

Some children are unable to associate a symbol – for example, a picture or sign – with a real thing in the world. In order to help their communication, adults can use 'objects of reference'. This will often start with encouraging the child to make a choice between two real objects. For example, you might say to a child, 'Do you want an orange?' and show the orange, then withdraw the orange from sight and say, 'Do you want an apple?' and show the apple. You would then repeat and follow up an indication of choice – for example, pointing or looking. So if a child made a movement when you showed the apple, you would then give the child a piece of apple.

It is important to follow through consistently, so that the child experiences this or her communication leading to a choice. In time, this will allow the child to start expressing choices.

Objects of reference may be developed into a larger system – for example, you might have a display that shows a small amount of sand in a jar (sand play), a cup (drink/snack), a Lego brick (construction play) and some grass (outdoor play). By pointing to the appropriate object, the child can make a choice about what he or she wishes to do next.

See http://www.communicationmatters.org.uk.

Think about ideas

Research the three approaches identified above and make a plan for introducing one into your setting. Discuss the benefits with your colleagues or study group.

The use of a sensory curriculum for profound needs

All teachers differentiate the framework/curriculum (that is, they provide different learning experiences) in order to meet the range of needs in their class. Children who are multisensory-impaired are likely to need the curriculum differentiated individually, because each child's combination of hearing impairment, visual impairment, other disabilities and learning characteristics will be different.

Some settings have a multisensory room which provides opportunities for children with a wide range of special needs. This room features a variety of lights, smells, sounds and touch sensations which help to stimulate each sense. Staff need to be trained in the use of a sensory room so that it works optimally for each child.

Further reading, weblinks and resources

Dickins, M (2014) *A – Z of Inclusion in Early Childhood*. Maidenhead: OUP / McGraw Hill Education.
Roffey, S and Parry, J (2014) *Special Needs in the Early Years: Supporting Collaboration, Communication and Co-ordination*. Oxon: Routledge.
Wall, K (2011) *Special Needs and Early Years: A Practitioner Guide*. London: Sage.

Department for Education

Guidelines for early years settings:
https://www.gov.uk/government/publications/send-guide-for-early-years-settings

British Dyslexia Association (BDA)

The BDA is a national charity working for a 'dyslexia-friendly society' that enables dyslexic people of all ages to reach their full potential.
www.bdadyslexia.org.uk

Department for Children, Schools and Families

The National Strategies Early Years, 2010, *Inclusion Development Programme Supporting Children with Behavioural, Emotional and Social Difficulties: Guidance for Practitioners in the Early Years Foundation Stage*. London: DCSF Publications
www.foundationyears.org.uk/eyfs-statutory-framework

The Dyspraxia Foundation

A national charity supporting children and adults with Dyspraxia.
www.dyspraxiafoundation.org.uk

Early Support

An example of good practice can be found here:
https://www.gov.uk/government/publications/a-partnership-approach-to-early-help-for-families-in-need-of-support

Equality Act 2010

This Act brings together all the legislation which makes it illegal to discriminate on the grounds of sex, gender, race, sexuality, age or disability.
http://www.legislation.gov.uk/ukpga/2010/15/contents

Every Child a Talker (ECAT)

The ECAT programme supported children's communication and language by focusing on developing an enabling environment and encouraging early years practitioners to listen to children and engage in conversation with them. The programme documents are now archived but can be accessed here:
http://webarchive.nationalarchives.gov.uk

National Autistic Society (NAS)

The NAS aims to champion the rights and interests of all people with autism, and to provide individuals with autism and their families with help, support and services.
www.nas.org.uk

Royal National Institute of Blind People (RNIB)

The RNIB is the UK's leading charity offering information, support and advice to over two million people with sight loss.
www.rnib.org.uk

Action on Hearing Loss formerly (RNID)

Action on Hearing Loss is the new name of RNID and is the largest charity in the UK offering a range of services for people who are deaf or have a hearing impairment, and providing information and support on all aspects of deafness, hearing loss and tinnitus.
www.actiononhearingloss.org.uk

Scope

Scope is a charity that supports people with disabilities and their families. Its vision is a world where people with disabilities have the same opportunities as everyone else. Scope specialises in working with people who have cerebral palsy.
www.scope.org.uk

SEBDA: Supporting the Social, Emotional and Mental Health of our Children and Young People.

SEBDA is a charitable organisation (registered charity number 258730), which exists to promote excellence in services for children and young people who have social, emotional and behavioural difficulties.
http://www.sebda.org

References

Clark, A., 2011, *Listening as a way of Life*, London: National Children's Bureau, The Young Children's Voices Network. Available at: http://www.ncb.org.uk/media/74018/an_introduction_to_why_and_how_we_listen_to_very_young_children.pdf.

Department for Education, 2015, *The Special Educational Needs and Disability Code of Practice*, available at: www.gov.uk/government/publications.

Dickins, M., with Denziloe, J., 2004, *All Together: How to Create Inclusive Services for Disabled Children and their Families. A Practical Handbook for Early Years Workers*, London: National Children's Bureau.

Dickins, M., 2011, *Listening to Young Disabled Children*, London: National Children's Bureau, The Young Children's Voices Network. Available at: http://www.ncb.org.uk/media/74018/an_introduction_to_why_and_how_we_listen_to_very_young_children.pdf.

Dickins, M., 2014, *A–Z of Inclusion in Early Childhood*, Maidenhead: Open University Press/McGraw-Hill Education.

Smith, C. and Teasdale, S., 2003, *Let's Sign Early Years: BSL Child and Carer Guide*, Bolton: Co-sign Communications.

Stobbs, P., 2015, *Disabled Children and the Equality Act 2010: What Early Years providers need to know and do, including responsibilities to disabled children under the Children and Families Act 2014*, London: Council for Disabled Children/ NCB.

Sylva, K., Melhuish, E.C., Sammons, P., Siraj, I. and Taggart, B., 2004, *The Effective Provision Of Pre-school Education (EPPE): Final Report*, London: DfES/Institute of Education, University of London.

Chapter 3

Working in partnership with parents and carers

Working in partnership with children's parents and other carers is a fundamentally important aspect of professional practice in early years practice. This chapter discusses issues that need to be considered when families are new to a setting and offers guidance on sharing information between practitioners and parents. We also consider different ways of involving parents in the life of the setting according to their needs and discuss some of the challenges that may arise when practitioners and parents have differing views. Addressing these successfully depends on good communication and practitioners having a clear understanding of their own values, so the chapter starts with a discussion about ideas about families and parenting.

Understanding the concept of 'family', roles and responsibilities of parents, and factors affecting family life

Different family structures

The starting point for working successfully in partnership with parents is for practitioners to be clear about their attitudes and ideas about what a family is and how it functions.

Children in early years settings and schools are likely to come from a range of family structures, including:

- children whose parents are married or in a civil partnership
- children whose parents live together, but are not married (cohabiting parents)
- children being brought up by a lone parent (usually, but not always, a mother) following a relationship breakdown
- children with a single parent who has chosen to have and bring up a child without a partner
- children in reconstituted families; where only one adult is a biological parent to the child, and where there may be children living together who have different biological parents. One of the parents in a family like this may be called a step-parent

- looked-after children living with foster parents; usually children who have been taken into care by the local authority for safeguarding reasons and placed with a foster parent or parents in the short or medium term
- children living in a family in a private fostering arrangement; when a child under the age of 16 is cared for by someone who is not their parent or a close relative for more than 28 days, as part of a private arrangement made between the parent and the carer
- children who live with their parents and members of their extended family all together
- children who live with grandparents or aunts and uncles
- children who have no siblings and no or few cousins
- children with many siblings and cousins.

The parents referred to above may be heterosexual, bisexual, lesbian or gay.

The traditional idea of the 'nuclear family'; that is, a heterosexual adult couple with dependent children has become idealised in our society, even though historically it did not always exist and even today, it does not represent the majority of families internationally (Clark 2010). In the UK today, two in every three marriages ends in a divorce, almost half of all children are born to unmarried parents, and a quarter of all children now live in a family headed by a lone parent.

There is not one way that a family 'should' be. Research shows that what matters in terms of children's health and well-being is not the structure but the quality of the relationships within the family (Golombok 2000). Children's life chances and outcomes are affected more by their relative wealth or poverty than their family form.

However, the idea of the 'nuclear family' has dominated policy and practice in the UK, so early years practitioners and settings should be aware of how this impacts on their thinking and practices. To take a more open approach it may be useful for practitioners to think about, 'who are the people around this child? Who interacts with them and affects how they are?' This may give a more inclusive view of who is significant in the child's family.

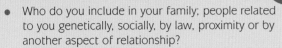

Think about ideas

- Who do you include in your family; people related to you genetically, socially, by law, proximity or by another aspect of relationship?
- Choose three children at random. Who is important to them? Do you know who the key people in their family are?
- What are your views of different kinds of families? Do you think differently about large or small families? Single or two-parent families? Families with heterosexual or homosexual parents? Poor or rich families?

Parent roles and responsibilities

In all family set-ups, parents will have a central role in their children's lives. Parents:

- are the first and most enduring carers and educators of their child
- know and understand their own child best
- have specific legal responsibilities towards their child
- give their child a strong sense of identity and belonging.

'Parental responsibility'

The Children Act 1989 (later updated 2004) replaced the term 'parental rights' with '**parental responsibility**'. Parents have responsibility for all aspects of a child's upbringing and welfare. While the law does not define in detail what parental responsibility is, the list below covers the key elements:

- physical and emotional care of the child
- naming the child and agreeing to any change of name
- ensuring that the child receives a full-time education, suited to his or her needs and abilities
- maintaining the child and providing a home
- disciplining the child
- consenting to the child being medically examined or receiving medical treatment
- accompanying the child on visits outside the UK and agreeing to the child's emigration, if that issue arises
- responsibility for the child's property
- appointing a guardian for the child, if necessary
- consenting to a private fostering arrangement (in which the child is cared for by a person who is not a close relative)
- allowing confidential information about the child to be shared and discussed by others.

KEY TERM

Parental responsibility – The legal conferment of responsibilities for a child on an adult.

Some aspects of parental responsibility require the consent of both parents of the child. These include:

- the authority to agree to the child being adopted
- the authority to remove the child from the UK.

Who has parental responsibility?

The mother always has automatic parental responsibility.

The father has parental responsibility if he was married to the mother at the time of the birth of the child. This is also true for a lesbian parent if they were married or in a civil partnership with the mother when the child was born.

An unmarried father (or lesbian or gay partner) has parental responsibility if the birth was jointly registered by both parents (from December 2003), or if he is named on a parental responsibility agreement made by a court.

The Children Act 1989 does not create any rights of consultation between a child's parents before action is taken in respect of a child. On the contrary, the Act says that each person with parental responsibility may act independently in meeting that responsibility, except where the law requires consent (e.g. adoption). Because of this, parental responsibility is no guarantee of cooperation. If the child is living with the mother, for example, a father with parental responsibility may find it very frustrating that he does not have to be involved in decisions regarding the child. If he disagrees very strongly with what the mother is doing, he has to apply to the court for either a 'prohibited steps order' or a 'specific issue order'.

- Parental responsibility is not lost as a result of separation or divorce.
- Parental responsibility cannot be surrendered or transferred. It can, however, be temporarily delegated or entrusted to someone else.
- Parental responsibility is not lost when another person acquires it. Rather parental responsibility is then shared. This is so even when a local authority acquires parental responsibility under a care order.
- Parental responsibility is lost when an adoption order is made; otherwise, it is lost only in exceptional circumstances.

The Children Act 2004 did not replace or change much of the 1989 version. However, it placed additional responsibilities on local authorities and partners to work together to safeguard and promote the well-being of children and young people.

Families and communities

Up to this point, we have discussed the structure of families as something that is determined by individual choices and actions. However, family life is also very much affected by external, social and economic forces, and by the wider culture. This is particularly the case in relation to wealth and poverty.

The Child Poverty Action group identify that the UK has a very high rate of **child poverty**: four million children (one in three) are currently affected. This is one of the highest levels in the industrialised world.

Children growing up in poverty are significantly more likely to:

- live in poor, overcrowded housing
- live in families where the worry about getting through each day and each week without running short of money can lead to high levels of stress and anxiety, reducing opportunities to enjoy family life (Jones et al. 2013).

Poorer neighbourhoods are significantly more likely to:

- have comparatively high levels of crime, especially violent crime
- have play areas of poor quality and vandalism, which may deter children and families from using them.

Taken together, the impact of poverty on a child's life chances can be substantial – for example:

- Children from poorer backgrounds lag behind at all stages of education.
- By the age of three, poorer children are estimated to be, on average, nine months behind children from more wealthy backgrounds.
- According to Department for Education statistics, by the end of primary school, pupils receiving free school meals are estimated to be almost three terms behind their more affluent peers.
- Children from low-income families often forgo events that most of us would take for granted. They may miss school trips, cannot invite friends round for tea, and cannot afford a one-week holiday away from home, for example.

Sometimes older people comment that although they were poor when they were young, they were happy because they did not know any different. There are two issues to think about here:

1 The middle part of the twentieth century was a time of great social mobility, when chances to improve your life situation were greater than they are now.

2 It is the gap between relative poverty and wealth that has the greatest impact on well-being. The gap between rich and poor in the UK has widened considerably in recent times, resulting in the well-being of children in the UK being amongst the lowest in Europe (Layard and Dunn 2009).

Asset-based community development

The facts about the impact of child poverty can make it seem that poorer neighbourhoods are hopeless places for children and their families which need to be fixed by large-scale government intervention. But it is very difficult to plan a programme for a particular community from central government offices in Whitehall. Such programmes are often rather disappointing, costing a great deal, but delivering few positive results.

An alternative approach is **asset-based community development** (Russell 2015). This approach builds on the strengths of neighbourhoods and communities, rather than just focusing on the problems and what is lacking. When working with parents, asset-based community development highlights the importance of:

- Finding out what the skills and capabilities of the parent group are – in every neighbourhood, however impoverished, there will be parents with skills in finance who can help run budgets; parents with practical skills in making clothes, cooking, gardening; and parents who are good with ICT. Other parents will have a good way with people, and will be able to organise meetings or distribute leaflets to local flats and houses.

KEY TERMS

Child poverty – There is no single agreed definition for 'child poverty' in the UK. But it is generally understood to describe a child living in a family that lacks the resources that would enable the child to participate in activities and have housing and material goods that are customary in the UK. Child poverty does not necessarily have to mean lacking physical necessities, like food and clothing.

Asset-based community development – An approach to community development which aims to discover and use the strengths already available in a local community. This is understood as a way of giving choice and power to local communities. It is in contrast to the usual model of trying to establish what is wrong in a community, and send people in (more social workers, more police) to fix it.

- Building on existing community groups and organisations – many neighbourhoods have a church, mosque or temple that is well attended, or a thriving community group, club or association. These organisations may offer help and advice to families with young children.
- Linking with and helping to improve local services – for example, health centres, schools and hospitals.

The Igbo tribe, who live in Nigeria, have a saying which roughly translates as, 'It takes a village to raise a child'. All local communities have the potential to offer better life chances to young children and early years provision has an important role to play here. The Mental Health Foundation (1999) says that one of the protective community factors that support children's mental health and resilience is good-quality early years provision.

Support available for families

Financial help for families with young children

Every parent is entitled to receive Child Benefit for children under the age of 16 years. Although this used to be a universal, tax-free payment, recent policy changes by the Government mean that if one of the parents earn over £50,000 p.a., they can only receive a taxed benefit.

There are also targeted benefits for families. To receive these, the family's income is assessed to find out if they are eligible for financial support. These means-tested benefits include:

- Sure Start Maternity Grant – this is a one-off payment to help pay for things needed for a new baby. To qualify for a Sure Start Maternity Grant there must be no other children in your family and you must already be in receipt of certain benefit payments. The Sure Start programme was launched in the late 1990s but still continues in the form of children's centres around the country.
- Child Tax Credit – If you are on a low income, you can get Child Tax Credit for each child you are responsible for if they are under 16 or under 20 and in approved education or training.
- Families with children with disabilities may also be eligible for extra Child Tax Credit for each child with disabilities they are responsible for or they may be able to receive Disability Living Allowance for children.
- Full-time higher education students with children can apply for a Childcare Grant. The grant helps with childcare costs for children under 15, or under 17 if they have special educational needs.

- Working Tax Credit – you can receive this if either of the following apply:
  - you are aged from 16 to 24 and have a child or a qualifying disability
  - you are 25 or over, with or without children.
  You must:
  - work a certain number of hours a week
  - get paid for the work you do (or expect to)
  - have an income below a certain level.
- Child maintenance – the Child Support Agency (CSA) is part of the Department for Work and Pensions (DWP). The CSA's role is to make sure that a parent who lives apart from his or her child contributes financially to the child's upkeep by paying child maintenance. Child maintenance is money paid to help cover the child's everyday living costs. The parent with whom the child does not normally live (the non-resident parent) is responsible for paying child maintenance to the parent or other person, such as a grandparent or a guardian, with whom the child normally lives.

These benefit payments are constantly being changed, for further and updated information visit: https://www.gov.uk/browse/childcare-parenting.

Community information for families

Families need information about a wide range of topics and, as an early years practitioner, you may be required to advise them on where they can access information. Much information can be gained from the media – radio, television and newspapers. The internet is also a valuable source of information, but not every family has easy access to computing and internet connections. The sources of information generally available are listed below.

Public library

This will usually have internet services, local information about a wide range of services for children and families, and also a reference section, with books giving information on benefits and other government services.

Citizens' Advice Bureau

Most towns have a Citizens' Advice Bureau (CAB); rural areas may have to access one by telephone. They offer independent legal and financial support.

Family and childcare information services

Local authorities provide information for parents about the range and costs of childcare in their area, often through local children's centres. The central government website (www.childcarelink.gov.uk) has links to all local authorities. Parents without internet access could write directly to their local authority for printed information.

Reflecting on practice

Partnership working

A mother comes to the setting to collect her child in the afternoon. She reads the weekly menu and looks angry and upset. You ask if anything is the matter, and she says, 'I've had enough. I've just been at the doctor's with Rhianna and been told to cut out cakes and puddings to help her weight. But I can see here that they have cake, custard and all sorts for pudding in nursery.' You try to explain that the nursery's menus have been checked with the dietician and that each meal is properly balanced, but she storms off.

- Think about why early years practitioners should work closely with healthcare professionals in order to help in a situation like this. Discuss your ideas with another learner or in a group.
- How should you have handled the situation differently?

Reflecting on practice

Taking a parent's view

If you are a parent, you can draw on your own experience for this exercise. If you are not a parent, you might either talk to a friend or relative who is, or imagine things as far as you can, from a parent's point of view.

- Why might a parent choose childcare?
- What are the things that might influence a parent's decision about using childcare?
- What help and support do you want from government policy as a parent?
- What community facilities best help and support you as a parent?

Benefits Agency

Most large towns have a Benefits Agency office with a wide range of leaflets – often printed in different languages – and experienced staff to explain what is available. The central government website offers general information on benefit payments: https://www.gov.uk/browse/benefits.

Early Support

Early Support is a Government programme for coordinated, family-focused services for young children with disabilities and their families in local authorities, hospitals and community-based health services across England. See Chapter 2 for more information.

Choosing childcare

The last Labour Government's 10-year childcare strategy was entitled 'Choice for Parents, the Best Start for Children' (HM Treasury 2004). This emphasis on choice is often heard but in reality even parents who we may think choose their childcare arrangements freely, in fact often do not get the type of childcare they wanted originally and many find themselves using the type they wanted least (Leach et al. 2006). This can impact on their levels of satisfaction with the setting.

Other parents have no choice at all; they may have been required to bring their child to a setting as part of a care plan to safeguard the child. This too will impact on how the parent views the setting and the practitioners. The recent Government initiative to fund places in early years settings for vulnerable two-year-olds (DfE 2011) means that many of these families, if not required to bring their child to a setting, will have

been strongly advised to do so and, by implication, they will have been given the message that their parenting is lacking in some way.

Parents choose different kinds of childcare and early education for many different reasons:

- Some parents want full-time childcare so that they can work, because they positively want to work.
- Other parents want full-time childcare because they have to work, for economic reasons.
- Some parents want part-time childcare. They may want their child to move in a wider social circle and to have new and interesting experiences away from them. And some parents need personal space away from their child for part of the day. This may be while the family adjusts to a new baby or while the parent catches up with chores or simply relaxes. It may also be because the parent's health means that looking after a child full-time is difficult.
- Other parents will want settings where they can join in with their child – perhaps not every day, but regularly.

Developing a partnership with parents

The EYFS places a specific duty on early years settings to build relationships with parents. The EYFS states that there should be a 'strong partnership between practitioners and/or carers'.

The ability to work closely with parents and to develop positive relationships with them is a key professional skill of the early years practitioner. Such relationships are built on respect and clear, regular, two-way communication.

If the partnership between parents, staff and child is going to develop well, each needs to be able to trust

▲ **Figure 3.1** Effective parent-practitioner partnerships are built on respect and clear, regular, two-way communication

and respect the other. The self-esteem and well-being of the people in the partnership are important when they are working together.

Early years practitioners need to bear in mind the following:

- Every family is different, with different needs and traditions.
- Parents generally want to do the best for their child, even if they are not always sure what this might be.

- Each one of us only really knows what it is like to grow up in our own family. Parents are likely to think fondly of some of the things about their own family and the way they were brought up; but they will just as certainly wish that other aspects of their upbringing had been different.
- Parents usually welcome help when trying out some alternative ways of doing things. They will not want to change too much, though, and they will not want rapid changes forced on them by other people. Early years practitioners need to respect parents' wishes.

Guidelines for good practice

Working with parents

✔ **Support parents** – begin by seeing yourself as a resource and support that can be used by parents to further their child's best interests.

✔ **Respect all parents** – the vast majority of parents love their children. It is important not to judge parents, and to respect their good intentions. Almost every parent wants to do the job well, even if on the surface they may not seem to be interested or loving.

✔ **Recognise the good intentions of parents** – work positively, with this understanding as a central focus. Concentrating on the good intentions of parents helps to give them a positive self-image.

Just as children need positive images reflected about themselves, so do parents. The attitude of the staff must therefore be to show parents respect; it is hard bringing up a child.

✔ **Reinforce the parents' sense of dignity and self-esteem** – showing parents respect and reinforcing their dignity demonstrates to them that their child also needs respect and a sense of dignity.

✔ **Use your experience** – if you are not a parent, you will not have experienced some of the things that parents have. If you are a parent, you will only know about being a parent of your own child; you will not know what it is like to be a parent of other people's children or their particular circumstances.

- All parents, whatever their sociocultural background, will need some support at some point in their parenting career.

Beginning the partnership and building trust

Parents and practitioners have one thing in common that is very important: they all want the best for the child. However, they have different but complementary roles and relationships with children:

- Staff have knowledge of general child development.
- Parents know their own child best.

The parent is a deeply important person to the child, and the relationship between parent and child is always very emotional. Emotional relationships can be a source of great strength, but they can also be demanding. It is important to recognise that parents and staff have different kinds of relationships with the children in their care.

Staff need to develop consistent, warm and affectionate relationships with children, especially babies, toddlers and two-year-olds, but they should not seek to replace the parents. Babies and young children need to be with the same people each day to develop social relationships. This is why the EYFS requires all early years settings and schools to implement a key person approach (Elfer et al. 2011).

Another important element of key working is building trusting relationships with parents. However, it is important to remember that although you will be *friendly*, you are not trying to make *friends* with parents – this is a professional relationship only. Friendships are about choosing each other; they are based on being interested in the same things – for example, the same sort of food, or an activity such as dancing or football. A professional relationship is one

▲ **Figure 3.2** The parent is a deeply important person to the child

Look, listen and note

Observe a child who is new to the setting. Note down how the key person builds a relationship with the child and the parent(s). How do they help the parent to feel confident in the care their child will receive?

Talk to a parent in the setting or to a friend or relative who has recently started taking their child to a setting. How do they feel? What did they need to help them manage this situation? What would they suggest should happen to support parents when leaving their child in a setting?

in which people come together because of the work they do. Early years practitioners and parents come together because they each spend time with and work with the child.

It is also important to consider that, however confident they may appear, or however positive their choice for someone else to look after their child might be, *all* parents will have ambivalent feelings about leaving their child. They will all have concerns and expectations about the relationships their child will form with their key person and others in the setting.

Goldschmied and Selleck (1996) discuss the complex feelings that are aroused in the triangle of care between practitioner, parent and child. Feelings of anxiety, rivalry, guilt, doubt and loss can arise, which can result in difficult practitioner–parent relationships rather than mutually respectful ones. So creating a 'triangle of trust' through clear, respectful communication is important.

This may be complicated further if parents have had bad experiences of school or other institutions or people in positions of authority. When their child joins a group setting, all those past feelings may come rushing back to the surface. As a result, parents may then be anxious and not feel good about themselves. They might expect your setting to be like the one they went to, and this may make them fear for their child. This is often the case when parents are required to bring their child to the early years setting under a care plan. Staff will need to be extra sensitive to the feelings of parents in this sort of situation.

For these reasons, it is very important that an atmosphere of trust is developed from the very first meeting or visit to the setting or child's home and then throughout the settling-in period. This is a crucially important aspect of practice that must be given a lot of care and consideration as it sets the tone for the rest of the time that child, parent and practitioner work together (Manning-Morton and Thorp 2006)

Guidelines for good practice

Communicating well with parents

✔ Maintaining eye contact helps you to give your full attention to a parent.

✔ Remember that your body language shows how you really feel.

✔ Try not to interrupt when someone is talking to you. Show positive attention and that you are listening.

✔ Every so often, summarise the main points of a discussion, so that you are both clear about what has been said.

✔ If you do not know the answer to a parent's question, say so, and say that you will find out. Do not forget to follow up!

✔ Remember that different cultures have different traditions. Touching and certain gestures might be seen as insulting by some parents, so be careful.

✔ If the parent speaks a different language from you, use photographs and visual aids. Talk slowly and clearly.

✔ If the parent has a hearing impairment, use sign language or visual aids.

✔ When you are talking together, bear in mind whether or not this is the parent's first child.

✔ Remember that the parents of a child with a disability may need to see you more often to discuss the child's progress.

✔ If the parent has a disability, make sure that when you talk together you are at the same level.

✔ Never gossip.

✔ Do not use jargon.

Guidelines for good practice

Welcoming parents and children to the early years setting

The following will help parents and children to feel welcome when they first arrive at the setting:

✔ Parents and visitors are given a friendly welcome by staff, who know they are coming if it is pre-arranged.

✔ Clearly signed entrance with arrows to the reception office.

✔ An attractive display in the entrance area, showing some of the recent activities that children have been involved in.

✔ Information showing the names of staff, with their photographs.

✔ Photograph albums, slide shows or videos that show children playing, learning and developing.

✔ The week's lunch menu.

✔ Positive images and messages about diversity – for example, different languages, ethnicities and genders, with examples of both boys and girls taking part in a full range of activities.

✔ Including something for children to do in a lobby or entrance area is helpful. One nursery school has a beautiful rocking horse in the entrance hall and this is very popular with the children. One family centre has an aquarium to look at and an interest table with baskets full of shells.

✔ Somewhere comfortable to sit.

Establishing a professional relationship

Home visits enable parents to meet staff on their own territory. The aims and practical arrangements for these visits are discussed in Chapter 10.

An advantage of home visits is that professionals can ask parents about their views on education and care. It is only by understanding how parents feel that professionals can share effectively what they know and have learned in their own training. This is especially important when working with families from different cultural backgrounds. The assumptions on both sides about what care and education is, and how it should be carried out, can be different.

Some parents may hope that their child will learn to read early, and might already have taught the alphabet to their three-year-old. Do not reject their ideas about how children learn to read, even though your own

point of view might be very different as a result of your training. Try asking the parents if they would like to know some of the other things children need to know in order to read. Stress that learning each of these things is valuable in itself and that there is no hurry to learn to read. It is more important that children learn at their own pace, and they are more likely to become avid readers as a result. This does not reject the fact that a parent has taught his or her child the alphabet, but it does open up all sorts of other possibilities for what the parent can do to help the child to read. The messages to the parent are that the staff also value reading, that they respect the intentions of the parent and that they can be a helpful resource for a family that is teaching a child to read.

Through mutual respect, trust is established. This brings with it a deep commitment on both sides to working together for the child.

Some early years settings and schools are unable to organise home visits, and there will be some parents who do not wish to be visited at home. For these parents, the reception they get on their first visit will be especially important. Parents may also come in to register their child, to visit an open day or because there is a 'Stay and Play' or other parent-and-child group offered.

Sharing information

Developing good communications systems between parents and practitioners means thinking carefully about how and when information is shared. Information sharing should be two-way and will be both formal and informal. Information sharing will happen at the beginning of the partnership, at regular set times during the year and on an ongoing daily basis. The younger the child, the more detailed and frequent information sharing should be.

Some of this information can be shared with parents by going through a photo album or watching a DVD about the setting together. This could show, in a very practical way, the philosophy, activities and timetabling of the day. Seeing the approach 'in action' can help to make sense of questions about how children learn through play, or the approach taken to meals and snacks.

The basic information record

Before the child is left in the setting without a parent or carer being present, a contact and basic information record must be filled in. All parents should be reassured that this record will be treated with confidentiality and that it will be stored safely. The record will then be reviewed regularly and kept up to date with the parents' help.

Guidelines for good practice

Sharing information with parents before the child starts in the setting

Parents need to know about:

✔ how the key person system works, and how their child will be helped if he or she becomes upset, angry, tired or needs a change of clothes

✔ what type of educational opportunities are offered and who is permitted to collect the child

✔ how they can keep up to date with their child's development and progress, and share any concerns that may arise

✔ meals, snacks and how allergies and other dietary requirements are catered for, particularly for babies and as regards religious considerations

✔ arrangements for outings and parental permissions

✔ policy on the use of photographs and video to record children's progress, and for use in displays and publicity.

✔ Collection and non-collection is referred to on page 50.

The key person, room leader or teacher collects all this information by chatting with the parents. If the family speaks a different language, you will need to arrange to have an interpreter present.

Writing reports

As part of your role, you may need to prepare reports. A report is a formal document which presents facts and findings, and can be used as a basis for recommendations. Certain reports that you may write will be a statutory requirement within the EYFS framework, and must be made available to any Ofsted inspection. These include accident reports, reporting of illnesses or injuries and any report of concerns about a child.

Reports you may be required to write include:

● **An accident or incident report**: this is quite straightforward, and will involve completing a standardised form.

Guidelines for good practice

Details to include on a basic information record

You need to include the following:

✔ the child's name, address and date of birth

✔ the full names and contact details of parent(s) with parental responsibility, identifying who the child usually lives with

✔ the child's ethnicity and gender and languages spoken at home

✔ the child's special educational need status. For most young children, where the parents or other professionals have a concern, a specific special educational need will not usually have yet been identified. This needs very sensitive handling

✔ emergency contact addresses and telephone numbers

✔ the child's GP's name, address and telephone number

✔ the child's health visitor's name, address and telephone number

✔ any important medical details – for example, in relation to diet, allergies, medicine

✔ information about social workers or other professionals working with the child – for example, a speech therapist

✔ the names of people who are allowed to collect the child, bearing in mind that other children (for example, older children) may not collect the child

✔ the contact details of any other registered childcare the child attends – for example, a childminder or another nursery setting

✔ details about the child's interests, fears, favourite toys and comforters, and any special words the child uses.

- **A CAF pre-assessment checklist or CAF form**: an official form which is focused and easy to complete.
- **A formal report about a project or plan**: for example, a plan to change the use of a room within the setting.

A formal report has a fairly rigid structure, and is usually divided into sections, probably with subheadings performing a very specific task. The language used should be straightforward and to the point, and the report's structure should make it easy to identify the various parts, and to find specific items of information quite quickly. The three general principles of a report are: Why was it done? How was it done? What does it mean?

Information sharing

The Government produced a '*Guide to information sharing*' (2008) for all practitioners working with children and young people. This outlined the important Acts that can be used to develop an information sharing policy in children's services:

- The Data Protection Act 1998 provides a framework to ensure that information is shared appropriately.
- The Children Act 2004 on the duty to safeguard and promote the welfare of children.
- Working Together to Safeguard Children (HMG, 2006): the statutory guidance that sets out how organisations and individuals should work together to safeguard and promote the welfare of children.
- What to do if you are worried a child is being abused (HMG, 2006).
- The Education and Inspections Act 2006, which sets out the duty to promote the well-being of pupils to governing bodies of maintained schools.
- The Child Health Promotion Programme (DH, 2008).
- Local Safeguarding Children Board (LSCB) policies, procedures, protocols and guidance. (LSCBs are organisations set up for each local authority area in order to make sure there is an agreement and plan for organisations that work with children to effectively work together to safeguard children).

Recording and storing information

Every setting must provide clear policies and procedures about the recording and storing of information. These are governed by the Data Protection Act 1998. Anyone who keeps records, whether on computers or on paper should comply with the Data Protection Act. It should be clear to service users (in this case parents or guardians) for what purpose the data is being kept. Information about a child should also be accessible to his or her parent or carer and shared with them. It is not necessary to do this 'on demand'. A convenient time

to be able to discuss the information can be arranged. Information should not be kept for longer than necessary, although accident and incident records will need to be kept for at least three years in case they are needed for reference at some time in the future. Records must also be stored securely.

Electronic recording and storing of information

If information is kept on computers or sent by email, steps must be taken to ensure that it could not fall into the hands of unauthorised people (for example, by the use of encryption software).

The National electronic Common Assessment Framework (eCAF) enables authorised, trained practitioners from across the children's workforce to electronically store and share CAF information quickly and securely, and to work together to build a holistic picture of a child's needs. The system reduces the need for children and families to repeat their story for different services.

Parent handbooks and brochures

Parents appreciate having booklets of their own to keep. There is a lot of information for new parents to retain, so practitioners should expect to go back over relevant points of information over the first six weeks or so. To support this, an introductory brochure can be given at the first meeting with the key person or teacher. This should contain:

- the address and telephone number of the early years setting or school, plus email and website, if appropriate
- the name of the child's key person and room leader or teacher
- a chart showing the names of all the staff, what they do and their qualifications
- information about the opening and closing times
- details of other services, such as parent-and-toddler groups, drop-ins, toy library, and the contact details for the local children's centre
- information about how the children are admitted, and about fees, if appropriate
- information about what to do if the child is to leave the setting
- information about the age range of the children
- information about what the parent needs to provide – for example nappies, spare clothes, snacks
- what would happen in the event of late collection, and if a child was lost/went missing
- information about policies on behaviour and bullying, administering medicines, equal opportunities and race equality, inclusion of children with special needs, safeguarding and making a complaint. Parents also need to be told

how to complain directly to Ofsted, should they wish to do so.

Early years settings and schools may develop a range of leaflets and brochures to share important information. Examples might cover the key person approach, learning outdoors, or the curriculum and planning.

Consolidating and extending the partnership with parents

Considerable research shows that children's development and learning can be greatly enhanced with the support of parents and the availability of play opportunities at home (Desforges 2003, Sylva et al. 2004).

But working with parents can follow different models:

- **A social control model** of teaching parents how to bring up their children. This means the staff show parents examples of what to do, hoping the parents will copy 'good models'. The parents and the home environment they provide are considered to be deficient; there will often be a list of resources and activities that parents are told they should provide.

- **A developmental partnership** in which professionals do not try to tell parents how to bring up their children. Instead, they seek to find out about the parents' perspectives. They respect parents' views and help them to build on what they already know about and want for their children, offering knowledge, information and discussion but also learning from the parents.

Different parents and families have different needs and expectations of their early years setting. There needs to be a whole range of ways for parents to access the setting and be involved in their children's learning, so that they can find the one that is most suitable for them.

- Some parents like to have regular home visits or telephone conversations because they need to collect their child quickly at the end of the day, without waiting about for a long chat with the key person.

- Some parents prefer to use a diary to communicate. For babies and toddlers, diaries are updated daily, but for older children this may be weekly or even monthly. Information sharing with families who have older children with special educational needs also needs to be daily. The diary is sent home with the child; parents can add to it and send it back. This is particularly helpful in monitoring the child's progress.

Think about ideas

A developmental partnership

Pen Green Centre for Children and their Families has led practice in involving parents in understanding and supporting their children's development (Whalley 2007). This programme includes:

- action for the parent – helping parents to reclaim their own education and build up their self-esteem
- action for the child – encouraging parents to child-watch, to be involved in and be respectful of their children's learning process and development.

In a system of parents involved in their children's learning (PICL), professionals and staff work closely together, sharing and shaping joint understandings. A parent's unique knowledge of the child is respected; and professional knowledge about child development is shared with the parent, including:

- understanding children's well-being and involvement as they play
- noticing and working with children's schemas
- video of the child, taken by parents in the family home and by staff in the nursery, provides a way of observing and reflecting on children's play.

Find out more about PICL by going to www.pengreen.org or search online for 'Parents involved in their children's learning'.

- Some parents like to come in to the nursery setting to talk to the key worker. However, staff may be very tired if they have worked a long shift, and it may be difficult to speak to the parent and to care for the other children who have not yet been picked up. So negotiation and understanding each other's point of view are needed.

- Some parents like to come to morning or afternoon sessions in the parents' or staff room. Many early years settings now make provision for this. Parents may come in to sit with one another and their babies, or to attend a session led by the local health visitor, for example. Subjects covered may include children's feeding routines, sleep patterns and other areas of concern. Other parents will be too busy to attend things like this or may find joining such a group intimidating.

Involving parents in the setting
Workshops

Parents often appreciate workshops run by the setting about different aspects of play provision. These usually take place in the evening; parents come to experience some of the things their children do and staff explain what the children get out of the activities.

▲ **Figure 3.3** It is important to make parents feel comfortable spending time with their children in the setting

Reflecting on practice

Planning a workshop

1 Plan a workshop for parents that will help them to understand how children learn through an activity such as cooking, sand play or painting. Plan the materials you would use for a demonstration, and make instruction cards with diagrams to help parents experiment with the materials.

2 Rehearse what you might say to parents in a presentation about one of the activities.

3 Advertise your workshop to parents and carry out your plan. Do not worry if not many people attend – even one parent taking part will give you valuable experience, and it is common to find that it takes several months of working with parents to encourage high levels of participation.

4 Evaluate how successful your workshop is. Include your own impressions, and information from parental feedback that you have obtained either by talking to the participants or by asking them to fill in an evaluation form.

For example, after a cooking activity Jamal's father said that he understood the link between doing division sums in mathematics and sharing the biscuits he had made. He had not previously seen this as doing a division sum in mathematics. He thought it was a very good way to learn mathematics. But he had also been shocked by his own feelings; he had not wanted to share the biscuits he had made and it made him understand how Jamal might feel when told that the biscuits must be shared.

Open days and evenings

These are often popular with parents. They can be purely social or may be a mixture of a social occasion and a workshop or talk. Many early years settings combine these.

Opportunities for parents to feedback on and shape services for children and families

Different early years settings will have a range of management systems:

● Maintained nursery schools, and primary schools, will have a legally constituted governing body that includes parent representatives. The governing body will have formal systems for reporting back to all parents and for acting on suggestions and complaints. There will also be systems to survey parents' views on a regular basis.

● Other settings may have a management committee made up of parents and other volunteers. Voluntary and community settings – for example, a preschool or a community nursery – will usually be led by parents of children currently or previously on roll, and be linked to other community and local groups.

● Children's centres will usually have a parents' forum, a gathering of parents who give feedback on the services offered and shape the future direction of the centre.

Parents keeping records

Staff may ask parents to complete a form about their child's current interests and needs, to help with the individual planning for the child. Parents might also be asked to take an observation sheet and complete it at home. Parents can draw, write about or take photographs of interesting things that their child does. Drawing helps parents and staff to have a dialogue without the need for words or skilled writing. It can involve, with sensitivity, parents who use a different language or who are not confident about writing.

In the past, many staff thought that parents would not want to be involved in record-keeping. However, in the 1980s, as part of the Froebel Early Education Project, the researcher Chris Athey found that parents (several of whom spoke Urdu, but not English) loved to keep observation notes – they drew in order that staff and parents could communicate with each other. Older brothers and sisters often enjoy filling in these observation sheets too. In many settings, parents are encouraged to fill in observation sheets and to meet with staff to discuss them.

Many early years settings and schools store each child's Profile Book in a place where it can be easily picked up and read by the child's parents. This can enable parents to keep up to date with the latest observations, assessments and planning for their child. Sometimes parents are encouraged to take the Profile Book home, share it with their child, and add to it themselves. Together with regular reviews when the parent and key person sit down formally together, this type of system can help parents feel that they are up to date and are active participants in planning for their child's development and learning.

Parent volunteers in the early years setting

Some parents welcome the opportunity to spend time in the early years setting, working alongside the staff. However, this can be very difficult for parents who work, so there should be no pressure to contribute. Sometimes parents agree to help on a rota system. However, this can be too formal an arrangement for some parents. On the other hand, it does help the staff to know that a particular parent is coming to work with them and they can make sure that the parent is made to feel welcome.

When parents come in to work in the early years setting, although they are giving, they also need to take – this is central to volunteer work. People must receive as much as they give when they volunteer to help; they must find the work rewarding in order to be motivated to volunteer. So, while understanding that the parent has come into the early years setting to help, it is very important not to expect parents to do chores that the staff dislike doing. Most parents have their own washing-up and cleaning at home. They do not necessarily want to come to the early years setting to clean up the paint pots!

Parents much prefer doing something that makes them feel relaxed and secure in what might be a new situation for them. They might be a bit nervous about the idea of cooking and tossing pancakes, sewing clothes or taking a group activity at song time. On the other hand, looking at books with individual children in the book area or helping children to sweep the garden leaves might be enjoyable for them.

If a parent is volunteering on a regular basis – for example, a parent who comes in to help every Monday morning – he or she will need:

- an induction (which should be friendly and informal) that explains the organisation, ethos and approach of the setting, including behaviour management, confidentiality and safeguarding
- to be registered with the Independent Safeguarding Authority (from November 2010 for new volunteers). This existed until 1 December 2012, when it merged with the Criminal Records Bureau (CRB) to form the Disclosure and Barring Service (DBS).

Reflecting on practice

Examples of parent volunteers

A father came in to make pancakes. The staff were very grateful because no one could toss a pancake as he could. Everyone had such fun. His commitment was great because he had taken the morning off work to do this on Pancake Day.

A mother, who was a home-based clothes-maker, came into the nursery and made costumes for the home area. She sat in the corner with a sewing machine that belonged to one of the staff. The children loved to watch and to try things on for her. Other parents brought in bits of material that she might be able to use, and they enjoyed chatting to her (in Urdu). She had been learning some songs at her English class, and at group time she enjoyed joining in and singing them. She also sang some songs in Urdu.

Make notes on what you would need to do to enable a parent to participate in your group in this way:

- How are parents involved in your setting?
- Are there particular groups of parents for whom it is difficult to be involved? Why?
- Identify what barriers there are to parents getting involved in your setting and how you might overcome these.

Additional services that settings may offer to parents

During the last decade, there has been a strong emphasis in the UK on offering a wider range of services to parents with young children. These services can be offered in a variety of different ways. A neighbourhood may have a 'full-service' children's centre, which is purpose-built, with a number of rooms and spaces available for group work with parents, confidential meetings, and large spaces for Stay and Plays for children and parents together.

In rural areas and more affluent areas, the model may be more like a 'virtual children's centre'. There will be no single, large building that is the focus of extended services for families with young children. Instead, there will be information points in places like GP practices and health clinics, libraries, post offices and schools, directing parents to where different services are offered. There may be a toddler group in the library one day a week, a group for toddlers in the church hall three days a week, and advice sessions in the health centre.

Children's centre services may also be coordinated with or linked to local extended schools services. Extended schools offer services in addition to the standard school day. These can include before- and after-school care, holiday care, sports clubs, cultural activities and clubs – for example, dance, music, art – and outreach services to support children and families who are experiencing difficulties.

Services that may be offered from a children's centre

Parent-and-baby and parent-and-toddler group (or Stay and Play group)

These groups introduce parents and children to being in a group setting in an informal way. Parents might bring their toddler to the group once a week. There will be drinks and healthy snacks for parents and children, together with activities appropriate for toddlers. Adults can talk, exchanging ideas and feelings. Babies can also be brought to the group. The group may have a regular programme of visits from a range of professionals – for example, a speech and language therapist and a clinical psychologist. Planning for the group may draw on best practice in early years education, offering high-quality treasure baskets for babies, a range of play and first-hand experiences, and outdoor play.

Toy libraries

These can be very beneficial to families, especially those on a low income. Instead of needing to spend a great deal of money on an expensive toy, families can see if the interest in a particular toy is short-lived. Children can get a broader play experience through regular borrowing, and can enjoy a range of high-quality toys and materials. A good toy library can show how open-ended equipment – for example, a Duplo set with bricks, animals and people – provides long-lasting and rich play opportunities. On the other hand, many 'educational toys' that are advertised on television and in catalogues – for example, an electronic toy that speaks the names of letters when you push the buttons – will not usually hold a child's interest for more than a few hours at best. Toy libraries can have a particular role in supporting families with a child who has disabilities, by offering specialist play equipment.

Book packs and activity packs

The BookStart programme, which began in Birmingham in 1992, initially aimed to provide a pack of free books to every family with a baby. The programme has now expanded to provide a free pack to every baby, toddler and 3- to 4-year-old, with bilingual packs, packs for children who are deaf, and packs for children who are blind or have visual impairments.

In addition, some children's centres have developed packs to help parents to provide opportunities for early language and literacy, and maths and science experiences in the family home, at no or low cost. They encourage parents to enjoy books and educational activities with their children. Children can begin to learn mathematics and science in a very natural way.

Challenges when working with parents

There is always potential for conflict and antagonism between parents and practitioners.

'These conflicts can arise from the different and varied expectations parents will have of settings and from differences in childcare approach between parent and practitioner. Issues such as setting limits and managing behaviour, gender roles and toilet learning and many others are all potential areas of disagreement.' (Manning-Morton and Thorp 2015).

Raising concerns

As an early years practitioner, your first duty is to promote the welfare, development and learning of each child. Sometimes this means raising difficult or sensitive issues with a parent. A key person might need to share a concern with parents that a child:

- has special educational needs
- is not getting sufficient support and help at home, or that his or her needs are being neglected
- is overweight, or not in good health.

All of these are sensitive issues. It is important that they are raised in a way that shows concern for a child, not criticism of a parent. However, parents feel highly responsible for their children and their initial reactions may well be defensive ('I do not know why you would think that') or hostile ('It is my business what my child has for breakfast and dinner'). In general, if a discussion is sensitively arranged in a confidential space and with a clear focus on the child's best interests, the vast majority of parents will be supportive, even if their first reaction is negative. It is always important to involve senior staff in such discussions – for example, the head teacher, setting manager or SENCO.

See Chapter 4 for information on the Common Assessment Framework (CAF) and Team Around the Child (TAC).

Reflecting on practice

Raising concerns

Ade had been attending nursery for six months. Aged two years six months, she was noticeably overweight. Her clothes did not fit her well – trousers were either far too long and rolled up or very tight around her waist, making her uncomfortable. She avoided outdoor play and indoor physical activities, but on the occasions when she did run, she would quickly become exhausted and would sometimes say her knees were hurting. Ade's mother and father were both very loving towards her. Her father was overweight.

After discussion at a staff meeting, Ade's key person – who was very experienced – spoke to Ade's mum. The key person was told that Ade's weight, and her dad's weight, were due to genetic factors and that the family all ate healthily.

Three months later, the nursery's SENCO felt that Ade was noticeably missing out in nursery and reopened discussions. She met both parents. Ade's key person explained how Ade often felt left out of games with her friends and that her clothes often hampered her. The parents explained that they could not find clothes to fit her properly. The SENCO asked if she could contact the health visitor for further advice, which the parents agreed to.

The health visitor met with the parents and explained that there was a special service locally for overweight children. She said that Ade and the family would be given extra help, and that Ade would not be put on a diet and expected to lose weight. Instead, the emphasis would be on eating healthily, being more active, and keeping her weight stable, so that as she grew, her body mass index (BMI) would reduce. She also explained that the weight on Ade's knees was already causing her discomfort, and that further ill-health might follow.

Over the next year, Ade's weight remained about the same. The family changed some of their eating habits, and organised to go swimming together once a week and started walking to nursery. Some clothes for three-year-olds were found that were a reasonable fit for her, and, with encouragement, she started using the nursery bikes. The health visitor and paediatric dietician were very pleased with Ade's progress, and predicted that within a couple of years her weight would be within the usual range. When Ade left for reception, her parents said that they could not have helped Ade without the help and support of the nursery.

Try to look at this scenario from each person's point of view. If you can do this in a group, each person can take on a particular perspective.

- How do you think each person is feeling?
- What does each person need to know or to happen?
- What would each person like the others to understand?

When you have made your notes discuss each perspective in turn. What have you learned about meeting with parents over sensitive issues?

Parents becoming angry or upset

Occasionally, parents might become upset and might shout at you. Many early years settings have a policy on how a member of staff can get help from a senior colleague if there is an emergency of any kind. Make sure that you know about this in advance! Call on the head teacher or manager if you are not sure how to handle a situation. When parents become upset, it is almost always because they are under emotional stress of some kind. For example, the paint spilt on the child's clothing may not seem serious to you, but it might be the last straw for a parent after a stressful day. Try to remain calm and polite; pointing, shouting or moving angrily towards a parent in a situation like this will almost always make things worse. Your line manager will encourage the parent to move away from the public area, and will help by offering a quiet place to talk.

Parents with different priorities

Sometimes it may appear that a parent prioritises other parts of his or her life at the expense of his or her child's welfare. A parent may work long hours and arrive at the end of the day, at the last minute (or even late), and expect to pick up the child, all ready for home. Meanwhile, the child might be tired out after a long day at nursery and need a few minutes of unrushed care before being ready to go home.

A key person can help by offering advice in a friendly and non-critical manner, perhaps pointing out how every evening there is a scene at picking-up time and suggesting some ways of avoiding this. However, there will always be times when staff do not see eye to eye with parents, but as long as the child is adequately cared for and is developing, staff need to accept that in a free society parents may not always act the way we might like them to.

Problems with discriminatory attitudes

When working with issues of equality, it is best to put the main emphasis on positive actions, rather than responding to problems. For example, the parent handbook should make it clear that the setting is positive about diversity, celebrates the different languages children speak, and actively opposes discrimination. This should be reinforced through displays and other methods, to establish an atmosphere that is welcoming to all, and opposed to racism and prejudice.

Occasionally, a child in nursery will show discriminatory behaviour that has come from the home environment – for example, a child may make a racist comment, and when this is discussed with the parent, he or she may display the same prejudice.

In these cases, the manager or head teacher will need to be clear about the legal and moral requirement to oppose discrimination, and to help children learn to be tolerant of others. The parent needs to be told clearly that such views are not acceptable in an early years setting or school.

Differences in rules and expectations

Families have a range of approaches to the problems they face. These approaches may contradict what is expected in an early years setting or school – for example, children may be made to stay at the table until they have finished their dinner at home, but an early years setting may allow children to choose what they eat, and how much.

The best approach to difficulties like these is to try to build bridges between home and the setting, while accepting that there are differences. Staff and parents can explain to a child that there is a different expectation or rule in nursery, for example. A key person, in response to a parent who does not want the child to play outside on a cold day, might first

 # Moving on

The Early Years Foundation Stage (DfE 2012) not only includes recommendations for working with parents, but *legally requires* partnership. It says:

- Educators '*must* explore the child's skills in the home language with parents and/or carers' (DfE 2012: 6).
- 'The key person *must* seek to engage and support parents and/or carers in guiding their child's development at home' (DfE 2012: 7).
- 'Providers *must* inform parents and/or carers of the name of the key person, and explain their role, when a child starts attending a setting' (DfE 2012: 7).

The use of the term 'must' in this statutory document means that these are not *suggested* practices but a *legal obligation*.

But it is not just what you do when working in partnership with parents, it is how you do it and there are different approaches that settings take. MacNaughton and Hughes (2003) look at three different ways of working with families: conforming, reforming and transforming; suggesting that the

transforming approach is the best way to share knowledge and power with parents.

- **Conforming:** the setting is seen as the expert and teaches parents and others the right way to care for and educate their children. For instance, a session informing parents on the best way to help children learn to read.
- **Reforming:** the setting involves parents and others in the care and education of their children – but on the setting's terms. For instance, meetings where practitioners and parents exchange information about the child so the setting can enhance their planning to better meet the child's needs. The parent also benefits by being better informed about the child's learning at the setting.
- **Transforming:** the setting collaborates with children, parents and others to change the relationships between them. In this model there is much closer involvement of parents. Parents and others are invited to work with practitioners to form policies, manage resources and evaluate services. Decisions about what and how children learn are also devolved to parents.

Think about ideas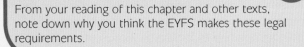

From your reading of this chapter and other texts, note down why you think the EYFS makes these legal requirements.

Reflecting on practice

Review the way in which you work in partnership and involve parents in your setting. Which of these approaches would you say your setting adopts?

show sympathy and understanding, then explain the policy on free flow, and finally meet the parent's needs halfway by undertaking to ensure that the child is really well wrapped up, and by arranging a further discussion, if necessary, to explain the nursery's approach.

Further reading, weblinks and resources

Abbott, L. and Langston, A. (Eds.) (2006) Parents Matter: Supporting the Birth to Three Matters Framework, Maidenhead: Open University Press.

Brunton, P and Thornton, L (2010) The Parent Partnership Toolkit for Early Years. London: Optimus Publishing.

Fitzgerald, D. (2004) Parent Partnership in the Early Years, London: Continuum.

MacNaughton, G and Hughes, P (2011) Parents and Professionals in Early Childhood Settings. Maidenhead: OUP.

Whalley, M and the Penn Green Team (2007) Involving Parents in Their Children's Learning. London: Paul Chapman Publishing.

Better Beginnings, Better Futures

A Canadian research project evaluating the effectiveness of early childhood services in low-income neighbourhoods.
bbbf.ca

Head Start

Head Start is a long-standing American programme to support the social and cognitive development of children through the provision of educational, health, nutritional, social and other services to enrolled children and families.
www.acf.hhs.gov/programs/ohs

Child Poverty Action Group

A campaigning group aiming to end child poverty.
http://www.cpag.org.uk/content/impact-poverty

Parents as Partners in Early Learning Project

Partnership with parents is shown in two ways in this project: parents become involved in bookmaking with their children, and they begin to learn about observing their children to see what interests them, and how they can extend their children's learning through their interests and patterns of learning.
www.peal.org.uk/media/1746/childright_article_nov07_PEAL.pdf
www.foundationyears.org.uk/wp-content/uploads/2011/10/

References

Athey, C., 1990, *Extending Thought in Young Children: A Parent-Teacher Partnership*, London: Paul Chapman.

Clark, R.M., 2010, *Childhood in Society for Early Childhood Studies*, Exeter: Learning Matters.

Department for Education, 2011, *Rolling out Free Early Education for Disadvantaged Two year olds: An Implementation Study for Local Authorities and Providers*, London: National Children's Bureau with National Centre for Social Research. Available at: http://www.natcen.ac.uk/media/26401/rolling-out-free-early-education.pdf.

Department of Health, 1991, *The Children Act 1989. Guidance and Regulations*. Available at: http://www.legislation.gov.uk/ukpga/1989/41/contents.

Desforges, C., 2003, *The Impact of Parental Involvement, Parental Support and Family Education on Pupil Achievement and Adjustment: A Literature Review*, Nottingham: DfES Publications.

Elfer, P., Goldschmied, E. and Selleck, D. Y., 2011, *Key Persons in the Early Years: Building Relationships for Quality Provision in Early Years Settings and Primary Schools*, London: Routledge.

Goldschmied, E. and Selleck, D., 1996, *Communication between Babies in Their First Year*. London: National Children's Bureau.

Golombok, S., 2000, *Parenting: What Really Counts?* London: Routledge.

Jones, E., Gutman, L. and Platt, L., 2013, *Family Stressors and Children's Outcomes*. London: Department for Education. Available at: http://www.education.gov.uk/rsgateway/DB/SFR/s000977/index.shtml.

Layard, R., Dunn, J. and the panel of The Good Childhood Inquiry, 2009, *A Good Childhood: Searching for Values in a Competitive Age*, London: Penguin.

Leach, P., Barnes, J., Nichols, M., Goldin, J., Stein, A., Sylva, K., Malmberg, L.-E., and the FCCC team, 2006, 'Child care before 6 months of age: A Qualitative Study of Mothers' Decisions and Feelings about Employment and Non-maternal Care', *Infant and Child Development*, 15:471–502, Wiley.

Manning-Morton, J. and Thorp, M., 2006, *Key Times: A Framework for Developing High Quality Provision for Children from Birth to Three Years*, Maidenhead: Open University Press.

Manning-Morton, J. and Thorp, M., 2015, *Two Year Olds in Early Years Settings; Journeys of Discovery*, Maidenhead: Open University Press.

MacNaughton, G. and Hughes, P., 2003, 'Curriculum Contexts: Parents and Communities', in MacNaughton (ed.), *Shaping Early Childhood: Learners, Curriculum And Contexts*, Maidenhead: Open University Press.

The Mental Health Foundation, 1999, *Bright Futures. Promoting Children and Young Peoples Mental Health*, London: The Mental Health Foundation.

Russell, C., 2015, *Asset Based Community Development (ABCD): Looking Back to Look Forward*: ebook.

Sylva, K., Melhuish, E., Sammons, P., Siraj-Blatchford, I. and Taggart, B., 2004, *Effective Pre-School Education: Final Report*, London: Institute of Education.

Whalley, M., 2007, *Involving Parents in their Children's Learning* (2nd edn), London: Paul Chapman.

Safeguarding children

All children have the right to be protected and safe from abuse. Everyone who works with children has a duty to safeguard and protect them. This chapter starts from the premise that the welfare of the child must always be the primary consideration. It will examine the key issues relating to safeguarding children and give clear guidance on how to recognise the potential and actual indicators of child abuse. It will also detail the procedures to follow if you suspect abuse, and examine when and how to share information while respecting confidentiality.

Keeping children safe is everyone's responsibility

There is one aspect of work with babies, toddlers and young children that must always come first: the requirement to keep them safe, and to protect them from significant harm. Children spend a considerable amount of their lives in schools and early years settings and early years practitioners are some of the most important adults that they will come across. As a team, practitioners can create an atmosphere and ethos which profoundly affects the child's experience of being cared for, listened to, valued, guided and stimulated. Early years settings and schools therefore play a considerable part in promoting – or, sadly, sometimes neglecting – children's best interests.

For some children, universal services like early years education and health visiting are not enough to ensure their healthy, safe and happy development. These children might, for periods of time, be vulnerable. They may experience emotional difficulties, fall behind in their development or learning, or suffer the adverse effects of poverty, poor housing or ill-health. There are also children in need, who due to their circumstances are judged to be unlikely to reach or maintain a satisfactory level of health or development unless they are offered additional services. This group includes children with disabilities, for example.

Finally, there are children who are subject to an inter-agency child protection plan. These children are judged to be at risk of significant harm without the provision of additional services as well as close and careful monitoring by specialist children's social workers.

The latest government guidance is 'Safeguarding is a term which means more than just protecting children from harm'. The Department for Education's statutory guidance 'Working together to safeguard children' (2013) defines safeguarding as:

- protecting children from maltreatment
- preventing impairment of children's health and development
- ensuring that children grow up in circumstances consistent with the provision of safe and effective care and taking action to enable all children to have the best outcomes.

We explore some of these complexities later in this chapter, and also explain how judgements might be reached by professionals on the basis of the best possible assessments. Although there is much that is complex and worthy of debate, it is a priority for professionals to take swift action where necessary.

This chapter attempts to offer concise but useful and accurate information about safeguarding. If you have any doubts or concerns about a child, however trivial you might think they are, we strongly advise you to speak to the manager or head teacher of the early years setting or school where you are working. Always ask for information and guidance.

Key issues in safeguarding

The child's interests are paramount

All the legislation and guidance in recent decades, including the Children Act 2004, make it clear that the child's interests must come first. All professionals must work together to promote the child's welfare before all else. For example, imagine that you found out that a father had slapped his child on the face, leaving a mark. You may have developed a very close relationship with this parent and you may be very sympathetic to the difficulties he is experiencing. You may feel that this incident will not happen again, that he genuinely loves and cares for the child, and that he would be devastated if you did not keep this to yourself. All the same, you are required to put the child's interests before your feelings about the family. The actions you might take are discussed later in this chapter on page 67.

Early intervention is best

Different professionals and agencies should work together to help the child and family early on when there are difficulties. They should not wait until something serious happens before taking action. For example, a health visitor might notice that a mother is getting very stressed by the behaviour of her toddler and is struggling to cope. **Early intervention** might involve talking to the mother, showing empathy, and perhaps finding some support for her at the local children's centre or setting up a programme of home visits. This would be much better than waiting to see if the situation gets any worse before doing anything.

Professionals should work positively with parents and other family members

Although there is still a common view that social workers intervene to take children away from their families, in reality, the vast majority of social work is about helping different agencies work together to support the family, so that the child's safety and well-being are assured.

Legal requirements for all settings

All early years settings and schools must nominate a member of staff to oversee safeguarding and child protection. This person must be specifically trained to undertake this role. The whole team (including volunteers and students) must work together to promote children's welfare and keep them safe. The whole team will need regular training and updating, and it is best practice that such training provides staff with time to explore different experiences, attitudes and opinions as steps towards agreeing policy and practice.

Go to the end of this chapter and pages 74–76 for a list of all the legislation that is relevant to this chapter.

Safeguarding covers a wide spectrum of activities and processes; we will explore some of these in the next section.

Ensuring that children feel safe and secure

Every adult working in the setting must be a *suitable person* to work with young children, and must have a full DBS clearance – see below. This includes students on placements and regular volunteers.

The Disclosure and Barring Service

The Disclosure and Barring Service (DBS) helps employers make safer recruitment decisions and prevent unsuitable people from working with vulnerable groups, including children. (It replaces the Criminal Records Bureau (CRB) and Independent Safeguarding Authority (ISA)). The DBS acts as a central access point for criminal records checks for all those applying to work with children and young people.

A safe environment, risk and challenge

The physical layout and organisation of the setting must keep children safe and secure. The working practices and culture of the setting must also contribute to children feeling safe and secure – for example, developing the key person approach (covered in Chapter 4), and helping children to feel appropriately confident and assertive. However, it is important that this emphasis on safety is balanced with opportunities for children to explore and take

KEY TERMS

Early intervention – This approach seeks to offer extra help and support to a family before the child starts to lag behind in development or experience neglect or abuse. Early intervention is about working cooperatively with parents and carers, giving them a chance to make choices about which services they need.
Safeguarding policy – A safeguarding policy is a statement that makes it clear to staff, parents and children what the organisation or group thinks about safeguarding, and what it will do to keep children safe.

▲ **Figure 4.1** Helping children to feel safe and secure is the cornerstone of safeguarding

risks. When children are placed in an environment that is too safe, they may lack the stimulation that comes from being challenged, and they may not develop the ability to evaluate risks and make judgements. If there is no challenging climbing equipment, for example, children will not learn the skills of judging how high they can go. So an appropriately safe and secure environment will include opportunities, inside and outside, for children to challenge themselves and take some risks. But it will exclude aspects that are merely hazardous, like a poorly designed, uneven surface, which is a trip hazard.

Actively promoting the well-being of each child

This involves making opportunities available to children to develop, learn, play, communicate and socialise with each other in the setting. Children also need healthy, nutritious and enjoyable food, and opportunities to move and exercise their bodies. Moreover, they need to be able to make decisions and develop a level of independence that is appropriate to their age and development.

Providing extra support, working with parents and other professionals

Some children in an early years setting may present with delayed development, or emotional and social difficulties. These may result from adverse early experiences, for example witnessing domestic violence, or growing up with a parent who has mental health difficulties. Extra support could include helping a mother join a 'Stay and Play' group, to make friends and find support, or

Look, listen and note

Spend some time observing the children at key points in the day, like dropping-off time, in the middle of the session, at lunchtime, in the afternoon and at the end of the day. What can you tell about the children's well-being from your observations?

Do children who are upset at the start of the day get help to manage their feelings, or are they just left to get on with things?

- Do children seem happy playing, or do they look lost or bored a lot of the time?
- Do they enjoy lunch?
- Are there times of the day when they are herded around in big groups, so that some children look stressed?
- How are children towards the end of the day?

working with the clinical psychology service to give advice about bedtimes or mealtimes. This work can be coordinated under the Common Assessment Framework (CAF), which is discussed later in this chapter (page 71).

Protecting children who may be at risk of significant harm as a result of their home and family circumstances

Some children are at risk because of the actions of their parents – for example, physical abuse like hitting, sexual abuse – or neglect because their parents fail to act to keep them safe and well. In these cases, the different agencies still work together to provide support and help to the parents, but there may also be actions that the parent is required to take, which can be checked through unannounced visits and compulsory medical, developmental and psychological assessments.

Different ways of understanding child abuse

There is no absolute definition of child abuse. It is a concept that is formed by history and culture, and is subject to change. (See page 64 for definitions of child abuse). For example, until quite recently, disciplining children in the family by smacking, slapping and hitting them was considered quite normal in Europe. Now it is illegal to hit children in 19 European Union countries, and although it is still legal in the UK, many campaigners regard it as abusive. The notion of 'child abuse' is contested by different groups of people, who have different opinions.

Reflecting on practice

What might it feel like to be a child here?

Safeguarding children begins with making sure that they feel safe and secure in their early years setting or school. Try to imagine how the children find being in your setting. Before the children arrive, go round the whole area on your knees, so your eyes are at child-height.

- Does the setting feel welcoming and accessible to you, or do you feel that lots of things are placed too high?
- Do you feel overwhelmed?
- Are you kept safe, or could you reach door handles and get out?
- Can you move freely and safely around the space?

Models for understanding child abuse

The medical model

This focuses on categories, symptoms and treatments. Child abuse is seen as a medical condition with certain symptoms – for example, shaken baby syndrome, where an adult has violently shaken a baby, causing brain damage and other internal injuries. This model is about diagnosing trauma and injury from a medical point of view, and does not prioritise relationships, social or emotional factors.

The feminist model

This sees child abuse as part of the overall structure of male power. The social system is regarded as giving power to men at the expense of women and children. This is understood to legitimise violence (men using violence against women and children) and to make it difficult for women to have their voices heard or to claim their rights. For example, in most cases of domestic violence, it is the woman who will flee the house with the children, therefore losing out on the family home and suitable housing. Feminist research would also point to the historic and continuing difficulties that women and children have convincing the authorities – for example, the police – to take action when they have been raped or assaulted.

The social model

This emphasises how social circumstances contribute to child abuse – for example, abuse might be understood to be more likely to occur in families living in stressful circumstances, poor and overcrowded housing, and where parents feel isolated and have no one to help them.

Thinking about ideas

The former United Nations Commissioner for Human Rights, Louise Arbour, believes that 'violence against children is a violation of their human rights, a disturbing reality of our societies. It can never be justified whether for disciplinary reasons or cultural tradition.'

However, the sociologist Frank Furedi argues that the government is trying to take too much control over family life. He has written that 'the campaign against smacking is driven by a wider agenda that seeks to undercut the right of parents to discipline their children. The assumption is that in most cases such parental punishment is likely to have a harmful effect. The principal objective of the campaign against smacking is to save children from their parents.'

What do you think?

The psychological model

This focuses mostly on the psychological disturbances in parents that can lead to them abusing children – for example, a parent who was mistreated as a child or who has drug or alcohol problems might be thought to have an 'abusive personality'.

A combination of factors inform our understanding of child abuse

It is now generally accepted that no single model 'explains' child abuse. Instead, a range of factors contributes to situations that might lead to a child being abused. These factors include:

● the family
● the local community, and
● the wider culture.

Family factors

It is thought that children with disabilities, and children who are more difficult to care for because they are hard to settle, sickly or very active, are more likely to be abused. However, the most important family factor is not the children, but the parents. Parents who may be more likely to mistreat their children include those who:

● **find it difficult to be authoritative with their children and help them to develop positive behaviour** – instead, there may be periods of time when the children's behaviour is hardly regulated at all, followed by a sudden harsh intervention. They may experience the child's behaviour very personally, as deliberate stubbornness and defiance. They may have unrealistic expectations about the child's development, expecting too much from a toddler or young child.

● **feel under stress because of problems with adult relationships** – for example, domestic violence, drug or alcohol misuse, poverty or bad housing. They may be easily 'tipped over the edge' by the demands of their children.

● **find it hard to imagine being a child** – this limits their ability to think through how different experiences might affect their child's development and health.

Once parents start behaving harshly towards children, a pattern of withdrawal can set in. The child may not seek contact for fear of being shouted at or hurt. This means that there is little enjoyable interaction between parent and child.

Community factors

Caring for young children is very hard work and can be emotionally draining. Parents need help, advice, a friendly ear and also practical support – for example, babysitting. Some parents are very isolated socially, either because they have moved or been rehoused away from friends and family, or because they find it hard to form relationships with others. There may be few facilities for children in the local area, such as parks and other play opportunities. This can lead to the parent feeling overwhelmed by the demands of the child, lacking places to go, people to see and any opportunity for time for themselves. This makes for a very stressful life, and can lead to a parent becoming exhausted and withdrawn.

Cultural values

The wider culture can prepare the ground for the mistreatment and abuse of children – for example, the campaigning group Children Are Unbeatable!, which opposes all forms of physical punishment, including smacking. It argues that 'smacking may initially stop a child misbehaving, but research has shown it does not make them behave better in the longer term, so the child is smacked again, and harder. A proportion of parents who smack today will go on to beat tomorrow'. (Gershoff 2002)

In other words, it is argued that allowing all parents the legal right to smack their children prepares the way for a small number of parents to beat and severely mistreat their children.

Difficult judgements

Safeguarding children requires practitioners to make difficult judgements, which must be consistent with the equal opportunities approach outlined in Chapter 1. Some specific issues to consider include the following:

Social class

Class bias can affect judgements. It is sometimes argued that safeguarding can take the middle-class child as the 'norm' and judge all other children as being deficient. Different parents have different ways of parenting, for example in the way they talk to their children, on their opinions about clothing, and where children can play at home. The important matter to consider is the impact on the child. A child could live in a lovely, well-decorated home with plenty of toys, but relationships in the family might be rather cold and distant. If the child is presenting as withdrawn and anxious, you would take steps to help. Another child could live in a cramped flat that seems rather chaotic to you, and the child's clothes might often be faded, old and haphazardly chosen. If the child is

developing well, and is confident and sociable, these things do not matter.

Cultural differences

Ethnic minority families have experienced appalling discrimination in countries such as the UK. In the 1960s and 1970s, for example, a disproportionate number of Afro-Caribbean children were judged to be 'educationally subnormal', and some childcare experts believed that their home culture and language were not good enough to ensure their healthy development. In countries like Canada and Australia, the children of indigenous people (Native Americans/American Indians, Australian Aborigines) were routinely taken into the care of the state because it was believed that their culture was inadequate. Many forms of discrimination persist. Unfortunately, in an attempt to take this into account, some professionals have held back from making any judgements about the well-being of black and ethnic minority children, for fear of being racist. This had tragic results in the case of Victoria Climbié. Some staff judged that the fear she displayed when she was around her abusive great-aunt was the traditional respect shown by children to adults in some Afro-Caribbean societies. She was eventually murdered by her great-aunt in 2000, having been failed by the medical and child protection services. You can find the inquiry report at https://www.gov.uk/government/uploads/system/uploads/attachment_data/file/273183/5730.pdf

Disability

Research indicates that children with disabilities are three times more likely to be abused than other children. Children with disabilities are more vulnerable for a number of reasons. They may need a considerable amount of intimate care, and if this care is undertaken by many people, it can be exploited by abusers. Their disability may make it difficult for them to tell someone they are being abused. Sometimes disturbed behaviour by children with disabilities is thought to be caused by their disability, while in other children such behaviour might prompt concern. The key person approach has a special role to play in safeguarding children with disabilities, because of its emphasis on seeking consent for intimate care, and restricting this care to the key person as far as possible. The key person is also in a good position to notice changes in behaviour and emotional well-being. It is important that no children, including those with disabilities, are left feeling that anyone can undress them at any time, as if they have no right to privacy.

Helping children to protect themselves against abuse

In recent decades, a number of attempts have been made to design programmes for children under five years to help them to protect themselves against abuse. These have included lessons on 'stranger danger', working with children in groups to explore times when they feel uncomfortable, and teaching children not to keep 'bad secrets'.

There is little or no reliable evidence that such programmes have protected children under five years from abuse, and it has been argued that the children merely end up feeling confused, frightened and alarmed. It has also been argued that these approaches can make young children feel some responsibility if they are being abused, because they were unable to do or say what they were taught.

It is worth remembering that children in the Early Years Foundation Stage (EYFS) do not generally learn effectively through group discussions, or through being shown pictures like one of a man in a car and being asked what they would do in that situation. These approaches are most suited to older children in the primary and secondary phases of their education. There are some tried and tested programmes available from the National Society for the Prevention of Cruelty to Children (NSPCC), Barnardo's and Kidscape for older children. In the EYFS, a more successful approach is likely to be one that is built into the daily lives of the children in their early years setting or school.

The key person approach

A strong key person approach supports safeguarding through:

- **Listening and tuning in to a child** – this will include noticing changes in a child's behaviour and emotional well-being, and developing a trusting relationship so that the child can tell you if things are upsetting him or her. Taking a child's concerns seriously is important. Often, when a child has been bullied or abused in some way, he or she will try to communicate what has happened. The child needs to know that you are there to listen and, most importantly, that you will believe what he or she tells you.

- **Allowing a child to express his or her feelings** – if a child is allowed to express sadness and anger, as well as happiness and enjoyment, he or she may feel more confident that it is all right to have a range of emotions. The child will be more likely to tell other people how he or she is feeling.

Guidelines for good practice

Working as a team

✓ Work in a team to help children feel safe and secure.

✓ Know about what measures early years settings and schools must have in place in order to safeguard children.

✓ Understand that there are different models which are used to explain child abuse.

- **Increasing a child's confidence** – this involves making a child feel a sense of belonging, and that he or she is special for his or her unique qualities. It is important to show a genuine interest in what a child has to say, and to praise him or her for any achievements. A quick 'That was good of you, Suhail', is really not enough to show a child that you value him. A better response may be 'That's very good, Suhail, you showed kindness and a real sense of responsibility when you helped Asha to find her missing shoes.'

- **Observing a child and keeping regular records of his or her behaviour** – you are in a strong position to note any changes of behaviour or signs of insecurity that could result from child abuse.

The emphasis in the key person approach on developing a close relationship with parents is also important. A key person can:

- help a parent to appreciate that a child is finding a particular situation upsetting or difficult

- support a parent with practical advice on general care and clothing

- offer emotional and practical support in cases of family conflict or domestic violence.

Definitions of abuse and neglect, and recognising signs of child abuse

'Working together to safeguard children' (2013) defines abuse as:

> *A form of maltreatment of a child. Somebody may abuse or neglect a child by inflicting harm, or by failing to act to prevent harm. Children may be abused in a family or in an institutional or community setting by those known to them or, more rarely, by others (e.g. via the internet). They may be abused by an adult or adults, or another child or children.*

There are four categories of abuse: physical, emotional, sexual abuse, and neglect:

Physical abuse

Physical abuse, or non-accidental injury (NAI), involves someone deliberately harming a child. This may take the form of:

- bruising – from being slapped, punched, shaken or squeezed
- cuts – scratches, bite marks, a torn frenulum (the web of skin inside the upper lip)
- fractures – skull and limb fractures from being thrown against hard objects
- burns and scalds – from cigarettes, irons, baths and kettles.

Often the particular injuries can be explained easily, but you should always be suspicious if a child has any bruise or mark that shows the particular pattern of an object (e.g. a belt strap mark, teeth marks or the imprint of an iron). Also look out for behavioural disturbances in the child, such as aggressiveness towards others or a withdrawn attitude.

Physical harm may also be caused when a parent fabricates the symptoms of illness in a child, or deliberately induces illness – for example, giving a child so much salt that he or she becomes very ill, so that medical staff think the child has a gastric illness or a brain condition.

Emotional abuse

Emotional abuse occurs when a child consistently faces threatening ill-treatment from an adult. This can take the form of verbal abuse, ridiculing, mocking and insulting the child. It is difficult to find out how common this form of abuse is, because it is hard to detect. It involves continual emotional mistreatment which results in significant damage to the child's emotional development. The child may come to feel worthless, unloved, inadequate or valued only if they meet the expectations or needs of another person. Emotional abuse includes:

- The parent having expectations that are well outside what is suitable for the child's age and development. This includes unreasonable expectations, like continuously trying to force a child to achieve more, and then constantly criticising the child for his or her failures. At the other end of the spectrum, some parents may fail to stimulate their child adequately – for example, keeping a two-year-old in a playpen with only a couple of baby toys.

- Preventing a child from participating in normal social interaction with other children, either by keeping the child at home, or by taking the child out but being so overprotective, fearful or controlling that the child cannot join in.

- Failing to protect the child from witnessing the mistreatment of others – for example, cases of domestic violence.

All children will experience some emotional difficulties as part of the ordinary processes of growing up. It becomes abusive if the result is significant damage to the child's emotional development. All cases of child abuse will include some degree of emotional abuse.

Signs of emotional abuse include:

- withdrawn behaviour – child may not join in with others or appear to be having fun
- attention-seeking behaviour
- self-esteem and confidence are low
- stammering and stuttering
- tantrums beyond the expected age
- telling lies, and even stealing
- tearfulness.

Emotional neglect means that children do not receive love and affection from the adult. They may often be left alone without the company and support of someone who loves them.

Sexual abuse

There is much more awareness today about the existence of sexual abuse. Sexual abuse means that the adult uses the child to gratify their sexual needs. This could involve sexual intercourse or anal intercourse. It may involve watching pornographic material with the child. Sexual abuse might also mean children being encouraged in sexually explicit behaviour or oral sex, masturbation or the fondling of sexual parts. Signs of sexual abuse include the following:

- bruises or scratches as in a non-accidental injury or physical injury
- itching or pain in the genital area
- wetting or soiling themselves
- discharge from the penis or vagina
- poor self-esteem and lack of confidence
- may regress and want to be treated like a baby
- poor sleeping and eating patterns
- withdrawn and solitary behaviour.

Neglect

Neglect means that the parent persistently fails to meet the child's basic physical needs, psychological needs or both. The result is that the child's health or development is significantly impaired.

Neglect can occur during pregnancy if the mother abuses drugs or alcohol, which can have serious effects. Neglect of babies and young children includes the failure to:

- provide adequate food, clothing and shelter
- keep the child safe from physical and emotional harm or danger
- supervise the child adequately, including leaving the child with inadequate carers
- make sure the child is seen promptly by medical staff when ill
- respond to the child's basic emotional needs.

Signs of physical neglect include:

- being underweight for their age and not thriving
- unwashed clothes, which are often dirty and smelly
- poor skin tone, dull, matted hair and bad breath; a baby may have a persistent rash from infrequent nappy changing
- being constantly tired, hungry and listless or lacking in energy
- frequent health problems, and prone to accidents
- low self-esteem and poor social relationships – delay in all areas of development is likely because of lack of stimulation.

Recognising the signs of child abuse

Early years practitioners are good at recognising when all is not well with a child. Historically, the biggest difficulty has not been in recognising problems, but in communicating concerns to others (including the child's parents) and acting on them. Often practitioners worry about the consequences of passing on information, and worry that it might lead to the family being split up. It is important to remember that in the vast majority of cases the different services will work with the family to ensure the child's safety. But the decision about what is best for the child should be made by a trained social worker, acting on the best possible information. When practitioners feel worried but do not communicate their concerns to others, a child can be put in danger.

The NSPCC finds that children and young people often find it very difficult to talk about the abuse they are experiencing. As adults, we have a vital role to play in looking out for the possible signs.

Think about ideas

How to recognise signs of child abuse

The NSPCC has a wealth of information on the signs of child abuse:

"The signs of child abuse aren't always obvious, and a child might not tell anyone what's happening to them.

Children might be scared that the abuser will find out, and worried that the abuse will get worse. Or they might think that there's no-one they can tell or that they won't be believed.

Sometimes, children don't even realise that what's happening is abuse.

The effects of abuse may be short term or may last a long time - sometimes into adulthood. Adults who were abused as children may need advice and support." (www.nspcc.org.uk).

Visit the NSPCC website (www.nspcc.org.uk/services-and-resources/) and find out more about the following aspects of recognising signs of child abuse:

- How to tell whether a child's behaviour is normal for his or her age
- How to recognise emotional neglect and emotional abuse in pre-school children
- How to identify bruises that may be the result of child abuse or neglect

Using the relevant Core Info leaflets, make a fact-file summarising the main points.

Actions to take if harm or abuse is suspected and/or disclosed/alleged

What happens if you are worried that a child is being abused?

If a child makes an allegation to you, or if you are worried for one or more of the reasons listed by the NSPCC (see page 66), follow the guidelines below.

(see page 66)

KEY TERM

Allegation/ Disclosure – This is when a child alleges (or discloses) information that is secret or private to them, that causes an adult to be concerned about the child's safety and well-being. This can happen through children talking, acting things out in their play, or drawing and painting. It is essential that early years practitioners listen and watch very carefully, but do not question the child or put words into the child's mouth.

Guidelines for good practice

Allegations or Disclosure

Sometimes a child may disclose or allege information that leads you to think that he or she is being abused. With young children, this may happen in a number of ways. A child might tell you something directly: 'Mummy and daddy went out yesterday, and me and Scarlet were scared because we were all alone.' Or a child might use play to communicate – for example, you might observe a child in the home corner shouting at and slapping one of the dolls.

In all cases, your role when a child discloses or alleges is to listen very carefully and show concern. Reaffirm that it is good for the child to tell you things that are worrying or upsetting him or her. Say that you believe the child. If you are not sure about something the child has said, then ask for clarification: 'I'm not sure I quite understood – did you say it was your arm that hurts?'

However, there are also some things that you must *not* do. You must not question or cross-examine a child or seem to put words into a child's mouth. So you would not ask a question like, 'Does this happen every day?' because the child might just agree with you, or repeat your words. You are there to listen and observe – you are not an investigator.

A child may make a disclosure or an allegation to anyone – his or her key person, the caretaker, the dinner supervisor, a student on placement. For that reason, it is very important that everyone who comes into contact with children has training on safeguarding and knows what to do if they have any reason to be worried about a particular child.

Guidelines for good practice

Reporting child abuse or neglect

✓ **Make a note that is as exact as you can make it**, recording exactly what the child said, and anything you noticed (signs of an injury, child seeming upset, stressed, angry or ashamed while talking to you). If you have had ongoing concerns, summarise what these are; again, be as accurate as you can.

✓ **Discuss your concerns** as a matter of urgency with the named member of staff for safeguarding, however busy that person seems to be.

✓ **Report the indicators** that have led you to suspect child abuse or neglect to your designated safeguarding and child protection officer. Your line manager will help you to follow the correct procedures, but you should know them too.

✓ **You will need to continue to keep carefully written observations.** This is because you may be required to make a report, and for this you must have written evidence.

✓ **In most cases, the named member of staff will discuss the concerns with the parent** and then make a judgement about what to do next. You should be told what action (if any) is being taken, and why.

✓ **If you have raised a concern and you think that the action being taken is inadequate**, meet the named person again. Explain your opinion, referring to what you have observed or heard. Although such conversations are very difficult, they are essential if we are to uphold to the principle that the child's welfare and safety comes first.

✓ **If you are a student, discuss your concerns in confidence with your tutor.** Any worried adult is also entitled to contact Children's Social Care or the NSPCC directly. If you have reason to believe your concern is not being acted on, you should do this.

After reporting child abuse or neglect

Responses might include:

- **No action** – for example, in a case where a parent gives a reasonable explanation for their child's injury or behaviour.
- **Advice given** – for example, a parent is advised on what sort of clothes will keep their child warm enough in winter. Staff can then check that the child is appropriately dressed on subsequent days.
- **Support offered** –for example, a parent might agree that she is finding it difficult to manage the

child's behaviour, and might welcome the offer of support from a parenting group or an appointment with a clinical psychologist.

- **Referral to family support at the local children's centre** – this will provide structured support and help for the family on a voluntary basis. A similar type of referral might be made to a specialist social work team (Disabled Children's Team, Domestic Violence Project).

- **Referral to Children's Social Care** (social services) – if the named person judges that the

child is at risk of significant harm, a written referral will be made to Children's Social Care.

The Challenge of Sexualised behaviour

Ofsted inspectors investigating an increase in exclusions from primary schools have discovered 'worrying' levels of sexual behaviour among very young children.

An inquiry into schools that have repeatedly suspended pupils as young as four has unearthed high incidences of children touching other children inappropriately and using sexually graphic language as well as swearing, attacking staff and throwing furniture.

(The Guardian, 23 June 2009)

Confidentiality and 'need to know'

In general, you must keep sensitive information confidential. Information about a child protection issue should only be shared with people on a 'need to know' basis. This means that only staff working directly with the child or the parents will have access to any information about a disclosure or investigation. Gossip and hearsay must be avoided. Names and identities must never be disclosed outside the group designated as having a 'need to know'.

Think about ideas

✔ What are the four categories of child abuse?

✔ What should you remember to do, if a child makes an allegation to you? What should you avoid doing?

✔ Why would early years staff share concerns about a child's welfare or well-being with the child's parents, rather than just keeping a record or making a referral?

For further information, visit www.education.gov.uk and search for 'What to do if you are worried a child is being abused'.

Reflecting on practice

The challenge of sexualised behaviour

In this case study, names and some details have been changed to maintain confidentiality.

Soon after Anthony started in nursery, staff became concerned about his sexualised behaviour.

He would make very sexual and suggestive dance moves, and seemed to be drawn to the toilets, where he would hang around. Staff concerns heightened when he seemed to be leading children into dens and other areas of out of staff sight, so they decided to monitor closely. Checking up one day, they found Anthony trying to put his hands down another child's trousers. The other child looked frightened. Anthony's behaviour was also becoming increasingly disruptive. He also pushed a girl up against a wall and forced his mouth over hers. The member of staff in charge of safeguarding spoke to Anthony's key person to build up a picture of his behaviour. In discussion, they agreed that while it was not unusual for children to play games like 'I'll show you mine if you show me yours', Anthony's behaviour was outside of ordinary childhood sexual play because he was forcing himself on others, and because of his persistence, which seemed almost obsessional.

The key person and safeguarding coordinator met Anthony's mother at the end of the day to outline their concerns. Anthony's mother was first very angry, and then dismissive, saying that all children played like that, and taking exception to the comments about his dancing. The key person explained that Anthony's behaviour was upsetting other

children and asked his mother if she could think of steps to take to help him understand what sort of behaviour was acceptable in nursery, and what was not.

Anthony's mother refused to continue the conversation.

That evening, as many staff as possible were brought together and a plan was agreed to make sure that the other children in the nursery would be kept safe. Staff arranged to be extra vigilant in areas where Anthony was playing. It was planned for Anthony's key person to be given some time with him individually the next day, to tell him clearly the types of behaviour and touching that were not allowed in nursery. Staff not present at the meeting were briefed first thing the next morning.

Later in the week, staff observed Anthony trying to climb up and look over toilet cubicle walls and saw him fondling a doll in the home corner in a sexual way. A referral was made to Children's Services because of the continuing concerns about Anthony's behaviour. However, staff were determined to maintain Anthony's place at nursery, fearing that if he was excluded then he would lose a place of safety.

1 Think about how you might feel if you were Anthony's key worker. To what extent would his behaviour upset, shock or anger you?

2 Talk in a small group or with another learner about your response, and what would help you to feel supported at work and able to relate positively to Anthony as your key child.

Guidelines for good practice

Recording suspicions of abuse and allegations

You should make a record – *as soon as possible* after the observation or conversation – of:

✔ the child's name

✔ the child's address

✔ the age of the child

✔ the date and time of the observation or the allegation

✔ a concise, objective and factual record of the observation: for example, if a child has physical injuries, these should be clearly recorded on a body outline figure. You should only record the facts as you see them and not draw any conclusions about the possible cause of the injury

✔ an objective record of the allegation: write down what the child or adult has told you, using their own words. Note also your own responses. Avoid making judgements and interpretations

✔ the name of the person to whom the concern was reported, with date and time

✔ the names of any other person present at the time

These records must be signed and dated and kept in a separate confidential file.

If information circulates too freely, parents can feel very exposed and vulnerable. They may stop sharing information with staff.

- **Where appropriate, seek consent before you share information** – you might find out on a home visit that a child's mother has a serious mental health difficulty, which is well managed by medication and therapy. However, the medication can make her feel rather tired first thing in the morning, and she tells you that she can struggle to take on information or hold a conversation then. So you might say, 'I'll need to tell my manager this, but shall we also let the staff team know, so they can talk with you at the end of the day and not in the morning?' The parent can then give or withhold consent freely.

- **Never disclose any information** – about a child's welfare in an inappropriate way to people outside the setting or school – for example, you would not tell friends or family about a child protection conference you had attended.

- **Put the child's interests first** – if sharing information will help to ensure a child's safety, you must do this. In nearly all cases, you would start by explaining to the parent why you wish to share the information and how this would help the child. If a parent refuses, ask for advice and guidance from the named person for safeguarding or the manager/head of the setting. If a parent says something like, 'I did smack her round the head, but you won't tell anyone will you? They'll take her into care,' you will need to explain clearly that you are legally required to pass on information like this.

Allegations made against staff

Schools and early years settings are usually some of the safest places for children to be. However, sadly there have been incidents when children have been harmed or abused by the adults who work with them and care for them. Cases include the murders of Holly Wells and Jessica Chapman by their school caretaker Ian Huntley in 2002, and the discovery in 2009 that a nursery nurse, Vanessa George, had taken and distributed indecent pictures of some of the children in her care.

Generally, an early years setting or school keeps children safe by having good procedures around safer recruitment, management and its general operating policy – for example, if children are encouraged to speak out when they feel unhappy or uncomfortable, they will be much less vulnerable to abuse. Children's intimate care – nappy changing, toileting, dressing and undressing – should be coordinated by a key person. This means that children do not have the experience that anyone can take them aside and undress them. Their right to privacy is upheld. It is good practice, where developmentally appropriate, to ask children to consent to offers of intimate care and to give them as much control as possible. So you might say to a toddler in the toilet, 'Would you like me to help pull your pants down?' rather than just going ahead and doing it.

However, no system alone can protect children: what matters, beyond good policies and procedures, is that practitioners are confident to raise concerns, and that children are encouraged to say if they are unhappy or uncomfortable with anything that happens to them.

All early years settings and schools are required to have a policy to deal with allegations made against staff. This will cover cases where a child makes a disclosure, or an adult is seen or overheard behaving in an inappropriate way. But there are other examples that might give rise to a concern, without a specific allegation being made:

- a child who seems fearful of a particular member of staff

- a member of staff seeming to try to develop a very close relationship with a child – for example, offering small presents and special treats, or arranging to meet the child outside of the setting or school

- a parent expressing a general concern about how a member of staff relates to their child, without being able exactly to say what is wrong.

In cases like these, you will need to discuss your concerns with the named person for safeguarding. Discussions like these are awkward, but it is important to share any concerns you have – the child's welfare is paramount.

Whistleblowing

Sometimes a person inside an organisation knows that something is going wrong and is being covered up. This could affect the safety and well-being of children. Examples of this in early years settings and schools include the following:

- A member of staff has reported a number of concerns about a child's welfare. The child's parents are on the management committee of the nursery, and the manager says, 'They are not the sort of people who would harm their child.'

- There are consistently too few staff on duty in the nursery. When the local authority come to visit, supply staff are hired, and during an Ofsted inspection, management and office staff are brought into the room so that legal ratios are met.

In cases like these, it is very important that action is taken before there is a serious incident. If a member of staff has spoken to the manager, head teacher or other appropriate person and made clear that a situation is dangerous and illegal, and no action is taken, it is necessary to 'blow the whistle' and report the concerns directly to an outside body, such as the local Children's Services, Ofsted or the NSPCC.

If you act to protect children or to keep them safe, you are clearly protected by the law. In general, employees who blow the whistle are legally protected against

KEY TERM

Whistleblowing – This means reporting concerns, for example, about abuse or unsafe practices to management and/or other authorities.

Guidelines for good practice

Understanding confidentiality

✔ Working in a team, you should discuss your concerns about children in meetings or with senior staff, as appropriate.

✔ Understand why you would ask a parent for consent before sharing confidential information with another professional.

✔ Understand that there are times when you would share information without consent.

being bullied, sacked or disciplined, if they have acted in good faith.

The Public Interest Disclosure Act 1998, known as the **Whistleblowing** Act, is intended to protect the public interest by providing a remedy for individuals who suffer workplace reprisal for raising a genuine concern, whether it is a concern about child safeguarding and welfare systems, financial malpractice, danger, illegality, or other wrongdoing.

Search online for 'Protection of whistle-blowers' or find out more at www.direct.gov.uk.

Safeguarding systems

Common Assessment Framework (CAF)

The Children Act 2004 requires different agencies – for example, across education, health, children's social care and housing – to cooperate in the best interests of children and young people. The CAF provides a structure to facilitate this cooperation. Although the CAF is specific to England, the same approach of working together is recommended in all the countries of the United Kingdom.

The CAF is informed by research which suggests that children and families can move in and out of difficult phases in their lives, and that early intervention can prevent longer-term or more serious difficulties arising.

Shared assessment

One of the many difficult issues when working with vulnerable children and families is making an assessment of what the needs of the child and the family are. In the example we will consider here, a health visitor may notice that a three-year-old girl presents as slightly more prone to infections than is usual, and appears a little low in energy. But her development may seem satisfactory in terms of number of words spoken and understood, walking and running, and building with blocks in the clinic.

However, the early years practitioners working with the child may have noticed that she appears sociable at first, but is not able to play with or alongside other children. It may have been observed that while the child remains playing in areas of the nursery for some time, this involvement is only superficial and she is merely repeating the same actions over and over again.

As a result of these concerns, the child's key person could arrange to meet with the parents and the health visitor to discuss the extent to which the child is:

- healthy
- safe from harm
- learning and developing well
- socialising and making positive relationships with others
- not significantly impaired by the effects of poverty.

Team Around the Child (TAC)

This type of meeting is called Team Around the Child (TAC). There is a pre-assessment checklist for the CAF which practitioners can consult before calling such a meeting. It is important to remember that meetings like this, and the process of drawing up a CAF, are voluntary. Practitioners should only proceed with the informed consent of parents.

Using our example of the three-year-old girl, in such a meeting, the mother might explain that her child sometimes gets very little sleep at night because her older brother, with whom the girl shares a room, is disabled and needs care through the night. The mother might explain that the family is feeling overwhelmed and very stressed, and that there is little time for positive attention for her daughter.

By bringing together the information from the health visitor, the early years practitioner and the parent, an assessment of needs can be made in the following areas:

- development of the child
- parents and carers
- family environment.

This assessment, and the action plan based on the assessment, will be recorded on a standard CAF form, or electronically (the eCAF). In this case, the possible benefits of the CAF could be:

- a referral to the children's centre family support service, in order to investigate whether the family could be entitled to disability carers' allowance with respect to the older sibling
- a local voluntary group might be contacted, to provide respite care for several hours a week so that the older brother who is disabled can be cared for while the rest of the family have some time together
- an application for more suitable housing could be made, supported by the different agencies.

The parent will be asked to nominate a **lead professional** to coordinate this plan. With the CAF, the parents will not constantly need to fill out different forms and repeat the same information to different agencies.

It is possible that without this support, the child's development and play could have fallen further behind that of her peers in nursery, leading to her becoming more isolated and unhappy. The stress of the family's situation could have led to the child's needs being neglected at home. In a small number of cases, stress of this kind can lead to mistreatment of one or both children.

Children in need

The CAF is intended to provide short-term help and support for children and their families. But sometimes a child's or family's needs are likely to be significant and long-term, although the child is not at immediate risk.

The Children Act 1989 (later updated in 2004) requires local authorities to provide services to such 'children in need'. These services aim to keep the child safe and well, and to support the child's development and well-being.

Government guidance states that a child in need may be:

- disabled
- unlikely to have a reasonable standard of health or development without services from a local authority
- likely to experience impairment of their health or development without services from the local authority.

Local authorities are required to coordinate inter-agency assessment of children who may be in need, and to provide the necessary services. These services might include:

- a nursery or childminder place for a baby or toddler, a short-break service or a holiday play scheme to provide opportunities for the child to play and socialise in a safe and stimulating environment, and to offer respite to the parents
- additional care at home
- some aids and adaptations – for example, adapting a house so a child with a disability can have a ground-floor bedroom and an accessible toilet and bathroom
- financial help – for example, to pay for the transport costs for hospital visits.

There is more infinoration on the Children Act 1989 and 2004 on page 76.

Inter-agency child protection

You may have heard about children being 'on the child protection register', but technically they should be described as having an **'inter-agency child protection plan'.**

Initial assessments

Initial assessments are undertaken by specialist children's social workers in response to referrals made by schools, doctors, nurses and early years settings, for example. The initial assessment informs the decision of what to do next. Possible decisions include:

- **Offering services to support the child and family**, if it is judged that the child is not at immediate risk of harm but is at risk of poor developmental outcomes.

- **Urgent action to protect the child from harm** – for example, applying for a court order to take the child into care. Social workers cannot take children away from their parents – only the courts can direct this. However, a police officer can take a child into police protection in an emergency.

- **Holding a strategy discussion** – this would happen where the assessment indicates that the child may be suffering significant harm. Other professionals who know the child and family, such as GPs, health visitors, teachers and early years practitioners, may be invited to this discussion. Specialist police officers must always be represented in strategy discussions. Where appropriate, a child protection conference will be arranged.

It is important to remember that staff in early years settings and schools should not investigate possible abuse or neglect. The role of the early years

KEY TERMS

Lead professional – The lead professional takes the lead to coordinate provision, and acts as a single point of contact for a child and their family when a TAC (Team around the Child) is required.

Child in need – Any child who has been assessed as needing extra services from the local authority in order to attain good health or good development is a 'child in need'. This includes children with a disability.

Inter-agency protection plan – If a child's health or development has been significantly impaired as a result of physical, emotional or sexual abuse or neglect, an inter-agency protection plan may be drawn up. The plan will identify the steps that the family needs to take to safeguard the child, with the support of Children's Services and other agencies. The child's safety, health, development and well-being will be regularly monitored throughout the plan.

practitioner is to refer concerns to children's social care, to contribute to the initial assessment and to attend meetings as requested.

The initial assessment can lead to:

- further work and assessment being undertaken by specialist children's social workers – this is called the **Core Assessment**
- help being offered to the child and family on a voluntary basis, usually coordinated under the **CAF**
- a child protection conference being convened – key staff working with the family, along with the child's parents, will be invited to this conference; the meeting will be organised by an independent chairperson who has not previously been involved in the case in any way, and who reports to the Director of Children's Services.

Child protection conference

The child protection conference seeks to establish, on the basis of evidence from the referral and the initial assessment, whether the child has suffered ill-treatment, or whether his or her health or development has been significantly impaired as a result of physical, emotional or sexual abuse, or neglect. A professional judgement must be made about whether further ill-treatment or impairment is likely to occur. It is possible to hold a child protection conference pre-birth if there are significant concerns that the newborn baby will be at risk of immediate harm – for example, in a family where there has been significant previous child abuse, or where a mother has abused drugs or alcohol during pregnancy.

If this is established, the child will be made the subject of an inter-agency child protection plan. The child's early years setting or school should be involved in the preparation of the plan. The role of the school or early years setting to safeguard the child, and promote his or her welfare, should be clearly identified. Examples of this role might include:

- carefully monitoring the child's heath or well-being in the setting on a daily basis
- making referrals to specialist agencies – for example, educational psychology

- offering support and services to the parents – for example, a parenting class at the setting
- monitoring the child's progress against the planned outcomes in the agreed plan.

The Core Group

The Core Group of professionals and the child's parents must meet within ten working days of a child being made subject to a child protection plan. The group will be called together by the child's social worker in the role of the lead professional (sometimes called the key worker), and will then meet regularly as required. This group should include a member of staff from the child's early years setting or school. The Core Group develops the child protection plan into a more detailed working tool, outlining who will do what and by when. Both this working plan and the overall child protection plan should be based on the assessments undertaken by the specialist social worker and others, and should address the issues arising in relation to:

- the child's developmental needs
- parenting capacity
- family and environmental factors.

There should be a review of the child protection conference within three months of the initial conference. Further reviews should be held at least every six months while the child remains subject to a child protection plan.

The plan may be ended if it is judged that there have been significant improvements to the well-being and safety of the child. These improvements might have taken place as a result of:

- a change in circumstances – for example, the abusing parent has moved out of the family home and no longer has unsupervised contact with the child

Reflecting on practice

One of your key children is subject to an inter-agency child protection plan, under the category of neglect. During the day, you notice that the child looks rather grubby. Other children are avoiding him because of his poor hygiene.

Discuss how you would talk to the parent at the end of the day and what information you would pass on to the child's social worker.

Guidelines for good practice

Understanding the roles of others in safeguarding

✔ Working in a team, you should help work towards the plan in a CAF, or offer additional help to a child who has been identified as being vulnerable.

✔ Know about the definition of a child in need.

✔ Know who can take children into protective care if they are in immediate danger.

✔ Understand why a child might be made subject to an inter-agency child protection plan.

- the family is responding positively to the requirements set out in the plan, and following advice given
- the child is being given the medical or other treatment that he or she needs.

At this stage, there might be no further involvement from Children's Services, or the family may continue to be offered further help and support by the different agencies, usually coordinated under the CAF. This only happens once Children's Services are satisfied that their involvement is not required because the child is no longer considered to be 'in need'.

Legislation and guidelines relating to safeguarding, protection, welfare of children

'Working together to safeguard children' (2013)

This document applies to those working in education, health and social services as well as the police and the probation service. It is relevant to those working with children and their families in the statutory, independent and voluntary sectors. The document covers the following areas:

- a summary of the nature and impact of child abuse and neglect
- how to operate best practice in child protection procedures
- the roles and responsibilities of different agencies and practitioners
- the role of Local Safeguarding Children Boards (LSCBs)
- the processes to be followed when there are concerns about a child
- the action to be taken to safeguard and promote the welfare of children experiencing, or at risk of, significant harm
- the important principles to be followed when working with children and families
- training requirements for effective child protection.

This document streamlines previous guidance documents to clarify the responsibilities of professionals towards safeguarding children and strengthen the focus away from processes and onto the needs of the child.

It replaces:

- 'Working together to safeguard children' (2010)
- 'Framework for the assessment of children in need and their families' (2000), and

- statutory guidance on making arrangements to safeguard and promote the welfare of children under section 11 of the Children Act 2004 (2007).

'What to do if you're worried a child is being abused' (2006) is a guide for professionals working with children which explains the processes and systems contained in 'Working together to safeguard children'.

See p. 60 for information on the Disclosure and Barring Service.

The Children Act 2004

This Act placed a duty on local authorities and their partners (including the police, health service providers and the youth justice system) to cooperate in promoting the well-being of children and young people and to make arrangements to safeguard and promote the welfare of children.

The Act gave the Local Safeguarding Children Boards powers of investigation and review procedures which they use to review all child deaths in their area, as required by the Working Together to Safeguard Children statutory guidance. The Act also revised the legislation on physical punishment by making it an offence to hit a child if it causes mental harm or leaves a lasting mark on the skin. This repealed the section of the Children and Young Persons Act 1933 which provided parents with the defence of 'reasonable chastisement.' See page 16 for more information on this.

Legislation relating to health and safety

Health and Safety at Work Act 1974

Employers have a duty to:

- make their workplace as safe as they are able
- display a Health and Safety Law poster or supply employees with a leaflet with the same information (available from the Health and Safety Executive (HSE))
- decide how to manage health and safety: if the business has five or more employees, this must appear on a written Health and Safety Policy.

As an employee, you have a duty to:

- work safely. If you are given guidance about how to use equipment, you should follow that guidance. You should not work in a way that puts other people in danger.

Regulatory Reform (Fire Safety) Order 2005

The advice from www.firesafe.org.uk, for a nursery to meet this legislation, includes the following points:

- There should be a designated person responsible for fire safety at the setting.

- There should be adequate escape routes, free from obstruction.
- The Fire Safety Officer in the setting is required to carry out a fire risk assessment for all those who are on or around the premises.
- Sufficient numbers of trained staff should be available to enable a **safe and efficient evacuation**, taking into account the need to assist or carry children.
- There should be an induction process for new staff and **regular training and fire drills** for all staff and children.
- Fire safety notices and procedures must be written and displayed for all staff and visitors.

Control of Substances Hazardous to Health Regulations 2002 (as amended 2004) (known as COSHH)

This requires employers to keep a record of substances that could be hazardous to health, where they will be kept, how they will be used and for what purpose, as well as what to do if they contact skin, eyes or are ingested. In a nursery setting, this mainly applies to cleaning chemicals and those used for general maintenance.

Solutions such as bleach or dishwasher powders, some solvent glues and other materials in your setting can be hazardous. You should have a risk assessment that tells you what these things are, and what to do to minimise the risks involved. Any new person coming to the team must be made aware of what to do.

Every workplace must have a COSHH file which lists all the hazardous substances used in the setting. The file should detail:

- where they are kept
- how they are labelled
- their effects
- the maximum amount of time it is safe to be exposed to them
- how to deal with an emergency involving one of them.

Never mix products together as they could produce toxic fumes. Some bleaches and cleaning products, for instance, have this effect.

Manual Handling Operations Regulations 1992

This covers jobs that involve lifting. In early years settings this will apply to lifting and carrying babies and young children, as well as furniture and large play equipment. It requires employers to ensure staff are trained to lift correctly, in order to reduce back strain and injury caused through work tasks.

Reporting of Injuries, Diseases and Dangerous Occurrences Regulations 2013 (RIDDOR)

This requires that the HSE are told about serious accidents which result in injuries needing treatment from a doctor. In addition, outbreaks of a serious disease, the death of a child or adult, or a dangerous occurrence, such as an explosion, are also reportable.

An **accident report book** must be kept in which incidents that happen to staff are recorded. (Accidents to children are recorded in a separate book – see Chapter 15, p. 330).

There are two accident books:

1. For accidents within the Provision to children, kept with the First Aid Box; and
2. For accidents to employers, paid or voluntary. If an incident occurs at work that is serious enough to keep an employee off work for seven or more days, employers will need to fill in the relevant paperwork and send the report to the HSE. The HSE may investigate serious incidents and give advice on how to improve practice if needed.

Health and Safety (First Aid) Regulations 1981

Employers should make sure that at least one person at each session has an up-to-date first aid qualification and is the 'appointed' first aider. In childcare settings regulated by Ofsted, there is also a requirement for a staff member to be trained in paediatric first aid. Methods of dealing with incidents to adults and children are not the same, particularly where resuscitation is involved. Recommendations change, and for this reason, first aid qualifications must be renewed every three years.

Food Hygiene (England) Regulations 2006

The food hygiene requirements in the statutory framework for the EYFS state that:

> *managers/leaders must be confident that those responsible for preparing and handling food are competent to do so. In group provision, all staff involved in preparing and handling food must receive training in food hygiene.*

Everyone involved in preparing food for young children, or helping them to eat, needs to understand the importance of food safety and hygiene, and be aware of the requirements of the Food Hygiene Regulations. These cover what might be seen as common-sense points:

- washing your hands before preparing food
- making sure that the surfaces and utensils you use are clean and hygienic
- making sure that food is stored safely at the correct temperature
- disposing of waste hygienically.

These regulations also include knowledge of safe practices in the use of chopping boards, having separate sinks for hand-washing and preparing foods, how to lay out a kitchen, and so on. There should always be people who have completed a Basic Food Hygiene certificate available to ensure that guidance is properly carried out.

Food Information Regulations (FIR) 2014

Under this general legislation, all early years settings in the UK that provide food for children must correctly state the ingredients in all the food that they prepare. They must also clearly state if any ingredients fall into one of 14 food categories that are likely to cause allergic reactions. The categories are listed in the legislation and include familiar ingredients such as nuts and milk, as well as less familiar things such as sulphur dioxide, which is used as a preservative. You and your setting must know about these.

The legislation also includes plans for nutrition labelling to be extended in 2016 – you must keep up to date with the details of these requirements by checking www.food.gov.uk. This website also has information on the allergen labelling rules that came into force in December 2014. Moreover, the School Food Standards, which were launched as part of the School Food Plan, became mandatory in schools from January 2015. More information is available online, at www.schoolfoodplan.com/standards.

Personal Protective Equipment at Work Regulations 1992

Under these regulations, employers must make sure that suitable protective equipment is provided for employees who are exposed to a health and safety risk while at work. This is considered a last resort, for the risk should be prevented wherever possible. In childcare the most important piece of personal protective equipment that is provided will be gloves, to be used when dealing with body fluids.

Employees and students should be made aware of the need to use these when changing nappies or dealing with blood spillage or vomit. Good hygiene protects both adults and children.

Data Protection Act 1998

Anyone who keeps records, whether on computers or on paper, should comply with this Act. It should be clear for what purpose the data is being kept. Information about a child should also be accessible to its parent/carer and shared with them. It is not necessary to do this 'on demand'. A convenient time to be able to discuss the information can be arranged. Information should not be kept for longer than necessary, though accident and incident records will need to be kept in case they are needed for reference at some time in the future. Records must also be stored securely.

Children Act 1989, 2004

The Children Act 1989 brought together several sets of guidance and provided the basis for many of the standards we maintain with children. It first outlined the amount of space that should be available as well as some of the principles that we now take for granted:

- The welfare of the child is paramount.
- Practitioners should work in partnership with parents.
- Parents should care for their children whenever possible.
- Children's opinions should be taken into account when matters concern them.

The 2004 Act did not replace or change much of the 1989 version, but placed additional duties on local authorities and partners to be responsible for the delivery of Children's Services, and safeguarding and well-being of children.

Childcare Act 2006

This sets out the statutory assessment of settings within the framework of the EYFS. Among other things, the EYFS covers the adult: child ratios for working with children aged under eight. This is based on the age of the children being cared for. The minimum ratios are set out below:

Age of children	Number of adults: children (ratio)
0–2	1:3
2–3	1:4
3–8	1:8

Some places have slightly different ratios depending on local conditions, such as the number of rooms used, or the location of the toilets if not directly off the main room. Local authority nursery classes and schools may also work on a ratio of one adult to 13 children for over threes, where a trained teacher is working directly with the children.

Children in Reception classes in maintained schools must have no more than 30 children per qualified teacher.

For a good summary of current relevant child protection legislation visit the NSPCC website at http://www.nspcc.org.uk/preventing-abuse/child-protection-system/ and follow the links to the legislation, policy and guidance page.

Munro Review of Child Protection 2011

This government-commissioned detailed review by Professor Eileen Munro recommended a number of further changes to the way in which child protection is organised and the associated inspection framework.

Moving on

Think about ideas

Exploring children's rights

Until recently, parents in the UK could use the legal defence of 'reasonable chastisement' when accused of harming their child through physical punishment. This legal term, which dated back to 1860, meant that parents were legally permitted to use a degree of force in order to discipline their children, including smacking and beating.

However, the European Court of Human Rights ruled that the British law on corporal punishment in the home failed to protect children's rights and in an amendment to the Children Bill agreed by the House of Lords in 2005, smacking was outlawed in England and Wales 'if it causes harm such as bruising or mental harm'.

Find out all you can about:

- the arguments against smacking children – in particular, investigate the work of the Children Are Unbeatable! Alliance, whose aims are (a) to seek legal reform to give children the same protection under the law on assault as adults and (b) to promote positive, non-violent discipline (www.childrenareunbeatable.org.uk).
- the arguments for parents' right to smack their own children – for example, look into the Parents Have Rights campaign, which is against any legislation that interferes with parents' right to punish their children as they see fit (www.families-first.org.uk).

Further reading, weblinks and resources

Lindon, J., 2009, *Safeguarding Children and Young People*, London: Hodder Education.

Lindon, J., Webb, J. 2016, *Safeguarding and Child Protection 5th edition: Linking Theory and Practice*, London: Hodder Education.

The British Association for the Study and Prevention of Child Abuse and Neglect (BASPCAN)

BASPCAN is a registered charity that aims to prevent physical, emotional and sexual abuse and neglect of children by promoting the physical, emotional, and social well-being of children.
www.baspcan.org.uk

Kidscape

Kidscape is the first charity in the UK established specifically to prevent bullying and child sexual abuse.
www.kidscape.org.uk

NSPCC National Society for the Prevention of Cruelty to Children

The NSPCC works directly with children and families in over 40 service centres across the UK. The NSPCC helpline is a free telephone service for anyone who needs advice, help or information about concerns for a child's welfare, or to those who want to report concerns they have about a child or young person at risk of abuse.
www.nspcc.org.uk/preventing-abuse/safeguarding/
www.nspcc.org.uk

Working together to safeguard children

This is the government's guide to inter-agency working to safeguard and promote the welfare of children.
www.gov.uk/government/publications/
working-together-to-safeguard-children -- 2

Children Act 1989, 2004

For more information about children in need, go to
www.direct.gov.uk or search online for 'Children Act 1989, 2004 and social care services'.

CAF

To read the guidance on the CAF, including the pre-assessment checklist, go to **https://www.gov.uk/ government/organisations/department-for-education** and search for 'every child matters CAF'.

Department for Education

Working together to safeguard children (2015): A guide to inter-agency working to safeguard and promote the welfare of children.
www.gov.uk/government/publications/working-together-to-safeguard-children

The Children are Unbeatable! Alliance

A campaign to make hitting children against the law.
www.childrenareunbeatable.org.uk

In this chapter we will look at observation as a fundamentally important aspect of early years practice. You will find out about how to develop your skills in observation and the different techniques and tools you can use. We will discuss how to interpret observations as a basis for informed assessments of children's development and learning and using observations and assessments as your starting point for planning.

We will consider the ethical and underpinning principles of parents' and children's rights in the observation and assessment process and how the different professionals who observe and assess children can work together.

We will also explore provision, and observation as a tool for evaluating practice.

Observation

The tradition of observational practice

There is a long tradition of using written observations to gather and record information about children's development. In the nineteenth century, the biologist Charles Darwin kept a notebook about his first son William, and wrote it up in his book *A Biographical Sketch of an Infant*. While in the early twentieth century, the psychologist Jean Piaget filled his early books with beautiful observations of his children Laurent, Jacqueline and Lucienne (Bartholomew and Bruce, 1993). At this time too, Susan Isaacs and Anna Freud, as psychoanalytically trained teachers, kept regular observations of the children in their care, not only to better understand the children but also as a training tool for their staff.

In this way traditional early years practice has always emphasised the careful observation of young children and has strong multi-disciplinary roots.

What is observation?

When working with young children we are observing all the time. Being attentive, noticing and tuning in to children are fundamentally important behaviours for practitioners. But when we talk of observation as a practice, we usually mean closely watching and listening in a focused and purposeful way to what a child is doing, and recording the observation as accurately as possible.

The role of observation, assessment and evaluation in early years settings

Becoming skilled in observation and assessment is one of the most important parts of your training and developing practice. Through careful observation, you can:

- get to know each child as an individual
- understand each child's growth, health and well-being
- think about each child's particular styles of play and learning, their interests and strengths
- reflect on each child's development and think about how to support their needs and extend their learning
- gather information to share with parents, and show how you value parents' observations of their own children
- gain an understanding of how children experience life in nursery, how they interact with others and how they behave.

Analysing and interpreting observations for assessment

You can make informed assessments of children's progress in their development and learning through using your knowledge and understanding of child development theory to make sensitive interpretations of your observations. Knowledgeable and balanced assessments can inform everyone's understanding of a child in a **multidisciplinary** context.

Your observations and assessments can identify how children's development and learning is progressing. You might notice, for example, that a child is making lots of progress in their communication, but you have no observations of their exploratory play and early scientific learning. You will need to plan to look out for the child's play and learning in that area and will then understand better what may be hindering an aspect of development or learning.

KEY TERM

Multidisciplinary approach – This is where professionals from different professional specialisations work together or where a topic is looked at from different academic disciplines.

Observation for planning

You might also notice, for example, that a child has a strong interest in carrying objects around in different containers and you may have interpreted this as a transporting schema (Nutbrown 2011). This will enable you to devise play opportunities that follow the child's interests and are a good match to their abilities. It will also help you to develop a play environment that is not only interesting and stimulating but also relevant and meaningful to the child.

Observation for evaluation

Sometimes settings might identify that there are patterns in their observations and assessments, which enable them to evaluate and adjust their practice and provision, for example:

● If there are many observations of boys in the block play area, but none of girls, you will need to think of how you will encourage girls to take part in construction play.
● If boys spend little time in the book area, you might need to change the types of books on display, or try adding home-made books about children's play and interests.
● If the bilingual children (those who speak more than one language) in the setting make less progress than those who speak English as a first language, you will need to focus on whether your setting is providing enough appropriate support.

Assessment

Assessment in early years education and care involves practitioners, parents and children. It is about establishing what children understand, feel, are interested in and what they can do. See page 93 for more information on assessment.

Assessment for learning

Assessment for learning means using assessment information to help plan for children's next steps of development and learning. This planning could include activities, resources, talking and playing, or trips out.

In England the Early Years Foundation Stage framework requires practitioners to engage in 'on-going assessment' as an integral part of the learning and development process. It states:

> *It involves practitioners observing children to understand their level of achievement, interests and learning styles, and to then shape learning*

experiences for each child reflecting those observations.

(DfE 2014:13)

See chapter 7 for information on schemas which will be useful to the understanding of this chapter.

The EYFS emphasises assessment and requires practitioners to complete a progress check for all children aged two years and then to assess each child's level of development against the early learning goals at the end of the foundation stage when they reach five years old by completing the EYFS profile (DfE 2014:14).

The frameworks for early years education in Scotland, Wales and Northern Ireland also emphasise the importance of practitioners closely observing children in order to assess their progress.

All these processes depend on the quality of your observations. If your observations are poor, you will not get any useful information from them. Some practitioners collect a great deal of information about children, through observations, photographs and drawings, but the value of their work is limited if they just collect information and do not put it to any use. Equally, other practitioners plan activities for children without any thought to what they have observed the children doing. They simply pluck ideas from the air— 'Let's do play dough with glitter on Wednesday; we haven't done that for a while.' This makes it unlikely that the children will be able to build on their learning over time.

Observation, assessment and planning are in a continuous cycle. Children are regularly observed by

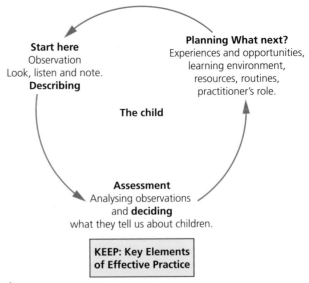

▲ **Figure 5.1** Observation, assessment and planning are a continuous cycle of activity in the early years

practitioners, and those observations are used to assess children's development and learning and to inform planning.

An overview of different approaches to observation

Tools used for observations

Different tools can be used for observation:

- photos, video, audio or written.

Practitioners are increasingly using video, photography and audio recording of children. There are many advantages that have come with new technology, especially as digital cameras and MP3 recorders are cheap and easy to use. If you want to study a child's language development and discuss it with parents, then an audio or video recording might be a very good way of doing this. Likewise, nothing records a child's construction or model as well as a carefully taken photograph. However the ethical issues in using these tools must be considered and a policy, agreed with parents, must be in place in the setting.

Written observations vary from short 'snap-shots' written on post-its or in note books or longer narrative style observations.

Different approaches to observation

- anecdotal observation – a brief note of the key point you observed (e.g. Charlie did a painting for the first time today)
- narrative observation – an account of what you saw when you observed a child for a period of time
- sampling – a focus on a particular activity or time
- longitudinal or child studies.

Anecdotal records

Practitioners in many early years settings make 'snap shot' observations of what children are doing and saying and record the details on post-it notes or similar. This would be a brief description of an incident written soon after it has occurred. This is a widely used method of observation and is useful because these notes can be easily placed with the child's file and provide the evidence which contributes to their profile. The practitioner records a significant piece of learning, perhaps the first steps a baby takes unaided, or an important development in relationships with other children.

Recent practice in early years settings seems to favour these short, 'snapshot' observations written to identify the 'Development Matters' progressive steps

(Early Education 2012). Although such notes can capture a significant new development for the first time, they cannot give the kind of **holistic** view of a child that is necessary for really understanding the 'unique child'.

Narrative observation

Narrative or '**naturalistic**' observations attempt to record exactly what is observed in the moment without being selective. They are usually written in the present tense and the reader should be able to visualise what happened, where it happened, and who said what. Sometimes a narrative observation may just include the context and time/date of the observation then a written piece where the observer records spontaneously what they see; as in a diary description method. Sometimes they have more structure, as in the target child method (Riddall-Leech 2005).

The advantage of using this approach is that it does not require any special preparation. You only need pen and paper. The method enables you to record what you see and hear. However, recording all the detail is difficult unless you have developed your own shorthand writing, so there is a chance that you might miss out on seeing something while writing.

Diary description

This is usually kept to monitor the learning and development of an individual child (but can also be used for a group) and provides a day-to-day account of significant events. It may include anecdotal records (see above) and other forms of observation. A diary is time-consuming to keep and you need to be sure that the information gathered is helpful and remains objective, rather than being mundane, repetitive and subjective. This type of observation can help to record the progress of every child in a group over time.

Target child observation

The target child observation (Painter, Roy and Sylva, 1980) is a technique based on narrative observation, which also includes a coding system to help you interpret your findings. The target child observation

KEY TERMS

Holistic approach – Adopting an holistic approach means thinking about children and their experiences in an integrated way rather than dividing the focus into different areas. This kind of integrated thinking is effectively developed through undertaking holistic, narrative observations.

Naturalistic observation – A research method that involves observing subjects in their natural environment.

RP = role play, SOL = solitary, SG = small group, LG = large group, TC = target child, C = child, A = adult, BC = book corner, SW = small world, W = waiting

Child initials: JG Gender: M Age: 3 yrs 10 mths Date/Time: 1/10/05 2.15 p.m.

ACTIVITY RECORD	LANGUAGE RECORD	TASK	SOCIAL
1 min TC on carpeted area, playing with farm animals and buildings.	TC→C My cow wants to come in your field. C→TC No. You'll have to wait till my tractor has finished.	SW	SG
2 min TC sitting at edge of carpet, looking at wall display.		W	SOL
3 min Now in dressing-up area, putting on a floppy hat and laughing.	C→TC You look funny in that. TC→C Let me see. Where's the mirror?	RP	SG
4 min Sitting in a small chair at a table, holding a knife and fork in his hands.	TC→C Where's my tea? I want my tea. Not fish fingers again!	RP	SG
5 min Standing at 'cooker' and stirring something in a pan.	A→TC What are you cooking? TC→A I'm a good cooker. it's basgetti.	RP	SG
6 min Taking off hat and tidying equipment.		RP	SOL
7 min Sitting in story corner, looking at book.		BC	LG

▲ **Figure 5.2** Example of a target child observation

involves observing individual children for 10 or 20 minutes, allowing you to gain in-depth information about each child. You will need time for the observation and then allow at least the same amount of time again for the coding and analysis of your results.

The target child observation approach was used in the Oxford Preschool Research project in the 1970s and the EPPE (Effective Provision of Preschool Education) project, which has been in progress since 1997.

Two other methods of narrative observation which not only include the context but also the social and emotional content of the scenario are the infant observation technique (Miller et al. 1989) and learning stories (Carr and Lee 2012).

The infant observation technique

The infant observation technique' was developed at the Tavistock Clinic in London for the training of psychotherapy and social work students. During their training, a student observes a child weekly from birth for a period of a year (or sometimes now a child aged between one and two), either at home or in a nursery setting. Unlike observations undertaken in early years settings, during the hour-long observation, the observer does not take any notes. Instead they are simply 'there', taking in everything that they see. Then, as soon as possible afterwards, the observer writes up their observation in as much detail as possible.

Important detail is perhaps lost this way but this technique actually provides a wealth of detail about the child and their experience because the observer notices every small example of a look, an expression, interaction or body language. It also highlights the emotional 'temperature' of the environment as what is retained in the observer's mind are their feelings about what was observed, as well as the incidents that resonated most with them.

The observer's interpretations of the observation and their emotional responses to it are then explored in a weekly discussion group. This not only helps the observer to understand what they have observed but also, because their feelings about the observation have been made explicit, they can be discussed and used to think about the child's emotional world rather than becoming overwhelmed by it or repressing their emotional response (Elfer 2005, Manning-Morton 2011).

Learning stories

The learning story approach was developed by Margaret Carr and colleagues in New Zealand to document a child's learning (Carr and Lee 2012). It uses storytelling (written and pictures) to describe a child's learning process, focusing primarily on children's dispositions and approaches to learning. A learning story starts with noticing something a child has initiated or responded to in their own particular way; this is the 'initiative' aspect.

It then describes how the experience or event unfolds, how the child interacts with others, objects and materials during the experience, their conversations and levels of interest etc. These are the 'engagement', 'intentionality' and 'relationships' aspects.

Learning stories focus on positive aspects; what the child can do rather than what the child cannot do and tells the story of this experience or event to the child, to the family, to the practitioner and to others.

Unlike other observation methods, learning stories often use direct speech in the way they are written.

The observer then writes about 'what this means' and 'what next', thus using the learning story as an assessment tool; interpreting a child's learning dispositions and evaluating and planning further

experiences. Practitioners who use this approach report not only that they discover even more wonderful things about the child but that using direct speech makes them feel closer to the child and also more ethically accountable for what they write. Learning stories also strengthen partnership working as the format includes the child's, their parents' and colleagues' views too (Manning-Morton and Thorp 2015).

Sampling methods

Time-sampling

Time-sampling involves making a series of short observations (usually up to two minutes each) at regular intervals over a fairly long period. The interval between observations and the overall duration is your decision, depending on exactly what you are observing and why. For example, you may choose to record at 20-minute intervals over the course of a whole day, or every 15 minutes during a half-day session.

It can be a useful way of finding out how children use particular toys or resources, to monitor how a new child has settled in or to observe the behaviour of an individual child. When observing an individual child's behaviour, time-sampling can raise awareness of positive aspects which may be overlooked in the normal run of a busy day. Staff can then make a point of noticing and appreciating the incidents of positive behaviour and encourage these as part of a strategy to reduce unwanted aspects.

A disadvantage of this method might be that it is difficult to keep stepping away at regular intervals from whatever else you are doing, in order to make

---

The poppy leaf: A learning story: Karin (two-and-a-half years)

Karin, today I saw you walk over to a bucket filled with rain water with leaves floating on the top; you crouched beside it for a better look. You looked at the floor around you and picked up a leaf, you threw it into the bucket and watched closely as the leaf slowly filled with water and sank. You then picked up another leaf which was red in colour and curled in shape. You stood up and turned to me. "Look!" you said, and I crouched down beside you. "Oh that is lovely, what have you found?" I asked. "A poppy," you said.

I realised you were comparing the leaf to the poppies we had talked about during group time last week. I felt proud that you had remembered and gave you a little cuddle before continuing, "It does look like a poppy, can you remember our song?" You nodded, then stared at me blankly.

I began to sing quietly so that you could join in. I could hear you singing, "eee memba, dis day, poppy on illside, far far away." Your mummy has told me that you are beginning to pick up more of the songs that we sing in nursery and are singing them at home for her.

"Well remembered Karin, can you remember what colour a poppy is?" I said. You hold the leaf up in the air, and say, "Red." "Yes, red just like your leaf." You laugh as you throw your leaf into the bucket of water. "Bye-bye poppy leaf," you say, looking into the bucket as the leaf sinks.

▲ **Figure 5.3** Example of a learning story

Child observed = HR   Teacher = T   Other children = A, B, C, D, E.

LG = large group, SG = small group, P = pair of children

Aim: To find out how well a child, newly arrived from another school, has settled in, looking particularly at interaction with other children.

Time	Setting	Language	Social group	other
9.00	Registration – sitting on carpeted area.	None	LG	At back of class group, fiddling with shoelaces and looking around the room.
9.20	At a table, playing a language game.	HR: 'It's *not* my turn.'	SG	One parent helper and 3 other children.
9.40	On floor of cloakroom.	HR: 'You splashed me first and my jumper's all wet, look.'	P	Had been to toilet and is washing hands.
10.00	In maths area, carrying out a sorting activity using coloured cubes.	T: 'Can you find some more cubes the same colour, HR?' HR: 'There's only 2 more red ones.'	SG	Concentrating and smiling as he completes the task.
10.20	Playground – HR is standing by a wall, crying.	Sobbing sounds – won't make eye contact with or speak to T on duty.	SOL	Small group of children look on.
10.40	Music activity – playing a tambour to beat the rhythm of his name.	Says his name in 2-syllable beats.	LG	Showing enjoyment by smiling – T praises him.
11.00	Tidying away instruments with another child.	A→HR: 'We have instruments every week. It's good, isn't it?' HR→A: 'Yeh, i liked it.'	P	
11.20	Playing with construction equipment with A and B.	B→HR + A: 'I've got loads of Lego at home.' HR→B + A: 'So have I. I like the technical stuff best.' B→HR: 'What's that like?'	SG	Children working together to build a garage for toy cars.
11.40	HR fetching reading book to read to T.	Humming to himself.	SOL	
12.00	Lining up with other children to go for lunch.		LG	Nudging A, who is standing in front of him. A turns round and grins.

▲ **Figure 5.4** Example of a time sample in a Year 1 class

the record. Negotiation with colleagues is essential so that children's safety is not put at risk.

You can choose your own headings for the chart format to match the detail you need to include. Usual headings are 'Time', 'Setting or location', 'Language' and 'Social group', but you may want to include 'Actions' and 'Other'.

Event sampling

This involves the observation of specific situations, incidents or behaviour. The event to be observed is usually decided in advance, and a chart format is most often used to record events as they happen. This method can be particularly useful in evaluating practice such as transitions or mealtimes or in investigating why two children keep arguing, for example. This method can help practitioners to understand better what is happening but requires them to be alert to when a spontaneous event, such as an argument, is about to occur.

Flow diagram (or movement chart)

This method allows you to present information about an individual child or a group of children, activities, safety in a work setting or use of equipment. It can be very

simple, with very basic information (see Figure 5.5), or more detailed to highlight more than one aspect (see Figure 5.6). If you want to track one child from one area or activity to another during the course of a morning session, it might help to have a prepared plan of the room on which to map her or his movement.

From this type of observation you can see:

- which activities the child visited
- the order in which he or she visited them
- how long he or she spent at each one
- which activities he or she visited on more than one occasion
- which activities he or she did not visit at all.

The more detailed version provides the following additional information:

- which activities had adult-led tasks
- which ones had an adult permanently supervising or helping
- which other children were at an activity when the observed child arrived.

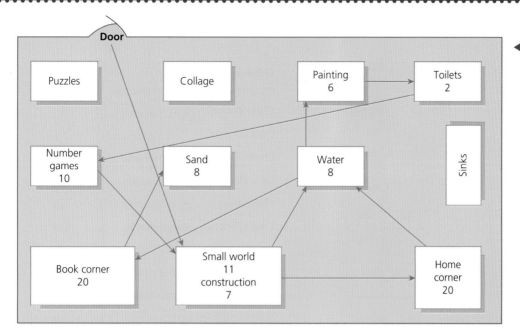

◀ Figure 5.5 Flow chart

From this level of detail you may gain further insight into the child's movements. Repeated observations may enable you to find out if the child never visits the sand, always heads for an activity with an adult present or always follows another child.

Sociogram

This is a diagrammatic method used to show an individual child's social relationships within a group, or to find out about friendship patterns between several children within a group. Identifying girls and boys separately can sometimes make it immediately clear whether girls play with girls, and boys with boys, or if they play in mixed gender groups. You should

record the ages of the children involved. You may find that an older child habitually plays with a group of much younger children. You will be able to identify any child who always plays alone or who always seeks the company of an adult. There are many factors that will affect play relationships—friendship of parents, proximity of homes, presence of siblings and, not least, pattern of attendance. These factors need to be taken into account when drawing your conclusions.

Growth charts

These can be used to plot the height and/or weight of an individual child over a period of time. Make sure you use one for the correct gender as

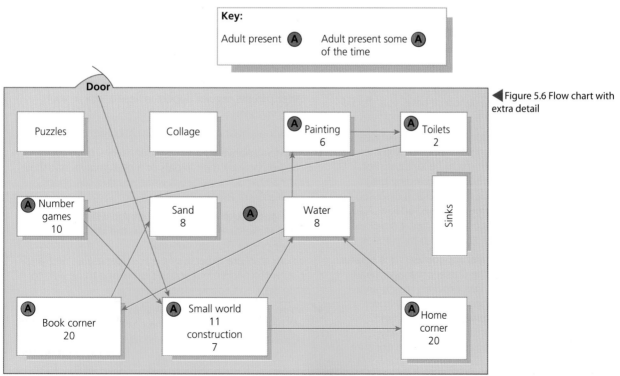

◀ Figure 5.6 Flow chart with extra detail

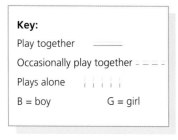

Key:

Play together ———

Occasionally play together = = = =

Plays alone ┊┊┊┊┊

B = boy   G = girl

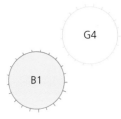

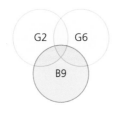

Children:	Ages:
Child B1 = boy	5 yrs 10 months
Child G2 = girl	6 yrs 1 months
Child G3 = girl	5 yrs 7 months
Child G4 = girl	6 yrs 0 months
Child B5 = boy	5 yrs 9 months
Child G6 = girl	5 yrs 6 months
Child B7 = boy	6 yrs 0 months
Child G8 = girl	5 yrs 11 months
Child B9 = boy	6 yrs 2 months
Child B10 = boy	6 yrs 0 months

▲ **Figure 5.7** Sociogram

there are variations between boys and girls. The chart cannot be used in isolation, but must be accompanied by your analysis of the information which makes reference to percentiles and shows your understanding. You must use the chart to interpret 'your' child's information. This type of chart is useful to include in a longitudinal study. Even if you are studying a child aged two years or over, it is quite likely that the parents will have a record of length/height and weight at birth and at some intervening intervals that you can plot.

Checklists

This form of recording should only be used in addition to other methods as it has many limitations. A checklist:

- gives no detail or supporting evidence
- is narrow in focus
- makes practitioners feel that they have more information than they really do
- is time-consuming to create.

Guidelines for good practice

Child studies

If you are on placement in a setting and you are going to observe a particular child over a period of time, you should take into account the following.

✔ First, speak to your supervisor or mentor: make clear the requirements of your course, and think together about which child or children might be suitable. For example, if a child is subject to a safeguarding plan, then he or she will already be observed and assessed by many different people, so would not be suitable. Also, some children are very self-conscious: being observed might stop them from playing. Ask for advice and help.

✔ Ask the parent or primary carer for consent: it is helpful if the child's key person or the nursery manager/head meets the parent with you. This provides reassurance. Explain the requirements of your course, and how having opportunities to observe children will help you to become a better practitioner. Answer any questions openly and honestly, and if you are not sure

of something, say so, and assure the parent that you will find out and answer the question in due course. Offer parents regular opportunities to look at your observations.

✔ Ask for a signature to show formal consent.

✔ Maintain anonymity and confidentiality – refer to children only by their initials or a pseudonym, not their full names; do not discuss what you find out about children with friends or family.

✔ Plan when, where and how often you will observe the child: make sure that everyone on the staff team is aware of this. You do not want to create a situation where staff are expecting you to supervise an area and play with children but you are expecting to be able to step back and spend time observing.

✔ Share your observations with staff in the setting: this will be a way you can help them with their record-keeping, assessment and planning.

Dear parent of [child's name]

My name is [your name] and I am on placement in [name of setting] for [dates of your placement].

One of the things I will be learning about is how children play, develop, learn and socialise with each other. To help me do this, I will be observing some individual children over time and I would like to ask for your consent to observe your child.

I would like to make it clear that:

- you are free to give or withhold your consent
- you can withdraw your consent at any time, without having to give a reason – just let me know
- you can ask to see my observations and notes at any time.

I will keep my observations and notes in a safe place where they cannot be read by other people. I will only share them with my tutors and with staff here at the nursery.

I will offer times to meet with you to share what I have observed. It will be very helpful if you are able to tell me about your child too, as you will know so much more than me.

Please sign below if you agree to allow me to observe your child.

Name:

Signature:

Date:

▲ **Figure 5.8** Example of a letter of consent

However, if these limitations are appreciated and the checklist is well thought out, it can be a very straightforward method of recording. It can also be useful for practitioners to help keep key points of development in mind.

Longitudinal or child studies

A longitudinal or child study consists of a series of observations of a particular child's development and learning, recorded using a variety of techniques over a period of time – a few weeks, months, a year or more. It provides opportunities to look at the 'whole' child by observing and assessing progress in all areas of development. As a student you are most likely to carry out such a study on a child whom you know well or whose family you know well. In this case, you may be given permission to include photographs and/or video footage.

The initial part of the study will involve gathering background and factual information, followed by observations carried out at agreed intervals (not necessarily regular). You may get the chance to observe special events, such as outings, birthdays,

clinic visits, as well as the child's time spent in a setting. When you have recorded all your observations you will collate the information and interpret your data according to the developmental theory you have learned. You might choose to present them in strict chronological order or in groups of observations of different developmental areas. This will depend on the focus of your study and the individual observations.

A longitudinal study can be useful in planning long-term strategies for a child with special needs.

Ethical considerations and underpinning principles in observation and assessment

An holistic approach

It is important to focus on children holistically, and think about their all-round development. The child who has a speech and language delay might be a strong and graceful mover. If we fail to think of the whole child, we can end up seeing children with problems that need fixing, rather than as individuals with strengths and special qualities as well as needs. Children's development is not even, orderly or predictable.

The Department for Education in England has produced non-statutory guidance to child development entitled 'Early Years Outcomes' (DfE 2013). This consists of a very simplified list of some elements of development against which practitioners are expected to observe children at each stage to see if they are developing typically for their age. However, these lists can be completely misunderstood if practitioners have had insufficient education in child development. They can also be misused, particularly if the main purpose of observation and assessment is seen to be to identify where children are not meeting the specified early learning goals (Manning-Morton and Thorp 2015).

The 'Early Years Outcomes' (DfE 2013) emphasises a normative view of children's development and learning. In reality, children's development is much more complex and less orderly, as can be seen from the examples below.

● **Children can become specialists for a time**: when a baby is just starting to lift him or herself and take a few steps, this might take up all of his or her energy for quite some time. Similarly, a four-year-old may become deeply interested in something like block play and spend a great deal of his or her time building constructions. So you might see a great deal of development in one area and not much in another.

● **Children have individual learning styles**: some babies are real 'doers' and are physically active all the time, while others might be 'communicators' and prefer to stay in close contact with parents and carers. The first baby will make a lot more progress in physical development, the second baby more in communication.

● **Some children have disabilities**: for example, a young child with a serious lung disease who uses oxygen to help his or her breathing. This means that the child's speech is very slow to develop, but in other areas his or her development is sound.

● **Some children have difficult early experiences**: if a baby is born prematurely and spends time in hospital, much of his or her early development will be delayed, and this delay might continue throughout their early years. The key question to ask is whether the child is making steady progress over time.

● **Some children have been neglected or abused**: if a young baby has been neglected by his or her parents, all aspects of development will be affected. Where children have witnessed domestic violence between their parents, they are likely to have difficulties with their emotional development. In cases like these, multi-agency assessment and planning, using the Common Assessment Framework (CAF – see Chapter 4 for more information) (CWDC 2009), will aim to support the child's development.

One of the key skills of an early years practitioner is to be able to work positively with children's diverse development and find individual ways of supporting each child to make progress. To do this it is necessary to understand the socio cultural contexts of children's development.

Objectivity and bias

When learning about observation, practitioners are taught to be as objective as possible in their observations, and this is important to ensure that observations are as unbiased as possible. However, as Elfer (2005) identifies, this can lead to observations being rather clinical and narrow; in contrast to the warm and enthusiastic way in which practitioners' talk about what they see their key children doing. The paradox is that to be valuable, observations need to be factual and without bias yet convey the qualitative atmosphere of a scenario which has emotional content. Therefore the recorded information must be both appropriate to what is being observed and use language that conveys

▲ **Figure 5.9** When observing children, practitioners should remain aware of how their own experiences will influence their interpretation of what they see and hear

the context and the quality of what was observed (Manning-Morton and Thorp 2015).

Personal bias

Another problem with objectivity is that it is impossible to see or hear something without having a thought and a feeling about it. When we observe a child we will have an emotional response to the situation and immediately form ideas in our minds about what is going on. These feelings and ideas will be influenced by our:

● own childhood experiences and how we feel about them

● personal values arising from our upbringing and family culture

● professional values based on our training and experience

● current personal and professional situation and how we feel about it.

The challenge for the observer is to be aware enough of their own responses to be able to work out whether their feelings are skewing their interpretation of what is happening or whether bringing their responses to the fore can help to understand the child or the situation better. The key way to do this is to spend time sharing and discussing your observations with skilled colleagues.

Sharing observations with colleagues and parents also helps to avoid the 'horn' or 'halo' effect, where we only notice things that fit with our already preconceived ideas about that child. This may result in overlooking a difficulty a child is having because we see them as generally competent or not noticing the achievements of a child about whom we have had negative reports.

Bias in the observation and assessment system

Child development charts, such as 'early years outcomes' or Mary Sheridan's charts of developmental progress (Sheridan 1997), can be criticised for trying to 'normalise' each child. In other words, instead of seeing development as varied and influenced by different cultures and backgrounds, charts can present an 'ideal child'. This is a problem if any child who develops differently is seen as abnormal and problematic.

For example, Laura E. Berk (2006: 333) summarises a large number of American research studies which suggest that the communication styles of some families from poorer minority ethnic backgrounds are very different to the styles that are expected and valued in schools. Observations indicated that wealthier, white families were likely to ask questions such as: 'How many beads have you got' and 'What colour is that car?' Children who are used to answering questions like this do well in schools where such exchanges are common.

On the other hand, in many of the minority ethnic families observed, 'real' questions were asked – where the parent genuinely does not know the answer. Often, questions asked by parents called for individual responses, not 'right' answers – for example, 'So, what do you think of that car then?'

Any observation and assessment system that focuses on children giving correct answers to questions would be likely to favour those from wealthier, white backgrounds. Children who could not answer lots of direct questions about the colour and numbers of things might be seen as deficient. But a more flexible observation and assessment system would be able to recognise the particular strengths of children with a range of conversational styles.

Observations that try to record accurately what children do and say will be less biased. One child's discussion of his views about a car can be valued just as much as another's correct description of the car's colour and features.

Bias in the setting

Bias can also arise in the observation system in a setting if the range of when and where observations are made is limited and if the focus of observation is skewed in the direction of only a few aspects of development and learning.

You can minimise bias by:

● focusing on what children actually do and say

● raising your awareness of cultural diversity

● learning from parents about how they play and talk with their children at home, and what they value

● involving children – ask them to tell you what their thoughts are about what you have noticed and heard

● avoiding drawing any conclusions while you are observing

● using holistic approaches to observation and assessment

● keeping a schedule of observations to check that all children are being observed in a range of contexts

● reflecting on the meaning of your observations with skilled colleagues.

Guidelines for good practice

Using cameras, camcorders and MP3 recorders

✔ Before you make an audio or video recording of a child, or take photographs, check the policy of the setting.

✔ Think about how you will store data safely and with parental consent. It is not advisable to download photos or video onto your personal computer, for example. Best practice would be to keep everything on a computer in the setting, with password protection or encryption.

✔ Think about how you will position yourself. You will need to be quite close to the children to pick up their voices clearly, for example.

✔ Analysing video and audio recordings is extremely time-consuming. You may get the best results if you record for just a minute or two at the right moment – when a child is really engaged in his play or in full conversational flow.

Accurately transcribing even a few minutes of children's conversation can take half an hour or more.

✔ Think about how you will display and share information:

✔ Digital slideshows of well-taken photos can be a powerful and accessible way of showing a child's learning story, for example, or how a range of children play and learn in a particular area.

✔ Many settings put together profile books of individual children. These usually consist of photos with written observations and assessments. You will need to take care that a profile book is not merely a scrapbook of photos, without any commentary on the child's learning and development.

No personal mobile phones or tablet computers should be used in a setting. If such devices are used to record observations, the setting will have their own device and the date will be stored securely

Involving parents and upholding their rights in the assessment process

Parents and primary carers will have a wealth of knowledge about their children. While you could just get on with observing and assessing children in the nursery, you will get a much more rounded picture if you also do the following.

Share observations with parents

Ask parents to tell you about what their children do at home

Ask parents about their child's favourite activities, special times and things that are difficult or cause problems. Parents often have a very good insight into how their child learns best: through movement, through conversation or by joining in with what adults do, for example.

Compare what children do in the nursery with what they do at home

Sometimes children play much more elaborately and for longer periods of time at home than they do in nursery. You could be in danger, then, of underestimating the child's development and learning, and you need help from parents to try to change or improve the nursery environment. Equally, sometimes parents are surprised and delighted by what their children are doing in nursery, and this can help them to think of more interesting and rewarding things to do at home.

Think aloud with parents to clarify your ideas

You might say something like, 'Jason seems to spend a lot of time at the play dough table, but he's very quiet and I'm not sure what he's up to.' Jason's mother might be able to tell you that Jason spends a lot of time in the kitchen while she is baking. Together, you might plan to give him more opportunities to practise rolling and cutting dough, and to talk about what he is doing.

Find out about children's home language development

If a child is learning English as an additional language (including the children of deaf parents who use British Sign Language (BSL) at home), it is important to find out about the child's language development at home. A child does not have a speech and language problem if their English is at a very early stage but they are talking fluently in their home language. On the other hand, if a child is hardly talking at home, it will be important to involve a speech and language therapist– otherwise you might wait a long time in vain for the child to start using English in the nursery. Where possible, bilingual support services should be used to aid communication between practitioners and parents.

Understand the child's family and culture

Some children's home cultures may emphasise showing respect for adults by listening, not talking back. A child may then be embarrassed or slow to talk to adults but if they show an interest in others and in nursery activities, there is no need for

Reflecting on practice

Sharing observations with parents

The best approach to working with parents is to develop a culture of mutual trust, respect and sharing of information. This principle is threaded through all curricula guidance and frameworks.

Review the framework you use in your setting and identify all the ways in which you are expected to involve parents and carers in the observation and assessment of their child.

- How do you implement these practices in your setting?
- Are there any that you think could be developed further?

concern. Gradually the child will manage to move between the different cultures of home and nursery, particularly if you support them by being sensitive and not pressurising them into having to answer direct questions.

However, if a child shrinks away, is afraid of adults or is generally fearful, you will need to discuss your concerns with the manager or nursery head.

The EYFS in England specifies the following:

- Practitioners should respond to their own day-to-day observations about children's progress and observations that parents and carers share.
- Practitioners must explore the child's skills in the home language with parents and/or carers.
- Parents and/or carers should be kept up to date with their child's progress and development.
- If a child's progress in any prime area gives cause for concern, practitioners must discuss this with the child's parents and/or carers and agree how to support the child.
- Providers must have the consent of parents and/or carers to share information directly with other relevant professionals.

The Welsh and Scottish curriculum frameworks also discuss the centrality of the assessment process to good quality teaching and learning. The Scottish 'Curriculum for Excellence' (for 3-18 year olds) framework and the Pre-birth to Three Guidance emphasise that assessment should be from the perspective of the child and be carried out in partnership with parents (educationscotland.gov.uk and http://gov.wales).

While this gives practitioners guidance on what they must do, successfully involving parents in the observation and assessment of their child means also

thinking about how to go about this. One consideration is how to make assessment records accessible while retaining their professional purpose. A folder full of long written observations is unlikely to engage most parents, especially if the observations are handwritten and hard to read. On the other hand, profile books that are carefully illustrated with photos, as well as including written observations, are much more inviting.

Video and slide shows of photos are another way to engage parents. The danger here is that the focus on the child's development, learning and well-being can get lost if parents are presented with something that looks like a scrapbook, family album or holiday slide show, full of posed images of smiling children.

Involving children and upholding their rights in the assessment process

It is very important to remember that everything that happens in the nursery must be in the children's interests. Children cannot give informed consent in the way that adults can, so you must take extra care to ensure that you are respecting their rights at all times.

If you think your observation might be causing distress or discomfort, you should stop. Look out for times where the child:

- keeps looking at you and seems inhibited from playing
- seems uncomfortable
- shrinks or looks away when you get close enough to observe
- indicates through body language or words that they do not want you to observe.

If a child asks you what you are doing or shows interest:

- explain that you are watching his or her play and that you are very interested in what he or she is doing
- show the child your notebook or paper and explain that you are writing things down
- wait patiently for the child to go back to his or her play or activity, without trying to shoo the child away; you will usually find that children get used to observations and stop noticing you.

If a child might be about to have an accident, or if you think a child is about to be hurt or bullied, you will need to stop your observation and intervene (or ask a member of staff to help).

It is also good practice to share your observations with children, taking account of their age and development. With very young children, you may want to look at photos together and consider the child's responses (smiles, frowns, lack of interest, etc.). Many children from the age of three years upwards will be able to talk to you for a time.

Listening to young children

Ensuring that young children are involved in the observation and assessment process and upholding their rights is central to the approach developed in the 'Listening as a way of life' project (Clark 2009). The project developed this approach so that children, as well as staff and parents, could be part of a specific consultation about a particular entitlement, choice, event or opportunity and also to ensure that all children feel confident, safe and powerful enough to express themselves (Lancaster and Broadbent 2003). This project advocates a '**mosaic**' approach (Clark and Moss 2011) to gathering information, involving children in using a range of different tools, including photography, drawing, play and storytelling.

Sharing information in a multi-professional context

It is extremely important that professionals working with the same child and family in different contexts share information appropriately, such as a social worker or health visitor sharing relevant information about a health issue in the family that is affecting the care of the child. This means always thinking about the impact and consequences for the child and family of sharing or not sharing information; being mindful of the parent/carer's rights but keeping the welfare of the child paramount.

See Chapter 3 p. 50 for more information on information sharing and relevant legislation.

Consent

Information on a child should only be collected and stored with the consent of the child's parents, who should have free access to this information on request. Information should only be shared between professionals with the express consent of parents, which should be gained formally with a signature. The only exceptions are cases where the child might otherwise be at risk of immediate and significant harm if you shared a piece of information with the parent.

Confidentiality

It is important that information is securely stored so that it cannot be freely accessed by anyone. Practitioners, including students, should not discuss or otherwise share this information – for example, when chatting in the staffroom or with friends at the weekend. If information is kept on computers or sent by email, steps must be taken to ensure that it could not fall into the hands of other people (through the use of encryption software for example).

However, where good, cooperative working is achieved between professionals, with clear consent, there are numerous benefits for parents:

- **Openness:** an assessment is shared, so parents can see what the different views of the professionals are, and can put across their own viewpoint too.
- **Not having to repeat the same information over and over again:** if information is shared, a parent will not have to tell each professional in turn about something distressing, like their baby's difficult birth. Parents only have to tell their story once.
- **Not being bombarded with different advice:** having a single agreed set of advice and action plan. Otherwise, a parent might find that everyone has a different opinion about how to help their child, and might feel overwhelmed or confused.

When professionals and parents cooperate well and share information in this way, children benefit.

- **They do not have to be constantly assessed by different people:** if a paediatrician has information about a child's development and learning in nursery, she or he will not need to undertake a long assessment at the clinic, but can focus instead on areas of particular importance.
- **Consistent programmes can be put together to help the child:** if a child has received speech and language therapy in a clinic, with the target of putting two words together, then consistent help with this at home and in nursery will provide significantly more benefit.

Assessment

Assessment is just one part of a cycle that sits most comfortably between observation and planning. High quality assessment and planning flow from observation and enhance the day-to-day experience of children. To be effective, assessments need to give an accurate, all-round picture of the child and should give a coherent view of the child's progress, so they need to be kept up to date and in chronological order.

By assessment, we mean interpreting what your observation says about the child's development, learning, health and well-being.

It is important to become skilled in interpreting your observations and assessing children so that you can:

- fully understand the children
- have purposeful discussions with parents, carers and colleagues
- think about what to plan next
- identify children's strengths and also their areas of difficulty
- monitor children's progress and offer help if a child does not seem to be accessing a particular area of the curriculum or does not seem to be making good progress
- reflect on the quality of your work as a practitioner and the overall quality of your setting.

The EYFS (DfE 2014) requires that:

- settings maintain and regularly update records of children's development and progress
- records must be securely stored
- records must be accessible to parents on demand.

Also providers must complete:

1   The EYFS profile:

> *All Early Years providers must complete an EYFS profile for each child in the final term of the year which the child reaches the age of five... The profile describes each child's attainment against the 17 early learning goals together with a short narrative about their learning characteristics.*

> **(DfE, 2013)**

2   The two-year-old progress check:

> *The Early Years Foundation Stage (EYFS) requires that parents and carers must be supplied with a short written summary of their child's*

▲ **Figure 5.10** It is essential to involve parents in the assessment process

> *development in the three prime learning and development areas of the EYFS: Personal, Social and Emotional Development; Physical Development; and Communication and Language; when the child is aged between 24–36 months.*

> **(National Children's Bureau, 2012)**

However, there are planned changes to these assessments in the EYFS so make sure that you are up-to-date with the latest requirements.

Interpretations and judgements in assessment

In the observation–assessment–planning cycle, it is necessary to have a good understanding of what you think your observations mean to be able to develop relevant play opportunities for children. But when we assess others, we have power over them so this has to be carried out ethically, sensitively and responsibly.

It is useful then to be clear about what we mean by making 'judgements' in assessment. This is not the kind of judgement that is a verdict or a conclusion about a child as a whole. Phrases such as 'Rohan is a very quiet boy' or 'Paulette is very popular' are judgemental and non-specific assessments, whereas informed and sensitive interpretations based on a sound knowledge of child development give much clearer information about the child, such as; 'Paulette shows pleasure at the other children's company; she enjoys being involved in the older children's games'. This kind of judgement is more about discernment or working out what the key issues are and your view of what that might mean.

This kind of approach does not mean that you hold back from making judgements. If you never make judgements about children's development, you will never notice which children are experiencing difficulties and therefore need extra help. But it does mean

Making links between your observations and what you are learning

Choose an observation that you have completed recently. Think about how this links to what you have learned in college or on courses about early years, childhood and child development, and what you have been reading about.

For example, you might have observed a group of children playing in the home corner:

Iqbal wants to start making the dinner, but Aaliya says to him, 'We can't start making dinner until the kitchen is tidy.' So Iqbal changes his plan and, together with Aaliya, starts clearing things away. You could write that this is an example of how 'group play offers children the opportunity to see things from other people's points of view' (Bruce, 2005: 192).

Now take one example from your observation and link it to a theory or idea about children's development. Remember to reference the ideas you use; who wrote about this theory?

approaching assessment with a spirit of enquiry asking, 'what am I learning about this child?' and avoiding using non-specific, judgemental and biased language.

The important thing is that you base your judgements on the information you have recorded, not merely on your opinions and impressions. You should also be open to the views of others – parents and your colleagues, for example. Be prepared to explain why you have formed your opinion, but be open to changing your mind.

What measures are we assessing children against?

In England, early years practitioners are expected to use the 'Early Years Outcomes' (DfE 2013) to measure children's progress. These scales present a normative view of children's development and learning. An outcomes or milestones perspective on assessment often relies on a task-based approach, whereby the child is presented with certain materials and encouraged to do certain activities. Test situations such as this can result in decontextualised, biased, unrepresentative and invalid results as children will often find them strange and bewildering (Manning-Morton and Thorp 2015).

It is also important to remember that the early learning goals set out the expected levels of achievement at the end of the Reception year. Unless you are completing

an EYFS profile, you will be considering children's progress in the light of the age bands set out in 'Development matters'. (Early Education, 2012)

Many researchers and practitioners have argued that the literacy targets in the early learning goals are inappropriate for five-year-olds. There has been a public campaign against these targets, with support from many public figures, including former children's laureate Michael Morpurgo and the author Philip Pullman. Evidence shows that only a minority of children achieve them. In addition, there can be as much as 11 months difference in age between the oldest and youngest children in the summer term of reception. So you would expect to see quite a significant difference in their progress against the early learning goals for this reason alone.

A useful way of avoiding the pitfalls of using checklists is to ask not 'Does this child show interest in illustrations and print in books and print in the environment?' for example, but to ask 'In what way…?' or 'What examples have I seen of…?'. This will recognise each child's individual way of doing things and give a more holistic picture of their development and learning.

In this approach, the assessment process will record the variety of ways the child demonstrates all they know and can do in the context of their everyday experiences. This is called **'formative assessment'**, wherein all aspects of the child's development are recorded and the way in which they interlink is made clear.

Different approaches to assessment

Different approaches to assessment are taken at different times and in different places. Like all aspects of practice and provision they have a historical and sociocultural context and a philosophical and pedagogical basis.

Documentation: the Reggio Emilia approach

In the infant/toddler and early years centres in Reggio Emilia in Northern Italy, documentation of children's learning is extensive. It will include many items that are familiar to practitioners in the UK such as samples of a child's work, photographs and comments from the practitioners and parents. But the approach is somewhat different. The practice in these settings is based on an **'emergent' curriculum** so documentation is focused more on the process of a child's work at several different stages of completion, rather than just the finished product. Also documentation is seen as a dialogue with the child so there will be transcriptions of children's discussions, comments, and explanations of intentions about the activity (Katz et al. 1996).

Project spectrum

Howard Gardner's theory of multiple intelligences challenges us to look at what we assess and how we value certain aspects of learning and development more than others.

In the USA, spectrum classrooms are based on Gardner's theory so their approach to assessment focuses on children's learning styles; their persistence, confidence, playfulness and how they respond to visual, auditory and kinaesthetic (movement) cues, for example. A key focus here is on the children's personal intelligences; their interpersonal and intrapersonal skills and understanding (of themselves and others) (Chen et al. 1998).

Profile books

Profile books are very influenced by the Reggio Emilia approach and also by the learning story approach, and many settings in the UK use profile books for formative assessments.

Profile books usefully include:

- Information provided by the parent/carer including information on the children's interests and favourite playthings at home, their physical care routines, cultures, languages and family compositions.
- Extracts from observations that illustrate actual achievements and interests with concrete examples collected by practitioners in the setting and parents/carers at home.
- Photographs and samples of artwork that are dated and annotated with specific comments such as 'David explored pushing the bottle under the water to make air bubbles come out' rather than general comments such as 'David had a lovely time playing with the water'.
- Pockets for objects made, found or brought from home.

Profile books should be stored so they are available to children and should be available for parents to take home, comment on and add contributions.

Profile books may also include summaries of a child's progress and next steps or these may be kept separately.

Profile books contain all the materials suggested for a 'learning journey', which is a collection of carefully chosen, dated and sequenced data that celebrate a child's achievements and interests during the time they spend in a setting and shows the journey of a child's learning and development.

Each of the above may focus mainly on formative assessments but will also include some summative assessments at key points, such as those outlined below:

Summative assessments

Summative assessments should be recorded at particular stages such as:

- a settling-in review with parents after the child's first six weeks in the setting
- regular parent conferences
- conferences with other professionals involved with the family
- when a child transfers to another group or setting.

These summative assessments should be written in consultation with parents, include their comments and points of view and only shared with other professionals with parental consent. They should use clear headings and everyday language rather than jargon. (Manning-Morton and Thorp 2006)

Observation and assessment of children on entry

It is important to start building up observations of each child and keeping good-quality records from the time they start in the setting.

- Collect information from parents on the home visit or at the pre-admission meeting.
- If the child has attended another setting or spent time with a childminder, ask for the parents' consent to have their records transferred.
- Observe how the child settles in. How do they manage the transition from parent to nursery? How is the relationship with the key person developing? Observe what sort of play they do in their early days and weeks, how long they remain involved, and whether they communicate with other children or adults.
- Some children are cared for by two or more EYFS providers – for example, a child may attend a playgroup in the morning and be picked up by a childminder who looks after him or her for the afternoon. The two providers will need to plan how they will update each other on their observations,

assessments and planning, allowing for common sense and realism. It will not be possible to have an extended daily update on the child, but it is a requirement that information is exchanged regularly.

It is not practical, and probably not even possible, to assess a child against all **seven areas of learning and development** when they start in a setting. Children who are just getting used to nursery are unlikely to show their best communication or immediately get involved in complex play for long periods. They are more likely to be a little quieter than usual, to hold back and watch others, or to seek reassurance by repeating favourite play activities or staying close to their key person.

Children who are starting in a setting are unlikely to take well to a practitioner quizzing them on their number and colour knowledge in order to fill out a baseline assessment form.

However, it is a requirement for all settings to track children's progress, so it is essential to establish a 'starting point' for each child. This should include at least:

● an observation and assessment showing the child's sense of security, emotional well-being and interest in taking part in nursery activities
● an observation and assessment of the child's communication, including verbal and non-verbal communication (smiling, crying, vocalising and gesturing)
● an observation and assessment of the child's play, in any area.

At the settling-in review, the key person can share these observations and assessments with the parent and learn about the child's development at home. Over subsequent months, it will be possible to chart the child's progress against these starting points. A child might begin in nursery quite upset and withdrawn for much of the day. But two months later, although the child still shows some distress when his or her parent leaves, he or she might usually be quick to approach a special friend and settle into play.

KEY TERM

Seven areas of learning and development – The EYFS uses the term 'learning and development' to describe seven areas of learning. They are divided into prime and specific areas. Prime areas are personal, social and emotional development, communication and language, physical development. Specific areas are literacy, mathematics, understanding the world, expressive arts and design.

So you can see the child's emotional development and his or her social development.

If you are not able to see development when you compare observations, you will need to consider whether the child might need some additional help or support. You should discuss this with your manager or head, and then talk over your concerns with the child's parents.

The Common Assessment Framework

This is

a standardised approach used by practitioners to assess children's additional needs and decide how these should be met.

(DfE, 2013a)

See Chapter 4 for more information on the CAF.

Other professionals and specialists involved in observation and assessment

For a long time it has been the role of health and medical professionals to carry out regular checks, measurements and assessments on children, initially as foetuses in the womb during pregnancy, through birth and into the early years.

● Health visitors oversee infant health, including immunisations, referring to paediatricians when necessary. They monitor weight, diet, general growth and development, usually until the child begins school.
● School health services continue sight and hearing tests, and may administer immunisations or vaccinations (e.g. in cases of hepatitis or meningitis outbreaks).
● Child clinics, family health centres and paediatric wards in hospitals also monitor children's health, relying on observation and assessment of children.

Historically, it was common for the professionals in different agencies – health, social services, child care and education – to keep their observations and records to themselves. But the Every Child Matters programme (DfES 2003) required professionals to work together more, and in closer collaboration with parents. The same theme is emphasised in the Scottish government's commitment to Early Intervention, Cymorth in Wales, and the Sure Start programme in Northern Ireland.

Although ECM is no longer a current government policy, the principle of working together remains in place.

In the past, a child's development at the age of two years would have always been assessed in a clinic by a health visitor using a tick-list. Clinics are unfamiliar places for children, and they are places we go to when we are sick – not the best places for children to play, talk and move around. But the recent development of the two-year-old check (DfE 2014) suggests a more integrated approach, with the early years practitioner and the health visitor working together with the child and the family in the early years setting to identify any issues with the child's progress.

Sometimes, a child is being helped by more than one agency. For example, an overweight child might be in nursery, and also under the care of a paediatric dietician. In these cases, the professionals will work together to assess the child's development, in partnership with parents, using the CAF. The CAF will help everyone to assess the child in a holistic way. For example, it will be just as important to find out how physically active the child is at home and in nursery, as it will be to find out what the child is eating. The CAF will then be used to agree a plan of action, involving the parents, to meet the child's needs.

Multi-professional working is important. But remember that it involves a team approach. As an early years practitioner, you will be able to observe how children:

- play and learn in nursery
- interact with other children
- move, inside and outdoors
- manage disputes and conflicts
- eat, drink, rest and sleep
- respond when they part from their parents and are reunited.

These observations will make an important contribution to a CAF. However, some children – especially those with medical conditions, disabilities and special educational needs – will also need to be observed and assessed by other specialist professionals. For example, a child with Down's syndrome may be observed in the nursery by an occupational therapist, a speech and language therapist, and an educational psychologist. Each of these professionals will be able to observe aspects of the child's development using their specific training and professional knowledge. It is also most important to remember that the child's parents will almost certainly be the people with the most knowledge and expertise.

Think about ideas

Find out more about the CAF by visiting www. education.gov.uk and search for 'Common Assessment Framework'.

Evaluation

One of the most important uses of your observations is to reflect on the effectiveness of your practice and provision. Sometimes a difficulty that is ascribed to an individual child can be easily addressed by reviewing how a particular aspect of the provision is organised and making small adjustments.

Evaluation of practice and provision helps you to:

- think about the quality of care routines and interactions
- evaluate the quality of the learning environment and the curriculum.

Different approaches to evaluation

Leuven involvement and well-being scales

The Leuven involvement and well-being scales were developed by Dr Ferre Laevers and colleagues at Leuven University and early years settings in Belgium in the Experiential Education (EXE) project. The theory underpinning the EXE project is that to assess the quality of a setting, it is necessary to focus on the process of children's experience, that is, their levels of emotional well-being and their levels of involvement. The project uses scales and indicators to measure these.

It also provides an 'Adult style observation schedule' (ASOS), which measures how the adult provides stimulation, sensitivity and gives autonomy. There are then ten action points, an inventory of ten types of practice and provision that favour well-being and involvement (Laevers and Moons 1997). Taken all together, these can give you valuable information about how effective your setting is. These scales were adopted by settings involved in the Effective Early Learning programme in the UK (Bertram and Pascal 1997).

The mosaic approach

The mosaic approach – devised by Clark and Moss (2011) – is a particularly well-known example of

▲ **Figure 5.11** Peer observation (observing each other) is a useful way to evaluate practice in settings

creative listening to children developed in order to gain an understanding of what children feel about their experiences in their early years setting. This is viewed as important in order that early years' settings improve their service in response to the views of all participants in a setting, not just the adult participants.

ECERS, ITERS and SSTEW

Thelma Harms and Richard Clifford and colleagues at the University of North Carolina, USA, developed three rating scales to measure the quality of both the physical and the social environments in group child care and home-based childcare settings. They are:

- The early childhood environment rating scale – revised (ECERS-R) (Harms et al. 2005)
- The infant-toddler environment rating scale – revised (ITERS-R) (Harms et al. 2003)
- The family child care rating scale – revised (FCCERS-R) (Harms et al. 2007).

The scales cover a wide range of aspects, including space and furnishings, personal care routines, activities and interaction, which are scored according to criteria across seven rating scales.

This method has been used extensively in the UK both by local authorities to evaluate settings and by researchers such as in the 'Quality Counts' evaluation of the Early Education Pilot for Two Year Old Children (Smith et al. 2009).

A recent addition to these scales in the UK, has been the sustained shared thinking and emotional well-being scale for provision for children aged between two and five years (Siraj et al. 2015). It aims to add to existing scales by focusing evaluation on the kinds of interactions that support well-being, self-regulation and focused thinking in children. See Chapter 17 for more information.

Further reading, weblinks and resources

Carr, M. and Lee, W. (2012) Learning Stories: Constructing Learner Identities in Early Education. London: Sage Publications.

Clark, A. and Moss, P. (2011) (2nd Ed.) Listening to young children: The Mosaic Approach. London: National Children's Bureau.

Fawcett, M. (2009) Learning through Child Observation. London: Jessica Kingsley Publishers.

The Welsh Government has produced a brief and helpful guide to observation in the Foundation Phase that will give you more ideas. You can find the guide by searching online for 'Foundation Phase Observing Children'.

EYFS documents

https://www.gov.uk/government/publications/ early-years-foundation-stage-framework--2

Early Years Foundation Stage Profile videos

Expertly selected video footage of children learning in the EYFS, together with notes and guidance. You can find these by searching for 'Early Years Foundation Stage Profile Videos.'

Every Child Matters

Although ECM is no longer a government policy, the Principle of working together remains in place. The policy paper, first published in 2003 can be found at

https://www.gov.uk/government/publications/ every-child-matters

Siren Films

High quality DVDs showing children playing and learning at home and in EYFS settings.
www.sirenfilms.co.uk

Moving on

Think about ideas

Use the reference list at the end of the chapter or search online to research an approach to observation, assessment or evaluation that you are not familiar with. Write a short account of this approach and identify its advantages and disadvantages. What ethical issues do you need to consider when using it?

What more have you been able to find out about the child as a result of using this method?

References

Bartholomew, L. and Bruce, T., 1993, *Getting to Know You: A Guide to Record-keeping in Early Childhood Education and Care*. London: Hodder & Stoughton.

Berk, L.E., 2006, *Child Development* (7th edn), Boston, MA: Pearson International Edition.

Bertram, T. and Pascal, C., 1997, *Effective Early Learning: Case Studies in Improvement*, London: Hodder & Stoughton.

Carr, M. and Lee, W., 2012, *Learning Stories: Constructing Learner Identities in Early Education*, London: Sage Publications.

Chen, J-Q. et al., 1998, *Building on Children's Strengths: The experience of Project Spectrum*, New York: Ablex Publishing Company.

Children's Workforce Development Council, 2009, *The Common Assessment Framework for children and young people: A guide for practitioners*. Available at: www.cwdcouncil.org.uk and www.dcsf.gov.uk/everychildmatters/strategy/deliveringservices1/caf/cafframework

Clark, A., 2009, *Listening as a way of Life*, London: National Children's Bureau, The Young Children's Voices Network. Available at: http://www.ncb.org.uk/media/74018/an_introduction_to_why_and_how_we_listen_to_very_young_children.pdf

Clark, A. and Moss, P., 2011, *Listening to Young Children: The Mosaic Approach* (2nd edn), London: National Children's Bureau.

Department for Education, 2013, *Early Years Outcomes. A non-statutory guide for practitioners and inspectors to help inform understanding of child development through the early years*. Available at: http://www.foundationyears.org.uk/eyfs-statutory-framework/

Department for Education, 2014, *Statutory Framework for the Early Years Foundation Stage*.

[Available at: http://www.foundationyears.org.uk/eyfs-statutory-framework/]

Department for Education and Skills, 2003, *Every Child Matters*, London: HMSO.

Early Education, 2012, *Development Matters in the Early Years Foundation Stage*. Available at: www.early-education.org.uk.

Elfer, P., 2005, 'Observation Matters', in Abbott, L. and Langston, A. (eds.), *Birth to Three Matters: Supporting the Framework of Effective Practice*. Maidenhead: Open University Press; McGraw-Hill Education.

Fawcett, M., 2009, *Learning through Child Observation*, London: Jessica Kingsley.

Harms, T., Cryer, D. and Clifford, R.M., 2003, *Infant/Toddler Environment Rating Scale – Revised*, New York: Teachers College Press.

Harms, T., Clifford, R.M. and Cryer, D., 2005, *The Early Childhood Environment Rating Scale – Revised*, New York: Teachers College Press.

Harms, T., Cryer, D. and Clifford, R.M., 2007, *Family Child Care Environment Rating Scale – Revised*, New York: Teachers College Press.

Katz, L.G. and Chard, S.C., 1996, *The Contribution of Documentation to the Quality of Early Childhood Education*. Available at: http://www.tru.ca/arts/literacies/reggio/reggioarticle1.htm

Laevers, F. and Moons, J., 1997, *Enhancing Well-Being and Involvement in Children: An Introduction in the Ten Action Points*, Leuven: Centre for Experiential Education.

Lancaster, Y.P. and Broadbent, V., 2003, *Listening to Young Children*, Maidenhead: Open University Press.

Manning-Morton, J., 2011. 'Not Just the Tip of the Iceberg: Psychoanalytic ideas and early years practice' in Miller, L. and Pound, L., *Theories and Approaches to Learning in the Early Years*, London: Sage.

Manning-Morton, J. and Thorp, M., 2006, *Key Times: A Framework for Developing High Quality Provision for Children from Birth to Three Years*, Maidenhead: Open University Press.

Manning-Morton, J. and Thorp, M., 2015, *Two Year Olds in Early Years Settings; Journeys of Discovery*, Maidenhead: Open University Press.

Miller, L., Rustin, M., Rustin, M. and Shuttleworth, J. (eds.), 1989, *Closely Observed Infants*, London: Duckworth.

Nutbrown, C., 2011, *Threads of Thinking* (4th edn), London: Sage.

Painter, M., Roy, C. and Sylva, K., 1980, *Childwatching at Playgroup and Nursery School*. London: Grant McIntyre.

Riddall-Leech, S., 2005, *How to Observe Children*, Oxford: Heinemann.

Sheridan, M., 1997, *From Birth to Five years. Children's Developmental Progress*, London: Routledge.

Siraj, I., Kingston, D. and Melhuish, E., 2015 *Sustained Shared Thinking and Emotional Well-being Scale for 2-5 year olds provision*, London: IOE Press.

Smith, Purdon, Mathers, Sylva, Schneider, La Valle, Wollny, Owen, Bryson and Lloyd, 2009, 'Early Education Pilot for Two Year Old Children Evaluation' *DCSF Research Report RR134*.

This chapter sets out an overview of approaches to studying and understanding babies and young children's development. It asks what we understand development and learning to be and why it is important for early years practitioners to study this subject. Key ideas about the development of young children are discussed and an overview of different theoretical perspectives on development given.

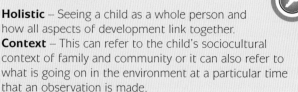

KEY TERMS

Holistic – Seeing a child as a whole person and how all aspects of development link together.
Context – This can refer to the child's sociocultural context of family and community or it can also refer to what is going on in the environment at a particular time that an observation is made.

Why study child development?

Child development is the essential subject of study for anyone who works with young children. Looking after other people's children gives you different responsibilities compared to having your own children. So people who work with other people's children need to be trained properly and carefully. They need to be informed about how children develop and learn. This is at the centre of your professional competence.

Having a good level of knowledge and understanding of child development theory will enable you to:

- be a more effective early years practitioner
- have a framework of knowledge that supports and informs your practice
- develop a **holistic** approach – this means seeing children in the round, as whole people
- understand each child's individual path of development
- make informed and effective assessments
- provide relevant and meaningful play opportunities
- identify any difficulties in a child's developmental progress
- provide useful information and guidance to parents about their child's development and learning
- liaise effectively with other professionals working with a child and their family
- enjoy your work and gain greater professional satisfaction.

The importance of context

It is very important to see the child in **context** when studying child development. Different family and community cultures value and promote different skills and behaviours, and different traditions of childcare will influence how and when developments happen.

Context also helps us to understand the interrelationship of aspects of development. For example: when children quarrel, in order to understand what is going on it is important to identify who or what made a particular child angry or started the quarrel; this is the context of the behaviour.

Researchers in the field of child development now realise that it is almost impossible to separate the different aspects of their behaviour, as the emotional (anger), physical (stamping with rage) and intellectual or language (what they say or do) all interact with each other.

By studying child development in context, we recognise that the biological part of development (physical development and genetic factors) is integrated with the cultural part of development (social, emotional, intellectual and linguistic factors).

What is child development?

Child development is a multidisciplinary subject, drawing on various academic fields, including psychology, neuroscience, sociology, paediatrics, biology and genetics. It is part of the science of developmental psychology, which is concerned with the study of change in humans over time.

Growth, development and learning

- **Growth**: Growth is the increase in size, knowledge and competence or capability in humans and therefore is a feature of the development and learning of babies and young children.
- **Development**: Development is more varied, it can be multidimensional and multidirectional (Schaffer 2006). Aldgate (2006: 19) defines development as 'changes over time in physical, neurological structures, thought processes and behaviour'. These changes are not haphazard or random, not temporary and not easily reversible. Developmental psychology focuses on how and why these changes take place.

- **Learning**: Development and learning are so intertwined that it is difficult to define them separately. However, it might be useful to understand learning as something that is provoked and that occurs in a specific situation, at a specific moment, or when a specific problem needs to be tackled. People help children to learn by creating environments and atmospheres that promote learning in the context of the child's all-round development. The idea of learning is usually associated with intellectual or cognitive development but learning takes place across all areas.

It is important to be clear about how development and learning interact. In the example below, Noah learns a new skill in the context of his physical development.

Most of children's learning happens while they are developing. We do not even notice that they are learning. It is one of nature's safety mechanisms. It is actually difficult to stop children learning as long as they are with people who encourage their general development – for example, if the adult knows and understands that two-year-olds need to run and jump.

Because of this, children can learn negatively as well as positively; they can learn NOT to learn, where their curiosity is discouraged through negative messages from adults or unsafe environments. Children are held back in their learning if they are not allowed to develop and a non-stimulating environment can hold back development.

It is important to take care that children with physical disabilities are not held back in their learning just because other aspects of their development are constrained in some way. For example, the child with a hearing impairment needs to communicate, otherwise learning about relating to other people will be held back. Use of facial expressions, gestures, sign language and finger spelling, as well as a hearing aid and help with lip-reading, will all help the child's general development. The child can then communicate, and learn to think and socialise in particular situations.

Development across the life-span

Development begins at conception and continues throughout life.

One question that developmental psychology explores is how much connection there might be between experiences in the earliest years and our personalities, abilities and behaviours later in life. What are the aspects that remain constant and what changes? And most importantly, what are the factors that influence those changes? Genetic processes or environmental influences?

An important idea here is that the experiences children have in their early years and their genetic inheritance (genes and features or attributes they have from their biological parents for example) are hugely *influential* on their future outcomes, but these experiences and their biological make-up do not *determine* these outcomes.

Development and the sociocultural context

Development has general patterns, but individual pathways happen in a **sociocultural** context.

As an early years practitioner/student, you will learn about the common features and patterns of development as set out by different theorists. However, within these patterns the development of each child is unique and will vary from child to child, family to family, culture to culture.

The paths that individual children follow in the course of their development are influenced by transition points or changes in circumstances during development. These may be biological, such as contracting a serious illness, or sociocultural/ environmental, such as being given piano lessons.

Researchers in child development now think more about how children develop in different cultures and in different types of society. They are asking two questions:

1 What is the same about all children?
2 What is different across cultures in the way that children are brought up?

Think about ideas

Noah, who is two-years-old, can run and jumps from one foot to the other.

Noah is taken to the fair, where he learns to jump in a new way. He watches the older children jumping high on an inflatable castle, lifting up both their knees at the same time and landing on their bottoms. Noah joins in by imitating them and is soon jumping with both feet off the ground.

Noah cannot yet hop or skip; learning to do so will be influenced by the growth and development of his muscles and nervous system, the opportunities he has had to practise running and jumping in order to develop his sense of balance, the sense of confidence he has in trying new things such as the bouncy castle, his mood, and whether he has seen someone else hop or skip so can think about the concepts of 'hop' or 'skip'.

Which, if any, of these factors do you think is less or more important than the others in the process of a child's development?

What opportunities do the children in your setting have to learn from older or more experienced children?

An important idea in developmental psychology is that development can be:

- **Equifinal**: there is more than one developmental pathway to a given outcome. So two children may grow up to be aggressive, for example, but the routes that their development took to this outcome may be different.

- **Multifinal**: identical early experiences do not necessarily result in the same outcome. Two children may experience the same early trauma such as bereavement, but the effect on their future lives will be different because they will respond to the experience each in their own unique way.

Development within and across different areas

Child development involves different aspects or domains. These are usually regarded as social, emotional, physical, cognitive and linguistic. Although these areas are often studied separately, it is important to emphasise that they are all interrelated in the holistic development of the child.

Key issues in child development

The nature–nurture debate

This debate is concerned with the extent to which development and learning are to do with the child's natural maturing processes, or as a result of experience.

This has long been debated within the world of philosophy and psychology. For example, Plato (427BCE–347BCE) and Rene Descartes (1596–1650) believed that children are born with some knowledge (**nativism**). On the other hand John Locke (1634–1704) believed that a child is born without any knowledge: the mind is a blank slate or empty vessel, and knowledge is only created by interaction with the environment (**empiricism**).

Today it is generally accepted that development is a product of both nature *and* nurture. It happens through the constant interaction between the growth and **maturation** of the body, the emerging structures of the brain, and the child's experience of the world and relationships with people.

However, theories and researchers may still favour an emphasis on one side of influence or the other. For example, in language development, Steven Pinker emphasises the role of biology and evolution while Jerome Bruner emphasises the influence of social interactions on language development (Schaffer 2006).

KEY TERMS

Sociocultural – The combination of social and cultural factors that influence personality and behaviour.
Equifinal – Different developmental pathways can lead to the same or similar outcome.
Multifinal – Similar or the same early experiences do not necessarily lead to the same outcome.
Nativism – Theories that stress the biological influences on development.
Empiricism – Theories that stress the environmental influences on development.
Maturation – The genetic or biologically determined process of growth that unfolds over a period of time.

Holistic development or separate areas of development?

Child development is usually divided into different areas or domains. It can be helpful to the adults involved in studying child development to have different areas in order to organise their thinking. It might also be useful for adults to further their knowledge by focusing on the detail of a particular area of development and to support the child; for example, looking closely at a child's language or emotional development to check that all is well, to celebrate progress, to see how to help the child with the next step of development and learning, or to give special help where needed.

Traditionally, child development has been looked at under six headings that make up the acronym PILESS:

- **Physical** development (see Chapter 9)
- **Intellectual** (cognitive) development (see Chapter 7)
- **Language** and communication development (see Chapter 8)
- **Emotional**, personal and **social** development (usually including cultural development) (see Chapters 10 and 11)
- **Spiritual** and moral development.

Advantages of separate areas of development

The advantages of using separate areas in the study of child development are that this approach provides:

- a useful framework for students to organise their studies
- a focus for the study of children – for example, in the use of observation techniques, case studies and the planning of activities for work with children.

Disadvantages of separate areas of development

- If different aspects of a child's development are seen as separated strands, each one isolated from the next, the child comes to be seen as a collection of bits and pieces, instead of a whole person.

- PILESS has been criticised for omitting 'C' for culture, thereby ignoring the context of children's development.

- It may be difficult to view the child as a whole person.

- It may be more difficult to contextualise the child if the categories are rigidly set out.

- Some areas may be prioritised over others or missed altogether (such as personal development).

In summary

So, even when focusing on one aspect of development to further your understanding, it is important not to forget that people are whole human beings from the very start of life. A person has a physical body, ideas, feelings and relationships – all developing and functioning at the same time. When we think of the complete child in this way, we are taking a holistic approach. This means understanding how each aspect of development relates and impacts on each other, and making links between different aspects in your observations and assessments.

 Theory and theorists: areas of the brain

A holistic approach is emphasised in perspectives on brain development. Although different parts of the brain are thought to be mostly responsible for processing certain information such as movement or language, many parts of the brain are simultaneously involved in processing the simplest piece of information; there is no single place where all the decisions are made or all the information is stored, which accounts for the flexibility and creativity of the human mind (Gopnik 1999, Carter 1999).

Sociocultural contexts of development

Development is deeply influenced by the child's environment. Although children across the world seem

Think about ideas

Research diagrams of the brain and learn about the different areas and which functions they are most concerned with. Then watch an online video of how the brain works and observe how the electrical impulses move around many different areas of the brain.

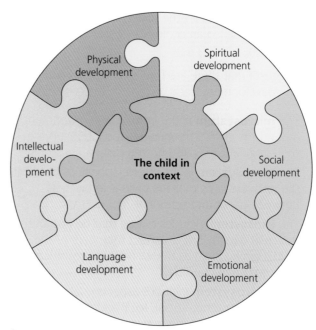

▲ **Figure 6.1** We can think of studying integrated development as looking at the pieces of a jigsaw

to pass through similar sequences of development, this happens in different ways and at different rates according to their sociocultural contexts.

This is sometimes called a '**developmental niche**' (Schaffer 2006); the multiple ways in which a particular community influence children's development through:

- the physical and social settings in which the child lives; the people he or she meets, the ideas, language and styles of communication in different situations

- the childcare customs in that culture

- the psychological characteristics of parents and family, and the way in which feelings and relationships are communicated and carried out.

Each of these experiences has a profound influence on a child's development.

See Chapter 14 for other factors that can influence a child's development.

 Theory and theorists: ecological systems theory

Urie Bronfenbrenner (1979, 2006) argued that development and learning are not limited to the individual child's biology or immediate experiences

KEY TERM

Developmental niche – A particular sociocultural context that influences children's development.

but are also affected by the wider social and political world. This is called an ecological systems model of development.

He suggests that there are four systems that affect human development:

1 The **microsystem** is the immediate environment around the child. This includes the interactions in the family but may also be the early years setting.

2 The **mesosystem** is the interrelationships between the microsystems that the child is in, such as between home and school.

3 The **exosystem** includes places that do not affect the child directly but do affect members of the child's family, such as the workplace, health centres and community facilities.

4 The **macrosystem** includes aspects such as the political, economic, social, legal and educational systems, which may be remote from the child but will still have an impact, for example through the level of provision of children's centres.

Bronfenbrenner developed a framework for illustrating the different environments that influence children's development; these are usually illustrated by a diagram of concentric circles as shown in Figure 6.2.

Think about ideas

Use Figure 6.2 to think about the different environments that affect a child in your setting or your family.

● Draw which microsystem settings they experience and the way they interact in the mesosystem.
● Then identify factors in the exosystem that are impacting on their family members and carers; perhaps an older sibling has just started secondary school a long way from home so they do not get to play together so much, or they might have had to move home due to their parent's work.
● Are there wider issues in the macrosystem that are apparent, such as the stress caused by a reduction in housing benefit?

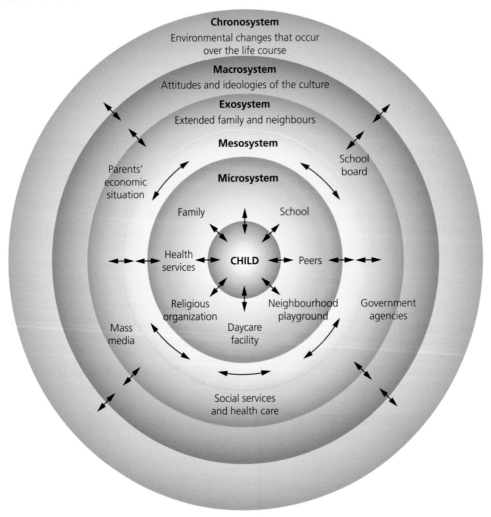

▲ **Figure 6.2** An ecological systems approach to thinking about children's development and learning (based on the Bronfenbrenner framework)

Developmental stages or continuous progression?

For some theorists, the process of human development happens in stages where there are distinctive shifts in development that are common to everyone (universal) and happen in a set order (invariant). These shifts mean that one developmental stage is qualitatively different to the next and characterised by a unique way of thinking or behaving.

Stage theories have been proposed by people writing from different disciplines. For example, Freud and Erikson from a psychoanalytic perspective on psychosexual and psychosocial development, Gesell from a biological perspective on maturation and Piaget's theory of cognitive development all adhered to the idea of stages of development. See pp. 107–119 for more information.

However, it is now thought that although **qualitative** changes in development do occur, they are not such a complete change as previously thought but are more gradual. Development is also continuous and involves **quantitative** changes; for example, children get bigger, they have more information about the world so can change their ideas as a result (Schaffer 2006).

So, to say that children develop according to age and stage is now regarded as rather out of date. This is because the age at which children do things varies enormously and does not depend on biological sequences alone. Developmental sequences are influenced by what they inherit from their family, nutrition, the opportunities that encourage their development, the people they meet, their life experiences and whether they have special needs or disabilities. For this reason it is now usual to talk about sequences of development.

Critical or sensitive periods?

A critical period is a biologically determined phase of development during which a child is maximally ready to acquire a new behaviour pattern (Schaffer 2006). This means that there are periods in a child's development when their bodies and minds are particularly suited to learning a new skill or understanding.

Until recently, it was thought that there were critical times for certain aspects of development; talking and developing attachment relationships, for example. It was believed that if a child missed out on key experiences at the right stage of development, the damage could not be repaired. However, recent research suggests that it is not always too late to catch up. This is a much more positive way of thinking about a child's development, although it is important to

remember that the development of the baby in utero (in the womb) remains a critical stage in most aspects of the child's development.

Optimal, sensitive and best times

Instead of 'critical periods', the term '**sensitive periods**' or '**optimal periods**' is now used to describe developmental phases when children are more likely to acquire or develop a new behaviour pattern than at other times. For example, the brain is particularly sensitive to the non-verbal emotional interactions that underpin attachment relationships and social understanding in the first three years of life. Children who for any reason are held back from developing during these sensitive periods will have more difficulty becoming skilled in these areas later on. However, this does not always mean that they cannot catch up after the best time has passed, but you should remember that it may take an older child longer to acquire or gain skills that they missed out on at the optimal stage, so patience is required.

The idea of '**brain plasticity**' shows us that, although there are some in-built functions in different parts of the brain at birth, the way in which the brain organises and reorganises itself means that different areas can take over the function of damaged or unused areas of the brain. So, as neuroscience (the study of the growth and development of the brain) develops, we are seeing that catching up is possible if the physical mechanisms are present, although they may have become latent, buried or weakened through being restrained.

Sensitive or optimal times can last for a number of months or even years, depending on the aspect of development involved. Arguably, it is as if children are designed so that there is plenty of time to learn things

KEY TERMS

Qualitative – Changes in the characteristics of an object. For example, Piaget proposed that a child's thinking in the sensory-motor stage of development was qualitatively different to their way of thinking in the pre-operational stage.

Quantitative – Changes in the size or amount of an object.

Sensitive period – A time when the mind may be particularly open to certain kinds of learning.

Optimal period – A time that might be the best time possible for learning a particular skill.

Brain plasticity – The ability of the brain to organise and reorganise itself according to life events so that different areas can take over the function of damaged or unused areas of the brain.

Reflecting on practice

Antonio (two years, three months old) started nursery as part of the English Government's funded two-year-olds scheme (DfE 2011). The nursery had only recently begun to cater for children under three, so the practitioners were more used to providing for the development and learning of children over three years of age.

Antonio had not been to an early years setting before and he approached this new experience by exploring everything very rapidly, using his whole body and all his senses; mouthing objects, drinking the water from the water tray, smearing paint on his body, climbing on furniture and moving constantly around the indoor and outdoor space, scattering objects as he went. Antonio had limited spoken language skills in both English and Italian, and was often unresponsive to the practitioners' verbal instructions and interactions.

Initially this led the practitioners to consider that Antonio might have learning difficulties. However, after learning

more about the development, behaviour and learning of babies and toddlers (and bilingual language development), they adjusted their expectations and provision. They made sure that Antonio had good support from his key person who also talked to his parents to get a better picture of Antonio at home and to rule out any hearing difficulties. Gradually they noticed that Antonio became more settled, responsive and focused in his play. Having had the opportunities to explore and learn in ways he would have done as a baby and young toddler, it was as if he had caught up on himself.

Review your age grouping in the setting:

- Does the age group structure allow for different children to function at different stages of development, or are all children of a certain age expected to behave, play and learn in the same way?
- How do you respond to children who seem to regress in their behaviour?

at every stage of their development. This is why it is so important not to rush children in their learning.

Early is not always best

The existence of 'optimum periods' does not mean that early is best for young children. In fact, neuroscientists think that a window of opportunity for a particular area of development is also a period of great vulnerability for the child's development in that area (Greenfield 2000). All practitioners need to develop the skill of observing children in enough detail to support them at the optimal or best moment for development, whenever this should come. This means not pushing children to do things too early, and it also means not waiting for maximum signs of readiness until it is rather late for children to attempt things – the window may have passed.

Children who are pushed on in advance of optimal times of development usually survive, but can also 'burn out' by eight or nine years of age; losing interest and motivation. When children are being pushed to do academic work (reading, writing and maths) too early and too fast, they may lose interest in an area they previously excelled at, and can be put off academic learning.

Children who are held back during optimal times of development through lack of stimulation may suffer low self-esteem because they cannot do things; they lack the competence or capability and skills that they know they need. In an extreme form, this lack of stimulation becomes neglect.

Children who are helped appropriately, at their optimal or best times of development, in a stimulating environment, by people who are sensitive and observant of what an individual child can manage (regardless of **norms** and average ages for doing things), flourish in their own unique way. Malaguzzi, the Italian who pioneered the Reggio Emilia approach, calls these 'rich' children (Edwards et al. 2012).

Practitioners need to know about child development so that they are informed enough to use their observations of children to encourage them into appropriate activity at the appropriate point of development. Because development is uneven and each child is a unique person, each child will need what is 'just right' for them. What helps one child will not necessarily help another. Different children need different sorts of help in learning.

Interpretation of experience: children effect their own development

Early theories of child development tended to see children as passive in the processes of growth, development and learning but constructivist theories introduced the idea of the child who is an active

KEY TERM

Norm – The usual or standard thing.

▲ **Figure 6.3** Development and learning happen through active interaction with people and objects

learner. Further to this, it is now acknowledged that children influence their development because they are active participants in their interactions with others. This idea is applied mainly to the socialisation of children, where, although it is clear that parents influence the child, who the child is also plays a part in this. The personality and characteristics of the child and the way they interact with their environment will have an impact on how they are perceived and, therefore, the expectations practitioners and adults in general have of them.

Individual children also respond differently to and interpret their experiences in different ways, so how they perceive the world around them will vary.

An important idea here is that development and learning occur through interaction with people and objects, and that the child is active in this process.

 Theoretical perspectives on child development

A theory of child development is someone's idea about how a child might grow, develop and learn. Theories may help to predict, for example, that before children talk, they usually babble; theorists will put forward an idea of why this happens. Theories about how children develop are products of research, so are influenced by the culture in which they are thought about. It is very important to remember this, because humans are not objective – they agree and disagree. There is no such thing as 'the truth' about child development. We always need to stop and ask: who is doing the research? Who is formulating the theory?

Two examples illustrate this point.

Guidelines for good practice

Thinking about child development

✔ Children are whole people. It can be useful to focus on one area of development – for example, communication and language – but it is not useful to isolate thinking about one aspect from thinking about the whole child's development.

✔ Children seem to go through the same sequences of development (see p. 105), but will vary in the exact way that they do.

✔ Milestones can be very misleading. Children with disabilities or talented/gifted children (children with a great talent or intellectual gift – for example, in dance, music or mathematics) may not go through the typical sequence of development.

✔ Cultural differences mean that norms vary across the world in terms of what young children are expected to do at different points. For example, in some cultures, children are expected to speak only one language, while in others they are expected to speak several languages from the moment they can form words.

✔ Normative development tends to make us compare children with each other. But it is more important to compare the child with his or her own previous development. We must not forget to ask: is this good progress for this particular child?

● The psychologist Vygotsky grew up in the former Soviet Union, where Communist ideas dominated. He came from a large family. Is it coincidence that his theory emphasises social relationships and the community?

● The psychologist Piaget grew up in Europe. He was an only child. Is it coincidence that his theory emphasises the child as an individual and as an active learner, trying to experiment and solve problems?

When analysing your observations and making assessments, you need to have an open mind and look at different theories, bringing together ideas that are useful from each one. You need to see in what ways theories like those of Vygotsky and Piaget are the same and in what ways they are different. Theories that are similar can be blended into a useful template for our work with children. But theories that are very different can cause tensions in practice as they advocate very different approaches.

The similarities that exist between many theories of child development can make categorising them difficult because there is so much that overlaps between them. What follows is an overview of the different perspectives that underpin the dominant theories of child development.

This is divided into three main perspectives:

1 nativist theories that emphasise maturation and nature
2 empiricist theories that emphasise experience and nurture
3 interactionist theories that stress both the biological and sociocultural influences on development.

Biological/nativist perspectives

In the eighteenth century, the French philosopher Jean-Jacques Rousseau (1712–78) thought that children developed and learned naturally; that the seeds of all their development and learning are innate, so they are biologically programmed to learn particular things at a particular time. He thought that just as a flower unfolds through the bud, so a child's learning unfolds – for example, babbling leads into language, and then on into reading and writing; and kicking the arms and legs leads to crawling and walking. See Chapter 8, p. 153 for more information.

Theories that focus on inborn biases (i.e. influenced by our genetic make-up), maturation, developmental sequences or normative scales/milestones of development emphasise a nativist perspective on development. This perspective sees development as predetermined by genetic and other biological factors, such as Chomsky's idea of an inborn language acquisition device, for example (see Chapter 8). From this perspective, it is biological processes that lead the course of growth (which is called maturation) as advocated by the American psychologist, Arnold Gesell (1880–1961). Gesell believed that development progressed according to a set sequence.

The work of Mary Sheridan (1889–1978) on developmental sequences is based on Gesell's theories, suggesting that children move through rigidly set stages that are linked to the child's age.

Theory and theorists: Gesell's maturation theory

In the 1930s, Gesell mapped out the sequence of development as he observed it and charted particular milestones in the child's development as it unfolded. Although Gesell was describing what he saw children doing, his milestones have become to be seen as developmental 'norms' (what children should be doing), and used to check that the pattern of development is 'normal'.

Gesell's developmental scales looked at motor, adaptive, language and personal–social areas. If children reached particular milestones, such as walking, within the 'normal' age range, then their development was said to be making 'normal' progress. This approach is depressing if used with children with special educational needs, as they are constantly labelled 'abnormal'. Indeed a major criticism of Gesell's research is that the children he studied came from a limited sociocultural group; therefore the 'norms' he defined are not universally applicable (Crain 1992).

The influence of both Gesell's and Sheridan's developmental milestones can be seen in current approaches to young children's development and learning such as the early learning goals and 'Development matters' (see Chapter 5) guidance in England and the Developmentally Appropriate Practice approach in the USA (see Chapter 19). The table of 'normative' development set in the appendix are an example of this approach.

Think about ideas

Read the case studies below. Using any of the frameworks identified above, identify how they would guide you to assess these children's developmental progress.

1 At 20 months old, Mark, who lives in urban England, moves around by bottom-shuffling. He does not yet walk.
2 Akinyi (three years six months) lives in rural Kenya. She is adept at estimating how much rice each of the baskets in her home can contain and can choose the best one for a particular task.

Consider this information:

- Although Mark did not walk until he was two years old, he went on to run, hop and skip at the normal times. Walking late was not a cause for concern, and he did not suffer from any developmental delay.
- Many African children living in rural villages estimate volume and capacity earlier than European children who live in towns. This is because they practise measuring out cups of rice into baskets from an early age, as part of their daily lives. Learning about volume and capacity early does not mean that children will necessarily go on to become talented mathematicians. Children who learn these concepts later might also become good mathematicians.

Review the frameworks you use to think about children's development. Do they help you to gain a holistic view of children and consider their cultural contexts, or is development and learning presented with no context?

Lilli Neilsen, a Danish specialist working with children who have multiple disabilities (complex needs), stressed the importance of carefully assessing the development of the whole child. For example, she observed a child with cerebral palsy, who was lying on his stomach on a mat, with toys around him. He looked at a toy, but each time he reached for it, his shoulder jerked involuntarily and he pushed the toy away. She gently weighted down his shoulder. He reached for the toy and was able to grab it. He smiled and made a contented sound.

It would have been easy to check his physical development and say, 'cannot reach and grasp'. Instead, we have a picture of a boy who:

● had an idea (to reach for the toy)

● knew what to do (but his body could not manage it)

● was given the right help (based on Nielsen's careful observation)

● experienced success and pleasure

● developed the motivation to have another go.

Intellectual, physical, emotional and social aspects all merge together.

1 Undertake some observations of two children, one of whom has additional needs, and use the tables in the appendix to analyse them.

2 Have you gained a clear view of each child's strengths or is the focus on what they cannot do or lack in some way?

▲ **Figure 6.4** The child's innate curiosity, growing physical skills and the surrounding environment all work together in the child's development and learning

Physical development, in particular, is often described within a nativist perspective, as maturation and genetic inheritance (the genes you inherit from your biological parents) are a major influence on motor, brain and nerve development. However, even at the level of our genes, environment has a part to play. For example, polluted air or water, and the excessive intake of alcohol or drugs can all affect the genetic unfolding of growth in the womb.

This is called 'gene-environment effects', a term which describes the interrelationships between genetic and environmental influences on behaviour and development. This happens in different ways: environments affect our genes, which in turn affect our responses to different environments, and we have particular experiences according to our genetic make-up (Schaffer 2006).

Thelen (in Schaffer 2006) suggests that there is no 'crawling gene' or 'walking gene' that somehow unfolds in a sequence. Instead, she argues, any new movement or motor skill is a result of a complex system of cognition, perception and motivation, as well as underlying physical change, operating together.

This idea is particularly important when considering the development and learning of children with SEN who often seem to 'dance the development ladder': they move through sequences in unusual and very uneven ways – for example, they might walk at the expected age, but they may not talk at the usual age.

Ideas of biology and maturation play a part in most of the major developmental theories, such as those of Freud and Piaget. However, the degree of biological influence they emphasise varies. In modern-day theory, evolutionary psychologists (i.e. those who focus on how useful the evolution of a behaviour is to humans) such as Steven Pinker prioritise genetic influences on development. But generally, the fact that both genes and environment are involved in virtually all aspects of psychological functioning is now accepted.

The nativist view of development suggests that children naturally do what they need to in order to develop and learn, and practitioners help children to learn by making sure that the environment supports the child's learning as it unfolds. Because adults

Advantages	Disadvantages
• Practitioners can learn about how to offer the right physical resources, activities and equipment for each stage of development. • Children can actively make choices, select, be responsible, explore, try things out and make errors without incurring reproach or a feeling of failure. • Practitioners value observing children and act in the light of their observations. This might mean adding more materials, and having conversations with children to help them learn more. • Practitioners are able to follow the child's lead and be sensitive to the child.	• Practitioners may hold back too much because they are nervous of damaging the child's natural development: for example, by not talking to a child while she is drawing or by holding back from playing with children. • Practitioners only support children in their learning, rather than extending the learning children do. • Children might be under-stimulated because adults are waiting for signs of readiness in the child. The signs might never come! Practitioners wait too long before intervening. • Children might not be shown how to do things in case it is not the right moment developmentally to teach them, which leaves them without skills. • Children with special educational needs or from different cultures might be labelled 'abnormal' or 'unready'. In fact, they might reach a milestone earlier or later, but still within the normal sequence. They might develop unevenly but in ways which make 'normal' life possible. Milestones in one culture might be different in another culture.

▲ **Table 6.1** Advantages and disadvantages of a nativist view and the laissez-faire approach

do not need to act, according to this theory, it is sometimes referred to as a laissez-faire (letting things take their own course) approach.

Environmental or empiricist perspectives

In the seventeenth century, the British philosopher John Locke thought that children were like lumps of clay or blank slates, which adults could mould into the shape they wanted or inscribe with the habits they wanted their child to develop. This is an 'environmental learning' perspective; this means development is influenced mainly by the external environment. That does not mean biology does not play a part, but it is given much less emphasis. It is children's experience and the consequences of their actions and behaviour that are the focus of these theories.

At the beginning of the twentieth century, a psychologist in the USA, John Watson (1878–1954), and a psychologist in Russia, Ivan Pavlov (1849–1936), were developing similar theories about how people develop and learn from this perspective. Influenced by these ideas, Burrhus Skinner (1904–90) and Albert Bandura (1925–) later developed their learning theories. These theories were welcomed at the time as they offered more potential for parents and teachers to have an impact on children than with biological theories. These theories, sometimes also called **behaviourist**, have had a strong influence on thinking about development.

Pavlov and classical conditioning

Classical conditioning is the way in which responses come under the control of a new stimulus. Pavlov experimented with conditioned responses in dogs. He liked to be described as a **physiologist** rather than as a **psychologist**, because he believed that psychological states (such as conditioning) are identical to physiological states and processes in the brain. He thought this approach was useful and scientific. In his experiments, there was a 'neutral conditioned stimulus (CS)', which was a bell ringing. This was paired with food, which was an 'unconditioned **stimulus** (UCS)'. The dogs were fed when the bell rang. This produced an unconditioned response (UCR), which was saliva flowing in the dog's mouth when the food appeared. Gradually, the sound of any bell would induce the dogs to salivate (a conditioned response (CR)) in the same way as if they were seeing or smelling food.

Watson and behaviourism

Watson emphasised the external behaviour of people and their reactions to given situations, which became known as behaviourism. He maintained that human behaviour could only be understood through the objective analysis of behaviours and reactions;

> ## KEY TERMS
>
> **Behaviourist** – Practices that are influenced by the observation and understanding of external behaviours only, rather than their underlying causes.
> **Physiologist** – Someone who studies biological activity.
> **Psychologist** – Someone who studies mental processes and behaviour.
> **Stimulus** – Something that causes a response.

he placed little value on people's internal, mental states and emotions. Like Pavlov, he also developed conditioning methods and asserted that with this approach any child, whatever their background, could be moulded into any kind of future adult.

One aspect of Watson's approach was to treat children like small adults and to avoid showing love and affection except to elicit the desired responses. He said:

> *Nearly all of us have suffered from over-coddling in our infancy ... the fact that our children are always crying and always whining shows the unhappy, unwholesome state they are in. There is a sensible way of treating children. Treat them as though they were young adults. Never hug and kiss them, never let them sit on your lap.*

(Watson, 1928)

These ideas are rightfully outdated but still influence ideas about childcare and parenting. Ideas that you will spoil a baby if you pick them up when they cry, and strategies such as 'controlled crying' programmes (where babies are left to cry for a set time in order to encourage them to sleep without their parent present) show this influence. You may have encountered this thinking in your personal experience of childcare and in your professional practice.

Skinner and operant conditioning

Skinner was a behavioural psychologist who worked in the USA; influenced by Pavlov and Watson, he developed what is known as operant conditioning theory. Bee and Boyd (2010: 16) define this as:

> *The process through which the frequency of a behaviour increases or decreases because of the consequences the behaviour produces.*

Whereas Pavlov fed his dogs when the bell rang whether they salivated or not, Skinner only fed his rats or pigeons if they behaved as he required. For example, Skinner gave rats a reward of food if they pressed a lever. This was reinforcement; the desired behaviour (how he wanted them to react) was rewarded.

 Theory and theorists: positive and negative reinforcement in behaviourism

Chris Rice, a lecturer in early childhood courses at Clydebank College in Scotland, explains positive and negative reinforcement in the following way:

Think about ideas

- Identify ways in which you reinforce behaviours in children, either as a parent or as a practitioner.
- Do you use praise and positive attention or star charts to encourage children to behave in certain ways?

Positive reinforcement is concerned with a child behaving in a certain way, leading to a pleasing outcome; then the behaviour will be repeated. For example, a baby points to a toy monkey and looks at the adult. The adult hands the baby the toy, making appropriate monkey noises, which they both find funny. The baby then repeats the behaviour with other objects, in order to be similarly amused.

Negative reinforcement is concerned with a child behaving in a particular way in order to avoid something unpleasant, to stop pain or to prevent discomfort. For example, the baby cries because he or she has a wet nappy and feels uncomfortable. The adult responds by changing the nappy and the baby feels better. The next time the baby feels discomfort he or she will repeat the behaviour – that is, repeat the crying – in order to stop the unpleasant feeling.

A reinforcer causes the behaviour to be repeated; it may be some form of reward for showing a desired behaviour or something that is linked to the avoidance of unpleasantness or pain.

As long as these responses occur, the baby will repeat the behaviour. If the adult ignores the behaviour instead of rewarding it, it will stop eventually (this is called extinction). See table 6.2.

Bandura and social learning theory

Bandura built on the thinking of Watson and Skinner by recognising the impact that adults' and other children's behaviour had on children. He noted how children do not always need a reinforcement to learn, they also look to others and imitate what they see. This is called 'observational learning'; learning new skills and behaviours through watching others perform them. He also acknowledged that children alter their behaviour according to intrinsic reinforcements such as feelings of pride or excitement.

Bandura revised his theory later on to also recognise a child's cognitive processes in learning. For example, children make meaning of what they observe; they understand the underlying rules of behaviours they observe, thereby learning abstract or non-concrete concepts such as values and attitudes, not just concrete behaviours. This led him to rename his theory 'social cognitive theory' in which people are seen more

Subject	Behaviour	Reinforcer	Outcome
Child	Has tantrum in supermarket	Gets sweets	Positive reinforcement: behaviour will be repeated
Salesperson	Meets sales target	Gets bonus	
Criminal	Pushes over old woman in street	Gets money from handbag	
Dog	Sits up and begs	Gets food	
Baby	Points to toy	Gets toy handed to her	
Holidaymaker	Puts on suntan oil	Avoids sunburn	Negative reinforcement: behaviour will be repeated
Tutor with headache	Takes aspirin	Stops headache	
Driver	Slows down before speed camera	Avoids speeding ticket	
Student	Hands in medical certificate	Avoids losing bursary	
Baby with wet nappy	Cries	Stops discomfort (adult changes nappy)	
Neighbour	Complains about loud music next door	Stops noise	

(With permission from Chris Rice, Clydebank College)

▲ **Table 6.2** Operant conditioning

Reflecting on practice

Scenario 1

A child is told that he can have a treat if he tidies up his toys. The child, understandably, thinks that he is being given a choice, and weighs the behaviour against the reward. Is it worth it? The child decides it is not and does not tidy his toys – he is baffled by the adult's displeasure with his choice. (An older child may see this as an opportunity to negotiate, asking for more treats!)

Scenario 2

A child is repeatedly told off for throwing his food on the floor; for the rest of the mealtime the adult is chatting to her friend. The child throws his food again and is told off again, with threats of removing the food. He throws the food again; the adult removes his plate, picks him up and sits him on her lap away from the dishes.

How do these two scenarios relate to behaviourism and operant conditioning?

Now consider this information:

Bribery and behaviour shaping

Scenario 1 illustrates bribery, which is quite different to behaviour shaping or behaviour modification; i.e. if we tell the child that he or she can have a treat if he or she tidies up, this is bribery. With bribery, the child learns that the point of the behaviour is to please the adult and gain the reward, not to contribute to the group or family by keeping his things tidy.

In behaviour shaping or modification, there is no 'if' and no mention of reward. The reinforcer comes only *after* the behaviour has appeared, usually in a way that is linked to the behaviour. 'Well done,' the adult might say, 'you have tidied that up quickly.'

The only time, when using behaviour shaping, that there is any mention of future outcome is in terms of what will be happening next – for example, 'When everyone is sitting quietly, then we can start the story.'

Punishment

Just as positive reinforcement must not be confused with bribery; negative reinforcement must not be confused with punishment. Although Skinner's initial definition of negative reinforcement was more similar to the idea of punishment or an 'aversive stimulant', he later redefined this to be the strengthening of behaviour by removing or avoiding an aversive event as in the removal of the uncomfortable nappy above.

In scenario 2, the child's negative behaviour was reinforced by the attention he received, even though it was negative attention. He learned that the only way to get the adult's attention was to misbehave.

Ignoring undesirable behaviour, together with clear and consistent reinforcement of desired behaviour, will lessen the behaviour and is more effective than punishment.

Review your interactions with children and reflect on how you can reinforce positive behaviours. Avoid bribery and attention that reinforces negative behaviour.

as self-organising, self-reflective and self-regulating rather than the passive recipients of external stimuli of environmental learning (Bandura 1986). So children do not just learn through copying – they think about how that behaviour relates to themselves and their particular situation.

The interactionist/constructivist/ social constructivist perspective

In the eighteenth century, the German philosopher Kant (1724–1804) believed that a child's learning was an interaction between the developing child and

Advantages	Disadvantages
• External behaviours are easily observable.	• The inner world of the child is not considered.
• Extrinsic reward systems such as star charts can give children and adults a framework for addressing negative behaviour that is easily understandable and may divert from negative punishing behaviours.	• The reasons for the child's behaviour may be overlooked and the child seen as a problem when it may be elements in the setting or the family that are the cause.
• Using such techniques may encourage practitioners and parents to discuss and be clear about which behaviours they want to encourage/discourage and why.	• The adult must make sure that what they intend is what actually happens, and that the child does not pick up an entirely different message. For example, a child may learn that if he says sorry within an adult's hearing and quickly enough after hitting another child, he may avoid punishment, irrespective of whether or not he has any feelings of remorse.
	• Often, adults ignore children when they are behaving appropriately, only giving them attention when they are disruptive. However, children need to realise the advantages (enjoyment and satisfaction) of cooperating with others in different situations, so that enjoyment and satisfaction become the reinforcers. Other kinds of reward are then not necessary.
	• Practice may become adult-led, with practitioner's deciding what children need to learn next, with no reference to the child's stage of development. This results in 'skills' sessions such as learning how to use scissors, that are not linked to observed need or interest.

▲ **Table 6.3** Advantages and disadvantages of behaviourist approaches

the environment. This is called an **interactionist** perspective.

Jean Piaget (1896–1980), Lev Vygotsky (1896–1934) and Jerome Bruner (b. 1915) all followed an interactionist view. In addition, central to their theories is the idea that children construct their own understanding and knowledge about things. This is called a **constructivist** view of how children develop and learn. In contrast to behaviourist perspectives, constructivist theories contain the belief that the mind actively participates in putting knowledge of the world together through the process of interacting with the environment, rather than passively acquiring or gaining knowledge through observation or instruction.

Interactionism is also an anti-nativist position as according to Piaget, the child arrives in the world

with little more than a few sensory-motor reflexes and proceeds from there to build up the mental apparatus. While retaining the belief that cognitive development is largely dependent on the child's constructive efforts, neo-nativists such as Annette Karmiloff-Smith consider that more account needs to be taken of the evidence from neuroscience, that babies are born with brains that are biologically prepared to make sense of the world in certain ways and to acquire or gain particular kinds of knowledge. They can then build on these in-built mechanisms through their own explorations and their experience of the world (Karmiloff-Smith 1992).

Jean Piaget's cognitive development theory

For Piaget (1952), knowledge is not accumulated or gained through passively soaking up information. When children try to master their environment they actively select and interpret the information available by bringing to it what they already know and with the use of whatever cognitive strategies they possess at the time. In the process they construct successively higher more sophisticated levels of knowledge. In this sense children are their own agents of development – they push forward their development; by struggling to understand their world they come to change that world as they perceive it.

KEY TERMS

Interactionism – Theories that stress both the biological and sociocultural influences on development.
Constructivism – Regarding children as actively involved in constructing their knowledge.

The important elements of Piaget's theory of how children learn are that they:

- go through stages and sequences in their learning
- are active learners
- use first-hand experiences and prior experiences in order to learn
- imitate and transform what they learn into symbolic behaviour.

Piaget took social and emotional development for granted and did not write about it in detail. Instead, his writing emphasises intellectual or **cognitive development** and learning. He did not explicitly emphasise the importance of the social and emotional aspects of learning or dwell on social relationships as much as the social constructivists such as Vygotsky. Piaget's theory is called constructivist (rather than social constructivist) for this reason.

Lev Vygotsky and social constructivism

Vygotsky (1978), while also seeing children as actively involved in constructing their knowledge, put a different slant on this process by emphasising the social context in which it takes place. This is called **social constructivism**; the idea that the meanings attached to experience are socially assembled, depending on the culture in which the child is reared and on the child's caretakers.

Vygotsky stressed the importance for development of someone who has more knowledge than the child and who can help the child to learn something that would be too difficult for the child to do on his or her own. Vygotsky described:

- The zone of proximal development; the space between what children know already and can do alone and what they might be able to do and learn with assistance from a more able peer or adult. This takes account of children's potential development; what the child can do with help *now* will be possible for him or her to do alone with no help *later in life*.

- The importance of play for children under seven years, allowing them to do things beyond what they can manage in actual life (such as pretend to drive a car).

- The zone of actual development – this is what the child can manage without help from anyone.

▲ **Figure 6.5** Vygotsky stressed the importance of children learning through the help of more knowledgeable and able peers

Bruner's social constructivist theory

Although a constructivist, Bruner emphasised the role of the adult in children's learning more. He believed that adults can tutor children and help them to learn. They do this by 'scaffolding' what the child is learning in order to make it manageable for the child. In Bruner's view children can learn any subject at any age but at an appropriate level. They can then revisit concepts at more complex levels as they grow, develop and learn; this is called a 'spiral curriculum'. For example, when a baby drops a biscuit over the side of the high chair, the baby can learn about gravity if the adult 'scaffolds' the experience by saying something like: 'It dropped straight down to the floor, didn't it? Let's both drop a biscuit and see if they get to the floor together.' Bruner's theory is also called a social constructivist theory, as social relationships are central to scaffolding.

Scaffolding

A mistaken understanding of scaffolding in practice is that the adult directs the direction of learning, whereas central to Bruner's idea is the emphasis on the child being given the right kind of help according to their understanding. He describes scaffolding as:

> *the process whereby a more expert partner offers help to a child in problem solving by adjusting both the amount and the kind of help to the child's level of performance.*

See Chapter 7, p. 133 for more information on scaffolding.

An important aspect of Bruner's theory is his identification of the different ways in which children learn through symbolic representations. The essence of Bruner's theory is that children learn through:

- doing (the enactive mode of learning)

Advantages	Disadvantages
● This approach is very rewarding and satisfying because adults and children can enjoy working together, struggling at times, concentrating hard, stretching their thinking and ideas, celebrating their learning, and sharing the learning together.	● It is very hard work compared with the other two approaches to learning that we have looked at in this chapter. This is because there is much more for practitioners to know about, more to think about, more to organise and do.
● Trusting each other to help when necessary creates a positive relationship between children, parents and staff. It means taking pride in the way that indoor and outdoor areas of the room are set up, organised, maintained and cared for.	● It is much more difficult for those who are not trained to understand how to work in this way.
● This approach requires teamwork by the adults, which is the way to bring out everyone's strengths in a multi-professional group of teachers and early years practitioners.	
● It means sharing with parents and children all the learning that is going on.	
● Practitioners need to go on learning about children's development. When adults continue to develop as people/professionals, learning alongside children, they have more to offer the children.	
● Practitioners and children respect and value each other's needs and rights, and help each other to learn.	
● Although it takes time, training and experience for practitioners to build up skills for working in this way, it is very effective in helping children to learn during their early years.	

▲ **Table 6.4** Advantages and disadvantages of the social constructive/interactionist view of learning

Reflecting on practice

Using a team approach to record-keeping in an early years setting, staff had built up observations of children. They noted that Damien (five years old) kept punching; he punched other children, furniture and other objects. It seemed to be his main way of exploring and communicating.

● Make notes on how you understand Damien's behaviour from a social constructivist perspective. Identify what you would do and provide for him from this perspective.
● Now read the section on psychoanalytic theory. How would this change the way you interpret Damien's behaviour? Would your approach change? If so, how?

Consider this information:

The staff in this setting decided to introduce activities that allowed punching.

● They put huge lumps of clay on the table.
● They made bread and encouraged energetic kneading.
● They sang songs like 'Clap your hands and stamp your feet' and 'Hands, knees and bumps-a-daisy'.

● They encouraged vigorous hand-printing and finger-painting.
● They helped children to choreograph 'dance fights' (a dance that represent a fight but there is no actual fighting) when acting out a story.
● Damien told the group about 'baddies' from another planet.
● He helped to beat the rug with a beater as part of spring cleaning.
● He spent a long time at the woodwork bench, hammering nails into his model.

How would you describe their approach?

Damien soon stopped hitting other children and began to talk about what he was doing in the activities with adults and other children. The use of observation and discussion enabled the practitioners to support Damien in educationally worthwhile ways that also contributed to his positive self-esteem.

Reflecting on practice

Undertake this activity to remind yourself of the holistic nature of children's development.

1 Draw circles of the same size; one for each of the following aspects of development: physical, cognitive, language and communication, emotional, personal and cultural, social and moral and spiritual development.

2 Cut them out, and write in the different aspects of development.

3 Thread the circles on a string.

4 Bunch them together to remind yourself these are seven parts of a whole.

5 Spread them out to focus on one aspect of the child, but return them to the whole at the end.

● imaging things that they have done (the iconic mode of learning)

● making what they know into symbolic codes – for example, talking, writing or drawing (the symbolic mode of learning).

(See Chapter 7 pp. 132–133 for definitions).

The notion that children are active contributors to their own development has come to be generally accepted. This perspective:

● is the approach currently most favoured by early years practitioners

● has the best support from research into child development in the western world

● draws on both the biological and the environmental influences on development and learning, rearranging elements of both into something that is helpful to those working with children.

See Moving on, p. 118 for information on the dynamic systems perspective.

Psychoanalytical theories

The discipline of psychoanalysis has many strands with slightly different theoretical emphases. Sigmund Freud (1856–1939) developed the fundamental theories in his work with adults. It was his daughter Anna Freud (1895–1982) and Melanie Klein (1882–1960) who adapted his theories to their work with children.

Melanie Klein observed, listened to and took seriously the anxieties of very young children, being the first to recognise play having a role in enabling children to explore their inner troubles and concerns. She devised a method of play therapy, arising from her view of play as being a child's talk.

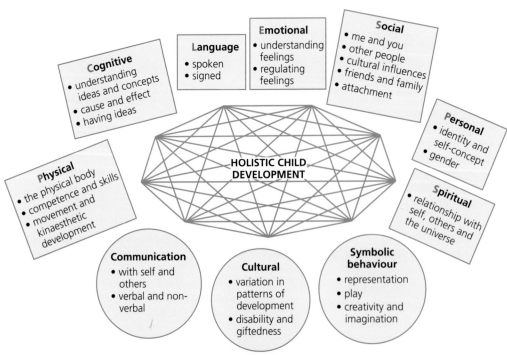

▲ **Figure 6.6** Holistic child development can be thought of as a web

Look, listen and note

1   Observe a baby between 6 and 15 months of age. Use the activity above to find out everything you can about the children under each heading, and then make links between each aspect of development.

2   Observe a toddler of 15 to 30 months in age. Again, use the activity above to find out everything you can about the child under those headings and then make links between each aspect of development.

3   Observe a child aged three to four years, and repeat the process.

4   Observe a child aged five to seven years, and repeat the process.

You might choose children from different cultural backgrounds, with different language backgrounds, or observe a child with a disability. Remember, it is not useful to do this just to see if children are behind or ahead of 'norms'. Instead, you are trying to build up a complete picture of each child. Then you can see how to facilitate and extend each child's development and learning.

Klein's work was further developed by Donald Winnicott (1896–1971) and John Bowlby (1907–1990) in the 'object relations' school of thought in psychoanalysis through their clinical work with children and families.

Psychoanalytic theory shares similarities with and diverges from both nativist and empiricist theories of development. Freud's ideas of the innate instinctual drives of the infant (for example, the instinct for self-preservation, including the drive to eat and drink and seek protection) can be understood as a nativist perspective, yet psychoanalytic theory is essentially concerned with how personality is shaped by childhood experiences. Freud linked thinking, feeling, and sexual and social relationships with early experiences, such as breastfeeding, toilet-training and separation from parents.

In this regard psychoanalytic theory has hugely influenced the idea of a causal link between early experience and later life; an idea shared with empiricists such as Watson. Both Freud and Watson believed strongly in developmental continuity; that the impact of what happens early in life can be seen in later personality and behaviour (Schaffer 2006).

However, unlike behaviourist or social learning theories, psychoanalytic ideas emphasise the fact that babies and young children have an inner life.

A fundamental idea in psychoanalytic theory is that of the unconscious mind; that human behaviour is determined by both conscious and unconscious thoughts. Therefore, a lot of what goes on in the mind is not observable. Like an iceberg, most of our motivations, conflicts and desires lie 70 per cent below the surface (Stevenson and Haberman 2004, cited in Manning-Morton 2011).

Psychoanalytic theory also shares similarities with Piaget's constructivist theory of cognitive development. In the same way that Piaget saw the purpose of assimilation and accommodation of new experiences is to maintain mental equilibrium (Piaget 1962), Freud suggested that we try to keep emotional and mental balance by pushing uncomfortable feelings into our unconscious mind.

Also, like Piaget, Freud set out his concept of personality development as a stage theory. For Freud though, they are stages of psychosexual development. (It is important to understand that 'sexual' in this context does not equate to adult sexuality but, for Freud, meant anything that produces bodily pleasure.)

He identified stages that relate to particular parts of the body. Each stage evokes certain conflicting feelings or tasks that the child has to resolve in order to reduce the tensions they experience. Over- or under-stimulation at each stage may lead to individuals becoming stuck at that stage and continuing to struggle in adult life with that unresolved emotional conflict (Bee and Boyd 2010).

Erik Erickson (1902–1994) further developed psychoanalytic stage theory in the context of cultural and societal influences rather than biological development. He called these '**psychosocial** stages'. Another difference between Erickson's and Freud's theories is that Erickson's stages of development continue into adulthood. However, they are similar in as much as each stage needs to be resolved satisfactorily for healthy mental development to take place.

KEY TERMS

Object relations – A perspective in psychoanalytic theory that emphasises relationships and babies and young children's actual experiences in their relationships and interactions with others, such as feeding, being held and being cleaned up.

Psychosocial – Psychological development in interaction with the social environment.

Approximate age	Encounter between child and society to be resolved	Social focus	Ego (self) strength that develops from positive resolution
0–1 year	Basic trust vs mistrust	Maternal person	Hope (and optimistic trust that the world will meet one's needs)
2–3 years	Autonomy vs shame and doubt	Parental persons	Will (the ability to exercise choice and self-restraint)
4–5 years	Initiative vs guilt	Basic family	Purpose (as sense of confidence in one's own abilities)
6–12 years	Industry vs inferiority	Neighbourhood/ school	Competence (a sense of confidence in one's own abilities)
13–18 years	Identity vs role confusion	Peer groups	Fidelity (the ability to freely pledge loyalty to others)
19–25 years	Intimacy vs isolation	Friendships	Love (romantic and erotic, the ability to commit to others and maintain the commitment through degrees of compromise and self-denial)
26–40 years	Generativity vs stagnation	The household	Care (a sense that certain things in life have meaning and importance, leading one to be productive in life)
41+ years	Ego vs despair	Humankind	Wisdom (a sense that one's life has been worthwhile, arrived at by integrating the outcomes of previous stages)

▲ **Table 6.5** Erickson's stages of psychosocial development

Moving on

Dynamic systems perspective

Dynamic systems theory takes interactionism in development and learning one step further. As well as interaction between the child's biology and the environment, a systems perspective emphasises the interactions that take place within the body and the mind in order to progress development.

A dynamic system is a complex organisation (such as a person or a family) that is made up of multiple parts. Each part has its own function (such as the nervous system or the parent in the family) but is also very much involved in the functioning of other systems. Therefore each part influences and impacts on each other part (Schaffer 2006).

The central ideas in dynamic systems theory are:

- wholeness: a system is an integrated whole that is greater than the sum of its parts

- complex systems are composed of subsystems, each of which is a system in its own right
- stability and change: a system can be open to outside influences
- within a system the pattern of influence is circular, not linear. each small development is influenced by as well as influencing another aspect of development.

In relation to child development, dynamic systems theory does not view a child's learning and development as something that can be divided and studied in discrete areas; e.g. physical, cognitive and social development. Rather it is a holistic view that focuses on the relationship and interconnectedness between the areas which connect them into a whole. Changes in one aspect of development have a direct impact or influence on that of another. For example, children, once able to talk, take leaps forward in their social development. As they initiate and respond to overtures or offers of friendship, their creativity as well as their ability to play imaginative games increases. And changes in one aspect of development are as a result of all aspects of the system working →

together. For example, physical change happens as a result of cognition, perception, motivation and children's social environments as well as biology.

As the system is open to outside influences, dynamic systems theory also takes account of the contexts of development. This theory is often also used in relation to family dynamics. A child does not develop as an individual in isolation; changes in the child impact on family members and changes that occur to family members in turn result in changes to the child (Schaffer 2006).

Dynamic systems also steers away from linear patterns of development. As researchers in this area learn more about child development, it is becoming more useful to think of a child's development as a network that becomes increasingly complex as the child matures and becomes more experienced in his or her culture. So, instead of thinking of child development and learning as a ladder, it is probably more useful to think of it as a web.

Think about ideas

Either research dynamic systems theory or one of the theoretical perspectives outlined in this chapter, and find out about it in more depth. The following texts will help you with this but you can also ask your tutor, colleagues or librarian for suggestions as well as searching online.

- Smith, P., Cowie, H., Blades, M., 2011, *Understanding Children's Development*, London: Wiley.
- Bee, H., Boyd, D., 2010, *The Developing Child* (12th edn), New York: Allyn and Bacon.
- Keenan, T., Evans, S., 2009, *An Introduction to Child Development*, London: Sage.

KEY TERM

Dynamic systems – Seeing development progressing as a result of the interactions that take place within the body and the mind.

Further reading, weblinks and resources

Siren Films

High-quality DVDs focusing on the development of children at different ages
www.sirenfilms.co.uk

Zero to Three

An American professional journal that discusses all aspects of the health, development and learning of children aged birth to three years.
www.zerotothree.org

References

Aldgate, J., 2006, 'Children Development and Ecology' in Aldgate, J., Jones, D., Rose, W., Jeffery, C. (eds), *The Developing World of the Child*, London: Jessica Kingsley Publisher.

Bandura, A., 1986, *Social Foundations of Thought and Action: A Social Cognitive Theory*, Englewood Cliffs, NJ: Prentice-Hall.

Bee, H., Boyd, D., 2010, *The Developing Child* (12th edn), New York: Allyn and Bacon.

Bronfenbrenner, U., 1979, *The Ecology of Human Development*, Cambridge, MA: Harvard University Press.

Bronfenbrenner, U. and Morris, P., 2006, 'The Bioecological Model of Human Development',

in R. M. Lerner (ed.), *Handbook of child psychology: Vol 1. Theoretical Models of Human Development* (6th edn), Hoboken, New Jersey: Wiley.

Carter, R., 1999, *Mapping the Mind*, London: Seven Dials.

Crain, W., 1992, *Theories of Development. Concepts and Applications*, New Jersey: Prentice-Hall.

Department for Education (2011) *Rolling out Free Early Education for Disadvantaged Two year olds: An Implementation Study for Local Authorities and Providers*, London: National Children's Bureau with National Centre for Social Research. Available at: http://www.natcen.ac.uk/media/26401/rolling-out-free-early-education.pdf

Edwards, C., Gandini, L., Forman, G. (eds), 2012, *The Hundred Languages of Children* (3rd edn), London, Ablex publishing.

Gopnik, A., Meltzoff, A., Kuhl, P., 1999, *How Babies Think*, London: Weidenfeld and Nicolson.

Greenfield, S., 2000, *The Private Life of the Brain*, London: Penguin Books.

Karmiloff-Smith, A., 1992, *Beyond Modularity. A Developmental Perspective on Cognitive Science*, Cambridge, MA: MIT Press.

Keenan, T., Evans, S., 2009, *An Introduction to Child Development*, London: Sage.

Manning-Morton, J., 2011, 'Not Just the Tip of the Iceberg: Psychoanalytic ideas and early years practice', in Miller, L. and Pound, L., *Theories and Approaches to Learning in the Early Years*, London: Sage.

Piaget, J., 1952, *The Origin of Intelligence in the Child*, London: Routledge and Kegan Paul.

Piaget, J., 1962, *Play, Dreams and Imitation in Childhood*, London: Routledge and Kegan Paul.

Schaffer, H. R., 2006, *Key Concepts in Developmental Psychology*, London: Sage.

Smith P., Cowie, H., Blades, M., 2011, *Understanding Children's Development*, London: Wiley.

Vygotsky, L. S., 1978, *Mind in Society*, Cambridge, MA: Harvard University Press.

Watson, J. B., 1928, *Psychological Care of Infant and Child*, New York: Norton Company, Inc.

This chapter sets out key aspects of babies and young children's **perceptual and cognitive development**. It emphasises the key role of the senses and movement in how children learn about and make sense of the world. Key aspects of cognition are discussed and the development of mental representations and early **concepts** is explored from the perspective of key theorists. This includes looking at **schemas** as a useful way of thinking about children's play and representation and reconsidering our understanding of intelligence as a way of understanding children's cognitive development.

Perceptual development: sensations and perceptions

Infants and young children come to understand the world primarily through their senses; sight, hearing, taste, touch, smell and movement. It used to be thought that babies experienced these sensations but did not really think about them. Now we understand that while processing sensory information in the brain (perception), babies and young children are extracting meaning or understanding from it **(cognition).**

Processing sensory information

The sense organs – ears/nose/eyes, mouth and skin – are the sensory systems that gather information, which the brain modifies and sorts. **Sensory stimuli** such as

KEY TERMS

Perceptual development – The processing in the brain of sensory information received through the sensory organs. The extraction of information from sensory experiences to make sense of the world.

Cognitive development – The development of the mind: the processes in the brain that enable us to recognise, reason, know and understand. It involves: what a person knows and the ability to reason, understand and solve problems; memory, concentration, attention and perception; imagination and creativity.

Concepts – Ideas that can be shared, such as fairness, weight and time.

Schemas – A pattern of thought or behaviour that organises categories of information and the relationships among them.

Cognition – The process of making sense and thinking about the world and experiences to develop ideas and form concepts.

a sound or a smell enter the brain through the sense organs as a series of electrical pulses, which then get processed through neural pathways to specific areas of the brain and thereby translated into visual, aural or other sensations.

For example, for audition (hearing) the sense organ is the outer/middle and inner ear and the specialised receptors in the ear gather sound and send it via the auditory nerve to the temporal lobe which is the specialised area of the brain which modifies and sorts sound. So the physical development of the sense organs can have a profound effect on other aspects of children's development. (Key aspects of the development of the senses are set out in Chapter 9.)

For some babies and children with complex needs, it can be difficult to be sure whether they are receiving messages through their senses, telling them they are having an experience. Observing this in children is always important, but it is particularly important in children with complex needs.

Very early on, babies have an awareness that goes beyond their immediate sensory feedback about people and things. Perception is the process of beginning to make sense of sensory information. What a baby, child or adult perceives is the result of the merging of different past experiences (physical, sensory, social and cultural) being interpreted. The neuroscientist Rita Carter (1999) points out that we never perceive the same thing in the same way twice because the sensory impact of something alters our subsequent perception of it; in turn that sensory impact and perception creates a different way of perceiving it the next time. So the second time we hear a piece of music, for example, we will hear it slightly differently because we bring to it our expectation of what it will sound like; we may hear elements we did not before because we can listen less attentively to the parts that are familiar and more to parts we missed previously.

So babies do not only take in sensory information, they also transform and rearrange it in their minds; they think about it! For example, touch is a key way in which babies and young children learn about objects. The skin is our largest sense organ, and in babies, the most sensitive area exists in their mouths. So babies mouth objects to find out about them. By using the more sensitive nerve ending around their mouths, they form a representation in their mind of the object. Babies who are given different shaped dummies to suck will look for longer at a picture of the dummy they were given. Gradually, as the palmar grasp develops into a pincer

▲ **Figure 7.1** Sensory experiences are fundamental to cognitive development

grip (see Chapter 9 for more information), babies can add the information they can get from their fingertips to their mouthing explorations.

As young infants' sensory perceptions develop, they are also able to use more than one sense to explore and understand their world. Particular parts of the brain are designed to respond to specific kinds of stimulation. For example, the cells in the retina of the eye send connections out towards the visual areas in the back of the brain rather than to the language centres on the side of the brain. But Rita Carter (1999) describes how in the early months of life there are still connections between auditory and visual areas that may give them the experience of 'seeing' sounds and 'hearing' colours; this is known as synaesthesia. Although this diminishes or weakens in most babies, the flexibility of brain growth enables the brains of babies with sight or hearing impairments, for example, to compensate for lack of stimulation in one area by growing an alternative area more and by employing the area less used for a different purpose. So the brains of babies who are blind will have many

more connections in the areas that process hearing, smell and touch, and the area that usually processes visual stimulation becomes sensitive to other sensory input.

In the process of development, it is the task of perceptual processing to both separate and link the different sensory stimuli. When babies process sensory information, their brains both separate the different stimuli and also link them together. For example, babies' well-developed sense of hearing enables them to tell from which direction the sound of their carer's voice is coming, so they can turn towards the sound and, when it is close enough, see the shape the mouth makes for that sound. They are then able to imitate that sound and action more effectively because they can integrate the different sensory stimuli.

Perceptual skills are fundamental to other aspects of development (Bee and Boyd 2010). For example:

● The inborn tracking reflex and interest in the human shape, faces and movement predisposes or prompts babies to be social.

● Babies' mature hearing enables communication development as they respond to mimicry or imitation of their own voices, which widens the range of vocal sounds they make.

● The stimulation of sensory information is fundamental to brain development. For example, touch helps babies and young children's brains to develop the systems that understand about tactile sensitivity. In other words, everything a baby hears, sees, smells, tastes and feels stimulates neural connections to be made in the brain.

● The experience of sensitive touch and holding comforts and calms babies, and aids their emotional development and sense of self.

● Positive touch contributes to good health as it helps the body to produce antibodies and boosts the immune system.

● Babies' social relationships are supported by their ability to differentiate between their primary carer and others through their sense of smell and their ability to hear the different sound of their voice.

● Through repeated and varied **sensory experiences**, babies learn that the shape, size and colour of categories of objects remain constant (**object constancy**). From this they learn to differentiate between objects and also learn about **object permanency**; the idea that an object still exists even when it cannot be seen, see p. 123 for more information. This ability is fundamental to cognitive learning.

KEY TERMS

Depth perception – The visual ability to perceive the world in three dimensions and the distance of an object.
Proprioception – Your sense of your body in space and how body parts relate to each other.
Kinaesthetic sense – Sense of movement; how to move your body for standing, sitting, running, crawling, jumping, dancing etc.

Think about ideas

Play 'where has it gone?' with a baby or young toddler using one or two objects and a cloth:

- Do they look for the object?
- Where do they look?

With two-year-olds this can be a simple 'hide and seek' game:

- How do they hide themselves?
- What are their responses to appearing and disappearing?

- Cognitive understanding is also supported by the ability to tell the difference between two and three dimensional objects, which also comes with experience.

- **Depth perception** helps the newly crawling baby to avoid crawling off the edge of the stairs. It is time spent on their tummies learning to creep and crawl that supports the development of depth perception. Babies who are put in baby walkers all the time cannot develop this ability so effectively.

It is important to give babies interesting sensory experiences, as well as the love and care that are essential. Babies will appreciate this, and will cry less when they are engaged with their senses. These kind of experiences lead to early concepts, and researchers are beginning to understand that concepts are formed earlier than was previously thought. Remember, all the senses are important – touch, taste, smell, hearing and seeing – along with **proprioception** and kinaesthesia. Our feelings, thoughts and physical selves all work together as we learn.

Theory and theorists: permanence of the object

Piaget used a test called 'the permanence of the object'. He would cover an object, and the baby had to sit and watch this. By nine months of age, the baby would reach for the object by uncovering it and picking it up; younger babies did not do this. It is now thought that babies have to realise that two objects (the object and the cover) can be in one place in order to complete the test.

Later researchers gave babies of five months of age an object which might be put in either their right hand or their left hand. When the light went out they found that the babies reached for the object as soon as it was dark. The object could not be seen, but the babies still reached out and almost always they reached out in the right direction. The babies seemed to know that the object was still there, even though they could not see

it in the dark. They also know that they only have one mother and so become disturbed if they are shown multiple images of her as early as five months old.

What is cognition?

Cognition is the process of knowing, using the senses to perceive how things are, and out of this, forming concepts (ideas that can be shared). Cognition includes the processes of attention, learning, memory, reasoning and problem-solving. The goal of cognition is to understand and manage the environment in the way that we need. To gain this kind of control we need to understand how things work and what causes things to happen.

Look, listen and note

Consider these three scenarios and note down the ways in which the child is perceptually physically and cognitively active:

- a six-month-old repeating 'ababa' when 'talking' to an adult, who smiles and mimics the baby
- a nine-month-old crawling after a ball
- a toddler pulling their truck up the steps.

Your notes will probably identify that these children are exercising muscles, experiencing new sensations, using their sight, hearing, touch, proprioception and **kinaesthetic senses**.

Did you also consider that they are thinking about cause and effect, about relative speed and distance and about spatial relationships and the manoeuvrability of solid objects?

They are also remembering past actions and experiences and recreating them, using their previous experience to plan their actions or to predict their outcome. These processes mean that they are cognitively active too (Manning-Morton and Thorp 2003).

Guidelines for good practice

Cognitive development in children who experience sensory impairment

Because learning through the senses and movement feedback is central to the development of thinking in young children, it is important to offer children with sensory impairments, such as visual or hearing impairments, the kind of support that allows them to do this as much as possible.

Hearing impairment

In order for children with hearing impairments to be supported as much as possible in developing their thinking and ideas, it is important to:

✔ have expert advice on the best kind of hearing aid for the child

✔ remember that a hearing aid does not mean the child will be able to hear normally

✔ work with the child in an enabling environment, without too much background noise as this is distracting, distorts sounds and makes it difficult to hear the child

✔ consider whether BSL may be helpful for the child to learn

✔ give the child broad and rich first-hand experiences in a variety of ways, so that learning has meaning and interests the child

✔ make sure that people talk to the child slowly but naturally, and on a one-to-one basis

✔ see that the child sits facing the adult directly at group time, with the light falling on the adult's face (which makes it easier to lip-read)

✔ avoid touching the child's face and turning it to draw their attention, as this is invasive and unpleasant for the child

✔ remember that when dancing and singing, the child sits on the floor to feel the vibrations, or can feel the rhythms through the floor with their feet in a physical way.

Visual impairment

In order for children with visual impairments to be supported in developing their thinking and ideas, it is important to:

✔ remember that wearing glasses will not give normal sight to a child with partial sight

✔ overcome the problem of losing things that go out of sight – it is helpful to put things on trays with raised sides

✔ bear in mind that a child with a visual impairment will often try to stay connected with people by engaging in conversation and chatting

✔ encourage the child to touch and hold so that he or she learns about the physical world around him or her

✔ tell the child when you are moving away from him or her, so that he or she is aware of this

✔ describe where food is on the child's plate (e.g. your peas are at the top of the plate and your potatoes are at the bottom)

✔ avoid suddenly taking a child's hand, as he or she is likely to be alarmed if this is done without warning.

Usha Goswami (1998) says that 'Cognitive development in a broad sense is thus the development of the set of processes that enable us to gain knowledge about causation.' In other words, it is the ability to put pieces of information together and understand how they affect each other.

The fundamental cognitive processes of learning, memory, perception and attention are available from, or even before, birth (Gopnik et al. 1999).

Problem-solving, understanding cause and effect, making hypotheses and theories, and predicting what will happen

Children are natural problem-solvers from the moment they are born. It used to be thought that, at first, children tried to solve problems through trial and error, and that only later could they develop a theory

or **hypothesis**. More recently, however, researchers have found that even newborn babies can make a hypothesis. This means having a theory that can be tested to see if it is right. It is amazing to think that babies can do this, rather than the cruder trial-and-error approach to solving problems.

Children can be very stubborn and inflexible about a theory they have! But testing out a hypothesis is a very important part of learning to solve problems. In order to learn about problem-solving, children need to test out their incorrect hypotheses as well as correct ones. The reasoning they employ is invaluable for intellectual development.

KEY TERM

Hypothesis – A hypothesis makes a prediction that something will happen and tests it out in a scientific way to see if it is true or not.

Think about ideas

Baby makes a hypothesis

This experiment, conducted in the 1970s, would be considered unethical today (because honey is now known to be dangerous to some babies under one year of age), but it does show how a baby makes a hypothesis. A newborn baby turned towards the sound of a buzzer and was given a honeyed dummy to suck on. The baby also turned to the sound of a bell, but was not given a honeyed dummy. Soon the baby turned only for the buzzer. Once the baby had tested the hypothesis – that the buzzer signified honey and the bell did not – the hypothesis was confirmed. Soon the baby was bored with confirming the hypothesis again and again, so the baby did not turn to either buzzer or bell.

Observe a baby at play. Can you see them testing out their ideas?

KEY TERMS

Abstract – A thought or idea that does not have a physical or concrete existence, such as beauty or fairness.
Semantics – The sense and meaning of language.

Babies and young children are fascinated by cause and effect.

- From as early as 12-weeks-old, a baby begins to understand the effect their crying causes and begins to anticipate a response; this is their first step towards **abstract** thought.
- Toddlers and two-year-olds are also experimenting with the effect of their behaviours on other people as well as objects and what they can cause to happen.
- Young children quickly find out what various buttons and levers do and often experiment with taking things apart to see how they work.
- Older children want to know why and how those levers and buttons work and use their experience and hypotheses to experiment with putting things together.

Memory

Memory is about the way experiences are stored, retained and recalled in the brain. There are different kinds of memory: short-term memory and long-term memory.

Short-term memory

When you make a phone call, you need to remember the number for long enough to dial. Remembering ten or so digits is quite hard to do. It becomes easier for the brain if the numbers are 'chunked', ideally into a maximum of three numbers per chunk, some chunks with two numbers.

Short-term memory relies hugely on hearing (acoustic) and quite a bit on seeing (visual). This is why it is difficult to remember words that sound similar (bog, dog, log, fog). The difference between 'dog' and 'cat' is easier for the brain to hear.

Short-term memories do not last long in the brain; they are limited. Neuroscientists now know that that our feelings, sensory perceptions and memories are all bound together in a seamless whole. This means that the feelings children have are of central importance in the way memory develops (Gopnik et al. 1999).

Long-term memory

We remember things that engage our interest and hold meaning for us. One famous example comes from Piaget's daughter Jacqueline when she was a toddler. She saw a friend (aged 18 months) have a temper tantrum. She was very impressed by this dramatic event, and the following day she tried it out for herself, imitating the tantrum.

Whereas short-term memory relies on sound and sight, long-term memory depends on meaning (**semantics**). Unless something makes sense, it cannot find its way into the long-term memory.

There are different kinds of long-term memory: declarative memory and procedural memory.

Declarative memory involves:

- consciously recalling something (where did I put the car keys?)
- semantic memory, which holds meaning independent of the context (remembering that the family name for your grandmother is 'Nana')
- episodic memory (including autobiographical memory), which depends on the context ('I remember that shop because I bought my shoes there')
- visual memory (having mental images of people's faces, objects, places, etc.).

Procedural memory involves:

- learning motor skills through repeating them (learning to sit, crawl, walk)
- topographic memory (positioning yourself or moving in space, recognising familiar places)

- being retrospective (remembering something from the past, happy moments, flashbacks or phobias)
- being prospective (remembering something to do in the future, such as remembering, in the morning, a doctor's appointment booked for 4 pm).

Memory in infants and young children

If you poke out your tongue at a newborn baby, they will imitate you. This means the baby is translating what they have seen into a movement in their own body. To do this requires memory and forming a representation of that action in your mind. So, imitation and memory are linked.

Newborn babies also demonstrate that they can remember things they have heard when in the womb, such as a television theme tune.

Six-month-old babies have been observed to form memories of events that they can retrieve two years later in the presence of the right reminders; usually sensory reminders such as a sound or a smell.

Between the ages of two and three years, children are able to remember more. The advantage of developing a longer-term memory is that they can organise their thinking a bit more. They remember what they have done before in similar situations with people, and they can use this memory to think about what to do in a new situation. This is called 'inhibition to the unfamiliar'. It means children begin to 'think before they do'.

Theory and theorists: infantile amnesia

The fact that many adults cannot retrieve memories from their infancy led to the concept of 'infantile **amnesia**' (Carter 1999, Gopnik et al. 1999). This is sometimes mistakenly interpreted as babies and young children forgetting their earliest experiences. However, it more specifically relates to the fact that our earliest memories (especially those with high levels of physical sensation or emotional content) are stored in the **limbic cortex**, the older part of our brain which is mature at birth. These memories tend to be unconscious.

Our conscious memories – ones that have language and a story attached to them – are stored in the **cerebral cortex** as the connections in the brain are further developed. These memories are more easily

> ### Think about ideas
>
> What is your earliest memory? Can you remember before you were two or three years old?
> Many people cannot. If you can, is this a memory that comes from what you have been told, or is it your 'own'?

> ## KEY TERMS
>
> **Amnesia** – Partial or total loss of memory.
> **Limbic cortex** – A group of interconnected structures deep in the brain that deal with emotions (such as anger, happiness and fear) as well as memories.
> **Cerebral cortex** – The outer layer of grey matter of the brain, largely responsible for higher brain functions, including sensation, voluntary muscle movement, thought, reasoning, and memory.
> **Centration** – The child cannot hold in mind several ideas at once, so focuses on one aspect.

retrievable through thinking and talking but our earliest memories are more often 'jogged' through sensory or bodily stimuli, especially touch and smell as they are the more mature senses in infancy (LeDoux 2002). For example, an adult might find the smell of hot chocolate drink nauseating because it reminds her of being expected to drink it as a toddler at nursery when he/she had disliked the feel and taste of the skin that had formed on the drink.

Going beyond the present, back to the past and into the future

One of the most important things about humans is our ability to think about the past and to imagine and plan the future. Researchers are beginning to find that chimpanzees – the closest relatives to humans in the animal world – can also do this to some extent.

Concepts of time are hard to understand for young children as they cannot be explored physically – time is an abstract concept, so they very much live in the present. As their understanding of object permanency grows though, they are more able to take themselves out of the here and now and can then begin to grasp sequences of events; 'after lunch we will go to the park'. As they get older young children can conceive of divisions of time such as 'morning' and 'afternoon', or 'last night'.

As children begin to walk, talk and imagine, they are able to think about the future. A child might decide that when they get to nursery they will do some cooking. The child might bake a cake and take it to eat with Grandma after nursery.

Young children become increasingly able to think forwards and backwards in time in quick succession. Because every event is a bit like a separate photograph, they need to focus (or centre) on one thing at a time: Piaget (1969) calls this **centration**.

As children begin to link their previous experiences more easily, the experiences they have become more like a moving film than a sequence of still photographs.

Cognition, representation and early concepts

Mental representation is central to cognition but the term is used in different ways; firstly to mean knowledge or the way in which humans store information in their minds, and secondly to mean the use of symbols to denote experience (Schaffer 2006). For example the word 'cat' may be used to represent a four-legged furry animal, a picture of a cat standing for the real cat, crawling on the floor saying 'miaow' 'being' a cat, and eventually understanding the marks written as CAT as also representing the four-legged furry animal. It is the way in which babies and young children organise their mental representations that leads to the formation of concepts, such as the characteristics that make cats different to other animals but similar to each other; 'catness'.

Andrew Meltzoff believes that the ability to form cognitive representations is innate. He suggests that when newborn babies imitate tongue protrusion (i.e. sticking out their tongue), they are not just copying and taking in information through their senses; they are also interpreting and reconstructing that action through their own actions, which requires **representational**

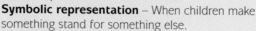

KEY TERMS

Representational capacity – The ability to form mental representations in the mind.
Symbolic representation – When children make something stand for something else.
Assimilation – This is the process by which new information is interpreted through existing schemas.
Accommodation – How the brain changes a schema to take account of new experiences.

capacity (Gopnik et al. 1999). In this way imitation can be seen to be an important part of the process of developing representations. Piaget (1962) suggests that imitation and the creation of internal mental images is the first step towards **symbolic representation**.

As they grow, develop and learn, children develop concepts of time, space, love, beauty and number (to name just a few), which continue to develop over the years. Concept formation is biological, social and cultural. Our brains quite literally change according to who we meet and the experiences we have. Also, it is through physically exploring the world through movement that enables children to understand concepts in a more abstract form. So spending time putting yourself in front and behind things helps to understand positional concepts of 'before' and 'after', which in turn helps children to deal with ideas such as writing from left to right.

As a child's cognition, representation and concepts emerge and develop, they begin to:

- develop memory, which helps them to know more
- organise their thinking
- link past, present and future around a particular idea
- predict things about the future
- understand sequences, with a beginning, middle and end
- understand transformations
- seriate (putting things into a series) and order, so that they understand the differences between things (different shapes, sizes, colours, objects and animals)
- classify, so that they see the similarities between things (e.g. cats and dogs are animals)
- organise previous experience – Piaget calls this **assimilation**
- take in new knowledge and understand it – Piaget calls this **accommodation**
- bring together their ideas, thoughts, feelings and relationships.

Reflecting on practice

With the children, look for some worms, ants, spiders and other mini beasts in the garden. Talk about the experiences as you do so, explaining what each creature is, how many legs it has and what it does – for example, worms turn the soil and aerate (introduce air into) it; ants live in colonies, with worker ants finding food and taking it back to the others; spiders eat flies.

Later in the day, show the children a book about mini beasts, with photos of them in it. Chat about this together. Let the children talk about what interests them in the photos. What do the children remember and enjoy talking about with you?

Make a book with simple cookery instructions and use it with a small group of children (two to four children aged between three and seven years). About a week later, have a chat with the children in a group and ask them how to make the recipe. What will they need? How will they do it?

Note what they say. What does this tell you about their thinking?

Think about ideas

An emerging concept of faces

Hannah cried when her Uncle Dan, who was bald, came to the house. This happened every time she saw her Uncle Dan for a month or so. She had to adjust to her new knowledge that some people do not have hair on the top of their heads.

Babies get to know the faces of people in their family and of their carers. They begin to develop an early concept of what faces look like. By the age of about six-to-nine months, typically, they find faces that seem different rather frightening because they do not fit with what they know. At first, Uncle Dan was very upset, but he was reassured when this was explained.

Observe a baby or young toddler responding to others.

- How do they differentiate between people?
- Which of their behaviours tells you that they recognise some people and not others?

As children's concepts begin to develop they begin to understand that things are not always as they appear. This typically occurs in middle childhood (7–12 years), according to Piaget. Children begin to be able to hold in mind several things at once, and they can run back and forth in their minds as they think. Their thinking is becoming more mobile at this point.

Theories of cognition, representation and early concepts

Different theorists have different views on how babies move from perceptual categorisations; for example, the feeling of being put in and out of the cot/bath, to meaning-based knowledge representations understanding the concept of in/out. What follows is a discussion of different theories about cognitive development and the development of representation and concepts.

Jean Piaget (1896–1980)

Piaget is often viewed as the elder statesman of child development study. He has left a rich description of how children develop in their thinking, and he has provided us with detailed observations that are very sensitively made. He deserves great respect for this.

There are several ways of exploring Piaget's theory. One is to look at the way he explores:

- biological sequences of development (the way children grow, develop and mature)
- social knowledge (other people and the way children relate to them)

Guidelines for good practice

Supporting cognitive development

- ✔ Remember that children are active learners.
- ✔ Observe children's thinking and the ideas they develop; carefully note your observations and share them with parents and colleagues.
- ✔ Remember the sequences of development in thinking, so that you can help the child in ways that tap into this.
- ✔ Develop your observation skills so that you tune in to children as unique individuals.
- ✔ Use what you have found in gathering observations of a child to plan experiences based on what interests them and helps their thinking and ideas to develop.
- ✔ Use your observations to make sure that you do not underestimate or overestimate a child's thinking. Try not to expect children to do things that are boring for them or expect them to perform tasks that are too difficult for them and therefore put them off.
- ✔ Offer a wide range of experiences through which they are able to develop and learn (not narrow activities and tasks that allow little choice on the part of the child).
- ✔ Ensure a wide range of experiences but make sure that you think of what would be of particular interest to individual children.
- ✔ Encourage children to have ideas and to be creative and imaginative; respect and show sensitivity to their ideas.
- ✔ Encourage children to try new things.
- ✔ Give children sensitive help in carrying out their ideas, helping only when needed.
- ✔ Adapt experiences to suit children with SEN, complex needs and disabilities.

- the **equilibrium** of learning (accommodating to new ideas and assimilating experiences into what is already known); because we are always learning, we are always balancing (as we do on a two-wheel bicycle)
- the importance of experience in development and learning – Piaget pioneered the idea that experience is important in the development of cognition (thinking).

KEY TERM

Equilibrium – This is the state of cognitive or mental balance that the mind tries to maintain. When a child's existing schemas are capable of explaining what they can perceive, they are in a state of equilibrium. New information upsets the balance until existing schemas change to accommodate the information and regain balance.

Usually, Piaget's work is looked at through the biological sequences of development rather than through the other aspects of his theory.

Piaget's stages of cognitive development

- Sensory motor stage (0 to about 18 months)
- Developing operations (about 18 months to 7 years)*
- Concrete operations (about 7 to 12 years)
- Formal operations (about 12 years to adulthood).

Although the exact ages vary, and are different in different cultures and for children with complex needs and disabilities, the sequences of Piaget's theory are still thought to be useful.

Recent research questions whether individual children go through these stages in the same way. It also questions whether all adults reach the stage of formal operations.

Piaget did not believe it was possible to teach concepts. He thought that children begin to develop concepts during the stage of concrete operations, through experience and social interactions with others, but mainly through the processes of biological maturing and conservation of concepts. Conservation of thinking means the child can hold in mind several things at once, and can think beyond how something looks. Two beakers might look as if the tall one holds more water than the wider one, but that is only because the height deceives the onlooker. The child needs to realise that width is as important as height in deciding which beaker holds the most water. Piaget's experiments looked at areas such as conservation of shape, weight, volume, speed, number and moral development.

Sensory motor development (birth to about 18 months)

Piaget (1962) describes that during the sensory motor period, babies build on their reflex actions through actively exploring and interacting with their own bodies, other people and objects around them. He uses the term 'schema' or 'schemata' to describe the cognitive structures in our minds that we use to make sense of experience. Babies and young children assimilate or integrate new experiences into their existing schemas, and thereby adjust or accommodate and develop more complex schemas. In this way they combine schemas to solve problems, achieve goals and

to learn about new objects according to their physical maturity (Goswami 1998). For example, schemas for reaching, grasping, coordinating hands and eye all work together for a baby to explore objects.

For Piaget, sensory motor behaviour becomes thought and children begin to make cognitive representations at the end of the sensory motor period, at about 18 to 24 months old. This view, that motor abilities have to be mature enough to be used to form cognitive representations, is challenged by evidence showing infants being able to understand aspects of cause and effect and object permanence as young as four months old, i.e. before they have the physical ability to explore that particular concept (Smith et al. 1998).

There are six sub-stages:

- Ready-made behaviours (reflexes) that the baby is born with are adapted and used – for example, the baby actively tries to reach for the nipple (teat) with his or her hands as soon as it touches the baby's lips.
- Hands become coordinated with sucking; sounds are looked for; objects are seen and reached for; hand-watching is important.
- Babies begin to show intention. They try to prolong or repeat something that interests them – for example, the baby bangs his or her foot against the side of the cot and the mobile moves, so he or she does this again, watching intently.
- Babies begin to experiment with making things happen. This is very clear when they throw things out of the pram. They begin to work out that although they do the same thing (throw) each time, the object they throw might behave in a different way – a ball will bounce, a biscuit will crumble and milk will spill. They imitate and they begin to play.
- Around the end of the first year, babies deliberately modify or change their actions in order to produce the result they want. They like trying out new things, and they follow through and search for a ball if it rolls under the sofa, expecting to find that it has rolled out the other side.
- They can think about the past and the future. They might imitate the action of eating a lollipop the day after they had one as a treat.

Pre-operational thinking: symbolic behaviour and intuition (18 months to 7 years)

From about 18 months to 7 years, we start to see the beginnings of what Piaget called the pre-operational period. The main features of this are that children are involved in:

- imitation (and increasingly imitating things after the event)

*Piaget calls this period of development 'pre-operational'. However, most early years practitioners do not like the idea that children are 'pre' anything, because it concentrates too much on what children cannot do, giving a negative image of the young child. It is much more useful to think in terms of developing operations, which provides a more positive emphasis.

- pretending (imagining things from the past or in the future)
- forming images inside their heads.

The first part of this phase is often called the period of symbolic behaviour, when children understand representation more and use objects to stand for something else. This is linked to play, imagination and creativity. We see the child becoming more and more able to think about and reflect on things he or she actively experiences.

Concrete operations (about 7 to 12 years)

Although children are beginning to be able to think in more abstract ways, they still need plenty of real and first-hand experiences in order to understand things. There is a Chinese proverb that says, 'I do and I understand'. During these years of middle childhood, children become increasingly able to:

- hold in mind several things at once
- deepen the way they use symbols as they draw, make models, dance, make music, write, read, make stories and use mathematical numbers and mark-making
- conserve ideas (be able to see beyond the superficial appearance of how things look) about shape, number, quantity, volume, and so on – for example, to work out that although five sweets look like more when they are spread out than when they are bunched up, there are still five sweets
- understand the rules of games, such as football or snakes and ladders.

Formal operations (about 12 years until adulthood)

In the stage of concrete thinking, children need real and present situations so that they can have their deepest thoughts – for example, they can understand a great deal about what is fair and unfair if one child is given a present and the other is not. But formal operations allow older children and adults to think in abstract ways. For example, the concepts of peace and justice are abstract ideas, we cannot see touch or feel them, just their effects.

Some adults never reach this stage, and for most of the time adults continue to rely on concrete, real

Think about ideas

Reflect on your own studying:
- What helps you to understand abstract ideas such as 'representation'?
- Does it help to have real examples, or to link the idea with your own experience?

situations when they think. It is hard to think in the abstract, without a real situation to help the thinking along, so we do not manage it all the time.

Further developments of Piaget's work

Piaget concentrated on children's thinking, intellectual development and ideas. This does not mean that he did not think that social, emotional and physical development were also important – he did. It is just that he did not make these his main area of study. Some people have argued that Piaget ignored social relationships and the cultural aspects of the child's life. In fact, Piaget thought they were so important that he took them for granted.

Social and cultural relationships

These are now thought to be just as central to a child's development as the other kinds of experience that Piaget emphasised more, such as the way that children build up an understanding of objects. Recent research is helping us to remember that it is important to have a balanced approach which emphasises:

- the importance of people and positive relationships for thinking and learning
- first-hand experiences that are physical, cultural and social
- learning and thinking in indoor and outdoor situations
- the importance of children having experiences that are of interest and that hold meaning for them
- that children are active learners, but they are not isolated learners – they need other children and adults to help them learn and think.

Children perform less well in test situations

When children are put into laboratory test situations, they find it harder to do their best thinking. They find it difficult to understand exactly what the 'experimenter' is asking them. When they are in a situation that makes 'human sense' to them – at home or in their early years setting with their mother or key person – they are in a familiar situation and they can think better.

Cultural sensitivities

Recent researchers look more at the importance of context. One of Piaget's conservation tests, to see if a child has a concept of looking at a view from different visual perspectives, involves asking a child to look at model mountains. The child is asked to say what a doll will see when placed at different points around the model. A child growing up in the Norfolk Broads for example, where the land is flat, will not experience the mountains of Switzerland in the way that the children whom Piaget studied did. The Swiss children saw views from different angles as they moved round the mountains, in a way that children living in Norfolk would not, so children living in flat countryside might appear to be less able according to the conservation test. In this example, the conservation test is culturally biased in favour of the Swiss children.

Barbara Rogoff (2003) explores the cultural contexts of children's development. She suggests that different cultural communities have different expectations of children participating in everyday life activities, which, therefore, have a different impact on the child's development. For example, in the USA, some families think that children are not capable of looking after themselves and others until they are 10-years-old. In the UK, children must not be left without adult supervision before the age of 14, and we give children plastic tools to play with rather than real tools to use. However, in many cultures, children are responsible for looking after themselves and others at a much younger age. In Kwara'ae of Oceania (Solomon Islands), children from the age of three are skilled workers in the family garden and are trusted to look after their younger siblings. Controversially, in the Efe of the Democratic Republic of Congo infants are allowed to use machetes safely, and in Fore (New Guinea) infants handle knives and fire safely from the moment they start walking.

This view suggests that a stage theory perspective on cognitive development might be problematic.

Transforming – you are never the same again

Piaget's stages of development are now seen as too linear. Instead, researchers look at the way networks of behaviour develop in sequences. Piaget's basic idea that one stage transforms as it changes into the next persists, but we now know that it is a very complex series of biological transformations, and we are trying to understand and learn about the detail.

Gaps in Piaget's theory

Although Piaget's is still the most overarching theory of cognition (thinking), it left a lot of gaps that recent researchers have been trying to fill. It is a bit like putting more pieces into a jigsaw puzzle so that we can have a fuller picture than the one Piaget gave us.

Lev Vygotsky (1896–1934)

Since the 1980s Vygotsky's work has become a major influence. He considered human development in terms of culture and interpersonal relationships as well as the development of the individual. The integration of these three determines the journey that each individual child takes (Schaffer 2004).

Vygotsky (1978) believed that the child is equipped with the innate abilities of attention, memory and perception, which he called elementary mental functions. These innate abilities can develop to some extent without the support of adults and others.

However, he placed great emphasis on social relationships and learning from others in his theory. In his view, children can have better ideas and do better thinking when an adult or child who knows more than they do is helping them – for example, an adult can help a child to experience a story like *Spot the Dog* by reading the book for the child; later, the child will be able to read for themselves.

In the same way, an older child might want to make lasagne, but could not do this alone. With help from an adult, they can share the instructions of the cookery book and together make the dish. Later on, the child will be able to do this without help.

So, for Vygotsky, cognitive development occurs through interaction with more knowledgeable adults and peers; what is shared becomes the child's knowledge and these interactions contribute to the development of higher mental functions such as voluntary attention, complex memory processes (such as using aids to remember things) and problem-solving.

Vygotsky therefore described both the zone of actual development – what the child can manage without help from anyone and the child's zone of proximal development; the space between what children know already and can do alone and what they might be able to do and learn with assistance from a more able peer or adult.

Vygotsky argued that learning takes place within a sociocultural context. Adults and peers are mediators who pass on the cultural tools of the social setting through interaction. For Vygotsky, culture comprises all the cultural tools, objects and skills that are used in a society and are handed down from generation to generation. Language is a key cultural tool that transmits knowledge, skills and values, and Vygotsky emphasises that it is necessary for intellectual activity and plays a major part in children's cognitive development because language enables children to access information and to understand other people (Vygotsky 1986).

Vygotsky suggested that language and thought develop independently from birth. He used the terms '**pre-intellectual speech**' and '**pre-linguistic thought**'. However, between two and three years

KEY TERMS

Pre-intellectual speech – The early vocalisations (vocal sounds) babies make to engage with others. Vygotsky called this 'primitive' speech and suggested that it did not involve any intellectual thought.

Pre-linguistic thought – Thought can take place without language, but for Vygotsky this was provided by and dependent on the interactions of the carer, whose responses provide the thinking about the experience.

language and thought merge and begin to function in a coordinated way. Vygotsky argued that children move from using language for social purposes to self-talk (monologue), which will help them to plan and sort out their thought processes. Gradually this external monologue becomes inner thinking – the child is now able to plan in their head without speaking out loud.

Vygotsky also believed that play is another way in which children can reach their highest levels of learning, that play creates a 'zone of potential development' where they are able to function at their highest level or learning. He emphasised imaginative play and suggested that this frees children from the here and now, allowing them to pretend. It is almost as if a child becomes, as Vygotsky described it, 'a head taller' than he or she really is, when he or she is deeply involved in imaginative play. Vygotsky believed that social relationships are at the heart of a child's learning, so his theory is called a social constructivist theory. See Chapter 6.

Vygotsky regarded the child's ability to make symbolic representations as the beginning of abstract thought. He noted how children use one object to represent another in imaginary play and described this as an ability to 'sever the object from its meaning' (Vygotsky 1966); they are able to suspend reality in their play. However, like Piaget, he has been criticised for underestimating the representational abilities of very young children as he suggested that using abstract symbols in play only emerged at about three years. Although the emergent pretend play of children under three years is often based in real situations with objects whose properties do relate to the thing they are imagining, they also use objects symbolically. For example, two-year-old Poppy picks up a stick in the garden and creeps it across the grass, singing 'incy wincy spider'.

Jerome Bruner (b.1915)

Bruner (1966, 1990) sees representation as the way in which we manage to keep hold of our experiences in an orderly way. He describes three modes of representation:

The enactive mode

Representation is based on actions: waving when parting, doing kangaroo jumping, spinning and dancing, Bruner believed this the most important mode.

a

b

▲ **Figure 7.2** Children might represent the concept of 'round and round' or circularity in both enactive and iconic modes

He believed in learning by doing – children cannot learn easily unless they do so through real experiences. They are active learners, and freedom of movement helps them to develop their ideas and helps them to think. Bruner calls this **enactive learning** – for example, riding a tricycle, watching how a snail moves and leaves a trail, pounding the clay and leaving marks on it, singing a song and doing the actions.

The iconic mode

The child holds experiences as impressions/pictures in their mind, and can be seen in children's drawing.

This helps children to remember experiences: they need books with pictures, displays on walls and interest tables with objects that remind them of prior experiences. After a visit to the park, there might be photographs on the wall of children splashing in puddles in their wellingtons, and on the table next to the wall, daffodil bulbs growing in a pot and a pair of wellies to help children remember what they saw and did. Bruner calls this **iconic thinking**.

The symbolic mode

This occurs when a child can represent the world through words, and later, through secondary symbols such as letters and numbers (Wood 1998).

Symbolic codes: In Bruner's theory a code is something that can be shared with other people. Languages are symbolic codes. The word 'dog' is not actually a dog; the word stands symbolically for a dog – it is a code meaning a dog. Learning to read and write are symbolic codes too, but at first children participate by learning to talk and use language, and by making marks on paper and being read to.

Scaffolding

Bruner drew on both Piaget and Vygotsky's thinking. He valued both the physical environment and social interaction as stimulators for children's learning but emphasised the way that children are helped by adults to participate in their culture. He built on Vygotsky's concept of the zone of proximal development to describe the adults' role as one of providing scaffolding. When a house is being built, scaffolding is put up so that the building can become increasingly higher. Think of the adult as the scaffolding and the building as the child whose knowledge and understanding is growing. Gradually, the scaffolding is removed as it is not needed anymore.

Bruner talks about the way adults can 'scaffold' a child's experience by tuning in to what the child is interested in, and then helping him or her. Gradually the adult gives less and less help as the child can manage without it – for example, a child learning to weave among the Zinacantecon people in southern Mexico is helped through six steps, from setting up the loom to finishing off the piece of weaving. The adult withdraws the help as the child takes over.

Practitioners can help develop children's thinking by being like a piece of scaffolding on a building. Scaffolding can be described as anything a teacher can provide in a learning environment that might help a child learn. This includes anything that allows the child to grow in independence as a learner – such as:

- clues or hints
- reminders
- encouragement
- breaking a problem down into smaller steps
- providing an example.

The same scaffolding may be provided to all children, or teachers may offer customised scaffolding to individual learners.

Information processing approach to cognitive development

Information processing focuses on how children perceive, store and retrieve information and the strategies they use to solve problems (Pound 2013).

In contrast to Piaget's stage theory of development, an information processing approach suggests that cognitive understanding happens by taking in more and more information and thereby creating more complex representations. As more information is processed in the brain, each piece of information is linked with other pieces of information and stored in memory. In this process perception, memory, knowledge and understanding are closely linked.

There are different models of the information processing approach. One of them is a multi-storey model. This is a model that explains how information enters the mind using the senses. The information is stored in the sensory register and is gradually transformed into mental representation and stored in the short-term (working) memory. The other model is connectionist which is related to neural networks (i.e. the firmed up connections in the brain). This model highlights that human cognition has different layers and networks when processing information. In this model, information results from stimulation involving active participation, i.e. taking part in the activity, this results in the connections being made.

Case (1992, cited in Berk 2012) combines an information processing approach with stage theory. He sees three factors contributing to cognitive change:

1 **Brain development** – the growth of connections and the firming up of reused connections and the dying away of unused connections that make processing information efficient.
2 **Practice** – the child works on the new information received (as in assimilation and accommodation); grouping and connections are made, releasing more room for other information.
3 **Forming central conceptual structures** – a network of concepts is formed, enabling the child to think about a wide range of circumstances in different ways.

See p. 138 for information on Annette Karmiloff-Smith and representational redescription.

Schemas – part of concept formation

The word 'schema' in developmental psychology can be used in slightly different ways. Schematic learning refers to the way that, from the beginning, babies organise their experiences into combinations that help them to distinguish between the familiar and unfamiliar. Jean Mandler (cited in Goswami 2008) suggests that babies categorise their perceptual experiences and use these to form representations of the key properties of objects and events. Babies then use this information to form what she calls 'image schemas'. For example, babies have many perceptual experiences of containment: in and out of the bath, pram and adult's arms; food in and out of the bottle, bowl, mouth and stomach; clothes on and off, etc. They recognise what is similar about the movements and spatial relations of these events and then categorise them by creating a containment image-schema, which becomes meaning-based knowledge about those objects and experiences, and the concept of 'containment'. This relates closely to Piaget's use of the word 'scheme' (sometimes schemata or schema) to describe the cognitive structures of the mind or the action or process of building concepts by categorising. In his later work Piaget distinguished between the terms 'schema'

(figurative thought; aspects such as perception and memory that are not entirely logical) and 'scheme' (operational thought; thinking logically about concrete objects and events). But generally, schemas are concepts which evolve and develop through the complementary systems of accommodation and assimilation to achieve equilibration when internal and external events or information are in balance in the mind.

According to Piaget, schemas are concerned with the whole child, embracing the physical, mental and emotional aspects of development. This is the theory that underpins our use of the word schema in early years practice.

Chris Athey (1990) developed Piaget's thinking on schemas and representation. She observed children exploring particular ideas or concepts in their play and identified patterns of behaviour. Athey called these observed patterns 'schemas' or 'themes of thought'. They are repeatable patterns that help children to take in experiences. Schemas become generalised and tried out in a variety of situations. They become coordinated with each other and grow increasingly complex as children develop and learn, forming clusters of coordinated schemas. Examples of schemas are transporting and enveloping (see Table 7.1). Children explore these themes over and over in all sorts of different ways. An enveloping schema may be explored at the drawing area wrapping crayons in paper, the home corner wrapping dolls in blankets: in fact all around the room and at home, a child might be wrapping things up, and this may be coordinated with a transporting schema where the wrapped objects are carried about.

Athey identified how schemas were observable dynamically through movements and actions such as dancing round, climbing up or crawling into, and configuratively through paintings, models or drawings. For example, building a model of a high tower (vertical trajectory schema) or painting around the edge of the paper (containment schema).

By focusing on the form of play, early years practitioners can see that the child's behaviour is purposeful, not flitting, idiosyncratic (individual) or mischievous. The practitioner's role is then to identify and provide a variety of opportunities for a child to explore their current schema and enrich their experience.

Children use schemas at four levels:

● 'Motor': at first, babies develop action schemas, using their actions, senses and movement. These develop out of the reflexes that they are born with, and include, for example, sucking and gazing. These remain throughout life.

- 'Symbolic representation': when they make something stand for something else.
- 'Functional dependency': exploring cause and effect and understanding that if I do this, then that will happen.
- 'Thought': when children talk about their schematic play.

(Athey 2007)

Knowing about schemas helps parents and practitioners to relate to children more easily and to enjoy their company more. It helps adults to understand some of the trying things children do too, and to work positively with children. Schemas, which are part of brain and cognitive development, help children to learn.

Symbolising

The beginning of children's use of symbols is seen in their first gestures, such as declarative pointing, signs and words. Then, as they use everyday objects in recreated scenarios such as talking on the telephone, their use of imagination begins to take off.

▲ **Figure 7.3** These children might be exploring a containment schema

Think about ideas

John Matthews (1994) observed his son Joel exploring arching trajectories at the motor level. He was 13-months-old at the time:

Joel likes to carry his cup of milk around with him. However, coordinating these two new skills is not easy and he frequently spills milk. On one occasion, the milk falls on to a smooth, shiny concrete floor. Joel, his jaw dropping, watches with great interest at the spreading shape. Then, he puts his right hand into the milk and starts to smear it, using the horizontal arching motion. He quickly brings his other hand into play, so that both hands are fanning to and fro in synchrony, meeting in the midline, until they become out of phase. In this way, he makes the two sectors of a circle in the spilt milk. Soon after this, his father introduced him to paint and Joel was able to explore this schema further with this new medium (Matthews 1994).

- How would you respond to a child making marks with their food or drink in this way?
- What concepts do you think Joel was learning?

How might his explorations of these movements and marks be useful to his later learning about writing?

Soon they begin to use objects that are unrelated to the real thing, such as a stick to be a spoon. Babies and young children often recreate an experience through action. Re-enacting the idea of moving along, for example, will include repeated patterns of

Look, listen and note

Observe a child throughout one day – either a baby, a toddler or a child up to five years old – using narrative observations and, if possible, photography (taking into account your setting's policy on photography). Then analyse your observations to see if you have any examples of consistent use of a schema or schema cluster (rotation is often strong when enclosure is present; the two schemas form a cluster). Use Table 7.1 to help you identify schemas.

1 Note the child's favourite experiences in the setting. Can you see if there are links with the child's schemas?

2 Ask the parent(s) what the child is interested in at home and share your observations with them. Are there any connections between what the child enjoys and finds interesting in the setting and at home?

3 What can you do to support and extend the child's schemas? For example, if the child is particularly interested in rotation, you might add whisks and spinners to the water tray.

Name of schema	Description
Transporting	A child may move objects or collections of objects from one place to another, perhaps using a bag, pram or truck.
Positioning	A child may be interested in placing objects in particular positions, for example on top of something, around the edge, behind. Paintings and drawings also often show evidence of this.
Orientation	This schema is shown by interest in a different viewpoint, as when a child hangs upside down or turns objects upside down.
Dab	A graphic schema used in paintings, randomly or systematically, to form patterns or to represent, for example, eyes, flowers or buttons.
Dynamic vertical (and horizontal)	A child may show evidence of particular interest by actions such as climbing, stepping-up and down, or lying flat. These schemas may also be seen in constructions, collages or graphically. After schemas of horizontality and verticality have been explored separately, the two are often used in conjunction to form crosses or grids. These are very often systematically explored on paper and interest is shown in everyday objects such as a cake-cooling tray, grills or nets.
The family of trajectories	**Vertical (up) and horizontal (down)** A fascination with things moving or flying through the air – balls, aeroplanes, rockets, catapults, frisbees – and indeed, anything that can be thrown. When expressed through the child's own body movements, this often becomes large arm and leg movements, kicking, or punching, for example. **Diagonality** Usually explored later than the previous schemas, this one emerges via the construction of ramps, slides and sloping walls. Drawings begin to contain diagonal lines forming roofs, hands, triangles, zig-zags.
Containment	Putting things inside and outside containers, baskets, buckets, bags, carts, boxes, etc.
Enclosure	A child may build enclosures with blocks, Lego or large crates, perhaps naming them as boats, ponds, beds. The enclosure is sometimes left empty, sometimes carefully filled in. An enclosing line often surrounds paintings and drawings while a child is exploring this schema. The child might draw circles, squares and triangles, heads, bodies, eyes, wheels, flowers, etc.
Enveloping	This is often an extension of enclosure. Objects, space or the child themself are completely covered. The child may wrap things in paper, enclose them in pots or boxes with covers or lids, wrap themself in a blanket or creep under a rug. Paintings are sometimes covered over with a wash of colour or scrap collages glued over with layers of paper or fabric.
Circles and lines radiating from the circle	**Semi-circularity** Semi-circles are used graphically as features, parts of bodies and other objects. Smiles, eyebrows, ears, rainbows and umbrellas are a few of the representational uses for this schema, as well as parts of letters of the alphabet. **Core and radials** Again common in paintings, drawings and models. Spiders, suns, fingers, eyelashes, hair and hedgehogs often appear as a series of radials.
Rotation	A child may become absorbed by things which turn – taps, wheels, cogs and keys. The child may roll cylinders along, or roll themself. The child may rotate their arms, or construct objects with rotating parts in wood or scrap materials.
Connection	Scrap materials may be glued, sewn and fastened into lines; pieces of wood are nailed into long connecting constructions. Strings, rope or wool are used to tie objects together, often in complex ways. Drawings and paintings sometimes show a series of linked parts. The opposite of this schema may be seen in separation, where interest is shown in disconnecting assembled or attached parts.
Ordering	A child may produce paintings and drawings with ordered lines or dabs; collages or constructions with items of scrap carefully glued in sequence. They may place blocks, vehicles or animals in lines and begin to show interest in 'largest' and 'smallest'.
It is important to remember that the sensory motor stage of the schema is at an earlier level, and that the cause and effect, together with the symbolic levels, both emerge out of this. In other words children need to explore these concepts physically first so they can then think about them symbolically.	

▲ **Table 7.1** Schema focus sheet

Reflecting on practice

Rearranging experiences

Ed and Elise (three years six months) were playing with wooden blocks. Elise made a row of blocks and said they were beds. She gathered three dolls and put them on the blocks, tucking them in as her parents do with her at bedtime. Ed decided to make a wall. He had watched a builder making a wall recently.

Review your play materials and resources. How much scope do they offer for children to recreate and rearrange their experiences?

movement such as throwing, running and carrying objects from one place to another. As they represent and re-enact their experiences, they are creatively transforming the original situation and expressing what they think and feel about it.

Over time young children externalise their ideas and feelings using different representational forms; through movement, drawing, constructing models, music and pretend play; and later through more abstract means such as writing or using numerical systems.

Cognition and intelligence

Cognition is sometimes called intellectual development. But the word 'intellectual' is often also used to mean clever, so cognition is sometimes mistakenly considered in terms of intelligence. This leads to misconceptions of a child being more or less able.

Some people believe that children are born intelligent (or not). There are others who feel equally strongly that children's life experiences, culture and the people they meet have a huge influence on how their intelligence develops. This is part of the nature–nurture debate discussed in Chapter 6, p. 102.

Intelligence quotient (IQ) tests

The idea that children are born with a fixed amount of intelligence, that can be given a score which is measured and which does not change throughout their lives, was not seriously challenged until the 1960s.

Before the 1960s, children were frequently tested to find their IQ, using scales such as the Stanford-Binet or Merrill-Palmer tests. Because these tests were usually developed by white, male psychologists with middle-class ways of looking at life, they favoured white, middle-class, male children, who therefore scored higher than other groups of children. This

began to worry some researchers, who found that IQ tests:

- favour children from the culture from which the tests emerged, which means the tests are not as objective as they were first thought to be
- measure particular types of intelligence, such as memory span and ability with numbers and language, so that intelligence is only looked at in a narrow way, which does not help us to consider outstanding ability in dancing, music or sensitivity to others, for example
- lead to children being labelled 'bright', 'average' or 'low ability'
- cause practitioners to have predetermined expectations of children (e.g. 'Well, she's only got an IQ of 80')
- are sometimes useful if used as part of a range of tests (especially for children with special educational needs), but they are not useful used in isolation from other forms of assessment
- do not show the motivation (will) a child has to learn; two children might have the same IQ, but the one with the greater will to learn is likely to do better.

Multiple intelligences

The psychologist Howard Gardner tried to overcome this with his concept of multiple intelligences (1993). He wanted to challenge psychometricians who believed that intelligence could be measured as a discrete entity through IQ tests and to move away from the narrow view of equating cognition with scientific thinking. He believes that this undervalues the arts and other representational media.

Gardner identifies seven kinds of intelligence:

- linguistic
- logico-mathematical
- bodily kinaesthetic
- social
- musical
- spatial
- personal (two personal intelligences termed 'interpersonal' and 'intrapersonal' intelligence).

Later, Gardner (1999) added other intelligences:

- naturalist intelligence
- spiritual intelligence
- existential intelligence
- moral intelligence.

Gardner's choice of the term intelligence to describe a collection of attributes was carefully considered.

He defines intelligence as 'the ability to solve problems or to create products that are valued within one or more cultural settings' (Gardner 1999: 33). This emphasises the sociocultural context in which a child's development takes place and the potential 'intelligence' of each child according to the cultural values and opportunities of that context.

Identifying separate intelligences as Gardner does may be seen as a 'domain-specific' view of development. However, he does acknowledge that people in particular areas of skill such as musicians, will draw on other intelligences as well as musical intelligence.

Other researchers also challenge Gardner's view as they emphasise the interconnection of brain processes. For example, Colwyn Trevarthen, a neuroscientist, suggests that intelligence is more organic, and argues, for example, that movement, sound and sight are interconnected or unified in the brain, and not separate domains of musical, social or kinaesthetic intelligence. Claxton (2008 cited in Pound 2013) and cognitive psychologists emphasise the underpinning cognitive abilities that need to be developed such as critical thinking, imagination, memory and problem-solving. In other words there are skills and abilities, such as problem-solving, that are needed across all intelligences.

Think about ideas

The Brooklands Experiment

A group of children with severe learning difficulties were taken from the wards of the Fountain Hospital in London in 1960. They were placed in a stimulating environment of people and first-hand interesting experiences. Their intelligence was found to develop rapidly. This research project, led by Jack Tizard of the University of London, was called the Brooklands experiment. Research like this led, in 1971, to children with special needs living in hospitals or attending day care centres, receiving education as well as care, by law.

Until then, it was considered impossible to educate children with IQs below 50.

Intelligence is elastic

Intelligence is not fixed and unchangeable, but elastic. This means it can stretch, grow and increase. It is shaped by the sociocultural context of the child.

The way in which cognitive tasks are interpreted and performed varies from culture to culture. The strategies used to perform the task are determined by the sociocultural context. Therefore, each community will interpret intelligence from a different perspective.

Moving on

Annette Karmiloff-Smith: Representational re-description

This is a complicated theory but is included as an example of how contemporary theories of cognitive development incorporate different elements of the 'grand' theories that we have discussed earlier.

Annette Karmiloff-Smith (1992, 1995) proposes a view of cognitive development that focuses on the ability to store, retrieve and use representations in memory, as in the 'information processing approach'.

She aims to explain how children's mental representations become more flexible as repeated experience leads to multiple representations. Experiences are 're-described' each time they are repeated and are then stored at different levels in the mind according to difficulty and levels of understanding. The re-described representations stay in the mind, which results in multiple representations with different levels of detail and complexity.

She gives the example of learning a tune on an instrument; at first you need to restart at the beginning each time you make a mistake but later when you have stored more of it in memory you can start in the middle. Later still, when you are an accomplished musician and can retrieve your stored representations from each level, you can play the same tune but in different styles perhaps.

Karmiloff-Smith suggests that representations can occur across the levels. This means that hers is not a stage theory of development. But neither is it purely an 'incremental' theory because she also describes qualitative differences between the representations at each level (Karmiloff-Smith 1992).

Karmiloff-Smith (1994) suggests that children's concepts of people, objects and words change because of what they find out about the world. She says:

This is what I think development is about. Children are not satisfied with success in learning to talk or solve problems; they want to understand how they do these things. And in seeking such understanding they become little theorists.

Look, listen and note

Focus on one of the following ideas
- perceptual development
- multiple intelligences
- schemas.

Read and research the topic further using the suggested reading below and/or searching online.

Then undertake some observations of children using these theories as your framework. What play opportunities can you provide to match the development and interests of the children?

For perceptual development:

Bee, H., Boyd, D., 2010, *The Developing* Child (12th edn), New York: Allyn and Bacon.

Gopnik, A., Meltzoff, A. and Kuhl, P., 1999, *How Babies Think*, London: Weidenfeld and Nicolson.

Smith, P. K., Cowie, H. and Blades, M., 1998, *Understanding Children's Development* (3rd edn), Oxford: Blackwell.

For multiple intelligence:

Gardner, H., 1993, *Frames of Mind: The Theory of Multiple Intelligences,* New York: Basic Books.

For schemas:

Arnold, C. and the Pen Green team, 2010, *Understanding Schemas and Emotion in Early Childhood,* London, Sage.

Louis, S., Beswick, C., Magraw, L., Hayes, L., Featherstone, S., 2008, *Again! and Again! Understanding Schemas in Young Children,* London: A&C Black Publishers.

Nutbrown, C., 2011, *Threads of Thinking* (4th edn), London: Sage.

For example, in a Ugandan village intelligence is interpreted as a person who is careful in decision making (Rogoff 2003), whereas, in some cultures intelligence can be related to speed and pace in making decisions when solving a problem.

The cultural context of intelligence is also highlighted by 'the Flynn effect'; the apparent rise in IQ scores since they were introduced. Flynn (2009 cited in Pound 2013) suggests that the more complex environments we now live in means that our brains are becoming more flexible and adaptable.

We now know that intellectual/cognitive development is helped if children:

- engage with adults and other children who are interesting to be with and who are interested in them
- experience a stimulating environment that encourages thinking and ideas, emotional intelligence and social interaction.

See Chapter 6 for information on theory of mind, positive and negative reinforcement.

Further reading, weblinks and resources

Siren Films

Siren Films produces high-quality DVDs covering a wide range of topics, such as the first year of life, two-year-olds, play, attachment and key person, three- and four-year-olds, early literacy and schemas in toddlers.
www.sirenfilms.co.uk

References

Athey, C., 2007, *Extending Thought in Young Children: A Parent/Teacher Partnership* (2nd edn.), London: Sage.

Bee, H., Boyd, D., 2010, *The Developing Child* (12th edn), New York: Allyn and Bacon.

Berk, L. E., 2012, *Child Development*, USA : Pearson Education.

Bruner, J. S., 1966, *Toward a Theory of Instruction*, Cambridge MA: Harvard University Press.

Bruner, J. S., 1990, *Acts of Meaning*, Cambridge, MA: Harvard University Press.

Carter, R., 1999, *Mapping the Mind*, London: Seven Dials.

Gardner, H., 1993, *Frames of Mind: The Theory of Multiple Intelligences*, New York: Basic Books.

Gardner, H., 1999, *Intelligence Reframed. Multiple Intelligences for the 21st Century*, New York: Basic Books.

Gopnik, A., Meltzoff, A. and Kuhl, P., 1999, *How Babies Think*, London: Weidenfeld and Nicolson.

Goswami, U., 1998, *Cognition in Children*, Sussex: Psychology Press.

Goswami, U., 2008, *Cognitive Development: The Learning Brain*, Hove: Psychology Press.

Karmiloff-Smith, A., 1992. *Beyond Modularity. A Developmental Perspective on Cognitive Science*, Cambridge MA: MIT Press.

Karmiloff-Smith, A., 1994, *Baby it's You*, London: Ebury Press.

Karmiloff-Smith, A., 1995, 'The Extraordinary Journey from Foetus through Infancy', *Journal of Child Psychology and Psychiatry*, 36, 1293–315.

Ledoux, J., 2002, *Synaptic Self: How our brains become who we are*, New York: Penguin.

Manning-Morton, J. and Thorp, M., 2003, *Key Times for Play, The First Three Years*, Maidenhead: Open University Press.

Matthews, J., 1994, *Helping Children to Draw and Paint in Early Childhood*, London: Hodder and Stoughton.

Piaget, J., 1969, *The Psychology of the Child*, London: Routledge and Kegan Paul.

Piaget, J. (1962), *Play, Dreams and Imitation in Childhood*. London: Routledge and Kegan Paul.

Pound, L., 2013, *Quick Guides for Early years: Cognitive Development*, London: Hodder Education.

Rogoff, B., 2003, *The Cultural Nature of Human Development*, Oxford: Oxford University Press.

Schaffer, H. R., 2004, *Child Psychology*, Oxford: Blackwell Publishing.

Schaffer, H. R., 2006, *Key Concepts in Developmental Psychology*, London: Sage.

Smith, P. K., Cowie, H. and Blades, M., 1998, *Understanding Children's Development* (3rd edn), Oxford: Blackwell.

Vygotsky, L. S., 1966, 'Play and its Role in the Mental Development of the Child', in Bruner, J. Jolly, A. and Sylva, K. (eds), 1976, *Play and its Role in Development and Evolution*, Middlesex: Penguin.

Vygotsky, L. S., 1978, *Mind in Society*, Cambridge MA: Harvard University Press.

Vygotsky, L. S., 1986, *Thought and Language*, Cambridge MA: The MIT Press.

Wood, D., 1998, *How Children Think and Learn*, Oxford: Blackwell.

Communication and language development

This chapter will outline the way in which verbal and non-verbal communication and language develops in babies and young children in the early years, and the different pathways that children take in becoming confident communicators. It emphasises the importance of language development for young children's learning and identifies how communication and language are related to other aspects of development and learning. Effective practice is explored with a focus on supporting children facing challenges in their communication and language development.

Communication

Communication is one of the most important aspects of development and learning in life. Babies, children and adults communicate all the time. Some communication is with ourselves and is an internal process. We communicate with ourselves about our feelings, relationships, thoughts and ideas. Communication with others is about the way we make this become external. A simple way of saying this is that we communicate in order to understand ourselves and develop a strong, confident sense of our identity but we also communicate to understand and relate to other people, their feelings, ideas and thoughts. In this way communication and **language** development is closely linked to social development. However, even when we are communicating verbally with others, 80 per cent of communication is without words.

Babies communicating

From the moment a baby is born, and even before, communication begins. During the last weeks of pregnancy the foetus develops a growing sensitivity to

> ### KEY TERMS
>
> **Communication** – The transmission of thoughts, feelings or information via body language, signals, speech or writing.
> **Language** – A recognised system of gestures, signs and symbols used to communicate.
> **Speech** – Verbal communication; the act of speaking; the articulation of words to express thoughts, feelings or ideas.

the unique qualities of its mother's voice and language (Karmiloff and Karmiloff-Smith 2001) and infants are tuned in to the human face and human movement from the beginning. They communicate with their gaze and can imitate facial and manual gestures in the first days and weeks of life (Bruner 1983).

When we converse with babies, we look at the baby and the baby looks at us. Eye contact is an important part of communication. When the baby has had enough of a chat, he or she will turn away his or her head and drop the eye contact, as if to tell us they are tired and need a break from the 'conversation'.

Babies listen to people's voices; they like the human voice more than other sounds. When we talk to babies, we tend to speak in a high-pitched tone, in short phrases, placing emphasis on the key words and using a great deal of repetition and exaggerated facial expressions. This is called 'child directed speech' or 'motherese' (Snow 1972) (or 'fatherese'). However, in some cultures adults do not speak to babies in motherese or fatherese. Instead, the babies watch their mothers working and talking with other adults and there is a lot of physical communication during physical care times (Schieffelin and Ochs 1987).

Babies with visual impairments respond to voices by becoming still and listening intently. Sighted babies 'dance' in response to **speech**. Adults will pause and be still when they have said something to the baby, and the baby will usually 'reply' in babble, moving as they do so. We move when we talk to babies too. Researchers such as Colwyn Trevarthen, call these early conversations 'proto-conversations' (2004). They have all the ingredients of a conversation, but without the words or signs.

Babies communicate with us in a range of ways, non-verbally through gazing at adults' faces, searching with their eyes, smiling, reaching out with their arms, pointing, craning their necks and kicking their legs, and they also use vocalisations such as babbling, laughing and shouting.

Crying is the primary means by which babies communicate and they have a different kind of cry for different situations: they cry with distress or pain for food and to say they are tired or bored. Babies 'call out' for company as they become lonely if they spend too much time alone.

▲ **Figure 8.1** Communication includes facial expression, voice tone and gentle touch

Young children and communication

Young children communicate in idiosyncratic (individual) and unique ways. These personal communications can include:

- particular gestures
- pointing at particular things at certain times
- props – the handbag that represents mother when she goes for coffee, and the child knows she is coming back because her handbag is there
- signals that give evidence – the footprint in the sand tells us someone was there
- links – the child has a teddy bear while mother is away that links the child to the absent mother; the communication is personal between this child and this particular mother.

Communication between babies, children and adults involves:

- facial expressions – smiling, frowning, raised eyebrow, eye contact
- gesture and body language – hugs, beckoning, clapping hands, shrugs, jumping with surprise, being stiff and ill at ease, feet and arms moving in response to someone talking to you
- movements of the hands and face – especially important for communication and language development

- moving together in synchrony – mirroring or imitating each other's movements and sounds
- pauses – these are very important; often we do not give babies and young children enough time to make their response
- the rhythms, tone and melody of a language – these are of great importance in developing communication and spoken language. Researchers have found that babies will finish a phrase in a musical way, adding a note that seems to complete it, when they respond to people talking to them; this seems to be cross-cultural (Malloch and Trevarthen 2010)
- intonation – tone of voice may be used to express fear, anger, pleasure, wanting to play, calm, reassurance, and so on
- spoken language and sign languages (such as BSL) – these are agreed codes that develop according to the cultures in which they arise
- communication systems such as Makaton that uses agreed and shared signs but is not a full language
- objects of reference – these build a personal communication system with an individual child, and are only shared between the child, the family and practitioners working with the child and the family.

Communicating feelings – finding the words to talk about feelings

Children experience difficulties when they are not able to put their feelings into words or express them in any way. This has a damaging impact on their sense of self and identity, and on their self-confidence. If children are full of anger, anxiety, frustration or fear, they need to express this. People express their emotions physically, through facial expression, gestures and actions. The younger the person, the more obvious and unrestrained this is. Toddlers and two-year-olds who cannot yet explain or put into words/signs how they feel often have temper tantrums or 'emotional collapses' (Manning-Morton and Thorp 2015). Older children with limited verbal expression or emotional understanding may show challenging behaviours. Learning how to talk about feelings is just as important as talking about ideas.

Features of language development

What are the features of a spoken/signed language?

Every language has:

- phonology – the sounds of the language (sign languages are visual)
- intonation – this gives the mood of the words (questioning tone, angry, joyous, upset) and the way the sounds go up and down
- grammar – the words of each language have a particular way of being ordered; grammar (sometimes called syntax) describes how language works; it is very important to remember that understanding grammar does not mean telling people how they ought to speak
- articulation – how words are spoken in order to be understood
- vocabulary – this is sometimes called the lexicon: the words that make up the language
- semantics – this is about the meaning of the words; unless language holds meaning for those involved and present, it is of no use

Look, listen and note

Sit with a child, either between one and three years, three and five years, or five and seven years. Note the communications you have between you that do not depend on words. Make a list of examples.

- conversations – ways for people to interact, share and exchange feelings and ideas, and relate to each other using language.

Receptive and expressive language

Communication and language development takes place through two strands:

- Receptive language – learning to listen and understand language. This means the child listens, watches people talking, and begins to understand what is being said. Children's understanding of language is always in advance of their expressive language.
- Expressive language – learning to speak and to use language to communicate. This involves using the face expressively, making gestures and speaking (or signing).

The Communicating Matters guidance (DfES 2005) identifies four strands of communication and language, integrating receptive and expressive language into the strands:

- knowing and using sounds and signs
- knowing and using words
- structuring language
- making language work.

Each of these strands is important but it is the last one, 'Making language work', that is the essence of communication.

Theories and theorists: Halliday and functions of talk

Halliday (1978) identified seven 'functions of talk':

1 Instrumental – being able to satisfy our needs and desires
2 Regulatory – being able to control or be controlled
3 Interactional – to establish and maintain contact
4 Personal – to express ideas and thoughts
5 Educational – to find things out
6 Imaginative – to create worlds
7 Representational – to inform.

Think about ideas

- Think back over your day and identify examples of when you or another person used each of Halliday's functions of talk.
- Listen to a group of children playing. Can you identify all seven functions? Is this different with older and younger children?

The sequence of communication and language development

Different children will learn about the various features of language at different points in their early lives. But generally they will tend to focus on particular aspects at particular ages. Babies focus a lot on listening to sound patterns and matching those to facial expressions and contexts. Toddlers are interested in matching words to objects and putting words together to convey meaning, and young children extend their skills by learning to communicate differently in different contexts.

Baby's first year

The first year of a baby's life is sometimes called 'pre-linguistic'. This is a rather misleading term. It is more positive and helpful to think of a baby as someone who communicates without words, and who is developing everything needed for conversations in spoken/signed language. This is sometimes called the period of emerging language. Bruner believed the basic schemas for developing language are developed very early in life. He suggests that early social games and interactions help babies grasp the turn-taking form of conversation and that this is a rich means of giving and receiving information.

Babies also use gestures in their early communications. When these are culturally shared gestures, the baby is using an agreed symbol. For example, a baby, towards the end of the first year typically, will often wave 'bye-bye' after someone has gone. When babies do this, it is cause to celebrate, and perhaps to say to the baby, 'Yes, you are right. Jill has gone, hasn't she, and we said bye-bye to her.'

Communication and emerging language development

- Babies show that they hear the difference between their language and any other language at four days old.
- Babies participate in communicative and conversational events; engaging in turn-taking behaviour.
- Babies identify patterns in adult speech from context, expressions, stance, gaze, gesture and action; from this babies soon recognise adult intentions.
- Babies learn to make links between objects and language from communicating in meaningful contexts.

- Babies respond to and recognise human voices and imitate human sounds.
- Babies communicate through crying, cooing; single repeated vowel sounds (aaahhh) and babbling; vowel sounds interspersed by consonants (dada).
- By the end of the first year intonation, imitative of adult talk, can be detected and children with different mother tongues sound different.

From one to four years

From the second year of the baby's life until about the age of four years, there is a period of language explosion. Two-year-olds may be acquiring between three and ten words a day and this rate increases between three and six years. Every aspect of language seems to move forward rapidly at this time. It is the best time to learn other languages, or to become **bilingual** or **multilingual**.

Receptive language development

- Toddlers listen carefully to the string of sounds they hear in conversations and try to segment them into identifiable chunks. To do this successfully, sighted children need to see the speakers face and for the conversation to happen in a meaningful context. A modern issue is that adults often talk to mobile phones more than they talk to babies and toddlers, and they have pushchairs which face forward, away from the adult pushing the baby or toddler along. This means that the child cannot see the speaker.
- Toddlers and young children understand a wealth of facial expressions and gestures and use them in their play and in everyday contexts.
- Toddlers and young children increasingly recognise words for common items and common phrases (e.g. cup, doggy, bye-bye, look at … , no). They always understand more language than they can produce.

Expressive language development

- Once children are beginning to move about, gesture and point, they often begin to name things.
- In the second year of life children use one word utterances. These are usually nouns and refer to things in the here and now. Children aged two to three years may have anything from 40 to 600 words in their vocabulary.

KEY TERMS

Bilingual – Having the ability to speak two languages.
Multilingual – Having the ability to speak a number of languages.

KEY TERMS

Holophrases – Using a single word to convey a more complicated meaning.
Telegraphic speech – Speech in which only the most important words are used.
Echolalia – The repetition or imitation of other people's vocal sounds.

Look, listen and note

Observe one of the following either in the home setting or the early years setting:
- baby aged 6 to 12 months
- child aged one to three years
- child aged three to five years
- child aged five to seven years.

Note down how the child:
- understands and uses sounds and signs
- understands and uses words (where appropriate)
- structures their language (where appropriate)
- makes their available language work to help them communicate.

- Individual words are simplified to enable pronunciation so words may be formed and used in a way that only close family understands what they are saying; for example 'dock' may mean 'sock'.

- They may use one word to convey different meanings (**holophrases**), for example, 'sock' may mean 'that's my sock', or 'Mummy, you've dropped the sock'.

- When children have between 50 and 100 words they will then begin to put two or three words together such as *Me down, Daddy gone* (**telegraphic speech**).

- At first, young children over-generalise their use of words; e.g. everything round is a *ball*. This helps them to communicate their meaning before they have all the available vocabulary.

- They will use **echolalia** (echoing prominent words/final syllables) as if they are practising the sounds and filing the language in their memory.

- Young children show their increasing understanding of the grammatical rules of language by using those rules where they do not apply. Saying 'I goed farm and saw sheeps' shows that the child understands the rules that generally apply in English (adding '-ed' to verbs in the past tense and 's' to the end of plural nouns) but do not in this instance. They start to be able to make language work by offering answers and explanations and to recount events and to initiate and maintain a conversation.

From four to eight years

- Children are consolidating their communication and language learning during these years.

- They build on what they know about communication with themselves, with other people, developing better articulation, and using more conventional grammar patterns.

- They think about who they are talking to, with greater sensitivity and awareness. They are also more attentive to the context in which they are talking, and the situation.

- They can put their ideas and feelings into words more easily than when they were toddlers.

- They use greater complexity in their language construction as the situations in which they communicate expand.

- Recounting stories becomes increasingly sophisticated and takes different perspectives, as does their ability to take account of the other person's knowledge, understanding and point of view in conversations.

To learn more about the detail of the sequence of communication and development, look at the charts of normative development in the appendix.

Bilingualism

Children need to feel a sense of belonging in an early years setting. It has been known for children to be labelled as having 'no' language, when in fact they simply speak a different language from English. It is an advantage to grow up learning more than one language.

It is important that children feel their bilingualism is valued and that they see it as the advantage that it is. In most parts of the world, it is common to speak three or four languages fluently. In fact, if we take the world as a whole, it is normal to be fluent in at least two languages. Bilingualism is a positive advantage for all sorts of reasons (Datta 2007):

- Learning a language means learning about a culture.

- Knowing about different cultures through living the language means that children who are bilingual experience cultural diversity in rich and important ways. For example, in Gujurati, 'thank you' is only used for special situations as an expression of deep gratitude; in English, people thank each other often, and it is just a form of everyday politeness.

- Bilingual speakers come at an idea from several directions, because different languages emphasise different things. This makes their thinking flexible and analytical.
- Children can think in different ways about the same thing when they speak different languages. For example, the Inuit language has several words for 'snow', which makes it possible to think about snow in greater detail than is possible in English.
- Children who are bilingual grow up understanding different ways of thinking. This helps them to respect and value differences between people.
- Children find it easier to understand that names for objects can be changed.
- Children who are bilingual are often more sensitive to the emotional aspects of intonation. They can interpret situations more easily.

Promoting bilingualism

Allow for a period of silence

Before children speak a language, they need to listen to it and tune in. They will make sounds with different tones as they try out the sounds of the language. It is difficult for children to work out what is being said (understanding and receptive language) or to see how to say things (expressive language) unless people actually look at them and talk to them. In order to learn to speak a language, it is important to see the shapes the mouth makes. The mouth looks different when the sound 'oo' is made compared with the sound 'ee'.

Comprehensible input

The researcher Stephen Krashen (2003) suggests that children need to make sense of what is being said. If an adult picks up a cup, points at the jug of orange juice and asks, 'Would you like a drink of orange juice?' the meaning is clear. If the adult just says the words, without the actions or objects being visible, the meaning is not at all clear. The adult could be saying anything.

Transitional bilingualism

In some early years settings, the child's home language has been valued only as a bridge into learning English. This is transitional (sometimes called subtractive) bilingualism. It is assumed that the child will no longer need to speak their home language once English begins to take over. For example, a child who speaks Punjabi at home might be expected to speak English at school and gradually to speak English rather than Punjabi at home.

In fact, children will need to continue their home language to help them transfer later on to reading and writing in English. If the child's home language is not valued alongside English, the opportunities for bilingualism and the advantages that bilingualism brings will be wasted. The home language is important for children to express their feelings and for thinking.

Additive and successful bilingualism

The home language (L1) is the language of thinking and feelings. English as an additional language (EAL) (L2) is only useful if the home language is strong. Then children think and manage feelings with deeper skill and understanding. This is called additive bilingualism.

Balanced bilingualism is when a child speaks more than one language, each with equal fluency.

Children need plenty of opportunity to listen to what is being said and to make sense of it before they begin to speak a language. This involves the child:

- understanding what is being said (comprehension)
- having a go at speaking (production) gradually becoming fluent (performance).

It is important to be aware that when children first begin to speak any language, they will not be fluent. They will make approximate sounds and communicate by intonation (tone of voice) rather than use words.

Children are helped in learning language if they spend their time with people who are fluent speakers and comfortable with the language. This is why children who are learning EAL are no longer taken out of the room to be 'taught' English. They learn much more effectively in a real-life situation that is relaxed and informal, with other children and adults who can already speak the language.

The EYFS (with regards to the English curriculum) gives specific advice with regard to bilingualism. Practitioners:

- should be aware of the needs of children learning EAL from a variety of cultures and ask parents to share their favourites from their home languages

> ### KEY TERM
>
> **Balanced bilingualism** – This is when a child speaks more than one language, each with equal fluency. In fact, the child's home language is usually more fluent than English. Very few children are completely balanced across two languages. For most, one language is more developed than the other.

- should give children opportunities both to speak and to listen, ensuring that the needs of children learning EAL are met, so that they can participate fully
- should value non-verbal communications and those offered in their home language for those children learning EAL.

Accents and dialects

Accent is mostly to do with the way the words are pronounced. Some accents may be difficult to understand for those who are not used to hearing them spoken.

Dialect is a variant form of a language. In the Caribbean, for example, a **patois** is spoken. It might seem to a standard English-speaker that a patois-speaker is speaking ungrammatical and poor English. However, patois here is actually a combination of French language with the local (mainly English) language, as used on the different islands. In Trinidad, it will be a combination of French and the particular way that English is spoken on that island. The words, phrases and speed of speaking will sound a bit like English, but patois is not English.

If children are to feel comfortable about themselves, it is important to value both accent and dialect.

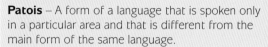

KEY TERM

Patois – A form of a language that is spoken only in a particular area and that is different from the main form of the same language.

Supporting and encouraging confident communicators

Every Child a Talker

Politicians and government departments in England have now been persuaded that the way children develop towards literacy (reading and writing) depends on the way they develop communication and language/sign language. This has led to an emphasis on encouraging communication and language development in the first five years.

Every Child a Talker (ECAT) (DCSF 2008) is a developmentally appropriate approach that emphasises the importance of a supportive and stimulating environment in which children are encouraged to develop communication and language. It was introduced in 2008 to support the work of the Early Years Foundation Stage in England, in home learning environments (childminders) and in group settings of all kinds.

Guidelines for good practice

Supporting children new to learning English

✔ Respect and value the child's home language. Think how you can make yourself understood using body language, gestures and facial expression, by pointing, using pictures and using actions with your words. Try asking children if they would like a drink using one of these strategies. You could use objects as props. It is important to be warm towards children. Remember to smile and to show that you enjoy interacting with them. Make sure that you are giving comprehensible language input.

✔ Try to accompany all children's actions with language by describing what is happening – for example, talk with the child and describe what they are doing when they cook or use clay.

✔ When telling stories you could:

　✔ use puppets and props, flannel boards, magnet boards, and so on

　✔ invite children to act out pictures as you go through the story

✔ use facial expressions, eye contact and body language to 'tell' a story and make it meaningful for the children.

✔ Use books in different languages and tell stories in different languages. Remember that there can be problems with dual-language textbooks because, although English, for example, reads from left to right, Urdu (the official language of Pakistan, also widely used in India) reads from right to left.

✔ Invite someone who speaks the child's language to come and tell stories – for example, ask a Hindi speaker to tell a story such as *Where's Spot?* in Hindi (an official language of India), using the book in that language but in a session that is for all the children in a story group. Then tell the story and use the book in English at the next session, again with all the children in the story group. Remember that grandparents are often particularly concerned that children are losing their home language as they become more fluent in English (transitional bilingualism). They may enjoy coming into the group and helping in this way.

The guidance is still available online and is very useful in helping practitioners to:

- identify what helps communication and language to develop
- audit their language provision and plan appropriately
- work positively with children with EAL
- make the most of everyday activities and experiences that promote communication and language
- develop a good partnership with parents and working with them to support their child's communication and language in the ways suggested in this chapter.

Encouraging conversations

Conversations need to:

- be two-way
- involve sharing feelings and ideas
- involve thinking of each other
- be a real exchange of feelings and ideas between children and other children, and between children and adults
- include turn-taking as the conversation flows
- involve thinking about what will be of interest to each other, as well as things that are of interest to oneself
- include a lot of active listening by the adult.

Small-group discussions

Children need help when taking part in group discussions. The younger the child, the smaller the number of people there should be involved in a conversation.

▲ **Figure 8.2** One-to-one situations in a cosy environment with an interesting object will offer good opportunities for communications in which children can hear and be heard

Look, listen and note

- Observe a group of children with an adult. Note examples of turn-taking and any of the things you would expect to find in a conversation that have been identified in this chapter.
- Note down who speaks, who listens and for how long.
- Be aware of differences of gender, ethnicity, (dis) ability and bilingualism: was there a difference in the number of times individual children spoke in the group? In what way?
- What was the size of the group? Evaluate how being in a small or large group impacts on communications.

So babies will usually be engaged in one-to-one interactions. Toddlers and two-year-olds will also experience a high level of one-to-one conversations and also some small-group discussions with two to three other children.

For children aged three to four years, groups should be no more than four to eight children, and wherever possible, small-group times for all children should be with the key person whom the children know well. In a small group, children can take part in the discussion more easily. Having to wait for a turn frustrates young children, and having to wait until everyone is sitting quietly does too. It is best to start a group time with a song or a dance with plenty of actions, so that everyone can join in from the beginning. Children are then much more likely to be willing to sit quietly for a story. Group times should be no longer than 10 to 15 minutes in length for older children, and for younger children should be spontaneous and flexible according to the children's interest.

Using language in different situations and contexts

It takes years for children to understand the difference between informal and formal situations. Going into school assembly or sitting at the table for a meal in a group are formal occasions. Children who have not experienced formal situations need sensitive help in this. Too much time spent in formal situations is not good for a child's development and learning. Assembly time is difficult for young children because they have to sit, often in an uncomfortable position, for a long time, and be passive (not make an active response). Fortunately, it is becoming unusual for children below five years to attend assemblies.

Even very young children readily learn about eating together in a group. They soon enjoy asking those next to them if they would like some vegetables passed to them, or saying thank you for their second helping, or talking about what they like to eat, making conversation. Mealtimes can be a very appropriate way of introducing children to formal gatherings in ways that allow them to enjoy participating. It is important that children are encouraged to be active, help each other and themselves, understand how to do this, enjoy chatting to people on their table and help with the clearing away.

Children learn by doing, so language is best learned when children are active in their learning. The practitioners might say to a three-year-old, 'You've got to the top of the slide, haven't you? Are you going to come down now?'

Children need to spend time talking with people they know

As developing language relies on social interactions between people, the most important resource for very young children who are learning how to communicate is the consistent, continuous care, of responsive practitioners who know them well. Each day children need to be with familiar adults who love them and whom they love – their family and key person. In this way they learn the subtle signals about how people talk to each other in different situations. Depending on the context, people comment, describe, give opinions, predict, give instructions, use formal phrases, and reminisce, and so on. Meaning changes accordingly. For example, 'Go into the hall!' means something different at home than it does in a school with a large room with a platform at one end.

Children are good at knowing the difference between someone who wants to talk to them and someone who is being patronising and puts on a 'talking to children', false sort of voice. Children appreciate adults who take their ideas and feelings seriously, and who respect and value them.

Children who are enabled to build trusting relationships develop self-confidence in expressing themselves and sharing their ideas. In such tried and tested relationships of mutual awareness and respect there is powerful motivation to interact, communicate and use language (Trevarthen 1998).

Children need to spend time with fluent speakers

It is important that children spend time with people who speak fluently, so that they hear the patterns of the language they are trying to learn. A stimulating environment, which encourages children to talk, is a

crucial part of this. Hearing other people speak fluently but with supporting gestures and context allows the child to experience 'comprehensible input'; i.e. interaction that is understandable through different communication methods. If the practitioner says, 'Oh dear, you've bumped your knee. Shall I rub it better?' and points at the child's knee and makes a rubbing mime, then the child has enough clues to understand what is being said. This is very important for very young children, children with language delay and children who are learning EAL.

Children need to be listened to

The Young Children's Voices network suggest that 'Listening to children is an integral part of understanding what they are feeling and what it is they need from their early years experience' (Williams 2009). They define listening as:

- an active process of receiving, interpreting and responding to communication. It includes all the senses and emotions and is not limited to the spoken word
- a necessary stage in ensuring the participation of all children
- an ongoing part of tuning in to all children as individuals in their everyday lives
- sometimes part of a specific consultation about a particular entitlement, choice, event or opportunity.

Active listening means tuning in to all the ways in which babies and young children communicate with us; their movements, facial expressions, gestures, actions and behaviours. It means showing a child that they have your full attention by using **open body language** and good eye contact, being at their level and nearby. To listen in an active way means giving a child time to express themselves and listening to the emotional content of the conversation, reflecting back what you interpret from the child's communication; 'Oh, so the dog barked very loudly, it seems like that frightened you.'

In this way an environment in which children feel confident, safe and powerful may be developed.

KEY TERM

Open body language – When your body language is 'open', you are turned towards the other person with your arms in a relaxed open position, showing interest and attentiveness. Your body language is closed when you have your arms and legs crossed, turn away and look away from the other person.

Language and gender

The ways in which language is used can discriminate and exclude or include. Often adults may not be aware of how the language they use conveys messages to children about the different expectations they have of boys and girls: saying 'Will you boys please be quieter' sends the message that you expect all boys to be noisy. It would be better to use children's individual names. Adults also often convey messages about what is acceptable in girls' and boys' speech and language. From a young age, girls get interrupted and talked over more by adults and boys, receiving the message that they should not take up verbal space (Pichler and Coates 2011).

How does spoken/signed language help us to develop and learn?

Language helps children (and adults) to:

● talk to ourselves – children and adults often talk out loud to themselves; as we develop our

Guidelines for good practice

Encouraging conversations

✔ It is important to remember that anybody in a group can start or end a conversation.

✔ Two speakers can talk together.

✔ In a good conversation there must be actions or props that show the meaning, as well as gestures and facial expressions. This is called 'comprehensible input'. The lack of 'comprehensible input' is probably one reason why many people dislike talking on the telephone, which provides intonation and other sound clues, but no visual clues.

✔ Children must not be rushed or pressurised to speak, and they must feel relaxed and listened to by someone genuinely interested in what they want to say.

✔ It is better to elaborate on what children say, rather than to correct their grammatical or pronunciation errors. This respects children's feelings and promotes their well-being. It helps them to be confident learners.

✔ The key person is important in encouraging children in conversations in a stable group, with familiar people, in a warm and affectionate atmosphere.

✔ Engaging in active listening enables practitioners to listen with their eyes and feelings as well as their ears and thereby understand the meaning of a child's communications.

Guidelines for good practice

Resources for supporting communication and language

✔ The environment should be full of interesting objects and materials that can be handled and discussed.

✔ Introduce and discuss new interesting objects during key group times.

✔ Visit new and interesting places.

✔ Invite interesting people to visit the setting.

✔ Play audio books and sing along to familiar songs on CD or mp3.

✔ Use books that:

  ✔ have a range of complexity of text and illustration

  ✔ have a range of themes and topics that will interest all children

  ✔ reflect all children's backgrounds and languages

  ✔ are board books, activity books, pop-up books, picture books, simple textbooks and encyclopaedias.

✔ Visit the local library, including special story sessions.

✔ Organise special events in the setting, such as festivals.

language skills, what we say out loud becomes 'internal speech', so that we are increasingly able to think of the words rather than saying them out loud

● move from the here and now into thoughts about the past or the future, and back again

● use and make different symbols, from spoken/signed language to the languages of dance, music, mathematical symbols, drawings, sculptures and models

● develop ideas, some of which become concepts, and put them into words

● express creative and imaginative thoughts and ideas

● express and communicate personal ideas

● think in abstract ways

● plan

● express feelings, think about their emotional responses and manage them, becoming increasingly self-disciplined.

Communicating ideas and thoughts – finding the words

As they begin to develop spoken or signed language, children are able to think about their own thinking. Thinking about your own thinking is called

metacognition. Children begin to say things like, 'I've got a good idea' or 'That was a bad idea', as they reflect on their own thought processes. Typically, by about four years they are beginning to think about what they say. This is called **metalinguistics**. Children make jokes and 'play' with words, devising nonsense words for fun.

Children often talk out loud to themselves (we do this as adults too) when they:

● feel frustrated and they are trying to understand something

● need to talk to themselves about how they feel

● are trying to organise an idea they are developing

● are trying out an idea and want to talk it through with themselves

● want to tell themselves what to do (give themselves an instruction).

Talking out loud to themselves is often described by researchers as 'egocentric speech'. This is where children talk aloud to themselves as if they were giving themselves guidance. It is helpful for children, as the bullet points above show. Gradually, children begin to be able to put themselves in someone else's shoes, providing that person's experience links with their own. They move from being self-centred to being self-relating to being other-people-centred. This does not mean the child is selfish; it just means they are becoming increasingly able to see something from someone else's point of view as well as their own.

The links between communication and language development and other aspects of development and learning

Language and feelings

Unless children develop the language of emotion, they will not be able to express their feelings in ways that others find acceptable. This will cause difficulties with relationships and will have a damaging influence on their social development.

▲ **Figure 8.3** Children increasingly use talk to convey their ideas, negotiate what they want and to think about what they are doing

Language and movement

The parts of the brain dealing with movement are near to each other, with interconnected networks developing, so that hands move as the baby makes sounds, for example. We use our hands as we speak as part of the way we communicate throughout our lives. We point a finger to show someone something. We wag a finger to show anger or when we are being insistent. We open out our hands when we welcome what others say.

Research shows that the way we move our head and hands is very important in communicating and speaking and listening (see p. 144 above for information on expressive and receptive language).

Language and vision and hearing

Babies love to look at faces. They stare at them and find them fascinating, and we love to look at the baby in response. If you talk to a baby, you will be helping him or her to learn that you make different shapes with your mouth, and they will gradually imitate these. Even at three months, if you say 'coo' and then pause, the baby will very likely say 'oo' back to you. Babies begin to work out that sounds come out of mouths.

KEY TERMS

Metacognition – Being aware of your own thinking and being able to analyse this.
Metalinguistics – Being aware of the structure of the language you use, such as something rhyming; for example, four-year-olds love to make nonsense words and to play with language rhymes of their own making.

Language and representing experiences

Language development is closely linked with the processes of representation. This means being able to keep hold of an experience. But it is more than just keeping an experience in our memory. Representation is about quite literally being able to 're-present' that experience in some way.

The 'hundred languages of children'

There are many ways of communicating, using different kinds of symbols other than spoken/signed language – for example, through dance, music, the visual arts, mathematical symbols and stories. The Italian educator Loris Malaguzzi called these the 'hundred languages of children' (Edwards et al. 1994). They are all important ways in which children begin to communicate their feelings, ideas and relationships.

A symbol is something that stands for something else. In order to 're-present' an experience, humans have developed the ability to use and make symbols. From the time children begin to walk, talk and pretend, they become symbol-users and makers. This means that children are increasingly able to represent and communicate their experiences in a variety of forms.

Spoken/signed language makes it easier for us to keep hold of (represent) experiences, and to share (communicate) them. Language is one kind of symbol system that helps us to develop **abstract** concepts, ideas and thoughts. Words stand for things. The word 'table' is not the real table; it is a symbol that stands for the table.

Language and thinking

Language and thinking are often considered to be particularly closely linked. Can we think without words? Some researchers have suggested that we cannot have concepts without having language (spoken or signed languages such as BSL). Certainly language is important for abstract thinking. It would be difficult to have an idea of what is fair or honest without any language. But some ideas can be expressed without words or sign language, and feelings and relationships often do not need language at an abstract or level.

KEY TERM

Abstract – A thought or idea that does not have a physical or concrete existence, such as beauty or fairness.

Look, listen and note

Observe a baby or young child's communications and language in a range of situations using either written narrative observations or audio recording. Identify all the ways in which this child's communication and language development links with all other aspects of development. Then make notes about how the child's communication and language is supporting their learning across different areas.

Theoretical perspectives on language development

There are different approaches to the study of language. Useful ones to consider are the normative, behaviourist, nativist and social constructivist approaches.

The normative approach

Vocabulary building

In the 1930s and 1940s, experts like Arnold Gesell studied the development of language in young children mainly by using vocabulary counts. They counted the number and types of words that children used. They looked at whether children used single words, phrases and different types of sentences. This approach tended to stress what children could do at particular ages, and it could be very misleading.

For example, recent research suggests that babies say words like 'up' and 'gone', but this is not recognised by adults. Instead, adults seize on babble like 'ma-ma-ma', as they are longing for babies to say, 'Mama'.

Research shows that in fact the first word children in different parts of the world say is usually a comment on how either objects or people have 'gone'. In Korea, when adults give babies a drink in a cup, they say, 'It's moving in'. In western cultures, adults are more likely to say something like, 'Here's your cup'. As a result, Korean babies say 'moving in' before they say 'cup', and western babies say 'cup' before they say 'moving in'. This shows that there is more to language development than vocabulary building (Mandler 1999).

Language-rich environments

In the 1970s researcher Basil Bernstein, in a paper called *Class, Codes and Control* (1971), introduced the idea that children from working class backgrounds developed what he called a restricted language code (using a more limited range of words and less complex forms of grammar). He thought that children from middle-class homes developed an elaborated language code (using a more wide range of words and more complicated grammar), and as a result they achieved better results academically.

As a result, in both the USA and the UK, programmes of education were developed with the aim of enriching the language and learning environments of young children, so that they would succeed in education.

But during the 1980s and 1990s it became clear that there is more to a language-rich environment than there seems. Gordon Wells found that it was important for practitioners working with young children to understand the background and culture of the children and families they were working with. Then they would be able to understand the richness of the child's own language and culture (1987).

Recent research shows that children growing up in Japan who are described as lower-class do badly in school compared with children described as upper-class. But if the family moved to the USA, they were simply thought of as Japanese. It did not matter what class they had been described as in Japan. In the USA there is a perception that Japanese children study well at school, and this positive attitude towards them seemed to influence things so that they did well in school. In other words, positive attitudes towards the children is essential if children are to develop good language skills.

The behaviourist approach

In 1913 James Watson, an American psychologist, established behaviourism. The idea was that human behaviour is a response to environmental stimuli. The behaviourists thought that language had to be 'put into' children, because they are rather like empty vessels. Children were thought to learn language by imitating the people who they were with, such as their parents and the practitioners working with them. This meant that they thought children would only learn the language they heard or were taught directly.

Social learning theory approach

This approach would also emphasise that children learn language through imitating the language they hear around them. Of course, the language environment is hugely important and very influential but it does not take account of how children are also thinking about the structure of language and trying to make sense of it, as can be seen in the 'mistakes' children make such as calling a group of sheep, 'sheeps'.

The nativist approach

Noam Chomsky

An exciting revolution occurred when the behaviourist view was challenged by Noam Chomsky (1975). He showed that young children invent sentences that they definitely have not heard before. He suggested that we are not like empty vessels, born with nothing inside us mentally. Instead, human babies are born with what he called a language acquisition device (LAD) inside their brain.

Chomsky said that:

- babies are born with the predisposition or tendency to learn, talk and listen
- children learn to talk because they are genetically equipped to do so; they learn partly through the people they meet, communicate and socialise with.

Researchers studied the mistakes or errors that children make when they talk. They found that these gave important clues about innate language rules that children all over the world seem to be born with (including children who use sign language).

Chomsky has been criticised because he ignores the context in which children learn to talk. He is not interested in what the words mean (the semantics). His focus is on the structure of the language (the grammar).

The social constructivist approach

Jerome Bruner

Although Bruner agrees with Chomsky that there is a LAD, he does not think this is enough. He argues that there also needs to be a language acquisition support system (LASS). By this he means that the child's family and the whole context in which the child learns language is important. Mealtimes, bedtimes and going shopping are all an important part of the way children learn to speak and socialise using language.

Bruner stresses the importance of relationships and a warm affectionate atmosphere in supporting language development. In games like peek-a-boo, for example, the child learns about 'here', 'gone', 'bye-bye' and the words to go with these situations, in a relaxed way, with people they love and who love him or her (Bruner 1983).

Jean Piaget

Piaget thought it was because of language development that children were able to think beyond the immediate situation. In his view, language also helps them to see that things are not always as they appear. But although he suggested that language is very important in developing thinking, it is not entirely responsible for this. He sees language as a social part of development, something that needs other people, so that ideas can be shared and developed. But he also stressed the importance of the very individual and personal symbols that appear at the same time as language emerges (Piaget and Inhelder 1969).

Piaget sees language as one kind of symbolic function that is socially interactive, and about sharing ideas, feelings and relationships. Another kind is more private and individual, and involves:

- symbolic play (a toddler pretending to go to sleep)
- deferred imitation (a young child re-enacting a temper tantrum the day after seeing a friend have one)
- mental images (which are internal).

Piaget therefore regarded thinking as coming before language. The roots of thinking are in the child's actions and the sensory motor period, which comes before language develops. But he also believed that when language emerges, it transforms thinking and takes it forward with a huge leap. In fact, it is not possible to think at a very high level without language. Language is necessary if thinking is to develop. Without language, a child's thoughts would remain at the level of personal and individual symbols, and they would not be able to share ideas and exchange thoughts with other people. It is important to remember that BSL is, like spoken languages, a recognised and official language.

Language helps our symbolic development so that we get the most out of our experiences, and it is crucial in developing our ability to think and cooperate with others.

Piaget stressed the importance of personal and individual ways of communicating through expressing thoughts, ideas, feelings and relationships, as well as the shared and agreed forms of language. His work has been particularly important in supporting the development of communication in children with disabilities such as profound deafness and for children with complex needs. His work is also useful in looking at babies and toddlers, who use personal language more than conventional spoken or signed language.

Lev Vygotsky

Vygotsky offered an interactionist explanation and thought that language emerged from social interactions and relationships. For example, Vygotsky's theory of the zone of proximal development fits in with the idea of the adult extending children's talk by modelling just one step beyond what the child is

Think about ideas

Observe a baby or young child. Can you see evidence of:

- imitation
- grammatical 'mistakes' that show an understanding of grammatical rules
- using language/gestures that relate to the social context
- using language to help their thinking.

currently saying. In that sense, language begins outside the child. But as the child takes part in the cultural life of the family, it becomes the way in which children begin to reflect on and elaborate on their experiences. Language development takes children on a personal journey in their individual thoughts, but it also gives them social experiences that are important in their culture and society (1986).

Vygotsky believed that language and thought were interrelated in profound ways. He thought that the talking aloud and to themselves that we see young children do gradually becomes internalised. It becomes inner speech, which is silent. In this way, children begin to gain control over their thoughts, so that they can plan, organise, remember and solve problems.

He suggested that this silent inner speech and spoken social speech are connected to the way concepts and the understanding of shared ideas develop together. In other words, there are two strands of development in learning to talk which have a deep influence on the way a child develops their ability to think:

- inner speech (silent and inside yourself)
- social communication using speech.

Difficulties in developing language

Not all human beings communicate through a spoken language, for one reason or another, but the vast majority of people in the world do. Not being able to talk or listen with ease can cause frustration, loneliness and a feeling of powerlessness. It can be very difficult for some children to listen and talk – for example, those who have a hearing impairment, severe learning difficulties, moderate learning difficulties or physical challenges such as cerebral palsy. It is very important that every child is encouraged to find ways of communicating with other people. A considerable minority of children are now helped to learn sign language or sign systems (Makaton) or to use personal references which help them to communicate.

It is important to remember that gestures and touch are effective forms of communication, as well as shared signs, finger spelling and computers and keyboards.

- BSL is an official language, using signs rather than words. Children with profound hearing loss are often taught BSL.

- Some children with disabilities and special educational needs are taught Makaton, which is a simpler communication system than BSL. It uses shared signs, but it is not a full language.

- Some children use PECS – pictures/symbols that help them to think ahead or think back about what they will do and what they have done. This is an example of a non-verbal augmentative communication system.

- A small number of children with disabilities and complex needs will not use a communication system that is understood by others. They will continue to use personal communication signs, which only those close to them will understand. They are helped to find ways to communicate that are right for them and their families and close friends through objects of reference, a system devised by Professor Adam Ockelford (2001, 2013).

Language delay

There are a variety of reasons why language may be delayed:

- The child may be growing up and spending time in environments that are not supporting the development of communication and language.

- The child may have a learning difficulty that makes it a challenge to process language – for example, aphasia, autistic spectrum disorder or Down's syndrome.

- The child may have a hearing or visual impairment.

For children with language delay, it may be necessary to support their language development with the help of a speech and language therapist, a specialist language teacher and other professionals, such as health visitors who work in the home context with families and young children.

Children who do not speak

It is important that children who do not speak (elective mute and some children who stammer) are not put under pressure to speak when they attend a group setting. But it is also important to create an environment that encourages children to communicate and talk/sign. This can be achieved by:

- making sure that the child is enabled to feel safe in a trusting relationship with their key person

- observing to see how the child spends the day in the setting – share your observations with your manager and the team

- checking that a silent child can see and hear – this is very important

- bearing in mind that a child under emotional stress may become withdrawn and will need sensitive encouragement to talk/sign

- inviting a child to talk about something during small group time, or perhaps in a one-to-one story, but respecting their decision if they turn down the invitation to speak, so that they do not feel bad about it

- using stories and rhymes with props and pictures to make them easy to understand

- making sure the child has understood what you have said – it may be necessary to try different ways of explaining something

- remembering that other children can often explain something to another child in a way that helps them to understand.

Guidelines for good practice

Supporting children's communication skills

✔ Speak to children as the individuals they are.

✔ They need to spend time with adults who are patient with them and who listen to them. It is hard for young children to put their feelings and thoughts into words, and it takes time, so adults need to be aware of this, giving them time. It is very tempting to prompt children and say things for them. Instead, try nodding or saying, 'Hmm'. This gives children time to say what they want to.

✔ Do not correct what children say. Instead, elaborate on what they have said, giving them the correct pattern. For example, Shanaz, at two years, says, 'I falled down.' The adult replies, 'Yes, you did, didn't you? You fell down. Never mind, I will help you up.'

✔ It is important that all children experience unrushed, one-to-one conversations with adults and with other children – for example, when sharing a drink together at the snack table, chatting while using the clay or sharing a book together.

✔ Value and respect the child's language and culture.

✔ Have genuine conversations with children, using gestures, eye contact and props.

✔ Encourage children to listen to and enjoy stories, including those of their own culture.

✔ Introduce 'book language', such as 'Once upon a time'.

Moving on

Think about ideas

Review the theoretical perspectives outlined in this chapter or in your further reading. Note three key messages from each theory and evaluate how applying that perspective in practice may support children's communication and language. Note also what limitations you can identify in each perspective.

Reflecting on practice

- Agree with a colleague to do a peer observation of each of you talking with a child/group of children.

- Note how your interactions support the children's communications.

- Use the guidelines for good practice in this chapter to identify your strengths and areas for improvement in your practice.

Further reading, weblinks and resources

Neaum, S., 2012, *Language and Literacy for the Early Years*, London: Sage.

Oates, J. and Grayson, A., 2004, *Cognitive and Language Development in Children*, Oxford: Blackwell Press.

Owens, R.E., 2014, *Language Development: An Introduction*, Boston: Ally and Bacon.

Whitehead, M., 2010, *Language and Literacy in the Early Years 0–7* (4th edn), London: Sage.

Talk to Your Baby

This organisation is part of the National Literacy Trust, and has campaigned for front-facing pushchairs which encourage adults to talk to children and show them exciting experiences.
ww.talktoyourbaby.org.uk

The Literacy Trust

http://www.literacytrust.org.uk/early_years

References

Bernstein, B. *Class, Codes and Control. Volume1: Theoretical Studies Towards a Sociology of Language*, London and Boston: Routledge and Kegan Paul, 1971. pp 266–xiv.

Bruner, J., 1983, *Child's Talk: Learning to Use Language*, Oxford: Oxford University Press.

Chomsky, N., 1975, *Reflections on Language*, New York: Random House USA Inc.

Datta, M., 2007, *Bilinguality and Literacy: Principles and Practice* (2nd edn), London: Continuum.

DfES, Sure Start, 2005, *Communicating Matters: Trainers pack*, London: DfES, HMSO.

Edwards, C., Gandini, L. and Forman, G., 1994 *The Hundred Languages of Children. The Reggio Emilia Approach to Early Childhood Education*, USA: Ablex Publishing.

Halliday, M.A.K., 1978, *Language as Social Semiotic*, London: Arnold.

Karmiloff, K. and Karmiloff-Smith, A., 2001, *Pathways to Language: From Fetus to Adolescent,* Cambridge MA: Harvard University Press.

Krashen, S. D., 2003, *Explorations in Language Acquisition and Use: The Taipei Lectures*, Portsmouth: Heinemann.

Malloch, S. and Trevarthen, C., 2010, *Communicative Musicality: Exploring the basis of human companionship*, Oxford: Oxford University Press.

Mandler, J. M., 1999, 'Pre-verbal Representation and Language' in Bloom, P., Peterson, M. A., Nadel, L. and Garrett, M. F. (eds), 1999, *Space and Language*, Boston: MIT Press.

Manning-Morton, J. and Thorp, M., 2015, *Two Year Olds in Early Years Settings; Journeys of Discovery*, Maidenhead: Open University Press.

Ockelford, A 2001, *Objects of Reference: Promoting Early Symbolic Communication* (Third Edition). Royal National Institute of the Blind, London.

Ockelford, A. (2013) *Music, Language and Autism*, London. Jessica Kingsley.

Piaget, J. and Inhelder, B., 1969, *The Psychology of the Child*, London: Routledge Kegan Paul.

Pichler, P. and Coates, J. (eds), 2011, *Language and Gender: A Reader*, West Susex: Blackwell.

Schieffelin, B.B. and Ochs, E., 1987, *Language Socialisation Across Cultures*, Cambridge: Cambridge University Press.

Snow, C.E. (1972) Mothers' speech to children learning language. *Child Development* No'43: pp.549–65.

Trevarthen, C., 1998, 'The Child's Need to Learn a Culture', in Woodhead, M., Faulkner, D. and Littleton, K. (eds), *Cultural Worlds of Early Childhood*, London: Routledge.

Trevarthen, C. and Aitken, K.J., 2001, 'Infant Intersubjectivity: Research Theory and Clinical Application', *Journal of Child Psychology and Psychiatry*, 42, 1, pp. 3–48.

Trevarthen, C., 2004, *Learning about Ourselves from Children: Why a Growing Human Brain needs Interesting Companions*, Edinburgh: Perception-in-Action Laboratories, University of Edinburgh.

Vygotsky, L.S., 1986, *Thought and Language*, Cambridge MA: MIT Press.

Wells, G., 1987, *The Meaning Makers. Children Learning Language and Using Language to Learn*, Portsmouth: Heinemann.

Whitehead, M., 2010, *Language and Literacy in the Early Years* 0–7 (4th edn), London: Sage.

Williams, L., 2009, *Listening as a way of life*, London: The Young Children's Voices Network, National Children's Bureau.

Physical development and movement

Physical development involves the ways in which babies and young children gain control of their bodies. It plays an important role in maintaining activity and health during childhood. As children develop motor skills and the skills of balance and coordination, they also learn to use equipment and materials successfully and safely. This chapter will help you to understand the importance of physical activity and exercise. It will also consider theoretical perspectives in relation to physical health and development, and the growth of Forest Schools.

The difference between growth and physical development

Growth

Growth refers to an increase in physical size, and can be measured by height (length), weight and head circumference. Growth is determined by:

- heredity
- hormones
- nutrition
- emotional influences.

Physical development

Physical development involves the increasing skill and functioning of the body, including the development of:

- motor skills (or skills of movement)
- skills of coordination (for example, hand–eye coordination)
- balance.

Common patterns in physical growth and development

Height

The most important factors controlling a child's growth in height are the genes and chromosomes inherited from the parents. From birth to adolescence there are two distinct phases of growth:

- **From birth to two years:** this is a period of very rapid growth. The baby gains 25 to 30 cm in length and triples his or her body weight in the first year.

- **From two years to adolescence:** this is a slower but steady period of growth. The child gains 5 to 8 cm in height and about 3 kg in body weight per year until adolescence.

Body proportions

As a child grows, the various parts of his or her body change in shape and proportion, as well as increasing in size. The different body parts also grow at different rates – for example, the feet and hands of a teenager reach their final adult size before the body does. At birth, a baby's head accounts for about one-quarter of the total length of his or her body, whereas at seven years old, the head will be about one-eighth of the total length. This difference in body proportions explains why newborn babies appear to have such large eyes, and also why adolescents often appear to be clumsy or awkward in their physical movements.

Measuring growth

Centile charts are used to compare the growth pattern of an individual child with the normal range of growth patterns that are typical of a large number of children of the same sex. The charts are used to plot height (or, in young babies, length), weight and head circumference.

The importance of newborn reflex movements

Newborn babies display a number of **reflex** actions. A reflex action is one made automatically, without needing a conscious message from the brain – such as swallowing, sneezing or blinking. The presence of some of the newborn's primitive reflexes is essential to survival. The most important of these reflexes is breathing, closely followed by the 'rooting' and 'sucking' reflexes that help them to search out the breast and to feed successfully. The reflexes are replaced by **voluntary** responses as the brain takes control of behaviour; for example, the grasp reflex has to fade before the baby learns to hold – and let go of – objects which are placed in his/her hand. Doctors check for some of these reflexes during the baby's first examination. If the reflexes persist beyond an expected time it may indicate a delay in development. (See page 161 for definitions).

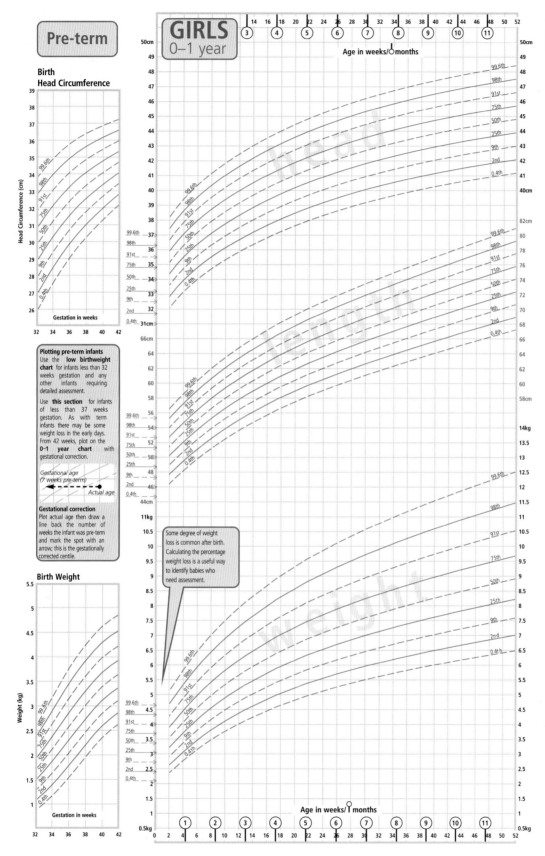

◀ Figure 9.1 Child growth chart: girls' weight (kg) birth to one year

The swallowing and sucking reflexes

When something is put in the mouth, the baby at once sucks and swallows; some babies make their fingers sore by sucking them while still in the womb! The swallowing reflex is permanent but the sucking reflex disappears after about four months.

The rooting reflex

If one side of the baby's cheek or mouth is gently touched, the baby's head turns towards the touch and the mouth purses as if in search of the nipple usually looking for food. This is very useful when learning to breastfeed a baby as it helps the baby to "latch on" well to the breast in the first weeks of life. This reflex should have disappeared by three to four months of age. See Figure 9.2(a).

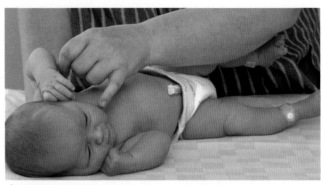

▲ **Figure 9.2** (a)

The grasp reflex

This is demonstrated by placing your finger or an object into the baby's open palm, which will cause a reflex or automatic grasp or grip. If you try to pull away, the grasp will get even stronger. This reflex should have disappeared by around three months of age. See Figure 9.2(b).

▲ **Figure 9.2** (b)

The stepping or walking reflex

When held upright and tilting slightly forward, with feet placed on a firm surface, the baby will make forward-stepping movements. This reflex is present at birth, disappears at around two to three months and then reappears when the child is ready to learn to walk later on. See Figure 9.2(c).

The startle reflex

This is the baby's generalised alarm reflex, which provides protection against danger before the brain is developed enough to determine what is and is not dangerous. When an adult fails to support or hold the baby's neck and head or if the baby becomes startled by a sudden loud noise, bright light or sudden touch, the arms of the baby will thrust outward and then curl in as to embrace themselves. This reflex should disappear between two to four months of age. See Figure 9.2(d).

The asymmetric tonic neck reflex (ATNR)

This reflex involves a coordinated movement of the baby's neck, arm and leg in conjunction with the head. If the baby's head is turned to one side, he or she will straighten the arm and leg on that side and bend the arm and leg on the opposite side. The ATNR reflex begins about 18 weeks after conception and should be fully developed at birth. Later this reflex plays an important role in hand–eye coordination and object and distance perception. See Figure 9.2(e).

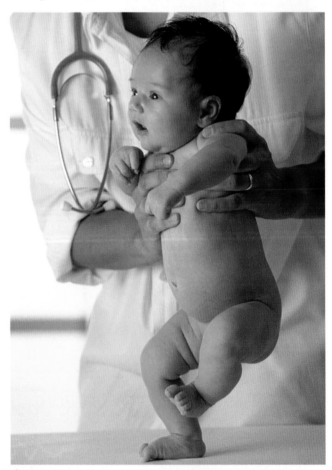

▲ **Figure 9.2** (c)

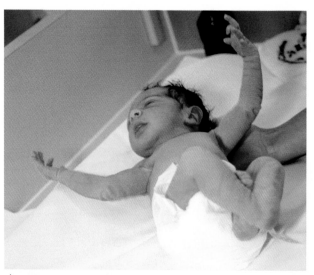

▲ **Figure 9.2** (d)

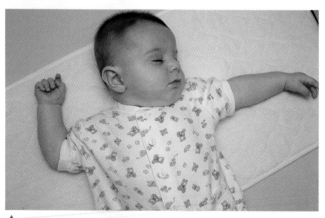

▲ **Figure 9.2** (e)

▲ **Figures 9.2 a-e** Primitive reflexes in a newborn baby

The falling reflex

This is often called the Moro reflex. Any sudden movement which affects the neck gives the baby the feeling that she may be dropped; she will fling out her arms and open her hands before bringing them back over the chest as if to catch hold of something. This reflex will disappear by four to six months.

What is physical development?

Physical development is the way in which the body gains skills and becomes more complex in its performance. It is the most visible of all the abilities shown in childhood and includes the less observable development of all the senses: hearing, vision, touch, taste and smell. Development follows a sequence:

● **From simple to complex** – for example, a child will walk before she can skip or hop.

● **From head to toe** – for example, head control is acquired before coordination of the spinal muscles. Head control is important from birth in order for the baby to feed.

● **From inner to outer** – for example, a child can coordinate his arms to reach for an object before he has learnt the fine manipulative skills necessary to pick it up.

● **From general to specific** – for example, a young baby shows pleasure by a massive general response (eyes widen, legs and arms move vigorously, etc.). An older child shows pleasure by smiling or using appropriate words and gestures.

As we saw in Chapter 6 on holistic child development, babies and young children follow standard basic patterns when acquiring physical skills, but there are wide variations between individuals. A child's range of physical skills or abilities has a major effect on other areas of development – for example, once the child has learnt to crawl or shuffle on his bottom, he will be more independent and will be able to explore things that were previously out of reach.

The responses of other people to a child who has developed new skills will also alter. Adults will make changes to the child's environment – putting now reachable objects out of harm's way – and they will say 'no' more often.

The development of motor skills

The sequence of physical development involves **gross motor skills** first – these involve control of large muscles in the body. This is followed by development of **fine motor skills**, which depend on small muscle coordination – these are sometimes called skills of movement, and include:

● **gross manipulative skills**, which involve single-limb movements, usually the arm – for example, throwing, catching and sweeping arm movements

● **fine manipulative skills**, which involve precise use of the hands and fingers for drawing, using a knife and fork, writing, and doing up shoelaces and buttons.

The ability to grasp

Grasping is the ability to hold onto objects and use them for specific purposes.

● **Reflex grasp**: very young babies have a reflexive grasp; their hands automatically close tightly when pressure or stimulation is applied to their palms.

● **Palmar grasp**: using the whole hand to grasp an object. From about four to six months a baby will start to 'rake' an object towards him or herself, and will start passing objects from one hand to the other, using the whole hand.

● **Inferior pincer grasp**: using the thumb and fingers to grasp an object. At around eight or nine months, a baby will be able to pick up small objects such as raisins by resting a forearm on a table and using the sides of thumb and the index finger.

● **Superior pincer grasp**: using the thumb and tip of the first finger to grasp an object. At around 12 months, a baby will be able to pick up and release a tiny object such as a piece of cereal by using the tip of the index finger and thumb while holding wrist off the surface.

● **Static tripod grasp**: the pencil is held between the thumb, index finger and middle finger (i.e. three fingers are touching the writing tool). Commonly seen between the ages of three and four years.

● **Dynamic tripod grasp**: the pencil is placed between the thumb and index finger. The side of the middle finger gently supports the pencil, with the third and little fingers lightly curled under. This is considered the most efficient grasp for handwriting and drawing, as intricate and detailed marks can be made.

Locomotion and balance

Locomotion is the ability to move around on one's own. It is central to the pattern of development changes that occurs at the end of the baby's first year, and it begins with crawling or bottom shuffling.

Balance is the first of all the senses to develop. It is crucial to posture, movement and **proprioception** (see page 165).

The eight-month-old child who rolls backwards and forwards across the floor, with no particular goal in sight, is preparing her balance for sitting, standing and walking.

The skills of locomotion

Babies go through the 'pre-walking' stage between birth and 11 months:

> **KEY TERMS**
>
> **Proprioception** – The ability to recognise and use the physical sensations from the body that give feedback on balance and the position of our limbs.
> **Locomotion** – Movement or the ability to move from one place to another.

▲ **Figure 9.3** (a) palmar grasp

▲ **Figure 9.3** (b) pincer grasp

▲ **Figure 9.3** (c) dynamic tripod grasp

● **Between birth and five months**, the baby is learning to turn from their side to their back and from their back to their side.

- **Between four and ten months**, the baby is developing the ability to roll from their back to his stomach.

- **Around 11 months**, the baby should reach the pre-walking progression of being on her hand and knees.

- Between the ages of **five and twelve months** the walking stage occurs. This stage begins with:
  - stepping movements, followed by the ability to walk while holding onto furniture, followed by
  - walking with help until he can walk alone. This ability is usually gained by around 17 months of age, and coincides with the development of the ability to walk well.

- **Up to the age of 20 months**: the final stages that the baby should go through in order to achieve locomotive abilities are:
  - developing the ability to walk sideways and backwards
  - walking up and down stairs with some help, which should develop until around 23 months of age, and finally the ability to walk with one foot on a walking board, which occurs up to around 24 months of age.

Walking

Walking develops further and becomes more efficient after the age of two. Children then become able to vary their walking by including a tiptoe action and a walking backwards action, and by being able to walk in different circumstances (i.e. uphill or downhill or on uneven surfaces) and at different paces.

As walking becomes an increasingly automatic function, children learn to multi-task and can carry out other actions while walking – for example, transporting objects when walking from one place to another.

Running

Another key development that occurs in the early years is that of the ability to run. Children begin to run at around 18 months and by the age of 2 years, most children can run. Between the ages of four and six years, children begin to be able to run with ease and begin to play running games.

Jumping and hopping

In the development of jumping, the age of achievement varies, but all children follow the same stages:

- At 18 months, the ability to step down occurs, which is then followed by the ability for two-foot take-off.

- At around two years, a key milestone for young children is the two-foot jump from the ground.

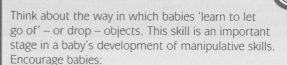

Think about ideas

Think about the way in which babies 'learn to let go of' – or drop – objects. This skill is an important stage in a baby's development of manipulative skills. Encourage babies:

- to use both hands together to pick up and to let go of objects – by providing a toy that is too large to pick up using only one hand; and

- to pass objects from one hand to another, by demonstrating the skill yourself.

In the development of hopping:

- by around three-and-a-half years: children can hop once

- by around five years, they can hop about ten times.

Hopping can lead to the development of other locomotor activities such as skipping and galloping. Skipping begins to develop at around three-and-a-half years (with the ability to skip on one foot) to five years (with the ability to skip on alternating feet). Researchers have found that there are gender differences in this ability; for example, 55 per cent of boys are able to enact five continuous skips at five-and-a-half years compared to 91 per cent of girls.

A sense of balance

Balancing is not always seen as a developmental skill, but rather as a means of developing skills such as running,

▲ **Figure 9.4** Jumping requires a good sense of balance

Gross motor skills (locomotion or movement)	Fine motor skills (manipulation)	Balance and stabilisation
walking	throwing	bending
running	catching	stretching
skipping	picking up	twisting
jumping	kicking	turning
hopping	rolling	balancing
chasing	volleying	squatting
dodging	striking	transferring
climbing	squeezing	landing
crawling	kneading	hanging

Table 9.1 A summary of activities related to physical skills development

Look, listen and note

Observing Isla

Isla walks towards a ball. She wants to pick it up. She leans over to touch the ball, but instead her foot hits it and the ball slides across the floor. She walks towards it again, and this time she tries to kick the ball on purpose. She misses the ball; her foot goes past the left side of the ball. Isla tries again and again. She kicks it and begins to run after the ball, tries to stop in front of it and falls forward. She stands up and kicks it to a new location and she laughs.

1   How old do you think Isla is?
2   What has Isla learnt during this activity? Try to list at least six things and then compare them with the list at the end of this chapter (page 177).

hopping, skipping and climbing. However, at around two years of age, a child can momentarily stand on one foot and can walk along a line on the ground. By three years of age, children can generally stand on one foot for around five seconds and can walk around a circular line on the ground. Finally, by age five, most children can stand alone on one foot for around ten seconds.

Eye–hand coordination

The ability to reach and grasp objects in a coordinated way requires months of practice and close attention:

- In the first months after birth, hand–eye coordination takes effort.
- By around nine months of age, a baby can usually manage to guide his or her movements with a single glance to check for accuracy – for example, when feeding themselves with a spoon.

Foot–eye coordination

The ability to execute actions with the feet, guided by the eyes, is necessary for many movement activities; for example, climbing stairs, and kicking or dribbling a ball.

There are several aspects of physical development, which are outlined in Table 9.1.

Sensory development

Sensation is the process by which we receive information through the senses. These include:

- vision
- hearing
- smell
- touch
- taste
- proprioception (see page 165).

Perception is making sense of what we see, hear, touch, smell and taste. Our perception is affected by previous experience and knowledge, and by our emotional state at the time. There are therefore wide variations in the way different individuals perceive the same object, situation or experience.

Visual development

A newborn baby's eyes are barely half the size of an adult's, and although they are structurally similar they differ in two ways:

1   A baby's focus is fixed at about 20 cm, which is the distance from the baby to his or her mother's face when breastfeeding. Anything nearer or further away appears blurred. The baby will remain short-sighted for about four months.

2   The response to visual stimuli is slower in babies because the information received by the eye takes longer to reach the brain via the nervous pathway. A newborn baby is able to fix his or her eyes on objects and follow their movement only poorly. Head and eye movement is also poorly coordinated; in the first week or two, the eyes lag behind when the baby's head is turned to one side – a feature known by paediatricians as the 'doll's eye phenomenon'.

Research has shown that babies prefer looking at:

- patterned areas rather than plain ones, especially stripes
- edges of objects in 3D
- anything that resembles a human face – babies will actually search out and stare at human faces during their first two months of life
- brightly coloured objects.

By around four months a baby can focus on both near and distant objects, and his ability to recognise different objects is improving steadily. By six months the baby will respond visually to movements across the room and will move his head to see what is happening. By one year the baby's eye movements are smoother and he can follow rapidly moving objects with his or her eyes – a skill known as **tracking**. A squint is normal at this point.

The development of hearing

- Newborn babies are able to hear almost as well as adults do.
- Certain rhythmic sounds – often called 'white noise' – seem to have a special soothing effect on babies. The drone of a vacuum cleaner or hairdryer is calming!
- The sound of a human voice evokes the greatest response, and the rhythms of lullabies have been used for centuries in all cultures to help babies to sleep or to comfort them.
- A baby can recognise his or her own mother's voice from the first week and can distinguish its tone and pitch from those of other people.
- Sudden changes in noise levels tend to disturb very young babies and make them jump.
- From about six months, a baby learns to recognise and distinguish between different sounds – for example, the sound of a spoon in a dish means that food is on its way.
- Babies can also discriminate between cheerful and angry voices, and will respond in kind.

The development of smell, taste and touch

The senses of smell and taste are closely linked. If our sense of smell is defective – for example, because of a cold – then our sense of taste is also reduced. A baby as young as one week old who is breastfed is able to tell the difference between his or her own mother's smell and other women's smells. From birth, babies are also able to distinguish the four basic tastes – sweet, sour, bitter and salty.

The sense of touch is also well developed in infancy, as can be demonstrated by the primitive reflexes (see page 158). Babies seem to be particularly sensitive to touch on the mouth, the face, the hands, the soles of the feet and the abdomen. Research has shown that babies would rather be stroked than fed.

Proprioception

The word proprioception comes from the Latin *proprius* – meaning 'one's own'. Proprioception – or

see page 158

> ### KEY TERM
>
> **Tracking** – The smooth movements made by the eyes in following the track of a moving object. These are sometimes called 'smooth pursuit'.

proprioceptive learning – means knowing the position of our bodies and where our bodies begin and end, without us having to look at them. When babies kick their legs repeatedly and wave their arms around, they are starting to develop the sense of proprioception as information is constantly sent to the brain from the muscles and joints to the brain, both when our muscles and joints are moving and when they are still.

Sensory deprivation

A congenitally blind baby (i.e. a baby who is born blind) will develop a more sophisticated sense of touch than a sighted baby, although they both start life with the same touch potential. As the sense of touch develops, so the area of the brain normally assigned to touch increases in size for the blind baby, and the area of the brain normally assigned to sight decreases.

Similarly, in a congenitally deaf baby, the part of the brain that normally receives auditory stimuli is taken over by the visual and movement input from sign language.

Factors affecting physical development

Children's physical development is influenced by their:

- growing confidence and sense of identity
- enjoyment of physical play
- increasing ability to control their own bodies through movement
- physical well-being and strength.

As children develop, they become faster, stronger, more mobile, more sure of their balance, and they start to use these skills in a wider range of physical activities.

There are many other factors that affect children's physical development:

- **genetic factors** – the genes children inherit from their parents affect both growth and development
- **nutrition** – family income, lifestyle and culture all affect the diet a child receives; children who are on poor diets are more susceptible to infection, as their immunity is affected by the lack of adequate minerals and vitamins

- **environmental factors**, which include:
  - overcrowded housing
  - air pollution (e.g. lead poisoning from traffic exhausts and adults smoking in the home)
  - lack of access to a play area or garden
- **social factors**, which include:
  - love and affection
  - stimulation
  - opportunities to play.

Healthy growth and development can be affected when a child receives too little (or too much) stimulation.

Normative physical development

All of the normative charts can be found in Chapter 6 on holistic child development. Below is a brief summary showing the *average* age at which children acquire motor skills – often referred to as milestones. Remember that every child is unique and these are only guidelines.

Also bear in mind that supervision is essential, and that toys suggested in the guidelines below should all be safe and age-appropriate; check with other staff members if you have any questions or concerns. See Chapter 14 for more information on health and safety.

Gross motor skills

- rolling over: six months
- sitting: nine months
- crawling: nine to ten months
- standing: one year
- walking: 12 to 15 months
- running: two years
- pushing and pulling wheeled toys: two years
- jumping: two to three years
- climbing: four years
- riding a trike: four years
- bouncing a ball: four years
- throwing and catching a beanbag ball: five years.

Fine motor skills

- hand and finger play: three months
- palmar grasp: six months
- turning pages in book: one year
- pointing to objects: 15 months
- primitive tripod grasp: 18 months
- fine pincer and tripod grasp: two years
- threading large beads: two years six months
- dynamic tripod grasp: three years
- threading small beads: four years
- dressing independently: five years.

▲ **Figure 9.5** The majority of babies start walking around the age of 1 year to 15 months, but this varies greatly

▲ **Figure 9.6** Threading large beads promotes hand–eye coordination, spatial awareness and the development of fine motor skills

Guidelines for good practice

Promoting development, birth to four weeks

✔ Encourage the baby to lie on the floor, to kick and experiment safely with movement.

✔ Provide an opportunity for the baby to feel the freedom of moving without a nappy or clothes on.

✔ Always support the baby's head when playing with him or her, as the neck muscles are not strong enough to control movement.

✔ Use bright colours in furnishings.

✔ Provide a mobile over the cot and/or the nappy-changing area.

✔ Feed on demand, and talk and sing to the baby.

✔ Provide plenty of physical contact and maintain eye contact.

✔ Talk lovingly to the baby and give her the opportunity to respond.

✔ Introduce the baby to different household noises.

✔ Provide contact with other adults and children.

✔ Encourage bonding with the main carer by enjoying the relationship.

✔ Expect no set routine in the first few weeks.

✔ Pick up the baby and talk to her face-to-face.

Guidelines for good practice

Stimulating development, four to eight weeks

✔ Use a special supporting infant chair so that the baby can see adult activity.

✔ Let the baby kick freely, without a nappy.

✔ Massage the baby's body and limbs during or after bathing.

✔ Use brightly coloured mobiles and wind chimes over the baby's cot and/or changing mat. Let the baby explore different textures.

✔ Light rattles and toys strung over the baby's pram or cot will encourage focusing and coordination.

✔ Talk to and smile with the baby.

✔ Sing while feeding or bathing the baby – allow him time to respond. Learn to distinguish the baby's cries and to respond to him differently.

✔ Tickling and teasing the baby may induce laughter.

✔ Talk to the baby and hold him close.

Guidelines for good practice

Stimulating development: 8 to 12 weeks

✔ Place the baby in a supporting infant chair so that he or she can watch adult activity.

✔ Encourage the baby to kick without a nappy.

✔ Massage and stroke the baby's limbs when bathing or if using massage oil.

✔ Use brightly coloured mobiles and wind chimes to encourage focusing at 20 cm.

✔ Place a rattle in the baby's hand and attach objects above the cot that make a noise when struck.

✔ Sing nursery rhymes to the baby.

✔ Talk sensibly to the baby and imitate her sounds to encourage her to repeat them.

✔ Hold the baby close and talk lovingly to strengthen the bonding process. Encourage contact with other adults and children.

✔ Respond to the baby's needs and show enjoyment in caring for her.

Guidelines for good practice

Stimulating development: three to six months

✔ Practise sitting with the baby on your knee.

✔ Play rough-and-tumble games such as rolling the baby to and fro on the bed.

✔ Play bouncing games on your knee while singing songs.

✔ Offer rattles and soft, squashy toys to give a variety of textures.

✔ Offer home-made toys (e.g. transparent plastic containers with dried peas inside or empty cotton reels tied together). Remember to check that lids are secure and always supervise play.

✔ Continue talking to the baby, particularly in response to his sounds. Provide different toys, with a range of textures and sounds.

✔ Sing nursery rhymes combined with finger play (e.g. 'This little piggy. . .').

✔ Give the baby the opportunity to find out things for himself and begin to choose play activities.

✔ Encourage playing alone and in the company of other children. Offer waterproof books in the bath.

Guidelines for good practice

Stimulating development: six to nine months

✔ Encourage confidence and balance by placing toys around the baby when she is sitting.

✔ Make sure furniture is stable and has no sharp corners when the baby is using it to pull herself up.

✔ Encourage mobility by placing toys just out of the baby's reach.

✔ Encourage visual awareness by providing varied experiences.

✔ Small objects, which must be safe if chewed by the baby, will encourage the pincer grasp (small pieces of biscuit are ideal, but always supervise).

✔ Build a tower of bricks with the baby and watch her delight when they all fall down.

✔ Look at picture books together and encourage the baby to point at objects by naming them.

✔ Talk to the baby about everyday things.

✔ Widen the baby's experiences by going on outings that include animals. Imitate animal sounds and encourage the baby to copy you.

✔ Allow plenty of time for play.

✔ Provide simple 'musical instruments' (e.g. xylophone or wooden spoon and saucepan).

✔ Use a safety mirror for the baby to recognise herself.

Guidelines for good practice

Stimulating development: 9 to 12 months

✔ Provide large-wheeled toys to push around – brick trucks serve the dual purpose of walking and stacking games.

✔ Ensure furniture is safe and stable for climbers.

✔ Take the baby swimming or walking in the park.

✔ Provide small climbing frames – closely supervised – to increase the baby's balance and coordination.

✔ Offer stacking and nesting toys.

✔ Roll balls for the baby to bring back to you.

✔ Provide sand and water play – always supervised.

✔ Make cardboard boxes and saucepans available to put things into and take things out of.

✔ Partake in plenty of talking to the baby that requires a response that will develop language ability.

✔ Encourage self-feeding – tolerate messes.

✔ Talk constantly to him and use rhymes and action songs.

✔ Offer lots of play opportunities with adult interaction – sharing, taking turns, and so on.

✔ Foster a feeling of self-worth by providing the baby with his own equipment and utensils (e.g. the baby will need his own flannel, toothbrush, cup and spoon).

Guidelines for good practice

Stimulating development: 12 to 15 months

✔ Provide stacking toys and bricks.

✔ Provide push-and-pull toys for babies who are walking.

✔ Read picture books with simple rhymes.

✔ Offer big empty cardboard boxes for the baby to play with.

✔ Provide thick crayons or thick paintbrushes.

✔ Arrange a corner of the kitchen or garden for messy play involving the use of water or paint.

Guidelines for good practice

Stimulating development: 18 months to 2 years

✔ Provide toys to ride and climb on, and space to run and play.

✔ Allow trips to parks and opportunities for messy play with water and paints.

✔ Encourage use of safe climbing frames and sandpits, always supervised.

✔ Provide simple models to build (e.g. Duplo) as well as jigsaw puzzles, crayons and paper.

✔ Provide picture books and glove puppets to encourage interaction and conversation.

Guidelines for good practice

Stimulating development: 15 to 18 months

✔ Provide push-and-pull toys – still popular at this age.

✔ Teach the child how to manage stairs safely.

✔ Provide threading toys, and hammer and peg toys.

✔ Encourage and praise early attempts at drawing.

Guidelines for good practice

Stimulating development: two to three years

✔ Provide a wide variety of playthings – dough for modelling, sand and safe household utensils.

✔ Encourage play with other children. Allow swimming and trips to the park; maybe even enjoy long walks, ensuring that they are supervised at all times.

✔ Read to the child and discuss everyday events.

✔ Encourage art and craft activities.

✔ Promote independence by teaching the child how to look after and put away their own clothes and toys.

✔ Encourage visits to the library and story times.

Guidelines for good practice

Stimulating development: three to four years

✔ Provide plenty of opportunity for exercise.

✔ Play party games (e.g. musical statues).

✔ Use rope swings and climbing frames.

✔ Obtain access to a bike with stabilisers.

✔ Provide small-piece construction toys, jigsaws and board games.

✔ Encourage gluing and sticking activities, as well as paint, sand, water and play dough.

✔ Prepare the child for school by teaching them how to dress and undress for games, and to manage going to the toilet by herself.

✔ Ensure all equipment is safe and appropriate for the ages of the children. Check with a senior team member if you are unsure and have any questions or concerns.

Guidelines for good practice

Stimulating development: four to five years

✔ Provide plenty of outdoor activities.

✔ Encourage non-stereotypical activities (e.g. boys using skipping ropes, girls playing football).

✔ Encourage team sports, which may be provided at clubs such as Beavers, Rainbows and Woodcraft Folk.

✔ Encourage the use of models, jigsaws, sewing kits and craft activities, as well as drawing and painting.

✔ Introduce tracing and image patterns.

Guidelines for good practice

Stimulating development: five to seven years

✔ Provide opportunities for vigorous exercise.

✔ Encourage team sports, riding a bike and swimming. Offer plenty of praise for new skills learnt and never force a child to participate.

✔ Provide books and drawing materials, board games and computer games.

✔ Encourage writing skills.

✔ Display the child's work prominently to increase his or her self-esteem.

Physical development in relation to other areas of development

Physical development is linked to other areas of development, such as emotional and social development and cognitive and language development. Each affects and is affected by the other areas. For example: once babies have mastered crawling, they are free to explore the world on their own – they become more independent and confident when away from their familiar adults.

The ability to reach and grasp objects (usually achieved at around six months) develops their understanding of the nature of objects. This often results in a surprise – for example, when they try to pick up a soap bubble or a shaft of sunlight. Babies are also interested in edges (e.g. of a book or a floor) and may wonder where does one object end and the next object begin?

Promoting physical development

Physical development is the easiest aspect of development to observe and measure. Parents are usually proud of their child's physical achievements, but children are often compared unfavourably with their peers and may also be judged by others.

Guidelines for good practice

Promoting physical development in children

✔ Children do not need lots of expensive toys and play equipment in order to grow and develop physically.

✔ Provide access to a rich outdoor environment, with a variety of natural obstacles, surfaces and structures.

✔ Provide a range of malleable play materials such as dough, clay and gloop, wet and dry sand, and water, to encourage manipulation and so support fine motor control.

✔ Provide opportunities for tummy-time play for babies.

✔ Plan activities which encourage children to use their whole bodies, including rough-and-tumble or active play, crawling, climbing, sliding, rolling, running, hopping and jumping.

✔ Plan activities which include lifting, carrying and tasks such as sweeping and digging.

✔ Ensure there are periods of rest and relaxation and opportunities for affectionate touch and physical comforting.

✔ Provide opportunities for children to be able to make their own risk assessments relating to their activities, for themselves, rather than removing all risk for them.

✔ Help children to see physical activities as fun, rather than as tests of competency. Encourage them to compete with themselves – can I do this better than I managed last time? – rather than comparing themselves with others.

✔ Help children to develop the ability to praise others' achievements without feeling degraded.

✔ Be fair to all children: encourage patience, understanding and teamwork.

✔ Recognise and allow differences between siblings and friends – try not to compare.

We should always stop and consider how the parents and their child might feel when the child is not able to perform certain physical tasks. Rather than feeling sorry for the child who has a physical disability or illness, we should aim to maximise their individual potential for development.

The importance of floor play and tummy time for babies

Floor play

Floor games which involve the pushing and kicking of legs help to promote motor skills for babies who are not yet walking. Once walking, toddlers can be provided with indoor and outdoor play surfaces of varying textures and slopes.

Tummy time

There are many physical benefits to building opportunities for tummy time. Placing babies on their tummies enables them to:

● develop their neck muscles so that they can hold up their head

● develop their back muscles, which are needed for rolling and for sitting

● use their hands to bear their own weight; this also helps to develop the full palm stretch, which is important for literacy skills as it promotes strength of grasp and fine motor skills

● learn to shift their weight – a crucial skill for later crawling and walking

● focus their eyes at close range and 'track' objects in their line of vision

● develop movement across the mid-line of the body. These cross-lateral connections are thought to be important for higher-level thinking and memory skills.

Promoting the development of fine motor skills

Children should be provided with a rich variety of opportunities to develop their skills, using different materials and a range of tools. They also need to develop the skills required to take care of their own bodies – for example, in washing and dressing themselves, cleaning their teeth and becoming more independent at mealtimes.

To strengthen the hands and promote the development of fine motor skills, you should provide:

● play dough or clay – for squeezing, rolling, squashing, making holes with fingers and tools

● newspaper – for scrunching up, using one hand at a time, or tearing into strips and crumpling them into balls

● safety scissors – when safety scissors are held correctly, and when they fit a child's hand well, simple cutting activities will exercise the same muscles that are needed to manipulate a pencil in a mature tripod grasp; the correct scissor position is with the thumb and middle finger in the handles of the scissors, the index finger on the outside of the handle to stabilise, with fingers four and five curled into the palm. For cutting, you should provide:

  ● junk mail or similar thick paper

  ● straws

  ● play dough.

- mark-making opportunities, with chunky pens, pencils and paintbrushes for drawing, writing, painting, tracing, and so on
- a peg game, which promotes the development of the pincer grasp – give each child a cardboard plate and provide lots of brightly coloured plastic pegs; using a sand timer or clock timer, see how many pegs the children can arrange around their plate (this activity is also good for learning their colours)
- a finger gym, which promotes the development of fine manipulative skills, such as pinching, screwing, threading, winding, and so on; provide a basket or box in which you have collected items that need small fingers to work, but that are also attractive and appealing to children – for example:
  - old clocks, radios, and so on
  - spinning tops
  - squeezy toys
  - eye-droppers to 'pick up' coloured water for colour mixing or to make patterns on paper
  - buttons, fasteners, and so on
  - dried pasta shapes and chopsticks for picking them up
  - wind-up toys
  - jar tops – opening and closing or other twisting toys
  - cotton reels, chunky beads (and smaller ones as the children get older) for threading
  - shape-sorters and 'posting' toys
  - pegs of various sizes with boards.

Promoting eye–hand coordination

This involves accuracy in placement, direction and spatial awareness. You can promote eye–hand coordination by ensuring children partake in activities such as:

- throwing beanbags or soft 'koosh' balls into a hoop placed flat on the floor (gradually increase the distance)
- play throwing and catching with a ball; start with a large ball and then work towards using a smaller ball
- practise hitting skittles with a ball; improvise by using weighted plastic bottles.

Promoting physical development in children with special needs

Although the sequence of physical development may remain the same for a child with a special need, the rate at which a 'stage' is achieved may be slower. The attitudes and actions of parents and early years practitioners will have a great influence on the child's behaviour and self-esteem.

All children should be appreciated and encouraged for any personal progress made, however small, and should not be compared to the normative measurements. This is because children with special needs often move through stages of development in unusual and uneven ways – for example, they might sit or walk at the usual time, but not talk.

Adults should recognise and understand that a child who is having difficulty acquiring a skill may become frustrated and may need more individual attention or specialist help; also, the child may not yet be ready to acquire the particular skill.

Every child must be seen as an individual first; activities and equipment should be tailored to the specific needs of that child. Plan activities to encourage exercise and movement of all body parts.

Sequence of development

Children across the world seem to pass through similar sequences (or order) of development, but in different ways and different rates according to their culture. The work of Mary Sheridan on developmental sequences has been invaluable, but she suggests that children move through rigidly prescribed stages that are linked to the child's age: the child sits, then crawls, then stands, then walks.

In fact, this is not the case. Not all children *do* crawl. Blind children often do not. Some children 'bottom-shuffle', moving along in a sitting position. A traditional approach to child development study has been to emphasise normative measurement. This is concerned with 'milestones' or stages in a child's development. These show what *most* children can do at a particular age. In reality, there is a wide range of normal development, and this will be influenced by genetic, social and cultural factors. Because of this, normative patterns of development should only be used as a guide. Children have been labelled as 'backward' or 'forward' in relation to the so-called 'normal' child, which is not always helpful.

Rate of development

It is important to be aware that normative measurements can only indicate general trends in development in children across the world. They may vary quite a bit according to the culture in which a child lives. It is important to understand that while the sequence of development is fairly general to all children, the rate – or speed – of development can vary a great deal. When children do things earlier than the milestones suggest is normal, it does not necessarily mean that they will be outstanding or gifted in any way. Parents sometimes think that

Promoting physical development in a child with special needs

Either:

- visit a school for children with special needs, or
- invite an early years practitioner with experience of working with children with special needs into college.

Prepare the questions you need to ask to find out:

- how a child with coordination difficulties can be helped to develop these skills
- what activities might be used to promote physical development in a child who uses a wheelchair
- what the role of the early years practitioners is in promoting physical development in children with special needs.

because their child speaks early, is potty-trained early or walks early, he or she is gifted in some way. Einstein did not talk until he was three!

Physical activity and exercise

Children need to be physically active in order to prevent harmful effects on their health, in both the long and short term. Physical activity and exercise are no longer regular features in many children's lives. Some children never walk or cycle to school, or play sport.

Effects on short-term health

Physical activity boosts energy, and helps to alleviate stress and anxiety. Children who are physically active are more likely to fall sleep easily and to sleep for longer. They are also less likely to develop infections, such as colds and flu, because their immune system is made stronger by having regular exercise and sufficient sleep.

Effects on long-term health

Physical activity in young children also helps in the long term, with:

- Controlling weight – and so preventing obesity. A recent study found that teenagers who carry a gene for obesity are less likely to become overweight or obese if they are physically active for an hour a day. If an overweight child becomes an overweight or obese adult, they are more likely to suffer from health problems, including diabetes, stroke, heart disease and cancer.
- Increasing bone density in children and helping to maintain strong bones in adolescents. It also slows down bone degeneration later in life. This can help

to prevent osteoporosis, a condition when bones become brittle and more prone to break.

- Reducing blood pressure: if you have high blood pressure, you are more likely to have a stroke or heart attack.
- Reducing the risk of diabetes: keeping active can help lower the risk of developing type 2 diabetes later on in life.
- Reducing the risks of some kinds of cancer.

Physical activity and general well-being

Children who are physically active have improved psychological well-being; it aids rest/sleep and even digestion. They gain more self-confidence and have higher self-esteem. Children benefit from playing outdoors in the fresh air and having lots of space in which to move freely. They also benefit socially from playing alongside other children and making friends. See Public Health England's paper *How healthy behaviour supports children's wellbeing* for more details on these ideas.

The importance of physical play

Through opportunities for physical play, children steadily become better at those skills requiring coordination of different parts of the body – for example:

- hands and eyes for throwing and catching
- legs and arms for skipping with a rope.

Physical play also helps children to:

- **Express ideas and feelings**. Children become aware that they can use their bodies to express themselves by moving in different ways as they respond to their moods and feelings, to music or to imaginative ideas.
- **Explore what their bodies can do** and become aware of their increasing abilities, agility and skill. Children's awareness of the space around them and what their bodies are capable of can be extended by climbing and balancing on large-scale apparatus, such as a climbing frame, wooden logs and a balancing bar, and by using small tricycles, bicycles and carts.
- **Cooperate with others in physical play and games**. Children become aware of physical play as both an individual and a social activity – in playing alone or alongside others, in playing throwing and catching with a partner, in using a seesaw or pushcart, or in joining a game with a larger group.

- **Develop increasing control of fine movements of their fingers and hands (fine motor skills)** – for example, playing musical instruments and making sounds with the body, such as clapping or tapping, helps develop fine motor skills in the hands and fingers, while also reinforcing the link between sound and physical movement. Helping with household tasks – washing-up, pouring drinks, carrying bags – also develops fine motor skills.

- **Develop balance and coordination**, as well as an appreciation of distance and speed. Energetic play that involves running, jumping and skipping helps children to develop these skills.

- **Develop spatial awareness** – for example, dancing and moving around to music develops spatial awareness while also practising coordination and muscle control.

Providing variety, risk and challenge in play

Play England states:

> *All children both need and want to take risks in order to explore limits, venture into new experiences and develop their capacities, from a very young age and from their earliest play experiences.*

Guidelines for good practice

Providing opportunities for physical play

Opportunities for physical activity should be provided both inside and out. Regular sessions of indoor physical play or visits to local sports and leisure centres are particularly important when the weather limits opportunities for outdoor play. The outdoors can provide a scale and freedom for a type of play that is difficult to replicate indoors – for example, outdoors there are opportunities for children to:

✔ dig a garden

✔ explore woodland

✔ run on the grass and roll down a grassy slope

✔ pedal a car across a hard surface.

Physically challenging activities that involve safe risk-taking help children to build and extend their strength and fitness levels. You need to plan activities that are interesting to children, and that offer physical challenges and plenty of opportunities for physical activity. When assessing risk and challenge in physical play, you need to decide whether the activity is developmentally appropriate. Children quickly become frustrated if activities are *too* challenging or difficult; but they also lose interest in activities that are lacking in challenge or that they find too easy.

Reflecting on practice

Taking your cue from children

Rebecca, Shana and Chris work in a nursery setting with children aged three to five years. On quieter days, they like to take the children to the local park. One day, they plan an outing with ten children. Rebecca, the room leader, ensures that they have drinks, first aid kit and mobile phones with them. She has checked that all the parents and carers have signed up-to-date outing permission slips.

As they walk through the park, four-year-old twins Chloe and Oscar run ahead to a fallen tree. The other children are delighted by their find and rush to join them. Rebecca decides that they will stop here to let the children play. The staff help the children to climb and balance, and encourage them to jump off the lower end of the tree trunk onto the soft grass. The children love the activity and it promotes much discussion when they return to the setting.

The next time they plan to go to the park, Rebecca includes Shana and Chris in thinking of ways to promote the children's movement skills as they play. They decide to take rubber rings, markers, and a canvas tunnel, and they set about making an obstacle course that incorporates the fallen tree as a central obstacle. The children are shown the course, how to complete it and are supported to have a go, one at a time. The children waiting for their turn join in with the staff, shouting encouragement. Chris decides to vary the course after every child has had a turn, and he involves the children in helping him. The children are encouraged to offer their ideas, and are supported in working as a team to put the objects in the right places.

- List the areas of development being promoted.
- How are the children being empowered during this activity?
- This activity can be extended in many ways to promote children's movement and balance skills. Think of other activities that could be used with the children, incorporating the children's interests, such as the fallen tree.

Theoretical frameworks in relation to children's physical development

Motor skills and learning: cause and effect

One of the most important cognitive skills to develop in the first two years of life is learning about cause and effect. Young babies have difficulty with determining cause and effect, but as they develop, they are increasingly able to understand the cause-and-effect relationship – and then can intentionally make the desired result of an action occur. Research shows that motor play contributes to this kind of causal thinking. For example, one study found that the longer seven-month-old babies played with a toy that produced an interesting result, the better they were able to cause that result to occur again in later play. In the study, babies were provided with a toy that made a noise when they pushed a button. When presented with the toy again after a period of time, the infants immediately and repeatedly pushed the button, suggesting that they had learnt how to perform an action to cause the sound.

'Back to sleep' and 'Prone to play'

Recent research has shown that *positioning* babies properly for play will improve their motor skills. The 'back-to-sleep' campaign, begun in 1992 to protect babies from sudden infant death syndrome (SIDS) has led to an unfortunate trend: some parents are placing their babies on their backs during waking periods as well. In addition, the increased use of car seats and bouncy chairs also mean that many babies are left with fewer opportunities for playing on their tummies or backs. The research shows that babies who are placed on their tummies to play have improved motor skills compared with those who spend a lot of their waking hours on their backs. Current advice use the phrases: 'back to sleep' and 'prone to play' to remind parents and practitioners of the importance of tummy time for babies.

Arnold Gesell (1880–1961): norms of development

In the 1930s Arnold Gesell mapped out some norms of development (normative measurement was discussed in Chapter 6). These Gesell Development Schedules were used with children between four weeks and six years of age to chart milestones in each child's development as they unfolded. Gesell believed that normal development progressed according to a set sequence. His milestones could be used to check that the pattern of development was 'normal'. Gesell's developmental scales looked at motor, adaptive, language and personal–social areas. If children reached particular milestones, such as walking, within the 'normal' age range, then their development was said to be making 'normal' progress. Gesell's theory has been criticised by other psychologists because he did not readily acknowledge that there are individual and cultural differences in child development, and his focus on developmental norms implied that what is typical for each age is also what is desirable.

Sally Goddard Blythe: *The Well-balanced Child*

Sally Goddard Blythe is a consultant in neurodevelopmental education and writer of many books, including *The Well-balanced Child*. She states:

> *without balance we could not stand, walk nor run. We couldn't see images in sharp detail as we move, or navigate without visual landmarks, or perhaps even think clearly.*

She describes the importance of balance for a child in the following ways:

- Balance is the first of the sensory systems to mature and is an essential player in how the brain interprets information from the other senses. How a child sees, hears and feels the world around him is all intimately connected to the functioning of balance.

- Balance provides the platform for the development of coordination, stable eye movements and visual perception – or how a child 'sees' the world. These abilities are crucial to all aspects of learning, from being able to control the body at sports to being able to sit still, track a moving object at speed such as catching a ball, or more slowly to control the eye movements needed to follow along a line of print when reading.

- Balance is 'the art of not moving'; the ability to remain totally still is the most advanced of all levels of movement. It is really hard for a young child to be still, because they have not done enough moving yet. It can take seven years for the vestibular pathways to be fully developed. A child who continues to have difficulty being still as they get older needs *more* opportunities for movement, rather than fewer.

- Balance is also important for emotional stability in order to feel secure, perceive the outside world as it is and to be in control of oneself. When balance is disturbed, this can result in physical and psychological feelings of anxiety with no obvious external cause. Just as the balance mechanism itself is hidden from view, so the origins of anxiety, avoidance and depression can also have a hidden cause.

Reflecting on practice

- How does the planning and layout of the environment in your setting facilitate physical development through the characteristics of effective learning?
- Is there room to run, jump, stretch and climb both indoors and out? If not, how can you achieve this, making sure, for example, that 15 minutes of walking to the park is balanced by 15 minutes of physical activity that leaves both practitioners and children out of breath?
- Are opportunities for physical activity balanced by opportunities for rest and quiet and provision of regular healthy snacks and drinks?

Forest Schools

In an attempt to raise standards of physical development, Forest Schools were introduced to Britain in 1995. The Forest School initiative was developed in Scandinavia in the 1950s and has been rapidly developing in England and Wales since 2000. The idea is to use a woodland setting as an 'outdoor classroom' as a way of helping young people learn about the natural world. A qualified Forest School leader devises a programme of learning that is based on the children's interests and which allows them to build on skills from week to week, at their own pace. The programmes are designed to give children a varied experience of the woodland through experimental and hand-on tasks and activities.

Forest Schools provide a safe woodland environment for the children to explore, embedded in routine that is established early within the programme. Forest Schools also place an emphasis on children assessing levels of risk and challenge for themselves. (See also Chapter 18 for information about Forest Schools.)

Moving on

Overview of the brain

Pre-birth

Brain development starts within a week of conception. The different parts of the brain, such as the brain stem, thalamus and cerebellum, are built during pregnancy. These provide the basic brain functions that help the baby live. If you think about the brain as a computer, these structures are the 'hardware'. By the time an embryo is eight weeks old, the cells which will develop into the neo-cortex (the grey matter on the outside of the brain) have developed and the lower parts of the brain are established.

The growth of the embryo's nerve cells are influenced by:

- genetically controlled messages the cells send to each other
- hormones and growth substances the cells produce
- nerve impulses sent through the nerve connection networks
- input from the wider environment through the mother's body.

At birth

The baby's brain contains an estimated 180 billion neurons (brain cells) but is the only body organ incomplete at birth because these neurons are mostly yet to be connected. This is like the 'software' of the brain.

As cells grow, connections are made through the development of synapses, which is called synaptogenesis.

- A neuron is a cell that is part of the brain.
- Each neuron has a cell body and develops an axon and dendrites.
- Axons are the part of the neuron that sends signals to another neuron.
- Dendrites receive the incoming signals from another neuron. Each neuron can have many dendrites. As the dendrites multiply, a more complex network develops.
- The synapse is the small space that separates the nerve cells from the dendrites. A synapse forms when the axon of one neuron hooks up with the dendrite of another neuron.
- When the neural connections are made, messages are sent and received through electrical impulses between neuron and through the release of chemicals and hormones, such as seratonin.
- Axons and dendrites do not quite touch; the electrical and chemical message jumps the synaptic gap.

As babies and young children have repeated experiences and practice actions, myelin sheaths are laid down around the axon which improve and hasten the connections between cells. Axons are like electrical wires and the myelin acts like insulation, without which signals would go astray. This is the 'wiring of the brain', an ongoing process of connecting neurons and consolidating trillions of synapses to form neural pathways.

A neural pathway is a series of synapses that have formed a network in the brain. The pathway is a reliable set of connections that can then be activated by a particular experience, such as buttoning your coat. The construction of these pathways are influenced by environmental factors and by genetic inheritance.

In the first two months of life, the brain is more active than it ever will be again, making connections a very rapid rate (there may be 1,000 trillion synapses in the brain by eight months). In the first 12 months it grows more rapidly than any other part of the body, to three-quarters of its adult size.

If the brain just continued to grow along with all the new connections, our brains would be far too big for our skulls. So, just as important as synaptogenesis is synaptic pruning (the dying off of cells). Synaptic pruning means that weaker pathways that are not used or are unnecessary disappear.

After the first birthday, pruning occurs quickly and by 10 years old a child has about 500 trillion synapses, which is the same as the average adult. Pruning occurs for about 12 years but the brain maintains flexibility for future learning.

During the first months of life the cerebral cortex gradually takes over more and more functions from the sub-cortex, which is the part of the brain controlling all reflex actions. This take-over by the cerebral cortex enables the baby to make more deliberate voluntary actions.

Also the two hemispheres of the brain will establish more interconnections through the corpus calloscum (the thick band of nerve fibres that join the two sides of the brain), with each hemisphere becoming more specialised. This process continues well into middle childhood

The brain continues to organise and develop specialist functions, for example the ability to read or to play an instrument. A post mortem on the brain of a musician, for example, would show that more of the brain was specialised to hear and reproduce music. This reflects the 'plasticity' of the human brain; the brain is malleable and the human mind is flexible and creative. Although areas may take the lead on a particular function (like speech for example), there is no single place where all the decisions are made or all the information is stored.

Neuroscience and early education

Because the brain grows so rapidly in the first years of life, ideas about critical periods of synaptic growth have developed. These ideas come from studies that showed that 'enriched' environments increased synaptic density in rats and have led to some people believing that 'earlier is better' in children's learning. For example, this has resulted in practices such as exposing babies to flash cards or listening to Mozart, thinking that this will increase synaptic growth and therefore lead to greater intelligence.

These ideas have been discredited as it has been shown that any initial spurt of synaptic growth evens out and reverts to 'normal' levels later on. As Gopnik et al. (1999) point out, in the early experiments, the rats 'enriched' environment was actually just more like their natural wild environment, whereas the laboratory was a 'deprived' environment, which is what is damaging to development. They emphasise that what babies and young children need is not 'hot-housing' but involvement in the activities of everyday life with an interested and nurturing adult.

The development of the brain and the young child's physical experience

The brain is tightly connected to the body through the spinal cord, the **autonomic nervous system** and the neuroendocrine system. These are vital in carrying messages to and from the brain. Neuroscience confirms Piaget's theory: sensory-motor experiences are a primary source of information for babies and young children and play an important role in their acquisition of knowledge about the world, other people and themselves. Feedback from the body (tension in the muscles, sensory information from the skin, eyes, nose, mouth, ears) tells the brain where we are, what we are experiencing and who we are.

Think about ideas

The following texts will support your learning in this area:

Carter, R., 1999, *Mapping the Mind*, London: Seven Dials.

Eliot, L., 1999, *Early Intelligence. How the Brain and Mind Develop in the First Five Years of Life*, London: Penguin.

Gopnik, A., Meltzoff, A., Kuhl, P., 1999, *How Babies Think*, London: Weidenfield and Nicolson.

Karmiloff-Smith, A., 1994, *Baby it's You*, London: Ebury Press.

Karmiloff-Smith, A., 1995, 'The Extraordinary Journey from Foetus through Infancy', *Journal of Child Psychology and Psychiatry*, 36, 1293–315.

Developmental movement play

The ideas introduced above are central to Jabadao's approach to developmental movement play (www.jabadao.org). They see movement play as enabling children to use their bodies as a way of knowing themselves and the world, through physical and sensory exploration.

Their approach is based on the idea that perceptual awareness, the development of the brain and the development of early movement patterns develop in parallel. For the higher levels of the brain (the cortex) to work, there needs to be sensory integration, which requires that the lower levels of the brain (the sub-cortex or mid-brain) sorts information accurately. Therefore developmental movement play emphasises two important aspects of movement:

1 opportunities for children to indulge in free-flow, child-led, spontaneous movement play

2 attention to specific early movement patterns and activities that appear to prompt neurological development.

They have identified the following as being neurologically significant activities:

Belly crawling:

● stimulates horizontal eye-tracking and the nerves that pull the eyes into alignment

● helps coccyx alignment and strengthens the arches in the feet

● promotes stability of the neck, spine and hips

● is connected to brain functions that ensure accurate perception of pain, heat, cold and hunger

● creates a feeling of 'vertical throughness', which helps the child to feel grounded.

Creeping/crawling:

● stimulates visual convergence and promotes eye–hand coordination

● helps shoulder, hip and wrist rotation

● supports the development of the corpus callosum and thereby the connections between the brain's two hemispheres, whose functions include memory retrieval, sorting and sequencing

● enables the integration of vestibular (nervous system), proprioceptive and visual systems.

Bette Lamont, a developmental movement consultant in USA, recommends that between the ages of two-and-a-half months and seven months, babies should spend at least an hour of their day on their tummies (www.developmentalmovement.org).

She also suggests that using 'containing' equipment such as baby walkers, lay back chairs and bouncy swings interfere with necessary physical and neurological connections; concerns that are shared in reports on brain development in the Zero to Three journal (www.zerotothree.org).

In this section, consider the idea that development is a constant interaction between the emerging structures of the brain and the child's experience of the world. Read the sections below and reflect on your practices that enable children to be involved in everyday learning experiences with an interested and nurturing practitioner and that support the integration of the senses and the body through movement.

Look, listen and note

Answers to Observing Isla (page 164)

1 Isla has just had her second birthday.

2 These are some of the things you may have listed (you might have found more). Isla has learnt:

● that you need to watch your feet as well as your hands

● if you hit something with your foot, it moves

● you have to aim at the ball, not just swing your leg

● not to give up, even when it is difficult

● not to run too fast when you go after a ball

● to slow down before trying to stop

● to start stopping at a certain distance ahead, depending on the speed at which you are moving

● how to assess speed, distance and force

● the connections between cause and effect

● to keep trying, because you can succeed

● that learning is fun.

Further reading, weblinks and resources

Meggitt, C., 2012, *An Illustrated Guide to Child Development* (3rd edn), Oxford: Pearson.

JABADAO

A national charity that works in partnership with the education, health, arts and social care sectors to bring about a change in the way people work with the body and movement.
www.jabadao.org

England

Learning, Playing and Interacting: Good practice in the Early Years Foundation Stage

A toolkit to support early years practitioners' work with advice on pedagogy, practice and assessment.
www.keap.org.uk/documents/ LearningPlayingInteracting.pdf

Start4Life and Play4Life (Department of Health)

The early years section of the Department of Health's Change4Life campaign, aimed at health care and childcare professionals. Active play resources are available which can be downloaded from:
www.dh.gov.uk (search Start4Life)

Play England

www.playengland.org.uk

Wales

Framework for Children's Learning for 3- to 7-year-olds in Wales (Welsh Government)

www.wales.gov.uk

Foundation Phase Child Development Profile Guidance

This helps practitioners observe children across all areas of learning, including physical development.
www.wales.gov.uk

Physical development

A booklet which provides guidance to support the physical development area of learning in the Foundation Phase Framework for Children's Learning for 3- to 7-year-olds in Wales.
www.wales.gov.uk

Scotland

Pre-Birth to Three. Positive Outcomes for Scotland's Children and Families

This replaces 'Birth to three: Supporting our Youngest Children' and gives guidance for students and staff working with or on behalf of the youngest children and their families in Scotland. Produced by Learning and Teaching Scotland.
www.ltscotland.org.uk/earlyyears

Curriculum for Excellence: health and wellbeing experiences and outcomes (Learning and Teaching Scotland)

www.curriculumforexcellencescotland.gov.uk

Northern Ireland

Understanding the Foundation Stage (Northern Ireland Council for Curriculum, Examinations and Assessment (CCEA))

www.nicurriculum.org.uk

Learning outdoors in the early years

A resource book (CCEA) which shows how the outdoor learning environment can be used for planning activities across all the areas of learning. You can also find this resource at the following link:
www.nicurriculum.org.uk

Learning through play in the early years

A resource book (CCEA) which provides guidance on provision and progression in play and is intended as a starting point for practitioners in planning activities. This can also be found at
www.nicurriculum.org.uk

References

Carter, R., 1999, *Mapping the Mind*, London: Seven Dials.

Eliot, L., 1999, *Early Intelligence. How the Brain and Mind Develop in the First Five Years of Life*, London: Penguin.

Gopnik, A., Meltzoff, A., Kuhl, P., 1999, *How Babies Think*, London: Weidenfield and Nicolson.

Karmiloff-Smith, A., 1994, *Baby it's You*, London: Ebury Press.

Karmiloff-Smith, A., 1995, 'The Extraordinary Journey from Foetus through Infancy', Journal of Child Psychology and Psychiatry, 36, 1293–315.

Chapter 10

Emotional, personal and social development: feelings, identity and relationships

This chapter looks at the fundamentally important areas of emotional, personal and social development, and emphasises how they are connected to each other and to all other aspects of development. It sets out key aspects of each area from birth through early years and considers the influence of both innate biological and environmental, cultural factors. The role of the practitioner in promoting positive emotional, personal and social development is explored, particularly in relation to **anti-bias practice**, the key person approach (see Chapter 4) and **transitions**.

KEY TERMS

Anti-bias practice – Actively working against bias, prejudice and discrimination in early years practice.
Transition – The movement and change from one group or setting to another or from one activity to another.

What is emotional, personal and social development?

Emotional, personal and social development involves helping children to:

- develop a positive sense of themselves and others
- form positive relationships and develop respect for others
- develop social skills and learn how to manage their feelings
- understand appropriate behaviour in groups; and
- have confidence in their own abilities.

The development of emotional, personal and social understanding are commonly written about and discussed together because they are so closely related to each other. For example, babies and young children learn about their emotions in their close relationships with others, and in these relationships they get feedback about who they are. This in turn helps them to understand other people and their feelings better.

Judy Dunn (1993: 2) says that 'Relationships are viewed as the contexts in which socialisation takes place ... in which communication skills are acquired ... in which the regulation of emotion develops and...in which the self-system has its origins'. In other words, learning about who you are, what feelings are, how to behave and interact with others, all happen in relationships. This reflects the interrelationship of personal, social and emotional development.

However, the danger in grouping these aspects together is that the depth and detail of each may be reduced, or one of them may be overlooked. So it is important, in practices such as observation and assessment, that each separate aspect is addressed specifically and also linked to the others.

Emotional development means how children come to recognise their feelings, how they begin to regulate or control their emotions and express them in socially accepted ways.

Emotional development involves:

- growth of feelings about, and awareness of, oneself
- development of feelings towards other people.

Personal (or personality) development is to do with a child's growing self-awareness and self-knowledge, and involves the development of identity and self-esteem.

Personal development includes:

- dispositions and attitudes: how children develop interest in – and become excited and motivated about – their learning
- self-confidence and self-esteem: how children have a sense of their own value and develop an understanding of the need for sensitivity to significant events in their own and other people's lives
- self-care and independence: how children gain a sense of self-respect and concern for their own personal hygiene and care and how they develop independence.

Social development is about understanding other people and how to build relationships with them. It includes social cognition: the ability to think about relationships and to understand how the social world works and how you are expected to behave within it.

Social development includes:

- forming relationships: this refers to the importance of children forming good relationships with others and working alongside others sociably
- behaviour and self-control: how children develop a growing understanding of what is right and wrong

and why, along with understanding the impact of their words and actions on themselves and others

- sense of community: how children understand and respect their own needs, views, cultures and beliefs and those of other people.

It is important to remember that it is not possible to separate emotional, personal and social development from other areas of development. Positive social interactions and relationships are now widely accepted as important in children's cognitive development, as the process of thinking and talking about emotions in social relationships includes the kind of problem-solving processes that are essential to cognitive understanding. Also, children's learning is deeply affected by their current emotional state, the relationships they have with the people around them and how they feel about themselves as learners.

The concept of well-being is often mostly related to positive emotional, personal and social states but also includes intellectual, physical, health and spiritual experiences, which makes it a useful concept for maintaining a holistic view of children's development and learning (Manning-Morton 2014).

Nature and nurture in children's emotional, personal and social development

In emotional, personal and social development, as in all areas of development, different theories emphasise the influence of biology or environment to different degrees. But as discussed in Chapter 6, it is now generally accepted that development happens as a result of both.

For example, during evolution, emotions developed to be useful in our survival. They prepare our bodies to respond to danger and threat, and cause physiological changes that underpin our behaviours, such as increasing the blood flow to our hands, or making it easier to grasp a weapon to fight off danger. However, our social learning will help us to think about and understand whether it is appropriate in the given situation to fight, and we will modify our behaviour accordingly! (Goleman 1996)

In personal development, it is clear that all children have unique personalities and will develop in different ways. This will reflect their genetic inheritance and innate temperament, and also the influence of the family and culture they are born into. Ideas about what constitutes an adequate or satisfactory person are socially and culturally constructed, with particular traits and social behaviours being encouraged accordingly. For example, in China inhibition or shyness is seen as

reflecting social maturity but in North America it is perceived to reflect immaturity (Cole 1998).

Social development is the area that is seen to be most influenced by children's environment, with behaviourism very influential on thinking in this respect (see Chapter 6, p. 110 for a definition and information on behaviourism). However the interpretation of social behaviour is also influenced by the responses of others to the child's biological make-up; their gender, ethnicity and abilities. And social understanding in children on the autistic spectrum (see Chapter 2, p. 32 for more information) is affected by how the connections in their brains work.

An interactionist view of development (see Chapter 6, p. 112 for more information on interactionist theory) would see babies and young children coming to understand their feelings, selves and other people through a combination of biological and social interactions: the physical system of the chemicals in the brain, the nervous system and muscles interacting with the social system of the child's experiences, relationships and communications with others in the family and community.

Children's feelings: developing emotional understanding

Primary and secondary emotions

Charles Darwin suggested that humans have an innate and universal range of facial expressions for the primary emotions of happiness, anger, disgust, sadness, surprise and fear (Darwin 1872 cited in Harris 1989). These primary emotions are then built upon through the child's sociocultural experience. In this way humans develop a range of secondary emotions such as hope, anxiety, excitement, frustration and so on that are blends of the basic emotions. These blended emotions take on slightly different meanings and modes of expression through growing up in a particular culture, with the result that there are even some named emotions that cannot be translated into another language as the meaning of the emotion is different (Wulff 2007).

Very young babies' emotions are unconscious; they are stored in the limbic system (an inner part of the brain which is responsible for *emotions and memories*) in the brain as the connections that process conscious feelings are still being made in the cerebral cortex (responsible for *higher brain functions, including sensation, voluntary muscle movement, thought, reasoning, and memory*). From about six-months-old, more connections are made between neurons (brain cells) as a result of the child's experience, and pre-existing feelings start to become conscious. It is through the connections in the cortex (the outer layer of the brain) that children start to be able to know and understand their emotional responses. These connections begin to be made at about six-months-old and reach maximum density about two years later but they are not all completely firmed up into neural pathways until early adulthood (Eliot 1999). Learning about emotions and how to regulate them is a long process!

Because the feelings of babies and very young children are not mediated by the connections in the cortex, they feel their emotions very immediately. Also, because babies and young children are totally dependent on others for survival, they feel their emotions intensely and therefore express them very directly. If they did not do so, their need for food, shelter, comfort and love could be overlooked and they might not survive (Manning-Morton and Thorp 2003, 2015).

Although babies communicate how they feel very powerfully through crying and screaming, their distress is often general so it can be hard to tell whether a baby is crying from hunger, cold or through wanting a cuddle. This is why the early years practitioner must know the baby very well, have good experience of young babies and be attuned to the baby's needs.

Older babies (approx. 8-15 months):

- start to show fear as they start to become mobile – for example, of heights when he or she is crawling, and of unfamiliar adults
- are now more likely to show signs of anger – for example, if a familiar practitioner or caregiver leaves the room briefly, or if the baby cannot get hold of something he or she wants or it does not respond in the way the baby expects
- are very affectionate when they are shown love
- start to become aware of other people's feelings as they become more aware of their own feelings.

Toddlers and two-year-olds' strong feelings can quickly overwhelm them. This can lead to:

- sobbing with sadness
- jealousy that makes a child want to hit out
- joy that makes a child literally jump and leap with a wildness that is unnerving to many adults
- frustration when something does not go well or they cannot make themselves understood
- tantrums that are full of anger and rage.

But rapidly increasing language skills mean that toddlers and two-year-olds start to be able to explain how they are feeling, especially if they are surrounded by people who talk to them about emotions; for example, 'Mummy, scared' when not enjoying a book about ghosts.

Young children (approx. three to six years) are:

- increasingly able to act in order to manage their emotional states: the child may cover his or her eyes to avoid seeing something he or she does not want to see, or use words to get through an emotionally difficult time; for example, muttering, 'I'll ask Dad to help me. This is hard,' rather than becoming angry and frustrated
- easily afraid at this time – for example, they might be afraid of the dark and so need a night light in their bedroom.

The fears children have are very real to them. Some (especially babies and toddlers) are afraid that their parents or carers might leave them. Some are afraid of loud noises like thunder, of heights (perhaps they do not like to come down from the climbing frame) or of sudden movements, such as a dog leaping up at them. Going to a strange place, like the clinic, might bring on feelings of fear, and many children are afraid of the dark. Sometimes children's fears seem strange to us as there is no clear reason for them. For example, why was two-year-old Poppy scared of the garden ornament with the happy face of the Sun on it, and two-year-old Levi scared of flowers? Whatever the reason, early years practitioners should recognise that the immature cognitive understanding (see Chapter 7 for more information) of the very young child often leads to such fears, which should be taken seriously and addressed kindly and sensitively.

See pp. 186–187 and 190–191 for information on the stages of personal, emotional and social development.

Emotional expression

Children need to express their feelings, and not just through words. They do so through:

- **physical actions** – like running away, stamping with rage, screaming with terror, hitting out, jumping with joy or seeking a cuddle
- **facial expressions** – a pout or blank eyes tell the adult the child is not happy, compared with eyes that are shining with joy
- **the position of the body** – playing alone with the dolls' house or hovering on the edge of a cooking session might indicate that the child wants to join in but does not know how; this may indicate shyness. Playing boats right in the centre of a group of children tells the practitioner something quite different; it may indicate confidence

- **body movements** – children who keep twisting their fingers together are not at ease, compared with children who sit in a relaxed way.

Children under emotional stress

When children are under emotional stress, they react differently according to their personality. They may:

- become aggressive
- be very quiet, watchful and tense
- begin bedwetting or soiling themselves
- find it difficult to eat
- return to babyish ways – regressing in development, they may want a bottle again or a comforter; they might want to be held and cuddled or carried about; they might want help with eating and dressing.

When children are under emotional stress, their behaviour can change quite quickly. It is important, therefore, that early years practitioners are alert to the changes listed above and that they respond sensitively and with understanding.

Because of their relatively immature neurological, linguistic and cognitive development, toddlers and two-year-olds are more prone to emotional stress and overload arising from everyday changes and frustrations; this can result in emotional collapses or tantrums (Manning-Morton and Thorp 2015).

However, if a child is frequently breaking down or exhibits changes in behaviour as described above, it is important to talk with your line manager about your observations. If there is an obvious cause at home or in the setting– for example, a change in key person, a new baby or a sick parent – the discussion will be taken further between the key person and the child's parents, and opened up to the staff team to agree what steps could be taken in practice.

Where children continue to experience such difficulties for more than a few weeks, and where there is no obvious cause, it may be important, in partnership with the parents, to involve another professional, such as a clinical child psychologist.

It is neither possible, nor desirable, to relieve a child of all his or her anxiety. If people did not feel anxiety, they might not hesitate before making a decision that could be bad for themselves or harm another person. Sometimes anxious energy is channelled into work, sport or art – without that anxiety, perhaps there would be no great artistic or sporting achievements. However, it is our job as caring practitioners to help a child learn to manage their anxiety and, when they are very young, that means managing the anxiety for them.

Guidelines for good practice

Dealing with children's fears and anxieties

Excessive or extreme anxiety can lead to a great deal of pain and suffering, and can prevent children from learning or enjoying the company of others. Early years practitioners can help in the following ways:

- ✓ developing trusting relationships with key children
- ✓ talking about fearful feelings and showing the child that you understand
- ✓ later on, you can help children to use imaginative play – for example, in the home area, dolls' house or toy garage – to face and deal with their fears and worries
- ✓ allowing a child to take out his or her aggressive feelings on a soft toy if they are feeling jealous and anxious about the arrival of a new baby at home. This channels the aggression, giving the child permission to express his or her feelings
- ✓ showing understanding, while remaining confident yourself – for example, soothe a child who is very fearful of loud noises, while showing by your own responses that the noises do not bother you
- ✓ creating cosy corners within the group room where children can feel safe and relaxed.

Putting feelings into words

It helps children to manage their feelings if they can put them into words. The child who can say, 'Stop hitting me! That hurts! I don't like it!' has found an appropriate way to deal with an unpleasant situation.

- The cries that a baby makes are early attempts to 'tell' others how he or she feels. By trying to 'tune in' to the baby and understand the cause of his or her distress, you help the baby's developing confidence by showing that he or she is understood by other people.
- Toddlers and two-year-olds (particularly those with limited language) will use physical means to express themselves. This may be hitting out, running away or curling up in a corner and hiding.
- Early on, children may shout a term of abuse in a difficult situation rather than using appropriate words. This may be a step forward along the way from physical hitting (via use of unacceptable language) to an appropriate expression of feelings in words. Introducing gestures and signing such as Makaton for 'No' or 'Stop' can help at this stage.
- It takes time, experience and adult support for young children to learn how to express their

feelings in words and to negotiate in dialogue with others. It can help to give them examples of sharp-sounding words, such as 'Stop it!' so that they can take control of situations. Children learn the language of feelings through real situations that hold great meaning and that engage their whole attention.

- Stories that relate to an area of difficulty for the child can help them to develop more understanding. Some children find it hard to say goodbye to their parents at the start of nursery. Hearing a story such as *Owl Babies* by Martin Waddell might be a way to start talking about those feelings of loss, and the relief the babies feel when their mother returns.

The role of the early years practitioner in promoting emotional development

From early babyhood, children need practitioners and adults generally who can 'tune in' to them and try to understand what they are communicating, and respond with understanding and empathy. The baby who cries, and is soothed by a carer who waits to see if he or she is hungry, tired or cold, learns that his or her needs can be understood by another, that crying can be understood as something with a meaning. On the other hand, the baby who experiences repeated anger from a carer when he or she cries, or is ignored and rejected, can learn that emotions are incomprehensible (i.e. that they cannot understand emotions) and that the world is unpredictable and harsh (Lieberman 1995).

Also, if carers do not think about what a child means when he or she cries or gets angry, the child, in turn, will be less able to think about how other people feel. Empathy is the ability to understand and share the feelings of another, and should not be confused with sympathy. Some people find it easy to appreciate how someone else is feeling by imagining themselves in that person's position.

At the same time as remembering the importance of 'tuning in', it is also crucial to hold on to the fact that the baby or young child is a separate being. It is important for young children to become their own people. Toddlers need to be allowed to do things for themselves. It might take five times as long for a toddler to put on their own shoes as it would for you to do it for him or her, but it is important to give them the time to do it. However, the strength of the feeling of frustration that may arise from not being able to put the shoes on may threaten to overwhelm or overcome the child; in which case they need practitioners who empathise, understand and support them in a way that

▲ **Figure 10.1** The role of the adult early years practitioner in promoting emotional development

will help them to learn to deal with the strength of their feelings. Feelings are hard to manage – even adults do not always succeed in dealing with how they feel.

Play

Play helps children to understand their feelings and to experiment with showing emotions. They can become the cross mum, the grumpy shopkeeper, the kind aunty when a child falls over, or the angry bus driver. It also helps them to experience what someone else might feel when someone is cross, grumpy, kind or angry towards them. A toddler pushing toy cars round and round a track can gain a great deal of comfort and a sense of control; equally, smashing trains into each other or into bridges can be a good way of expressing and gaining control over feelings of anger and violence.

Being actively involved in social play opportunities with children means practitioners can name and suggest a wide range of emotional states thereby expanding children's emotional vocabulary.

 Theory and theorists: Bion (1897–1979), containment

From psychodynamic theory comes the notion of **containment**, developed by Wilfred Bion (1962).

In Bion's model, a baby will have an experience of frustration, such as hunger. If an adult – for example, the baby's mother – can receive this unprocessed emotion from the child and think about it, by interpreting the cry as meaning hunger, then the understanding is 'given back' to the baby.

Bion conceptualised this by saying that the baby projects the sensation or feeling into the mother. The mother processes this through what he calls her **reverie**, and returns the projection in a way that the baby can manage. A parent picking up a distressed infant and helping the infant to cope with the feeling by singing, feeding, repositioning or talking to the baby is an example of containment. A parent becoming angry or distressed with a baby's communication (crying, 'whinging', seeking attention, and so on) is probably failing to contain the baby.

The regular experience of containment helps the baby to develop the capacity to think, to turn the raw experience of discomfort into a thought: 'I am hungry.' On the other hand, if the baby's raw experience is rejected – for example, the adult is cross at the constant crying and shouts angrily at the baby – then the baby is simply given back the raw emotion and does not develop the structures for thinking.

According to this theory, if the baby experiences enough containment, he or she becomes increasingly able to manage frustration by thinking. Those thoughts might include being confident that she will be fed soon, or being able to communicate hunger. If the baby constantly experiences the raw emotion being returned, thinking will not develop and the baby will be terrified by powerful emotion.

The baby's needs can never be met fully. There will be times when it is not possible for the practitioner to offer the function of containment. If the frequency or intensity of these times is not overwhelming, the child manages it through symbolisation – representing things in play or in language, for example. So a toddler who is angry about parting from his or her mother at nursery might direct this angry energy into very focused play in the home corner and not wish anyone to disturb or interrupt him or her.

KEY TERMS

Containment – This refers to an adult or practitioner's state of mind in relation to a baby or young child. Through containment, the adult can receive the baby's communications of anxiety, pain, distress or pleasure.

Reverie – The adult can process the baby's communications and hand them back to the baby, either sharing the pleasure in a loving and intimate interaction, or handing back distressing thoughts in a way that the baby can manage.

Reflecting on practice

Containment

Jaydeen is three years old. It is five o'clock in the afternoon on a hot day. Her key person, Tara, sees out of the corner of her eye that Jaydeen is struggling to put the marble run (construction set) together. After a few minutes, Jaydeen flings a piece to the floor in frustration and shouts so loudly that the child playing next to her starts to cry.

Tara comes over and sits close to Jaydeen, comforting the child who is crying. Then she says to Jaydeen, 'I think you're probably fed up because you're hot and tired. Shall we all sit together and have a cuddle and a story?' Jaydeen puts her thumb into her mouth and snuggles up to Tara.

1 How does Tara provide a containing function for Jaydeen's emotions?

2 How might this change things for Jaydeen?

The pattern of this development is formed in the baby's early experiences, and remains as a pattern through childhood and into adult life. So Bion's theory is not just about very young babies; you can use it when thinking about older children, too.

Who am I? Developing a sense of self

The development of self is a central aspect of children's development. Indeed some neuro-scientists such as Blakemore (1998) would suggest that this aspect is a main focus for the brain in the early years of development.

Babies and young children enter the world already with certain abilities and characteristics that are unique to them and that will influence who they become; they are not blank slates or empty vessels. Each of us is born with genetically determined physical features and also biologically influenced ways of responding to the environment and to other people (Schaffer 2006). These characteristic patterns are our temperaments, which continue through childhood and into adulthood. It used to be thought that personality was fixed at birth (just as it used to be thought that intelligence was fixed at birth and unchangeable thereafter). But, as in other areas of development, a child's personality development may be partly biological, but is also hugely influenced by environmental factors such as:

- life experience
- community culture

- physical challenges, including special needs and disabilities
- the people children meet.

Personal development is often discussed using these ideas:

- The 'I' self; one's private inner self and awareness of your own distinctiveness that continues over time. This comes from your subjective of experience and how you interpret it; this is self-awareness.
- The 'me' self; our self as shown and known by other people. This is our self-concept; the mental representations we have of ourselves which answer the question, 'Who am I?'
- The 'looking glass-self'; our understanding of ourselves as others see us. We internalise the views of others and attempt to integrate them into our self-concept.

(Schaffer 2006)

Learning about who you are continues through life with all the experiences it brings. Although the influence of genetic inheritance and early experiences resonate or resound throughout, self-concept can change over the life-span.

Sequences of development

Young babies

- From the first day of life, babies have the beginnings of a sense of self. Their ability to imitate adult gestures such as tongue protrusion (sticking their tongue out) means that they are able to differentiate between what they see another doing and an action they make with their own body (Gopnik et al. 1999). This indicates early self-awareness.
- In their earliest days babies become aware of where their bodies begin and their mother's/ carer's ends through being held. This, along with the physical experiences of suckling, digestion and defecation (excretion), is an infant's earliest experience of their physical self.
- As they develop the ability to control their limbs and make deliberate physical actions, babies experience the impact of their actions on objects; this gives them feedback about themselves.
- The baby comes to know their own feet, hands and limbs through their proprioceptive (see Chapter 7, p. 123 for definition) sense.
- Babies' ideas about who they are come mainly through experiencing the effect of their behaviours on other people (such as crying, cooing and smiling) and the responses from those people towards them.

Older babies

- They like to look at themselves in the mirror.
- They know their name and respond to it.

 Theory and theorists: the mirror test

The mirror test sets out to show the development of physical self-recognition. The test suggests that before three months old, babies show little interest in their reflection, but at about three to four months old they reach out to touch the reflection they see. At this stage they do not appear to recognise the reflection as themselves. At 10 months babies will look around on seeing an adult approaching in the mirror, which indicates that they understand that what is in the mirror is only a reflection. Then at 15–18 months old children will touch their own noses in the 'rouge' test rather than their reflection when some red powder is surreptitiously (secretly) put on their nose; indicating that they recognise the reflection as themselves (Smith, Cowie and Blades 1998).

Toddlers and two-year-olds

At this stage, children:

- understand themselves principally through their physical selves; they explore what their bodies can do and produce and enjoy using their developing physical skills
- recognise themselves initially through current movements or expressions, but very soon this is diminished and they recognise themselves in photographs in which they have different clothes or hair styles
- increasingly show that they have minds of their own. They love to do things for themselves – this is called **autonomy**. The toddler's growing autonomy goes hand-in-hand with increased **social referencing** (See page 187 for definitions)
- become increasingly self-conscious – for example, feeling pride, embarrassment, shame and guilt
- love their efforts to be appreciated: 'You've found Martha's coat for her, thank you.' They are sensitive to feedback from familiar adults. This feedback can make the child feel securely loved and capable of doing lots of things; 'Wow, you've put out all the

Think about ideas

Observe a baby between 4 and 18 months old playing with a mirror. Do you see any of the evidence of self-awareness discussed in the mirror test above?

KEY TERMS

Autonomy – Being able to do things for yourself, without needing help or waiting for permission.

Social referencing – This is when a baby or young child checks an adult's emotional response before taking action. An example would be a baby who sees something on the grass in a park and looks back at her mother before deciding whether to crawl confidently forward to grab it, or to stay away and watch warily.

Reactivity – This refers to the intensity and speed of the child's emotional responses, the child's ability to focus attention and the child's movement.

cups on the table ready for snack time!'. It can also lead them to feel incompetent and anxious about doing anything new in case they get it wrong; for example it is not a good idea to say 'Careful, don't drop them,' or 'No, the cups don't go there.'

- are beginning to form their social identities, understanding for example that they are a girl or a boy.

Young children (approx. three to six years)

At this age, children:

- are establishing a stable self-concept and are less in need of adult praise or feedback to feel emotions like pride or disappointment
- have a terrific desire to be accepted by other children and adults, but also need to be an individual in his or her own right; children with a strong sense of identity learn to be strong people
- begin to be able to describe aspects of their personality such as 'shy' and identify roles such as 'a big sister'
- are developing an understanding of themselves as part of different social categories
- are beginning to understand that their gender identity remains stable and does not change.

Personality and temperament

Temperament is the style of behaviour that is natural to the child. So the child's temperament influences the personality that emerges.

Laura E. Berk (2006: 412) summarises Mary Rothbart's theory that babies and young children have differing levels of emotionality, sociability and **reactivity**. Reactivity describes their:

- levels of activity
- capacity to pay attention for a time
- fearful distress, especially when faced by new situations
- irritable distress, especially finding it difficult to get comfortable, 'fussing'

- positive emotional response and state: how often they appear to be happy and experiencing pleasure.

This way of measuring children's responses led to the identification of three types of temperament:

- The 'easy child' who responds positively to new events and has regular physical functions.
- The 'difficult child' who is irritable has irregular patterns and responds negatively to new events.
- The 'slow to warm up child' who displays passive resistance and has few intense reactions positive or negative but once adapted is more positive.

(Thomas and Chess 1980)

These categories have been broadened recently but can be useful for understanding individual children in our settings as they can help us to have a better understanding of their responses to events. It is very important that early years practitioners do not favour smiling children at the expense of those children who seem more 'difficult' or seem inactive and 'slow to warm up', and it is critical that they do not form negative opinions of children with more difficult temperaments, as each temperament has its positives and negatives. The 'easy' baby who is content to lay back may be very fearful about exploring and crawling, while the 'fussy', wriggly baby who never seems to settle may love the physical sensations of movement and enjoy getting around.

Although there is evidence of the biological source of temperament, it does not mean that our personalities are entirely determined by our genes. As children grow, their temperament can change with their development. Our temperamental 'pre-dispositions' are shaped, strengthened or counteracted through relationships and experiences as we interact with the environment in ways that will change or adjust our basic temperamental patterns.

And of course these interactions are reciprocal (mutual or shared): the cultural context will impact on a baby's temperamental disposition and a baby's behaviours will affect the adults' responses to them and the choices they make for the child (Schaffer 2006).

Developing a social identity

Part of their self-concept is the child's identification with particular social groups or categories. Sex or gender, disability and ethnicity are core issues in identity, and young children are exploring how they are the same and different to others from an early age.

In considering what determines both our individuality and our 'sameness' with others, much of the discussion still centres on the nature versus nurture debate. See Chapter 6, p. 102 for more information.

Clearly there is a biological basis for identity: children are born with particular **chromosomes** and genital differences that categorise them into being male or female, and they are born with different skin tones, hair textures and physical or mental abilities that mean they are more like some groups of people and less like others. But of course these categories of ability and ethnicity are **socially constructed** (as discussed in Chapter 1), as are the different expectations held by different societies about how boys and girls should behave. So the environment we are born into, including the belief systems, values and social and cultural frameworks hugely influences who we become.

Gender identity development

Gender development can be roughly divided into two components. Cognitive understanding begins early on and is about children becoming aware that they and others are biologically male or female. The second aspect is behavioural; how children work out the appropriate roles for themselves and others based on gender expectations in their culture (Derman-Sparks and Edwards 2010). Babies and children understand gender in a number of ways:

- Babies distinguish between male and female voices and faces.
- Toddlers label themselves according to their gender; they know if they are boys or girls and can make that distinction between others. However, they rely on visual cues to make these judgements, and as these cues are culturally determined this can let them down. For example, both men and women can have long and short hair.
- Two-year-olds develop an understanding of gender as a social category but think that their sex can change.
- Children aged between three and six years develop stereotypical behaviour (how girls and boys behave) but also a better understanding of gender and that their own gender will always remain the same.

Racial identity development

Identity development in terms of 'race' or ethnicity, like gender, includes awareness of biological traits and also learning about culturally accepted roles.

- Babies seem to focus more on pictures of faces that are more similar to their own.
- Toddlers and two-year-olds are aware of the physical differences and variations between people and start to think about where they fit in.
- By the age of two-and-a-half, children are beginning to be aware of the cultural aspects of ethnic identity; for example, the different roles men and women play in their families.
- At around the age of three, children may want to know how they got their skin colour, hair texture and eye colour.
- Children will wonder if skin colour, hair colour and texture and eye colour remain constant.
- Children may get confused about racial group names, the actual colour of skin, and why two people of different skin tones are considered part of the same group.

However, in many societies around the world, racial identity formation also means coming to understand the different value ascribed to different groups of people as discussed in Chapter 1.

- From as early as two-and-a-half years, children may show signs of pre-prejudice, that is, discomfort with physical differences.
- Around the age of four, children from minority ethnic groups may express unhappiness with their appearance as they realise that being white is given greater value.
- White children may express discriminatory views.

(Derman-Sparks and Edwards 2010)

The role of the early years practitioner in promoting personal development

The most important practice in supporting babies' and young children's personal development is to know each child really well. This is enabled by:

- implementing an effective key person approach
- working closely with parents
- observing children regularly
- providing play opportunities that are personalised
- implementing an anti-bias approach.

By knowing each child very well, early years practitioners can plan to support different children in different ways.

The shy or withdrawn child

Although it is important for every child to have his or her own personal space and be allowed opportunities to do things alone, some children have difficulty socialising with other children or with adults. There are a number of things that you can do to help a child to overcome his or her shyness.

- Making introductions: when an adult is new to the child, you can introduce them. 'Michael, this is Jane. Jane wants to do a painting. Can you help her to get started? Can you tell her how to find the colours she wants?' The same approach can be taken by asking another more experienced child to help.

- Being welcoming: if a child is shy with adults it can be helpful to join the child with a warm smile, but to say nothing. You might find that a welcoming gesture, such as handing the child a lump of clay if they join the clay table, reassures them.

- Observing children: keeping good observations of children's social relationships is important. If a child who is normally outgoing suddenly becomes quiet, withdrawn and solitary, this should be discussed with the team and parents. Multi-professional help from outside may be required if the problem cannot be solved within the team.

The demanding child

Children can be demanding for many different reasons. Some children – for example, children with no brothers or sisters – are the main focus of their family and are given one-to-one attention by adults most of the time. These children may not have experienced having to share space, playthings or adult attention with other children so may appear over-demanding of adult attention, insecure or ill at ease with other children. These children need sensitive help to become involved in parallel, associative and cooperative social behaviour with other children. Having a negative image of these children as 'spoilt' is not helpful.

Some children are afraid of losing control of situations, maybe because events in their own lives feel out of control. These children may take over the play scenarios; for example in the home area, they may control the other children by saying what the storyline is going to be and by making the other children do as they say. These are the so-called 'bossy' children. But this is another negative and unhelpful label. Such children need an adult to help them to see that the 'story' will be better if other children's ideas are allowed in. It takes a bit of courage for the child to dare to let the play

'free-flow', because no one knows quite how the story will turn out. See p. 377 for more information on free-flow play.

Sibling jealousy can also be a source of demanding behaviour. When a new baby is born, it can be hard for a child who is used to having a lot of attention. Sibling jealousy often results in very demanding behaviour, which may last for some time, until the family adjusts to its new relationship pattern. Recent research shows that the older child needs to feel that he or she is being treated in exactly the same way as the new baby – for example, getting some special attention at times.

An anti-bias approach

All settings are required to have policies that uphold equal opportunities, so that all children and families are given an equal chance to use the setting and access its services. As discussed in Chapter 1, many early years practitioners argue that it is important to go much further than that, and actively oppose bias and discrimination.

Reflecting on practice

Name-calling and harassment can damage a child's positive self-esteem. It is important to help children to develop positive ideas about difference and diversity. Because young children are very interested in differences in physical appearance, they are also very aware of differences in skin colour or clothing.

When Jason, who is mixed-race, met Marcia, who had recently arrived from the Caribbean, he called her 'chocolate face'. The early years practitioner who overheard this first made it clear to Jason that it was not kind to use that sort of language, and that it could make Marcia sad. But the practitioner knew that to really engage with this, she needed to do much more than just deal with the incident then and there. So she set up an area of the nursery with mirrors, skin-tone paints and skin-tone paper, and talked proactively and positively with Jason and other children about their skin colour. A large display of children's self-portraits – some painted with the paints, some drawn in pencil on the skin-tone paper – celebrated the whole range of different skin tones and colours. The message was powerful: everyone was different, but together in one nursery community.

- How do you actively address children's comments such as this in your setting?

- Do you have skin-tone paints and papers – are they always available?

When children are learning English as an additional language, it is important that the child's first language and home languages are valued.

Children with disabilities

The child who has special needs can also quickly lose a good self-image. Children who use a wheelchair, wear glasses, use a hearing aid, walk differently or think differently (e.g. a child with a learning difficulty) would all need to be supported so that they develop a good self-image and positive self-esteem. Other children also need support to understand how and why children are different, and what this involves. They need to understand that when everyone makes it a priority to learn how to help each other and be well informed, the whole community gains and everyone in it can then make a strong and positive contribution.

Because of the embarrassment and ignorance of many people, children with a disability have to come to terms not only with their disability, but also with the way people react to it. It is very important that all children meet a wide range of people so that this kind of 'stranger fear' gradually disappears from society. Children are naturally inquisitive (ask questions) and often talk bluntly or frankly. For example, when Jayda started at nursery, children immediately commented on her standing frame and were curious when the physiotherapist came in to set up her exercise programme. So practitioners let the other children use the standing frame, with Jayda's permission, and allowed them to join in with the exercise sessions too. Children's questions about Jayda's legs were answered honestly, and they were shown how they could help Jayda to enjoy moving around the nursery and how they could help her to join in. This was a much more positive experience for Jayda and her family than the usual stares and embarrassed silence they had experienced when out shopping and in the playground.

Understanding other people and developing social relationships

Humans are social beings; we live in groups. Learning the skills that enable us to do this successfully are crucial and babies, it seems, are born ready to relate to others and with skills that predispose them to being part of a social group. How they learn to do that though is determined by the sociocultural context (discussed on p. 103) into which they are born.

Sequences of development

Young babies (approx. birth to six months)

Young babies:

- take an interest in the human face and voice from birth
- respond to others and make their own communications from birth
- recognise people they know well
- like to be held in the arms of someone they know and love
- smile when interacting with familiar people
- turn to a familiar person's voice, especially their mother
- react when they hear, see or feel their carer's presence (the baby may stop crying, for example). Babies who have a visual impairment often become very still, as if listening and waiting for more information

Older babies (approx. 6–15 months)

At this age, babies:

- are interested in others and want to gain people's attention and respond to them
- enjoy the company of other babies. When they sit together, they touch each other's faces; they look at each other, vocalise and smile at each other
- enjoy the company of older children
- enjoy peek-a-boo games. This is an early example of cooperative social behaviour; it involves turn-taking and is the foundation of having a conversation with someone else
- delight in having a shared idea
- laugh with pleasure
- respond to others' distress by becoming distressed themselves
- begin to expect patterns in face-to-face communication: if the baby smiles, they expect a smile in return; if the baby makes a noise, they are starting a conversation of babbling, in which turn-taking, varying pitch and using facial gestures occur just as much as they do between adults conversing with words
- engage in **social referencing**: this means that they make use of other people's emotional responses in order to make a decision or to evaluate a situation. If a baby approaches a new toy across the room, he or she may look back to check the response of his or her carer, and this response – pleasure, anxiety, lack of interest – will influence the baby's decision to play with that toy or not

KEY TERMS

Joint attention – A baby and their parent/carer or practitioner following or directing each other's attention to an object or event. An example might be the baby making sounds and when the adult looks at them, the baby looks towards the fridge where the milk is, waving her arms. The adult immediately understands that the baby wants more milk.

Theory of mind (ToM) – The idea that because you have a mind and have thoughts, others have too but they think different thoughts to you – for example, a child sees her friend choosing an apple every day at snack time, and says to you, 'I think Jamal loves apples.' See page 192 for more information on Theory of mind.

- imitate other people – for example, clapping hands or copying sounds
- cooperate when he or she is being dressed
- engage in **joint attention** by following other's gaze at objects or directing their carer's attention to something with their own gaze and by pointing.

Toddlers and two-year-olds

At this age, children:

- imitate what other people do
- are very interested in other children; imitating and following each other. One child might pick up a toy and another will copy. They laugh together. There is plenty of eye contact. One drops the toy intentionally, and the other copies. They laugh with glee. They have a shared idea that they can enjoy together
- enjoy the company of others but need support with managing new social experiences
- show empathy (see Chapter 12, p. 000 for definition) to others in distress by offering them what they know they would want themselves, such as a comfort blanket. Later on they will offer what they know the other child would want
- can only manage to socialise cooperatively or willingly for a small part of their day: it is too much to expect them to cooperate with others for large parts of the day. Indeed, children who are just settling-in might not manage to socialise at all; instead, all their energy is going into adjusting to the new social setting.

Young children (approx. three to six years)

Children at this age:

- begin to develop a more complex **theory of mind (ToM)** as they try out what it is like to be someone else through imaginative role play

- use words like 'think' and 'know' as they talk about their own thoughts and beliefs and those of others
- are interested in having friends and are becoming more influenced by each other. They love to use 'silly talk' and to laugh together
- often have one special friend. They value companionship, but they also value being alone. This means that they need:
  - solitary or 'alone' times
  - times to do things in parallel; alongside others
  - times to be cooperative
- sometimes follow the lead of another child and sometimes show leadership
- love to feel power and to have control – over things and people
- sometimes negotiate at their own level
- are beginning to think about things that are right and wrong; they are developing moral values
- often argue with adults in a dogmatic way, and will not shift their position.

Older children (approx. six to eight years)

Children at this age:

- are increasingly influenced by other children of the same age, as well as by familiar adults
- take in and internalise the social rules of the surrounding culture
- have begun to work out the difference between:
  - social rules – these vary from culture to culture (e.g. the way to greet somebody)
  - display rules – these govern how we show or hide our feelings (e.g. hiding disappointment that a present is not what we hoped for)
  - moral values – these are to do with what is deemed right or wrong (e.g. not hitting people)
- start to have a wider social understanding, and may be troubled by news programmes reporting violence and natural disasters
- are able to follow a series of events from beginning to end, and to be sensitive to the needs of other people as they do so
- are able to take considerable responsibility, and enjoy helping other younger children.
- need to be accepted by other children and adults.

A key way in which children develop and hone their social skills is through imaginative and socio-dramatic play. Although children can practise social skills when playing with adults, play with peers offers more challenge as they have to adapt their behaviour to a less socially skilled play partner (Rogoff 1990).

Theories and theorists: ToM, mindsight or mentalisation

Although he admitted it was an unfortunate description, Piaget (1956) maintained that children are 'intellectually egocentric' (unable to take other's point of view) until the age of about four or five years. However, Margaret Donaldson, using laboratory techniques in the late 1970s, demonstrated that children perform at a more advanced level when a situation makes what Donaldson called 'human sense' to them (1978).

Judy Dunn, observing children in their homes in the 1980s, found that even toddlers know how to annoy or comfort other children. From the time they walk, talk and pretend, children are able to understand other people's feelings, particularly when in surroundings that they know and feel comfortable and when they are with people they know and love (Dunn 1988).

So developing the ability to understand other people starts much earlier than previously thought. Instead of talking, as Piaget did, about children gradually shedding intellectual egocentricity, we now talk about developing ToM, which is more positive.

ToM develops from the early behaviours of joint attention and social referencing, which form the basis of babies' awareness of other people's feelings, thoughts, wishes and beliefs. It is called having ToM because it is not possible to actually know what is in someone else's mind; we can however create a theory in our own minds, based on our own previous experience in similar circumstances, our existing knowledge of that person and our reading of their body language and emotional state.

Obviously the younger the person, the less experience they have so the harder it is to do this. Being able to think of someone else's needs and adjust their own behaviour accordingly takes enormous effort for young children. It is an ability that will come and go depending on the situation, the people involved and the child's well-being. Children who become skilled in this area have usually had their own thoughts and feelings attended to sensitively by their parents/carers or early years practitioner. These children are often popular leaders and other children want to be with them.

Daniel Siegel calls the capacity to perceive or observe the mind of the self and others, '**mindsight**'. He links this growing ToM to security of attachment, identifying that where parents/carers do not focus on the mental states of the child or where their own mental states are intrusive on the child's, the acquisition of

ToM is impaired (Siegel 1999). This could happen, for example, when a parent continues a game with their baby, even though the baby is showing anxiety or protesting, or the state of mind of a depressed parent means they do not respond to the baby's communications.

Being able to appreciate another person's way of thinking from their point of view is an incredible thing to be able to do. The neuroscientist Sarah-Jayne Blakemore outlines key aspects of this development:

- Until they walk, talk and pretend, babies concentrate on what they see, want and feel.
- Once they pretend, they begin to have some understanding of what is real and unreal.
- Gradually, they begin to talk about their beliefs (for example that the biscuits are in the kitchen cupboard).
- By the end of the first five years, typically they are beginning to know that people can have different beliefs to theirs, and that theirs can be changed too.

Peter Fonagy et al. uses the term '**mentalisation**' (2004) to describe the ability, through imagination, to interpret what other people do and say. Mentalisation is needed to develop friendships, which depend on being able to imagine how another person is feeling; and it is also needed in order to take part in role play, enjoy books and a whole host of other experiences. For example, Julia Donaldson's book, *The Gruffalo* (1999), depends on the reader or listener being able to imagine that the animals are afraid of a mysterious big monster in the forest.

The ability to understand what is real and what is imagined is part of developing ToM. This is illustrated by the 'false-belief' test, which is usually a laboratory based research experiment as described below.

The Sally and Anne false-belief task

The Sally-Anne experiment involves placing a doll on a table and telling the child that this is Sally. Sally has a basket. Then a doll called Anne is introduced and she is placed next to Sally. Anne has a box.

KEY TERMS

Mindsight – the ability to understand your own mind and the minds of others.
Mentalisation –The ability to understand another person's mental state through observing their behaviour; for example, a child saying, 'I think Sophie wants to be my friend; she is trying to hold my hand.'

Look, listen and note

Observe a baby, toddler, young and older child. Note examples of how they show empathy, understand another child's needs or desires, or the ability to take someone else's viewpoint.

Sally has a marble, which she places in her basket. She goes for a walk. Anne takes the marble out of the basket while Sally has gone. Anne puts the marble in her box. Sally comes back. She wants to play with the marble. The child is asked, 'Where will Sally look for the marble?'

The child may or may not realise that Sally will not know that Anne has moved the marble to her box while she is away. The answer the child gives will show whether the child understands what it is like to see things from either Sally's or Anne's point of view in terms of their 'knowledge' of the situation. If the child says that Sally will look in Anne's box for the marble, it shows they do not understand that Anne has moved it there, but that Sally would not know this as she had left the room when this was done. They are not yet looking at this from Sally's point of view.

Theory and theorists: (John Bowlby 1907–1990) attachment theory

Bowlby developed the theory of attachment from the idea that human babies have a biological need to have a close loving bond with their mother or caregiver, not only for physical survival but also for positive mental health. In Bowlby's view, if this bond is not allowed to form or is broken, emotional and personality development will be disrupted. He stressed that it is the security and sense of safety provided by the parent that are the foundations of emotional attachment.

Bowlby (1988:121) suggests that the framework for attachment is the coordination of 'care seeking 'and 'care giving'. Attachment behaviours such as care or proximity seeking are triggered by separation or threatened separation from someone with whom the child has an attachment relationship. This **separation anxiety** is eased by gaining proximity (i.e. becoming closer); this might range from just being in sight or hearing soothing words to the physical closeness of being held.

Responsive 'care giving' behaviours from the adult that are complementary to the child's attachment behaviours and that are focused on maintaining the stability of the relationship, provides the child with a '**secure base**'. As carers support both children's urge to explore and play and their need to be close,

the child gradually develops an inner trust in the possibility of feeling safe while also being outgoing, competent and independent. Secure-base behaviours such as running away and then clinging when anxious are the essence of the second year of life but can be observed in children throughout their early years. How the carer balances their task of protecting the child with the need to let them go, will also influence the child's mental model of how to balance intimacy and independence in later life.

Through these interactions, the child forms what Bowlby described as an internal working model of the attachment figure, which helps sustain the child for periods when they are separated from this person. This model also sets a '**blueprint**' for what they can expect from close relationships and is thereby used to recreate and predict later relationships (Holmes 1993).

Where a parent or other caregiver offers a high degree of sensitivity and is generally responsive to a child's needs through engaging in consistent patterns of behaviour, the child will usually develop a secure attachment to them (Holmes 1993). In other words, a child will usually be closer to a parent/carer or practitioner who is sensitive to their needs.

Mary Ainsworth et al. (1978) identified that attachment relationships can also be insecure because the adult is unavailable, inconsistent or rejecting. Children with insecure attachment patterns feel intense love and dependency but also fear rejection. They may either be very clinging or unhealthily independent; unable to expect, ask for or accept help or support (Holmes 1993). Children with these patterns are often identified later on as difficult in some way; they may seek attention and emotional support in socially unacceptable ways or have difficulty focusing calmly on their learning in school. Clarke and Clarke (2000) claim that the basis of their difficulties lies in their lack of emotional security or strong affectionate ties to anyone.

KEY TERMS

Separation anxiety – A normal part of development in babies and young children that arises at times when the child perceives itself as separated from the mother/carer and is unable to do anything that will bring them back into proximity.

Secure-base – The feeling of safety and security that close caring adults provide for children through being physically and emotionally available. This allows the child to go off and explore.

Blueprint – A design or plan which determines how something is built.

▲ **Figure 10.2** The key person's role is to develop a close trusting relationship with their key children

Supporting children's emotional, personal and social development through the key person approach

A key person is sometimes thought of as the person who collects observations and updates records for a specific child. Although it is important for settings to have systems and procedures like these, they do not constitute a key person approach.

A key person is:

- a named member of staff who has more contact than others with the child
- someone who builds a trusting relationship with the child and parents
- someone who helps the child become familiar with the provision
- someone who meets children's individual needs and care needs (e.g. dressing, toileting etc.)
- someone who responds sensitively to children's feelings, ideas and behaviour
- the person who acts as a point of contact with parents.

(from Dearnley, Elfer, Grenier, Manning-Morton and Wilson 2008)

Background

From the 1920s onwards, an interest in the work of Sigmund Freud and the other early psychoanalysts began to influence English nursery childcare, with specific attention paid to children's emotional development.

Anna Freud

Freud's daughter, Anna, was a nursery teacher; she set up a residential nursery school in Hampstead in London during the Second World War, to help care for children whose parents were working or otherwise

absent. She arranged for each child in the Hampstead Nursery to have a constant 'maternal figure', later writing that

> *repeated experience proves the importance of the introduction of this substitute mother relationship into the life of the residential nursery. A child who forms this kind of relationship to a grown-up not only becomes amenable to educational influence in a very welcome manner, but shows more vivid and varied facial expressions, develops individual qualities, and unfolds his whole personality in a surprising way.*

> **(Freud 1973)**

In other words, children flourish as a result of the care that a good key person is able to offer.

Susan Isaacs

At around the same time, another early psychoanalyst and teacher, Susan Isaacs, wrote of her worries that if a child was in an institution like a hospital or nursery where there was inadequate or sub-standard care, 'this does not mean to him the mere absence of the good he requires, a merely neutral place; it means the actual presence of positive evil' (Isaacs 1945: 218). She wrote of her despair when faced with the 'rigid routine and emotionally barren life in an institution', and proposed instead that each child 'should feel himself to be the member of a small family group' in care settings (Isaacs 1945: 225).

John Bowlby

A third major theorist of children's early emotional development in this period was John Bowlby, who drew on ideas from animal studies, psychology and psychoanalysis to develop attachment theory as discussed above (Bowlby, 1969). Following the Second World War, Bowlby was concerned about the numbers of children who had not been able to form such attachments, and his work proposed that in order to secure good mental health in children mothers must stay at home (instead of working, as many did in the war), to develop secure relationships with their babies and young children.

Although Bowlby's work was primarily motivated by his concern for the well-being of young children, he overstated the idea that mothers must always stay at home with their babies. Subsequent research has demonstrated that there are other, equally successful approaches to caring for babies and infants, involving people in addition to the mother and the immediate family. All the same, his compassion and care for babies and their well-being is a reminder that poor quality childcare can lead to unhappiness and suffering.

Bowlby, Isaacs and Anna Freud all argued (though in different ways) that the child's experience of a close, emotionally warm relationship is internalised, and becomes part of the child's developing personality. On the other hand, if children are neglected or treated harshly, they will internalise these early experiences and are likely to become aggressive and unhappy.

Care assignment and the development of the key person approach

In the 1970s, an important action research study was carried out in a London day nursery by Alastair Bain and Lynne Barnet, and published in 1980 as *The Design of a Day Care System in a Nursery Setting for Children under Five*. Working with the nursery team, Bain and Barnett (1980: 72–3) developed what they called a 'care assignment system', which they described in the following terms:

> *each child was predominantly cared for during the day by his nurse whom he could turn to for love, attention and help, at meal times, in play, when he needed comfort and affection, being changed, being helped on the lavatory, and washing.*

These ideas were then developed by Elinor Goldschmied and Sonia Jackson in their book *People Under Three* (2004), where the term 'key person' was coined. Continuing research and experience both suggest that the key person approach is an effective way of organising nursery care (Bain and Barnet, 1980; Manning-Morton and Thorp 2003, 2006; Elfer and Dearnley, 2007).

The continuing role of the key person

The role of the key person should continue throughout the child's time in nursery. It is useful to think about how this can be planned – for example, Goldschmied and Jackson (2004) suggest that instead of grouping all the children together for story or song times, children could instead be in a smaller group (which they call an island of intimacy) with their key person.

Planned regular review meetings between the key person and parent, in addition to informal, ongoing discussion, provide a time and place for thinking together about the child's development and needs.

If children are moving from one room to another in the nursery, or from the nursery to reception, the role of the key person in supporting the child with this transition, and liaising with parents and receiving practitioners, is crucial, and many of the suggestions made about initial settling-in can be adapted for this period too.

It is also important to balance the individualised nature of the key person relationship with the social experience of group care. This means thinking of ways in which the whole nursery environment can help the child. A key person needs to balance being close to key children and giving support through their relationship, with the benefit children gain through being helped to make and maintain friendships with others and from taking part in play.

Challenges within the key person approach

Anna Freud and Elfer, Goldschmied and Selleck (2005) write about the challenges of implementing a key person approach. These include:

- Jealousy and envy – other key children may find it difficult to share their key person and colleagues may envy a practitioner's ability to get on well with a particular child.
- Sadness and protest on separation – sometimes children have a very close relationship with their key person which leads to them crying when their key person goes for lunch and being unsettled if their key person is not present at the start of the

day. This is a natural response and can be eased by establishing a 'buddy' or 'secondary key person' system.

- Competitive feelings between parents and practitioners – sometimes a key person might feel that the child is better with him or her than with the parents, and say things like, 'I just wish I could take him or her home with me.' Practitioners should never express this verbally and should avoid expressing it non-verbally too. Equally, some parents feel it is wrong for their child to have such a close relationship with a practitioner and might worry about being displaced. Practitioners should always make sure that they make it clear to parents that they value the parent–child relationship as the most important one.

- Practical arrangements – shifts, holidays and going on courses can become stressful when children miss their key person. Arrangements for support are necessary.

- Getting out of your depth – the key person approach can stir up strong feelings in practitioners, children and parents. Managers and practitioners need to be clear about the strengths and limitations of their knowledge and skills, and not confuse care and education with therapy and get into situations they are not able to deal with. Situations that do arise need thoughtful and careful handling, and external expert help and support as necessary.

There is no simple, reassuring paragraph we can write to answer the concerns around these complications. The success of the system depends on staff being able to communicate openly and honestly with each other, in a professional manner, and being able to work together to overcome difficulties. Staff need regular time and space to talk about being a key person, with their manager or another appropriate individual. Parents also need to know that their worries will be sympathetically heard if they are experiencing difficulties.

Helping children's emotional, personal and social development through settling children into nursery

Once it was common to think that the best way to start children in nursery was simply to leave them with the staff on day one, and that having a parent around would only lead to distress and confusion.

▲ **Figure 10.3** Being in a large group, having to share resources and space all day can be very demanding for young children. Having duplicates of materials and plenty of space and time to move around freely can reduce conflict

However, as early as the 1950s, James and Joyce Robertson showed, in a sequence of brilliant and harrowing documentary films, how damaging it was when children were simply left in hospital and nursery, following the conventional thinking of the time. Their films show children lapsing into a state of withdrawal and depression, not wanting to eat, becoming fretful and finally despairing that anyone will be there for them.

Settling new children into the nursery is one of the most important roles practitioners undertake. It is important that times of transition are as positive as possible for both the individual child and the family as a whole. Transitions can be painful and cannot always be happy experiences for children or those who love them. However, it is always possible to ease the impact of difficult separations through thoughtful, sensitive support. But this needs to be well thought out and organised.

The first meeting with the family

This might take place when the family visits the early years setting or through a home visit. It is important that parents do not feel forced into accepting a home visit from staff. Often home visits are welcomed by families as an opportunity to get to know the early years practitioner. A home visit, or a visit to the setting before the child starts there, gives staff the chance to find out what the parents are expecting from the setting.

Sharing and exchanging information provides an opportunity to clear up any misunderstandings and can reassure parents, children and staff. Staff may discuss:

- routines of the day
- what equipment the children will use

Guidelines for good practice

Conducting home visits

✔ Do not to go alone, for your own safety, especially in the evenings. Tell colleagues the time and location of the home visit.

✔ Make an appointment, as the parent may not want to open the door to a stranger.

✔ Where necessary, take an interpreter with you, to make sure that parents with limited English do not miss out on important information.

✔ Staff usually find that if one person concentrates on the parent(s) and the key person gets to know the child, everyone enjoys the visit. The child has the full attention of one adult, with a bag of carefully chosen books and toys. The parents and staff are free to get to know each other, and can fill in the basic information records together without the pressure of being in a busy setting.

✔ Parents should not feel judged or tested. They need to be sure that their home is not being inspected to see if it is clean, tidy, fashionable or tasteful.

✔ It is important to give time to the parent, so that he or she can ask any specific questions or raise any particular concerns. Make time to listen, as well as to explain about the nursery.

✔ Ensure that you discuss and record accurately essential information – for example, about the child's health, allergies and other dietary information.

✔ Not all parents will accept the invitation to be visited. Parents' wishes should be treated with respect.

- outings and permission for children to take part
- photographing and videoing the children, and ethics and parental permission for this
- the key person system
- photographs and captions in a brochure or leaflet from the setting.

When families have a home visit, they will come to the setting and see at least one familiar face and know that someone knows them and their child.

The settling-in period

This is a very important time for everyone. Parents will not necessarily know what sort of approaches will help their child, and what will hinder the process of

Think about ideas

Watch *Life at Two: Attachments, Key People and Development* (from www.sirenfilms.co.uk), which shows Eva as she first visits and then settles in to her nursery. What did the nursery staff do to help Eva and her mother?

settling in. Equally, practitioners will not know the child well or be familiar with what the child finds soothing or upsetting. So it is important to maintain good communication with parents throughout the process. A parent knows his or her child best; the practitioner has the most experience of helping children to settle in – it is by combining their knowledge, that they can help the child best.

Every child and every family is unique. Children's responses to starting nursery will vary from full-on enthusiasm, to wariness, to a great deal of crying and clinging. None of these responses is a cause for concern in itself, and it is helpful to reassure parents about this. No child's needs can be met fully by a key person: there is bound to be some unhappiness or uncertainty.

 Theory and theorists: Donald Winnicott (1896–1971)

Donald Winnicott who was an English paediatrician and psychoanalyst, proposed two ideas that may be helpful when thinking about transitions:

- Being good enough – Winnicott (1964) came up with the notion of the 'good-enough' mother, as opposed to the 'perfect mother'. By extension, we could think of the 'good-enough key person', who is available to the child and responds to his or her needs enough of the time for the child to feel secure, but allows some space and time when the child needs to find his or her own way (which will usually happen because of the demands of other children).

- The object of transition – this is an object that a child uses to maintain a connection with the parent or carer who is no longer present when the child is in nursery. For some children, this may be a teddy or other special toy. Others may have a special blanket or an object from home like a pillow to use at sleep times.

Leaflet on settling-in for parents from Kate Greenaway Nursery School and Children's Centre

The settling-in period

The settling-in period is the time when you are here with your child in the nursery school. It is a time for your child to get to know his or her key person – with the reassurance of having you here too. As the relationship develops, your child will be able to trust that:

- the key person and the other staff in the nursery are able to meet her or his needs
- they can be helpful, comforting and deal positively with any problems
- they can provide interesting experiences which make it worthwhile to come to nursery.

The settling-in process gives you a chance to check out:

- what type of nursery this is
- how the staff work
- what kinds of experiences we offer to the children.

Our aim is to settle children in at their own pace – when children are ready to move away from their parents, we will encourage and support this. We have found that in the long run, this means more settled and happier children – and parents!

The settling-in process

1 **The home visit** (if you chose to have one). This can be very special for a child – often children remember it for a long time. The home visit helps your child to begin an attachment with the key person on 'home territory'.

2 **Your child spending time in the nursery room with you**. During this time, you are available to support your child and to help staff get to know your child. It is best to be available to your child but not too interesting! We are aware that both you and your child may be feeling stress, and your child may not be on 'best behaviour'. Please do not worry about this.

3 **Your child spending time in the nursery room while you are in another part of the building**. It will be up to you and your key person to decide when your child is ready.

This might be for quite a short period of time at first, and then for longer stretches of time. Please note that it is always very important that you say clearly to your child that you will be leaving the nursery room. It is tempting to nip out when your child is busy, but if your child turns round a few minutes later to find you have unexpectedly gone, she or he may be really upset.

4 Finally, it is for you to judge – with the support of the key person – when your child is ready to be left in the nursery with the staff. Your child might be very sad or angry at the moment of parting, but if the settling-in process has gone well, she or he will be able to manage this with the support of the key person and other members of staff. If your child continues to be upset after you have gone, please be reassured that we would contact you and would not put your child through an ordeal.

When saying goodbye, some parents find it easiest to set a limit on how long they will stay (e.g. 'I'll read two books with you and then it will be time for me to go'). Other parents like to have a special ritual like:

- going to the sofa and reading a book
- waving goodbye through the glass doors
- kiss-cuddle-high five.

It is up to you how you manage this, but please do ask for support or advice if it will be helpful.

Please make sure that you always bring your child right into the nursery room and make your key person or another member of staff aware before you leave.

It is not uncommon for a child to settle very well into the nursery, and then unexpectedly a few weeks later to find it difficult to come in. This might be for any one of a variety of reasons, and again we will offer our support or help if you would like it. You are always welcome to phone and ask how your child is getting on at any time of the day.

▲ **Figure 10.4** Leaflet on setting in for parents from Kate Greenaway Nursery School and Children's Centre.

Guidelines for good practice

Supporting the personal, social and emotional well-being of children

✓ Implement an effective key person approach: children need love, security and a feeling of trust. They also need consistent care from people they know. All early years settings are required to have a key person system that provides continuity.

✓ Children need to have a feeling of trust that their basic needs for food, rest and shelter will be met. Rigid rituals are not helpful, but days do need a shape or routine. This will give children a predictable environment within which they can develop a sense of belonging and contribution through helping in setting the table, for example.

✓ Children and their families need to be shown respect first, in order that they can develop self-respect. So children, parents and staff need to speak politely and respectfully to each other.

✓ Children have strong and deep feelings. They need help, support and care from adults.

✓ Children need clear, consistent boundaries or they become confused. When they are confused they begin to test out the boundaries to see what is consistent about them.

✓ Value children for *who they are*, not for what they do or how they look.

✓ Look at the book area and the displays on the walls in your setting. Are you giving positive messages? People who give children positive images about themselves (in terms of skin colour, language, family form, gender, disability, culture and economic background) help children to develop good self-esteem.

✓ Visitors to the nursery can provide positive images too. The people children meet occasionally or on a daily basis will all have a strong influence on them. If children almost never see men working in early years settings or women mending pieces of equipment, they form very narrow ideas about who they might become. Books, pictures, outings and visitors can all offer positive images that extend children's ideas of what sort of person they might be and what they might do in the future.

✓ Children need to feel some success in what they set out to do. This means that practitioners must avoid having unrealistic expectations of what children can manage – for example, dressing, eating or going to the lavatory. It is important to appreciate the efforts that children make. They do not have to produce perfect results. The effort is more important than the result.

✓ Practitioners help children's self-esteem if they are encouraging. When children make mistakes, do not tell them they are silly or stupid. Instead, say something like, 'Never mind, let's pick up the pieces and sweep them into the bin. Next time, if you hold it with two hands it will be easier to work with.'

✓ Children benefit from being given choices in their lives and being consulted about changes, too. Some practical approaches to this are suggested by Alison Clark and Peter Moss in their book, *Listening to Young Children: The Mosaic Approach*.

Moving on

Theoretical perspectives on gender development

Psychoanalysis

In psychoanalytic terms the acquisition of sex roles is a process of identification with the same sex and rejection of the opposite sex. Identification is the process of incorporating into ourselves the thoughts and feelings of others. Freud argued that gender identity was flexible at first because the child thinks their biological traits can change, specifically for Freud through gaining or losing a penis. This is resolved through the Oedipus complex at about the age of five or six years.

Social learning theory

Social learning theorists such as Bandura (Bandura and Bussey 1999) explain differences in gender roles as attributable to the effects of socialisation. Children come to know what is 'masculine' or 'feminine' through observation. They imitate the behaviour of role models of the same sex, for example girls imitating the nurturing behaviour of female figures.

Think about ideas

There are different theoretical perspectives on the development of gender and related behaviours. To extend your understanding further, read about these perspectives. Make notes on the strengths and limitations of each of them and research them further.

In this model of gender development children are moulded into developing what is considered to be sex-appropriate behaviour through the reinforcement or reward of behaviours that conform to socio-culturally appropriate norms, such as boys being boisterous (or noisy) and sanctioned for behaviours not acceptable in that culture, as in the phrase, 'big boys don't cry'.

MacNaughton (2000: 21) calls this explanation the 'sponge model' of identity formation as it ignores the complexity of gender identity and the many different messages that children receive from different sources, some of which are actively resisted.

Cognitive developmental theories

Laurence Kohlberg (Kohlberg 1966) proposed a cognitive developmental view of the emergence of gender identity; that children develop their gender identity in line with their level of cognitive understanding. His theory reflected Piaget's stage theory of cognitive development (see p. 129).

He suggested that children go through three developmental stages to reach the essential understanding that gender remains constant and cannot be changed.

These stages are:

- gender identity: the ability to label one's own sex and identify other people as boys, girls, men or women
- gender stability: an understanding that people will have the same gender throughout life
- gender constancy: an understanding that biological sex stays the same whatever the external cues of hair length, clothes worn or occupation are.

(Bee and Boyd 2010)

Kohlberg argued that gender development involves active participation. He stated that children are motivated to adapt to their environment, and that gender-typed environments influence the development of gender and gender identity. But Kohlberg's theory does not take into account individual differences in gender role development.

You may also want to look at other aspects that affect the emotional, personal and social development of children. These are covered in Chapters 11 (social behaviour and developing self-discipline), 6 (holistic development), 15 (effects of ill-health) and 16 (diet and nutrition).

Further reading, weblinks and resources

Robertson Films
Website about the classic and harrowing films made in the 1950s by James and Joyce Robertson, about children going into hospital and to nursery.
www.robertsonfilms.info

Siren Films
High-quality DVDs showing the importance of attachments and key people in the EYFS.
www.sirenfilms.co.uk

The 'strange situation'
Video clips of the method devised by Mary Ainsworth and colleagues to identify qualities of attachment relationships.
https://www.youtube.com/watch?v=s608077NtNI

Attachment theory and key person role
Secure Attachment and the Key Person in Daycare: a series of four video clips presented by Richard Bowlby.
https://www.youtube.com/watch?v=s608077NtNI

The Bobo doll experiment
This is a link to a YouTube video on the Bobo doll experiment:
https://www.youtube.com/watch?v=dmBqwWIJg8U

References

Ainsworth, M., Blehar, M., Waters, E., and Wall, S., 1978, *Patterns of Attachment: Assessed in the Strange Situation and at Home*. New Jersey: Erlbaum.

Bain, A. and Barnett, L., 1980, *The Design of a Day Care System in a Nursery Setting for Children under Five*, London: Tavistock Institute for Human Relations.

Bandura, A. and Bussey, K., 1999,' Social Cognitive Theory of Gender Development and Differentiation', *Psychological Review*, 106(4), Oct, 676–713.

Bee, H. and Boyd, D., 2010, *The Developing Child* (12th edn), New York: Allyn and Bacon.

Berk, L. E., 2006, *Child Development* (7th edn), Boston, MA: Pearson International Edition.

Blakemore, C. 1998, *The Mind Machine*, London: BBC Books.

Blakemore, S. J. and Frith, U., 2005, *The Learning Brain: Lessons for Education*, Oxford: Blackwell.

Bowlby, J., 1969, *Attachment and Loss. Vol. I: Attachment*, London: Hogarth Press.

Bowlby, J., 1988, *A Secure Base: Clinical Applications of Attachment Theory*, London: Routledge.

Clarke, A. and Clarke, A., 2000, *Early Experience and the Life Path*, London: Jessica Kingsley Open Books.

Clark, A. and Moss, P., 2001, *Listening to Young Children: The Mosaic Approach*, London: National Children's Bureau.

Cole, M., 1998, 'Culture in Development', in Woodhead, M., Faulkner, D. and Littleton, K. (eds), *Cultural Worlds of Early Childhood*, London: Routledge.

Dearnley, K., Elfer, P., Grenier, J., Manning-Morton, J. and Wilson, D., 2008, 'Appendix 1: The Key Person in Reception Classes and Small Nursery Settings', in *Social and Emotional Aspects of Development: Guidance for Practitioners Working in the Early Years Foundation Stage*, Nottingham: DCSF Publications. Available at http:// nationalstrategies.standards.dcsf.gov.uk/ node/132720.

Derman-Sparks, L. and Olsen Edwards, J., 2010, *Anti-Bias Education for Young Children and Ourselves*, Washington DC: NAEYC.

Donaldson, J., 1999, *The Gruffalo*, London: Macmillan Children's Books.

Donaldson, M., 1978, *Children's Minds*, London: Fontana.

Dunn, J., 1988, *The Beginnings of Social Understanding*, London: Blackwell.

Dunn, J., 1993, *Young Children's Close Relationships, Beyond Attachment*, New York: Sage.

Elfer, P., Goldschmied, E. and Selleck, D., 2005, *Key Persons in the Nursery: Building Relationships for Quality Provision*, London: David Fulton.

Elfer, P. and Dearnley, K., 2007, 'Nurseries and Emotional Well-being: Evaluating an Emotionally Containing Model of Continuing Professional Development', *Early Years: An International Journal of Research and Development*, 27(3): 267–79.

Eliot, L., 1999, *Early Intelligence. How the Brain and Mind Develop in the First Five Years of Life*, London: Penguin.

Fonagy, P., Gergely, G. and Jurist, E. L., 2004, *Affect Regulation, Mentalization and the Development of the Self*, London: Karnac Books.

Freud, A., in collaboration with Dorothy Burlingham, 1973, *The Writings of Anna Freud. Vol. III: Infants without Families [and] Reports on the Hampstead Nurseries, 1939–1945*, New York: International Universities Press.

Goldschmied, E. and Jackson, S., 2004, *People Under Three, Young Children in Day Care* (2nd edn), London: Routledge.

Goleman, D., 1996, *Emotional Intelligence: Why it can matter more than IQ*, London: Bloomsbury Publishing.

Gopnik, A., Meltzoff, A. and Kuhl, P., 1999, *How Babies Think*, London: Weidenfeld and Nicolson.

Harris, P., 1989, *Children and Emotion. The Development of Psychological Understanding*, Oxford: Blackwell.

Holmes, J., 1993, *John Bowlby and Attachment Theory*, London: Routledge.

Isaacs, S., 1945, *Childhood and After: Some Essays and Clinical Studies*, London: Agathon Press.

Kohlberg, L., 1966, 'A Cognitive Developmental Analysis of Children's Sex Role Concepts and Attitudes', in Maccoby, E., *The Development of Sex Differences*, Stanford CA: Stanford University Press.

Lieberman, A. F., 1995, *The Emotional Life of a Toddler*, New York: Free Press.

Manning-Morton, J. (ed.), 2014, *Exploring Well-being in the Early Years*, Maidenhead: Open University Press.

Manning-Morton, J. and Thorp, M., 2003, *Key Times for Play, The first three years*, Maidenhead: Open University Press.

Manning-Morton, J. and Thorp, M., 2006, *Key Times: A Framework for Developing High-quality Provision for Children from Birth to Three*, Maidenhead: Open University Press.

Manning-Morton, J. and Thorp, M., 2015, *Two Year Olds in Early Years Settings; Journeys of Discovery*, Maidenhead: Open University Press.

MacNaughton, G., 2000, *Rethinking Gender in Early Childhood Education*, London: Paul Chapman.

Piaget, J. and Inhelder, B., 1956, *The Child's Conception of Space*, London: Routledge, Kegan Paul Ltd.

Rogoff, B. (1990) *Apprenticeship in Thinking*, New York: Oxford University Press.

Schaffer, H. R., 2006, *Key Concepts in Developmental Psychology*, London: Sage.

Siegel, D. J., 1999, *The Developing Mind*, New York: Guilford Press.

Smith, P. K., Cowie, H. and Blades, M., 1998, *Understanding Children's Development* (3rd edn), Oxford: Blackwell.

Thomas, A. and Chess, S., 1980, *The Dynamics of Psychological Development*, New York: Bruner/Mozel.

Waddell, M., 1995, *Owl Babies*, London: Walker Books.

Winnicott, D. W., 1964, *The Child, the Family and the Outside World*, London: Penguin Books.

Wulff, H., 2007, *The Emotions: A Cultural Reader*, London: Bloomsbury Academic.

Understanding social behaviours and developing self-discipline

This chapter builds on key issues discussed in Chapter 10 to focus on how children develop an understanding of how the social world works. This means developing social cognition, which is based on children developing empathy and theory of mind, and includes learning social rules and accepted forms of behaviour. The **sociocultural** contexts of socialisation are emphasised throughout. Different kinds of behaviour and their possible causes are discussed, and different approaches to helping children to develop self-discipline are explored.

Social cognition

Social cognition is how we develop understanding of how the social world works; its customs and rules. Babies are born ready to become part of the social world, and how they are helped to do so has a major influence on all other aspects of their development, learning and their future lives. Although children's learning about the social world takes a similar path to their learning about the physical world, there are important differences; people can be unpredictable, they respond in unexpected ways as our relationships and interactions are reciprocal or mutual, and not one-way. Other people also have motivations and intentions that are not obvious, so 'reading' other people is a very important social skill.

This is called developing '**Theory of Mind**' (ToM), which is fundamental to social cognition, as discussed in Chapter 10. In Chapter 10 you can read about this and other important developments in emotional, personal and social understanding that influence and underpin children's ability to form positive social relationships, including the impact of biological and environmental influences. For example, children's temperament may predispose or influence them to being very active, but how that activity is displayed will be determined by their **sociocultural** experiences. Children tend to behave according to the way they experience life. If they are ridiculed or smacked, for example, they are likely to laugh at and hit others, especially children younger or smaller than themselves. On the other hand, a child who is helped to develop confidence and the ability to

understand and tell the difference between emotions, develops **social competence**.

 Theory and theorists: the development of empathy

An important social skill, related to ToM, is the development of **empathy**.

Hoffman (1988 cited in Bee 2000) identifies four stages in the development of empathy:

- Stage 1 – global empathy. In the first year of life, babies will match others' strong emotions, such as crying when another baby cries.
- Stage 2 – egocentric empathy. When a child begins to develop a separate sense of self at around 12–18 months, they will still become distressed when someone else is distressed but will also attempt to comfort the other person by offering them what they would find comforting themselves, such as a dummy or toy.
- Stage 3 – empathy for others' feelings. From toddlerhood through to the early school years (approximately one to seven years), children note others' feelings, and partially match them; they also respond to the other's distress in non-egocentric ways by offering comfort that they know the other person would like.
- Stage 4 – empathy for another's life condition. From late childhood on (approximately 8–12 years), children recognise that the sadness of the other person may not be momentary but an ongoing feeling associated with an event or circumstance.

KEY TERMS

Sociocultural — The combination of social and cultural factors that influence personality and behaviour.
Theory of mind – The ability to understand that you have beliefs, desires and knowledge, and that others have beliefs, desires, intentions and perspectives that are different from your own.
Social competence – A child's ability to get along with other people and communicate with other children and with adults.
Empathy – Awareness of another person's emotional state, and the ability to share the experience with that person. To see the world from someone else's point of view.

The development of empathy and concern for others is based on children's development of ToM or 'mindsight' (see Chapter 10, p. 192). Daniel Siegel (1999) links this to attachment theory because children with some types of **insecure attachment** are not enabled to gain ToM as readily as some other children. This can occur where the parent or carer does not focus on the needs of the child, and focuses more on their own needs. The parent/carer's mental state then becomes intrusive, meddling or disorganising in the relationship, which can impair the acquisition of mindsight. Although children are resilient and strong, and can be helped to recover or develop these capacities at a later stage, this is more difficult than establishing mindsight early in life.

Such a breakdown in developing secure attachment may also have wider implications as it may compromise children's moral development. Children develop a model in their minds of how to behave in relationships with others through their attachment relationships with the adults who care for them. If that model is shaky or unsound as a result of an insecure attachment, some children will have no clear model in their heads of what their close adult would do in a particular situation. Because of this, they are unable to make sound moral judgements about the best course of action to take. Gopnik et al. (2001) emphasise that morality is very closely linked to social development because it requires empathy.

Morality refers to ethics and principles, and the way we tell the difference between what is right and what is wrong.

Learning social rules

A key feature of social cognition is learning the rules about social interactions. This includes:

- how to talk to different people in different situations
- how to be polite
- who is allowed to talk and when
- which behaviours are allowed in some situations and not others
- the different behaviours allowed in and by some people and not others.

All of these social rules will reflect sociocultural ideas of who is more powerful/dominant and/or due higher or lesser levels of respect and consideration. They also change over the lifespan and from setting to setting, which means that this kind of social learning can be very tricky for the child and that it continues throughout life.

Early in development, children are faced with the dilemma of satisfying their own needs or meeting the demands and restrictions placed on them by their parents and society. With age, these conflicts change from basic 'dos and don'ts' that are learned by repetition or habit, such as remembering to say please and thank you, to more complex and abstract rules such as that it is wrong to steal or hurt others. As they develop, children learn to control their behaviour by adopting standards of conduct for themselves and feeling guilt when they fail to meet these standards. They develop into adolescents and adults who can appreciate the logic or reasoning behind society's rules, which are based on mutual respect for others.

Learning about social rules begins with **social referencing** (see Chapter 10, p.190 for more information): how children refer back to the adult's expressions and pay close attention to their tone of voice and what they say, to make sense of situations. In practice, this can be used to help children understand situations and to reinforce behaviours – for example, a smile for a child as they explore reinforces their inner sense of confidence and enjoyment. This is most effective where the child has a trusting relationship with the adult.

In the process of learning social rules, there can be conflict between adults and children. Adults can become frustrated by the inconsistency of children following a 'rule'. This is particularly true of younger children who sometimes appear to understand that something is not allowed but are unable to resist doing it. This relates to their immature emotional regulation, i.e. managing their feelings as discussed below, but is also related to the complexity of social rules that are hard for very young children to understand. For example, when asked if they would like some fruit, a child may not understand that the social rule is that you only take one piece. Also confusing may be the way adults approve of a behaviour in one situation but not in another; for example, throwing a ball is praised, yet throwing other toys causes censure. Practitioners

> ### KEY TERMS
>
> **Insecure attachments** – Children form insecure attachments to carers who are insensitive to or reject their needs, or are unpredictable in the care they offer. These children may either be very clingy or unhealthily independent.
>
> **Morality** – is our ethics and principles and the way we tell the difference between what is right and what is wrong.
>
> **Social referencing:** Social referencing refers to the tendency of a child to look to an adult in an ambiguous or unclear situation in order to obtain information that would clarify things.

should approach such situations with understanding and calm explanation rather than criticism (Manning-Morton and Thorp 2015).

There are many social rules to learn, some of which are emphasised more by adults at home and less by practitioners in the early years setting and vice versa. This can make going to nursery or a childminders a difficult step for a child to take as they need to manage following expectations, routines and rules, which may be unfamiliar and very different to their home experience. This is particularly difficult for very young children who are only at the beginning of understanding social rules. It is also difficult for older children who have had limited experience of wider social situations before coming to nursery.

Practitioners often concentrate on the ability to share and take turns as the focus of social learning, yet these skills are only part of developing social understanding. Instead, think carefully about how to facilitate or enable thoughtfulness, kindness and empathy in young children as this needs to come first. Then the young child will come to understand that sharing and taking turns is positive because it aids their social relationships. This means finding the 'teachable moment' (a moment when a situation is 'live' and children can relate your explanations to an actual event, so can understand the reasons for following these rules) in everyday interactions, noticing children's acts of kindness and thoughtfulness, and modelling such behaviours. This helps the younger child who is still developing ToM and the older child who has had limited experiences of interacting in a group of other children, to learn these skills in a deep way rather than just following adults' instructions.

Children's friendships

Children's friendships are a key way in which they hone their social skills because although they can practice social skills with adults, play with peers requires them to adapt more to a less socially skilled play partner (Rogoff 1990).

Early friendships are important; they may last throughout life or they may be brief. As children's interests change and they go off in different directions, old friendships may fade. Early friendships are like adult ones – they are based, at least in part, on people sharing the same interests. As children become more able to play imaginatively together, the possibilities grow for sharing and enjoying each other's company. This is because, in play, children can rearrange the real world to suit themselves – you can pretend anything

Reflecting on practice

Sharing and taking turns

An experienced early years practitioner sees a child snatch a toy train from another child, who starts to cry. She goes over to the children calmly and says, 'I can see you really wanted that train, Harry. But Iqbal really wants it too.' After a moment, she asks Harry, 'Can you see that Iqbal is sad?' Harry nods, so she asks, 'What could we do to make him feel better?' Harry is not sure and does not answer. So she asks Iqbal, who points at the train. After a minute or so, Harry hands the train to Iqbal.

The practitioner says, 'I wonder what you could do next time when you really want something like the train.' Harry does not reply, so she suggests, 'Maybe you could say, "Can I have a turn next?" Or perhaps you could look for another train?' Then she checks to see if Iqbal is all right, and suggests, 'Next time, if someone grabs something off/from you, you could say, "No, it is mine," or "Stop it. I do not like that." Shall we try saying that together?'

1 How has the practitioner helped the children to acknowledge their feelings?

2 How has the practitioner given the children ideas to manage their behaviour in the group?

3 This approach would take a lot longer than just telling Harry off and making him give the train back to Iqbal. Do you think the extra time and attention is worthwhile?

4 What might be the longer-term benefits of dealing with the incident in this way?

when you play! This kind of social, creative play is a prime mechanism for children's learning.

Socially competent children who know how to get on with other children have good access strategies for joining in:

● First, a child will tend to circle around the edge of an activity, perhaps on a tricycle, trying to work out what is happening, or will watch what is happening from the safe viewpoint of being at the sand tray or water tray.

● Then they will imitate what the other children are doing – for example, pouring sand in and out of pots and laughing as each pot is upturned. We call this using a side-by-side strategy. Doing the same helps the child to join in with other children.

● The child may then add another feature to the imitated play action, which acts as an indicator that

▲ **Figure 11.1** Children's friendships are important for their learning and well-being

they want to be friends. If the offer to be friends is accepted, this is adopted by the new friend(s) who then transforms it again into something new.

How you can help a child to join in

Some children need a great deal of support to play well and get on with other children. You might say to the child, 'Do you want to join in? Let's look at what they are doing, shall we? Don't ask if you can do the same as them; just do the same as them.' This advice is given because if children ask if they can join in, they are usually rejected. If, on the other hand, children simply do what the other children are doing, they are very likely

to be accepted into the group. This is an important access strategy that practitioners can help children to develop. It is also a useful strategy for practitioners to use if they are joining a group of children. Practitioners can also help young children by modelling phrases such as, 'Can I have a go next?' or 'Can I have that when you're finished?', which can help children to find a way between being left out and never getting a turn, or being impulsive, rash and grabbing things to force their way in.

Understanding social behaviour

What is behaviour?

Behaviour is everything we do; it is our actions in response to stimuli in the environment or to internal urges and needs. So we are all 'behaving' all the time. As humans, we use our behaviours to communicate with others, as they can observe our actions and thereby understand something of our thoughts and feelings. From this perspective we can see that all children's behaviour has meaning and is communicating something to us, so the child who is lying on a cushion may be telling us they are tired, feeling reflective or fed up; the child running around the room may be bored, anxious, frustrated or happy. So practitioners need to keep their eyes, ears and emotions open to understanding what a child is trying to tell them through their behaviour.

When we talk about behaviour in the context of children's development and learning, we are referring

---

Guidelines for good practice

Supporting children's social cognition

All children will have difficulties socialising with others at some point, but some difficulties may be more extreme and long-lasting than others. This may be because of the child's temperament or because they have had difficult early experiences, or it might be a combination of the two. Practitioners can help children a great deal, both through their reassuring presence in children's lives and through following specific strategies to help children.

✔ Give children the words they need: teach them to say, 'I need some help'.

✔ Help children to understand social rules: 'Throwing cars may hurt someone, cars are hard. But it's OK to throw these balls because they are soft. Let's throw them in the basket'. 'At nursery we sit down together to have dinner so we can have a nice chat and make sure that you don't get hungry'.

✔ Adopt and model a problem-solving approach: 'If you stamp your feet and cry, I can't help you. I need to know the problem. Can you show me the problem?' 'Can you see my face? It is easier for us to listen to each

other if I look at your face. You look unhappy. How can I help?'

✔ Show understanding, empathy and concern: 'I can see that made you really angry, but pushing people to get the car is not OK. Shall we see if there is another car for you to play with?'

✔ Support children's friendships; plan for their shared play interests, and organise so they can be with each other.

✔ Focus on enabling the children to enjoy each other's company and on helping and learning from each other.

✔ Look at what the children are doing and find things in the room and outdoors that you think make a good fit with their interests and moods. Children who are constantly frustrated in what they do can become angry children who are very challenging to work with.

✔ Remember that children have different temperaments: while one child can accept waiting a few minutes, another might be more restless and impulsive or spontaneous. Adapt your approach but be consistent about boundaries.

to the way children learn about behaviours that are socially acceptable in a particular cultural context. Often, when we refer to children's behaviour in practice, we are talking about behaviour that is seen as 'difficult' or 'challenging' and how to 'manage' it. But much behaviour in children or adults is not' totally 'good' or totally 'bad', so it is useful to see it as part of the whole range of skills and behaviours that make up social development.

Everyday behaviours

If we see children's behaviour as part of their overall social cognition, we can understand that there are behaviours that are a result of their development. Children can only behave according to their developmental abilities: their ability to sit still, to say what is wrong, to apologise with understanding, to wait and to share, all depend on their stage of development in all areas.

For example, toddlers are beginning to establish a sense of self, which is why 'possession' is important to them and their favourite words are often 'no' and 'mine'. Although toddlers often turn their backs and say 'No!' to a suggestion, they do in fact take up and imitate the idea offered to them. Practitioners need to be aware of this, and to realise that when a toddler says 'No!' they really mean they want to do something for themselves, and to make the decision for themselves, rather than feeling controlled. It is all part of developing a strong sense of self.

Similarly, expecting young children to sit still without fidgeting or becoming restless is unrealistic. Being able to be still is the peak of physical development only achieved by the development of muscles through movement; prolonged 'carpet times' undermine children's efforts to master control of their bodies.

Everyday behaviours of conflict, non-compliance/ refusal or teasing, for example, may arise from feelings of frustration, excitement or boredom. The first consideration for practitioners in such situations is to evaluate your own practice and provision. For example, you should consider the following points:

- The way the indoor and outdoor areas are set up may be causing boredom and frustration in the children. In cases where the practitioners seem to lack interest and enthusiasm, it is hardly surprising that children resort to challenging, aimless or silly behaviour.
- Where there are inappropriate play opportunities and resources, children may get discouraged and frustrated; there may be lots of activities but they may be too difficult for some of the children to access or enjoy. For example, presenting fiddly puzzles to toddlers will often result in frustration and tantrums.
- Additionally, unsuitable expectations are sometimes made of young children – for example, to sit quietly through long school assemblies or to line up and wait for long periods of time. Lining up and waiting often lead to pushing and shoving, and it is only to be expected that a young child, for example who cannot see or really understand an assembly or a long story session, will start to fidget, become restless and talk.
- Children can also get irritable as a result of hunger, thirst, tiredness and physical discomfort.

It is important to bear in mind that children need:

- a good choice of activities, and interesting people to be with
- interesting and exciting things to do
- new and challenging activities
- familiar things to do
- opportunities to make choices and decisions during the day
- resources and equipment that are clearly stored with picture/word labels for easy identification and selection
- water available to drink throughout the day and regular healthy snacks and meals
- space to be quiet and away from others
- rest and sleep
- space and opportunity to move freely
- the consistent attention of trusted and interested practitioners and adults generally.

Conflict

Squabbles, conflicts and disagreements are all an important part of growing up – you cannot be yourself if you never disagree with anyone else. What is important is that children learn how to resolve disagreements in a way that is not destructive to the other person or to their own self-esteem.

Conflict often arises over issues of sharing space, objects or people. The younger the child, the harder this is for them to do and the greater the chance of tussles happening. For very young children, particularly two-year-olds for example, their understanding of possession is closely bound up with using an object and their developing sense of self. Therefore, if a child has been playing with the dumper truck to make tracks or transport sand, the creative process they experience is felt to be part of them and the truck becomes 'mine' and remains so, even if they leave it while they explore something else, resulting in conflict when another child picks up the truck (Manning-Morton and Thorp 2015).

Arguments and hostility between friends can arise from conflicting interests or different children with different schemas (see Chapter 10) being expected to play with the same equipment in the same area. Older children can compete with each other for friendship, resulting in conflict.

Conflicts also arise because being sociable all day long can be hard work. The social skills required to operate in a large group all day can tax the patience of many practitioners even with well-honed social skills, let alone a young child who is in the early stages of developing such skills.

When beginning to explore social relationships it is important that children are not frightened by aggressive and demanding behaviour from their peers, so practitioners have an important role in participating in the play of very young children and modelling positive communication and negotiation or cooperation. Children need help to learn how to reconcile or 'make up' when they have hurt someone else. Insisting children say 'sorry' can lead to a half-hearted apology, while putting the problem back to the child and saying, 'How can we make Iqbal feel a bit better now?' can be more productive.

Supporting children to work alongside others

Many children are growing up in a culture that emphasises competition, individuality and getting things just right or winning at any cost. Some children will therefore need a great deal of support from adults to learn alongside others and to be helped to turn difficult situations into positive ones. Learning to get along with others presents a series of problems for children to solve. They need practitioners to step in gently, explain and help, and give them the chance to come up with their own solutions. When children are in conflict, practitioners might intervene sharply to say 'No', or to reprimand or tell a child off with terms like 'naughty' and 'nasty'. These responses can lead children to associate those situations with anger and criticism, and a cycle of difficult behaviour can arise. When children just hear 'No', they are unlikely to learn

▲ **Figure 11.2** Suggesting tasks children can do together can foster cooperation, responsibility and contribution to the group

how they could have acted or thought differently, in order to avoid a quarrel or a fight next time, or to make up afterwards. An alternative approach is to try to help the children to understand what has happened and what they might be feeling. This means approaching an incident of difficult behaviour rather like a problem to be solved together.

Guidelines for good practice

Helping children to relate positively to others

No one gets on with everyone all the time. Children are just like adults in this way. But unlike adults, children do not have years of experience to draw on and, in general, children have stronger and more impulsive emotions than adults. Every child needs:

✔ the personal space to do things on his or her own, without interruptions or pressure from anyone else – imagine if you were trying to do something tricky, like drill a hole in some wood, and you kept having to share the drill and move out of the way for other people

✔ to feel nurtured and loved as a person in his or her own right

✔ to be able to choose who to be with and what to do for most of the day (always having to do adult-led tasks is a great pressure for young children)

✔ his or her difficulties to be addressed with sensitivity and care by adults – imagine if every time you felt angry, you were told off by people around you and no one ever showed any sympathy or understanding

✔ individual attention so that he or she feels there is enough time to talk and share without the pressure of being in a group (a child might appreciate a one-to-one story, for example); individual attention is especially important for younger children (aged up to three years).

Strategies for reducing conflict include having open-ended flexible resources and materials, such as sand, cornflour and paint, corks, lengths of fabric or cartons, which will effectively cater for children's different play agendas and choices to play alone or together. Such materials reduce the need to share and therefore reduce conflict. Having duplicates of books, wheeled toys and components in construction sets also reduces competition and conflict (Manning-Morton and Thorp 2015).

It is very important that children are encouraged to learn about being cooperative, positive and caring towards each other. Practitioners need to help children to have a go at things, to take risks and not to be anxious about making errors.

Ensuring all children have opportunities for being in small groups also helps with learning about cooperation, and even more so for younger children. Communicating, relating, concentrating and relaxing are all more difficult when surrounded by a lot of people. Employing strategies such as making small, enclosed dens from large cartons and lengths of material for two or three children to be together and having regular small '**key group**' times will encourage easier social interactions between children.

As practitioners, and adults generally, if we feel criticised, misunderstood, blamed or otherwise under attack, we are unlikely to be able to take responsibility for something we have done wrong or to make amends. So it is with young children too, and practitioners need to consider their voice tone and body language when addressing anti-social behaviour.

KEY TERM

Key group – The group of children allocated to the same key person.

Look, listen and note

Model ways to solve conflicts. For example: talking to a pair of children who have been fighting, a practitioner might say, 'I wonder how Jason could have said he wanted the train, instead of grabbing it?' or 'Serena, I wonder how you could stop Jason grabbing the train, without hitting him?'

There are some good examples of turning children's conflicts into opportunities for learning social development in the High/Scope DVD Supporting Children in Resolving Conflict. See the weblinks section on p. 221.

- Always speak calmly; you can still be firm without raising your voice.
- Make sure you are close enough at the child's level and use gentle touch to show concern when appropriate.
- Make eye contact if possible but if not, make sure the child can hear you.
- It is useful to acknowledge the feelings of the child (for example, 'I can see you're angry that you cannot have all the cars to yourself.')
- Repeat what needs to happen in a positive way. For example, 'It's important that you sit down when using the scissors.' That way, children hear 'sit down' rather than (don't) 'run around' and they are clearer about what you want them to do.

Guidelines for good practice

Responding to everyday incidents

Where there are incidents (as there always will be!), practitioners should consider the following:

✔ Are your expectations of behaviour developmentally appropriate for *this* child? What is this child's social context? Can they understand the language you are using?

✔ Are your communications clear? For example, rather than 'play nicely', it is better to say 'Throwing the sand can hurt people's eyes; when you are playing near the other children it's better to pour it through the tube together.'

✔ Are your directions/explanations too obscure, long or confusing? Remember that young children may only hear key words in sentences that are above their comprehension or understanding, and therefore may misunderstand the meaning of what is being said. So keep what you say brief and to the point; for example, 'Please take just one cracker for now.'

✔ Also, it is never nice to feel nagged into doing something, so when giving instructions do not repeat the instruction too many times – wait for the child to process what you have said and give them a chance to comply or follow before you check that they have heard and understood or ask again.

✔ Help children to make sense of what you want them to do.

✔ Try to ensure that children see you as someone who wants to help, who does not nag, who is warm and encouraging, and who does not stop what the children are doing by saying 'no' all the time. Be positive.

✔ Provide alternatives and redirection to a different context in which a child's actions would be acceptable.

- Aim to be firm and clear but avoid a power struggle by giving the child some choice within the boundary you have set; for example, 'I can wait one minute for you to finish on the bike and then you need to come for lunch.'
- Sanctions or making the consequences clear should be used only if absolutely necessary and then must be immediate and understandable. Consequences should be explicit and immediate: 'I need to take the scissors now because running with them is dangerous. When you are sitting down, then I can give them back to you.' Threats and bribery are not appropriate.

Loss and grief

Children will sometimes become aware for the first time of death and dying when they are in an early years setting or school; a child's grandparent may die, for example.

People say different things when someone dies – for example, they may tell children that the person has:

- gone to heaven
- gone to sleep
- gone away
- turned into earth.

Children can become very confused. They get frightened that they will be taken away to this place called heaven, or that if they go to sleep they might not wake up. Children need honest, straightforward explanations of death that make it clear that the person will not come back and that it is not their fault that the person has died.

Children need to grieve, just as adults do. If they are not helped to grieve, they may experience difficulties at the time and later on in adult life. If they are helped,

Reflecting on practice

Dealing with loss

Anna is a four-year-old child in your setting. She has missed a few days of nursery; as you are her key person, you phone home to find out if everything is all right. Anna's mum, Doreen, answers the phone and soon breaks down into tears. 'Her great-aunt has died. She was old and not very well, but it's still been a shock,' she says. 'I do not want to upset Anna, so I have not told her; it will make her too sad. But she does not seem to want to go anywhere and I cannot get her to nursery.'

With a partner or in a small group, discuss what you would say to Doreen.

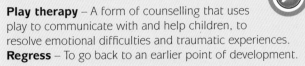

KEY TERMS

Play therapy – A form of counselling that uses play to communicate with and help children, to resolve emotional difficulties and traumatic experiences.
Regress – To go back to an earlier point of development.

however, they will experience positive relationships with other people and come to terms with their loss in a positive way.

What is difficult behaviour?

When discussing 'difficult' or 'challenging' behaviour, it is necessary to be clear about what we mean.

- Is the behaviour seen as 'difficult' because the practitioner finds it so, even though it might be a common behaviour for a child of a particular age? Children can only behave according to their

Guidelines for good practice

Helping children to grieve

- ✔ Explain things – for example, if someone is terminally ill, that parents are separating or divorcing or that a person is going to prison, children need to be told of the reality of the situation. Make sure the child does not feel responsible for what has happened.
- ✔ Do not exclude the child – let them be part of the family. If someone has died, let the child go to the funeral or visit the grave and share the sadness.
- ✔ Be especially warm and loving; cuddle the child, be calm and quietly be there for them.

- ✔ Give the child reassurance that it is okay to feel grief. Help the child to know that, although these feelings will last for a while, they are normal. Tell them that the pain will ease over time.
- ✔ Find photographs and evoke memories. Some children are helped by **play therapy**.
- ✔ Be prepared for the child to **regress**; do not demand too much of the child. When the child begins to show an interest in things once more, gently encourage them.

developmental understanding and abilities. The 'difficulty' or 'challenge' often lies in practitioners' unrealistic expectations or may arise from the practitioner's cultural perspective on what is acceptable.

- Is the behaviour 'difficult' because it is anti-social, showing a lack of care for others or the environment?
- Is the behaviour 'difficult' because it is disturbing and raises concerns about the child's well-being?

Where do difficult behaviours come from?

Children can display difficult behaviour for many reasons, including the following:

- Feeling insecure and having low self-esteem – if a child has experienced early neglect at home, for example, he or she might not feel confident that anyone is thinking about him/her and will respond to his/her needs. The child may feel that the only way to get attention, or to get what he or she needs, is to demand it or fight for it. Children who are running off or clinging to their key person will be communicating how confident or insecure they are feeling at that particular time.
- Feeling unsure – if there are different rules depending on whether a child is at home, with grandparents or at nursery, the child may genuinely be unsure of what is expected of him or her.
- Lack of appropriate care in the early years setting – examples of this include young reception children being sent into the playground for long lunch periods, without any familiar staff being available. While some children will respond by becoming sad or withdrawn, others may become rather wild and disobedient.
- Being hungry, tired, cold, hot, sick, hurt or anything that causes children discomfort can cause them to be irritable, uncooperative and sometimes to lose control and act aggressively. Very young children may not realise what the source of their unhappiness is and are less able to express their ill feelings in words. It is up to the practitioner to think about what might be causing negative behaviour and to address children's comfort needs promptly and with empathy.

Angry behaviour

Emotions such as anxiety, fear and anger trigger the **fight or flight response**, so children who are often running around manically or hitting out may be communicating these feelings through their physical behaviour. Children can feel losses very intensely, such as the departure of their mother or father at the start of the day. Some children become sad or withdrawn,

but others may feel angry at being left, and may express this through angry behaviour. **Psychodynamic** theories argue that if a child cannot tolerate a feeling, he or she will try to get rid of it by passing it on to someone else. So the child who cannot bear feeling sad might hit another child to make him or her sad, thereby moving the sad feeling away from him or herself and on to another person. Spitting is very effective in rejecting people and may arise from a child's feelings of rejection and abandonment; biting may also give the biter temporary relief from feelings of stress, anger and frustration.

Hitting, kicking, spitting, biting, swearing and disrupting other children's activities are behaviours that children use to gain the adult's attention. When children behave like this, they can soon become labelled as naughty or impossible to manage, and it is only a short step to these children starting to live up to their label and staff starting to speak and act towards them in an anxious or aggressive way. So it is important to break this cycle, to try to hold on to the positive aspects of the child's behaviour and appeal to these. The following strategies may help:

- Try to imagine what it might be like to be a child in the setting. Does it sometimes feel like there is a great mass of children, all demanding attention and seeking the same equipment? You can help by taking time with individual children, listening to them and observing them, treating them as special individuals and not just one of many in the group.
- Try to become aware of your own feelings. Angry children can provoke angry responses from practitioners. Can you work on your responses and become calmer and clearer, and reduce confrontations? Saying, 'I can wait a minute, but then I really do need you to come and sit down,' will often work much better than demanding 'Sit down now!'
- Respond in a balanced way to bad behaviour, explaining simply and clearly why a particular behaviour is unacceptable and making it clear that it is the behaviour that is unacceptable, not the child.

KEY TERMS

Fight or flight response – Physical changes in the body (such as increased heart rate) in response to stress, such as fear.

Psychodynamic – Theories in psychology that explain personality in terms of conscious and unconscious processes.

- It is very useful to look for patterns in a child's difficult behaviour. This can be done by using the **ABC approach** to observation. If difficulties largely occur at the same time, or in the same area, or with the same children, you may be able to plan ahead and avoid those 'triggers' by guiding the child elsewhere, to play with other children, or by ensuring that the child has a rest or something to eat.

Different kinds of behaviour can show themselves at different times of the day, in different situations and according to the child's mood, personality, physical comfort and previous experiences of relating to people. It is important for adults to create and sustain a calm, orderly environment and help children to regulate their impulses by helping them to shift their focus and energy into play and enjoying materials like sand, clay and water.

It is important that you do everything you can to establish a good relationship with the child's parents. If a child has similar difficulties at home, and behaviour remains difficult over time in the early years setting or school, you may decide that this is a special educational need and seek help and support from the special educational needs coordinator (SENCO).

What is self-discipline?

Self-discipline refers to the ability to manage your responses, actions and behaviours in line with sociocultural expectations for the given situation. Internalising these expectations results in being able to 'self-manage' your behaviour rather than having to rely on others to guide you. This is a sophisticated skill to develop and one at which most adults fail at least some of the time (you only have to think about

keeping up with work or study schedules, exercise or diets to realise how difficult self-discipline, or **effortful control** can be).

The development of self-discipline, or **self-regulation** as it is called in developmental psychology, is also very complex as it arises from physical and neurological or brain developments, cognitive understanding and, crucially, developments in emotional and social understanding and positive early relationships.

Theory and theorists: developing emotional regulation

Self-discipline and regulating our behaviour relies on our ability to understand and regulate our emotions. Children will not be happy and cooperative all the time. Being a person is about having an emotional range, being able to feel happiness and sadness, calmness and anger. It is useful to understand the neurological basis for this.

Our consciously felt and understood emotions, for example recognising that you feel happy, are processed in the **pre-frontal lobes** of the cortex of the brain, while our unconscious basic emotions (fear, anger, joy, sadness, disgust) are governed by the limbic system at the centre of the brain. The **limbic system** includes the **amygdale**, which Joseph LeDoux (2002) describes as our 'emotional sentinel'. When the brain receives information that is threatening in some way, rather than being transmitted to the **cortex** for consideration, it travels directly to the amygdale which releases hormones and chemicals that trigger the fight or flight response. (See page 213 for definitions).

Look, listen and note

If the behaviour of a particular child in your setting is difficult, observe the child considering the following factors:

- Does the child have a strong relationship with a key person?
- Are there plenty of stimulating things to do which match the child's interests?
- Are routines and demands appropriate for the child's development and age?
- Might the child feel tired or hungry?
- Have there been any recent changes in the child's family life that may have unsettled him or her?

You could share your thoughts with other members of staff in your setting and discuss how you might improve the situation for the child.

KEY TERMS

ABC approach – The ABC model of behaviour analysis can be very useful in identifying the causes of negative behaviour and ways in which the issue can be addressed. In the approach, A represents the antecedent, which means the conditions or stimulus that are present before a behaviour occurs; B is for the behaviour or response to the stimulus; and C represents the result of the behaviour.

Effortful control – This is children's capacity to override their immediate wants, desires and responses with a more socially acceptable and effective response. Children who can see that there are cakes on the table but wait for the practitioner to say that they can have one, are showing high levels of effortful control.

Self-regulation – In terms of behaviour, self-regulation is the ability to act in your long-term best interest, consistent with your values. Emotionally, self-regulation is the ability to calm yourself down when you are upset and cheer yourself up when you are down.

KEY TERMS

Pre-frontal lobes – The part of each hemisphere of the brain located behind the forehead that processes complex cognitive, emotional, and behavioural functions.

Limbic system – The inner part of the brain which is responsible for emotions and memories.

Amygdale – A structure in the brain that is linked to emotions. It deals with emergency fear responses and the formation of emotional memories

Cortex – The outer part of the brain, the grey matter, that is responsible for higher brain functions, including sensation, voluntary muscle movement, thought, reasoning, and memory.

Chemical inhibitors – The brain produces chemicals that either allows an impulse from one nerve cell to pass to another nerve cell or inhibits or stops it.

The development of the connections in the cortex happens gradually throughout childhood and adolescence. As these neural pathways are firmed up though, as a result of the child's experiences of the world and relationships, they send **chemical inhibitors** to the amygdale, thereby gradually developing the capacity for emotional control (Gerhardt 2004). However, while this neurological development is happening in the cortex, children are less able to regulate their emotional responses. This means that their emotional states can change quickly and that they are more prone to lose control of their emotions and behaviours.

Even as adults we can experience what Daniel Goleman calls 'emotional hijacking'; where an event provokes the immediate and overpowering fight or flight response, when information such as hearing a strange noise in the house in the middle of the night, goes straight to our limbic cortex and causes

▲ **Figure 11.3** Being in a large group, having to share resources and space all day can be very demanding for young children. Having duplicates of materials and plenty of space and time to move around freely can reduce conflict

us to freeze in fear or leap out of bed, ready to scare the intruder away, even before we know what we are doing! These kinds of emotional and physical responses are much more frequent in young children.

Approaches to helping children develop self-discipline

The aim of managing children's behaviour should be to move away from the outer control of the practitioner to children having inner control. But there are many different views on how to manage children's behaviours and to help them develop self-discipline.

Parents and practitioners may have different views about this based on their:

- own childhood experience and how their parents disciplined them
- sociocultural traditions
- knowledge and understanding of children's development
- professional experience.

In modern-day western society, families are generally smaller and often live long distances from their extended family members, so the advice and support and customs about how to manage their children's behaviour, previously handed down through the generations, is less available to parents than it used to be. In the United Kingdom there is no shortage of advice being given out to fill this gap, from television 'nannies' to numerous journalists and authors, who promise solutions to age-old problems like sleep difficulties and temper tantrums. All this advice may seem helpful, but it can be simplistic, may contradict other advice parents may have received and so can be confusing and overwhelming. Practitioners are not immune to these influences either.

A lack of general agreement about how best to approach children's socialisation means that developing clarity between practitioners and parents about how children should behave is a challenge that is crucial to address. It seems that a key focus of this challenge should be how to encourage children's altruism or consideration for others in the group or in society as a whole. This is to counter-balance the modern, western cultural tendency to prioritise individual wants, desires and needs instead, which it seems, does not support social well-being.

Behaviour policies

It is important that settings develop policies and procedures to ensure that children's behaviour is be managed in a way that is appropriate for their stage of development and particular individual needs. Schools are also legally required to have policies and

Guidelines for good practice

Developing an effective behaviour policy

✔ The policy should be developed by the whole team, ideally with specialist advice – for example, from an educational psychologist.

✔ Members of the staff team should have the opportunity to explore and discuss their opinions and values about children's behaviour.

✔ Approaches to promote positive behaviour should be the starting point of the policy.

✔ Members of the team should agree on what rules and boundaries are going to be upheld and how this will be done consistently – for example, it is very important that all staff uphold the setting's or school's values around opposing racism; if this is not the case, individual members of the team can feel under a great deal of pressure to make an individual judgement.

✔ The policy should be brief, easy to read and should be shared with parents.

You can find an example of a setting's behaviour policy at www.kategreenaway.org.

procedures in place to identify and prevent bullying. See p. 217 for more information on bullying.

However, writing a policy alone will not ensure consistent appropriate practice in responding to children's behaviour. Practitioners working in a team need to develop a shared pedagogical approach. This is crucial at this time as unacceptably large numbers of young children in the early years are being excluded from nursery or school. The *Independent* newspaper reported in 2012 that in 2011, 2000 children aged 4 and 5 years old were excluded from schools for committing acts of violence or disrupting lessons.

Exclusion

Practitioners sometimes blame poor parenting and exposure to unsuitable media such as video games for the behaviours leading to exclusion. These issues may play a part in this but other factors also need to be considered, especially when the statistics show that certain groups of children are more likely to be excluded than others. For example, children on free school meals were four times more likely to be excluded, and pupils of black Caribbean origin nearly three times more likely than the average. Research by Ambitious About Autism (2015), which campaigns on behalf of autistic children and young people, found that 4 in 10 children with autism are subject to informal (just being sent home on a regular basis) – and therefore illegal – exclusions. See weblinks on p. 221 for more information on statistics concerning the exclusion of pupils with autism.

As well as these issues, other contributory factors might be:

● diverse ideas about what is appropriate behaviour and how to manage it, resulting in inconsistency of approach and confusion for the child

● a 'top-down' approach where whole school behaviour policies are drawn up with older children in mind and then applied to children as young as four because of the early school starting age in the UK

● the formalisation of learning in nurseries, leading in some settings to age-inappropriate expectations of and provision for play; particularly restricted provision for movement play and free-flow imaginative play.

Excluding a very young child is a drastic step to take, which could have long-term consequences. Therefore an ongoing joint approach where practitioners and parents share their views must be developed.

Words or terms in relation to behaviour, such as discipline, boundaries or managing behaviour have different meanings for different people and often are thought to be just about rule-keeping or reward and punishment. Gerber (2005:42) uses a much more helpful definition, seeing discipline as:

> *a social contract, in which family or community members agree to accept and obey a particular set of rules.*

What is important is that this 'social contract' really reflects the needs of the particular members of the community, that is, the age and development of all the children it is applied to.

A partnership approach

What young children learn from well-handled discipline has a major effect on their ability to succeed in life later on. Practitioners who appreciate this will prioritise promoting positive behaviour as a key aspect of practice; developing a policy and strategies that focus on enabling the children to enjoy each other's company, on helping and learning from each other and on taking care of themselves, others and their surroundings.

If we want children to develop inner control (self-regulation or self-discipline) and become adults who understand *why* certain types of behaviour are anti-social or why an action is wrong, then we need to implement ways of guiding children's behaviour that keep safe boundaries and are consistent yet can be flexible enough to accommodate particular circumstances. For example, we want children to learn to cooperate but we do not want children to become mindless followers of instructions, so we have to bear in mind that resisting pressure and saying 'no' is sometimes a necessary life skill.

Developing this kind of flexibility that is not too rigid and not too lenient or soft is a key professional skill. For example, when practitioners or adults generally can accept that they have made a mistake, or change their opinions as a result of hearing what someone else says, they help children to understand about compromise and negotiation. If practitioners never seem to get anything wrong, children will not learn how to accept that they have made an error, and will not learn how to make up for this.

Where there is a successful partnership approach, the practitioner is able to show fairness, flexibility and reasonableness but is also able to take charge of difficult situations so that all children know that they can rely on her or him to keep them safe and to ensure that justice and fairness is maintained. Manning-Morton and Thorp (2015:131) claim that in this way, practitioners show

> *benevolent authority rather than control because they are interested in working alongside children, not in having power over them.*

Key aspects of a partnership approach:

- There is a balance of responses made between major and minor transgressions (for example). Children who are constantly shouted at to stop doing something or removed for minor issues will not appreciate the difference and may either become withdrawn, resentful and fearful or increasingly disobedient and uncooperative.

- The focus is on enabling the children to enjoy each other's company and on helping and learning from each other. This means emphasising what children can do and not just what they cannot do, and showing appreciation of their efforts at pro-social behaviour; for example, their acts of kindness and care towards others and the environment.

 Theory and theorists: behaviour modification

Learning theory is often applied to the management of children's behaviour (see Chapter 6). In a behaviourist model, behaviour is understood as a response to positive reinforcements – for example, if a child has a tantrum and is given sweets to help him or her to calm down, the sweets become a positive reinforcement, so the child may start to throw tantrums in order to get sweets. If the parents stop giving the sweets, the learned behaviour will no longer be reinforced and will

wither away. This approach is often called **behaviour modification** (See page 216 for definition), and it is used a great deal in early years settings and schools. It is underpinned by the following ideas:

- Most behaviour – good or bad – is learned.
- If behaviour is reinforced when it occurs, it will increase.
- If behaviour is ignored when it occurs, it will decrease.

In this view, behaviour can be changed if consequences are always applied immediately. Rewards will increase the desired behaviour, and negative consequences (e.g. time out, ignoring) will decrease the undesirable behaviour. The timing of the reinforcements is crucial, especially for young children: it has to be immediate, otherwise the reward or consequence will not be associated with the behaviour (adapted from Sylva and Lundt 1982: 198.)

This approach to managing behaviour can work well in certain circumstances – for example, parents often use it successfully to manage difficult issues like going to bed, using star charts linked to rewards (if you go to bed on time, you get a star; if you get five stars, you will get a reward, like a small toy). In an early years setting or school, it may be an effective strategy when cooperative behaviour (such as managing to play alongside another child for two minutes) is consistently rewarded with praise, and special time on a favoured activity like the computer. This approach is often used with children with learning difficulties or other SEN.

Behaviour modification also has drawbacks that need to be considered:

- ***Adults use punishment*** or negative consequences (such as a 'naughty chair') other than ignoring to try to reduce the child's behaviour. However, negative behaviour can also be reinforced by negative attention. Children quickly learn that the way to get an adult's attention is to misbehave.

- ***Children might not be able to generalise***. For example, a child might stop drawing on books at home but then goes to his or her grandparents' house and draws on the walls. The child has stopped the specific behaviour, but does not understand the general requirement to be careful and avoid doing damage.

- ***Children might start doing things only for rewards***, which will affect their curiosity and general motivation.

- ***It takes no account of the child's inner world***. A child's behaviour may be difficult because of current difficulties, witnessing domestic violence for example, or previous experiences – for example, experiencing the trauma of losing a parent in early

- using comments such as, 'Ooh, tell me about your painting,' or 'Wow, you've climbed all the way to the top, that's the first time I've seen you do that!'

This approach ensures that children are given strong messages that their efforts, perseverance and concentration are valued; messages that contribute positively to children's dispositions to learning (Katz 1995).

 Theory and theorists: a therapeutic approach

In contrast to the behavioural modification approach outlined above, a therapeutic approach will generally involve trying to find the underlying causes of the child's difficult behaviour.

The therapeutic approach is based on psychoanalytic theory, which sees play as having a key role in enabling children to explore their inner troubles and concerns, and to express or work through anxieties. This view of play is apparent in early years practice when we provide clay to pummel or dolls for a child with a new sibling. Through play, art, music or talking in a free way, the child can be helped to express his or her feelings (Manning-Morton 2011).

In a more formal play therapy session the child's play is self-directed and takes place within a protected, uninterrupted time and space, with the non-directive but full reflective attention of the therapist. The therapist helps by giving the child a safe space for expression, and by interpreting the child's communications in a way that makes it more possible for the child to live with feelings of anger, loss or unhappiness. As the child is increasingly able to express and find ways of living with difficult emotions, he or she becomes more able to develop and grow through childhood, instead of being 'stuck'.

Some of the professionals who may work with a child in a therapeutic way are art, music or play therapists, and child psychotherapists.

In early years practice, the challenge is to balance our understanding of individual children's difficulties

KEY TERMS

Behaviour modification – This is an approach to working with children who have BESD and draws on the theory of behaviourism. In order to change the child's behaviour, the adult focuses on and is observable and tries to change it using rewards such as praise or stickers.

Behavioural, emotional and social difficulties (BESD) – Signs that a child may have BESD include withdrawn or isolated behaviour, highly disruptive or disturbing behaviour, hyperactivity and significant difficulties with social interactions. It is difficult to assess whether a young child has BESD, and an educational psychologist or clinical child psychologist should always be involved.

Behaviourism – A perspective on child development which understands human behaviour only through the objective analysis of behaviours and reactions and does not consider people's internal mental states and emotions.

childhood. Behaviour modification would only seek to control the child's behaviour, rather than seeking to help the child to grieve and find ways of expressing his or her feelings of sadness and anger.

Praise

Practitioners often use praise as a reinforcer of children's pro-social behaviours. However, empty, indiscriminate praise such as 'well done' or 'good girl' tell a child nothing about what they have done and so do not help the child to understand and therefore repeat their positive behaviour in other situations. In this way, praise can lead children to rely only on an authority figure's evaluation of right and wrong, rather than develop self-direction and self-control.

Also, praise for completed tasks such as 'well done' or 'aren't you clever' can lead to children working only in order to achieve adult recognition rather than from their inner interest or motivation. Such comments are shown to invite comparison and competition and, at a time when self-knowledge is forming, can lead to a child just producing what the practitioner deems is valuable rather than developing their own ideas about the value of their efforts and achievements. Children who come to rely on adult's evaluations can develop a fear of failure and achieve less well in school later on (Dowling 2010).

This does not mean that children's positive behaviours are ignored but are noticed and acknowledged in more thoughtful and direct ways, using strategies such as:

- participating in children's play
- encouraging children to describe their efforts and products

Think about ideas

To find out more about therapeutic help, read *Dibs: In Search of Self*, by the American play therapist Virginia Axline.

Find out more about how therapeutic ideas can be used in mainstream early years settings and schools by reading *Wally's Stories*, by Vivian Gussin-Paley.

with the needs of the whole group to feel safe and comfortable. Understanding children's emotional states is not the same as permitting them to act out their emotions however they want. Young children have powerful urges, for good and for ill. Their loving and forgiving ways go along with intense feelings of rivalry, aggression and hatred. Children often need adults to help them, by standing up against these intense feelings. If, for example, Chloe keeps shouting at children, it will be important for the practitioners to make it very clear that this is not allowed, and that she must find some other way of expressing her anger. Practitioners should not permit children to be aggressive through a misplaced belief that they are being caring. The practitioner is needed to come in on the side of the child's urge to be sociable, the desire to relate to others, to belong and to be liked.

Dealing with temper tantrums

Temper tantrums or emotional collapses are everyday behaviours for very young children (usually aged 15 months to about three years) who often find the world confusing, overwhelming and frustrating. Where this kind of behaviour persists in older children, practitioners need to discern whether this is due to underlying emotional, physical or communication difficulties or is a learned behaviour for getting what they want.

Temper tantrums can be:

● noisy – the child might hurl themselves about, perhaps hurting themselves, usually in rather a public way

● quiet – the child holds their breath and might even turn blue.

It is almost always best to deal with temper tantrums in a calm way, however much you sense your own feelings boiling up. Try to give as little attention as possible to the tantrum and encourage other children to stay away. It is important to stay near the child, offering quiet reassurance, such as, 'I can see you are very upset, I will sit with you until you feel a bit better.' But other than this it is usually best not to talk; the child is in no state for discussion. At the end, you might say something like, 'Now you are calmer, we can talk about this and see what we can do about it', and help the child return to playing with others.

Practitioners should also review their practice and provision to see if there are triggers for tantrums. Ask yourself:

● Are the routines of the day flexible? Are children warned about changes in activity and given time to finish what they are doing or the choice to return to it later?

● Is the environment over stimulating? Is it a large noisy group? Where can a child go for some quiet time or solitude?

● Are key persons consistently available to their key children, playing with them at their level?

● Do all adults engage in positive interactions with children, noticing pro-social behaviours?

Dealing with bullying

Some young children bump into others, grab for equipment first, give others an aggressive look or generally act so that others are afraid to get in the way of what they want. Other children say things to make others feel left out or foolish; for example, 'You are not coming to my party' or 'Do not play with stupid Eleanor'. Behaviour like this can quickly intensify to more serious forms of bullying like open aggression, which is either physical (hitting, pushing) or verbal (name-calling). It is important that practitioners look out for this sort of behaviour and encourage other children to say confidently how it affects them.

Firm action should be taken when necessary. You may have to tell a child something like, 'Pushing like that is not allowed. Do you remember yesterday when Jason said he felt sad when you pushed him? So I am going to have to take you away from the trains for two minutes.' You can help the child by saying clearly which part of their behaviour is not acceptable, while not being negative towards the child personally. This is why you would not say, 'You're being naughty.' It is important that you follow this up by settling the child back into the play. 'We can go back to the trains, but I need you to remember that there is no pushing', and then spend time in that area, helping the children to play together.

In any group, there are likely to be instances of bullying. Helping children to become **assertive** and to resolve conflicts can help to minimise bullying. But remember that, in the end, it is the practitioner's responsibility to uphold acceptable behaviour – some children may not be able to stop others from being aggressive and domineering or forceful, however much they try to be assertive. If bullying is persistent despite your attempts at positive management, you will need to seek advice from the SENCO in your setting or school.

KEY TERM

Assertive/assertiveness – Expressing thoughts, feelings and beliefs in direct, honest and appropriate ways and also respecting the thoughts, feelings and beliefs of other people.

Children might bully others because they feel bad about themselves, or because others have bullied them. They can pick on weaker children or children who are different – for example, they tease or make insults with regard to race, gender or disability. Teaching all children to value the way others are different, rather than to mock or be nervous, and to be assertive in their response to name-calling or hitting, can help to prevent bullying.

Do not use negative labels like 'bully' or 'disruptive'. These can give a child a reputation or bad name that the child will then live up to – and often children do not really understand what these words mean anyway. Instead, talk to children in ways they understand, about what they can see or feel – for example, 'When you shout like that, it makes Adam sad. Can you see he is crying now? What would be a better way to get your turn on the bike?'

In this way you can help both children to develop assertive rather than passive or aggressive ways of getting what they want. You could teach children to use phrases like 'Can I have a turn when you're finished?' Encourage children to respond to things they do not like, by saying 'No thank you' or 'Stop that, I don't like that'.

Practitioners can help to prevent bullying in the following ways.

- Encourage a culture where children can say how they are feeling.
- Sometimes it may feel like particular children, or a particular child, keep coming to you for help. It is important that on every occasion you listen with sympathy and sensitively try to help the child.
- Develop good communication with parents.

Reflecting on practice

It has been a difficult week in the nursery. There seems to be a lot of conflict between the children, and a small group of older children seem to be snatching things from the younger ones. One of your colleagues says, 'As soon as we see anything we should get straight in there and clamp down on them. We need to stop this bullying.'

Using the theories and ideas explained in this chapter, note down how you think this approach will or will not help the children to learn about sociable behaviour? Discuss your thoughts with another learner or in a group.

- If a child is being bullied, it may be the parent who first notices that there is something the matter at home. By working together, you may be able to find out what is happening and take steps to help the child.
- Clearly explain and tell children when their behaviour is not acceptable.
- Help children to develop assertiveness.

You can find out more about bullying by going to www.kidscape.org.uk or searching online for 'kidscape'.

Dealing with biting

In babies and toddlers, biting may arise from the need to relieve the discomfort of teething. In these circumstances the baby does not differentiate between biting their teething ring or biting a person and there is no aggression involved. However, if this behaviour gets a huge reaction from others, the child may seek to repeat the behaviour, In which case, it may become problematic.

Biting by young children out of aggression is a serious and often upsetting form of behaviour that can occur in groups of young children. When a child is bitten, the child's parents will often be very angry and upset at seeing the injury. Equally, the parents of a child who is biting may feel a great deal of shame, and may feel upset and helpless. A child whose behaviour is attention-seeking may often bite, because these reactions provide so much attention. You can help in this difficult situation in the following ways:

- **Use your regular approaches to behaviour management** – clear and consistent behaviour management will help to minimise biting incidents. If practitioners become distressed and angry, this can make things worse. Encourage the parents of the child who is biting to use the same approaches as you, so the child gets a consistent response and message.
- **Look out for patterns** – if biting generally occurs at a particular time, in a particular place or with a particular combination of children, practitioners can take steps to reduce those occasions and be very vigilant when they do occur.
- **Be honest with parents** – explain to parents that biting is something that young children do, and is almost always a phase the child grows out of. Explain the steps you are taking, but be honest that you will not be able to stop every incident.

Dealing with swearing

This is another behaviour that young children can develop, to the distress of practitioners, parents and adults in general. However, as with biting, when practitioners respond with great emotion, shock or upset, this can encourage a child to continue to swear in order to gain attention. You can help by doing the following:

- Using your judgement – if a child is very frustrated and swears in imitation of what he or she hears adults do at home, you can quietly but firmly say, 'That's not a word we use here; it can upset other people.' Helping children to express their feelings of anger or frustration in ways that are allowed can also help.

- Where swearing is repeated, use your regular approaches to behaviour management – this ensures that undue attention is not given to the swearing.

- Communicate effectively with parents – if a child is swearing, explain the problem this is causing in the setting. Encourage the parents to take care about what they say around their child, and to use the same approach as you do if their child swears. If a parent is upset because their child has never experienced swearing at home, but has learned swear words through nursery, show your sympathy, explain your approach and explain that as children grow up they will be exposed to bad language and behaviour. Think with the parent about how they can help their child to cope with this.

Swearing can create similar problems to name-calling. Often it is simply the case that swearing is an everyday part of the child's language experience. However, it is quite a different thing when children swear in order to shock. Any child who swears needs help in:

- learning which words they cannot use in the early years setting

- finding new words to replace the swear words (they still have to be able to express their thoughts and feelings)

- building up their vocabulary so that they have wider choice of words.

Dealing with racist name-calling and incidents

This type of behaviour between young children links to the wider structures and realities of society, in which black and minority ethnic people may experience discrimination, lack of access to jobs and training, poorer housing and racist violence (see Chapter 1). Opposing racism and developing positive attitudes towards diversity are positive contributions that early years education and care can make towards building a fairer and more just society. Children may come into a school or setting with racist or prejudiced attitudes from their family or local community. While you cannot change the views of other adults, you can clearly state your values and help the child to understand that there are different opinions, and that certain behaviour and comments are not allowed in a school or early years setting.

You can help in the following ways:

- **Develop positive attitudes to difference and diversity** – you can do this through the curriculum, resourcing and planning that you put in place. (There are more details on this in Chapter 1.)

- **Make clear that you are opposed to/against bias, discrimination and racism** – never ignore these incidents, as ignoring can be understood as permission. You might say something like, 'We do not use words like that here; it makes people feel very sad and angry.' Put across a different point of view: 'I like the way we all have different skin colours. Let's put our hands together and see what differences we can see.'

- **Use good judgement** – if children giggle when they hear an unfamiliar language for the first time on a CD, this may simply be part of the general way that children respond to the unknown. Show the children how you are interested in what you are hearing, and show that you are listening carefully. A child may comment on the appearance, skin colour or hair of another child, because children do notice new things and remark on them. Instead of being embarrassed, pick up confidently on what the child has said – for example, 'It's true, Annalise does have darker skin than you Liz, and her hair is really curly, isn't it? I think curly dark hair is lovely.'

- **Discuss incidents openly with parents** – if a child has been called by a racist name, explain to the child's parent exactly what happened and how you dealt with it. This builds confidence and it helps families to offer further support at home. You will need to meet the parents of any child who is using racist language or behaving in a discriminatory way, and explain exactly what you have seen, why you think it is unacceptable, and what your policy is when children behave like this.

To find out more about racist name-calling and other incidents, go to www.education.gov.uk and search for 'promoting race equality in early years'.

Similar difficulties may arise around gender and sexuality issues, and the same responses are also appropriate in these situations. If boys are excluding girls from an area or activity, you could challenge them by saying, 'All the activities here are for boys and girls. Let's see if we can help Jessica learn to use the hammer, shall we?' Or children might use 'gay' as a term of contempt towards another child, but you could respond by putting forward a different point of view: 'You know what, I do not think there is anything bad about someone being gay.'

Dealing with sexualised behaviour

It is an ordinary part of young children's development to explore sexual feelings and each other's bodies. This might involve taking a great interest in other children during nappy changing or in the toilets for example. Generally, this is best responded to in a matter-of-fact spirit of openness. Try to avoid showing feelings like embarrassment, shame or nervous giggling, which can stop children from feeling confidence and pride in their bodies. So you might for example say, 'Yes,

Jessica, little boys do have willies, just like you said. They are different to girls, aren't they?'

However, it is also important to make sure that children always feel safe and protected. If a child indicates a desire for privacy during toileting or having his or her clothes changed, do everything you can to uphold this. You could tell other children, 'Jay does not like people to see her undressed. It is okay to be private. Let's all move away and let her be on her own for a while.'

If a child shows knowledge beyond that which would be expected for their age and persistent sexualised behaviour that ignores the feelings of other children, you will need to act promptly and with the support of senior managers and other agencies.

See Chapter 4 for more information on this subject.

 # Moving on

Thinking about ideas

Focus on one of the following practice ideas:

- the High/Scope approach to resolving conflict (*see* the High/Scope DVD *Supporting Children in Resolving Conflict*).
- the use of praise
- the ABC observation technique.

Read and research the topic further using the suggested reading/viewing below and/or searching online.

Then discuss your findings with colleagues and fellow students.

What changes would you suggest making to your practice as a result of what you have read?

For the High/Scope approach to resolving conflict:

High/Scope DVD, *Supporting Children in Resolving Conflict* available from http://www.highscope.org. There are also written guidelines on their website and some short clips online but make sure they are from High/Scope.

For the use of praise:

Henderlong, J. and Lepper, M. R., 2002, 'The Effects of Praise on Children's Intrinsic Motivation: A Review and Synthesis', *Stanford University Psychological Bulletin*, 128: 5, 774–95.

Tompkins, M., 1991, 'In Praise of Praising Less', *Extensions*, 6: 1 (this is the High/Scope newsletter)

Dowling, M., 2010, *Young Children's Personal, Social and Emotional Development* (3rd edn), London: Sage Publications.

For the ABC observation technique:

Lindon, J., 2012, *Understanding Children's Behaviour: 0-11 Years: Linking Theory and Practice*, London: Hodder Education.

Nicolson, S. A. and Shipstead, S. G., 2001, *Through the Looking Glass: Observations in the Early Childhood Classroom* (3rd edition), New York: Pearson.

Further reading, weblinks and resources

Anna Freud Centre

The centre was established in 1947 by Anna Freud to support the emotional well-being of children through direct work with children and their families, research and the development of practice, and training mental health practitioners.
www.annafreud.org

HighScope

High/Scope is an American approach to early education and care, with several decades of research into its effectiveness. The website includes books, DVDs and news of training events and conferences in the UK. There are also some good examples of turning children's conflicts into opportunities for learning social development in the High/Scope DVD *Supporting Children in Resolving Conflict*.
www.highscope.org

Kidscape

This charity was established specifically to prevent bullying and child sexual abuse. The website includes resources for parents, children and professionals, and details of campaigns and training events.
www.kidscape.org.uk

The National Strategies (Early Years)

The government's programme for developing practice in the early years, including statutory requirements, advice on best practice, and research findings. The National strategies are no longer in place and this is archived content.
www.education.gov.uk and search for early years, or go to www.nationalarchives.gov.uk/webarchive

Poverty.org

These websites cite the statistics regarding black and minority ethnic children, and Ambitions about Autism discusses the exclusion of autistic pupils.
http://www.poverty.org.uk
http://www.irr.org.uk
http://www.theguardian.com/education/2015

Ambitious about Autism

The national charity for children and young people with autism.
www.ambitiousaboutautism.org.uk
The moving on section covers further reading useful to the understanding of this chapter.

References

Ambitious about Autism, 2015, *The Illegal Exclusion of Children with Autism*. Available at: http://www.ambitiousaboutautism.org.uk

Axline, V., 1971, *Dibs, In Search of Self: Personality Development in Play Therapy*, London: Penguin.

Bee, H., 2000, *The Developing Child* (9th edn), New York: Harper Collins.

Dowling, M., 2010, *Young Children's Personal, Social and Emotional Development* (3rd edn), London: Sage Publications.

Gerber, M., 2005, 'RIE Practices and Principles', in Petrie and Owen (2005) *Authentic Relationships in Group Care for Infants and Toddlers – Resources for Infant Educarers (RIE)*, London: Jessica Kingsley Publishers.

Gerhardt, S., 2004, *Why Love Matters. How Affection Shapes a Baby's Brain*, Hove/New York: Brunner-Routledge.

Gopnik, A., Meltzoff, A. and Kuhl, P., 2001, *How Babies Think: The Science of Childhood*, London: Weidenfield and Nicolson.

Katz, L., 1995, *Talks with Teachers of Young Children: A Collection*, Norwood, NJ: Ablex Publishing.

Ledoux, J. (1998) *The Emotional Brain: The mysterious underpinnings of emotional life*. New York: Touchstone.

Ledoux, J., 2002, *Synaptic Self: How our Brains become Who We Are*, New York: Penguin.

Manning-Morton, J., 2011, 'Not Just the Tip of the Iceberg: Psychoanalytic Ideas and Early Years Practice', in Miller, L. and Pound, L., *Theories and Approaches to Learning in the Early Years*, London: Sage.

Manning-Morton, J., 2014, 'Young Children's Personal, Social and Emotional Development: Foundations of Being', in Mukherji, P. and Dryden, L. (eds), 2014, *Foundations of Early Childhood: Principles and Practice*, London: Sage.

Manning-Morton, J. and Thorp, M., 2003, *Key Times for Play, The First Three Years*, Maidenhead: Open University Press.

Manning-Morton, J. and Thorp, M., 2015, *Two Year Olds in Early Years Settings; Journeys of Discovery*, Maidenhead: Open University Press.

Paley, V.G., 1981, *Wally's Stories*, Cambridge, MA: Harvard University Press.

Rogoff, B., 1990, *Apprenticeship in Thinking*, New York: Oxford University.

Siegel, D.J., 1999, *The Developing Mind*, New York: Guilford Press.

Sylva, K. and Lunt, I., 1982, *Child Development: A First Course*, Oxford: Blackwell.

The Independent, 2012, 'Primary Schools Exclude 89 Pupils a Day over Violence'. Available at: http://www.independent.co.uk/news/education/education-news

Chapter 12

Caring for babies in the first year of life

Caring for babies involves much more than attending to their physical needs. An understanding of development of the baby from conception to the age of one year is important when providing individualised care. Every baby's family will have its own methods and preferences regarding their care, and these must always be respected. This chapter will enable you to understand how to fulfil a baby's needs for food, hygiene and safety, the prevention of ill-health and accidents – and most importantly, a baby's need for love and emotional security.

Development from conception to end of gestation

Conception

The human reproductive system contains all the organs needed for reproduction or producing babies. Conception occurs in the fallopian tube when a male sperm meets the female egg (the ovum) and fertilises it. The fertilised ovum now contains genetic material from both mother and father – a total of 46 chromosomes (23 pairs) – and conception has taken place: a new life begins.

Fertilisation

Fertilisation happens when an egg cell meets with a sperm cell and joins with it. This happens after sexual intercourse. Sperm cells travel in semen from the penis and into the top of the vagina. They enter the uterus through the cervix and travel to the egg tubes. If a sperm cell meets with an egg cell there, fertilisation can happen. The fertilised egg divides to form a ball of cells called an **embryo**. This attaches to the lining of the uterus and begins to develop into a **foetus** and finally a baby.

Genes and inheritance

Each cell in the human body contains 23 pairs of **chromosomes** – i.e. 46 chromosomes in total (except the sex cells – sperm and ova – which have

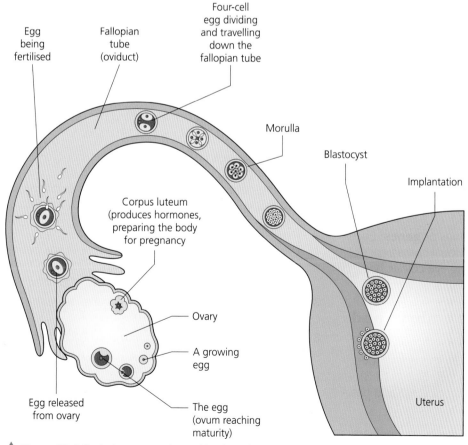

Egg being fertilised

Fallopian tube (oviduct)

Four-cell egg dividing and travelling down the fallopian tube

Morulla

Blastocyst

Implantation

Corpus luteum (produces hormones, preparing the body for pregnancy

Ovary

A growing egg

Egg released from ovary

The egg (ovum reaching maturity)

Uterus

▲ **Figure 12.1** Ovulation, conception and implantation

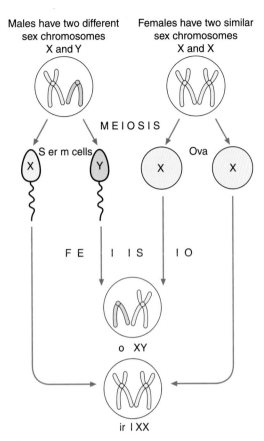

Figure 12.2 Sex determination

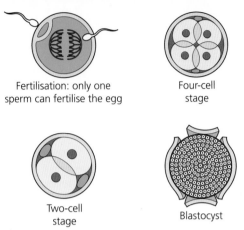

Figure 12.3 The early days of life

23 chromosomes). When fertilisation takes place, the male and female chromosomes from these sex cells join together to form a new cell, called a zygote, which has its full 23 pairs.

Girl or boy?

In humans, sex is determined by the male. Sperm cells contain an X or a Y chromosome but egg cells contain only X chromosomes. If a sperm cell carrying an X chromosome fertilises the egg, the resulting baby will be female; if the sperm cell is carrying a Y chromosome then the baby will be male.

Each chromosome contains thousands of **genes**. Each gene is responsible for certain individual characteristics inherited from the parents, including eye colour, hair colour and height.

The development of the embryo and foetus: the early days of life

Within about 30 hours of fertilisation, the egg divides into two cells, then four, and so on (see Figure 12.3); after five days it has reached the 16-cell stage and has arrived in the uterus (womb).

Sometimes a mistake happens and the ovum implants in the wrong place, such as in the fallopian tube; this

is called an ectopic pregnancy and it is not sustainable. By about the tenth day, the cell mass forms a tiny ball of new tissue called a **blastocyst** and has embedded itself entirely in **endometrium**, and the complex process of development and growth begins. The outer cells of the blastocyst go on to form:

- the placenta (called chorionic villi during early development). The placenta (afterbirth) provides the foetus with oxygen and nourishment from the mother via the **umbilical cord** and removes the foetal waste products. The placenta also acts as a barrier to certain microorganisms, but some may cross this barrier and cause damage to the embryo or foetus.
- **amniotic sac** (or membranes). This sac is filled with amniotic fluid (mostly composed of water) and provides a protective cushion for the foetus as it develops and becomes more mobile.

The inner cell mass goes on to form the embryo proper. Until eight weeks after conception the developing baby is called an embryo; from eight weeks until birth the developing baby is called a foetus. The embryonic cells are divided into three layers:

1 The **ectoderm** – forms the outer layer of the baby, the skin, nails and hair; it also folds inwards to form the nervous system (brain, spinal cord and nerves).

2 The **endoderm** – forms all the organs inside the baby.

3 The **mesoderm** – develops into the heart, muscles, blood and bones.

Development of the embryo

At **4–5 weeks**, the embryo is the size of a pea (5 mm) and yet the rudimentary heart has begun to beat, and the arms and legs appear as buds growing out of the sides of the body (Figure 12.4).

◀ **Figure 12.4** Embryo at 4–5 weeks

At **6–7 weeks**, the embryo is 8 mm long and the limb buds are beginning to look like real arms and legs; the heart can be seen beating on an ultrasound scan (Figure 12.5).

◀ **Figure 12.5** Embryo at 6–7 weeks

At **8–9 weeks** the unborn baby is called a foetus and measures about 2 cm. Toes and fingers are starting to form and the major internal organs (brain, lungs, kidneys, liver and intestines) are all developing rapidly (Figure 12.6).

◀ **Figure 12.6** Foetus at 8–9 weeks

At **10–14 weeks** the foetus measures about 7 cm and all the organs are complete. By 12 weeks the unborn baby is fully formed and just needs to grow and develop. The top of the mother's uterus (the fundus) can usually be felt above the pelvic bones (Figure 12.7).

◀ **Figure 12.7** Foetus at 10–14 weeks

At **15–22 weeks**, the foetus is large enough for the mother to feel its movements. A mother who has had a child before may feel fluttering sensations earlier as she is able to identify them. At 22 weeks the greasy, white protective film called **vernix caseosa** has begun to form and the foetus is covered with a fine, downy hair called **lanugo** (Figure 12.8).

◀ **Figure 12.8** Foetus 15–22 weeks

At **23–30 weeks**, the foetus is covered in vernix and the lanugo has usually disappeared. From 28 weeks the foetus is said to be **viable** – that is, if born now, he has a good chance of surviving, although babies have survived from as early as 23 weeks. The mother may be aware of his response to sudden or loud noises and he will be used to the pitch and rhythm of his mother's voice. At 30 weeks the foetus measures 42 cm (Figure 12.9).

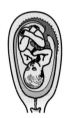

◀ **Figure 12.9** Foetus at 23–30 weeks

At **31–40 weeks**, the foetus begins to fill out and become plumper; the vernix and lanugo disappear and the foetus usually settles into the head-down position ready to be born. If his head moves down into the pelvis it is said to be 'engaged', but this may not happen until the onset of labour (Figure 12.10).

◀ **Figure 12.10** Foetus at 31–40 weeks

Factors influencing the health of a newborn baby

There are many factors that can influence the health of a newborn baby. These include preconceptual care, antenatal care, care around the time of birth and post-natal care.

The potential effects on development of pre-conception experiences

Preconceptual care means both partners work to reduce known risks before trying to conceive in order to create the best conditions for an embryo to grow and develop into a healthy baby – in other words, actively planning for a healthy baby. Caring for the *woman's* health is particularly important because in the very early weeks of pregnancy she may not even know she is pregnant – but the first 12 weeks of life in the womb (or uterus) are the most crucial as this is when all the essential organs are being formed. A balanced

Fertilisation – Fertilisation is the moment when sperm and egg meet, join and form a single cell. It usually takes place in the Fallopian tubes. The fertilised egg then travels into the uterus, where it implants in the lining before developing into an embryo and then a foetus.

Embryo – The unborn child during the first eight weeks after conception

Foetus – The unborn child from the end of the eighth week after conception until birth.

Chromosome – An organised structure containing most of the DNA of a living organism.

Genes – The individual instructions that tell our bodies how to develop and function. They govern our physical and medical characteristics, such as hair colour, blood, type and sustainability to disease.

Blastocyst – The rapidly dividing fertilised egg when it enters the woman's uterus.

Endometrium – The lining of the womb that grows and sheds during a normal menstrual cycle and which supports a foetus if a pregnancy occurs.

Umbilical cord – The cord connecting the foetus to the maternal placenta. It contains blood vessels that carry nutrients to the placenta and remove waste substances from the placenta.

Amniotic sac – Often called 'membranes' or the 'bag of waters', the amniotic sac is the bag of amniotic fluid that surrounds and cushions the foetus.

Vernix – A protective white greasy substance that often covers the skin of the newborn baby.

Lanugo – Downy, fine hair on a foetus. Lanugo can appear as early as 15 weeks of gestation, and typically begins to disappear sometime before birth.

Viable – Able to maintain an independent existence – to live after birth.

Chromosomal abnormality – An abnormality in the number or structure of chromosomes. Chromosomes are the structures that hold our genes.

Think about ideas

- Where does fertilisation take place?
- When does the embryo become a foetus?
- At what stage is the foetus considered to be viable – i.e. capable of independent life outside the womb?

this is not good advice. Research shows that it is the quality (not quantity) of a baby's nutrition before birth that lays the foundation for good health in later life. Therefore, during pregnancy, women should eat a well-balanced diet, and also should do the following:

- ***Avoid pre-packed foods*** and any foods that carry the risk of salmonella or listeria (such as soft or blue-veined cheeses, pate, liver and raw meat). Listeria can cause miscarriage, premature labour or severe illness in a newborn baby.

- ***Take folic acid tablets and have a diet rich in folic acid***: when taken both pre-conceptually and in pregnancy, folic acid helps the development of the brain and spinal cord, and also helps to prevent defects such as **spina bifida**. Sources of folic acid include broccoli, nuts and whole grain cereals.

The mother's age

The best age to have a baby from a purely physical point of view is probably between 18 and 30 years. Complications of pregnancy and labour are slightly more likely above and below these ages.

- ***Younger mothers***: under the age of 16 years there is a higher risk of having a small or premature baby, of becoming anaemic and suffering from high blood pressure. In addition, emotionally and socially, very young teenagers are likely to find pregnancy and motherhood hard to cope with, and they will need a great deal of support.

- ***Older first-time mothers***: first-time mothers over the age of 35 run an increased risk of having a baby with a **chromosomal abnormality**. The most common abnormality associated with age is Down's syndrome. A woman in her 20s has a chance of only one in several thousand of having an affected baby, but by 40 years the risk is about 1 in every 110 births, and at 45 the risk is about 1 in every 30. Amniocentesis can detect the extra chromosome which results in Down's syndrome; it is usually offered routinely to women who are 37 or over.

Number of pregnancies

Some problems occur more frequently in the first pregnancy than in later ones, e.g. breech presentation, pre-eclampsia (see below), low birth weight and neural

diet is important in allowing the woman to build up reserves of the nutrients vital to the unborn baby in the first three months. The known risks to the baby's development are similar to those during pregnancy – for example, if the mother-to-be smokes or drinks alcohol or takes recreational drugs, the unborn baby's development can be impaired.

The potential effects on development during pregnancy

Different factors may affect the growth and development of the foetus while in the womb.

Diet during pregnancy

Every pregnant woman hears about 'eating for two', but the best information available today suggests that tube defects. First babies represent a slightly higher risk than second and third babies do. The risks begin to rise again with fourth and successive pregnancies; this is partly because the uterine muscles are less efficient, but it also depends to a certain extent on age and on the social factors associated with larger families.

Maternal health

Pre-eclampsia is a complication of later pregnancy that can have serious implications for the well-being of both mother and baby. The oxygen supply to the baby may be reduced and early delivery may be necessary. It is characterised by:

- a rise in blood pressure
- *oedema* (swelling) of hands, feet, body or face, due to fluid accumulating in the tissues
- protein in the urine.

In severe cases, pre-eclampsia may lead to *eclampsia*, in which convulsions (seizures) can occur. This can occasionally threaten the life of both mother and baby. If pre-eclampsia is diagnosed, the woman is admitted to hospital for rest and further tests.

Smoking

Smoking during pregnancy cuts the amount of oxygen supplied to the baby through the placenta. Babies born to mothers who smoke are more likely to be born prematurely or to have a low birth weight. (It is also important to continue not to smoke after the baby is born, as babies born into a household where there is a smoker are more at risk of cot death, chest infections and asthma.)

Alcohol

Alcohol can harm the foetus if taken in excess. Babies born to mothers who drank large amounts of alcohol throughout the pregnancy may be born with **foetal alcohol syndrome**. These babies have characteristic facial deformities, stunted growth and mental retardation. Even moderate drinking may increase the risk of miscarriage. It is best to avoid alcohol when trying to conceive, during pregnancy and whilst breastfeeding.

Substance misuse

Most drugs taken by the mother during pregnancy will cross the placenta and enter the foetal circulation. Some of these may cause harm, particularly during the first three months after conception:

- **Prescription drugs**: drugs are sometimes prescribed by the woman's doctor to safeguard her health during pregnancy, such as antibiotics or anti-epilepsy treatment. This has to be very carefully monitored to minimise any possible effects on the unborn child.

KEY TERMS

Foetal alcohol syndrome – The physical and mental problems that can develop in a baby as a result of the mother consuming alcohol during the pregnancy.
Congenital – A trait, habit or physical abnormality present from birth.
Intellectual disability (ID) – intellectual development disorder (IDD) or general learning disability is a neurodevelopmental disorder. People who have intellectual and adaptive function which is significantly impaired can be said to have ID.

- **Non-prescription drugs**: drugs such as aspirin and other painkillers should be checked for safety during pregnancy.
- **Illegal drugs**: recreational drugs such as cocaine, crack and heroin may cause the foetus to grow more slowly. Babies born to heroin addicts are also addicted, and suffer painful withdrawal symptoms. They are likely to be underweight and may even die.

Infection

Viruses and small bacteria can cross the placenta from the mother to the foetus, and may interfere with normal growth and development. During the first three months of a pregnancy, the foetus is particularly vulnerable. The most common problematic infections are:

- **Rubella (German measles)** – a viral infection which is especially harmful to the developing foetus as it can cause **congenital** defects such as blindness, deafness and mental retardation. All girls in the UK are now immunised against rubella before they reach childbearing age, and this measure has drastically reduced the incidence of babies affected or damaged by rubella.
- **Cytomegalovirus (CMV)** – this virus causes vague aches and pains, and sometimes a fever. It poses similar risks to the rubella virus such as blindness, deafness and **ID**, but – as yet – there is no preventive vaccine. It is thought to infect as many as 1 per cent of unborn babies, of whom about 10 per cent may suffer permanent damage.
- **Toxoplasmosis** – an infection caused by a tiny parasite. It may be caught from eating anything infected with the parasite, including:
  - raw or undercooked meat, including raw cured meat such as Parma ham or salami
  - unwashed, uncooked fruit and vegetables

● cat faeces and soil contaminated with cat faeces

● unpasteurised goat's milk and dairy products made from it.

In about one-third of cases, toxoplasmosis is transmitted to the foetus and may cause blindness, hydrocephalus (see page 229) or ID. Infection in late pregnancy usually has no ill effects.

● **Syphilis** – a bacterial sexually transmitted disease (STD). It can only be transmitted across the placenta after the 20th week of pregnancy, and causes the baby to develop congenital syphilis or even lead to the death of the foetus. If the woman is diagnosed as having the disease at the beginning of pregnancy, it can be treated satisfactorily before the 20th week.

Antenatal care

The main aim of antenatal care is to help the mother deliver a healthy baby. Women are encouraged to see their family doctor (General Practitioner or GP) as soon as they think they might be pregnant. The team of professionals – midwife, doctor, health visitor and obstetrician – will discuss the options for antenatal care, delivery and post-natal care with the mother.

Antenatal care has the following principles or aims:

● a safe pregnancy and delivery, resulting in a healthy mother and baby

● the identification and management of any deviation from normal

● preparation of both parents for labour and parenthood

● an emotionally satisfying experience

● promotion of a healthy lifestyle and breastfeeding.

The women most at risk of developing complications during pregnancy are those in poor housing, on a poor diet or whose attendance at antenatal clinics is infrequent or none at all. The midwife and health visitor will be aware of the risks that such factors pose for both mother and baby, and will target such individuals to ensure that preventive health care, such as surveillance and immunisation, reaches them.

Signs of pregnancy

The signs and symptoms of pregnancy occur after the fertilised ovum has implanted in the lining of the uterus. Pregnancy (sometimes referred to as the period of 'gestation') normally lasts from 37 to 42 weeks from the first day of the woman's last period, and is usually confirmed by a simple urine test.

Parentcraft classes

Childbirth preparation classes are available, usually in later pregnancy; these are held in hospitals, health centres, community halls and private homes. They usually welcome couples to attend and aim to cover the following areas:

● all aspects of pregnancy – diet and exercise; sexual activity; how to cope with problems such as nausea, tiredness and heartburn

● labour – what to expect; pain control methods; breathing and relaxation exercises

● birth – what happens at each stage and the different methods of delivery

● the new baby – what to expect and how to care for a newborn; common problems, including post-natal depression.

Diagnostic tests in pregnancy

Diagnostic tests confirm whether a baby has a certain condition and are offered if the screening tests predict an increased risk of a problem. Unlike the screening tests, these tests do carry a slight risk of miscarriage.

Amniocentesis

Amniocentesis is a diagnostic test that is usually used between 15 and 19 weeks of pregnancy. It is offered to any woman who has a higher risk of carrying a baby with **Down's syndrome** – either because she is in the higher age group (over 35) or because prior tests (such as the **maternal serum screening** test or MSS) have detected a higher risk of abnormality.

A fine needle is inserted into the amniotic fluid surrounding the baby. Ultrasound is used to guide the positioning of the needle. The amniotic fluid contains some cells from the baby that are cultured in the laboratory and then analysed in detail. Full results can take up to four weeks.

This is an accurate way of finding out whether the baby has a number of genetic or inherited disorders, such as Down's syndrome or **cystic fibrosis**. Amniocentesis carries a slight risk of harming the baby or causing a miscarriage. It is usually only offered to women when screening tests show they may be at a higher risk of having a baby with a genetic disorder, or to women over 37 years old.

KEY TERMS

Alpha-fetoprotein (AFP) – A protein, produced by the foetus's liver, which can be detected in the mother's blood most accurately between the 16th and 18th weeks of pregnancy. High levels of AFP may be associated with **spina bifida**; low levels may be associated with **Down's syndrome**.

Down's syndrome – A genetic disorder resulting from the presence of an extra chromosome; children usually, but not always, have learning difficulties.

Spina bifida – This occurs when the spinal canal in the vertebral columns is not closed (although it may be covered with skin). Individuals with spina bifida can have a wide range of physical disabilities. In the more severe forms the spinal cord bulges out of the back, the legs and bladder may be paralysed, and obstruction to the fluid surrounding the brain causes hydrocephalus (which is an abnormal amount of cerebrospinal fluid in the brain, often called 'water on the brain').

Maternal serum screening (MSS) – A blood test offered to pregnant women if they want to find out if they have a greater risk of having a baby with downs syndrome, neural tube defects (such as spina bifida) or Trisomy 18 (which is a chromosomal abnormality).

Cystic fibrosis – A condition that affects certain organs in the body, especially the lungs and pancreas, by clogging them with thick sticky mucus. New treatments mean people with cystic fibrosis can live relatively healthy lives.

Neural tube defects – This term includes anencephaly, encephalocoele and spina bifida. These conditions occur if the brain and/or spinal cord, together with its protecting skull and spinal column, fail to develop properly during the first month of embryonic life.

Think about ideas

- Why are some women offered diagnostic tests in pregnancy, and what disorders may they diagnose?
- Should prospective parents be able to obtain whatever genetic information they want about their foetus?

Chorionic villus sampling (CVS)

For CVS, a fine instrument is inserted through the woman's cervix into the uterus and a sample of the chorionic villi (tiny finger like projections found in the placenta) is removed. These have the same genetic material as the baby. This test looks for similar problems as amniocentesis, although it does not test for **neural tube defects**. CVS is performed earlier – usually between 10 and 12 weeks of pregnancy, and the results are usually available within a few days. The results are not quite as accurate as amniocentesis, the procedure is technically quite difficult and it is not always successful. There is a slightly higher risk of miscarriage with CVS than with amniocentesis.

The birth and the potential effects on development of birth experiences

The majority of babies are born safely, usually in hospital, but sometimes in a special midwife-led unit or at home. Giving birth is a momentous event; everyone reacts differently, and while many mothers feel an immediate rush of love and excitement, others can feel quite detached, needing time to adjust. Early contact with their newborn baby is equally important for fathers as for mothers, and learning how to care for a newborn baby can make couples feel closer. Many mothers experience the 'baby blues' – a feeling of mild depression caused by hormonal changes, tiredness and reaction to the excitement of the birth. If these feelings persist for longer than a few days, the mother may develop a more serious condition, post-natal depression, and she will need medical help.

Most women give birth vaginally (called a normal delivery), but sometimes the delivery is **assisted** medically, using forceps, vacuum delivery or a **Caesarean section** (see page 230 for definition).

Forceps delivery

Forceps are like tongs that fit around the baby's head to form a protective 'cage'. They are used during the second stage of labour to help deliver the head under the following circumstances:

- to protect the head during a breech delivery (when the baby presents bottom first)

- if the mother has a condition, such as heart disease or high blood pressure, and must not over-exert herself
- if the labour is very prolonged and there are signs of foetal distress
- if the baby is very small or **preterm (premature)**.

Vacuum delivery (ventouse)

This is an alternative to forceps, but can be used before the cervix is fully dilated; gentle suction is applied via a rubber cup placed on the baby's head.

Caesarean section

A Caesarean section is a surgical operation performed under either a general or an epidural anaesthetic; the baby is delivered through a cut in the abdominal wall. The need for a Caesarean section may be identified during pregnancy and is called an elective (planned) operation; for example, when the woman is expecting twins or triplets. A Caesarean section may be performed as an emergency in the following circumstances:

- when induction of labour has failed
- when there is severe bleeding
- when the baby is too large or in a position (such as breech) which makes vaginal delivery difficult
- in *placenta praevia* – when the placenta is covering the cervix
- in cases of severe foetal distress
- if the mother is too ill to withstand labour.

Birth trauma

Occasionally, a baby may suffer from foetal distress during the birth process. This is usually caused by a lack of oxygen to the baby's brain (anoxia). During labour, midwives and doctors look out for signs of foetal distress and will often accelerate the delivery by using forceps.

Premature and multiple birth

Babies who are born before the 37th week of pregnancy are premature babies. Around 10 per cent of babies are born before 38 weeks of pregnancy, and most of them weigh less than 2,500 g. The main problems for premature babies are as follows:

- **Temperature control** – heat production is low and heat loss is high, because the surface area is large in proportion to the baby's weight, and there is little insulation from subcutaneous fat (which is found directly under the skin).
- **Breathing** – the respiratory system is immature and the baby may have difficulty breathing by himself; this condition is called respiratory distress syndrome (RDS). This is caused by a deficiency in

surfactant, a fatty substance that coats the baby's lungs and is only produced from about 22 weeks of pregnancy.

- **Infection** – resistance to infection is poor because the baby has not had enough time in the uterus to acquire antibodies from the mother to protect against infection.

The extent to which prematurity and multiple births affect the healthy development of the foetus and baby varies a great deal and is linked to how *early* a baby or babies are born: the earlier they are born, the more help they are likely to need in these areas.

Advances in the medical and nursing care of babies born prematurely have meant that many babies born after 35 weeks are able to breathe and feed independently, and their healthy development is not usually affected. However, babies who are born very early – such as around 25 weeks – require intensive neonatal care and have a higher risk of developing hearing and sight problems and learning difficulties, than those who are born at full term.

KEY TERMS

Caesarean section – A Caesarean or C-section is when the baby is delivered through an incision in the mother's abdomen and uterus. It is used when a woman cannot give birth vaginally or if the baby is in distress or danger.

Premature (or preterm) baby – A premature baby is one who is born before 37 weeks of gestation.

Post-term babies

Babies born after the expected date of delivery (after 40 weeks of pregnancy) may also experience problems with breathing, feeding and keeping warm. This is because the placenta stops functioning after about 42 weeks, and so fails to provide the larger baby with enough oxygenated blood.

Sources of support for parents following the birth of a baby

After the baby has arrived, it is the role of midwives and health visitors to help parents look after their baby as well as themselves. All families receive a visit from a health visitor around two weeks after their baby is born, to check that the baby is healthy and developing well and to support parents with the challenges of early parenthood.

The role of the health visitor

The health visitor is a qualified registered nurse, midwife, sick children's nurse or psychiatric nurse with specialist qualifications in community health which includes child health, health promotion and education. The health visitor's role is to offer support and encouragement to families through the early years from pregnancy and birth to primary school and beyond. They work closely with GPs and cover the geographical area of the GP practice.

Every family with children under five has a named health visitor. Health visitors offer help and advice to parents on the following:

- their child's growth and development
- common infections in childhood
- common skin problems
- behaviour difficulties
- sleeping, eating, potty training, temper tantrums and teething
- breastfeeding, weaning, healthy eating, hygiene, safety and exercise
- post-natal depression, bereavement and violence in the family.

Health visitors are also involved in:

- working in partnership with families to tailor health plans to their needs
- coordinating child immunisation programmes
- organising and running baby clinics
- breastfeeding support groups
- parent support groups, and parenting courses.

The GP

This is a doctor who has taken further training in general practice. Every family should be registered with a GP, and he or she is the first port of call in cases of illness in the family.

The paediatrician

This is a doctor who has specialised in the care of children up to the age of 16 years. Paediatricians attend all difficult births in case the baby needs resuscitation. The GP may refer a baby or child to a paediatrician for specialist support.

Self-help groups

Often just talking to others helps the carer to feel less isolated. Self-help groups such as Cry-sis or the National Childbirth Trust Post-natal Support System can help by offering support from someone who has been through the same or similar problems.

Routine developmental checks from birth to 12 months

The first question usually asked by parents is, 'Is the baby okay?' The doctor and midwife will observe the newborn baby closely and perform several routine tests which will show whether the baby has any obvious physical problem.

Immediately after birth: the Apgar Score

This is a standard method of evaluating the condition of a newborn baby by checking five vital signs (see Table 12.1). The Apgar Score is assessed at one minute and five minutes after birth; it may be repeated at five-minute intervals if there is cause for concern. Most healthy babies have an Apgar Score of 9, losing one point for having blue extremities; this often persists for a few hours after birth. A low score at five minutes

Apgar score	Interpreting the Apgar score
10	The baby is in the best possible condition.
8–9	The baby is in good condition.
5–7	The baby has mild **asphyxia** and may need treatment.
3–4	The baby has moderate asphyxia and will need treatment.
0–2	The baby has severe asphyxia and needs urgent resuscitation.

▲ **Table 12.1** The Apgar Score

KEY TERMS

Asphyxia – Lack of oxygen in the blood.
Centile charts – Also known as percentile charts or growth charts, these are used to monitor a child's growth regularly and are contained in the child's PCHR.

is more serious than a low score at one minute. In hospital, the paediatrician will be notified if the score is six or under at 5 minutes. Dark-skinned babies are assessed for oxygenation by checking for redness of the conjunctiva (this is the mucous membrane that covers the front of the eye and lines the inside of the eyelids) and inside the mouth.

Developmental reviews during the baby's first year

Personal Child Health Record (PCHR)

All parents are issued with a PCHR (or Red Book) that enables them to keep a record of their child's development. This form is completed by doctors, health visitors and parents, and is a useful source of information if the child is admitted to hospital or is taken ill when the family are away from home. (See figure 12.11).

Centile growth charts

Each child's growth is recorded on a **centile chart** in the child's PCHR. This allows parents and health professionals to see how their height and weight compare to other children of the same age. Boys and girls have different charts because boys are on average heavier and taller, and their growth pattern is slightly different. Since May 2009, the centile charts in the PCHR or red book have been based on measurements taken by the World Health Organization from healthy, breastfed children with non-smoking parents from a range of countries. The charts are used to plot height (or, in young babies, length), weight and head circumference. See Chapter 9, Figure 9.1.

- The 50th centile (or percentile) is the **median**. It represents the middle of the range of growth patterns.
- The 15th centile is close to the bottom of the range. If the height of a child is on the 15th centile, it means that in any typical group of 100 children, 85 would measure more and 15 would measure less.
- The 85th centile is close to the top of the range. If the weight of a child is on the 85th centile, then in any typical group of 100 children, 85 would weigh less and 15 would weigh more.

Developmental reviews

Parents will want to know as soon as possible if their child has problems: it is easier to come to terms with a serious problem in a young baby than in an older child. Early years practitioners are usually very astute in recognising abnormalities in development because of their experience with a wide variety of children.

Do you feel well yourself?	yes ☐	no ☐	not sure ☐
Do you have any worries about feeding your baby?	yes ☐	no ☐	not sure ☐
Do you have any concerns about your baby's weight gain?	yes ☐	no ☐	not sure ☐
Does your baby watch your face and follow with his/her eyes?	yes ☐	no ☐	not sure ☐
Does your baby turn towards the light?	yes ☐	no ☐	not sure ☐
Does your baby smile at you?	yes ☐	no ☐	not sure ☐
Do you think your baby can hear you?	yes ☐	no ☐	not sure ☐
Is your baby startled by loud noises?	yes ☐	no ☐	not sure ☐
Are there any problems in looking after your baby?	yes ☐	no ☐	not sure ☐
Do you have any worries about your baby?	yes ☐	no ☐	not sure ☐

Any other issues you would like to discuss? ....
....
....

Results of newborn bloodspot screening

Condition	Results received? yes / no / not done	Follow-up required? no / yes & reason	If follow-up, outcome of follow-up
PKU			
Hypothyroidism			
Sickle Cell			
Cystic Fibrosis			
Other			

▲ **Figure 12.11** Personal Child Health Record

The face is examined for cleft palate – a gap in the roof of the mouth, and facial paralysis – temporary paralysis after compression of the facial nerve, usually after forceps delivery

Eyes are checked for cataract (a cloudiness of the lens)

Hands are checked for webbing (fingers are joined together at the base) and creases – a single unbroken crease from one side of the palm to the other is a feature of Down's syndrome

The head is checked for size and shape: any marks from forceps delivery are noted

The heart and lungs are checked using a stethoscope; any abnormal findings will be investigated

The neck is examined for any obvious injury to the neck muscles after a difficult delivery

Feet are checked for webbing and talipes (club foot), which needs early treatment

Genitalia and anus are checked for any malformation

Skin – vernix and lanugo may still be present, milia may show on the baby's nose; black babies appear lighter in the first week of life as the pigment, melanin, is not yet at full concentration

The spine is checked for any evidence of spina bifida

Hips are tested for cogenital dislocation using Barlow's test

The abdomen is checked for any abnormality, e.g. pyloric stenosis, where there may be obstruction of the passage of food from the stomach; the umbilical cord is checked for infection

▲ **Figure 12.12** Examination of the newborn baby

6- to 8-week check			
Parental concerns	**Observation**	**Measurement**	**Examination**
The doctor will ask the parent about: • feeding • bowel actions • sleeping • micturition (passing urine).	While the parent is undressing the baby for examination, the doctor will look out for: • the responsiveness of the baby – smiles, eye contact, attentiveness to parent's voice, etc. • any difficulties the parent has holding the baby – which may indicate maternal depression • jaundice and anaemia. The general appearance of the baby will give an indication of whether he or she is well nourished.	The baby is weighed naked and the weight is plotted on the growth chart. The head circumference is measured and plotted on the growth chart.	The eyes are inspected using a light – the baby will turn his or her head and follow a small light beam. An ophthalmoscope is used to check for a cataract. • The heart is auscultated (i.e. listened to with a stethoscope) to exclude any congenital defect. • The hips are manipulated, again to exclude the presence of congenital dislocation of the hips. • The baby is placed prone and will turn his or her head to one side; hands are held with the thumbs inwards and the fingers wrapped around them. • The posterior fontanelle is usually closed by now; the anterior fontanelle does not close until around 18 months.
Hearing			
Most babies will have been screened soon after birth. There is no specific test at this age. The parent is asked if or she thinks the baby can hear. A baby may startle to a sudden noise or freeze for some sounds.			
Health education points			
The doctor will discuss the following health topics, give the first immunisation and complete the personal child health record. • Nutrition: breastfeeding, preparation of formula feeds, specific feeding difficulties. • Immunisation: discuss any concerns and initiate a programme of vaccinations. • Passive smoking: babies are at risk of respiratory infections and middle ear disease. • Illness in babies: how to recognise symptoms. • Crying: coping with frustration and tiredness. • Reducing the risk of cot death (SIDS: sudden infant death syndrome).			

▲ **Table 12.2** Developmental checks in the first six to eight weeks

Six-to-nine-month check			
Parental concerns	**Observation**	**Measurement**	**Examination**
The doctor or health visitor will enquire again about any parental concerns.	The doctor will look out for: • socialisation and attachment behaviour • visual behaviour • communication – sounds, expressions and gestures • motor development – sitting, balance, use of hands, any abnormal movement patterns.	Head circumference and weight are plotted on the growth chart.	Manipulation of the hips is carried out. • The heart is listened to with a stethoscope. • The testes are checked in boys. • The eyes are checked for a squint – if this is present, the child is referred to an ophthalmologist (eye specialist); visual behaviour is checked. • Hearing is sometimes tested by the distraction test.
Health education points			
• Nutrition: weaning; control of sugar intake. • Immunisations: check they are up to date. • Teeth: regular brushing once teeth appear; information on fluoride; visit the dentist. • The need for play and language stimulation. • Accident prevention.			

▲ **Table 12.3** Developmental checks at six to nine months

Two-year check
This check is similar to the previous tests. It is often easier for the health visitor to carry out the check during a home visit. The parent is asked about any general concerns. A physical examination is not normally carried out at this age.

• The height is measured if the child is cooperative.
• Weight is only checked if there is reason for concern.
• The parent is asked if there are any concerns about vision and hearing, and the child is referred to a specialist if necessary.
• A check is made that the child is walking and that the gait (manner of walking) is normal.
• Behaviour and any associated problems are discussed (e.g. tantrums, sleep disturbance, poor appetite or food fads).
• The possibility of iron deficiency is considered. It is common at this age and may be a cause of irritability and developmental and behavioural problems, as well as anaemia.

Health education points

• Nutrition and dental care: the child will be referred to the dentist if teeth are obviously decayed.
• Immunisations: check they are up to date.
• Common behavioural difficulties, such as temper tantrums, sleep disturbance, toilet training.
• Social behaviour: learning to play with other children and to share possessions.
• Accident prevention.

Parental concerns	**Observation**	**Measurement**	**Examination**
This check is usually carried out by the GP and the health visitor. The parent is asked if there are any general concerns about the child's progress and development, or any behavioural or emotional problems.	Motor skills – can the child walk, run and climb stairs? Does the child tire more quickly compared with other children? • Fine manipulative skills – can the child control pencils and paintbrushes? • Behaviour – parents are asked about the child's ability to concentrate, to play with others and to separate from his or her parents without distress. • Vision, language and hearing – observation and discussion with the parent will determine any problems that may need specialist assessment.	Height and weight are measured and plotted on the growth chart.	The heart is listened to for any abnormal sounds. • The lungs are listened to for wheezing. • In a boy, the testes will be checked again; if still not descended, he will be referred to a surgeon. • The spine is inspected for signs of curvature or spina bifida occulta. • Blood pressure is usually measured only if the child has a history of renal disease or growth problems.

Health education points
• Immunisation: pre-school booster.
• Dental care: diet – danger of sweets and snacks; brushing teeth; dental decay; visits to the dentist.
• The child's needs for play, conversation and social learning.
• The recognition and management of minor ailments.
• Accident prevention.

▲ **Table 12.4** Developmental checks at two years

Eight-year check
This is carried out by the school nurse, and parents are encouraged to attend the sessions at school. It involves the following:
• a general review of progress and development; the parent may voice concerns such as bedwetting (enuresis) or food fads
• height and weight are measured
• vision is tested and, if a problem is found, the child is referred to an ophthalmologist or optician.

Health education points
• Accident prevention: particularly safety on the roads and awareness of 'stranger danger'.
• Diet.
• Exercise.
• Dental health.

Hearing
Parents who are concerned that their child is not hearing properly should have access to hearing testing. This is particularly important if the child has had:
• meningitis
• measles
• mumps
• recurrent ear infections or glue ear.

▲ **Table 12.5** Developmental checks at eight years

(Continued from page 232).

Developmental reviews give parents an opportunity to say what they have noticed about their child. They can also discuss anything that concerns them about their child's health and behaviour. Child development is reviewed by doctors and health visitors, either in the child's home or in health clinics. The areas that are looked at are:

- **gross motor skills** – sitting, standing, walking, running
- **fine motor skills** – handling toys, stacking bricks, doing up buttons and tying shoelaces (gross and fine manipulative skills)
- **speech and language** – including hearing
- **vision** – including squint
- **social behaviour** – how the child interacts with others, such as family and friends.

Early detection is important as:

- early treatment may reduce or even avoid permanent damage in some conditions
- an early diagnosis (of an inherited condition) may allow genetic counselling and so avoid the birth of another child with a disabling condition.

Features of the newborn baby

Size

All newborn babies are weighed and their head circumference is measured soon after birth; these measurements provide vital information for professionals when charting any abnormality in development.

- **Length**: it is difficult to measure accurately the length of a neonate and many hospitals have abandoned this as a routine; the average length of a full-term baby is 50 cm.
- **Weight**: the birth weight of full-term babies varies considerably because:
  - first babies tend to weigh less than brothers and sisters born later
  - boys are usually larger than girls
  - usually, but not always, large parents have larger babies and small parents have smaller babies.

The average weight for a baby born at full term in the UK is 3.5 kg (7 lb 7 oz).

- **Head circumference**: the average head circumference of a full-term baby is about 35 cm.

Appearance

The baby will be wet from the amniotic fluid and she may also have some blood streaks on her head or body, picked up from a tear to the **perineum** or an **episiotomy**: this is a small surgical cut in the perineum, the area of skin between the vagina and rectum.

- The head is large in proportion to the body, and may be oddly shaped at first, because of:
  - **moulding** – the head may be long and pointed as the skull bones overlap slightly to allow passage through the birth canal
  - **caput succedaneum** – a swelling on the head, caused by pressure as the head presses on the cervix before birth; it is not dangerous and usually disappears within a few days
  - **cephalhaematoma** – a localised blood-filled swelling or bruise caused by the rupture of small blood vessels during labour; it is not dangerous but may take several weeks to subside.
- **Vernix** (literally, varnish) – or protective grease – may be present, especially in the skin folds; it should be left to come off without any harsh rubbing of the skin.
- **Lanugo**, or fine downy hair, may be seen all over the body, especially on dark-skinned babies and those who are born preterm.
- **Head hair**: the baby may be born with a lot of hair or be quite bald; often the hair present at birth falls out within weeks and is replaced by hair of a different colour.
- **Skin colour**: this varies and depends on the ethnic origin of the baby. At least half of all babies develop **jaundice** on the second or third day after birth; this gives the skin a yellow tinge – usually no treatment is necessary.
- **Mongolian spot**: this is a smooth bluish-black area of discoloration commonly found at the base of the spine on babies of African or Asian origin; it is caused by an excess of **melanocytes**, the brown pigment cells, and is quite harmless.

- **Milia**: sometimes called milk spots, these are small whitish-yellow spots which may be present on the face; they are caused by blocked oil ducts and disappear quite quickly.
- **Birthmarks**: the most common birthmark is a pinkish mark over the eyelids, often referred to as 'stork marks'; they usually disappear within a few months. Other birthmarks, such as strawberry naevus, persist for some years.

Neonatal screening tests

Three screening tests are carried out on the newborn baby to check for specific disorders that can be treated successfully if detected early enough.

- **Barlow's Test**: this is a test for congenital dislocation of the hip and is carried out soon after birth, at six weeks and at all routine developmental testing opportunities until the baby is walking. There are varying degrees of severity of this disorder; treatment involves the use of splints to keep the baby's legs in a frog-like position.
- The **newborn bloodspot test**: all babies are screened for phenylketonuria and congenital hypothyroidism; in some areas babies are also screened for cystic fibrosis, sickle-cell disorders and some other conditions. A small blood sample is taken from the baby's heel and sent for analysis.
  - **Phenylketonuria** is very rare, affecting 1 in 10,000 babies; it is a metabolic disorder that leads to brain damage and learning delay. Early diagnosis is vital since treatment is very effective. This involves a special formula protein diet that has to be followed throughout the person's life.
  - **Congenital hypothyroidism** (CHT) affects 1 in 4,000 babies in UK. Babies born with this condition do not have enough **thyroxin**; untreated babies develop serious, permanent, physical and mental disability. Early treatment with thyroxin tablets prevents disability and should start by 21 days of age.

Screening for hearing impairment

The Otoacoustic Emissions Test (OAE)

Newborn babies are usually screened using the otoacoustic emissions (OAE) test. A tiny earpiece is placed in the baby's outer ear and quiet clicking sounds are played through it. This should produce reaction sounds in a part of the ear called the cochlea, and the computer can record and analyse these. It is painless and can be done while the baby is asleep. Sometimes clear results are not obtained from the

KEY TERMS

Perineum – The skin between the vagina and the rectum.
Episiotomy – A small surgical cut in the perineum.
Jaundice – caused by immaturity of the liver function.
Milia – Small whitish-yellow spots which may be present on the face at birth.
Puerperium – The period of about six weeks which follows immediately after the birth of a child.

KEY TERMS

Retinopathy of prematurity – An abnormal growth of blood vessels in the retina at the back of a premature baby's eye; when severe it can cause loss of vision.
Orthoptist – A professional who investigates, diagnoses and treats defects of vision and abnormalities of eye movement.

OAE test. Then a different method can be used, called the automated auditory brainstem response (AABR): Small sensors are placed on the baby's head and neck, and soft headphones are placed over the ears. Quiet clicking sounds are played through the earphones and a computer analyses the response in the brain, using information from the sensors.

Screening for visual disorders

Screening tests for visual problems are carried out on all children at: the newborn examination, the six-to-eight-week review, and the pre-school (or school-entry) vision check.

The newborn examination and six-to-eight-week review

The eyes of newborn babies are examined for any obvious physical defects, include cross-eyes, cloudiness (a sign of cataracts), and redness. This includes:

- **The red reflex**: this test uses an ophthalmoscope. Light is directed into the baby's eyes and a red reflection should be seen as the light is reflected back. If the reflection is white instead, the child will be referred to a specialist immediately, as it can be a sign of a cataract or other eye condition.
- The **pupil reflex** is checked by shining a light into each eye from a distance of 10cm. The pupils should automatically shrink in response to brightness.
- **General inspection of the eyes** may suggest other conditions. For example, one eye larger than the other may indicate glaucoma.
- A **specialist examination** is indicated in babies who:
  - have an abnormality detected in the above routine examinations, or
  - have a known higher risk of visual disorders.

For example, low birth weight babies at risk of **retinopathy of prematurity**; babies who have a close relative with an inheritable eye disorder; and babies with known hearing impairment.

Developmental reviews are also discussed in Chapter 14, p. 289.

Common neonatal problems and disorders

Jaundice

Jaundice is a common condition in newborn infants that usually shows up shortly after birth. In most cases, it goes away on its own; if not, it can be treated easily. A baby gets jaundice when **bilirubin**, which is a yellowish pigment found in bile, a fluid produced naturally by the body (the liver), builds up faster than the newborn's liver can break it down (usually it would be excreted in the baby's stool or poo). Too much bilirubin makes a jaundiced baby's skin look yellow. This yellow colour will appear first on the face, then on the chest and stomach and, finally, on the legs. Older babies, children, and adults get rid of this yellow blood product quickly, usually through bowel movements.

How is jaundice treated?

Mild to moderate levels of jaundice do not require any treatment. If high levels of jaundice do not clear up on their own, the baby may be treated with special light (phototherapy) or by another treatment. The special light helps to get rid of the bilirubin by altering it to make it easier for the baby's liver to excrete. Another treatment is to give more frequent feeds of breast milk or formula to help pass the bilirubin out in the stools. Increasing the amount of water given to a child is not sufficient to pass the bilirubin because it must be passed in the stools.

Common skin problems in babies

A newborn baby's skin has a unique tender quality, as it has not been exposed to the environment and to ultraviolet radiation. Table 12.6 shows certain common disorders that may affect the newborn child.

Maintaining body temperature

From birth, babies have a heat-regulating mechanism in the brain which enables them to generate body warmth when they get cold. However they can rapidly become very cold for the following reasons:

- they are unable to conserve body warmth if the surrounding air is at a lower temperature than normal
- they have a large surface area compared to body weight
- they lack body fat, which is a good insulator.

Maternity units are always kept at a high temperature (usually about 29°C or 80°F) to allow for frequent undressing and bathing of newborn babies. At home, the room temperature should not fall below 20°C

Common skin disorders in babies	
Dry skin	**Urticaria**
Some babies have dry skin that is particularly noticeable in cold weather. It can be treated by using a water-soluble cream (e.g. E45 cream) instead of soap for washing and by applying Vaseline to lips, cheeks or noses – the most commonly affected skin areas.	In newborns, urticaria presents as red, blotchy spots, often around a small white or yellow blister. They usually appear from around the second day after birth and disappear within a few days. They are harmless to the baby.
Sweat rash	**Milia**
A baby's sweat glands are immature and they do not allow heat to evaporate from the skin. This can lead to a rash of small red spots on the face, chest, groin and armpit. The baby should be kept cool and the skin kept dry; calamine lotion will soothe the itching.	Milia – often called 'milk spots' – occur in 50 per cent of all newborn babies. They are firm, pearly-white pinhead sized spots which are really tiny sebaceous (oily, greasy or fatty) cysts. They are felt and seen mostly around the baby's nose, and will disappear without scarring in three to four weeks.
Peeling	**Cradle cap**
Most newborn babies' skin peels a little in the first few days, especially on the soles of the feet and the palms. Post-mature babies may have extra-dry skin, which is particularly prone to peeling. Babies of Asian and Afro-Caribbean descent often have drier skin and hair than babies of European descent. No treatment is necessary.	This is a type of seborrhoeic dermatitis (a common skin disease which makes your skin, red inflamed and itchy) of the scalp and is common in young babies. It is caused by the sebaceous glands on the scalp producing too much sebum or oil. The scalp is covered with white or yellowish-brown crusty scales which, although they look unsightly, rarely trouble the baby. It may spread as red, scaly patches over the face, neck, armpits and eyebrows. Treatment is by applying olive oil to the affected area overnight to soften the crusts and by special shampoo.
Infantile eczema	
Infantile eczema (or atopic dermatitis) presents as an irritating red and scaly rash, usually on the baby's cheeks and forehead, though it may spread to the rest of the body. It is thought to be caused by an allergy and appears at two to three months. It causes severe itching, made worse by scratching. It should be treated by rehydrating the skin with short, cool baths, using an unscented cleanser and frequent application of special moisturisers. If the eczema is severe, the doctor may prescribe special cortisone creams. The baby's fingernails should be kept short and scratch mittens worn. Cotton clothing should be worn and antibiotics may be used to treat any infection. It is not contagious.	

▲ **Table 12.6** Common skin disorders that affect the newborn child

(or 68 °C). A preterm or light-for-dates baby (who is underweight for his or her age or height) is at an even greater risk of hypothermia.

The importance of loving, secure relationships

The way in which babies are cared for has a huge impact on how they will respond to difficulties and relationships later in life. Babies learn and begin to make sense of the world through **responsive care** and loving, secure relationships. If they learn to feel and enjoy their parents' love, care, comfort and protection, they will start to feel secure and understood. Being in warm, loving surroundings, with plenty of physical contact, is the single most important factor for improving a baby's physical and emotional well-being. Babies and toddlers are more likely to feel safe and loved when the same familiar people are looking after them each day. As early years practitioners, you need, above all, to have 'empathy' – to be able to appreciate the world from a baby's point of view. See sections on attachment in this chapter, p. 60 and in Chapter 10, pp. 193–195. See also Chapter 11, p. 203 for a definition of empathy.

During the first year of life, babies mostly play with objects, with someone they love, or by themselves (solitary play). There are many ways in which you can play with a baby; babies do not need a room full of expensive toys in order to play. The most important part of a baby's development is to experience continuous attention and affection from their parents, caregivers, relations and other significant adults. Any toys and activities that you use with the babies in your care should be chosen carefully (see box below).

> **KEY TERM**
>
> **Responsive care** – Building close relationships with babies and children, being observant of them and meaningfully involved with them. Adults need to demonstrate a sensitive and caring approach through words and facial expressions.

The importance of play

Play is important because it helps babies to:

- learn about and understand the world around them
- socialise and form relationships with their primary carers.

From a very early age babies learn best by exploring the world through their senses – touch, sight, hearing, taste and smell – and through their movements. In other words they learn by:

- doing
- seeing
- listening
- tasting

- smelling
- touching.

Look, listen and note

Observing a baby who is becoming more mobile

Plan to observe a baby, who is beginning to be more mobile – for example, starting to crawl, to bottom-shuffle, to stand or to walk. Aim to observe the baby's use of gross motor skills in achieving mobility. Evaluate your observation by:

- assessing the baby's use of gross motor skills
- defining any areas of difficulty
- identifying ways to overcome any difficulty and thus promote development.

Guidelines for good practice

Promoting physical development

Babies master the physical skills of rolling over from front to back, crawling or bottom shuffling, bear walking and standing during their first year. Some babies walk unaided by the age of one year, and 70 per cent of babies walk by the age of 13 months. You can help babies in the following ways:

1 **Sitting**: by about six or seven months, most babies can balance in a secure sitting position for a short while. You can help them by:

   ✔ providing a protective 'ring' so that any sudden overbalancing is safe and painless

   ✔ placing the baby on the floor with legs wide apart for balance and then arranging cushions or rolled-up blankets all around her

   Never leave babies sitting alone on the floor, even for a few minutes, as they could fall and trap their arms awkwardly.

2 **Crawling**: by about nine months, babies are usually starting to crawl, even if they cannot always control their direction. You can help by, for example,:

   ✔ protecting their knees against friction on rough textured carpets etc. (for example, by dressing them in light trousers or dungarees)

   ✔ foreseeing possible dangers, such as steps, splintery floors or unsuitable objects left lying around.

3 **Standing**: most babies can stand for a few moments at around 10 months, but are not able to balance and may suddenly sit down again. You can help them by ensuring that:

   ✔ furniture is stable, i.e. not likely to topple over when babies hold on to pull themselves up

   ✔ there are no dangling cords, electrical flexes or tablecloths which the baby could pull on and cause themselves harm

   ✔ they go barefoot as much as possible, (it helps when babies can feel the floor and so can make sensitive adjustments with their toes to achieve balance).

4 **Walking**: towards the end of the first year, babies are usually standing alone and are able to cruise around the room holding onto furniture. You can help them by:

   ✔ kneeling down one or two paces away from the baby and encouraging them to toddle into your arms

   ✔ letting them walk in bare feet whenever possible; avoid slippery floors and use socks with non-slip soles, rather than shoes, until the baby is walking confidently

   ✔ protecting them from falls and by keeping older, most boisterous children out of their way when they are feeling unsteady and need to practise in a calm environment.

These 'milestones' of physical development are all dependent on the individual baby's confidence and motivation, as well as on their muscles and coordination. You should never try to hurry a baby towards being able to stand or walk. You may hold their development back if, for example, they become afraid of falling over.

Guidelines for good practice

Selecting toys for small babies

1   Is the toy or plaything clean and safe?

✔ no rough or broken edges

✔ no small parts which could become loose and swallowed, for example check the eyes on a soft toy

✔ no strings to become tangled around a baby's neck

✔ not so heavy that a young baby could be injured

✔ no toxic paint

✔ complies with safety standards (if a bought toy, see p. 388).

2   Is the toy or activity appropriate for the child's developmental stage?

✔ if using household objects – wooden spoons, saucepans, keys or empty plastic containers – check that the baby is closely supervised

✔ once the baby is able to walk, even if 'cruising' by holding onto furniture, new safety checks will need to be made.

See Chapter 14 for information on maintaining the safety of babies' toys and equipment.

Think about ideas

Designing a mobile

1   Think of two or more designs for making a mobile.

2   Compare your ideas, considering the following factors:

- availability of resources and materials
- skills and time required
- costs of materials
- appropriateness of the design for its purpose
- safety of the design.

3   Select one of the designs; if possible use a computer graphics program to prepare patterns and write or type up a set of instructions for making the mobile.

4   Follow your instructions and make the mobile. Evaluate both the instructions – were they easy to follow or did you have to modify the plan? – and the mobile. If appropriate, offer the mobile as a gift to a baby known to you (perhaps in family placement) and conduct a detailed observation on the baby's reaction to the mobile and his or her associated behaviour.

Guidelines for good practice

Promoting language development

Talking to babies is easier for some people than for others; this applies to the baby's parents as well as to carers. Some people are naturally chatty; others are naturally quiet and may feel silly talking to a baby who cannot 'talk' back to them. While you cannot change your personality, there are a number of ways in which you can communicate effectively with babies:

✔ Always listen to babies; when they smile at you or make cooing sounds, try to answer in words. You do not have to keep up a running commentary – you just have to be responsive to the baby's efforts to communicate.

✔ Try to talk normally, without trying to simplify your language, so that it feels natural and like a real conversation with a friend.

✔ Tell babies what you are doing whenever you are handling them; e.g. if you are feeding a baby, talk about the food and about what the next course will be.

✔ Ask questions, such as 'Was that nice?' and 'Where's it gone?' The baby will answer with a gesture or a facial expression that speaks as clearly as any words.

✔ Bath time is a good time to talk to babies; talk to them and tell them what you are doing: 'I'm just going to put some soap on your tummy now.'

✔ Read picture books to babies; point to the pictures and name them. Even though young babies cannot understand what is going on in the book, they will be very responsive and will enjoy taking part in the experience.

✔ Learn some simple nursery rhymes and action songs; babies love to hear the old favourites such as 'This little piggy went to market'. Try to find out some simple rhymes or songs from other cultures too.

See Chapters 6 to 10 for information on promoting development of babies.

Promoting development and learning in babies

The normative development of babies is discussed in Chapter 6. You need to have a thorough knowledge of these norms of development in order to:

- be reassured that babies are developing as expected
- identify those babies who, for some reason, may not be following these normative stages
- build up a picture of a baby's progress over time
- anticipate – and to respond appropriately to – certain types of age-related behaviour
- guide you in providing for the baby's developmental needs.

As well as knowing about babies' developmental milestones, you need to know how to promote a baby's development in a wider, holistic sense.

Positive overall care and safe practice

In Chapter 13, the factors that make up a safe, stimulating and caring environment for children over one year are described. The same principles apply when caring for babies in domestic and

in nursery settings. The **key person system** is particularly important for providing continuity of care. Babies need to be cared for by just one person most of the time, so that they can form a close relationship. This also helps to minimise the difficulty of separation for babies from their parents or primary carers. The baby's key person is responsible for:

- the routine daily hands-on care, e.g. feeding, washing, changing etc.
- observing the baby's development
- encouraging a wide range of play activities tailored to the baby's individual needs
- recording and reporting any areas of concern
- liaising with the baby's primary carers or parents and establishing a relationship which promotes mutual understanding.

Any setting which uses the key person system should have a strategy for dealing with staff absence or holidays.

Hypothalamus – This functions to regulate body temperature, certain metabolic processes, and other autonomic activities.

(See also Chapter 19 for information on the key person role and the lead professional role.)

The importance of routines

Routines – for example around mealtimes and bedtimes – can be very useful in helping babies and toddlers to adapt both physically and emotionally to a daily pattern, which suits both them *and* those caring for them. This is especially helpful during times of transition and change in their lives, such as starting nursery or moving house. If certain parts of the day remain familiar, they can cope better with new experiences. Having routines for everyday activities also ensures that care is consistent and of a high quality. This does not mean that caring for babies is, or should be, in itself a routine activity. Anyone looking after babies should be able to adapt to their individual needs, which will change from day to day. Therefore, you need to be flexible in your approach and allow, whenever feasible, the individual baby to set the pattern for the day – as long as all the baby's needs are met.

Care for a baby's skin

A baby's skin is soft and delicate, yet forms a tough pliant covering for the body. The skin has many important functions:

- **protection** – it protects underlying organs and, when unbroken, prevents germs entering the body

- **sensation** – each square centimetre of skin contains up to 250 nerve endings called receptors. These detect different feelings, such as touch, cold, warmth, pressure, pain and hair movement

- **secretion of oil** (sebum) – this lubricates the skin and gives hair its shine

- **manufacture of vitamin D** – vitamin D is made when the skin is exposed to sunlight and is essential for healthy bones and teeth. Black skin protects against sunburn but is less efficient at making vitamin D, and black children may need a supplement of vitamin D in the winter

- **excretion** – the skin excretes waste products in sweat

- **temperature regulation** – the **hypothalamus** in the brain controls body temperature by causing the skin to release sweat. This evaporates from the skin's surface, cooling the body.

A topping and tailing routine

1. Wash your hands.
2. Remove the baby's outer clothes, leaving on her vest and nappy.
3. Wrap the baby in the towel, keeping her arms inside.
4. Using two separate pieces of cotton wool (one for each eye; this will prevent any infection passing from one eye to the other), squeezed in the boiled water, gently wipe the baby's eyes in one movement from the inner corner outwards.
5. Gently wipe all around the face and behind the ears. Lift the chin and wipe gently under the folds of skin. Dry each area thoroughly by patting with a soft towel or dry cotton wool.
6. Unwrap the towel and take the baby's vest off, raise each arm separately and wipe the armpit carefully as the folds of skin rub together here and can become quite sore – again dry thoroughly and dust with baby powder if used.
7. Until the cord has dropped off, make sure that it is kept clean and dry using special antiseptic powder supplied by the midwife.
8. Wipe and dry the baby's hands.
9. Take the nappy off and place in lidded bucket.
10. Clean the baby's bottom with moist swabs, then wash with soap and water; rinse well with flannel or sponge, pat dry and apply protective cream.
11. Put on clean nappy and clothes.

Topping and tailing

A young baby does not have to be bathed every day because only his/her bottom, face and neck, and skin creases get dirty and her skin may become dry or tend to dryness. If a bath is not given daily, the baby should have the important body parts cleansed thoroughly – a process known as 'topping and tailing'. This process limits the amount of undressing and helps to maintain good skin condition. Whatever routine is followed, the newborn baby needs to be handled gently but firmly, and with confidence. Most babies learn to enjoy the sensation of water and are greatly affected by your attitude. The more relaxed and unhurried you are, the more enjoyable the whole experience will be.

Babies do not like having their skin open to the air, so should be undressed for the shortest possible time. Always ensure the room is warm, no less than 20°C (68°F) and that there are no draughts. Warm a large, soft towel on a not-too-hot radiator and have it ready to wrap the baby afterwards.

Guidelines for good practice

A bathing routine

1 Undress the baby except for her nappy and wrap her in a towel while you clean her face, as for 'topping and tailing'.

2 Wash her hair before putting her in the bath: support her head and neck with one hand, hold her over the bath and wash her head with baby shampoo or soap; rinse her head thoroughly and dry with second towel.

3 Unwrap the towel around her body, remove her nappy and place it in bucket.

4 Remove any soiling from the baby's bottom with cotton wool; remember to clean baby girls from front to back to avoid germs from faeces entering the urethra or vagina.

5 Lay the baby in the crook of one arm and gently soap her body front and back with baby soap. (If preferred, use baby bath liquid added to the bath beforehand.)

6 Lift the baby off the towel and gently lower her into the water, holding her with one arm around the back of her neck and shoulders and holding the far arm to stop her slipping.

7 Talk to the baby and gently swish the water to rinse off the soap, paying particular attention to all skin creases – under arms, between legs and behind knees. Allow time for the baby to splash and kick, but make sure that the water does not become too cold.

8 Lift the baby out and wrap in a warm towel; dry her thoroughly by patting, not rubbing.

9 Baby oil or moisturiser may now be applied to the skin; do not use talcum powder with oils as it will form lumps and cause irritation.

10 Check if fingernails and toenails need cutting. Always use blunt-ended nail scissors and avoid cutting nails too short.

11 Dress the baby in clean nappy and clothes.

Collect all the equipment you will need before you start:

- changing mat
- water that has been boiled and allowed to cool
- cotton wool swabs
- lidded buckets for soiled nappies and used swabs, and clothes
- bowl of warm water
- protective cream, e.g. Vaseline
- clean clothes and a nappy

Bathing the baby

When the bath is given will depend on family routines, but it is best not to bath the baby immediately after a feed, as he/she may be sick. Some babies love being bathed; others dislike even being undressed. Bath time has several benefits for babies (see box below).

Benefits of bath time

Bath time provides:

- the opportunity to kick and exercise
- the opportunity to clean and refresh the skin and hair

- the opportunity for the carer to observe any skin problems, such as rashes, bruises etc.
- a valuable time for communication between the baby and the carer
- a time for relaxation and enjoyment.

Before you start ensure the room is warm and draught-free, and collect all necessary equipment:

- small bowl of boiled water and cotton swabs (as for 'topping and tailing' procedure)
- changing mat
- two warmed towels
- brush and comb
- baby bath filled with warm water – test temperature with your elbow, not with hands as these are insensitive to high temperatures; the water should feel warm but not hot
- lidded buckets
- clean nappy and clothes
- toiletries and nail scissors.

Guidelines for good practice

Keeping babies clean

✔ Cultural preferences in skin care should be observed; cocoa butter or special moisturisers are usually applied to babies with black skin and their bodies may be massaged with oil after bathing.

✔ Always put cold water in the bath before adding hot – many babies have been severely scalded by contact with the hot surface of the bath.

✔ Do not wear dangling earrings or sharp brooches and keep your own nails short and clean.

✔ Never leave a baby or child under 10 years alone in the bath, even for a few seconds.

✔ Do not top up with hot water while the baby is in the bath; make sure that taps are turned off tightly as even small drops of hot water can cause scalds.

✔ From a few months old, babies may be bathed in the big bath, keeping the water shallow and following the same guidelines regarding temperature and safety. A non-slip mat placed in the bottom of the bath will prevent slipping.

✔ Avoid talcum powder because of the risk of inhalation or allergy; if it is used, place on your hands first and then gently smooth it on to completely dry skin.

✔ Do not use cotton wool buds – they are not necessary and can be dangerous when poked inside a baby's ears or nose, which are self-cleansing anyway.

✔ Nail care should be included in the bathing routine. A young baby's nails should be cut when necessary. Do this after a bath when they are soft.

✔ Hair should be washed daily in the first few months, but shampoo is not necessary every day. A little bath lotion added to the bath water could be gradually worked into the baby's scalp until a lather forms and may then be rinsed off using a wrung out flannel.

✔ If the baby dislikes having her hair washed, try to keep hair washing separate from bath time so that the two are not associated as unpleasant events.

Nappy changing

The first 'stool' a newborn baby passes is **meconium** – a greenish-black, treacle-like substance which is present in the baby's bowels before birth and is usually passed within 48 hours of birth. Once the baby starts to feed on milk, the stools change:

- A breastfed baby has fluid, yellow mustard-coloured stools which do not smell unpleasant.

- A bottle-fed baby has more formed stools which may smell slightly.

Babies pass urine very frequently; bottle-fed babies tend to pass stools less often than breastfed babies. Constipation can occur in bottle-fed babies but can be relieved by giving extra boiled water to drink.

Nappies

The choice of nappies will depend on several factors: convenience, cost, personal preference and concern for the environment. There are two main types of nappy:

1 **Fabric nappies** – these are made from cotton terry towelling and come in different qualities and thickness. Two dozen are required for everyday use. Fabric nappies may be squares or shaped to fit. The latest style is similar in shape to the disposable nappy and has popper fastenings. If using fabric squares, you will also need special nappy safety pins and six pairs of plastic pants. Disposable one-way liners may be used with towelling nappies to keep wetness away from the baby's skin and to make solid matter easier to dispose of, by flushing down the toilet.

2 **Disposable nappies** – these are an all-in-one nappy, liner and plastic pants and are available in a wide range of designs. Some have more padding at the front for boys and there are different absorbencies for day and night-time use. Some brands have resealable tapes so that you can check if the nappy is clean.

Nappy changing

Nappies must be changed regularly to avoid nappy rash, and should always be changed immediately after they have been soiled. You must wear appropriate personal and protective equipment (PPE) when changing nappies – case disposable gloves and aprons. See Chapter 13 and 14 for more information on PPE. Whenever possible, the baby's key person should change the baby's nappy as this helps to develop a close, trusting relationship and enables the key person to report any concerns to the parents. Young babies will need several changes of nappy each day, whenever the nappy is wet or soiled. As with any regular routine, have everything ready before you begin:

a plastic-covered padded changing mat	a bowl of warm water(or baby wipes)
baby lotion	barrier cream, such as zinc and castor oil cream
nappy sacks for dirty nappies	cotton wool
baby bath liquid	new, clean nappy

Guidelines for cleaning the nappy area

1 Disposable gloves and disposable plastic aprons must be worn.

2 Wash your hands and put the baby on the changing mat or secure changing unit.

3 Undo the clothing and open out the nappy. It is quite common for baby boys to urinate just as you remove the nappy, so pause for a few seconds with nappy held over the penis.

4 Clean off as much of the faeces as possible with the soiled nappy. Safely dispose of the nappy and soiled wipes in line with your setting's hygiene policy.

5 **Boys**: moisten cotton wool with water or lotion and begin by wiping his tummy across, starting at his navel. Using fresh cotton wool or baby wipes, clean the creases at the top of his legs, working down towards his anus and back. Wipe all over the testicles, holding his penis out of the way. Clean under the penis. Never try to pull back the foreskin. Lift his legs using one hand (finger between his ankles) and wipe away from his anus, to buttocks and to back of thighs.

6 **Girls**: use wet cotton wool or baby wipes to clean inside all the skin creases at the top of her legs. Wipe down towards her bottom. Lift her legs using one hand (finger between her ankles) and clean her buttocks and thighs with fresh cotton wool, working inwards towards the anus. Keep clear of her vagina and never clean inside the lips of the vulva.

7 Dry the skin creases and the rest of the nappy area thoroughly. Let the baby kick freely and then apply barrier cream if required.

8 Dispose of soiled nappies and wipes according to your setting's hygiene policy. For information on PPE go to Chapter 14.

Guidelines for good practice

Procedure for changing nappies in a group setting

Nappy changing is an important time and you should ensure that the baby feels secure and happy. Singing and simple playful games should be incorporated into the procedure to make it an enjoyable experience. Every setting will have its own procedure for changing nappies. The following is an example:

✔ Nappies should be checked and changed at regular periods throughout the day.

✔ A baby should never knowingly be left in a soiled nappy.

✔ Collect the nappy and the cream needed. Put on apron and gloves. Ensure that you have warm water and wipes. Follow the procedures for nappy changing in close liaison with parents/carers. Carefully put the baby on the changing mat, talking to them and reassuring them.

✔ Once the baby has been changed, dispose of the soiled nappy and discard the gloves in accordance with the policy and procedures of the setting.

✔ Thoroughly clean the nappy mat and the apron with an antibacterial spray.

✔ Wash your hands to avoid cross-contamination.

✔ Record the nappy change on the baby's **Nappy Chart**, noting the time, whether it was wet or dry or if there were any faeces from a bowel movement. Also note any change you have observed – such as in colour or consistency of the stools, or if the baby had difficulty in passing the stool. Also, note if there is any skin irritation or rash present.

✔ Check nappy mats for any tears or breaks in the fabric and replace if necessary.

Never leave a baby or toddler unsupervised on the changing mat or changing unit.

For information on disposing of waste in the early years setting, see your setting's Health and Safety policy on disposal of waste.

Think about ideas

What sort of nappies?

Research the advantages and disadvantages of terry towelling and disposable nappies, including the following information:

● costs – initial outlay for purchase of nappies, liners, pants and continuing costs of laundry

● the effects of each method on the environment – chemicals used in laundering; disposal in landfill

● convenience and suitability for the purpose.

(Continued from page 244).

It is important to pay attention to the differences between boys and girls when cleaning the nappy area – see the guidelines below. If you are using a special changing table or bed, make sure the baby cannot fall off.

Never leave the baby unattended on a high surface. As long as there are no draughts and the room is warm, the changing mat can be placed on the floor.

Nappy rash

Almost all babies have occasional bouts of redness and soreness in the nappy area. This may be caused by leaving wet and dirty nappies on too long, poor washing techniques, infections, skin disorders such as eczema or seborrhoeic dermatitis, or reaction to creams or detergents.

The most common types of nappy rash are:

Candidiasis or thrush dermatitis

This is caused by an organism called candida albicans, a yeast fungus which lives naturally in many parts of the body. The rash is pink and pimply and is seen in the folds of the groin, around the anus and in the genital area; it is sometimes caused in breastfed babies whose mothers have taken a course of antibiotics, or in bottle-fed babies where the teats have been inadequately cleaned and sterilised.

Treatment

- Use a special anti-fungal cream at each nappy change. This is prescribed by the doctor.
- Do not use zinc and castor oil cream until the infection has cleared as the thrush organism thrives on it.
- If oral thrush is also present a prescribed ointment may be used.

Ammonia dermatitis

This produces the most severe type of nappy rash. It is caused when the ammonia present in the baby's urine and stools reacts with the baby's skin; it is more common in bottle-fed babies because their stools are more alkaline, providing a better medium for the organisms to thrive. The rash is bright red, may be ulcerated and covers the genital area; the ammonia smells very strongly and causes the baby a lot of burning pain.

Treatment

- Wash with mild soap and water, and dry gently.
- Expose the baby's bottom to fresh air as much as possible.
- Only use creams if advised and leave plastic pants off.

- If using towelling nappies, a solution of 30 ml vinegar to 2.5 litres of warm water should be used as a final rinsing solution to neutralise the ammonia.

Care of the feet

- Feet should always be washed and dried thoroughly, especially between the toes, and clean socks should be put on every day.
- All-in-one baby suits must be large enough not to cramp the baby's growing feet.
- Toenails should be cut straight across, not down into the corners.

Care for a baby's teeth

Although not yet visible, the teeth of a newborn baby are already developing inside the gums; a baby's first teeth are called deciduous teeth or milk teeth and these start to appear at around 6 months (see Chapter 10). Dental care should begin as soon as the first tooth appears, with visits to the dentist starting in the child's second year. Teeth need cleaning *as soon as they appear*, because **plaque** (see page 247 for definition) sticks to the teeth and will cause decay if not removed. Caring for the temporary first teeth, even though they are temporary, is important because:

1 It develops a good hygiene habit which will continue throughout life.
2 Babies need their first teeth so that they can chew food properly.
3 First teeth guide the permanent teeth into position. If first teeth are missing the permanent teeth may end up crooked.
4 If milk teeth decay, they may need to be extracted; this could lead to crowding in the mouth, as the natural gaps for the second teeth to fill will be too small.
5 Painful teeth may prevent chewing and cause eating problems.
6 Clean, white shining teeth look good.

Cleaning a baby's teeth

Use a small amount – a smear – of baby toothpaste on a soft baby toothbrush or on a piece of fine cloth (e.g. muslin) to clean the plaque from the teeth. Gently smooth the paste on to the baby's teeth and rub lightly. Rinse the brush in clear water and clean her mouth. Brush twice a day – after breakfast and before bed.

It is also important to keep any foods containing sugar to feed times.

Teething

Some babies cut their teeth (i.e. their teeth appear through their gums) with no ill effects; others may experience:

- general fretfulness (they may rub the mouth or ears)
- red or sore patches around the mouth
- diarrhoea
- a bright red flush on one or both cheeks, and on the chin
- dribbling.

Teething should not be treated as an illness, but babies will need comforting if in pain. Teething rings and hard rusks usually provide relief. Teething powders and gels are not advised, as they are dangerous if given in large quantities. Infant paracetamol may be helpful in relieving pain but is unsuitable for babies under three months unless advised by the doctor.

Fresh air and sunlight

Babies benefit from being outside in the fresh air for a while each day. When air is trapped in a house it becomes stale, the level of humidity rises and there is an increased risk of infections spreading. Carers working in nurseries should ensure that rooms are well ventilated and that there are opportunities for babies

to go outside. Sunlight is beneficial too, but care should be taken with babies and young children:

- Keep all children out of the sun when it is at its most dangerous, between 11 am and 3 pm; carers of young children should plan outdoor activities to avoid this time unless children are well protected by hats and sun protection cream. Permission must be obtained from the child's parent or guardian before applying sunscreen creams.
- Specialists advise keeping babies up to 9 months of age out of direct sunlight altogether to prevent the risk of developing skin cancer in later life.
- Use sun hats with a wide brim that will protect the face, neck and shoulders on older babies.
- Use sun protection cream on all sun-exposed areas.
- Use sunshades or canopies on buggies and prams.

See Chapter 13 for more information on protecting children in the sun.

Sleep and rest

Everyone needs sleep, but the amount that babies sleep varies enormously, and will depend on the maturity of the brain (the preterm baby may sleep for long periods) and on the need for food. Sleep is divided into two distinct states:

1. **Rapid eye movement (REM)**, which is termed active sleep
2. **Non-rapid eye movement (NREM)**, which is termed quiet sleep.

In REM sleep the mind is active and is processing daytime emotional experiences. In NREM sleep the body rests and restoration occurs. In babies under one year, more of the sleep is active (REM). It is important not to wake babies during deep sleep, as it plays a vital part in restoring energy levels.

A baby aged six weeks

Newborn babies tend to sleep a great deal. At around six weeks old, a baby will probably sleep for shorter spells during the day and longer periods at night. The baby will have more deep, non-REM sleep and less light sleep, but will probably still wake for a feed or more than one feed at night. Sleep and rest periods are spread throughout the 24-hour period, usually comprising four to five periods of rest and sleep, lasting between two and three hours each.

A baby aged six weeks needs to sleep and rest for approximately 15 hours in a 24-hour period.

Guidelines for good practice

Encouraging a baby's sleeping routine

✔ Allow the baby time to settle alone so that she begins to develop her own way of going to sleep. Some babies do cry for a short period as they settle; leave the baby but stay within hearing distance and check after five minutes to see if she is comfortable.

✔ Give the baby plenty of stimulation during the day by talking and playing with her when she is awake.

✔ Try to make night-time feeds as unstimulating as possible; feed, change and settle the baby in her cot.

✔ Make bedtime at night into a routine; by repeating the same process each night, the baby is made to feel secure and comfortable. These are both good aids to sleep.

A baby aged seven months

From four-and-a-half months onwards, most babies are capable of sleeping for eight hours at night without needing a feed. By seven months, babies may have two to three daytime sleeps, each between one-and-a-half and two hours.

A baby aged seven months needs between 13 to 14 hours sleep and rest in a 24-hour period.

See Chapter 13, p. 269 for information on sleep and rest needs of children older than seven months.

Few aspects of parenthood are more stressful than months of broken nights. Carers could try the strategies suggested in the guidelines box above to encourage babies to adopt different sleep patterns for day and night.

Guidelines for good practice

A bedtime routine for babies

Between three and five months, most babies are ready to settle into a bedtime routine.

✔ Give the baby a bath or wash and put on a clean nappy and nightwear.

✔ Take her to say goodnight to other members of the household.

✔ Carry her into her room, telling her in a gentle voice that it is time for bed.

✔ Give the last breast- or bottle-feed in the room where the baby sleeps.

✔ Sing a song or lullaby to help settle her, while gently rocking her in your arms.

✔ Wrap her securely and settle her into the cot or cradle, saying goodnight.

✔ If she likes it, gently 'pat' her to sleep.

The routine can be adapted as the baby grows. Advice from the NHS and The Lullaby Trust is that the safest place for a baby to sleep is in a cot in the parents' room for the first six months.

Reflecting on practice

Contented little babies

Two parents in your nursery are following the advice given in *The Contented Little Baby Book* by Gina Ford, and one of the pieces of advice is that all babies should be placed in a darkened room to have a sleep at 11 am each day. They have each asked their baby's key person to make sure that this happens every day.

1 Do you think the nursery could – or should – accommodate the parents' wishes?

2 What would happen in your own setting if such a request were made?

Think about ideas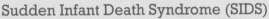

Sudden Infant Death Syndrome (SIDS)

In groups, prepare a display which details the risk factors implicated in SIDS. Using the information provided, make a poster for each risk factor and state clearly the precautions that should be taken to prevent cot death. Access the NHS website: http://www.nhs.uk/conditions/pregnancy-and-baby/pages/reducing-risk-cot-death.aspx for up-to-date recommendations. Also see www.lullabytrust.org.uk

SIDS is covered on pp. 251–252.

Exercise

Exercise strengthens and develops muscles. It also helps to promote sleep, as the body needs to relax after physical activity. Carers of young babies can provide opportunities for exercise in the following ways:

● Give plenty of opportunities for the baby to practise each new aspect of physical development as she becomes capable of it.

● Allow times for wriggling on the floor without being hindered by nappy or clothes.

● Allow freedom to look around, to reach and to grasp.

- Give opportunities to roll, crawl and eventually walk around the furniture safely.
- Provide objects and toys to exercise hand–eye coordination.
- After she has had her first 5-in-1 vaccination, the baby can be taken to special baby sessions at the local swimming pool.

Crying in young babies

Crying is a baby's way of expressing her needs. Finding out why a baby is crying is often a matter of elimination, so it is important that all carers should understand the physical and emotional needs of a baby at each stage of development (see Table 12.7).

Hunger
This is the most common cause of crying. It is quite likely unless the baby has just been fed. Breastfed and bottle-fed babies should be fed on demand in the early weeks. By the age of six months, the baby will probably need solid foods.
Being undressed
Most new babies hate being undressed and bathed, because they miss the contact between fabric and bare skin. One solution is to place a towel or shawl across the baby's chest and tummy when she is naked.
Discomfort
Until they can turn themselves over, babies rely on an adult to change their position. Babies show marked preferences for sleeping positions.
Nappy needs changing
Some babies dislike being in a wet or dirty nappy and there may be nappy rash.
Twitches and jerks
Most new babies make small twitching and jerking movements as they are dropping off to sleep. Some babies are startled awake and find it difficult to settle to sleep because of these twitches. Wrapping a baby up firmly – or swaddling – usually solves the problem.
Overtired or overstimulated
Some babies can refuse to settle if there is too much bustle going on around them, e.g. loud noises, too much bouncing or bright lights in a shopping centre; take her somewhere quiet and try rhythmical rocking, patting and generally soothing her.
Pain or illness
A baby might have a cold or snuffles and be generally fretful or may have an itchy rash, such as eczema. (For signs and **symptoms of illness** in babies, see Table 12.8.)
Allergy
An intolerance of cow's milk could cause crying; seek medical advice.
Thirst
In particularly hot weather, babies may be thirsty and can be given cool boiled water. Breastfed babies may be offered an extra feed as breast milk is a good thirst-quencher.
Feeling too hot or too cold
Temperature control is not well developed in the young baby. If too hot, he or she will look red in the face, feel very warm and may be sweaty around the neck folds; loosen clothes and wrappings and remove some layers of bedding, but watch for signs of chilling. If too cold, he or she may also have a red face or may be pale. To check, feel the hands, feet, tummy and the back of the neck. Cuddle the baby, wrap a blanket around him or her and try a warm feed.
Boredom/need for physical contact
Babies find being cuddled or carried reassuring; talk to her and provide interesting objects for her to look at and a mobile; put pram under a tree or near a washing line so that he or she can see movements (NB: remember to fix a cat net to prevent insects and other unwanted visitors).
Colic
If the baby cries after being fed or has long bouts of crying, especially in the evening, he or she may be suffering from colic.

▲ **Table 12.7** Causes of crying

Guidelines for good practice

Helping a crying baby

✔ Make sure the baby is not hungry or thirsty.

✔ Check that the baby is not too hot or cold.

✔ Check that the baby is not physically ill (see p. 253 for signs of illness in babies).

✔ Check if the baby's nappy needs changing.

✔ Treat colic or teething problems.

✔ Cuddle the baby and try rocking gently in your arms (the most effective rate of rocking is at least 60 rocks a minute; the easiest way to achieve this rapid and soothing rocking without getting exhausted is to walk while rocking her from side to side).

✔ Rock the baby in a cradle or pram.

✔ Talk and sing to the baby.

✔ Take the baby for a walk or a car ride.

✔ Leave the baby with someone else and take a break.

✔ Play soothing music or a womb sounds recording.

✔ Talk to a health visitor, GP or a parent's helpline.

✔ Accept that some babies will cry whatever you do.

✔ Remember that this phase will soon pass.

If the crying ever feels too much to bear:

✔ Take a deep breath and let it out slowly. Put the baby down in a safe place, like a cot or a pram. Go into another room and sit quietly for a few minutes, perhaps with a cup of tea and the television or radio on to help take your mind off the crying. When you feel calmer, go back to the baby.

✔ Ask a friend or relative to take over for a while.

✔ Try not to get angry with the baby. She will instinctively recognise your displeasure and will probably cry even more.

✔ Never let things get so bad that you feel desperate. There are lots of organisations that can help at the end of a telephone line.

Persistent crying

Some babies do cry a great deal more than others, and are difficult to soothe and comfort. Parents and carers can feel quite desperate through lack of sleep and may develop personal problems; they may suffer guilt at not being able to make their baby happy or lack confidence in caring for her. Such feelings of desperation and exhaustion can unfortunately result in physical violence to the baby – throwing her into the cot, shaking her or even hitting her. Parents experiencing such stress need a great deal of support.

Colic

Some babies keep on crying even when you have tried everything and there are no obvious signs of illness. Colic is excessive crying or extended and repeated periods of crying or fussing in babies who are otherwise healthy and thriving. Common symptoms in babies usually begin within the first few weeks of life and generally end by around three months.

Reflux

Excessive crying might also be caused by reflux, which occurs when the stomach contents – food (milk) and acid – come back up into the throat or into the mouth. Most babies have reflux to a certain degree because the muscular valve at the end of their food pipe, which acts to keep food in the stomach, has not developed properly yet. This is painful for only a small proportion of babies.

Help and advice

Often just talking to others helps the carer to feel less isolated. Self-help groups such as Cry-sis or the National Childbirth Trust Post-natal Support System can help by offering support from someone who has been through the same problem. Talking to the health visitor or GP may help, and some areas run clinics with a programme to stop the 'spiral' of helplessness.

Reflecting on practice

Safety at sleep and rest times

Early years settings should have a policy and procedure for minimising the risk of sudden infant death when babies are resting or sleeping. Staff supervision is the most important factor in ensuring safety at these times. Other considerations include:

- Sleep mats must be placed away from windows and radiators to ensure that babies and children do not overheat during sleep.
- Sleep mats must have at least one inch between them.
- Babies and children will be positioned head to toe – to reduce the risk of spread of infection.

Think about the practice in your setting. If you feel there are any possible risk factors, discuss your concerns with your manager or supervisor.

In pairs, rehearse the procedure to follow if a young baby is found 'apparently lifeless' in his cot. Use a baby resuscitation mannequin test each other's skills.

NB: Professional supervision will be required. First Aid procedures are described in Chapter 15.

KEY TERMS

Possetting – The regurgitation (or bringing back) of a small amount of milk by babies after they have been fed.

Signs of illness – These can be directly observed, for example, a change in skin colour, a rash or a swelling.

Symptoms of illness – These are experienced by the child, for example, pain or discomfort or generally feeling unwell.

Signs and symptoms are covered on page 253.

Sudden infant death syndrome

Sudden infant death syndrome (SIDS) is often called 'cot death'. It is the term applied to the sudden unexplained and unexpected death of an infant. The reasons for cot deaths are complicated and the cause is still unknown. Although cot death is the most common cause of death in babies up to 1 year old, it is still *very rare*, occurring in approximately 2 out of every 1000 babies. Recent research has identified various risk factors.

Guidelines for parents from the NHS

- ✔ Cut smoking in pregnancy – fathers too!
- ✔ Do not let anyone smoke in the same room as your baby.
- ✔ Place your baby on the back to sleep.
- ✔ Do not let your baby get too hot.
- ✔ Keep baby's head uncovered – place your baby with their feet to the foot of the cot, to prevent wriggling down under the covers.
- ✔ If your baby is unwell, seek medical advice promptly.
- ✔ The safest place for your baby to sleep is in a cot in your room for the first six months.
- ✔ It is dangerous to share a bed with your baby if you or your partner:
    - ✔ are smokers (no matter where or when you smoke)
    - ✔ have been drinking alcohol
    - ✔ take drugs or medication that makes you drowsy
    - ✔ feel very tired.
- ✔ It is very dangerous to sleep together on a sofa, armchair or settee.

Guidelines for good practice

Reducing the risk of SIDS

✔ The chance of SIDS is higher in babies who get too hot. The room where an infant sleeps should be at a temperature that is comfortable for lightly clothed adults (16–20°C). Use a room thermometer if necessary and check the baby's temperature by feeling his tummy, making sure your hands are warm beforehand.

✔ Babies should never wear hats indoors, as small babies gain and lose heat very quickly through their heads.

✔ If the baby is a natural tummy-sleeper, keep turning her over onto her back. A musical mobile may help to keep her happy while lying on her back.

✔ Place the baby on a firm, flat mattress that is clean and in good condition. The mattress should be brand new, even if the baby's cot is second-hand. Avoid soft or bulky bedding, including pillows, quilts and duvets.

✔ Never allow the baby to come into contact with smoky rooms; ask visitors not to smoke in the house. The risk factor increases with the number of cigarettes smoked.

✔ Learn to recognise the signs and symptoms of illness and know how to respond. Learn and practise on a special baby resuscitation mannequin how to perform artificial ventilation and cardiac massage. This should always be practised under the supervision of a qualified first-aid trainer.

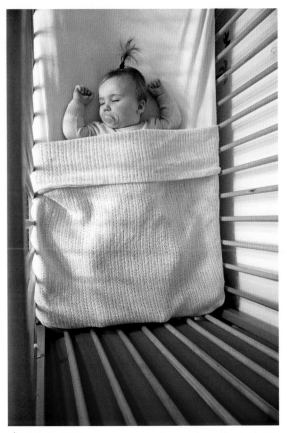

▲ **Figure 12.13** Preventing SIDS: the feet-to-foot position

Common signs of illness in babies	
Raised temperature or fever The baby may look flushed or be pale but will feel hot to the touch. Black babies and those with dark skin tones may look paler than usual and their eyes may lose sparkle. Occasionally a very high temperature may trigger a seizure (fit) or febrile convulsion.	**Refusing feeds/loss of appetite** A young baby may refuse feeds or take very little. An older baby may only want milk feeds and refuse all solids.
Diarrhoea Persistent loose, watery or green stools can quickly dehydrate a baby. Dehydration means that the baby is losing important body salts.	**Vomiting** If persistent or projectile (i.e. so forceful that it is projected several feet from the baby) and not the more usual **possetting** (see page 251 for definition).
Excessive and persistent crying If the baby cannot be comforted in the usual way or if the cry is very different from usual crying.	**Lethargy or 'floppiness'** The baby may appear to lack energy and lack the normal muscle tone.
Dry nappies If the baby's nappies are much drier than usual because he or she has not passed urine, this could be a sign of **dehydration**.	**Persistent coughing** Coughing in spasms lasting more than a few seconds. Long spasms often end with vomiting.
Difficulty with breathing If breathing becomes difficult or noisy with a cough, the baby may have bronchitis or croup.	**Discharge from the ears** Ear infections may not show as a discharge, but babies may pull at their ears and may have a high temperature.
Sunken anterior fontanelle A serious sign of dehydration, possibly after diarrhoea and vomiting. The anterior fontanelle is a diamond-shaped soft spot at the front of the head just above the brow measuring about 4cm to 5cm across. It remains visible in babies up to 12 to 18 months. In dehydrated babies, this area is sunken and more visible.	**Seizures (also called convulsions or fits)** During a seizure the baby either goes stiff or else jerks his or her arms or legs for a period lasting up to several minutes. The eyes may roll upwards, the skin and lips may become blue. The baby may dribble and will be unresponsive to you.

▲ **Table 12.8** Common signs of illness in babies

(this table relates to the text on p. 253)

Look, listen and note

Observing babies

Observe a baby's head, so that you can identify the anterior fontanelle and understand how it should appear in healthy babies. (It is normal in young babies for the anterior fontanelle to bulge slightly when the baby is crying, but this should be temporary).

General signs and symptoms of illness in babies

Babies are not able to explain how they are feeling to their carers, so it is important to recognise some of the general signs that accompany illness. Some babies may cry in a 'strange' way – in a way that is different from their usual cry – indicating pain, hunger or thirst. They may refuse feeds or become unusually listless or lethargic. If the baby has an infection, there will be a raised temperature (or fever).

Some of the common signs of illness in babies are shown in Table 12.8 on page 252.

Identifying signs of illness in babies and children with different skin tones

Both within and between different ethnic groups there is a wide variety of skin tones and colours affecting the way skin looks during illness. When dark-skinned children are ill they may show the following signs:

- **Skin appearance**: normal skin tone and sheen may be lost; the skin may appear dull and paler or greyer than usual. You must pay attention to those parts of the body with less pigmentation – the palms, the tongue, the nails beds and the **conjunctiva** (the insides of the bottom eyelids) — all of these will be paler than usual.

- **Rashes**: in children with very dark skin, raised rashes are more obvious than flat rashes.

- **Bruising**: the discoloration that is obvious in pale skin may not be easily observed in darker-skinned children. When bruised, the skin may appear darker or more purple when compared with surrounding skin.

- **Jaundice**: in a fair-skinned child, gently press your finger to his forehead, nose, or chest, and look for a yellow tinge to the skin as the pressure is released. In a darker-skinned child, check for yellowness in his gums or the whites of his eyes.

When to call the doctor

If you think the baby's life is in danger, **dial 999** if you are in the UK. Ask for an ambulance urgently and explain the situation.

Contact the GP if the baby has any of the symptoms shown in Table 12.9. If the doctor cannot reach you quickly, take the baby to the accident and emergency (A&E) department of the nearest hospital.

Contact the GP if a child shows these symptoms	
Has a temperature of 38.6°C (101.4°F) that is not lowered by measures to reduce **fever**, or a temperature over 37.8°C (100°F) for more than one day	Has **convulsions,** or is limp and floppy
Has severe or persistent **vomiting** and/or **diarrhoea**, seems **dehydrated** or has projectile vomiting	**Cannot be woken**, is unusually drowsy or may be losing consciousness
Has symptoms of **meningitis**	Has symptoms of **croup**
Is pale, listless, and **does not respond** to usual stimulation	**Cries or screams** inconsolably and may have severe pain
Has bulging **fontanelle** (soft spot on top of head of a baby) when not crying	Appears to have severe abdominal pain, with symptoms of **shock**
Refuses two successive feeds (babies)	Develops **purple-red** rash anywhere on body
Passes bowel motions (stools) containing **blood**	Has jaundice
Has a suspected **ear infection**	Has been injured, e.g. **by a burn which blisters and covers** more than 10% of the body surface
Has inhaled something, such as a peanut, into the air passages and may be **choking**	Has swallowed a **poisonous** substance, or an object, e.g. a safety pin or button
Has bright pink cheeks and swollen hands and feet (could be due to **hypothermia**)	Has difficulty in **breathing**

▲ **Table 12.9** When to call a doctor or take the baby to A&E

Your role in reporting and recording illness in early years settings

Nannies and childminders should always contact the baby's parents directly in the case of accident or illness.

In schools and nurseries, you should notify a senior member of staff, who will then decide if and when to contact the baby's parents.

Recording procedures in early years settings are discussed in Chapter 14.

Clothing and footwear

The layette

The layette is the baby's first set of clothes. Many shops specialising in baby goods supply complete layettes, and there is a vast range of clothing available. Baby clothes should be:

- **loose and comfortable** to allow for ease of movement; as babies grow rapidly, care should be taken that all-in-one stretch suits do not cramp tiny feet – there should always be growing space at the feet to avoid pressure on the soft bones

- **easy to wash and dry**, as babies need changing often; natural fibres (e.g. cotton and wool mixtures) are more comfortable; any garment for babies up to three months old must carry a permanent label showing that it has passed the low flammability test for slow burning

- **easy to put on and take off** – avoid ribbons, bows and lacy-knit fabrics which can trap small fingers and toes

- **non-irritant** – clothes should be lightweight, soft and warm; some synthetic fibres can be too cold in winter as they do not retain body heat, and too hot in the summer as they do not absorb sweat or allow the skin pores to 'breathe'.

Footwear for babies

Babies' feet are very soft and pliable. When choosing footwear bear in mind that:

- there must be room for the baby to wiggle his or her toes in a baby stretch suit or in socks or tights

- socks should have a high cotton content so that moisture from the feet can escape; make sure that socks are not too loose as the friction can cause blisters

- soft corduroy shoes called padders keep a baby's feet warm when crawling or walking, but should not be worn if the soles become slippery

- outside shoes should not be worn until the baby has learnt to walk unaided, and then should be fitted properly by a trained shoe fitter.

Equipment for a young baby

Babies need somewhere to sleep, to be bathed, to feed, to sit, to play and to be transported.

For sleeping

Cradles and 'Moses baskets' (wicker baskets with carrying handles) can be used as beds for a young baby, but are unsuitable for transporting the baby outside or in a car.

Prams and carrycots come in a wide variety of designs; safety mattresses are available which are ventilated at the head section to prevent the risk of suffocation. Whether the pram is new or second-hand, it must meet the following safety requirements:

- brakes should be efficient and tested regularly
- when shopping, a shopping basket should be positioned underneath to prevent shopping bags being hung on the handles and causing overbalancing
- there must be anchor points for a safety harness
- the vehicle must be stable, easy to steer and the right height for the carer to be able to push easily without stooping
- the mattress must be firm enough to support the baby's back.

Cots

Often a baby will move into a cot for sleeping when he has outgrown his carrycot, but cots are also suitable for newborn babies. Cots usually have slatted sides – which allow the baby to see out – with one side able to be lowered and secured by safety catches. Safety requirements are:

- bars must be no more than 7 cm apart
- safety catches must be childproof
- the mattress should fit snugly with no gaps
- cot bumpers (foam padded screens tied at the head end of the cot) are not recommended for babies who may be able to untie the strings, but research on this is equivocal

- if the cot has been painted, check that lead-free paint has been used.

Travel cot

This is a folding cot with fabric sides, suitable for temporary use only; it is especially useful if the family travels away from home a lot and it can double as a playpen when the mattress is removed.

Blankets and sheets

These should be easy to wash and dry as they will need frequent laundering. The ideal fabric for sheets is brushed cotton; blankets are often made from cellular acrylic fabric, which is lightweight, warm and easily washable.

For bathing

Baby baths are easily transportable (when empty) plastic basins that can be used with the fixed base bought for a carrycot, or within the adult bath. After a few months, the baby can be bathed in the adult bath; carers should guard against back strain, cover hot taps because of the risk of burns and always use a non-slip rubber mat in the base of the bath.

NB Never leave a baby alone in any bath, even for a few seconds.

For feeding

If the baby is being bottle-fed, eight to ten bottles and teats, sterilising equipment and formula milk will be required. If she is being breastfed, one bottle and teat is useful to provide extra water or fruit juice. A high chair, with fixed safety harness, is useful for the older baby. (Feeding babies is also discussed in Chapter 16).

Hygienic practice is very important when working with babies. A baby's immune system is not as strong or as well developed as an adult's. This means that babies are much more likely to get ill and develop infections. Therefore, good hygiene is essential when making up a formula feed and sterilising equipment. Hygienic practice is making sure that all equipment that you use when feeding, and the surfaces that you are working on, are clean and sterile. You must also make sure that your hands are thoroughly washed and clean before touching the equipment.

Guidelines for good practice

How to prepare a formula feed

✔ Fill the kettle with at least 1 litre of *fresh* tap water (do not use water that has been boiled before).

✔ Boil the water. Then leave the water to cool for no more than 30 minutes so that it remains at a temperature of at least 70°C.

✔ Clean and disinfect the surface you are going to use.

✔ **Wash your hands**: this is very important.

✔ If you are using a cold water steriliser, shake off any excess solution from the bottle and the teat, or rinse the bottle with cooled boiled water from the kettle (not the tap).

✔ Stand the bottle on a clean surface.

✔ Keep the teat and cap on the upturned lid of the steriliser. Avoid putting them on the work surface.

✔ Follow the manufacturer's instructions and pour the correct amount of water that you need into the bottle. Double check that the water level is correct. Always put the water in the bottle first, while it is still hot, before adding the powdered infant formula.

✔ Loosely fill the scoop with formula, according to the manufacturer's instructions, and level it off using either the flat edge of a clean, dry knife or the leveller provided. Different tins of formula come with different scoops. Make sure you use only the scoop that is enclosed with the powdered infant formula that you are using.

✔ Holding the edge of the teat, put it on the bottle. Then screw the retaining ring onto the bottle.

✔ Cover the teat with the cap and shake the bottle until the powder is dissolved.

✔ It is important to cool the formula so it is not too hot to drink. Do this by holding the bottom half of the bottle under cold running water. Make sure that the water does not touch the cap covering the teat.

✔ Test the temperature of the infant formula on the inside of your wrist before giving it to your baby. It should be body temperature, which means it should feel warm or cool, but not hot.

✔ If there is any made-up infant formula left after a feed, throw it away.

Guidelines for good practice

Bottle-feeding

✔ Always wash hands thoroughly before preparing feeds for babies.

✔ As manufacturers' instructions vary as to how much water and powder to use, it is important to follow the instructions on the product very carefully.

✔ Do not add extra powdered infant formula when making up a feed. This can make the baby constipated and may cause dehydration. Too little powdered infant formula may not provide the baby with enough nourishment.

✔ Never add sugar or salt to the milk, and never make the feed stronger than the instructions state – this could result in too high a salt intake which can lead to severe illness

✔ Never warm up infant formula in a microwave as it can heat the feed unevenly and may burn the baby's mouth.

✔ Always check the temperature of the milk before giving it to a baby.

✔ Always check that the teat has a hole of the right size and that it is not blocked.

✔ Never prop up a baby with a bottle – choking is a real danger.

✔ Do not use bottled water: it is not recommended to make up a feed as it is not sterile and may contain too much salt (sodium) or sulphate. If you *have* to use bottled water to make up a feed, check the label to make sure the sodium (also written as 'Na') level is less than 200 milligrams (mg) per litre, and the sulphate (also written as SO or SO_4) content is not higher than 250 mg per litre. It is not usually sterile, so it will still need to be boiled, like tap water, before you prepare the feed.

Bacteria in infant formula

Always make up each feed as the baby needs it. Hygienic practice (such as using water at 70°C and only using fresh water) is vital when preparing formula milk. (Water at this temperature will kill any harmful bacteria that may be present).Even when tins and packets of powdered infant formula are sealed, they can sometimes contain bacteria such as Cronobacter sakazakii and, more rarely, Salmonella. Although these bacteria are very rare, the infections they cause can be life-threatening. Bacteria multiply very fast at room temperature. Even when the feed is kept in a fridge, bacteria can still survive and multiply, although they do this more slowly.

Sterilising equipment

There are several ways of sterilising the feeding equipment. For example, by:

● using a cold water sterilising solution

● steam sterilising or

● sterilising by boiling.

Remember, before sterilising, **always**:

- Clean the feeding bottles, teats, caps and covers in hot, soapy water as soon as possible after a feed, using a clean bottle brush. Teats may be cleaned using a special teat cleaner; turn teats inside-out to ensure all milk deposits are removed and wash in the same way as the bottles.
- Rinse **all** the equipment in clean, cold running water before sterilising.

Cold water sterilising solution

- Follow the manufacturer's instructions.
- Change the sterilising solution every 24 hours.
- Leave feeding equipment in the sterilising solution for at least 30 minutes.
- Make sure that there are no air bubbles trapped in the bottles or teats when putting them in the sterilising solution.
- Keep all the equipment under the solution with a floating cover.

Steam sterilising (electric steriliser or microwave)

- It is important to follow the manufacturer's instructions as there are several different types of sterilisers.
- Make sure the openings of the bottles and teats are facing down in the steriliser.
- Manufacturers will give guidelines on how long you can leave equipment that you are not using immediately (straight after sterilising) before it needs to be resterilised.

Sterilising by boiling

- When using this method, care must be taken to ensure safety and prevent scalds or burns. Hot pans and liquids should not be left unattended, especially if children are present.
- Make sure that whatever you sterilise in this way is safe to boil.
- Boil the feeding equipment in water for at least 10 minutes, making sure that all items stay under the surface of the water.
- Remember that teats tend to get damaged faster with this method. Regularly check that teats and bottles are not torn, cracked or damaged.
- Wash your hands thoroughly. Clean and disinfect the surface where you will put together the bottle and teat.
- It is best to remove the bottles just before they are used.

NB: Once sterilised, if the bottles are not being used immediately, they should be put together fully with the teat and lid in place. This is to prevent the inside of the

Reflecting on practice

Babies have different dispositions and preferences and there are natural variations in the ways in which they learn as well as the pace of learning. Think about the ways in which you establish responsive care and reflect on how you can improve your practice:

For example, do you give close attention to:

- method of feeding: *how* individual babies like to be fed
- food preferences: what individual babies *like* to eat
- comfort and security: *how* individual babies prefer to be comforted.

sterilised bottle from being contaminated, along with the inside and outside of the teat.

See Chapter 13, pp. 271–272 for information on meal times, which also include advice for meal times for babies. Also see Chapter 16 for information on breastfeeding.

For sitting

Bouncing cradle

This is a soft fabric seat which can be used from birth to about six months; it is generally appreciated by babies and their carers as it is easily transported from room to room, encouraging the baby's full involvement in everyday activities. It should always be placed on the floor, never on a worktop or bed, as even young babies can 'bounce' themselves off these surfaces and fall.

For playing

Babies like to be held where they can see faces clearly, especially the carer's face; they prefer toys which are brightly coloured and which make a noise. In the first three months, provide:

▲ **Figure 12.14** A bouncing cradle

- mobiles, musical toys and rattles
- soft balls and foam bricks
- toys to string over the cot or pram.

From about three months, provide:

- cradle gym, bath toys and activity mat
- chiming ball and stacking beakers
- saucepans and spoons
- building bricks
- rag books.

See Chapters 17 and 18 for ideas about providing toys, equipment and activities to promote holistic development.

For transport

Baby slings

Baby slings, used on the front of the carer's body, enable close physical contact between carer and baby, but can cause back strain if used with heavy babies; child 'back carriers' which fit on a frame like a rucksack are suitable for larger babies.

Pram, buggy or 'travel system'

A newborn baby can be transported in a special buggy with a tilting seat (the baby must be able to lie flat). This can then be used for as long as the baby needs a pushchair; the buggy has the advantage of being easier to handle than a pram, easier to store at home and to take on public transport. It is not possible to carry heavy loads of shopping on a buggy and lightweight buggies are not recommended for long periods of sleeping. Travel systems usually include either a carrycot, pushchair and car seat, or a pushchair and car seat, and are suitable for babies from birth. Some models have fully reversible seat units so that the baby can face the person pushing the pushchair.

▲ **Figure 12.15** A travel system

Car seats

A baby should never be carried on an adult's lap on the front seat of a car. Small babies can be transported in a sturdy carrycot with fixed straps on the back seat or in a rearward-facing baby car seat – if the car has a passenger airbag, the baby seat should always be fitted in the back seat; for babies under 10 kg, these seats can be used also as a first seat in the home.

Positive relationships with primary carers

The diversity of child-rearing practices

Child-rearing practices vary across different cultures, and can differ within cultural groups. Respecting cultural values and practices as they relate to the care of young children is not just a matter of having appropriate insight and a positive attitude towards diverse cultural practices. It may also demand a willingness to modify the routines in an early years setting in order to accommodate the needs of a particular child and their family.

Examples of different customs around the birth of a baby include:

- 'wetting the baby's head' (a euphemism for having an alcoholic drink to celebrate the birth)
- baby 'showers' and the giving of gifts and cards
- restricted visiting by male members for the family for up to ten days following the birth
- preparing special foods for the mother to eat
- a Christian family may wish to have the baby christened
- a Muslim family may wish that a male relative whisper the Islamic call to prayer into the baby's ear.

Weaning is also an important milestone in many cultures and the progression from milk feeds to solids may be marked by specific ceremonies:

- For Hindus, there is a rice feeding ceremony at six months of age when various members of the family, usually starting with the grandparents, feed the baby its first rice.
- Congee, a traditional Chinese weaning food of rice boiled in watery meat broth, is introduced at six to ten months.

See Chapter 16 for information on feeding babies.

Avoiding stereotypical attitudes

It is important not to make assumptions about any individual – as this can lead to stereotyping (see Chapter 1). It is very important that you get to know the children in your care and their parents, and that you consider each child as an individual with his or her own unique needs.

Families under pressure

Families come under a lot of pressure from friends, from advertising companies and from television programmes to provide the very best clothing and equipment for their new baby. The idealised picture of happy, smiling parents cuddling their precious bundle of joy is hard to resist; advertisers use these images to bombard the new parents with a dazzling array of objects that are deemed 'essential' to happy parenthood. You are in an important position to advise on the basic principles when choosing equipment. Parents should prioritise their needs by considering all factors relevant to their circumstances:

- **Cost**: how much can the parents afford to spend? What may be available on loan from friends whose children are past the baby stage? Can some equipment, e.g. the pram, be bought second-hand or hired cheaply?
- **Lifestyle**: is the family living in a flat where the lifts are often out of action, in bed and breakfast accommodation, or in a house with a large garden? These factors will affect such decisions as pram or buggy, and where the baby will sleep.
- **Single or multiple use**: will the equipment be used for a subsequent baby – in which case the priority may be to buy a large pram on which a toddler can also be seated? It may be worth buying new, high-quality products if they are to be used again.
- **Safety and maintenance**: does the item of equipment chosen meet all the British Safety Standards? What if it has been bought second-hand? How easy is it to replace worn-out parts?

Factors that may cause stress to parents

- **Financial**: if both parents have to go out to work, this can be stressful. One or both parents may need to reduce the hours of work or they may need to pay for childcare.
- **Age of parents and support available**: very young parents or parents who are at the upper end of the childbearing age range may have less support from their peers and find the adjustment to parenthood more stressful. Some parents lack support from the extended family who may live a long way away.

- **Tiredness**: having a young baby can disrupt parents' sleeping patterns; this is particularly stressful if both parents have to get up to go to work.
- **Responsibility**: some parents find the responsibility of looking after a young baby overwhelming; they may worry that they cannot cope or find that 'the baby' has completely taken over their life.
- **Conflict**: parents may have several other children to care for, all with their own needs. The needs of the new baby may conflict with the established routine within the family.

Providing information for parents

When caring for babies – whether as a nanny in their home or in a nursery – you need to ensure that parents have information about their baby on a daily basis; most settings provide a daily record chart which helps to make sure the parents are involved in their child's care. Information includes:

- **Feeding**: what, when and how much their baby has consumed
- **Excretion:** nappy changing information
- **Health**: any concerns – e.g. nappy rash, unexplained rashes, teething symptoms etc.
- **Holistic development**: all aspects of development should be noted – physical, intellectual, language. emotional and social
- **Behaviour**: what the baby has been doing during the session; how happy; any problems etc.

You need to be available to discuss any concerns a parent may have about their baby – ideally each key person will hand over to 'their' baby's parent or carer at the end of each session, reporting on the child's progress during the day and inviting any questions.

Access to health care and support

There are many voluntary organisations that can offer help and support to parents of young children. The health visitor will be able to advise parents about local groups, such as parent-and-toddler groups and Home-Start, which is a voluntary organisation that provides trained volunteers to work with families under stress.

Potential problems

Occasionally you might come across parents who have difficult or challenging attitudes towards the staff and the setting generally. You should always be patient, even when *you* are exhausted at the end of a busy day! There could be any number of reasons for a sudden, angry outburst and you need to react in a professional and caring manner. Several factors – including competition, guilt and time constraints – may affect the relationship between a working parent and staff in an early years setting. For example:

- **Competition**: The parents may feel they are competing with you for the baby's affection, since both you and they have formed strong **attachments** to the baby.
- **Jealousy**: Parents may feel jealousy if their baby takes her first steps in your presence, rather than at home.
- **Guilt**: Parents often feel guilty; they may resent having to 'abandon' their children by leaving them while they work. This is even more difficult when separating from their baby causes *each* of them distress.
- **Time**: Employed parents may feel that they have many roles and duties to perform but not enough time to perform them. Consequently, they often feel overwhelmed when they turn up to collect their children.

Respecting differences

All babies need respectful and individual care. Within the early years setting, physical care arrangements should allow for individual differences; for example:

- **Food**: provide a variety of foods – do not expect each child to eat the same thing
- **Sleep**: allow babies to sleep when they need to, rather than having a set group time
- **Anti-discriminatory practice**: books, toys and ceremonies should reflect the cultural diversity of the nursery and should be positively non-sexist and against violence (see Chapter 1)
- **Stereotyping**: staff must avoid stereotyping language.

Attachment and separation

When children receive warm, responsive care, they feel safe and secure. Secure attachments are the basis of all the child's future relationships. Because babies experience relationships through their senses, it is the expression of love that affects how they develop and that helps to shape later learning and behaviour. They will grow to be more curious, get along better with other children and perform better in school than children who are less securely attached.

- **Primary attachments**: babies usually develop close attachments to those who care for them – at first with their parents or primary caregivers.
- **Multiple attachments**: babies can, and often do, make several attachments, often with other family members, close friends of the family and other carers.

- **Separation anxiety**: a baby may show signs of separation anxiety – typically at around six months; this may happen even when the primary carer, usually the mother, leaves the baby just for a few moments. The baby does not have certain feeling that the parent will return and can become very distressed in a short space of time. They might become tearful, uneasy or even filled with panic.

Read more about the importance of early attachments in Chapter 7.

Your role in meeting the needs of babies in group and domestic care

Most parents are understandably anxious when they decide to leave their baby with a stranger. Unless their baby has had some experience of being left for long periods of time with anyone other than the primary carers, the parents will not be certain of their reaction. Some common worries include:

- What will happen if my baby will not stop crying?
- Will my baby settle to sleep immediately but then be panic-stricken when she wakes up and finds that Mummy is not there?
- How will the nanny or key person handle such a situation?
- Will the nursery staff get annoyed with me if I want to know everything that has gone on in my baby's life since I left this morning?

It takes time for staff to get to know a parent but you can help to alleviate some of their concerns, and to provide quality care and education for babies by:

- **Showing empathy** – try to put yourself in the parent's shoes and follow the guidelines on p. 196 for settling-in new children.
- **Welcoming parents** and making time for them – make friendly contact with the child's parents. You need to be approachable. Try not to appear rushed even when you have a really busy nursery.
- **Helping parents to separate from their baby** – when a baby is handed from the parent to a new carer, it is best if:
  - you approach slowly
  - you talk gently before picking up and taking the baby from the parent
  - the baby is held looking at the parent during the handover.
- Explaining how you will be **caring for the baby** – for example, describing the daily routines and the layout of the setting.

- Being aware of your particular situation and your responsibilities – you need to maintain a **professional relationship** with parents (even if they also happen to be your friends) and work as a team member in an early years setting.

- Showing that you **enjoy** being with the baby – physical contact is important; encourage 'conversations' with babies; smile and talk to them.

- Always act in the **interests of the baby** – use your knowledge of holistic development and your powers of observation to enable you to tailor the care you give to the individual baby's needs.

- Keeping parents and other staff members **informed** – you need to know how and when to pass on information to parents about their baby's care; and to observe the rules of confidentiality (see p. 68).

Moving on

Respectful care for babies and toddlers

Babies, toddlers and 2-year-olds spend a lot of time being physically handled by people who are bigger and stronger than them and have much more power than they do. They are also learning a lot from non-verbal interactions and communications so will understand the practitioner's mood, intention and something of what the practitioner thinks of the child through the way they are approached, touched, looked at and handled. Therefore, the physical care of babies and young children must be sensitive and respectful.

Emmi Pikler (1902–1984) was a paediatrician in Budapest, Hungary, who founded the Loczy Institute for Residential Nurseries and developed practice based on these principles:

- Babies' independent physical activity is supported by attuned practitioners
- Babies need a close relationship with a practitioner
- The environment should support the babies' awareness of themselves and others
- Good physical health underpins the other three elements

These principles were put into practice through close and regular observation of the babies, which enabled the practitioners to become tuned into their needs.

Pikler's approach was taken to the USA by Magda Gerber who developed an organisation called Resources for Infant Educarers (RIE) to promote the respectful care of infants (Petrie and Owen 2005).

This approach includes the following elements:

- being attuned to the child's responses and cues, such as movement and gestures as well as vocalisations

- using slow paced gestures, such as gentle touch, affectionate touch and sensitive signalling touch as key ways in which practitioners and children will indicate their meaning to each other
- the practitioner will respond sensitively to the child's cues and follow the child's lead in setting the pace of the interaction

Practitioners at the Childspace Ngaio Infants and Toddler Centre in New Zealand identify the following key elements of what they call a 'peaceful caregiving' style (Dalli and Kibble 2010):

- Language that describes and explains
- Hand and other bodily gestures
- Facial expressions and cooperative / turn-taking behaviour

They implement a pattern of care they call ISE:

- Invite: This means helping the child to identify what needs doing 'is your nappy wet? Would you like to have a dry nappy now?' and letting the child know what we intend to do, 'I'm just going to wipe your nose with a tissue'
- Suggest: 'I think you might be feeling grumpy because you're hungry, shall we find a piece of banana? Or a breadstick?'
- Engage: Approach the child slowly and be at their level, be calm and offer reassurance, follow the child's non-verbal communications, make opportunities for the children to do things for themselves as much as possible.

Think about ideas

Research the RIE approach and review your practice:

Do you enable free physical movement for babies, toddlers and young children?

Are your physical care routines, peaceful, unhurried and respectful?

How much do practitioners 'invite, suggest and engage' children in their physical care?

Further reading, weblinks and resources

Meggitt, C. (2012) *An Illustrated Guide to Child Development* (3rd edn), Oxford: Pearson.

NHS

The NHS have advice about reducing a baby's risk of SIDS:
http://www.nhs.uk/conditions/pregnancy-and-baby/pages/reducing-risk-cot-death.aspx

The Lullaby Trust

The Lullaby Trust promotes expert advice on safer baby sleep and provides special support for anyone bereaved through SIDS
www.lullabytrust.org.uk

References

Dalli, C. and Kibble, N. (2010) *Peaceful Caregiving as Curriculum: Insights on primary caregiving from action research*. In Meade, A. (2010) (Ed) Dispersing Waves: Innovation in Early Childhood Education. New Zealand: NZCER Press.

Petrie, P and Owen, S (2005) *Authentic Relationships in Group Care for Infants and Toddlers – Resources for Infant Educarers (RIE)*. London: Jessica Kingsley Publishers.

13 Caring for children

Caring for children involves understanding their holistic needs. This chapter discusses their physical care and health needs, and includes basic care of children's skin, hair, teeth, feet and clothing. This chapter will also explore the importance of establishing routines when caring for children including routines for hygiene, sleep and rest, toilet training and the development of self-care skills.

Basic physical and health needs of children

From the moment they are born, all children depend completely on an adult to meet almost all their needs, but the way in which these needs are met will be different, depending on family circumstances, culture, the child and the caring adult.

For healthy growth and development – that is, physical, intellectual, emotional and social development – certain basic needs must be met. These are:

- food
- cleanliness
- sleep, rest and activity
- protection from infection and injury
- intellectual stimulation
- relationships and social contact
- shelter, warmth, clothing
- fresh air and sunlight
- love, and consistent and continuous affection

▲ **Figure 13.1** The needs of babies and children

KEY TERM

Routine – The usual way in which tasks or activities are arranged.

- access to health care
- appreciation, praise and recognition of effort or achievements
- security and nurture.

It is difficult to separate these basic needs from practical care, as they all contribute to the holistic development of a healthy child.

Care of babies (from birth to one year) is covered separately in Chapter 12.

Personal care routines

One aspect of children's need for love and security is the need for **routine.** This is why having daily routines is so important in all aspects of childcare. By meeting children's need for routine, parents and carers are helping the child to:

- feel acknowledged
- feel independent
- increase self-esteem.

All settings that provide care and education for children have routines for daily activities. This does not mean that every day is the same; rather, it means that there is a recognised structure to the child's day – one that will help children to feel secure and safe. Such routines include:

- hygiene – changing nappies and toileting older children; ensuring that there is a hand-washing routine after messy activities and before eating and drinking
- health and safety – tidying away toys and activity equipment; making regular checks on equipment for hazards
- safety at home times and trips away from the setting – ensuring that there is a correct ratio of adults to children, permission from parents and contact numbers, etc.
- meal and snack times: serving of meals and drinks under close supervision
- sleep and rest
- outdoor play.

Supporting hygiene routines

All children benefit from regular routines in daily care. You need to encourage children to become independent by helping them to learn how to take care of themselves. Ways of helping children to become independent include:

- teaching children how to wash and to dry their hands before eating or drinking
- making sure that children always wash and dry their hands after going to the toilet and after playing outdoors
- providing children with their own combs and brushes and encouraging them to use them every day
- providing a soft toothbrush and teaching children how and when to brush their teeth
- ensuring that you are good role models for children; for example, when you cough or sneeze, you always cover your mouth
- devise activities which develop an awareness in children of the importance of hygiene routines; for example, you could invite a dental nurse to the setting to talk to children about daily teeth care
- make sure that children are provided with a healthy diet and that there are opportunities for activity, rest and sleep throughout the nursery or school day.

Meeting the care needs of children in ways that maintain their security and respect their privacy

It is important that children have their rights to privacy respected when having their care needs met. Intimate, personal care such as nappy changing, toileting, dressing and undressing should be coordinated by a key person. When they are at the right level of development, young children should be asked to *consent* to offers of intimate care. You might say, for example, to a toddler in the toilet: 'Would you like me to help pull your pants down?' rather than just going ahead and doing it. Similarly, a child who has had a toileting accident should be encouraged sympathetically to help when changing his or her clothing.

Planning routines to meet individual needs

Anyone looking after children should be able to adapt to their individual needs, which will change from day to day. You therefore need to be flexible in your approach and allow, whenever feasible, the individual child to set the pattern for the day – as long as all the child's needs are met. Obviously, parents and carers have their own routines and hygiene practices and these should always be respected. (For example, Muslims prefer to wash under running water and Rastafarians wear their hair braided and so may not use a comb or brush.)

Whenever you are caring for children, you should always treat each child as an individual. This means that you should be aware of their individual needs at all times.

- Sometimes a child may have special or additional needs.
- Children may need specialist equipment or extra help with play activities.
- Routines may need to be adapted to take into account individual needs and preferences.

Guidelines for good practice

Everyday routines for babies and young children

- ✔ Be patient – even when pressed for time, try to show children that you are relaxed and unhurried.
- ✔ Allow time for children to experiment with different ways of doing things.
- ✔ If you work directly with parents, encourage them to make a little extra time in the morning and evening for children to dress and undress themselves. Children could be encouraged to choose their clothes the night before from a limited choice; the choosing of clothes to wear is often a fertile ground for disagreements and battles of will.

- ✔ Try not to take over if children are struggling, since this deprives them of the sense of achievement and satisfaction of success.
- ✔ Show children how to do something and then let them get on with it. If they ask for help, they should be shown again. If adults keep doing things for children that they could do for themselves they are in danger of creating 'learned helplessness'.
- ✔ Offer praise and encouragement when children are trying hard, not just when they succeed in a task.

Children like to feel independent, but sometimes they need an adult's encouragement to feel that they are capable and that adults believe that they can do it. Teaching independence with self-care skills such as hand-washing, brushing teeth, and dressing and undressing is an important step in development. It can be achieved when children are supported in a positive and encouraging way.

Basic care of children (one to eight years)

By around 12 to 15 months, babies can hold a cup in both hands and drink from it, and will recognise themselves in the mirror.

By 18 months most children go through a period of saying 'NO'; it is their way of asserting their new feelings of self-identity.

Between **one and four years,** children can:

1 *Use a fork and spoon*: most children have mastered this skill by 17 or 18 months.
2 *Take off their own clothes*: children usually learn to do it between 13 and 20 months.
3 *Brush their teeth*: they may start wanting to help with this task as early as 16 months, but probably will not be able to do it on their own until they are between three and four.
4 *Wash and dry their hands*: this skill develops between 19 and 30 months and is something children should learn before or at the same time as using the toilet.
5 *Get dressed*: they may be able to put on loose clothing as early as 20 months, but will need a few more months before they can manage a T-shirt, and another year after that before they are able to get dressed all by themselves. By 27 months, they will probably be able to pull off their shoes.
6 *Use the toilet*: most children are not physically ready to start toilet training until they are at least 18 to 24 months old, and some will not be ready to begin for as much as a year after that. Two key signs of readiness include being able to pull their own pants up and down, and knowing when they have to go before it happens.
7 *Prepare their own breakfast*: children as young as three may be able to get themselves a bowl of cereal when they are hungry, and most can do it by the time they are four-and-a-half.

Children aged four to eight:

1 Children aged four and five can eat skilfully with a knife and fork, for example, and can undress and dress themselves, except for laces, ties and back buttons.
2 By six to seven years old, children are completely independent in washing, dressing and toileting skills.

Care and protection of the skin and hair

As children grow and become involved in more vigorous exercise, especially outside, a daily bath or shower becomes necessary. Most young children love bath time, and adding bubble bath to the water adds to the fun of getting clean.

Guidelines for good practice

Caring for the skin, nails and hair

✔ Wash face and hands in the morning.

✔ Always wash hands after using the toilet and before meals – young children will need supervision.

✔ Girls should be taught to wipe their bottom from front to back, to prevent germs from the anus entering the vagina and urethra.

✔ Each child should have his or her own flannel, comb and brush, which must be cleaned regularly.

✔ Skin should always be dried thoroughly, taking special care with areas such as between the toes and under the armpits. Black skin tends to dryness and may need massaging with special oils or moisturisers.

✔ Observe skin for any defects, such as rashes, dryness or soreness, and act appropriately.

✔ Nails should be scrubbed with a soft nailbrush and trimmed regularly by cutting straight across.

✔ Hair usually needs washing twice a week; children with long or curly hair benefit from the use of a conditioning shampoo which helps to reduce tangles. Hair should always be rinsed thoroughly in clean water and not brushed until it is dry (brushing wet hair damages the hair shafts). A wide-toothed comb is useful for combing wet hair.

✔ Afro-Caribbean hair tends to dryness and may need special oil or moisturisers; if the hair is braided (with or without beads), it may be washed with the braids left intact, unless otherwise advised.

✔ Rastafarian children with hair styled in dreadlocks may not use either combs or shampoo, preferring to brush the dreadlocks gently and secure them with braid.

✔ Devout Sikhs believe that the hair must never be cut or shaved, and young children usually wear a special head covering.

Hand-washing

Babies and toddlers need to have their hands washed frequently. This is because they are constantly picking things up and putting their hands in their mouths, which means they may pick up an infection. It is important to build regular hand-washing into routine care.

Hand-washing is also an important skill that children need to learn. It can be made into a fun activity by singing 'This is the way we wash/dry our hands … on a cold/hot and frosty/sunny morning'. Children soon learn that hand-washing is a routine task that must always be done after going to the toilet, before and after meals and after playing outdoors.

Washing the face

Most young children dislike having their faces washed as they feel they are being suffocated. Always use a clean cloth and wipe each part of the face separately and gently. Dry thoroughly with a soft towel.

Protection from sun

Apart from ensuring that babies and children's skin is kept clean, it is also important that they are protected from the sun. Babies benefit from being outside in the fresh air for a while every day. When air is trapped in a building it becomes stale, the level of humidity rises and there is an increased risk of infections spreading. When working in nurseries, practitioners should ensure that rooms are well ventilated and that there are opportunities for babies to go outside. Sunlight is beneficial too, but care should be taken with babies and young children:

1   Keep all children out of the sun when it is at its most dangerous, between 11 am and 3 pm; those caring for young children should plan outdoor activities to avoid this time unless children are well protected by hats and sun protection cream. Permission must be obtained from the child's parent or guardian before applying sunscreen creams.

2   Specialists advise keeping babies up to nine months of age out of direct sunlight altogether to prevent the risk of developing skin cancer in later life.

3   Use sun hats with a wide brim that will protect face, neck and shoulders on older babies.

4   Use sun protection cream on all sun-exposed areas.

5   Use sunshades or canopies on buggies and prams.

See Chapter 15 for information on skin conditions such as eczema, and for more information on hair care and head lice. See Chapter 16 for information on mealtimes.

Oral hygiene

During the first year of life, babies eat their first solid food with the help of their primary teeth (or milk teeth). These 20 teeth start to appear at around the age of six months (see Figures 13.2 and 13.3).

There are three types of primary teeth:

1   incisors – tough, chisel-shaped teeth, with a sharp edge to help when biting food

2   canines – pointed teeth, which help to tear food into manageable chunks

3   molars – large, strong teeth, which grind against each other to crush food.

Teeth need cleaning as soon as they appear: see Chapter 12, p. 246 for guidelines on caring for a baby's teeth.

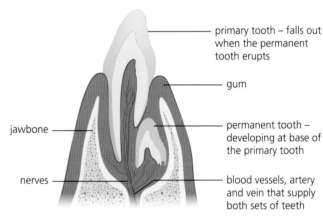

▲ **Figure 13.2** Structure of a primary tooth

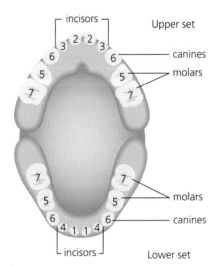

▲ **Figure 13.3** The usual order in which the primary teeth appear

There are 32 permanent teeth. These replace the milk teeth and start to come through at about the age of six years. The milk teeth that were first to appear become loose and then fall out as the permanent teeth begin to push through the gums.

Fluoride

Some toothpastes contain fluoride, which is a mineral that can help prevent dental decay. The British Dental Association advises cleaning twice a day with a specially formulated children's toothpaste, which has fluoride pitched at the right level for children who are not only smaller, but also have a tendency to swallow toothpaste.

Diet

For healthy teeth we need calcium, fluoride, vitamins A, C and D, and foods that need chewing, such as apples, carrots and wholemeal bread. Sugar causes decay and can damage teeth even before they have come through – 'dinky feeders' and baby bottles filled with sweet drinks are very harmful.

The best snacks are fruit and raw vegetables. Try tangerines, bananas, pieces of cucumber or carrot sticks. Other good snacks include toast, rice cakes and plain popcorn. Dried fruits – for example, raisins and apricots – are high in sugar and very sticky. They can be bad for teeth, so only ever give it to children with meals (for instance, as a dessert) and never as a snack between meals.

Guidelines for good practice

Caring for teeth

✔ Children should brush their teeth with soft-bristle brushes using fluoride toothpaste (1,000 parts per million to start with) *as soon as they have milk teeth.*

✔ Parents or carers must brush the teeth – or supervise brushing – for the first few years (sitting the child on your lap and brushing from behind is good for toddlers) and should then supervise until at least the age the age of seven.

✔ Brushing should be done for two minutes in the morning and evening and children should be shown how to brush (a circular action that starts and finishes in the same place on each tooth) by looking in the mirror, and be taught to spit rather than rinse as this retains the benefits of fluoride.

✔ Avoid sugary drinks, sweets and snacks between feeds or mealtimes.

✔ Teeth are at most risk at night because there is less saliva in the mouth to protect them.

✔ Water is the best drink to give at bedtime, but if giving milk, do not add anything to it.

Think about ideas

A dental hygiene routine

Plan a routine for a toddler that will cover all aspects of dental hygiene:

✔ brushing teeth

✔ dietary advice

✔ education about teeth/visits to the dentist.

Include examples of books that could be used to help prepare a child for a visit to the dentist. Remember to give a reason for each part of the routine.

Visiting the dentist

Children need to see a dentist once they have milk teeth. The dentist will suggest follow-up visits usually between three months and a year. NHS guidelines say that, as a minimum, children should have at least one visit to the dentist before the age of two. This is not only for children to get used to the whole dental surgery experience but also because preventive treatments for decay are now available, such as painting teeth with fluoride varnish to strengthen enamel.

Care of the feet

While a baby is in its mother's womb, a tough, flexible material called **cartilage** begins to form where harder bones will eventually grow. As the baby grows, cartilage is continually replaced with bone in a process called ossification. This takes place in the shafts (or long sections) and heads (or ends) of all bones. There are 26 bones in the adult foot; a baby's foot has only 22 bones (see Figure 13.4).

A child's feet are very soft and supple because the bones are not yet rigid and they are spaced wide apart; as the feet grow they change shape, and often one foot tends to be slightly longer or wider than the other.

Parents and carers should be aware that a child's feet can easily be distorted for life, so foot care must be treated seriously, just like dental hygiene.

KEY TERM

Cartilage – This is a connective tissue which is found in areas of the body such as joints including those between the elbows and knees. It is a firm but softer and more flexible tissue than bone.

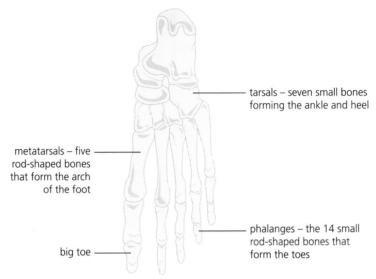

metatarsals – five rod-shaped bones that form the arch of the foot

tarsals – seven small bones forming the ankle and heel

phalanges – the 14 small rod-shaped bones that form the toes

big toe

▲ **Figure 13.4** The bones of the foot

Foot problems

1 **Club foot** (talipes) is fairly common and is caused by the foot being fixed in the same position in the womb for a prolonged time. Sometimes the condition corrects itself without treatment, but the foot may need gentle manipulation and/or strapping; eventually a surgical operation may be needed.

2 **Flat feet** are caused by ligaments and muscles that have not developed fully. The condition is very rarely seen in children; parents sometimes misdiagnose flat feet because children's footprints often look completely flat.

3 **Pigeon toes** is a minor abnormality in which the leg or foot is rotated, forcing the foot and toes to point inwards. It is fairly common in toddlers and generally requires no treatment, correcting itself by about the age of seven years.

4 **Chilblains** are red, itchy, swollen areas on toes that can be very painful. They usually heal without treatment, but could be prevented by keeping the feet warm and exercising to improve the circulation.

5 **Corns** are small areas of thickened skin on a toe, caused by pressure from ill-fitting shoes; they are easy to prevent but difficult to remove.

6 **Athlete's foot** and **verrucae** are fungal skin conditions of the feet (see Chapter 15).

Footwear

Parents and carers should always go to a shoe shop where trained children's shoe-fitters can advise on a wide selection of shoes. Second-hand shoes should never be worn as all shoes take on the shape of the wearer's foot.

Guidelines for good practice

Choosing the correct footwear for children

✔ When shoes are fitted, there should be at least 1 cm between the longest toe and the inside of the shoe.

✔ Both feet should be measured for length, width and girth.

✔ Shoes must fit snugly around the heel and fasten across the instep to prevent the foot sliding forward.

✔ The soles of the shoes should be flexible and hard-wearing; non-slip soles are safer.

✔ Leather is the ideal material for shoes that are to be worn every day, as it lets the feet 'breathe' and moisture can escape.

✔ Padders – soft corduroy shoes – keep a baby's feet warm when crawling or toddling, but should not be worn if the soles become slippery with wear.

✔ Shoes should never be bought a size too large as they can cause friction and blistering.

✔ Wellington boots should not be worn routinely because they do not allow the feet to breathe. However, they are very useful for outdoor play, with socks worn underneath.

The need for rest and sleep

Children need more sleep than adults because the brain is developing and maturing and they are physically growing as well. Sleep is important to child health because:

- it rests and restores our bodies
- it enables the brain and the body's metabolic processes to recover (these processes are responsible for producing energy and growth)
- during sleep, growth hormone is released; this renews tissues and produces new bone and red blood cells
- dreaming is believed to help the brain sort out information stored in the memory during waking hours.

Children vary enormously in their need for sleep and rest. Some children seem able to rush around all day with very little rest; others will need to 'recharge their batteries' by having frequent periods of rest. You need to be able to recognise the signs that a child is tired; these may include:

- looking tired – dark rings under the eyes and yawning
- asking for their comfort object
- constant rubbing of the eyes
- twiddling their hair and fidgeting with objects
- showing no interest in activities and in their surroundings
- being particularly emotional – crying or being stubborn
- withdrawing into themselves – sucking thumb and appearing lethargic or lacking energy.

Getting the right rest is crucial for the learning of babies and young children. Not all babies will need to sleep at the same time, and it is very worrying to find practice where all babies are expected to have their nappies changed at the same time and to sleep at the same time. These are very individual things. It is important for babies to feel that they are near someone when they sleep. Some babies sleep best on a mat, with a cover to keep them warm, on the floor of a quiet area that is gated. Others sleep better in a darkened room in a cot kept for them. This area should not be too full of stimulation. It is important to relax and let go when falling asleep. Neutral colouring is best, and the room should not be cluttered.

It is also important to keep to the sleep-time rituals and patterns that are familiar to the baby at home. Some babies need to have a cuddle, being lowered into their cot as they fall asleep. Others might never go to sleep on a lap, but need to be in a cot, in a quiet room, with their teddy, in order to fall asleep.

The sleep and rest needs at different ages

See Chapter 12, p. 247 for the sleep needs of babies under a year old.

A baby aged 15 months

From 12 months up until the age of two, babies tend to sleep for approximately 11 hours at night. The rest of their sleep will be in daytime naps. At around 15 to 18 months, many babies have just one longer daytime sleep, rather than two shorter naps.

A baby aged 15 months needs 14 hours sleep and rest in a 24-hour period.

A child aged two-and-a-half years

Most children between the ages of two and three years still need one nap a day, which may range from one to three-and-a-half hours. At this age children usually go to bed between 7 and 9 pm and wake up between 6 and 8 am.

A child aged two-and-a-half years needs a total of 13 hours sleep and rest in a 24-hour period.

A child aged four to five years

By the age of four years, most children meet all their sleep and rest needs at night, although a few may still need a short daytime rest or sleep.

A child aged four to five years needs a total of 11 to 11½ hours sleep and rest in a 24-hour period.

A child aged six to seven years

By this age, the need for daytime sleeps has disappeared, and all the sleep needs are met at night-time.

A child aged six to seven years needs a total of 10½–11 hours sleep and rest in a 24-hour period.

Guidelines for good practice

Establishing a routine for rest and sleep

Children will only sleep if they are actually tired, so it is important that enough activity and exercise is provided. Some children do not have a nap during the day but should be encouraged to rest in a quiet area.

When preparing children for a daytime nap, rest or bedtime sleep, you need to:

✔ treat each child uniquely; every child will have his or her own needs for sleep and rest

✔ find out all you can about the individual child's sleep habits; for example, some children like to be patted to sleep, while others need to have their favourite **comfort object**

✔ be guided by the wishes of the child's parents or carers; some parents, for example, prefer their child to have a morning nap but not an afternoon nap, as this routine fits in better with the family's routine

✔ reassure children that they will not be left alone and that you or someone else will be there when they wake up

✔ keep noise to a minimum and darken the room; make sure that children have been to the lavatory – children need to understand the signals which mean that it is time for everyone to have a rest or sleep

✔ provide quiet, relaxing activities for children who are unable, or who do not want to sleep; for example, jigsaw puzzles, a story tape or reading a book.

Different views about sleep and rest

There are cultural differences in how parents view bedtime and sleep routines. In some cultures it is normal for children to sleep with parents and to have a much later bedtime as a result. Some families who originate from hot countries where having a sleep in the afternoon is normal tend to let their children stay up in the evening. Such children are more likely to need a sleep while in your care; as long as the overall

amount of sleep is sufficient for the child, and fits in with the schedule of the setting it does not matter. It is always worth discussing bedtime routines with parents. Some areas have sleep clinics managed by the health visiting service to help parents whose children have difficulty sleeping.

Even after they have established a good sleep routine, children's sleep patterns can become disrupted. There may be a number of factors influencing children's sleep.

Some children prefer to rest quietly in their cots rather than have a sleep during the day; others will continue to have one or two daytime naps even up to the age of three or four years.

Guidelines for good practice

Establishing a bedtime routine

In the context of modern life in the UK, children benefit from a regular routine at bedtime; it helps to establish good habits and makes children feel more secure. A child will only sleep if actually tired, so it is vital that he or she has had enough exercise and activity. The stress on parents of a child who will not sleep at night can be severe (about 13–20 per cent of very young children have some sort of sleep problem); establishing a routine that caters for the child's individual needs may help parents to prevent such problems developing. The principles involved are:

✔ ensuring that the child has had enough exercise during the day

✔ making sure that the environment is conducive to sleep – a soft nightlight and non-stimulating toys might help, with no activity going on around bedtime

✔ following the precept 'never let the sun go down on a quarrel' – a child who has been in trouble during the day needs to feel reassured that all is forgiven before bedtime

✔ warning the child that bedtime is approaching and then following the set routine (see Guidelines below)

✔ reducing anxiety and stress – it is quite natural for a small child to fear being left alone or abandoned; the parents should let the child know they are still around, for example, by talking quietly or having the radio on, rather than creeping around silently.

All childcare must take into account any cultural preferences, such as later bedtimes, and family circumstances – for example, a family living in bed and breakfast accommodation may have to share bathroom facilities, or bedtime may be delayed to enable a working parent to be involved in the routine.

KEY TERM

Comfort object – Often a soft toy or blanket to which a child becomes attached, a comfort (or transitional) object is used by a child to provide comfort and security while he or she is away from a secure base, such as parents or home.

Guidelines for good practice

A bedtime routine for young children

✔ Warn the child that bedtime will be at a certain time (e.g. after a bath and story).

✔ Take a family meal about one-and-a-half or two hours before bedtime; this should be a relaxing, social occasion.

✔ After the meal, the child can play with other members of the family.

✔ Make bath time a relaxing time, to unwind and play gently; this often helps the child to feel drowsy.

✔ Give a final bedtime drink, followed by teeth cleaning.

✔ Read or tell a story: looking at books together or telling a story enables the child to feel close to the carer.

✔ Settle the child in bed, with curtains drawn and night light on, if desired. Then say goodnight and leave.

Think about ideas

Bedtime routine

Arrange to visit a family with a young child (ideally, your family placement) to talk about the child's bedtime routine. Devise a questionnaire to find out the following:

✔ Are there any problems settling the child to sleep?

✔ Are there any problems with the child waking in the night?

✔ Are any strategies used to address the problems?

Using the answers from the questionnaire to help you, devise a bedtime routine for a three-year-old girl who has just started nursery school and whose mother has three-month-old twin boys.

Points to include are:

✔ how to arrange one-to-one care for the three-year old

✔ how to avoid jealousy.

See Chapter 12 for information on sudden infant death syndrome (SIDS) in babies.

Mealtimes routines

Meal and snack times should be enjoyable occasions for both staff and children. The following safety guidelines should be followed to ensure health and safety at these times:

● **Hygiene**: wipe all surfaces where food will be served, before and after meals and snacks. Refer to

Look, listen and note

Observe a snack or meal time session in your setting. Note particularly how children interact when eating and how they express their preferences.

your setting's policy and clean the surfaces in the recommended way – often this is done using an antibacterial spray and disposable cloth. Make sure that children have washed and dried their hands before eating.

● **Serving food**: check that the food you are giving children is appropriate for them; check they have no allergies, for example to milk or wheat. Never give peanuts to children under four years old as they can easily choke or inhale them into their lungs, causing infection and lung damage. Food should be cut up into manageable pieces and should be served at the correct temperature – not too hot or too cold.

● **Seating**: babies should be securely strapped into high chairs, using a five-point harness.

● **Supervision**: supervise children carefully – never leave children unattended with drinks or food in case they choke. Never leave a baby alone, eating finger foods. Babies can choke silently when eating soft foods such as pieces of banana, so you should make sure that you know what to do if choking occurs. Never leave babies propped up with a bottle or feeding beaker.

● **Routines for mealtimes** for toddlers should allow time for them to feed themselves and include some planning to make the experience as enjoyable as possible. **Special dietary needs** and parental preferences must always be taken into account.

● **Feeding babies**: The advantage of family groups in early years settings is that babies can easily be part of mealtimes.

KEY TERM

Special dietary needs – When considering special dietary needs, you will need to think about things like allergies, intolerances, medical conditions, religious requirements, and social and cultural requirements. There is more information on this in chapter 16.

- When a whole row of babies all need feeding together, there are often tears and staff become anxious and frustrated, because it seems impossible to get each baby fed quickly enough. Meals become times of stress instead of times of pleasure.

- Babies learn more if they are given finger foods as soon as this is appropriate. A carrot stick is a wonderful learning experience, and makes a good contrast with a metal teaspoon. Observing a baby's learning at mealtimes is fascinating – for example, does the baby pass the spoon from one hand to the other? Is the spoon held with a palmar grip? Does the baby try to pick up the carrot stick with a pincer grip?

Signs and symptoms of potential concern

You are in an ideal position to notice when a child has any signs or symptoms of illness. Young children are particularly vulnerable to infection, which can occur within the body (e.g. **gastroenteritis**) or on the skin (e.g. **impetigo**). The incidence of the more common infectious diseases, such as chickenpox and measles, rises rapidly in nurseries and schools.

Such illnesses and infections are covered in depth in Chapter 15; see pp. 322–323 for signs and symptoms of acute illness.

Clothing for children

The same principles that apply to clothing for babies (see Chapter 12) apply to the selection of clothes for children. Parents and carers should expect children to become dirty as they explore their surroundings, and should not show disapproval when clothes become soiled.

Clothes for children should be:

- hard-wearing
- comfortable
- easy to put on and take off, especially when going to the toilet
- washable.

Types of clothes

- **Underwear** should be made of cotton, which is comfortable and sweat-absorbent.

- **Sleep suits** – all-in-one pyjamas with hard-wearing socks are useful for children who kick the bedcovers off at night. These must be the correct size, to prevent damage to growing feet.

- **Daytime clothes** should be adapted to the stage of mobility and independence of the child – for example, a dress will hinder a young girl trying to crawl; dungarees may prove difficult for a toddler to manage when being toilet-trained. Cotton jersey tracksuits, T-shirts and cotton jumpers are all useful garments that are easy to launder.

- **Outdoor clothes** must be warm and loose enough to fit over clothing, and still allow freedom of movement; a shower-proof anorak with a hood is ideal, as it can be washed and dried easily.

- **Choose clothes that are appropriate for the weather** – for example, children need to be protected from the sun and should wear wide brimmed-hats with neck shields; they need warm gloves, scarves and woolly or fleece hats in cold, windy weather and waterproof coats and footwear when out in the rain.

Caring for children's clothes

Many nannies have total responsibility for the care of children's clothes and bed linen. When caring for clothes, you should:

- look at the laundry care labels on each garment and make sure that you are familiar with the different symbols

- check and empty all pockets before laundering

- be guided by the parents regarding choice of washing powder – some detergents can cause an adverse skin reaction in some children

- dry clothes thoroughly before putting away

- label children's clothes with name tapes before they go into group settings.

Think about ideas

Children's clothing

Plan a wardrobe of clothes suitable for a child aged three years, to cover a whole year. For each garment, state:

✔ the reason you have chosen it

✔ how it should be laundered or cleaned

✔ how it may promote the child's independence.

The development of bowel and bladder control

Newborn babies pass the waste products from eating automatically – in other words, although they may go red in the face when passing a stool or motion, they have no control over the action. Parents used to boast with pride that all their children were potty-trained at nine months, but the reality is that they were probably lucky in their timing! Up to the age of 18 months, emptying of the bladder and bowel is still a totally automatic reaction – the child's **central nervous system** (CNS) is still not sufficiently mature to make the connection between the action and its results.

Recognising that a child is ready to move out of nappies and toilet training

There is no point attempting to start toilet training until the toddler shows that he or she is ready, and this rarely occurs before the age of 18 months. The usual signs are:

● increased interest when passing urine or a motion – the child may pretend-play on the potty with their toys

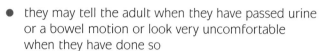

KEY TERM

Central nervous system (CNS) – This is comprised of the brain and spinal cord. It is the network of nerve tissues that controls the activities of the body.

● they may tell the adult when they have passed urine or a bowel motion or look very uncomfortable when they have done so

● they may start to be more regular with bowel motions, or wet nappies may become rarer.

When to start toilet training

Toilet training should be approached in a relaxed, unhurried manner. If the potty is introduced too early or if a child is forced to sit on it for long periods of time, he or she may rebel and the whole issue of toilet training will become a battleground. Toilet training can be over in a few days or may take some months. Becoming dry at night takes longer, but most children manage this before the age of five years.

Children need to learn that going to the toilet is a private activity, so you should withdraw by partially closing the door; remain nearby in case help is needed.

Guidelines for good practice

Toilet training

✔ **Be positive and supportive to the child's efforts:** be relaxed about toilet training and be prepared for accidents.

✔ **Structure the physical environment to help training:** have the potty close at hand so that the child becomes familiar with it and can include it in his or her play. It helps if the child sees other children using the toilet or potty. It is also helpful if children are dressed in clothes that are easy for them to manage by themselves, such as pull-up trousers rather than dungarees.

✔ **Work in partnership with parents and carers:** it is important to work closely with parents so that everyone takes a similar approach to toilet training, otherwise the child may become anxious. If a parent starts training their toddler when there is a new baby due, be prepared for some accidents. Many children react to a new arrival by regressing or going back to baby behaviour.

✔ **Encourage and praise:** always praise the child when he or she succeeds and do not show anger or disapproval if the opposite occurs; the child may be upset by an accident. It is important not to over-encourage children as this can make them worried about letting you down.

✔ **Treat a child with respect and avoid feelings of guilt:** do not show any disgust for the child's faeces. He or she will regard using the potty as an achievement

and will be proud of them. Children have no natural shame about their bodily functions (unless adults make them ashamed).

✔ **Establish a routine:** offer the potty regularly so that the child becomes used to the idea of a routine, and learn to read the signs that a child needs to use it. Cover the potty and flush the contents down the toilet. Always wear disposable gloves. Encourage good hygiene right from the start, by washing the child's hands after every use of the potty.

✔ **Flexible personalised approach:** some children feel insecure when sitting on a potty with no nappy on – let them try it first wearing a nappy or pants if they show reluctance. The child may prefer to try the 'big' toilet seat straightaway; a toddler seat fixed onto the normal seat makes this easier. Boys need to learn to stand in front of the toilet and aim at the bowl before passing any urine; you could put a piece of toilet paper in the bowl for him to aim at. Some children are frightened when the toilet is flushed; be tactful and sympathetic. You could wait until the child has left the room before you flush.

✔ **Provide plenty of fluids and fibre to prevent hard stools:** children need to drink plenty of water or other drinks in order for them to learn what having a full bladder feels like. They also need to be given foods that contain fibre (such as fruit and vegetables) to prevent **constipation** (see page 274 for definition).

Dealing with accidents

Even once a child has become used to using the potty or toilet, there will be occasions when they have an 'accident' – that is, they wet or soil themselves. This happens more often during the early stages of toilet training, as the child may lack the awareness and control needed to allow enough time to get to the potty. Older children may become so absorbed in their play that they simply forget to go to the toilet.

You can help children when they have an accident by:

- remaining calm and reassuring the child; let the child know that it is not a big problem, just something that happens from time to time
- reassuring the child in a friendly tone of voice and offering a cuddle if he or she seems distressed
- being discreet – deal with the matter swiftly; wash and change the child out of view of others and with the minimum of fuss
- an older child could be supervised discreetly and encouraged to manage the incident themselves, if they wish to do so; but always check tactfully afterwards that they have managed this
- following safety procedures in the setting – for example, wear the correct personal and protective equipment (PPE) and disposable gloves to deal appropriately with soiled clothing and waste.

Enuresis (bedwetting)

Enuresis is a common occurrence; about one in ten children wets the bed at the age of six years, and many continue to do so until the age of eight or nine years. It is more common in boys than in girls, and the problem tends to run in families. In the majority of children, enuresis is due to slow maturation of the nervous system functions concerned with control of the bladder; very rarely, it occurs because of emotional stress or because of a physical problem such as a urinary infection.

Guidelines for good practice

Managing bedwetting

✔ Investigate possible physical causes first, by taking the child to the doctor.

✔ Protect the mattress with a plastic sheet.

✔ Do not cut down on the amount that a child drinks during the day. A bedtime drink could be given earlier, but never let a child go to bed feeling thirsty.

✔ Encourage the child to pass urine just before going to bed. It sometimes helps to 'lift' the child just before adults go to bed, taking him or her to the toilet. It is important, however, that the child is thoroughly awake when passing urine; this is because he or she will need to recognise the link between passing urine on the toilet and waking up with a dry bed.

✔ Some parents find that a 'star chart' system of rewards for a dry bed encourages the child to become dry sooner, but there are problems with all reward systems (see Chapter 11). This should only be used if physical problems have been excluded.

✔ If the child continues to wet the bed after the age of seven years, a special night-time alarm system can be used: a detector mat is placed under the sheet. This triggers a buzzer as soon as it becomes wet; eventually the child will wake before he or she needs to pass urine (this system is said to succeed in over two-thirds of children).

Reflecting on practice

Toilet training

1 Arrange to interview a parent or carer who has recently toilet-trained a child.

2 Try to find out the methods they used and any problems they encountered.

3 Write a report of the methods used.

In small groups, make a colourful, eye-catching wall display that provides tips for parents and carers on toilet training.

Encopresis (soiling)

Encopresis is a type of soiling in which children who have no physical problems with their bowel motions deliberately pass them in their pants or on the floor. It occurs after the age at which bowel control is usually achieved and in children who know the difference between the right and wrong place to go. Fortunately, it is a rare condition, but one which needs very sensitive treatment. Encopresis may occur because of emotional problems and stress; if it persists, advice should be sought from the health visitor or doctor.

Think about ideas

Toilet training

In class, discuss the problems that can arise with toilet training and compare the strategies used by different families.

Hygiene and health

Providing a healthy and hygienic environment for children is vital to their development. A balance also has to be struck so that a child is allowed to get dirty when playing, but understands that he or she will need to wash afterwards.

Developing good hygiene routines is important because:

- **It helps to prevent infection and the spread of disease** – children who play closely together for long periods of time are more likely than others to develop an infection, and any infection can spread very quickly from one child to another.

- **Being clean increases self-esteem and social acceptance** – generally, people do not like to be close to someone who appears dirty or has poor personal hygiene.

- **It helps to prepare children in skills of independence and self-care** – all children benefit from regular routines in daily care. Obviously, parents and carers have their own routines and hygiene practices, and these should always be respected.

Being a good role model

You need to set a good example by always taking care of your appearance and your own personal hygiene. Often your early years setting will provide you with a uniform – usually a sweatshirt and trousers – but if not, choose your clothing carefully, bearing in mind the sort of activities you are likely to be involved in.

Providing a hygienic indoor environment

Children need a clean, warm and hygienic environment in order to stay healthy. Although most large early years settings employ a cleaner, there will be many occasions when you have to take responsibility for ensuring that the environment is kept clean and safe – for example, if a child has been sick or has had a toileting accident.

Guidelines for good practice

Personal hygiene

Personal hygiene involves regular and thorough cleaning of your skin, hair, teeth and clothes. The following are particularly important:

✔ Hand-washing: the most important defence against the spread of infection is hand-washing; wash your hands frequently, especially before eating, and before and after touching your mouth or nose. You should not use the kitchen sink to wash your hands.

✔ Parents and carers must wash their hands after they blow the nose or wipe the mouth of a sick child.

✔ Use paper towels to dry your hands if possible; if cloth towels are used, make sure they are washed daily in hot water.

✔ Keep your nails clean and short, as long fingernails harbour dirt. Do not wear nail varnish, because flakes of varnish could chip off into a snack you are preparing, for example.

✔ Avoid jewellery other than a simple wedding ring and a watch.

✔ Avoid contact with the secretions (especially on stray facial tissues) of somebody with a runny nose, sore throat or cough.

✔ Cover any cuts or sores on your hands with a clean, waterproof plaster. Use a new plaster each day. Note that plasters should only be used where permission has been given.

✔ Do not share utensils or cups with somebody who has a cold, sore throat or upper respiratory tract infection.

✔ Wear the correct PPE and disposable gloves when changing nappies or when dealing with blood, urine, faeces or vomit.

✔ Hair should be kept clean, be brushed regularly and be tied back, if long.

All early years settings should have set routines for tidying up and for cleaning the floors, walls, furniture and play equipment; details may be found in the setting's written policy for health and hygiene issues.

Providing a hygienic outdoor environment

Children benefit from playing in the fresh air, as long as they are dressed appropriately for the weather. All early years settings should be checked regularly to make sure a safe and hygienic environment is being provided.

Guidelines for good practice

Providing a safe and hygienic indoor environment

✔ Adequate ventilation is important to disperse bacteria or viruses transmitted through sneezing or coughing. Make sure that windows are opened to let in fresh air to the nursery – but also make sure there are no draughts.

✔ All surfaces should be damp-dusted daily. Floors, surfaces and the toilet area must be checked on a regular basis for cleanliness.

✔ All toys and play equipment should be cleaned regularly – *at least* once a week. This includes dressing-up clothes and soft toys. Use antiseptic solutions such as Savlon to disinfect toys and play equipment regularly; toys used by babies under one year should be disinfected daily.

✔ Check that sandpits or trays are clean and that toys are removed and cleaned at the end of a play session; if the sandpit is kept outside, make sure it is kept covered when not in use. Keep sand trays clean by sieving and washing the sand regularly.

✔ Water trays should be emptied daily, as germs can multiply quickly in pools of water.

✔ The home area often contains dolls, saucepans and plastic food; these need to be included in your checking and regular washing routines.

✔ Apart from routine cleaning, you should always clean up any spills straightaway; young children and adults can slip on wet surfaces.

✔ Use paper towels and tissues, and dispose of them in covered bins.

✔ Remove from the nursery any toy that has been in contact with a child who has an infectious illness.

✔ Throw out any plastic toys that have cracks or splits in them, as these cracks can harbour germs.

✔ Particular care should be taken to keep hats, head coverings and hairbrushes clean in order to help prevent the spread of head lice.

✔ Animals visiting the nursery or nursery pets must be free from disease, safe to be with children and must not pose a health risk. Children should always be supervised when handling animals and make sure they always wash their hands after touching any pet.

✔ A no-smoking policy must be observed by staff and visitors.

Guidelines for good practice

Ensuring a hygienic outdoor environment

✔ Check the outdoor play area daily for litter, dog excrement and hazards such as broken glass, syringes or rusty cans.

✔ Follow the sun safety code: provide floppy hats and use sun cream (SPF 30) to prevent sunburn (if parents give their permission).

✔ Check all play equipment for splinters, jagged edges, protruding nails and other hazards.

✔ Supervise children at all times.

✔ Keep sand covered and check regularly for insects, litter and other contamination.

✔ Keep gates locked and check that hinges are secure.

Policies relating to health and hygiene issues

All early years settings must have written policies for dealing with health and safety issues. This includes policies and procedures for:

- Food hygiene
- Administration of medicine
- Health and hygiene
- Evacuation procedures
- Safe disposal of waste
- Risk assessment
- Fire safety
- Safety at arrival and departure times, and on outings
- Infection control and prevention of illness
- First aid
- Accidents and emergencies

The 'Addressing health and hygiene issues' guidelines on page 277 include points which are often part of the policy document. Check with your setting for a comprehensive document about their health and hygiene policy.

Using correct PPE

The term 'PPE' includes single-use disposable gloves and single-use disposable plastic aprons. PPE is used as a preventive measure as part of infection control. It is used to protect people from exposure

Guidelines for good practice

Addressing health and hygiene issues

✔ Always wear disposable gloves when dealing with blood, urine, faeces or vomit.

✔ Always wash your hands after dealing with spillages – even if gloves have been worn.

✔ Use a dilute bleach (hypochlorite) solution (or other product specified by your setting's policy) to mop up any spillages.

✔ Make sure paper tissues are available for children to use.

✔ Always cover cuts and open sores with adhesive plasters.

✔ Food must be stored and prepared hygienically.

✔ Ask parents to keep their children at home if they are feeling unwell or if they have an infection.

✔ Children who are sent home with vomiting or diarrhoea must remain at home until at least 24 hours have elapsed since the last attack.

✔ Parents must provide written authorisation for early years workers to administer medications to children.

Guidelines for good practice

Safe disposal of waste

✔ Staff should *always* wear PPE when handling any bodily waste (blood, urine, vomit and faeces). Always dispose of the gloves and wash your hands after dealing with such waste, even though gloves have been worn.

✔ When dealing with water spillages – ensure when clearing them up that the surface is left completely dry.

✔ When dealing with body fluids – *before* clearing them away, ensure that you are wearing the correct PPE: mop up any spillages using a dilute bleach solution or use the resources provided by your setting's policy, and clean the surface until it is completely dry.

✔ Different types of waste should be kept in separate covered bins in designated areas; for example, food waste should be kept well away from toilet waste.

✔ Soiled nappies, dressings, disposable towels and gloves should be placed in a sealed bag before being put in a plastic-lined, covered bin.

✔ Always cover any cuts and open sores with waterproof adhesive plasters.

to blood, body fluids and infectious diseases. Whether you need to use PPE will depend on you coming into contact with blood and body fluids. Remember:

● Always wash your hands before putting on and after taking off PPE.

● Disposable gloves and disposable plastic aprons must be worn where there is a risk of splashing or contamination with blood or body fluids – for example, dealing with a nosebleed or nappy changing.

● Some larger settings supply disposable aprons in different colours – for example, red gloves may be used for dealing with blood.

See the 'Safe disposal of waste' guidelines above.

Promoting children's hygiene

All children need adult help and supervision to keep their skin, hair and teeth clean. You should not expect children to be forever worrying about personal cleanliness, but by encouraging hygiene routines, you will help to prevent the spread of infection.

Children are more likely than adults to develop an infection because:

● they have immature immune systems

● they are not usually aware of the need for hygiene – they need to be taught and reminded to wash their hands

● they tend to play closely with other children for long periods of time.

Good hygiene routines will help to prevent infection. Children will take their cue from you, so you need to ensure that you are a good role model by setting a high standard for your own personal hygiene.

Food hygiene

Food hygiene is important to everyone. The food we eat is one of the key factors in good health. If you are caring for children, you need to know the principles of food hygiene. Young children are particularly vulnerable to the bacteria that can cause food poisoning or gastroenteritis. Bacteria multiply rapidly in warm, moist foods and can enter food without causing the food to look, smell or even taste bad. So it is very important to store, prepare and cook food safely, and to keep the kitchen clean.

What is food poisoning?

Any infectious disease that results from consuming food or drink is known as food poisoning. The term is most often used to describe the illness, usually diarrhoea and/or vomiting caused by bacteria, viruses or parasites.

What causes food poisoning?

Most cases of food poisoning result from eating large numbers of pathogenic (or harmful) bacteria that are living on the food. Most food poisoning is preventable, although it is not possible to eliminate the risk completely.

At risk – babies and young children

Babies and very young children are at particular risk from food poisoning, partly because they have immature immune systems. Also, infection can spread very quickly in young children, if there is a lack of supervised thorough hand-washing after using the toilet and before eating, and from touching contaminated toilet seats and tap handles. Many young children also put their hands, fingers and thumbs in their mouths frequently, so hands should be kept clean.

How bacteria from food sources make you ill

Bacteria (germs) found in food can lead to food poisoning, which can be dangerous and can kill (though this is rare). They are very hard to detect since they do not usually affect the taste, appearance or smell of food.

Bacteria can either be present in food, or can come from other people, surfaces or equipment, or from other food through cross-contamination. The main causes of bacterial food poisoning are:

- **Undercooking** – for example, when the oven is not hot enough (or used for long enough) to ensure that the inside of a chicken is completely cooked. It is essential that frozen raw meat and poultry is adequately thawed, followed by thorough cooking to ensure that any pathogenic bacteria are destroyed.

- **Food prepared too far in advance and then not refrigerated** – for example, when a ham sandwich is left out of the fridge (uncovered or covered) for several hours. Food-poisoning bacteria can multiply rapidly at room temperature. All food prepared in advance must be refrigerated to ensure minimal bacterial growth. For this reason, fridges should operate below 5°C.

- **Poor personal hygiene** – for example, when a person prepares food without washing their hands properly. Poor personal hygiene can result in food becoming contaminated with bacteria. Hands must be washed as frequently as necessary but definitely:
  - before handling food or equipment
  - after visiting the toilet
  - in-between handling raw and cooked food
  - after handling waste food or refuse.

- **Cross-contamination** – for example, when a knife that has been used to cut raw meat is not washed and is then used to cut cooked or ready-to-eat food. Food-poisoning bacteria may be present in raw food such as meat and poultry. If these bacteria are allowed to contaminate food that is to be eaten without further cooking, food poisoning can result. Cross-contamination from raw food may happen as a result of poor storage, when the juices from raw meat are allowed to drip on to cooked food, or via a chopping board or utensils used for both raw and cooked food.

- **Infected food handlers** – for example, a person who returns to work after a brief episode of vomiting and diarrhoea may still be a carrier of food-poisoning bacteria. Any person suffering from vomiting and/or diarrhoea should not prepare or serve food until they are totally clear of the symptoms for at least 48 hours. Even then, extra attention to hand-washing is essential. Septic boils and cuts are another potential source of **pathogens**. Uninfected wounds should be completely covered and protected by a waterproof dressing.

- **Failure to keep cooked food hot** – for example, serving food that has been allowed to stand and become cool (under 63°C) – after cooking. As thorough cooking does not destroy spores, hot food kept below 63°C can allow the spores to germinate and produce food-poisoning bacteria. For this reason, it is important to keep hot food above 63°C.

- **Eating food from unsafe sources** – for example, buying food from a shop that does not refrigerate its products properly.

The prevention of food poisoning

Even healthy people carry food-poisoning bacteria on their bodies. These can be spread to the hands through touching parts of the body that contain them, such as the nose, mouth or bottom, and then from the hands to the food.

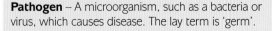

KEY TERM

Pathogen – A microorganism, such as a bacteria or virus, which causes disease. The lay term is 'germ'.

Guidelines for good practice

Food hygiene

When serving food and clearing away after meals and snacks, you should observe the general rules of food hygiene:

✔ Wash the backs of hands, wrists, between the fingers and under fingernails with soap and warm water, and then dry them thoroughly.

✔ Wear clean protective clothing such as disposable apron and gloves.

✔ Ensure any washing-up by hand is done thoroughly in hot water, with detergent; you should use rubber gloves.

✔ Cover cups/beakers with a clean cloth and air-dry where possible.

✔ Drying-up cloths should be replaced every day with clean ones.

✔ Never cough or sneeze over food.

Did you know?

✔ The number of bacteria on fingertips doubles after using the toilet.

✔ Bacteria can stay alive on our hands for up to three hours.

✔ 1,000 times as many bacteria spread from damp hands than from dry hands.

✔ Even after thorough washing, bugs (such as E. coli) can remain under long fingernails.

✔ Millions of bacteria can hide under rings, watches and bracelets.

✔ A 1mm hair follicle can harbour 50,000 bacteria.

Storing food safely

● Keep food cold. The fridge should be kept as cold as it will go without actually freezing the food (1–5 °C or 34–41 °F).

● Cover or wrap food with food wrap or microwave cling film.

● Never refreeze food that has begun to thaw.

● Do not use foods that are past their sell-by or best-before date.

● Always read instructions on the label when storing food.

● Once a tin is opened, store the contents in a covered dish in the fridge.

● Store raw foods at the bottom of the fridge so that juices cannot drip onto cooked food.

● Thaw frozen meat completely before cooking.

Preparing and cooking food safely

● Always wash hands in warm water and soap, and dry on a clean towel, before handling food and after handling raw foods, especially meat.

● Wear clean, protective clothing that is solely for use in the kitchen.

● Keep food covered at all times.

● Wash all fruits and vegetables before eating. Peel and cut tops off carrots and peel fruits such as apples.

● Never cough or sneeze over food.

● Always cover any septic cuts or boils with a waterproof dressing.

● Never smoke in any room that is used for food.

● Keep work surfaces and chopping boards clean and disinfected; for example, use separate boards for raw meat, fish, vegetables, to avoid cross-contamination.

● Make sure that meat dishes are thoroughly cooked.

● Avoid raw eggs. They sometimes contain salmonella bacteria, which may cause food poisoning. (Also avoid giving children uncooked cake mixture, home-made ice creams, mayonnaise or desserts that contain uncooked raw egg.) When cooking eggs, the egg yolk and white should be firm.

● When reheating food, make sure that it is piping hot all the way through, and allow it to cool slightly before giving it to children. When using a microwave, always stir and check the temperature of the food before feeding children, to avoid burning from 'hot spots' i.e. when some parts of the food remain too hot if not thoroughly stirred.

● Avoid leftovers – they are a common cause of food poisoning.

Keeping the kitchen safe

● Teach children to wash their hands after touching pets and going to the toilet, and before eating.

● Clean tin openers, graters and mixers thoroughly after use.

● Keep flies and other insects away – use a fine mesh over open windows.

● Stay away from the kitchen if you are suffering from diarrhoea or sickness.

● Keep the kitchen clean – the floor, work surfaces, sink, utensils, cloths and waste bins should be cleaned regularly.

● Tea towels should be boiled every day and dishcloths boiled or disinfected.

● Keep pets away from the kitchen.

● Keep all waste bins covered and empty them regularly.

- Keep sharp knives stored safely where children cannot reach them.

See Chapters 14 and 16 on diet, nutrition and food for legislation regarding food safety and hygiene.

See Chapter 12 for hygienic practice when preparing formula feeds and sterilising equipment

Moving on

The art and skill of caregiving

Manning-Morton (2000) suggests that the division between 'care' and 'education' and the emphasis in curriculum guidance on the importance of early learning (influenced by theories of brain development) for later outcomes, has led to a decline in focus on the physical and emotional care of babies and young children and what is called 'disembodied' practice (Tobin 1997, Pound 2005), for example not cuddling children or letting them sit on your lap. She also suggests that this has led to a view of an early years professional as someone whose focus is expected to be on developing children's cognitive skills rather than their physical and emotional well-being, resulting in the 'care' of children being undervalued.

However, as emphasised throughout this book, care and education are indivisible and all aspects of children's development and learning are interconnected and equally important. And effective caregiving requires a good knowledge and understanding of children and important professional skills as much as effective teaching does.

Reflecting on practice

Review your curriculum guidance: how much does it discuss the feeding, washing, toileting and dressing of babies and young children?

Review your observations and planning: how much do you focus on children's physical or emotional learning? Do you review and plan for physical care times?

Reflect on the views you and your colleagues have about the physical care of children; is it seen as less important in your practice?

Further reading, weblinks and resources

Meggitt, C., 2003, *Food Hygiene and Safety,* Oxford: Heinemann Educational Publishers.

Food Standards Agency

The Food Standards Agency carries out a range of work to make sure that food is safe to eat, including funding research on chemical, microbiological and radiological safety, and on food hygiene and allergy.
www.food.gov.uk

Foundation Stage Forum

The Foundation Stage Forum shares information on all aspects of Foundation Stage education, from childminding to Reception and Year 1, and from practical to theoretical and research.
www.foundation-stage.info

There are many factors affecting health in infancy and childhood. This chapter focuses on the promotion of child health, through active educational campaigns, child health surveillance programmes and immunisation. The relevant health and safety legislation is described and your role and responsibilities in preventing accidents, understanding the importance of risk and challenge and emergency procedures in the setting.

The promotion and maintenance of health

What is health?

The World Health Organization (WHO) defines health as a 'state of complete physical, mental, and social wellbeing, and not merely the absence of disease or infirmity'. Health and social well-being can best be viewed as a holistic concept, encompassing the different aspects of a person's health needs. These are described below.

Aspects of health

- **Physical health** – this is the easiest aspect of health to measure; it is concerned with the physical functioning of the body.
- **Emotional health** – how we express emotions such as joy, grief, frustration and fear; this includes coping strategies for anxiety and stress.
- **Mental health** – this relates to our ability to organise our thoughts coherently, and is closely linked to emotional and social health.
- **Social health** – how we relate to others and form relationships.
- **Spiritual health** – this includes religious beliefs and practices, as well as personal codes of conduct and the quest for inner peace.
- **Environmental health** – an individual's health depends also on the health of the society in which they live – for example, in famine areas, health is denied to the inhabitants, and unemployed people cannot be healthy in a society that only values those who work.

Factors affecting health in infancy and childhood

There are many factors that affect the healthy growth and development of children. These factors work in combination, so it is often difficult to estimate the impact of any single factor on child health. Factors include:

- nutrition
- infection
- poverty and social disadvantage
- housing
- homelessness
- accidents
- emotional and social factors
- environmental factors
- lifestyle factors.

Many of the factors that adversely affect child health are closely interrelated, and make up a *cycle of deprivation* – for example, poorer families tend to live in poorer housing conditions and may also have an inadequate diet; lack of adequate minerals and vitamins as a result of poor diet leads to an increased susceptibility to infectious diseases, and so on.

Nutrition

Milk, whether human or formula, is the fuel that makes babies grow more rapidly during the first year than at any other time. Both human and formula milk provide the right nutrients for the first months of life, with just the right balance of carbohydrates, proteins, fats, vitamins and minerals. Eating habits that are developed in childhood are likely to be continued in adult life. This means that children who eat mainly processed, convenience foods will tend to rely on these when they leave home. There are various conditions that may occur in childhood that are directly related to poor or unbalanced nutrition; see Chapter 16, p. 365.

Infection

During childhood, there are many infectious illnesses that can affect health and development. Some of these infections can be controlled by childhood **immunisations**; these are diphtheria, tetanus, polio, whooping cough, measles, meningitis, mumps and rubella (definitions are on p. 287). Other infections can have long-lasting effects on children's health.

Poverty and social disadvantage

According to The Child Poverty Action Group, there are 3.7 million children living in poverty in the UK today (that is 28 per cent of children).

Poverty is linked with the health of children for the following reasons:

- **Healthy eating costs more** – it costs more to provide a nutritionally balanced diet than one that is based on foods that tend to be high in sugar and fats.
- **Poor housing conditions** – families on a low-income s tend to live in poorer housing, which may also be overcrowded, compared with those who are better off.
- **Unemployment** – parents who are unemployed have a higher incidence of mental health problems, long-term physical illness and disability, and also higher mortality rates.

All these factors can have a lasting impact on the physical, emotional and social well-being of the child and family. Poverty is closely linked with social disadvantage; this means that families who have low incomes are likely to have fewer physical and personal resources to cope with illness. They will be at a disadvantage socially. They are also less likely to attend health clinics and are therefore less likely to receive adequate medical care, both preventive and in response to illness.

Housing

Poor housing is another factor that puts people at a social disadvantage. Low-income families are more likely to live in:

- homes that are damp and/or unheated – this increases the risk of infection, particularly respiratory illnesses
- neighbourhoods that are unattractive and densely populated, with few communal areas and amenities – children without access to a safe garden or play area may suffer emotional and social problems
- overcrowded conditions – homeless families who are housed in hotels or bed and breakfast accommodation often have poor access to cooking facilities and have to share bathrooms with several other families; often, children's education is badly disrupted when families are moved from one place to another.

Homelessness

More than 90,000 children in England, Scotland and Wales were without a permanent home in 2014.

Most of them will be living in temporary hostel accommodation or bed and breakfast housing. The vast majority of these children are in single-parent families, with very little financial or extended family support. Most of these families become homeless to escape from violence from a male partner or ex-partner, or from neighbours. The experience of homelessness causes many health problems for the children of such families including:

- mental health problems, including delays in social or language development
- behavioural problems
- disruption of social relationships and difficulty forming new friendships
- experience of marital conflict and domestic violence.

Accidents

Some childhood accidents have lasting effects on a child's healthy growth and development, and many are preventable (see p. 294).

Emotional and social factors

A child who is unhappy is not healthy, although he or she may appear physically healthy. Children need to feel secure and to receive unconditional love from their primary carers. Child abuse, though not common, is bound to affect a child's health and well-being, and can have long-lasting health implications. (See Chapter 4 for information about child abuse.)

Environmental factors

Pollution of the environment can have a marked effect on children's health and development. The three main threats to health are water pollution, air pollution and noise pollution.

Lifestyle factors

Smoking

Children who live in a smoky atmosphere are more likely to develop:

- coughs and colds
- asthma
- chest infections
- ear infections and glue ear.

Every year, around 17,000 children are admitted to hospital with respiratory infections; research has found that many of these children are exposed daily to cigarette smoke. There is also an increased risk of children taking up smoking themselves if one or both of their parents smoke.

Exercise

Some children take no regular physical exercise, apart from at school, and this is often because of the family's attitude and habits. Taking regular exercise allows children to develop their motor skills and to 'run off' any pent-up feelings of frustration or aggression. Exercise is important for many reasons. For example:

- Coronary heart disease is the greatest single risk to health in the UK.
- Adults who are physically inactive have about double the chance of suffering from coronary heart disease.
- Children who do not take much exercise tend to become inactive adults.
- Obesity is more common in children who take little exercise.

The promotion of community health

Health education

Health education is a method of self-empowerment; it enables people to take more control over their own health and that of their children. The aims of health education are to:

- provide information and to raise awareness
- change people's behaviour and attitudes
- meet national and local health targets – for example, promoting self-examination of the breasts to aid in the early detection of breast cancer.

Health education can be divided into primary, secondary and tertiary categories.

Primary health education

Primary health education is directed at healthy people. It is a prophylactic (or preventive) measure that aims to prevent ill-health from arising in the first instance. The areas of primary prevention in children are:

- sound nutrition and diet – that is, healthy eating
- immunisation
- the prevention of emotional and behavioural problems
- dental prophylaxis – that is, the prevention of tooth decay
- the prevention of childhood accidents
- basic hygiene.

Secondary health education

Secondary health education is directed at people with a health problem or a reversible condition. It emphasises the importance of the early detection of

defects and ways in which people can make lifestyle changes to improve their condition.

- **Screening** – by routinely examining apparently healthy people, screening aims to detect either those who are likely to develop a particular disease or those in whom the disease is already present but has not yet produced symptoms. Screening may detect a problem with hearing, sight or physical, emotional or behavioural development.
- **Reducing behaviours likely to damage health** – for example, overweight people can be encouraged to change their dietary habits, or a smoker to quit smoking.

Tertiary health education

Tertiary health education is directed at those whose ill-health has not been, or could not be, prevented and who cannot be completely cured. However, the quality of their lives can still be influenced. For example:

- Children with brain damage can achieve their own potential, with good support in communication and structured play.
- Patients dying of cancer can do so with dignity if their pain is kept under control.
- Rehabilitation programmes are chiefly concerned with tertiary health education.

Five approaches to health education

1 **The medical approach** – this approach promotes medical intervention to prevent or improve ill-health; it uses a persuasive and authoritarian method – for example, persuading parents to take their children for immunisation.

2 **The behaviour change approach** – this approach aims to change people's attitudes and behaviour, so that they adopt a healthy lifestyle – for example, teaching people how to give up smoking.

3 **The educational approach** – this approach aims to give information and to ensure understanding of health issues. Information is presented in as value-free a way as possible, so that the people targeted feel free to make their own decisions – for example, clients are given information about the effects of smoking and can then make a choice to stop smoking if they want to.

4 **The client-directed approach** – this approach aims to work with clients so that they can identify what they want to know about, and make their own decisions and choices – for example, the anti-smoking issue is only considered if the client identifies it as a concern.

5 **The social change approach** – this approach aims to change the environment in order to facilitate the choice of healthier lifestyles – for example, the drive for healthier school dinners and the no-smoking policy being implemented in restaurants, pubs, bars and workplaces.

Advertisers often use scare tactics to get the message across; this has been called the 'fear creation' approach.

Health education campaigns

Recent health education campaigns of particular relevance to children include the following:

- **Change4Life and LazyTown:** Change4Life teamed up with superhero Sportacus from children's television show LazyTown to create a range of games and activities encouraging children aged two to five to be more active and eat healthier food. The aim was to challenge them to become as healthy and active as Sportacus.
- **The Water is Cool in School Campaign** aims to improve the quality of provision and access to fresh drinking water for children in UK primary and secondary schools.
- **The School Fruit and Vegetable Scheme (SFVS)** is part of the 5-a-day programme to increase fruit and vegetable consumption. Under the SFVs, all four-to-six-year-old children in LEA-maintained infant, primary and schools for special educational needs are entitled to a free piece of fruit or portion of vegetables each school day.
- **'Safer Sleep for Babies'** is a campaign from the Lullaby Trust; leaflets and posters have been sent to all midwives and health visitors.
- **Birth to Five** is a comprehensive guide to parenthood and the first five years of a child's life. It covers child health, nutrition and safety and is given free to all first-time mothers in England.

Health education by private companies

Manufacturers of 'healthy' products, such as wholemeal bread or high-protein-balanced foods for babies, often promote their products both by advertising and by using educational leaflets. Such leaflets are offered free in health clinics, post-natal wards and supermarkets. Examples of this type of health promotion are:

- booklets on feeding your baby published by formula milk manufacturers
- leaflets on child safety on the roads produced by manufacturers of child car seats and harnesses

▲ **Figure 14.1** Safer sleep for babies

- the promotion of herbal remedies to encourage a stress-free lifestyle.

See Chapter 16 for more information on initiatives regarding children's diets.

There are strict controls over the claims that manufacturers can make about the health-giving properties of their products.

Health education leading to preventive action

All immunisation programmes are an attempt to prevent disease and, therefore, to promote health – both in the individual and in the general population. The campaign to prevent sudden infant death syndrome is another example of an important health message reaching those who need it.

Your role in child health education

There are many ways in which you can contribute to health education programmes in early years settings. The most important part of your role is to be a good role model for children.

Preventing ill-health through immunisation

Immunisation is a way of protecting children against serious disease. Once children have been immunised, their bodies can fight those diseases they come into contact with. If a child is not immunised, he or she will be at risk from catching the disease and will rely on other parents/carers immunising their children to avoid becoming infected.

An immunisation programme protects people against specific diseases by reducing the number of people getting the disease and preventing it being passed on. With some diseases – such as smallpox or polio – it is possible to eliminate them completely.

Guidelines for good practice

Teaching children about health and safety

✔ Be a good role model by, for example, always looking neat and tidy, washing your hands, wearing an apron during messy activities, etc.

✔ Supervise children's hand-washing throughout the day.

✔ Encourage children to cover their mouths when coughing.

✔ Choose books and displays which reinforce healthy lifestyles.

✔ Use drama and music sessions to encourage children to express their feelings in a safe environment.

✔ Create interesting board games with a healthy theme – for example, how to avoid accidents when playing outside.

✔ Welcome visitors to talk about their work in health care – for example, invite a health visitor or dentist to explain the importance of good hygiene routines.

✔ Demonstrate safety and hygiene routines – for example, a road safety officer or police officer could visit the setting to teach children how to cross the road safely.

✔ Make the home area into a hospital ward and encourage role-play as patients, nurses and doctors.

How immunity to disease and infection can be acquired

Babies are born with some natural **immunity**. They are:

● able to make their own infection-fighting cells

● further protected by antibodies and other substances found in breast milk.

A child's own experiences of infection boost his or her immunity. For some infections – e.g. measles – immunity is lifelong, while for others it is short-lived. Certain illnesses, such as the common cold, are caused by one of several strains of virus, which is why having one cold does not automatically prevent another one later. Sometimes the immune system does not work properly, as in the case of HIV/AIDS infection and some other rare conditions. Sometimes it *over*-works and causes allergy. It can also be affected by emotional distress and physical exhaustion.

As discussed above, immunity can be induced by contact with an infection. It can also be induced by immunisation against certain infective agents.

Active immunity

Active immunity is when a **vaccine** triggers the immune system to produce **antibodies** against the disease as though the body had been infected with it. This also teaches the body's immune system how to produce the appropriate antibodies quickly. If the immunised person then comes into contact with the disease itself, their immune system will recognise it and immediately produce the antibodies needed to fight it.

Passive immunity

Passive immunity is provided when the body is given antibodies rather than producing them itself. A newborn baby has passive immunity to several diseases, such as measles, mumps and rubella, from antibodies passed from its mother via the placenta. Passive immunity only lasts for a few weeks or months. In the case of measles, mumps and rubella it may last up to one year in infants – this is why MMR is offered just after a child's first birthday.

Herd immunity

If enough people in a community are immunised against certain diseases, then it is more difficult for that disease to get passed between those who are not immunised—this is known as herd immunity. Herd immunity does not apply to all diseases because they are not all passed on from person to person. For example, tetanus can only be caught from spores in the ground.

Advantages and disadvantages of immunisation

The **advantages** of immunisation include:

● Children who are not immunised run a risk of catching diseases and having complications.

● Immunisation is the safest way to protect children from particular diseases which may have long-lasting effects.

● Having children immunised at an early age means they are well protected by the time they start playgroup or school, where they are in contact with lots of children.

- Immunisation also protects those children who are unable to receive immunisation, by providing herd immunity.

The **disadvantages** of immunisation include the possibility of side effects. The possible risks that follow certain childhood immunisations must be weighed up against the possible risks of complications of the childhood illness. For example, with the MMR vaccine there is a risk of 1 in a 1,000 of febrile convulsions (fits). However, if a child catches the measles disease, the risk of convulsions is 1 in 200 people with the disease.

The immunisation schedule

Not every disease that affects children can be immunised against. There is no routine vaccination for chicken pox or scarlet fever in the UK although the chicken pox vaccine is offered with the MMR in some other countries. The following diseases are all included in the NHS programme of routine immunisation (2014).

- **Diphtheria:** a bacterial infection which starts with a sore throat but can rapidly get worse, leading to severe breathing difficulties. It can also damage the heart and nervous system.

- **Tetanus:** a bacterial infection caused when germs found in soil and manure get into the body through open cuts and burns. Tetanus is a painful disease which affects the muscles and can cause breathing problems.

- **Pertussis** (or **whooping cough**)**:** a bacterial infection that can cause long bouts of coughing and choking, making it hard to breathe. It is not usually serious in older children, but it can be very serious and can kill babies under one year old. It can last for up to 10 weeks.

- **Polio:** it is a highly infectious viral disease spread mainly through close contact with an infected person. The polio virus attacks the nervous system and can paralyse muscles permanently. If it attacks the muscles in the chest, or those that control swallowing, it can be fatal.

- **Hib:** Hib *(Haemophilus influenzae type b)* is an infection that can cause a number of major illnesses like blood poisoning, pneumonia and meningitis. All of these illnesses can kill if not treated quickly. The Hib vaccine protects the child against only *one* type of meningitis (Hib). It does not protect against any other type of meningitis.

- **Meningococcal disease:** this is one of the serious causes of meningitis—an inflammation of the lining of the brain – and serious blood infections in children. Although fairly rare now, before the introduction of the vaccine it was the most common killer in the one-to-five-years age group. The Men C vaccine protects the child against only *one* type of meningitis (meningococcal).

- **Measles:** the measles virus is highly contagious and causes a high fever and rash. Around 1 in 15 of all children who get measles are at risk of complications including chest infections, fits and brain damage. In very serious cases, measles kills. In 1988 (the year before the MMR vaccine was introduced in the UK) 16 children died from measles.

- **Mumps:** mumps is caused by a virus which can lead to fever, headache, and painful, swollen glands in the face, neck and jaw. It can result in permanent deafness, viral meningitis (swelling of the lining of the brain) and encephalitis (also inflammation of the brain). Rarely, it causes painful swelling of the testicles in males and the ovaries in females.

- **Pneumococcal disease:** this is the term used to describe infections caused by the bacterium *Streptococcus pneumoniae*. It can cause pneumonia, septicaemia (blood poisoning) and meningitis, and is also one of the most common bacterial causes of ear infections. The bacterium is becoming increasingly resistant to antibiotics in the UK and worldwide.

- **Rotavirus:** rotavirus is a highly infectious stomach bug that typically strikes babies and young children, causing an unpleasant bout of diarrhoea, sometimes with vomiting, tummy ache and fever. Most children recover at home within a few days, but nearly one in five will need to see their doctor, and 1 in 10 of these end up in hospital as a result of complications such as extreme dehydration. A very small number of children die from rotavirus infection each year.

- **Rubella:** (German measles) is caused by a virus. In children it is usually mild and can go unnoticed. Rubella infection in the first three months of pregnancy causes damage to the unborn baby in nine out of ten cases; it can seriously damage their sight, hearing, heart and brain. In the five years before the MMR vaccine was introduced, about 43 babies a year were born in the UK with congenital rubella syndrome – that is, the babies had developed the condition at or before birth.

Immunisations are usually carried out in child health clinics. The doctor will discuss any fears the parents may have about particular vaccines. No vaccine is completely risk-free, and parents are asked to sign a consent form prior to immunisations being given. Immunisations are only given if the child is well, and

Routine childhood immunisations
from summer 2015

When	Diseases protected against	Vaccine given and trade name		Usual site[1]
Eight weeks old	Diphtheria, tetanus, pertussis (whooping cough), polio and *Haemophilus influenzae* type b (Hib)	DTaP/IPV/Hib	Pediacel or Infanrix IPV Hib	Thigh
	Pneumococcal (13 serotypes)	Pneumococcal conjugate vaccination (PCV)	Prevenar 13	Thigh
	Meningococcal group B (MenB)[2]	MenB[2]	Bexsero	Left thigh
	Rotavirus gastroenteritis	Rotavirus	Rotarix	By mouth
Twelve weeks old	Diphtheria, tetanus, pertussis, polio and Hib	DTaP/IPV/Hib	Pediacel or Infanrix IPV Hib	Thigh
	Meningococcal group C disease (MenC)	Men C	NeisVac-C	Thigh
	Rotavirus	Rotavirus	Rotarix	By mouth
Sixteen weeks old	Diphtheria, tetanus, pertussis, polio and Hib	DTaP/IPV/Hib	Pediacel or Infanrix IPV Hib	Thigh
	Pneumococcal (13 serotypes)	PCV	Prevenar 13	Thigh
	MenB[2]	MenB[2]	Bexsero	Left thigh
One year old	Hib and MenC	Hib/MenC	Menitorix	Upper arm/thigh
	Pneumococcal	PCV	Prevenar 13	Upper arm/thigh
	Measles, mumps and rubella (German measles)	MMR	MMR VaxPRO[3] or Priorix	Upper arm/thigh
	MenB[2]	MenB booster[2]	Bexsero	Left thigh
Two to six years old (including children in school years 1 and 2)	Influenza (each year from September)	Live attenuated influenza vaccine LAIV[4]	Fluenz Tetra[3]	Both nostrils
Three years four months old or soon after	Diphtheria, tetanus, pertussis and polio	DTaP/IPV	Infanrix IPV or Repevax	Upper arm
	Measles, mumps and rubella	MMR (check first dose given)	MMR VaxPRO[3] or Priorix	Upper arm

[1] Where two or more injections are required at once, these should ideally be given in different limbs. Where this is not possible, injections in the same limb should be given 2.5cm apart. For more details see Chapters 4 and 11 in the Green Book. All injected vaccines are given intramuscularly unless otherwise stated.

[2] Only for infants born on or after 1 May 2015

[3] Contains porcine gelatine

[4] If LAIV (live attenuated influenza vaccine) is contraindicated and child is in a clinical risk group, use inactivated flu vaccine

Selective childhood immunisation programmes

Target group	Age and schedule	Disease	Vaccines required
Babies born to hepatitis B infected mothers	At birth, four weeks, eight weeks and Boost at one year[1]	Hepatitis B	Hepatitis B vaccines (Engerix B / HBVaxPRO)
Infants in areas of the country with TB incidence >= 40/100,000	At birth	Tuberculosis	BCG
Infants with a parent or grandparent born in a high incidence country[2]	At birth	Tuberculosis	BCG

[1] Take blood for HBsAg to exclude infection.

[2] Where the annual incidence of TB is >= 40/100,000 see https://www.gov.uk/government/uploads/system/uploads/attachment_data/file/393840/Worldwide_TB_Surveillance_2013_Data_High_and_Low_Incidence_Tables____2_.pdf

All vaccines for use in the routine childhood programme are available free of charge at www.immform.dh.gov.uk

▲ **Table 14.1** NHS Immunisation schedule for children from Summer 2015

© Crown copyright 2016 Available as a pdf only. Published by Public Health England 2016.

For information on when to immunise girls aged 12–13 years, and for children aged fourteen years old, visit the NHS website. These have been omitted from the table above.

Make sure you stay up-to-date with the NHS website for any updates to the schedule.

may be postponed if the child has had a reaction to any previous immunisation or if the child is taking any medication that might interfere with their ability to fight infection. The effects of the disease are usually far worse than any side effects of a vaccine.

Why some children are not immunised

In the UK, the childhood immunisation programme is not compulsory, and therefore parental consent has to be obtained before the child is immunised. Although primary immunisation uptake in the UK is relatively high (95 per cent of children are immunised by the age of two years, not including MMR), a small percentage of children are not immunised. Reasons why children may not be immunised include:

- parental preferences – e.g. for homeopathy
- religious reasons
- an unwell child when first immunisations were due
- general lack of belief in the validity of immunisation
- fear of being responsible for any possible side effects to the immunisation
- previous diagnosis with the disease.

Fear of side effects

In the past, children with epilepsy or a family history of epilepsy were not given the pertussis (whooping cough) vaccine. There were concerns that the vaccine could directly cause febrile convulsions and epilepsy. Studies since then have shown there is no link. The whooping cough vaccine is now routinely given to children with epilepsy

A study in 1998 by Dr Andrew Wakefield suggested that the MMR immunisation could cause autism. This is not the case. The study was flawed and has since been discredited. Extensive research since then has shown that there is no link between MMR and autism. The recent epidemic of measles – mostly in Swansea, Wales – was thought to have been caused by a severe drop in the number of children receiving the MMR jab, possibly because of the now discredited research into links with autism.

Child health surveillance

See Moving on section for definition of child health surveillance, the inverse care law, and priority groups for health surveillance.

Personal child health record

All parents are issued with a personal child health record that enables them to keep a record of their child's development. This form is completed by doctors, health visitors and parents, and is a useful source of information if the child is admitted to hospital or taken ill when the family is away from home.

Each child's growth is recorded on a centile chart. This allows parents and health professionals to see how their height and weight compare to other children of the same age. Boys and girls have different charts because boys are on average heavier and taller and their growth pattern is slightly different. See Chapter 12 p. 232 for more information.

Developmental reviews

See Chapter 12, p. 231 for more information on developmental reviews.

When do developmental reviews take place?

Parents are usually invited to developmental reviews when their child is:

- six to eight weeks old
- six to nine months old
- 18 to 24 months old
- three years to three-and-a-half
- four-and-a-half years to five-and-a-half years (before or just after the child starts school).

In some parts of the UK, the age at which children are reviewed may vary slightly from those given above, especially after the age of three years. During a developmental review, some health visitors may ask parents or carers questions about their baby; others may ask the child to do simple tasks, such as building with blocks or identifying pictures; others may simply watch the child playing or drawing, getting an idea from this observation and from the adult's comments of how the child is doing. If the child's first language is not English, parents may need to ask if development reviews can be carried out with the help of someone who can speak their child's language.

After the child has started school, the **school health service** takes over these reviews.

Primary, secondary and tertiary health care

- **Primary care services** are provided at the first stage of treatment when you are ill—by family doctors, dentists, pharmacists, optometrists and ophthalmic medical practitioners, together with district nurses and health visitors.
- **Secondary care** is the second stage of treatment when you are ill, and is usually provided by a hospital.
- **Tertiary care** is the third and highly specialised stage of treatment, usually provided in a specialist hospital centre.

6- to 8-week check			
Parental concerns	Observation	Measurement	Examination
The doctor will ask the parent about: • feeding • bowel actions • sleeping • micturition (passing urine).	While the parent is undressing the baby for examination, the doctor will look out for: • the responsiveness of the baby – smiles, eye contact, attentiveness to parent's voice, etc. • any difficulties the parent has holding the baby – which may indicate maternal depression • jaundice and anaemia. The general appearance of the baby will give an indication of whether he or she is well nourished.	• The baby is weighed naked and the weight is plotted on the growth chart. • The head circumference is measured and plotted on the growth chart.	• The eyes are inspected using a light– the baby will turn his or her head and follow a small light beam. An ophthalmoscope is used to check for a cataract. • The heart is auscultated (i.e. listened to with a stethoscope) to exclude any congenital defect. • The hips are manipulated, again to exclude the presence of congenital dislocation of the hips. • The baby is placed prone and will turn his or her head to one side; hands are held with the thumbs inwards and the fingers wrapped around them. • The posterior fontaneile is usually closed by now; the anterior fontaneile does not close until around 18 months.

Hearing
Most babies will have been screened soon after birth. There is no specific test at this age. The parent is asked if or she thinks the baby can hear. A baby may startle to a sudden noise or freeze for some sounds.

Health education points
The doctor will discuss the following health topics, give the first immunisation and complete the personal child health record. • Nutrition: breastfeeding, preparation of formula feeds, specific feeding difficulties. • Immunisation: discuss any concerns and initiate a programme of vaccinations. • Passive smoking: babies are at risk of respiratory infections and middle ear disease. • Illness in babies: how to recognise symptoms. • Crying: coping with frustration and tiredness. • Reducing the risk of cot death (SIDS: sudden infant death syndrome).

▲ **Table 14.2** Developmental reviews during childhood

6- to 9-month check			
Parental concerns	Observation	Measurement	Examination
The doctor or health visitor will enquire again about any parental concerns.	The doctor will look out for: • socialisation and attachment behaviour • visual behaviour • communication – sounds, expressions and gestures • motor development – sitting, balance, use of hands, any abnormal movement patterns.	Head circumference and weight are plotted on the growth chart.	Manipulation of the hips is carried out. • The heart is listened to with a stethoscope. • The testes are checked in boys. • The eyes are checked for a squint – if this is present, the child is referred to an ophthalmologist (eye specialist); visual behaviour is checked. • Hearing is sometimes tested by the distraction test.

Health education points
• Nutrition: weaning; control of sugar intake. • Immunisations: check they are up to date. • Teeth: regular brushing once teeth appear; information on fluoride; visit the dentist. • The need for play and language stimulation. • Accident prevention.

2-year check
This check is similar to the previous tests. It is often easier for the health visitor to carry out the check during a home visit. The parent is asked about any general concerns. A physical examination is not normally carried out at this age. • The height is measured if the child is cooperative. • Weight is only checked if there is reason for concern. • The parent is asked if there are any concerns about vision and hearing, and the child is referred to a specialist if necessary. • A check is made that the child is walking and that the gait (manner of walking) is normal. • Behaviour and any associated problems are discussed (e.g. tantrums, sleep disturbance, poor appetite or food fads). • The possibility of iron deficiency is considered. It is common at this age and may be a cause of irritability and developmental and behavioural problems, as well as anaemia.

Health education points
• Nutrition and dental care: the child will be referred to the dentist if teeth are obviously decayed. • Immunisations: check they are up to date. • Common behavioural difficulties, such as temper tantrums, sleep disturbance, toilet training. • Social behaviour: learning to play with other children and to share possessions. • Accident prevention.

▲ **Table 14.2** *(Continued)*

4 to 5-year check for 'school readiness'			
Parental concerns	**Observation**	**Measurement**	**Examination**
This check is usually carried out by the GP and the health visitor. The parent is asked if there are any general concerns about the child's progress and development, or any behavioural or emotional problems.	• Motor skills – can the child walk, run and climb stairs? Does the child tire more quickly compared with other children? • Fine manipulative skills – can the child control pencils and paintbrushes? • Behaviour – parents are asked about the child's ability to concentrate, to play with others and to separate from his or her parents without distress. • Vision, language and hearing – observation and discussion with the parent will determine any problems that may need specialist assessment.	Height and weight are measured and plotted on the growth chart.	• The heart is listened to for any abnormal sounds. • The lungs are listened to for wheezing. • In a boy, the testes will be checked again; if still not descended, he will be referred to a surgeon. • The spine is inspected for signs of curvature or spina bifida occulta. • Blood pressure is usually measured only if the child has a history of renal disease or growth problems.

Health education points

- Immunisation: pre-school booster.
- Dental care: diet – danger of sweets and snacks; brushing teeth; dental decay; visits to the dentist.
- The child's needs for play, conversation and social learning.
- The recognition and management of minor ailments.
- Accident prevention.

8-year check

This is carried out by the school nurse, and parents are encouraged to attend the sessions at school. It involves the following:

- a general review of progress and development; the parent may voice concerns such as bedwetting (enuresis) or food fads
- height and weight are measured
- vision is tested and, if a problem is found, the child is referred to an ophthalmologist or optician.

Health education points

- Accident prevention: particularly safety on the roads and awareness of 'stranger danger'
- Diet
- Exercise
- Dental health.

Hearing

Parents who are concerned that their child is not hearing properly should have access to hearing testing. This is particularly important if the child has had:

- meningitis
- measles
- mumps
- recurrent ear infections or glue ear.

Speech discrimination test

Any child who is suspected of having any hearing loss or whose language development is delayed may have the speech discrimination test. This involves using a set of toys, each with a single-syllable name- for example, dog, horse, key, tree, spoon, house, cup – which will test the child's ability to hear different consonants – for example, d, g, p, m, s, f and b. The child is gently encouraged to cooperate with the tester and together they name the toys using a normal voice. The child is then asked to find the toys with decreasing voice intensity – for example, 'Show me the house', 'Put the duck in the box'. Each ear is tested through the complete range of sounds.

▲ **Table 14.2** (*Concluded*)

The primary health care team

The primary health care team (PHCT) is made up of a team of professionals which generally includes one or more of the following:

- GP or family doctor – cares for all members of the family and can refer patients for specialist services.
- Health visitor – carries out developmental checks and gives advice on all aspects of childcare.
- Practice nurse – works with a particular GP; provides services such as immunisation, and asthma and diabetes clinics.
- Community midwife – delivers antenatal care and cares for the mother and baby until 10 to 28 days after delivery.
- District nurse – cares for clients in their own homes.
- Community paediatric nurse – a district nurse with special training in paediatrics to care for sick children at home (employed by some health authorities).

Services offered by the PHCT

Services will include some or all of the following:

- child health clinics (see below)
- antenatal clinics
- immunisation clinics
- specialist clinics (e.g. for asthma, diabetes)
- family planning clinics
- speech and language therapy
- community dieticians
- community physiotherapists
- community occupational therapists
- community paediatricians
- clinical medical officers (CMO)
- community dental service.

Child health clinics

Child health clinics are often held at the health centre or in a purpose-built centre. In rural areas, the clinic may take turns with other community groups in village halls or community centres. Depending on the population served, clinics may be weekly or fortnightly, and are run by health visitors, health care assistants and nursery nurses. A doctor or community paediatrician is usually present at specified times. Services provided at a child health clinic include:

- routine developmental surveillance (or reviews)
- medical examinations
- immunisations
- health promotion advice
- antenatal and parent craft classes.

School health service

The school health service is part of the community child health service and has direct links with those who carry out health checks on children before they start school. The aims of the school health service are to:

- ensure that children are physically and emotionally fit, so that they can benefit fully from their education and achieve their potential
- prepare them for adult life and help them achieve the best possible health during their school years and beyond.

Services provided by the school health service

The school nurse may work with one or more schools, and provides an important link between the school and health services. School nurses provide the following services:

- growth measurements – height and weight
- advice on management of health conditions – for example, if a child has a long-term illness or special educational need, the nurse will discuss possible strategies with the child's teacher
- enuresis (bedwetting) support and advice, including providing an enuresis alarm
- immunisation
- advice on health and hygiene, sometimes running workshops or similar sessions
- advice for parents on specific health issues – for example, treating head lice or coping with asthma (covered in Chapter 15)
- routine testing for vision, hearing or speech – to discover which children may need further tests or treatment; if treatment is thought to be required, the child's parents will be informed and consent requested
- liaison with the school doctor.

The attention of the school doctor is drawn to any possible problems, and parents and the GP are informed if any further action is considered necessary. The school doctor visits the school regularly and meets with the school nurse (or health visitor) and with teachers, to find out whether any pupils need medical attention. In addition, the doctor reviews the medical notes of all children in Year 1 and of all new pupils transferring to the school.

Parents are usually requested to complete a health questionnaire about their child at certain stages, and are asked if they would like their child to have a full medical examination. In addition, the school doctor may ask for parental consent to examine a child if his or her medical records are incomplete or if the doctor particularly wishes to check on the child's progress.

Parents are invited to be present at any medical examination and kept informed if the school doctor wishes to see their child again or thinks that they should be seen by the family doctor or a specialist.

The audiometry team checks children's hearing on a number of occasions before the age of 13 or 14 years. The school doctor will be told if a child seems to have a hearing problem. The doctor will then examine the child and let the family doctor know the result.

The speech and language therapist can provide assessment and treatment if the parent, a teacher or the school doctor feels that a child may have a speech or language problem.

Your role in child health screening and surveillance

Throughout your training, you will have learned about child development and the importance of knowing what to expect from children at each developmental stage. When working with children, you can use this knowledge, and your powers of skilled observation, to detect any developmental or health problems. Increasingly, trained early years practitioners are being employed in child health clinics, to assist doctors and health visitors in carrying out routine screening tests, and to offer parents advice on all aspects of child health and development.

Health and safety legislation relevant to working with children

See Chapter 4 for comprehensive information on health and safety legislation relevant to working with children.

Policies and procedures for health and safety

Each early years setting will have policies and procedures which reflect the way the setting is run.

Policies and procedures convey clear messages to staff members about their roles and responsibilities and set the boundaries within which they are expected to work. Standard sets of policies and procedures may be adopted, but it is important that such 'universal' policies are carefully adapted to reflect precisely what happens in each particular setting. For example, the procedure for evacuation will be very different between settings, according to the layout of the building and the surrounding physical environment.

Policies and procedures must be shared with everyone and each person must be allowed to contribute to them. They should never be compiled by just one person and they should be regularly reviewed. Each setting will develop its own policies and procedures and these may be covered under different headings from those outlined below.

Health and safety legislation is constantly being updated, in response to new research into accident prevention and increased knowledge about health and safety issues. For example, it is hard to imagine that only 25 years ago, children were allowed to sit unrestrained in the backs of family cars, but the laws since then regarding seat belts and restraints have saved countless lives. All early years settings are bound by these laws and legislation, and by the EYFS statutory framework. These laws and guidelines provide a framework within which practitioners can work as a team to provide an environment that is as safe and healthy as possible, while still allowing children the freedom to explore their environment in an active way.

The EYFS statutory framework

The EYFS places an obligation on providers to conduct a risk assessment and review it regularly.

- There is a duty to balance keeping children safe with encouraging them to learn actively.
- When children undertake a challenging physical activity successfully, they grow in confidence and capability; their skills develop well for their future when they will have to make risk assessments for themselves.

See p. 301 for advice on how to carry out a risk assessment.

Guidelines for good practice

Health and safety in early years settings

An early years setting or school keeps children healthy and safe by:

✔ having effective procedures around safety of equipment, hygiene guidelines and accident prevention

✔ ensuring that all practitioners have an understanding of the legislation that informs good practice

✔ developing risk assessments that protect children from incurring accidents in the setting.

Main policies and procedures relating to health and safety of children	
Health and safety	
• risk assessment • food safety • health and hygiene • infection control and prevention of illness • fire safety	• first aid • accidents and emergencies • safety at arrival and departure times, and on outings • evacuation procedures • administration of medicine
Safeguarding children	**Record-keeping**
• child protection • missing child • critical incidents • non-collection of child • death of a child • complaints against the registered provider or a member of staff	• sharing information • confidentiality • children's records
Staffing	**Partnership with parents and carers**
• staffing ratios • recruitment and deployment • volunteers and parent helpers • disciplinary and grievance procedures • students and induction • whistleblowing	• working in partnership with other agencies • key person system
Equality and inclusion	**Childcare practices**
• valuing diversity • special educational needs (SEN)	• behaviour management • identification and assessment of children with special educational needs • settling-in • daily routines • play and learning

▲ **Table 14.3** The main policies and procedures relating to health and safety

Infection control

Children who play closely together for long periods of time are more likely than others to develop an infection, and any infection can spread very quickly from one child to another, and to adults who care for them. Your setting's health and safety policy will establish procedures to reduce the risk of transferring infectious diseases. These include:

- providing staff members and parents with information on infection control policies and procedures
- stating the exclusion criteria that will apply when a child or a staff member is sick
- providing training for staff members so they understand and can use the infection control procedures
- providing adequate supervision to make sure everyone follows the policies and procedures

- providing adequate supplies of protective equipment
- providing adequate facilities for hand-washing, cleaning and disposing of wasteproviding safe work practices for high-risk activities – for example, dealing with blood and body fluids, nappy changing and toileting, handling dirty linen and contaminated clothing, and preparing and handling food.

Teaching children about safety issues

Children under five years of age tend to be absorbed in their play and focus on the 'here and now'. However, young children do tend to avoid any hazard that has been identified for them. It is important that safety issues are talked about at the setting and that learning opportunities are structured into the everyday play curriculum. A variety of materials are available to support safety work with children, including books,

Guidelines for good practice

Health and safety in the work setting

A safe environment is one in which the child or adult has a low risk of becoming ill or injured. Safety is a basic human need.

✔ Children should be supervised at all times.

✔ The early years environment and all materials and equipment should be in a safe condition.

✔ There must be adequate first aid facilities and staff should be trained in basic first aid.

✔ Routine safety checks should be made daily on premises, both indoors and outdoors.

✔ Fire drills should be held twice a term in schools and nurseries and every six weeks in day nurseries.

✔ Children should only be allowed home with a parent or authorised adult.

Think about ideas

Health and safety policies

● Find out where the health and safety policies are kept in your setting.

● How often are they reviewed?

● Who is responsible for keeping them up to date?

---

pictures, posters, plays and puppets. These can support the development of awareness about road safety, water safety and fire safety in children.

However, not all teaching needs to be planned. You can use any opportunities that arise naturally, such as an accident or a near miss that has happened to someone the children know. If children – even very young children – understand why the rules have been made, they will be more likely to abide by them. When teaching young children about safety, you will need to find ways to communicate with each child according to their needs – for example, children with hearing difficulties will need both children and adults to face them so that they can see any signs and can lip-read, if the hearing loss is severe.

Things you should teach children include:

● to carry things carefully

● never to run with anything in their mouths – this includes sweets and other food

● never to run while carrying a glass, scissors or other pointed objects; if a child falls, he or she can stab him or herself with something as simple as a pencil. Something in the child's mouth can choke him or her.

You also need to explain the reasons behind the rules you give them – for example, by saying:

> 'You must not throw sand because you will hurt your friend.'

> 'Never run into the road, because you could be hit by a car.'

> 'Do not run with a stick in your hand, as it would hurt you if you fall.'

For most children, you need to repeat these fundamental safety rules over and over again, so that they remember them.

Supporting children's safety when they move in and out of the setting

Every setting should have clear systems (policies and procedures) in place to ensure the safety of children:

● when being received into the setting

● when departing from the setting, and

● during outings (off-site visits).

During these times, there is often a lot of movement and activity. When children are received into the setting, several children may arrive at once, parents may be in a rush to get to work, and children are keen to rejoin their friends. When leaving the setting, again many children will be leaving at the same time, parents chatting with others and children eager to say goodbye to their friends. During outings, there is usually a great deal of excitement about being in a new place with lots to see and do. Every practitioner should be aware of the policy and procedures in their setting at these times, and should be clear about his or her own role and responsibility.

Receiving children into the setting

All settings must register children on arrival. A daily register of the names of all the children in the setting at any given time is essential, not only in case of an emergency evacuation of the setting, but also so that adequate staff supervision (or staffing ratios) is provided. Many early years settings have door entry phones and a password system for parents and staff to enter the premises. The entrance should be secure so that the door cannot be left open for people to wander in and out. In some settings, one member of staff is at the door, greeting and sharing information with each family as they arrive. Some settings have a designated dropping-off area where a calm atmosphere can be created as parents and carers 'hand over' their child to their key person.

Think about ideas

Receiving children into the setting

Find out about the system for receiving children in your setting:

- Who is responsible for registering the children?
- How does the setting ensure that the entrance door is kept shut between arrivals?
- How smooth is the transition from reception into the setting to each child being with his or her key person?

Ensuring safety on departure

Every setting will have a policy about correct procedure for when parents and carers come to collect their child. Again, the register must be kept so that it is clear which children are in the setting in case of an emergency. At home time:

- A member of staff must ensure that every child is collected by the appropriate person: the person registered as the child's own parent or carer, or a person who has written authorisation from the parent or carer.
- If parents know that they will not be able to collect their child on a particular occasion, they should notify the setting, giving permission for another named person to collect their child.
- The child's key person should, where possible, be responsible for handover at home times.
- Within the setting's safeguarding children policy, there should be a written statement of the procedures in place for an uncollected child.

Safety during outings

Any outing away from the children's usual setting (such as trips to farms, parks and theatres) must be planned with safety and security issues as a top priority. When taking part in off-site visits, all practitioners (including volunteers) have a duty to take reasonable

Reflecting on practice

Safety at arrival and departure

- Do you know the procedures for arrival and departure in your setting?
- How do you ensure that the person who arrives is authorised to collect the child?
- Do you know what to do if an unknown adult arrives to collect a child?
- Think about the most welcoming and safe way to greet families when they arrive.

Reflecting on practice

Problems at home time

Anna is a three-year-old child who attends a private nursery group four days a week. Her key person, Leanne, has developed a good professional relationship with Anna's mother and suspects that she and her partner are having problems balancing their home life with their work commitments. Anna's mother, Kirsty, often arrives late to collect Anna; she is always very flustered and apologetic about it. Anna's father, David, works long hours as a sales rep and is often away from home for weeks at a time. He has only collected Anna on a couple of occasions before, and only when Kirsty had given prior permission.

One Friday afternoon, David arrives at the nursery and explains to Leanne that Kirsty had rung him to say she was running very late and asked if he could collect Anna on this occasion. When Leanne replies that she must check with the nursery manager before allowing him to take Anna, David becomes very angry and starts to shout about his rights as a father. As Leanne is trying to reason with him, he suddenly pushes his way past her into the nursery room and scoops Anna up, grabbing her coat from her peg as he rushes out. Five minutes later, Kirsty arrives and becomes very distressed when she hears what has happened. She tells Leanne that she and David had had an argument that morning and that he had threatened to leave her.

Discuss this case study in class and answer the following questions:

- If you were Leanne (Anna's key person), what should you do?
- What are the main issues involved in this case study?
- How can the nursery ensure every child's safety at home time?

care to avoid injury to themselves and others, and to cooperate to ensure that statutory duties and obligations are met. Practitioners have a common law duty to act as would a reasonably prudent parent, and should not hesitate to act in an emergency and to take life-saving action in an extreme situation. As a safeguard to children, volunteer helpers on off-site visits must be:

- appropriate people to supervise children
- trained in their duties and must not be left with children, unsupervised by staff.

Unqualified staff or volunteers must not be left in sole charge of children except where it has been previously agreed as part of the risk assessment. Practitioners and volunteers should not be in a situation where they are alone with one child away from the rest of the group.

Risk assessments for outings

There is a legal requirement for settings to carry out risk assessments for outings. (See p. 301 for information on risk assessments). The EYFS makes it clear that this should include an assessment of the ratios of adults to children needed for outings, and it must include an assessment of the risks and hazards that might arise for the children. Each type of outing will carry its own particular risks and practitioners must assess the risks and hazards that may arise and the steps to be taken to remove, minimise and manage them – including an appropriate adult to children ratio.

Planning the outing

- Visit or find out about the place beforehand and discuss any particular requirements, such as what to do if it rains, or specific lunch arrangements. A risk assessment should be carried out to include consideration of potential risks in the environment, such as traffic, dogs, ponds or rivers etc.

- A copy of the children's contact information should be taken on the outing, and the person in charge should regularly check the names of the children against the day's attendance list.

- Parents should be informed of what is involved on the outing, such as what the child needs to bring (such as packed meal, waterproof coat), spending money if necessary (state the advised maximum amount). Information about the child's specific needs while out on a trip, such as any medical needs, must be found out. Parents must sign a consent form that gives the setting permission to take their child off the premises.

- There should always be trained staff on any outing, however local and low-key. Usually, help is requested from parents so that adequate supervision is ensured. If the children are under two years old or have special needs, then you would expect to have fewer children per adult than the minimum ratios.

- Swimming trips should be attempted only if the ratio is one adult to one child for children under five years old.

- The younger the children, the more adults are required, particularly if the trip involves crossing roads, when an adult must be available to hold the children's hands.

Head counts

Make sure that you all count the children regularly. . Always accompany children to public toilets, telling a colleague how many children you are taking with you.

Transport

If a coach is being hired, check whether it has seat belts for children. By law, all new minibuses and coaches must have seat belts fitted, and minibus drivers must pass a special driving test.

Safety at mealtimes and snack times

This is covered in Chapter 13 on p. 271.

Safety at sleep and rest times

This is covered in Chapter 13 on pp. 269 and 270.

Reflecting on practice

A breach of health and safety regulations

Ana, a happy and lively 14 month old toddler, died as a result of getting her neck trapped in the drawstring of a bag that had been left hanging on the side of the playpen that she had been placed in. The staff had failed to check on her for 20 minutes and when they did check on her, she appeared lifeless.

The verdict of the inquest jury was of unlawful killing, after hearing that the toddler was in the care of an 18-year old student and another unqualified member of staff. They heard that staff at the nursery had been warned by the child's parents that she had previously wrapped objects around her neck.

The judge in the case said that the nursery staff had shown 'gross incompetence' and staff should have realised that leaving a bag with a drawstring near a child who had a history of wrapping things around her neck clearly put the child at risk. The staff should have acted in a more responsible manner and should have known better. Staff should have checked on the child every 10 minutes but there had been a misunderstanding over this. Moreover, a risk assessment had not been done, and the other objects that could put children at risk were left near the playpen and play area.

The nursery regretted the incident and expressed their remorse. During the court case, the judge noted that the tragic accident should have been foreseen. The nursery had breached health and safety regulations but it was not manslaughter. The nursery received a fine for breaching health and safety regulations.

- What factors led to the toddler being unsafe while in nursery care?

- What sort of risk assessment could have helped to prevent the toddler's death?

- On a wider subject, do you think that all accidents are preventable?

Your role and responsibilities in relation to health and safety

Your setting's health and safety policy will contain the names of staff members responsible for health and safety. All practitioners are responsible for health and safety in any setting. Your responsibilities include:

- taking reasonable care for your own safety and that of others
- working with your employer in respect of health and safety matters
- knowing about the policies and procedures in your particular place of work – these can all be found in the setting's health and safety policy documents
- not intentionally damaging any health and safety equipment or materials provided by the employer
- reporting all accidents, incidents and even 'near misses' to your manager. As you may be handling food, you should also report any incidences of sickness or diarrhoea. If you are unable to contact the sick child's parents or carer (or other emergency contact person), then you will need to seek medical advice. Always ask your supervisor or manager if in doubt.
- reporting any hazards immediately, as soon as you come across them.

Apart from your legal responsibilities, knowing how to act and being alert and vigilant at all times can prevent accidents, injury, infections and even death – this could be in relation to you, your fellow workers or the children in your care.

Moving and handling: protecting yourself

Lifting and carrying children and moving the equipment used in childcare settings could lead to manual handling injuries such as sprains and strains. If you do have to lift something or somebody from the ground, you should follow these rules:

- Keep your feet apart.
- Bend your knees and keep your back upright.
- Use both hands to get a secure hold.
- Keep your shoulders level, your back upright and slowly straighten your legs.
- To put the load down, take the weight on your legs by bending your knees.

How to identify hazards to the health and safety of children, colleagues and visitors

Practitioners need to be conscious of any risks in the working environment and the potential impact of these risks. They can then plan ahead to avoid hazards and incidents.

Guidelines for good practice

Your roles and responsibilities in keeping children safe

- ✔ Know and work within the policy/procedures of the setting.
- ✔ Know when and how to respond when concerns are raised.
- ✔ Appreciate the guidance of the relevant Local Safeguarding Children Board.
- ✔ Supervise children within set ratios.
- ✔ Be up to date with safeguarding training.
- ✔ Appreciate the limits and boundaries of your role and know the reporting process for successful referral
- ✔ Have the knowledge and expertise to make clear and appropriate judgements and ensure that they are passed to the most appropriate local agencies, in line with the Munro Review of child protection.
- ✔ Identify behavioural changes in the children you care for.

- ✔ Observe and monitor children to ensure they are growing in confidence.
- ✔ Work as a key person alongside others and actively engage with the family in order to develop positive relationships and develop trust.
- ✔ Work as part of a professional team.
- ✔ Engage in positive partnership working.
- ✔ Contribute to a safe and stimulating environment where all children develop and learn.
- ✔ Monitor children's health and general well-being.
- ✔ Role-model positive behaviour.
- ✔ Be suitably qualified with full DBS clearance.
- ✔ Promote healthy practice and healthy living.
- ✔ Protect children from harm from social media, the internet etc.
- ✔ Maintain attendance records.
- ✔ Maintain safe collection procedures for children.

How to identify hazards in the setting

In the early years setting a **hazard** may be a substance, a piece of equipment, a work procedure or a child's condition. Examples of hazards in settings include:

- toys and play equipment
- chemical hazards, such as cleaning materials and disinfectants
- biological hazards, such as airborne (those that can be transmitted or passed on through air) and blood-borne (that can be spread through blood and other bodily fluids) infections, food hygiene infections
- the handling and moving of equipment and of children
- unsupervised children
- security of entry points and exits
- administration of medicines
- visual or hearing impairment of children

Types of hazard

- Physical hazard – something that may cause physical harm – like an object left on the floor that someone might trip on, or a sharp object left where children may grab it and cut themselves.
- Security hazard – something that might endanger the security of the children or practitioners, for instance a door to the street left open so that strangers can access the premises
- Fire hazard – any objects or set of circumstances that might either cause a fire or might endanger people in the event of a fire, e.g. an escape route being blocked by toys.
- Food safety hazard – any danger associated with food. This might be undercooked meat, unwashed vegetables, contamination of food that causes an allergy or intolerance, or the risk of choking.
- Personal safety hazard – often related to a physical hazard; it can mean any danger to someone's safety. Children do not have a very good concept of their own personal safety so practitioners must plan to minimise it for them.

The environment in which these hazards may occur include the indoors environment, where you probably spend most time, but also the outdoors environment; this may be an outdoor play area or the general outdoors when you go on an outing. The hazards listed above are likely to be different in indoor and outdoor environments.

The difference between risks and hazards

Risk is defined as the chance or likelihood that harm will occur from the hazard. The likelihood is described as 'the expectancy of harm occurring'. It can range from 'never' to 'certain' and depends on a number of factors.

Example 1: A door

The main entrance to a nursery or primary school may present a hazard. The risks are:

- that a child might escape and run into the road, or go missing, or
- that a stranger might enter the building.

The likelihood of the hazard of the entrance/door posing a risk will depend on a number of factors:

- the security of the entrance – for example, can it only be opened by using a key pad or entry phone system, and is the door handle placed high up, out of a child's reach?
- policies and procedures being known to parents and other visitors, such as at collection times.

Example 2: A damaged or uneven floor surface

This may present a hazard. The risk is:

- that someone may trip over and become injured.

The likelihood of the hazard of the damaged floor posing a risk will depend on a number of factors:

- the extent of the unevenness or damage
- the number of people walking over it
- the number of times they walk over it
- whether they are wearing sensible shoes
- the level of lighting.

Babies and young children are at particular risk of harm because they:

- lack any appreciation of danger
- are naturally inquisitive
- love to explore and test the boundaries of their world.

You need to help young children to explore within safe boundaries, but to adjust those boundaries according to their capabilities and increasing skill. Useful skills to employ when dealing with inquisitive toddlers include recognising the value of distraction – guiding attention

> **KEY TERMS**
>
> **Hazard** – A source of potential harm or damage, or a situation with potential for harm or damage.
> **Risk** – The possibility of suffering harm, loss or danger.
> **Risk assessment** – The assessments that must be carried out in order to identify hazards and find out the safest way to carry out certain tasks and procedures.

away from something dangerous and towards something potentially more interesting, physically removing the child: 'Harry, come with me – I want to show you something ...'.

Even so, no environment, however carefully planned and designed, can ever be totally without risk to children.

Older children face different risks. For example, they are more likely to travel to school independently and need to be aware of the principles of road safety. They also need to be aware of the risks involved in using the internet.

Protecting children from common hazards

Remember that *you* could be a risk to children's health. For example, if you have a heavy cold or have suffered from diarrhoea or vomiting within the previous 48 hours, you must not attend work as you could pass on a serious infection to the children.

All areas where children play and learn should be checked for hygiene and safety at the start of every session and again at the end of each session – this is often called the safety sweep (see below) – but do be alert at all times. Look at your setting's written policy for health and hygiene issues. Find out how to clean toys and other equipment from your manager, and remember that many objects (plastic toys and soft toys) end up in children's mouths, which is a good way of passing on and picking up an infection.

Safety sweeps

Most practitioners carry out a safety sweep, both indoors and outdoors, on a daily or twice daily basis – often at the start and end of a session. This is a very useful way to assess risk. The checks are often done informally and not always recorded unless the safety sweep has identified a risk that then requires formal assessment. For example, a safety sweep at the beginning of the day may involve checking the outdoor area for the following hazards:

- Is the 'safer' surfacing in the play area in good condition – e.g. no loose or uneven tiles? Rubberised surfaces can get an almost invisible build up of algae which can make them very slippery when wet, so always check surfaces for slipperiness.
- Are pathways undamaged and free from obstructions?
- Is the area free from litter, glass or any other dangerous objects?
- Is the area free from animal fouling?
- A **risk assessment** (see page 300 for definition) would be required if a safety sweep revealed problems regarding any of the above checks. Any faults should be recorded and reported to the relevant person.

Reflecting on practice

- Find out how safety is promoted in your setting.
- Do staff perform regular safety sweeps?
- Are risk assessments routinely carried out for new activities or scenarios?

Managing risk: a balanced approach

Children need a safe but challenging environment. Almost every human activity involves a certain degree of risk, and children need to learn how to cope with this. They need to understand that the world can be a dangerous place, and that care needs to be taken when they are negotiating their way round it. For example, when a child first learns to walk, he or she will inevitably fall over or knock into things. This is a valuable part of their learning and a natural part of their development.

Children who are sheltered or overprotected from risk and challenge when young will not be able to make judgements about their own strengths and skills, and will not be well equipped to resist peer pressure in their later years. Also, a totally risk-free environment lacks challenges and stimulation; this leads inevitably to children becoming bored and deteriorating behaviour. Simply being *told* about possible dangers is not enough: children need to see or experience the consequences of not taking care.

The risk assessment process

Risk assessment is a method of preventing accidents and ill-health by helping people to think about what could go wrong and devising ways to prevent problems. Risk assessments on aspects such as security of the building, fire safety, food safety, toilet hygiene and nappy changing, outings, and personal

Reflecting on practice

- Do you agree that it is important for children to take risks?
- How can you balance this with the need to promote their safety?
- Can you remember being allowed to take risks when you were a young child?

If you would like to learn more about children's need for risk and challenge, read Tim Gill's Blog: Rethinking Childhood, www.rethinkingchildhood.com.

safety of staff should already exist. Other examples of activities where risk assessments are required include:

- cooking activities
- supervising children's use of climbing equipment
- a visit from somebody outside the setting who may be bringing equipment – or a pet animal – to show the children as part of a topic
- making reasonable adjustments for children with disabilities or children with additional needs, staff or visitors.

It is important to note that 'setting' in this context means anywhere you go on trips and outings, as well as any outdoor space. It does not just mean the indoor space of the setting.

Whatever the reason for the risk assessment, the process remains the same. The Risk Assessment Process identifies five steps that you need to take:

- Step 1: Identification of risk or hazard – where is it and what is it?
- Step 2: Decide who is at risk and how – for example, childcare staff, children, parents, cooks, cleaners.
- Step 3: Evaluate the risks and decide on precautions – can you get rid of the risk altogether? If not, how can you control it?
- Step 4: Record your findings and implement them – prioritise and make a plan of action if necessary.
- Step 5: Monitoring and review – how do you know if what has been decided is working, or is thorough enough? If it is not working, it will need to be amended, or maybe there is a better solution.

It is usually the responsibility of the manager or person in charge to devise the format of the risk assessment using the above points; they must then ensure that they are carried out and that the completed forms are kept to inform procedures that guide your work on a day-to-day basis.

Look, listen and note

A risk assessment

1 Carry out a risk assessment for a visit by a parent who is bringing in her pet rabbit to show the children and talk to them about pets in general. Remember to include possible hazards – e.g. allergies, over-excited children, hygiene issues etc.

2 Observe the activity and note any further steps which would improve the safety of the experience in future.

How health and safety risk assessments are monitored and reviewed

It is important to monitor and review risk assessments as there may have been changes – for example, new equipment introduced or new procedures. After completing an initial risk assessment, a date should be set for the next one. This could be once a term, twice a year or annually, depending on the size of the setting, the number of staff changes, changes to the physical environment, additional equipment or resources. When new equipment arrives, a new risk assessment should be completed and the findings added to the original document.

The process of review includes answering the following questions:

- Have there been any changes?
- Are there improvements you still need to make?
- Have you or your colleagues identified a problem?
- Have you learned anything from accidents or near misses?

Supporting children to manage risk

An important aspect of teaching children about risk is to encourage them to make their own *risk assessments* and think about the possible consequences of their actions. Rather than removing objects and equipment from the environment in case children hurt themselves, adults should teach children how to use them safely. It is important to strike the right balance: protecting children from harm while allowing them the freedom to develop independence and risk awareness.

If a child seems at risk of harming him/herself in some way, the practitioner *must* intervene. Then, using language appropriate to the age and understanding of the child, the adult could ask open-ended questions for the child to identify why she could come to harm. In this way, the adult and the child work together to reach a solution and children gain a better understanding of why they were stopped from playing and how to identify dangers. (They can then carry on, if appropriate.)

As children become older, talk to them about keeping safe and about how to avoid accidents and injury. Children may also be encouraged to assess risks by being given reasons why they may be asked to do something. For example, when asking children to put the cars and trucks back into the box, the adult asks why it should be done and the child learns that if they are not collected, someone may trip over them and could hurt themselves.

Reflecting on practice

Supporting children to assess and manage risk

Four children are playing in a den they have made in the outdoor play area, using a frame and some cloth. The den looks rather crowded and the children are finding it difficult to carry out their play. Angela, a practitioner, asks them: 'How many children do you think should be in the den? How many of you are in the den? How is it making you feel? What could we do to make it less of a squash?' The children all join in with answers, and after a lively debate, two of the children decide to set up a den for themselves. Angela helps them fetch the equipment and the play resumes.

1 What are the hazards when too many children are playing in a confined space?

2 How did Angela support the children in making their own risk assessments?

3 Think of ways in which you could support children in your care to assess and manage risk for themselves.

Reflecting on practice

Your role in managing risk

Step five of the risk assessment process is monitoring and review. This part of the risk assessment process allows practitioners to reflect upon:

● actions taken against the risks that are identified

● the effectiveness of those actions

● any further amendments required.

By building the skills of reflective practice into your everyday work, you will develop the skills of identifying any adjustments that are required in order to minimise risks during an event or experience.

Managing risk means keeping children safe; but you must also ensure that the learning environment is an enabling one and provides challenges for children. Non-statutory guidance produced by Early Education to support the 2014 EYFS, states as a *Characteristic of Effective Learning*, that a unique child is one 'seeking challenge' and 'taking a risk, engaging in new experiences, and learning by trial and error'. Adults should 'Encourage children to try new activities and to judge risks for themselves.'

The guidance also suggests that, for instance, for children aged 22–36 months, adults should 'ensure children's safety, while not unduly inhibiting their risk-taking'.

Practitioners must also remember health and safety needs that may change or be different day-to-day – for instance, the application of sun-cream at appropriate times is an important health and safety need that might not exist for some part of the year.

You have a responsibility to report all accidents, incidents and even 'near misses' to your manager. As you may be handling food, you should also report any personal incidences of sickness or diarrhoea. Most early years settings keep two separate accident report books – one for staff and other adults and one for children. These should always be filled in as soon after the incident as possible (see Chapter 15, p. 330).

Coping with sudden illness

Provide comfort and reassurance

If a child becomes ill while at nursery, he or she may have to wait a while to be taken home. In the meantime you should:

● offer support and reassurance to the child, who may feel frightened or anxious

● always notify a senior member of staff if you notice that a child is unwell; that person will then decide if and when to contact the child's parents or carers

● ensure that a member of staff (preferably the child's key person) remains with the child all the time and keeps them as comfortable as possible.

You must deal with any incident of vomiting or diarrhoea swiftly and sympathetically to minimise the child's distress and to preserve their dignity. All settings have an exclusion policy that lets parents know when it is safe for their sick child to return to the group.

Chapter 15 includes a table on p. 324 on exclusion periods for common infections.

Serious conditions

A child who has sustained a serious injury or illness will need to be seen urgently by a doctor. A serious injury or illness includes:

● a head injury or any loss of consciousness

● a wound that continues to bleed after first aid treatment is given

● suspected meningitis (see Chapter 15, p. 309)

● an asthma attack not relieved by child's inhaler

● fracture or suspected fracture, burns and scalds, foreign bodies

● life-threatening incidents such as seizures, poisoning, choking, anaphylaxis, loss of consciousness, respiratory and cardiac arrest.

See Chapter 16, p. 366 for information on dealing with anaphylaxis.

Emergency procedures: what to do in the event of a non-medical incident or emergency

There are many different types of emergency (apart from a medical emergency when a person is seriously injured or ill) and it is important to know what procedures to follow, for example:

- if a child goes missing
- in case of fire
- if there is a security incident.

Missing children

Strict procedures must be followed to prevent a child from going missing from the setting. However, if a child *does* go missing, an established procedure must be followed, for example:

- The person in charge will carry out a thorough search of the building and garden.
- The register is checked to make sure that no other child has also gone astray.
- Doors and gates are checked to see if there has been a breach of security whereby a child could wander out.
- The person in charge talks to staff to establish what happened.

If the child is not found, the parent or carer is contacted and the missing child is reported to the police.

In case of fire

In the case of fire or other emergency, you need to know what to do to safely evacuate the children and yourselves. You must follow the procedures set out in your setting. In general though you should note the following rules for fire safety:

- Smoking is not allowed in any early years setting.
- Handbags containing matches or lighters must be locked securely away out of children's reach.
- The nursery cooker should not be left unattended when turned on.
- Fire exits must be clearly signed.
- Fire drills should be carried out regularly; registers must be kept up to date throughout the day.
- Fire exits and other doors should be free of obstructions on both sides.
- Instructions about what to do in the event of a fire must be clearly displayed.
- You should know where the fire extinguishers are kept and how to use them.
- Electrical equipment should be regularly checked for any faults.

Evacuation procedures

A plan for an escape route and the attendance register must be up to date so that everyone – children and staff – can safely be accounted for at the meeting point of safety. The attendance record must be taken by the person in charge when the building is evacuated. Clearly written instructions for fire drills and how to summon the fire brigade must be clearly visible and posted in an obvious place in the setting.

Security issues and violence

Early years settings and schools should be secure environments where children cannot wander off without anyone realising. But they also need to be secure so that strangers cannot enter without a good reason for being there. Occasionally, you might encounter a problem with violence – or threats of violence – from a child's parents or carers. Your setting will have a policy that deals with this issue.

Recording and reporting illness, accidents and emergencies

If a child becomes ill while in a group setting, you should *first* report it to your manager or supervisor and then record the following details in the child's Daily Record Book or similar:

- when the child first showed signs of illness
- the signs and symptoms: for example, behaviour changes, a high temperature or a rash
- any action taken: for example, taking the temperature or giving paracetamol (with parental permission agreed beforehand)
- progress of the illness since first noticing it: for example, are there any further symptoms? Chapter 15 includes a table on signs and symptoms of illness.

Reflecting on practice

Missing from a nursery

A two-year-old girl walked out of her pre-school nursery one winter morning, leaving her coat behind, and crossed a busy road as she wandered half a mile to her home. The first that the nursery knew of her disappearance was when her furious father turned up demanding to know why he had found his tearful daughter struggling to open their garden gate.

Fortunately, potentially dangerous events like this are very rare, but they should be preventable.

1   How do you think that this could have happened?
2   Consider your own setting and assess whether it could happen there.
3   How could such incidents be prevented?

What to do in case of serious illness or injury

1 Call for help: Stay calm and do not panic! Your line manager (or designated first aider) will make an assessment and decide whether the injury or illness requires medical help, either a GP or an ambulance. He or she will also contact the parents or carers to let them know about the nature of the illness or injury.

2 Stay with the child; comfort and reassure him or her.

3 Treat the injury or assess the severity of the illness and treat appropriately. You are not expected to be able to *diagnose* a sudden illness, but should know what signs and symptoms require medical treatment.

4 Record exactly what happens and what treatment is carried out.

What to do when an accident happens

If a child has had an accident, they are likely to be shocked and may not cry immediately. They will need calm reassurance as first aid is administered, together with an explanation of what is being done to them and why. Parents or carers must be informed and the correct procedures for the setting carried out. If the child needs emergency hospital treatment, parental permission will be needed.

If you work in a setting with others such as a daycare facility or school, there is likely to be a designated person who is a qualified in first aid; they should be called to deal with the situation.

Remember! It is essential that you do not make the situation worse, and it is better to do the minimum to ensure the child's safety such as putting them into the recovery position. The only exception to this is if the child is not breathing or there is no heartbeat.

Make sure you know what to do if a child becomes ill or has an accident. Find out where the records are kept in your setting and how they should be completed.

See Chapter 15 for information on illnesses.

Moving on

Child health surveillance

Surveillance is defined as close supervision or observation, and its primary purpose is to detect any abnormality in development so that the child can be offered treatment. For example, early detection of a hearing impairment gives the young child a better chance of receiving appropriate treatment and/or specialist education.

The inverse care law

The families who are most in need of child health surveillance are often those who are least likely to make use of the services provided – this is known as the inverse care law. Although children in the UK today enjoy better health than at any other time, the provisions of a National Health Service have not led to equality of health experience. Below is a list of people who might be seen as priority groups by health visitors and the primary health care team when organising caseloads and targeting resources. The health care of such priority groups is difficult and often involves a working partnership with other community services, such as social services or housing departments.

Priority groups for health surveillance

- Very young or unsupported parents, particularly those with their first baby.
- Parents thought to be at particular risk of abusing their children.
- Parents who are socially isolated, due to mental health problems or linguistic or cultural barriers.
- Families living in poor housing, including bed and breakfast accommodation or housing where there is overcrowding.
- Parents with low self-esteem or a lack of confidence.
- Parents with unrealistic expectations about the child, or with a poor understanding of the child's needs.
- Parents and/or children suffering significant bereavement (or separation as a result of a recent divorce).
- Parents who have experienced previous SIDS (sudden infant death syndrome) in the family.

Thinking about ideas

Investigating child health surveillance

Arrange to visit a child health clinic and find out the following information:

- What surveillance programmes are routinely carried out, and by whom?
- If further tests are necessary, to whom is the child referred?
- What records do health visitors maintain?
- How do health personnel try to ensure equality of access to health surveillance?

Further reading, weblinks and resources

British Red Cross

For information on first aid for children and how to become a qualified first aider.
www.redcross.org.uk

Child Accident Prevention Trust

This is the UK's leading charity, working to reduce the number of children and young people killed, disabled or seriously injured in accidents.
www.capt.org.uk

NHS Immunisation Information

For up-to-date information on the current immunisation schedule.
www.immunisation.nhs.uk

Royal Society for the Prevention of Accidents

For all child safety advice and information.
www.rospa.com

Health and Safety Executive (HSE)

HSE is the national independent watchdog for work-related health, safety and illness.
www.hse.gov.uk

RIDDOR

RIDDOR puts duties on employers, the self-employed and people in control of work premises (the Responsible Person) to report certain serious workplace accidents, occupational diseases and specified dangerous occurrences (near misses).
www.hse.gov.uk/riddor

Ofsted

Ofsted is the Office for Standards in Education, Children's Services and Skills. Ofsted inspect and regulate services which care for children and young people, and those providing education and skills for learners of all ages.
www.ofsted.gov.uk

EYFS 2014

www.gov.uk/government/publications/early-years-foundation-stage-framework--2

This chapter focuses on understanding the effects of ill-health on children and families. The more common illnesses are described within a framework of children's holistic needs. As some practitioners care for children within the family home, guidelines for caring for sick children are included. It is essential that all early years practitioners have a thorough understanding of how to administer first aid, and so current first aid techniques are discussed.

The causes of ill-health

Infection

Infectious diseases are extremely common in childhood and are caused by both bacteria and by viruses. Infection enters the body in several ways – directly and indirectly.

Direct infection

- Touch – skin that is unbroken (that is, with no cuts or grazes) provides an effective barrier to most organisms, although diseases such as impetigo can be transferred onto skin already infected by eczema. Scabies, for example, is also spread by skin contact.
- Droplet or airborne infection – if a person coughs or sneezes without covering their nose and mouth, the droplets may be carried several metres. Droplets are inhaled by people in the room; similarly, infection may be spread in this way by talking closely with others.
- Kissing – organisms are transferred directly from mouth to mouth; glandular fever (mononucleosis) is often referred to as the 'kissing disease'.
- Injection – the sharing of needles and syringes by drug addicts may cause infection to be transmitted by the blood. HIV infection and hepatitis B may both be transmitted in this way.
- Sexual contact – the transmission of diseases such as syphilis, gonorrhoea, HIV and non-specific genital infection (NSGI) is via sexual intercourse.

Indirect infection

- Water – the contamination of water used for drinking is a major cause of the spread of diseases – for example, typhoid fever, cholera and viral hepatitis A. Swimming in polluted water

may cause ear infections. Eating shellfish that live in polluted water may cause food poisoning or tapeworm infestations.

- Food – animals that are kept or caught for food may harbour disease organisms in their tissues. If meat or milk from such an animal is ingested without being thoroughly cooked or pasteurised, the organisms may cause illness in the human host – for example, food poisoning.
- Insects – many types of fly may settle first on human or animal excrement and then on our food, to lay eggs or to feed. Typhoid fever and food poisoning are two diseases spread in this way. Biting insects can spread serious infections through their bites – for example, the mosquito (malaria and filariasis), the tsetse fly (African trypanosomiasis), the rat flea (plague) and the sand fly (leishmaniasis).
- Rats – these rodents may harbour the leptospirosis bacterium which is excreted in their urine and may be transmitted to humans. (Leptospirosis is also known as Weil's disease.)

The body's natural barriers to infection

We are all born with natural immunity – this is the body's ability to resist infection. The body has a complex immune system which works in partnership with other protective body systems:

- The skin forms a physical barrier against germs entering your body. Skin is tough and generally impermeable or resistant to bacteria and viruses. The skin also secretes antibacterial substances – most bacteria and spores that land on the skin die quickly.
- Nose, mouth and eyes are also obvious entry points for germs. Tears and mucus contain an enzyme that breaks down the cell wall of many bacteria. Saliva is also antibacterial. Since the nasal passage and

KEY TERMS

Cilia – The fine hair-like projections from certain cells such as those in the respiratory tract that help to sweep away fluids and particles.

Pathogen – A bacteria, fungus, virus, infestation or prion (see page 308 for definition) that produces disease.

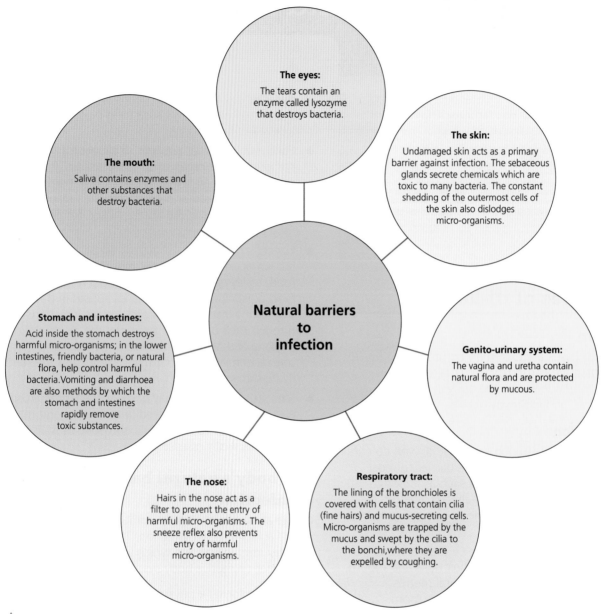

The eyes:
The tears contain an enzyme called lysozyme that destroys bacteria.

The skin:
Undamaged skin acts as a primary barrier against infection. The sebaceous glands secrete chemicals which are toxic to many bacteria. The constant shedding of the outermost cells of the skin also dislodges micro-organisms.

The mouth:
Saliva contains enzymes and other substances that destroy bacteria.

Natural barriers to infection

Stomach and intestines:
Acid inside the stomach destroys harmful micro-organisms; in the lower intestines, friendly bacteria, or natural flora, help control harmful bacteria. Vomiting and diarrhoea are also methods by which the stomach and intestines rapidly remove toxic substances.

Genito-urinary system:
The vagina and uretha contain natural flora and are protected by mucous.

The nose:
Hairs in the nose act as a filter to prevent the entry of harmful micro-organisms. The sneeze reflex also prevents entry of harmful micro-organisms.

Respiratory tract:
The lining of the bronchioles is covered with cells that contain cilia (fine hairs) and mucus-secreting cells. Micro-organisms are trapped by the mucus and swept by the cilia to the bonchi, where they are expelled by coughing.

▲ **Figure 15.1** Natural barriers to infection

KEY TERM

Prion – A protein that can fold in multiple, structurally distinct ways, at least one of which is transmissible to other prion proteins. It is this form of replication that leads to disease that is similar to viral infection.

lungs are coated in mucus, many germs not killed immediately are trapped in the mucus and soon swallowed.

- The respiratory system uses **cilia**, mucus and coughing to rid the body of inhaled microbes and pollutants.
- Acid in the stomach and enzymes in the intestines destroy many **pathogens**.

Recognising general signs of illness in babies and children

Small children are not always able to explain their symptoms, and may display non-specific complaints such as headache, sleeplessness, vomiting or an inability to stand up. Babies have even less certain means of communication, and may simply cry in a different way, refuse feeds or become listless and lethargic. With many infectious illnesses, there will be fever.

See Chapter 12, p. 253 for advice on identifying signs of illness in children with different skin tones.

The responsibility of caring for a baby who becomes ill is enormous; it is very important that early years

In babies under 12 months:	In older children:
Tense or bulging fontanelles.	Headache.
A stiffening body with involuntary movements, or a floppy body.	Inability to tolerate light.
Blotchy or pale skin.	Neck stiffness and joint pains – the child may arch the neck backwards because of the rigidity of the neck muscles.
A high-pitched, moaning cry.	Fever.
High temperature.	
The baby may be difficult to wake.	
The baby may refuse to feed.	
Red or purple spots (anywhere on the body) that do not fade under pressure – do the glass test.	

▲ **Table 15.1** Signs and symptoms of meningitis

practitioners should know the signs and symptoms of illness and when to seek medical aid. See Chapter 12 for general signs of illness in babies.

Meningitis in babies

Meningitis is an inflammation of the lining of the brain. It is a very serious illness, but if it is detected and treated early, most children make a full recovery. The early symptoms of meningitis – such as fever,

irritability, restlessness, vomiting and refusing feeds – are also common with colds and flu. However, a baby with meningitis can become seriously ill within hours, so it is important to act quickly if meningitis is suspected.

The glass test involves pressing the side or bottom of a glass firmly against the rash – you will be able to see if the rash fades and loses colour under the pressure. If it does not change colour, call for medical aid immediately. If spots are appearing on the child's body, this could be septicaemia, a very serious bacterial infection described as the 'meningitis rash'.

General signs and symptoms of illness in children

When a child feels generally unwell, you should ask the child if he or she has any pain or discomfort and treat it appropriately. Take the child's temperature and look for other signs of illness, such as a rash or swollen glands. Often, feeling generally unwell is the first sign that the child is developing an infectious disease. Some children can also show general signs of illness if they are anxious or worried about something, either at home or at school.

Emotional and behavioural changes

Children react in certain characteristic ways when they are unwell. Some of the more common emotional and behavioural changes include:

- being quieter than usual
- becoming more clingy to parents or primary carer
- attention-seeking behaviour
- changed sleeping patterns – some children sleep more than usual, others less
- lack of energy

▲ **Figure 15.2** The 'glass' test for meningitis

Condition	Signs and symptoms	Role of the carer and treatments
Colic	This occurs in the first 12 weeks. It causes sharp, spasmodic pain in the stomach, and is often at its worst in the late evening. Symptoms include inconsolable high-pitched crying, drawing her legs up to her chest, and growing red in the face.	Try to stay calm and seek medical intervention. Gently massage his/her abdomen in a clockwise direction, using the tips of your middle fingers.
Diarrhoea	Frequent loose or watery stools. Can be very serious in young babies, especially when combined with vomiting, as it can lead to severe dehydration.	Give frequent small drinks of cooled, boiled water containing glucose and salt or a made-up sachet of rehydration fluid. If the baby is unable to take the fluid orally, they must be taken to hospital urgently and fed intravenously, by a 'drip'. If anal area becomes sore, treat with a barrier cream.
Gastroenteritis	The baby may vomit and usually has diarrhoea as well; often has a raised temperature and loss of appetite. May show signs of abdominal pain, i.e. drawing up of legs to chest and crying.	Reassure baby. Observe strict hygiene rules. Watch out for signs of dehydration. Offer frequent small amounts of fluid, and possibly rehydration salts.
Neonatal cold injury – or hypothermia	The baby is cold to the touch. Face may be pale or flushed. Lethargic, runny nose, swollen hands and feet. Pre-term infants and babies under 4 months are at particular risk.	Warm *slowly* by covering with several light layers of blankets and by cuddling. Do not use direct heat. Offer feeds high in sugar and seek medical help urgently.
Reflux	Also known as gastro-intestinal reflux (GIR) or gastro-oesophageal reflux (GOR). The opening to the stomach is not yet efficient enough to allow a large liquid feed through. Symptoms include 'grizzly' crying and excessive possetting after feeds.	Try feeding the baby in a more upright position and bring up wind by gently rubbing her back. After feeding leave the baby in a semi-sitting position. Some doctors prescribe a paediatric reflux suppressant or antacid mixture to be given before the feed.
Tonsillitis	Very sore throat, which looks bright red. There is usually fever and the baby or child will show signs of distress from pain on swallowing and general aches and pains. May vomit.	Encourage plenty of fluids – older babies may have ice-lollies to suck. Give pain relief, e.g. paracetamol. Seek medical aid if no improvement and if fever persists.
Cough	Often follows on from a cold; may be a symptom of other illness, e.g. measles.	Keep air moist. Check the baby has not inhaled an object. Give medicine if prescribed.
Croup	Croup is an infection of the voice box or larynx, which becomes narrowed and inflamed. Barking cough (like a sea lion), noisy breathing, distressed; usually occurs at night.	If severe, seek medical help. Reassure the baby and sit them up, reassuring them and remaining calm. Increasing the humidity using a room humidifier will help to create an appropriate atmosphere. While there is little scientific evidence to support it, some people have found that allowing their child to breathe in steam from a hot bath or shower in a closed room has eased symptoms. Steam treatment should only be used under careful supervision as there is a risk of scalding your child. (Source: NHS website)
Bronchiolitis	A harsh dry cough which later becomes wet and chesty; runny nose, raised temperature, wheeze, breathing problems, poor feeding or vomiting. May develop a blue tinge around the lips and on the fingernails (known as cyanosis).	Observe closely. Seek medical help if condition worsens. Increase fluids. Give small regular feeds. Give prescribed medicine. Comfort and reassure.

▲ **Table 15.2** Illness in babies

Condition	Signs and symptoms	Role of the carer and treatments
Febrile convulsions (high temperature)	Convulsions caused by a high temperature (over 39°C, 102°F) or fever are called febrile convulsions. Baby will become rigid, then the body may twitch and jerk for one or two minutes.	Try not to panic. Move potentially harmful objects out of the way and place the baby in the recovery position. Loosen clothing. Call doctor. Give tepid sponging. Comfort and reassure.
Otitis media	Will appear unwell; may have raised temperature. May vomit, may cry with pain. May have discharge from ear.	Take to doctor, give antibiotics and analgesics (or painkillers). Increase fluids; comfort and reassure.
Conjunctivitis	Inflammation of the thin, delicate membrane that covers the eyeball and forms the lining of the eyelids. Symptoms include a painful red eye, with watering and sometimes sticky pus.	Take to doctor who may prescribe antibiotic eye drops or ointment. Bathe a sticky eye gently with cool boiled water and clean cotton wool swabs. Always bathe the eye from the inside corner to the outside to avoid spreading infection.
Common cold	Runny nose, sneeze; tiny babies may have breathing problem.	Keep nose clear. Give small frequent feeds. Nasal drops if prescribed.
Meningitis	Raised temperature, may have a blotchy rash; may refuse feeds; may have a stiff neck; may have a seizure; bulging fontanelle, may have a shrill, high-pitched cry.	Seek medical help urgently. Reduce temperature. Reassure.

▲ **Table 15.2** (*continued*)

- crying – babies cry for a variety of reasons (see Chapter 12); older children who cry more than usual may be physically unwell or you may need to explore the reasons for their unhappiness
- regression – children who are unwell often regress in their development and behaviour; they may:
- want to be carried everywhere instead of walking independently
- go back to nappies after being toilet-trained
- start to wet the bed
- play with familiar, previously outgrown toys.

See page 322 for a list of the signs and symptoms of acute illness.

High temperature (fever)

The normal body temperature is between 36°C and 37°C. A temperature of above 37.5°C means that the child has a fever. A child with a fever may:

- look hot and flushed; the child may complain of feeling cold and might shiver – this is a natural reflex due to the increased heat loss and a temporary disabling of the usual internal temperature control of the brain
- be either irritable or subdued

- be unusually sleepy
- go off his or her food
- complain of thirst.

Children can develop high temperatures very quickly. You need to know how to bring a child's temperature down (see p. 312) to avoid complications, such as dehydration and febrile convulsions.

How to take a temperature

All family first aid kits should contain a thermometer. There are many types, but the most widely used in the home are digital thermometers and temperature strips.

Digital thermometers

These are battery-operated and consist of a safe narrow probe with a tip sensitive to temperature. They are easy to read via a display panel and are available as in-ear thermometers, under the armpit or in the mouth thermometers:

1 Place the narrow tip of the thermometer in the ear or under the child's armpit – or for older children, place under their tongue.

2 Read the temperature when it stops rising; some models beep when this point is reached.

  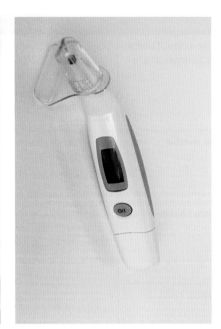

▲ **Figure 15.3** Forehead temperature strip and digital thermometers

Guidelines for good practice

Bringing down a high temperature

✔ Offer cool drinks – encourage the child to take small, frequent sips of anything he or she will drink (though preferably clear fluids like water or squash, rather than milky drinks). Do this even if the child is vomiting because, even then, some water will be absorbed.

✔ Remove clothes – keep the child as undressed as possible to allow heat to be lost.

✔ Reduce bedclothes – use a cotton sheet if the child is in bed.

✔ Sponge the child down – use tepid water (see Guidelines below for tepid sponging to reduce a temperature).

✔ Give the correct dose of children's paracetamol – make sure you have written consent from the parents to use this in case of emergency, otherwise medicines cannot be given. Contact the parents and try to obtain consent if you do not already have it.

✔ Cool the air in the child's room – use an electric fan or open the window.

✔ Reassure the child – he may be very frightened. Remain calm yourself and try to stop the baby from crying, as this will tend to push the temperature higher still.

✔ If the temperature will not come down, call the doctor. Always consult a doctor if a high fever is accompanied by symptoms such as severe headache with stiff neck, abdominal pain or pain when passing urine.

Forehead temperature strip

This is a rectangular strip of thin plastic which contains temperature sensitive crystals that change colour according to the temperature measured. It is placed on the child's forehead. It is not as accurate as other thermometers but is a useful check.

1 Hold the plastic strip firmly against the child's forehead for about 30 seconds.
2 Record the temperature revealed by the colour change.

Whatever the cause of a high temperature, it is important to try to reduce it. There is always the risk a fever could lead to convulsions or fits.

Common infectious childhood illnesses

Everyone concerned with the care of babies and young children should be aware of the signs and symptoms of the common infectious diseases, and should know when to summon medical aid.

There is more information on exclusion in this chapter on p. 323.

When to call a doctor or call for an ambulance

If you think the child's life is in danger, dial 999 if you are in the UK, ask for an ambulance urgently and explain the situation. Contact the family doctor (GP) if the child has

Guidelines for tepid sponging to reduce a temperature

✔ Make sure the air in the room is comfortably warm – not hot, cold or draughty.

✔ Lay the child on a towel on your knee or on the bed and gently remove his or her clothes; reassure them by talking gently.

✔ Sponge the child's body, limbs and face with tepid or lukewarm water – not cold; as the water evaporates from the skin, it absorbs heat from the blood and so cools the system.

✔ As the child cools down, pat the skin dry with a soft towel and dress only in a nappy or pants; cover the child with a light cotton sheet.

✔ Keep checking the child's condition to make sure that he or she does not become cold or shivery; put more light covers over the child if he or she is shivering or obviously chilled.

✔ If the temperature rises again, repeat sponging every 10 minutes.

Disease and cause	Incubation/ exclusion period	Signs and symptoms	Rash or specific sign	Treatment	Possible complications
Common cold (coryza) Virus	1–3 days	Sneeze, sore throat, running nose, headache, slight fever, irritable, partial deafness		Treat symptoms. Apply a product such as Vaseline to nostrils	Bronchitis, sinusitis, laryngitis
Chickenpox (varicella) Virus	10–14 days to develop. Exclude for 5 days from the onset of the rash	Slight fever, itchy rash, mild onset, child feels ill, often with severe headache	Red spots with white centre on trunk and limbs at first; blisters and pustules	Rest, fluids, calamine to rash, cut child's nails to prevent secondary infection	Impetigo, scarring, secondary infection from scratching
Food poisoning Bacteria or virus	1½ to 36 hours	Vomiting, diarrhoea, abdominal pain		Fluids only for 24 hours; medical aid if no better	Dehydration, can be fatal
Gastroenteritis Bacteria or virus	Bacterial: 7–14 days Viral: 1½ to 36 hours Exclusion: 48 hours after the last episode of diarrhoea or vomiting	Vomiting, diarrhoea, signs of dehydration		Replace fluids – water or Dioralyte; medical aid urgently	Dehydration, weight loss, death
Measles (morbilli) Virus	7–15 days Exclusion – 4 days from the onset of the rash	High fever, fretful, heavy cold – running nose and discharge from eyes; later cough	Day 1: Koplik's spots, white inside mouth. Day 4: blotchy rash starts on face and spreads down to body	Rest, fluids, tepid sponging. Shade room if photophobic (dislikes bright light)	Otitis media, eye infection, pneumonia, encephalitis (rare)
Meningitis (Inflammation of the meninges which cover the brain) Bacteria or virus	Variable Usually 2–10 days Exclusion: until fully recovered	Fever, headache, drowsiness, confusion, photophobia (dislike of bright light), arching of neck	Can have small red spots or bruises	Take to hospital, antibiotics and observation	Deafness, brain damage, death

▲ **Table 15.3** Common childhood infections

Disease and cause	Incubation/ exclusion period	Signs and symptoms	Rash or specific sign	Treatment	Possible complications
Mumps (epidemic parotitis) Virus	14–21 days Exclusion period – 5 days after the onset of swollen glands	Pain, swelling of jaw in front of ears, fever, pain when eating and drinking	Swollen face	Fluids: give via straw, hot compresses, oral hygiene	Meningitis (1 in 400) Orchitis (infection of the testes) in young men
Pertussis (whooping cough) Bacteria	7–21 days Exclusion: 5 days from start of antibiotic treatment	Starts with a snuffly cold, slight cough, mild fever	Spasmodic cough with whoop sound, vomiting	Rest and assurance; feed after coughing attack; support during attack; inhalations	Convulsions, pneumonia, brain damage, hernia, debility
Rubella (German measles) Virus	14–21 days Exclusion: 4 days from the onset of the rash	Slight cold, sore throat, mild fever, swollen glands behind ears, pain in small joints	Slight pink rash starts behind ears and on forehead. Not itchy	Rest if necessary. Treat symptoms	Only if contracted by woman in first 3 months of pregnancy: can cause serious defects in unborn baby
Scarlet fever (or scarlatina) Bacteria	2–4 days Exclusion: 5 days after the start of antibiotics	Sudden fever, loss of appetite, sore throat, pallor around mouth, 'strawberry' tongue	Bright red pinpoint rash over face and body – may peel	Rest, fluids, observe for complications, antibiotics	Kidney infection, otitis media, rheumatic fever (rare)
Tonsillitis Bacteria or virus	2–4 days Exclusion: none	Very sore throat, fever, headache, pain on swallowing, aches and pains in back and limbs	Throat reddened, tonsils swollen and may be coated or have white spots on them	Rest, fluids, medical aid antibiotics, iced drinks to relieve pain	Quinsy (abscess on tonsils), otitis media, kidney infection, temporary deafness

▲ **Table 15.3** (*Continued*)

Contact the GP if a child shows these symptoms	
Has a temperature of 38.6°C (101.4°F) that is not lowered by measures to reduce fever, or a temperature over 37.8°C (100°F) for more than one day	**Has convulsions,** or is limp and floppy
Has severe or persistent **vomiting** and/or **diarrhoea,** seems **dehydrated** or has projectile vomiting	**Cannot be woken,** is unusually drowsy or may be losing consciousness
Has symptoms of **meningitis**	Has symptoms of **croup**
Is pale, listless, and **does not respond** to usual stimulation	**Cries or screams** inconsolably and may have severe pain
Has bulging **fontanelle** (soft spot on top of head of a baby) when not crying	Appears to have severe abdominal pain, with symptoms of **shock**
Refuses two successive feeds (babies)	Develops **purple-red** rash anywhere on body
Passes bowel motions (stools) containing **blood**	Has jaundice
Has a suspected **ear infection**	Has been injured, **e.g. by a burn which blisters and covers** more than 10% of the body surface
Has inhaled something, such as a peanut, into the air passages and may be **choking**	Has swallowed a **poisonous** substance, or an object, e.g. a safety pin or button
Has bright pink cheeks and swollen hands and feet (could be due to **hypothermia**)	Has difficulty in **breathing**

▲ **Table 15.4** When to contact the GP

any of the symptoms listed in Table 15.4. If the doctor cannot reach you quickly, take the child to the accident and emergency department of the nearest hospital.

Disorders of the digestive tract

One of the most common signs that something is wrong with the digestive system is diarrhoea, when the bowel movements are abnormally runny and frequent. Other symptoms of infection or illness are vomiting and abdominal pain. Although these symptoms are often distressing – both to the child and to his or her carer – they are rarely a serious threat to health. See p. 316.

Vomiting

Vomiting is the violent expulsion of the contents of the stomach through the mouth. A single episode of vomiting without other symptoms happens frequently in childhood. It could be a result of overeating or too much excitement. Vomiting has many causes, but in most cases there is little warning, and after a single

bout the child recovers and quickly gets back to normal. Table 15.5 details possible causes of vomiting in children over one year old and what to do about it.

Guidelines for good practice

Helping a child who is vomiting

- ✔ Reassure the child, who may be very frightened.
- ✔ Stay with the child and support his or her head by putting your hand on the child's forehead.
- ✔ Keep the child cool by wiping his or her face with a cool, damp cloth.
- ✔ Offer mouthwash or sips of water after vomiting.
- ✔ Give frequent small drinks of cold water. You may be advised by your doctor to give special rehydrating powders.
- ✔ Encourage the child to rest lying down, with a bowl by their side. Do not leave the child until he or she has fallen asleep – and stay within call in case the child vomits again.

Possible causes of vomiting with accompanying symptoms	What to do
Gastroenteritis The child also has diarrhoea	See the doctor within 24 hours Prevent dehydration (see p. 316)
Intestinal obstruction The child's vomit is greenish-yellow	Call an ambulance; do not give the child anything to eat or drink
Meningitis The child has a fever, a stiff neck or flat, purplish spots that do not disappear when pressed	Call an ambulance
Head injury The child has recently suffered a blow to the head	Call an ambulance; do not give the child anything to eat or drink
Appendicitis The child has continuous abdominal pain around the navel and to the right side of the abdomen	Call an ambulance; do not give the child anything to eat or drink
Infection The child seems unwell, looks flushed and feels hot	Reduce the fever; see the doctor within 24 hours
Hepatitis The child has pale faeces and dark urine	See the doctor within 24 hours
Travel sickness When travelling, the child seems pale and quiet and complains of nausea	Give the child a travel sickness remedy before starting journey; take plenty of drinks to prevent dehydration
Migraine The child complains of a severe headache on one side of the forehead	See the doctor if accompanied by severe abdominal pain – it could be appendicitis
Whooping cough (pertussis) The child vomits after a bout of coughing	See the doctor within 24 hours

▲ **Table 15.5** Possible causes of vomiting and what to do

Diarrhoea

Most children have diarrhoea at some time, usually after an infection involving the digestive tract – for example, gastroenteritis. If the fluid lost through passing frequent, loose, watery stools is not replaced, there is a danger that the child will become dehydrated. Babies become dehydrated very quickly and can become seriously ill as the result of diarrhoea. Diarrhoea can also be caused by:

- emotional factors – overtiredness, excitement and anxiety
- allergy
- reaction to certain drugs and medicines.

Toddler's diarrhoea

Toddler's diarrhoea occurs when an otherwise healthy child (between one and three years) passes loose, watery faeces. The cause is uncertain, but it is thought to be the result of poor chewing of food. Signs and symptoms are:

- loose, watery faeces, often containing recognisable pieces of food – for example, raisins, corn, carrots and peas
- nappy rash if the child is in nappies.

What to do

- Consult a doctor to exclude other causes of diarrhoea, such as an infection.
- Encourage the child to chew foods thoroughly.
- Mash or liquidise foods that are difficult to chew and digest.

Children generally grow out of toddler's diarrhoea by three years of age. As it is not an infectious condition, there is no need for the child to be kept away from friends or from nursery.

Guidelines for good practice

Caring for a child with diarrhoea

- ✔ Reassure the child, who may be very distressed.
- ✔ Prevent dehydration by giving regular drinks of water.
- ✔ Keep a potty nearby.
- ✔ Be sympathetic when changing soiled underwear; soak any soiled clothing in a nappy sterilising solution before washing.
- ✔ Maintain a high standard of hygiene; hand-washing by both you and the child is vital in preventing the spread of infection.
- ✔ Unless it is toddler diarrhoea, keep child away from other children; early years settings will have an exclusion policy in the case of infectious illness, such as gastroenteritis.

Dehydration

Children can lose large amounts of body water through fever, diarrhoea, vomiting or exercise; this is called dehydration. In severe cases, a child may not be able to replace this water simply by drinking and eating as usual. This is especially true if an illness stops the child from taking fluids by mouth or if he or she has a high fever.

Signs of dehydration in babies

- sunken fontanelles – these are the areas where the bones of the skull have not yet fused together; they are covered by a tough membrane and a pulse may usually be seen beating under the **anterior fontanelle** in a baby without much hair
- fretfulness
- refusing feeds
- dry nappies – because the amount of urine being produced is very small.

Signs of dehydration in children
Mild to moderate dehydration

- dry mouth
- no tears when crying
- refusing drinks
- at first thirsty, then irritable, then becomes still and quiet
- inactive and lethargic
- increased heart rate
- restlessness.

Severe dehydration

- very dry mouth
- sunken eyes and dry, wrinkled skin
- no urination for several hours
- sleepy and disorientated
- deep, rapid breathing
- fast, weak pulse
- cool and blotchy hands and feet.

What to do

If you think a baby or child might have dehydration, do not try to treat them at home or in the early years setting. Call the doctor immediately or take the child to the nearest accident and emergency department.

KEY TERM

Anterior fontanelle – A diamond-shaped soft area at the front of the head, just above the brow. It is covered by a tough membrane and you can often see the baby's pulse beating there under the skin. The fontanelle closes between 12 and 18 months of age.

The doctor will prescribe oral rehydrating fluid to restore the body salts lost.

Infestations of the digestive tract

Threadworms

Threadworms are tiny white worms that infest the bowel. People of any age can get threadworms, but they are most common in children between 5 and 12 years old. They cannot be caught from animals.

- They are highly contagious, and pass easily from one person to another.
- The eggs are usually picked up by the hands and then transferred to the mouth.
- The eggs hatch in the small intestine, and the worms migrate downwards to the rectum, where they emerge at night.
- They cause intense itching – the child will then scratch, eggs will be caught under the nails and the cycle may repeat itself.
- The whole family will need to take medication prescribed by the doctor.
- Strict hygiene measures – scrubbing the nails after a bowel movement, the use of separate flannels and towels, and daily baths – help to prevent infestation.

Toxocariasis

This is an infection of the roundworms that usually live in the gut of dogs and cats. The eggs of the worm are excreted in the faeces of the animal, and young children may pick them up and transfer them to their mouths. Infection can, occasionally, be serious, leading to epilepsy or blindness. Prevention is through public awareness: all dog and cat owners must regularly worm their pets, and dogs should not be allowed in areas where young children play.

Skin disorders

Up to three million micro-organisms exist on each square centimetre of skin. Most of these are commensals (literally 'table companions', from the Latin) and are harmless to their host. These commensals have become adapted through evolution to live off human skin scales and the slightly acid secretions produced by the skin. Some important points to note regarding skin conditions are:

- Newborn babies are particularly prone to skin infection.
- Micro-organisms thrive in moist conditions – for example, at the axillae (the armpits) and the groin.
- The skin can never be sterilised. Iodine preparations used to prepare skin for surgical operations kill a large percentage of organisms, but cannot remove the bacteria that colonise the hair follicles.
- To provide a defence against infection, the skin must be intact – that is, unbroken.

There are two main reasons why the skin should be kept clean:

1 to prevent infection by microorganisms via the sweat pores
2 to prevent the accumulation of oil, sweat and micro-organisms, which will encourage insect parasites.

Parasitic skin infections

The two most common causes of parasitic skin infection in the western world are:

- the head louse
- the scabies mite.

Head lice

Head lice are a common affliction. Anybody can get them, but they are particularly prevalent among children.

Head lice:

- are tiny insects with six legs
- only live on human beings – they cannot be caught from animals
- have mouths like small needles, which they stick into the scalp and use to drink the blood
- are unable to fly, hop or jump
- are not the same as nits, which are the egg cases laid by lice. Nits may be found 'glued' on to the hair shafts; they are smaller than a pinhead and are pearly white
- are between 1 and 4 mm in size – slightly larger than a pinhead (see Figure 15.4)
- live on, or very close to, the scalp; they do not wander down the hair shafts for very long
- are caught just by coming into contact with someone who is infested – when heads touch, the lice simply walk from one head to the other
- do not discriminate between clean and dirty hair, but tend to live more on smooth, straight hair.

If you 'catch' one or two lice, they may breed and increase slowly in number. At this stage, most people have no symptoms. Many people only realise that they have head lice when the itching starts, usually after two to three months. The itching is due to an allergy, not to the louse bites themselves. Sometimes a rash may be seen on the scalp, or lice droppings (a black powder, like fine pepper) may be seen on pillowcases.

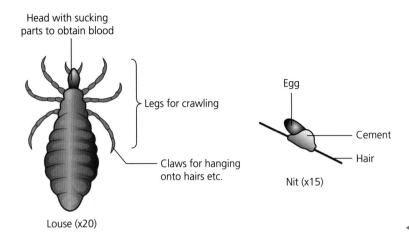

Head with sucking
parts to obtain blood

Legs for crawling

Claws for hanging
onto hairs etc.

Louse (x20)

Egg

Cement

Hair

Nit (x15)

Figure 15.4 A head louse and egg case (or nit)

The life cycle of the head louse

The female head louse lays six to eight eggs a day; these eggs are dull, well camouflaged and glued to the base of hair shafts. Hatching increases in warm, moist atmospheres. Once the eggs have hatched, the empty egg cases (called nits) remain glued to the hair and grow out with it at a rate of 1 cm per month, so distracting attention from the live eggs and lice. The nits are white and shiny and may be found further down the scalp, particularly behind the ears. They may be mistaken for dandruff but, unlike dandruff, they are firmly glued to the hair and cannot be shaken off.

Prevention

The best way to stop infection is for families to learn how to check their own heads. This way, parents can find any lice before they have a chance to breed. Families can then treat the lice and stop them being passed around. If a living, moving louse is found on one of the family's heads, the others should be checked carefully. Any of them who have living lice should be treated at the same time.

How to detect head lice

You will need a plastic detection comb (from the chemist), good lighting and an ordinary comb. Lice are most easily detected by combing wet hair with a fine-tooth comb. Some parents find that using a hair conditioner helps to lubricate the hair and ease the combing process; others report that such lubricants make it more difficult to see the eggs.

Treatment

Treatment should only be used if you are sure that you have found a living, moving louse. Special head louse lotions should never be used 'just in case', or as a preventative measure, since the lotions may be harmful to young children when used repeatedly. You

Guidelines for good practice

Detecting head lice

✔ Brush and comb the child's hair daily, preferably at night and in the morning, until the child is old enough to do it alone.

✔ Comb thoroughly. Contrary to popular belief, head lice are not easily damaged by ordinary combing. However, regular combing may help to detect lice early and so help to control them.

✔ Inspect the child's hair prior to washing it; pay special attention to the areas behind the ears, the top of the head and the neckline.

✔ Examine the child's hair closely if he or she complains of an itchy scalp or if there is a reported outbreak of head lice at school or nursery.

should check the heads of all the people living in your home, but only treat those who have living, moving lice. Treat them all at the same time, using a special lotion or aromatherapy mixture, not a shampoo. There are two main methods of treatment for head lice:

Insecticide lotions – lotions and rinses that are specifically formulated to kill lice and their eggs are available from pharmacists and from some child health clinics. Your school nurse, health visitor or pharmacist will advise you on which lotion to use. The lotion is changed frequently, as the lice become resistant to it and it no longer works. If you cannot afford the lotion, you can ask your GP for a prescription. Follow the instructions on the product carefully.

Aromatherapy lotions – these have been found to be effective by some parents in treating head lice. They are based on essential oils (containing extracts from plants such as rosemary, lavender, eucalyptus, geranium and tea tree).

Think about ideas

Awareness of head lice

Prepare a pamphlet for a parent whose five-year-old child has head lice. Include the following information in an easy-to-read format:

- what head lice are
- where to go for treatment
- how to prevent a recurrence
- how to treat the condition.

KEY TERMS

Head lice – Head lice are tiny grey/brown insects that live on the scalp and neck. Although they may be embarrassing and sometimes itchy and uncomfortable, head lice do not usually cause illness.

Scabies – Scabies is an itchy rash caused by the human scabies mite. It is spread easily through close physical contact.

The Community Hygiene Concern charity (www.chc.org) has developed the Bug Buster Kit, which contains specially designed combs that can rid a child of head lice without having to subject them to chemical treatments. This method has been approved by the Department of Health.

Scabies

Scabies is largely a disease of families and young children. The scabies mite differs from the louse in that it does not have a recognisable head, thorax and abdomen.

The scabies mite:

- has a tortoise-like body, with four pairs of legs
- is about 0.3 mm in size
- lives in burrows in the outer skin – these can be mistaken for the tracks made by a hypodermic needle (which is a hollow needle used with a syringe to inject substances into the body or extract fluids)
- is usually found in the finger webs, wrists, palms and soles
- is transmitted mainly by body contact, which must last for at least 20 minutes
- is not prevented from causing an infestation by cleanliness
- produces a widespread itchy rash, which is most irritating at night.

If untreated, secondary sepsis may occur, with boils and impetigo.

Treatment

Insecticide lotion is applied to the whole body below the neck; treatment is usually repeated after 24 hours. Calamine lotion may be used to soothe the itch that often lasts after treatment.

Eczema – an allergic skin condition

Eczema (from the Greek 'to boil over') is an itchy and often unsightly skin condition that affects millions of people to some degree. The most common type which affects children is atopic eczema. About one in eight of all children will show symptoms at some time, ranging from a mild rash lasting a few months, to severe symptoms that persist over years.

- Eczema is not infectious – you cannot 'catch' eczema from someone.
- It often starts as an irritating red patch in the creases of the elbows or knees, or on the face.
- It can spread quickly to surrounding skin, which becomes cracked, moist and red.
- In severe cases, it can blister and weep clear fluid if scratched.
- Later, the skin becomes thickened and scaly.
- Skin damaged by eczema is more likely to become infected, particularly by a bacteria called staphylococcus aureus, which produces yellow crusts or pus-filled spots.

Causes

There is no single known cause, but certain factors predispose a child to suffer from eczema:

- an allergy to certain foods – for example, cows' milk (see Chapter 16 on p. 350 for more information on milk)
- an allergy to airborne substances – for example, pollen, house dust, scales from animal hair or feathers, or fungus spores
- environmental factors – for example, humidity or cold weather
- a family history of allergy
- emotional or physical stress.

In severe cases, the GP will refer the child to a skin specialist (dermatologist).

Guidelines for good practice

Managing eczema

In mild cases where the child's life is not disrupted, the following measures are usually advised:

✔ **Do not let the child's skin get dry** – apply a moisturising cream or emollient to the skin several times a day. Aqueous cream is a good moisturiser and can also be used for washing instead of soap. Apply the cream with downward strokes – do not rub it up and down. (Try to put some cream on when you feed the baby or change a nappy.)

✔ **Identify triggers** – identify and avoid anything that irritates the skin or makes the problem worse – for example, soap powder, pets and other animals, chemical sprays, cigarette smoke or some clothing.

✔ **Avoid irritants** – that is, substances that dry or irritate the baby's skin, such as soap, baby bath, bubble bath or detergents, and bathe the child in lukewarm water with a suitable skin oil added. Avoid wool and synthetics – cotton clothing is best.

✔ **Prevent scratching** – use cotton mittens for small children at night; keep the child's nails short.

✔ **Foods to avoid** – do not cut out important foods, such as milk, dairy products, wheat or eggs, without consulting the GP or health visitor. Citrus fruits, tomatoes and juice can be avoided if they cause a reaction.

✔ **House dust mite** – the faeces of the house dust mite can sometimes make eczema worse. If the child has fluffy or furry toys in the bedroom, the house dust mite collects on them. Limit these toys to one or two favourites, and either wash them weekly at 60 °C or put them in a plastic bag in the freezer for 24 hours to kill the house dust mite.

✔ **Apply steroid creams** as prescribed by the GP – These must be used sparingly, as overuse can harm the skin.

See page 321 for guidelines on caring for children with eczema in the early years setting.

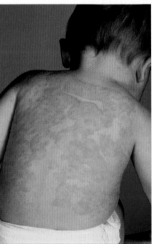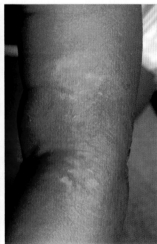

▲ **Figure 15.5** Eczema appears as a dry, scaly rash which becomes red and may start to 'weep'

Other common skin disorders

Impetigo

Impetigo is a highly contagious bacterial infection of the skin. The rash commonly appears on the face, but can affect the rest of the body. The rash consists of yellowish crusts on top of a reddened area of skin. The child should not mix with others until the condition is treated. Impetigo is easily spread by contact with infected flannels and towels, so scrupulous attention to hygiene is necessary. Treatment is with antibiotic medicines and creams.

Warts

Warts are the most common viral infection of the skin. They appear as raised lumps on the skin and are quite harmless. Most warts occur in children between the ages of 6 and 12 years, and disappear without treatment. If they become painful, the local hospital's outpatient department will arrange for their removal, usually by freezing with liquid nitrogen (a form of cryosurgery).

Verrucae

Verrucae (or plantar warts) are warts on the sole of the foot, and may hurt because of pressure. They are picked up easily in the warm, moist atmosphere of swimming baths. Treatment is by the application of lotions or by freezing. Tincture of thuja is an effective homeopathic remedy.

Molluscum contagiosum

This is a viral infection which consists of clusters of small, whitish-yellow, pearl-like spots on any part of the body. No treatment is necessary, as the spots disappear within a few weeks or months.

Pytiriasis rosea

This is an unidentified viral infection that affects mainly school-aged children. The rash is scaly, consisting of beige-coloured oval patches that appear on the chest, back and limbs. Sometimes the rash will cause irritation and can be controlled by use of a mild steroid cream.

Ringworm

This is not due to a worm at all – it is a fungal infection, often acquired from an animal. On the body,

Guidelines for good practice

Caring for a child with eczema in the early years setting

✔ **Food allergies** can create problems with school lunches, and the cook having to monitor carefully what the child eats. Ensure that you check with parents/carers about any allergies that the child may have.

✔ **Clothing** – wearing woolly jumpers, school uniforms (especially if these are not cotton) and football kits can all make the eczema worse.

✔ **A special cleaner** may be needed rather than the school soap; the child may also need to use cotton towels, as paper towels can cause a problem.

✔ **Extra time and privacy** may be needed for applying creams at school; children may need to wear bandages or cotton gloves to protect their skin.

✔ **Changes in temperature** can exacerbate the condition – getting too hot (sitting by a sunny window) or too cold (during PE in the playground).

✔ **Difficulty holding a pen** – if the eczema cracks, the child may not be able to hold a pen.

✔ **Pain and tiredness** – eczema may become so bad that the child is in pain or needs to miss school, due to lack of sleep, pain or hospital visits.

✔ **Irritability and lack of concentration** can result from tiredness – sleep problems are very common, as a nice warm, cosy bed can lead to itching and therefore lack of sleep.

✔ **Using play dough, clay and sand** – some children with eczema may have flare-ups when handling these materials.

Early years practitioners should find out from the child's parents or specialist nurse which activities are suitable and which should be avoided; alternatives should be provided, so that the child is not excluded from the normal daily activities in the setting.

---

it forms a reddish patch, with a ring of small pimples at the edge. Usually it affects the scalp, causing the hair to break and sore, bald patches to appear. Treatment is by medicine (griseofulvin), and the hair does grow again.

Athlete's foot

This is the name for ringworm that grows on the skin of the feet. It appears as a pink, flaky rash, particularly between the toes, and is intensely irritating. Treatment is by powder or cream.

Cold sores

These are small, painful blisters that develop on or around the lips. They are caused by the *herpes simplex* virus and are caught by close contact with an infected person. They can be triggered by illness, cold winds, bright sunlight and emotional upset. Treatment is by an antiviral cream.

Asthma – a respiratory disorder

Asthma is a condition that affects the airways – the small tubes that carry air in and out of the lungs. If you have asthma, your airways are almost always sensitive and inflamed. When you come into contact with something you are allergic to, or something that irritates your airways (a trigger), your airways will become narrower, making it harder to breathe. The muscles around the walls of your airways tighten. The lining of the airways becomes inflamed and starts to swell; often, sticky mucus or phlegm is produced.

Asthma in children

About one in ten children will have an asthma attack (or episode) at some time. There are 1.2 million children in Britain who are currently receiving treatment for asthma. In general, children who have mild asthma are more likely to be free of symptoms once they grow up, but this is not guaranteed. Some people find that their asthma goes away when they are teenagers, but comes back again when they are adults.

Although there is no guarantee that symptoms will go away, they can usually be controlled with medication. Asthma should never be left untreated in the hope that a child may grow out of it.

Causes of asthma

There is no single cause of asthma. Most children who develop asthma have several triggers, or predisposing factors, and these vary from one child to another. Triggers include the following:

- colds and viruses
- pollen – from grass
- pet hairs and feathers
- tobacco smoke
- stress and excitement
- weather changes
- exercise
- mould
- dust and house dust mites
- certain types of medication

- chemicals and fumes – for example, from car exhausts, paints and cleaning fluids
- certain foods – for example, peanuts, eggs.

It is important to try to identify possible triggers, so that they can be avoided. Generally, the more triggers present, the worse the attack. Typically, a child's first attack will follow one or two days after the onset of a respiratory illness, such as a cold.

Symptoms of asthma

- wheezing (although some children with asthma do not experience wheezing)
- elevated breathing rate (the normal rate is under 25 breaths per minute; over 40 is cause for calling the doctor)
- coughing, especially in the early morning
- longer expiration (breathing out) than inspiration (breathing in)
- sweating
- the child may appear very frightened
- the child becomes pale; a darker-skinned child may also appear drained of colour, particularly around the mouth.

Attacks may build over days or occur within seconds. There are two types of asthma:

1. **Acute asthma (or an asthma attack or episode)** – This may require medical stabilisation within a hospital setting.
2. **Chronic asthma** – This produces symptoms on a continual basis, and is characterised by persistent, often severe symptoms, requiring regular oral steroid medication.

What to do when a child has an acute asthmatic attack

Not all asthma attacks can be prevented. When the child is having an acute attack of wheezing (the difficulty is in breathing out rather than in catching one's breath), he or she needs a reliever drug (a bronchodilator, usually in a blue inhaler case). Most children will have been shown how to deliver the drug by an aerosol **inhaler** or a **nebuliser**.

Prevention of asthma

Where possible, avoid the likely triggers of asthma (see above).

Preventer inhalers are usually brown and contain corticosteroids. These have to be taken regularly every day, even when the child is feeling well; they act by reducing the inflammation and swelling in the airways. Corticosteroid drugs should not be confused with the

---

Guidelines for good practice

Helping a child who is having an asthma attack

- ✔ If the attack is the child's *first*, call a doctor and the child's parents.
- ✔ Stay calm and reassure the child, who may be very frightened. Encourage the child to sit up, to increase lung capacity.
- ✔ If the child has a reliever inhaler or nebuliser, supervise him or her while he or she is using it.
- ✔ Never leave the child alone during an attack. Try not to let other children crowd round.
- ✔ If these measures do not stop the wheezing and the child is exhausted by the attack, call a doctor. He or she will either give an injection of a bronchodilator drug or arrange admission to hospital.

Think about ideas

Promoting awareness about asthma

Design a poster, for use in a nursery or primary school, which presents the following information in a lively style:

- the main factors known to trigger an asthma attack
- what to do when a child has an asthma attack
- how preventers and relievers – via inhalers – work.

KEY TERMS

Inhaler – (or puffer) is a medical device used for delivering medication into the body via the lungs.
Nebuliser – Is a machine that changes liquid medicine into a fine mist. This can then be inhaled through a mask or mouthpiece.

---

anabolic steroids taken by athletes to improve their performance.

Acute illness

An acute illness is one that occurs suddenly, often without warning. It is usually of short duration. Examples are:

- gastroenteritis
- otitis media (inflammation of the middle ear)

- appendicitis
- tonsillitis
- an acute asthmatic attack.

Symptoms of acute illness in a child

Signs of such illness in a child include:

- anorexia or loss of appetite
- a lack of interest in play
- unusual crying or screaming bouts
- diarrhoea and vomiting
- abdominal pain – babies with colic or abdominal pains will draw their knees up to their chest in an instinctive effort to relieve the pain
- lethargy or listlessness
- fever
- irritability and fretfulness
- pallor – a black child may have a paler area around the lips, and the conjunctiva (the mucous membrane that covers the front of the eye and lines the inside of the eyelids) may be pale pink instead of red
- dehydration – any illness involving fever or loss of fluid through vomiting or diarrhoea may result in dehydration; the mouth and tongue become dry and parched, and cracks may appear on the lips (the first sign in a baby is a sunken anterior fontanelle – see p. 316).

Policies and procedures for infection control

There are some general rules about excluding children from early years settings:

- Children who are ill should *not* attend a childcare setting. If a child becomes ill while in childcare, a parent or guardian should be asked to take the child home as soon as possible.
- Children with diarrhoea or vomiting illnesses should not be in childcare settings. Parents should contact their GP for advice regarding the child's illness and possible need for collection of samples. The exclusion period should last until at least 48 hours after the last episode of diarrhoea or vomiting.
- Parents should be advised if there are known cases of infection within the childcare setting. It is particularly important that the parents of children whose immunity may be impaired due to illness or treatment (such as leukaemia, HIV) are given this information. It is also important that mothers who are pregnant are made aware of the following infections: chicken pox/shingles, rubella, slapped

cheek syndrome and measles. See Chapter 14 for definitions and more information.

- It is good practice that a child requiring antibiotics does not come into the childcare setting for 48 hours after they have begun treatment. This is so that the child's condition has an opportunity to improve, and that in the unlikely event of a reaction to antibiotics, the parent or carer can be with the child and is able to seek further help or advice from the GP. It is possible that some infections may take the child much longer to recover from and feel well enough to attend childcare. Other infections are subject to specific exclusions advice.

Exclusion policies

The 2010 Health Protection Agency (HPA) orange poster 'Guidance on Infection Control in Schools and other Child Care Settings' details the current guidelines for if – and when – to exclude a child with an infectious disease from the setting. Every early years setting must have an **exclusion policy** for infectious diseases, and parents should be informed of their responsibilities. The exclusion criteria for some of the more common infections are given in Table 15.6 on page 324. The HPA is now part of Public Health England.

Caring for sick children at home

Wherever possible, children should stay at home when ill, within the secure environment of their family and usual surroundings. The child will want their primary carer to be available at all times. The parents may need advice on how to care for their child, and this is provided by the family GP and primary health care team – some health authorities also have specialist paediatric nursing visiting services.

Limiting infection

If the illness is infectious, advice may be needed on how it spreads – for example, visits from friends and relatives may have to be reduced. The most infectious time is during the incubation period, but the dangers of infecting others remain until the main signs and symptoms – for example, a rash – have disappeared.

Reflecting on practice

- Find out about your setting's policy relating to excluding children when they have an infectious illness.
- Think of ways in which you could help to prevent the spread of infection in an early years setting.

Infectious illness	Recommended period for exclusion from the setting
Chicken pox	For 5 days from onset of rash. (See also section on female staff and pregnancy below.)
Diarrhoea and/or vomiting	For 48 hours from last episode of diarrhoea or vomiting. Exclusion from swimming should be for 2 weeks following last episode of diarrhoea.
Hand, foot and mouth	None. Exclusion is ineffective as transmission takes place before the child becomes unwell.
Impetigo	Until lesions are crusted or healed, or 48 hours after commencing antibiotic treatment.
Measles*	For 4 days from onset of rash.
Meningococcal meningitis*	The local Health Protection Unit (HPU) will give advice on any action needed. There is no reason to exclude from school siblings and other close contacts of a case.
Non-meningococcal meningitis*	None. Once the child is well, infection risk is minimal. Meningitis C is preventable by vaccination.
Meningitis due to other bacteria*	Exclude until recovered. There is no reason to exclude from school siblings and other close contacts of a case. Hib meningitis and pneumococcal meningitis are preventable by vaccination.
Mumps*	For 5 days from onset of swelling.
Rubella* German measles	For 6 days from onset of rash. (See section on female staff and pregnancy below.)
Shingles	Exclude only if rash is weeping and cannot be covered. (See section on Female staff and pregnancy below.)
Scabies	Child can return after first treatment has commenced.
Slapped cheek disease (Fifth Disease /Parvovirus)	None. Exclusion is ineffective as nearly all transmission takes place before the child becomes unwell. (But see section on female staff and pregnancy below.)
Whooping cough*	For 5 days from commencing antibiotic treatment.

Note: the diseases marked* are *notifiable*. This means that under the Public Health (Infectious Diseases) Regulations 1988, these infections and *all cases of food poisoning* must be reported to the Local Authority Proper Offices.

▲ **Table 15.6** Exclusion periods following illness

A child attending nursery or school will usually be kept at home until the GP says he or she is clear of infection.

The needs of sick children

Children who are sick have:

- physical needs – food and drink, rest and sleep, temperature control, exercise and fresh air, safety, hygiene and medical care
- intellectual and language needs – stimulation, appropriate activities
- emotional and social needs – love, security, play and contact with others.

The most important part of caring for sick children is showing that you care for them and responding to all their needs. If a child is going to be nursed for some weeks, it is often useful to draw up a plan of care, just as nurses do in hospital. This has the following benefits:

- It helps you to keep a record of any changes in the child's condition and to ask for outside help if necessary.
- It reassures you that you are providing for all the child's needs.

- It enables you to plan a simple programme of activities to keep the child entertained and occupied.
- It enables another family member or colleague to assist in the general care, allowing you to take a break.

Meeting physical needs

Bed rest

Children usually dislike being confined to bed and will only stay there if they are feeling very unwell. There is no need to keep a child with a fever in bed; take your lead from the child. Making a bed on a sofa in the main living room will save carers the expense of extra heating and tiring trips up and down the stairs. The child will also feel more included in family life and less isolated. The room does not have to be particularly hot – just a comfortable temperature for you. If the child does stay in bed in his or her own room, remember to visit often so that he or she does not feel neglected.

Hygiene

All children benefit from having a routine to meet their hygiene needs, and this need not be altered drastically during illness.

Guidelines for good practice

Safety when caring for a child at home

✔ Keep all medicines safely locked away in a secure cupboard.

✔ Supervise the child at all times – watch out for any sudden changes in their condition.

✔ Be aware of any potential complications of the child's condition and look out for warning signs.

Guidelines for good practice

Caring for a child in bed

✔ Use cotton sheets – they are more comfortable for a child with a temperature.

✔ Change the sheets daily if possible – clean sheets feel better. Leave a box of tissues on a table next to the bed.

✔ If the child has bouts of vomiting, pillows should be protected and a container should be kept close to the bed. This should be emptied and rinsed with an antiseptic or disinfectant such as Savlon after use.

✔ Wet or soiled bed linen should be changed to prevent discomfort. Paper tissues that can be disposed of by sealing in disposal bags are useful for minor accidents.

✔ A plastic mattress cover is useful, as a sick child's behaviour may change and cause him or her to wet the bed.

Guidelines for good practice

A hygiene routine for a sick child

✔ The child's room should be well ventilated and uncluttered. Open a window to prevent stuffiness, but protect the child from draughts. Provide a potty to avoid trips to the lavatory.

✔ Protect the mattress with a rubber or plastic sheet.

✔ A daily bath or shower is important. During an acute phase of illness, this can be done in the form of a bed bath – an all-over wash in bed.

✔ Brush hair daily.

✔ Clean teeth after meals and apply Vaseline to sore, cracked lips.

✔ Keep the child's nails short and clean, and prevent scratching of any spots.

✔ Dress the child in cool, cotton clothing; put a jumper and socks or slippers over pyjamas if the child does not want to stay in bed the whole time.

Guidelines for good practice

Encouraging sick children to drink

✔ Provide a covered jug of fruit juice or water; any fluid is acceptable, according to the child's tastes – for example, milk, meaty drinks or soups.

✔ If the child has mumps, do not give fruit drinks because the acid causes pain to the tender parotid glands (these are the large salivary glands situated just in front of each ear).

✔ A sick toddler who has recently given up his or her bottle may regress. Allow the child to drink from a bottle until he or she is feeling better.

✔ Try using an interesting curly straw.

✔ Give the child an 'adult' glass to make him or her feel special.

✔ Try offering drinks in a tiny glass or an eggcup, which makes the quantities look smaller.

✔ Offer fresh fruit juices, such as pear, apple or mango; dilute them with fizzy water to make them more interesting, but avoid giving more than one fizzy drink a day. Vary the drinks as much as possible.

✔ If the child does not like milk, add a milkshake mix or ice cream.

Guidelines for good practice

Encouraging a sick child to eat

✔ Most children with a fever do not want to eat, so while you should offer food, you should never force a child to eat.

✔ Allow the child to choose his or her favourite foods.

✔ Give the child smaller meals, but more often than you would normally.

✔ If the child has a sore throat, give ice cream or an iced lolly made with fruit juice or yoghurt.

✔ If the child is feeling slightly sick, you could offer mashed potato for example.

✔ Offer snacks regularly and always keep the child company while he or she eats.

✔ Most children who are sick do not find ordinary food very appetising, but may be tempted to eat with 'soldiers' of fresh bread and butter, slices of fruit or their favourite yoghurt.

✔ Try to make food as attractive as possible. Do not put too much on the plate at once, and remember that sick children often cope better with foods that do not require too much chewing – for example, egg custard, milk pudding, thick soups, chicken and ice cream.

Temperature control

If the child has a fever, you will need to take his or her temperature regularly and use tepid sponging to reduce it (see p. 313).

Feeding a sick child and providing drinks

Children who are ill often have poor appetites – a few days without food will not harm the child, but, as a general rule, fluid intake should be increased.

Drinks should be offered at frequent intervals to prevent dehydration – the child will not necessarily request drinks.

Meeting children's intellectual, emotional and social needs

See moving on section on page for information on play and the sick child.

Dignity and respect

When caring for young children, it is important to preserve their dignity and to show respect. This can be achieved by:

- recognising each child as a unique individual whose best interests must be paramount, while considering their physical, psychological, social, cultural and spiritual needs, as well as those of their families
- listening to the child and providing a means for them to express their opinions and feelings – and using these to guide decisions about the way they are cared for
- promoting and protecting the individual rights of children in all settings where they receive care
- ensuring privacy and confidentiality at all times
- respecting the right of children, according to their age and understanding, to appropriate information about their care.

Observation and monitoring

Careful observations of the child's behaviour, and regular monitoring of the child's symptoms – body temperature, evidence of pain and drowsiness should be carried out and recorded on a timed chart. If the child's condition deteriorates, be prepared to call a doctor or an ambulance.

Guidelines for good practice

Giving medicines to children

Here is a list of essential points to bear in mind when medicines are prescribed for a child:

- ✔ Store all medicines out of reach of children and in childproof containers.
- ✔ Ask the doctor for as much information as possible about the medicines – for example, if there are likely to be side effects, or if certain foods should be avoided.
- ✔ Measure doses of medicine accurately, using a marked medicine spoon for liquid – teaspoons are not equivalent to a 5 ml spoon.
- ✔ Always follow instructions carefully.
- ✔ Most medicines for young children are made up in a sweetened syrup to make them more palatable.
- ✔ Remember that your attitude is important – if you show anxiety when giving medicine to a child, he or she will be anxious too.
- ✔ Store medicines at the correct temperature – for example, in the fridge or away from direct heat if that is the direction on the bottle.

- ✔ Make sure you understand the instructions for giving the medicine before leaving the chemist – for example, how much, how often and when; check whether it should be given before, with or after meals.
- ✔ Make sure that all the medicine is swallowed – this can be difficult with babies (see below, Giving medicines to a baby or young child).
- ✔ Throw away any leftover prescribed medicines on completion of treatment.
- ✔ If a child needs to take medicine contained in syrup regularly, remember to brush his or her teeth afterwards to prevent tooth decay.
- ✔ Never put medicines into a child's drink or food, as the child may not take it all.
- ✔ DO NOT give aspirin to any child under the age of 16 years, because of the risk of **Reye's syndrome**.
- ✔ Always obtain written consent from the child's parents before giving any medicines.

Reye's syndrome – A very rare condition that causes serious liver and brain damage. Many children who develop Reye's syndrome have previously taken the painkiller aspirin to treat their symptoms. It is recommended that no child under 16 years should be given aspirin.

Giving medicines and tablets to older children

Older children do not seem to mind taking medicine, and often want to pour it out for themselves. Always supervise children and make sure that they take the medicine exactly as prescribed. After giving any medicine to a child, write down the time and the dosage.

Guidelines for good practice

Giving oral medicines

✔ Most medicines for children are given as sweetened syrups or elixirs. They can be given with a spoon, tube or dropper.

✔ Wash your hands before giving any medicine.

✔ Always check the label on the bottle, and the instructions. If the medicine has been prescribed by the doctor, check that it is for your child and follow the instructions exactly – for example, some medicines have to be taken with or after food. Generally, oral medicines are best given before meals, as they enter the bloodstream quickly.

✔ Shake the bottle before measuring the dose. Always pour any medicine bottle with the label uppermost, so that the instructions remain legible if the medicine runs down the side of the bottle.

✔ Some medicines do not taste good – for example, iron preparations. Always be truthful when the child asks, 'Does it taste bad?' You could answer, 'The medicine does not taste good, but I will give you some juice as soon as you have swallowed it.'

✔ If the child is reluctant, you should be prepared to offer a treat for taking the medicine if necessary – for example, a favourite story or a chocolate. Never punish or threaten a child who refuses to take medicine.

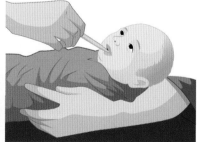

▲ **Figure 15.6** Giving medicines to a baby (a) by spoon (b) by dropper (c) by syringe

Guidelines for good practice

Giving medicines to a baby or young child

✔ If possible, get someone to help you in case the baby wriggles.

✔ Cradle the baby comfortably on your lap, in the crook of your arm, so that she is slightly raised, with the head tilted back. (Never lay a baby down flat while giving medicine, because of the risk of inhalation.)

✔ Put a bib on the baby and have some baby wipes or a flannel close at hand to wipe her clean.

✔ If you are on your own, wrap a blanket around the baby's arms so that you can stop her from wriggling.

✔ Only put a little of the medicine in the baby's mouth at a time.

✔ You can use a spoon, a dropper, a tube or a syringe to give medicine to a baby.

✔ Using a spoon – if the baby is very young, sterilise the spoon by boiling it or placing it in sterilising solution. Gently pull down the baby's chin if she will not open her mouth, or get someone else to do this. Place the spoon on the baby's lower lip, raise the angle of the spoon and let the liquid run into her mouth.

✔ Using a dropper – take up the required amount of medicine into the dropper. Place the dropper in the corner of the baby's mouth and release the medicine gently.

✔ Using a tube – Pour the required dose into the tube. Place the mouthpiece on the baby's lower lip and let the medicine run gently into her mouth.

✔ Using a syringe – Fix the special adapter to the bottle and withdraw the required dose. Place the end of the syringe in the child's mouth, pointing towards the cheek, and slowly squeeze in the dose.

How to give eye, ear and nose medication

Guidelines for good practice

Giving eye medication

An important part of the healing process after an eye operation or an injury to the eye is the administering of the prescribed eye drops and/or ointment. This is often a new experience for most children and their parents or carers, and the following guidelines may be useful.

Preparation

✔ A simple and honest explanation of what you are about to do, and perhaps a demonstration on the child's favourite doll or teddy, will help.

✔ It may be easier for you if the child lies flat, on a bed or settee, with his or her head tilted back.

✔ A baby or young child may wriggle and put his or her hands up to his or her face – try wrapping the baby in a blanket so that he or she feels secure and his/her arms are tucked out of the way.

✔ Try to distract the child afterwards. This will reinforce the idea that having eye drops is quick and easy, and there is nothing to be afraid of.

General directions

✔ Read the label on the bottle or tube for directions.

✔ Wash your hands.

✔ Position the child.

✔ Gently pull down the lower lid with one finger and squeeze one drop into the eye. If using ointment, squeeze about 1 cm of ointment into the lower surface of the inside of the lower eyelid.

✔ Try not to allow the end of the bottle or tube to touch the child's eye.

✔ Replace the top of the bottle or tube immediately after use.

✔ Discard the medicine once treatment is completed; otherwise use a fresh bottle or tube every four weeks.

✔ Do not save the medicine or use it for anyone else.

Guidelines for good practice

How to give ear drops

✔ The child should lie down on one side – on a bed or on your lap – with the affected ear uppermost. Place a pillow under the child's head to keep it steady and comfortable.

✔ Pull the pinna (the top of the outer ear) gently backwards towards the back of the head; this straightens out the ear canal.

✔ Hold the filled dropper just above the canal entrance. (Many eardrops are supplied in plastic bottles with pointed nozzles. If so, invert the bottle and squeeze gently.)

✔ Release the required number of eardrops into the ear.

✔ Gently massage the base of the ear to help disperse the liquid.

✔ Encourage the child to remain lying down in the same position for a few minutes.

✔ Put a piece of cotton wool loosely in the outer ear to prevent any leakage; do not pack it in too tightly, as it may cause harm and be difficult to remove.

✔ Eardrops can be warmed slightly to make them more comfortable; stand the bottle in warm (not hot) water for a few minutes.

Guidelines for good practice

How to give nose drops

To a baby

✔ Put the baby on a flat surface before you begin and get someone to help you, if possible.

✔ Tilt the baby's head backwards slightly and gently drop liquid into each nostril.

✔ Count the number of drops as you put them in; two or three drops are normally sufficient – any more will run down the throat and cause the baby to cough and splutter.

✔ Keep the baby lying flat for one or two minutes.

To an older child

✔ Ask the child to blow his or her nose and to lie down on a comfortable surface with his or her head tilted slightly backwards.

✔ Gently release the prescribed number of drops into each nostril. Encourage the child to stay lying down for one or two minutes.

✔ Do not let the dropper touch the child's nose – this will transfer the germs back to the bottle. If the dropper does touch the child, wash it thoroughly before replacing it in the bottle.

✔ Nose drops can be warmed slightly to make them more comfortable; stand the bottle in warm (not hot) water for a few minutes.

First aid for babies and children

Everyone who works with children should attend a first aid course. There are now specialist courses, such as the St John's **Early Years First Aid** (paediatric) and the British Red Cross's **Paediatric First Aid**.

Childminders must have attended a training course within six months of registration and must hold a current paediatric first aid certificate at the point of registration. It is useful and vital to learn how to respond to an emergency, and knowing how means that you could save a life one day. This chapter explains the major first aid techniques, but should not be used as a substitute for attending a first aid course with a trained instructor.

The role and responsibilities of the paediatric first aider

First aid is an important skill. By performing simple procedures and following certain guidelines, it may be possible to save lives by giving basic treatment until professional medical help arrives. Also remember that practice makes perfect. If you have memorised some of the most basic procedures – and, more importantly, practised them – you will be able to react quickly and efficiently.

The key aims of first aid can be summarised in three key points:

1 **Preserve life**: the overriding aim of all medical care, including first aid, is to save lives.

2 **Prevent further harm**: this is also sometimes called **prevent the condition from worsening**. It covers both external factors – such as moving a patient away from any cause of harm – and applying first aid techniques to prevent worsening of the condition, such as applying pressure to stop a bleed from becoming dangerous.

3 **Promote recovery**: first aid also involves trying to start the recovery process from the illness or injury, and in some cases might involve completing a treatment, such as in the case of applying a plaster to a small wound.

Each emergency situation is unique, but the aims of first aid remain the same. Your responsibilities are to:

● assess the emergency situation
● maintain your own safety
● contact the emergency services
● give accurate and useful information to the emergency services
● support the casualty physically and emotionally
● appreciate your own limitations
● know when to intervene and when to wait for more specialist help to arrive.

Guidelines for good practice

Basic hygienic measures in first aid

✔ Wash your hands with soap and water before and immediately after giving first aid. If gloves are available for use in first aid situations, you should also wash your hands well before putting them on and after disposing of them. (Plastic bags can be used when gloves are unavailable.)

✔ Avoid contact with body fluids when possible. Do not touch objects that may be soiled with blood or other body fluids.

✔ Be careful not to prick yourself with broken glass or any sharp objects found on or near the injured person.

✔ Prevent injuries when using, handling, cleaning or disposing of sharp instruments or devices.

✔ Cover cuts or other skin breaks with dry and clean dressings.

✔ Chronic skin conditions may cause open sores on hands. People with these conditions should avoid direct contact with any injured person who is bleeding or has open wounds.

How to minimise the risk of infection to self and others

First aid equipment

All first aid boxes should have a white cross on a green background.

The Health and Safety Executive advises:

There is no mandatory list of items to put in a first-aid box. It depends on what you assess your needs to be. As a guide, where work activities involve low-level hazards, a minimum stock of first-aid items would be:

- a leaflet giving general guidance on first aid (e.g. HSE's leaflet Basic advice on first aid at work…);
- individually wrapped sterile plasters (of assorted sizes), appropriate to the type of work (you can provide hypoallergenic plasters if necessary);
- sterile eye pads;
- individually wrapped triangular bandages, preferably sterile;
- safety pins;
- large, individually wrapped, sterile, unmedicated wound dressings;
- medium-sized, individually wrapped, sterile, unmedicated wound dressings;
- disposable gloves (you can find more advice at www.hse.gov.uk/skin/employ/gloves.htm).

This is a suggested contents list only. The contents of any first-aid kit should reflect the outcome of your first-aid needs assessment. It is recommended that you don't keep tablets and medicines in the first-aid box. (HSE, http://www.hse.gov.uk/)

Large nurseries and schools may have more than one first aid box and the contents will vary according to individual needs; for example, a nursery setting will have a larger number of small adhesive dressings or plasters.

- The first aid box must be a strong container that keeps out both dirt and damp.
- It should be kept in an accessible place, but one that is out of reach of children.
- All employees should be informed where the first aid box is kept and it should only be moved from this safe place when in use.
- Supplies must be replaced as soon as possible after use.
- It is recommended that you do not keep tablets and medicines in the first aid box.

Accident reports and incident records

Chapter 14 describes the recording and reporting procedures of accidents in early years settings (see p. 304). If a pupil is injured while at school the staff are obliged by law to record the injury in the **pupil accident book**. An accident record must be completed immediately following an incident providing as much information as possible.

For many incidents it is only necessary to complete an accident record but in some circumstances the Reporting of Injuries, Diseases and Dangerous Occurrences Regulations 1995 (RIDDOR) requires you to report an incident to the Health & Safety Executive.

Definition of an infant and a child for the purposes of first aid treatment

- An infant is under one year old
- A child is aged from one year to puberty

Reflecting on practice

Accident and incident reporting

Find out about policies and procedures relating to first aid in your work setting. In particular, find out the following:

- Where is the first aid kit kept, and is it easy to reach quickly?
- Who is responsible for replenishing the first aid box?
- Where is the accident report book kept?
- In what circumstances do you have to report an incident or accident at your work setting to the Health and Safety Executive?

How to assess an emergency situation and act safely and effectively

Safety first: At the scene of any accident, your first thought should always be safety, both for yourself and the victim. There is already one casualty, do not make yourself another.

Firstly look around and **survey the scene**: Is it safe? Look for any potential hazards; these could be anything that puts either of you at risk, from falling objects and running engines to oncoming traffic. Only when you are sure it is safe should you take action and begin to carry out first aid.

The primary survey

If you happen to come across a casualty, you will need to **assess the situation** before doing anything else.

It can be useful to remember **DR ABC**, which stands for Danger, Response, Airway, Breathing and Circulation.

When and how to call for help

1 **Assess the situation**: stay calm and do not panic.
2 **Minimise any danger to yourself and to others:** for example, make sure someone takes charge of other children at the scene.
3 **Send for help**. Notify a doctor, hospital, parents etc. as appropriate. If in any doubt, call an ambulance: dial 999. Be ready to assist the emergency services by providing the following information:
   - your name and the telephone number you are calling from
   - the location of the accident. You should know the address of the setting, and if on an outing, try to give as much information as possible, e.g. street names, familiar landmarks such as churches or pubs nearby
   - explain briefly what has happened: this helps the paramedics to act speedily when they arrive
   - tell them what you have done so far to treat the casualty.

First aid for an infant and a child who is unresponsive and breathing normally

A child's heart and/or breathing can stop as a result of lack of oxygen (e.g. choking), drowning, electric shock, heart attack or other serious injury. If an infant or child has collapsed you need first to find out if he/she is conscious or unconscious.

1 Can you get a response? Check if **conscious**.
   - *For an infant:* call their name and try tapping them gently on the sole of their foot.
   - *For a child:* call their name and try tapping them gently on their shoulders.

2 If there is no response you need to **check for breathing**.
   For both *infants and children*:
   - **Open the airway:** place one hand on the forehead and *gently* tilt the head back. Then using your other hand lift the child's chin. Take a quick look and remove any *visible* obstructions from the mouth and nose.

D	Danger	Firstly - ensure that neither you nor the casualty is in any danger. Make the situation safe and *then* assess the casualty.
R	Response	If the casualty appears unconscious, check this by shouting: *'Can you hear me?' 'Open your eyes,'* while gently tapping their shoulders. (See below for how to check for a response in infants and children.)
		If there is a **response**: if there is no further danger, leave the casualty in the position found and call for/get help if needed. Treat any condition found and monitor vital signs - level of response, pulse and breathing. Continue monitoring the casualty either until help arrives or he/she recovers.
		If there is **no response**: shout for **help**. If possible, leave the casualty in the position found and open the airway. If this is not possible, turn the casualty onto their back and open the airway.
		Check for other life-threatening conditions such as severe bleeding and treat as necessary.
A	Airway	**Open the airway** by placing one hand on the casualty's forehead and gently tilting the head back. Then lift the chin using 2 fingers only. This will move the casualty's tongue away from the back of the mouth.
B	Breathing	Look, listen and feel for **no more** than 10 seconds to see if the casualty is breathing normally. Look to see if the chest is rising and falling. Listen for breathing. Feel for breath against your cheek.
		If the casualty is **breathing normally**, place them in the **recovery position**.
C	Circulation	If the casualty is **not breathing normally** or if you have any doubt whether breathing is normal begin **CPR (Cardio-pulmonary Resuscitation)**
		Check for other life-threatening conditions such as severe bleeding and treat as necessary.

- **Look, listen and feel** for normal breathing: Place your face next to the child's face and listen for breathing. You can do this while looking along the child's chest and abdomen for any movement. You may also be able to feel the child's breath on your cheek. Allow up to 10 seconds to check if the child is breathing or not.

- If the infant or child is unconscious but breathing normally, place him or her into **the recovery position** – see below.

The recovery position

If a child is unconscious this means that they have no muscle control; if lying on their back, their tongue is floppy and may fall back, partially obstructing the airway. Any child who is breathing and who has a pulse should be placed in the recovery position while you wait for medical assistance. This safe position allows fluid and vomit to drain out of the child's mouth so that they are not inhaled into the lungs.

Recovery position for an infant (from birth to one year approx.)

Cradle the infant in your arms, with his head tilted downwards to prevent him from choking on his tongue or inhaling vomit.

Recovery position for a child (from one year onwards)

1. Place arm nearest to you at a right angle, with palm facing up.
2. Move other arm towards you, keeping the back of their hand against their cheek.
3. Get hold of the knee furthest from you and pull up until foot is flat on the floor.
4. Pull the knee towards you, keeping the child's hand pressed against their cheek.

Think about ideas

The recovery position

In pairs, practise placing each other in the recovery position you would use for a child.

5. Position the leg at a right angle.
6. Make sure that the airway remains open by tilting the head back, then check breathing by feeling and listening for breath.

Continuous assessment and monitoring of an infant and a child while in your care

Remember your **ABC** and continue to monitor the infant or child in your care until you can hand over to a doctor or paramedic.

- **A is for AIRWAY:** check that the airway remains open. Always monitor a child while in recovery position.

- **B is for BREATHING:** check that breathing is normal and regular.

- **C is for CIRCULATION:** check the pulse (*if you are trained and experienced*) **but ensure you take no more than 10 seconds to do this:**

  - *In a child over 1 year*: feel for the carotid pulse in the neck by placing your fingers in the groove between the Adam's apple and the large muscle running from the side of the neck.

  - *In an infant*: feel for the brachial pulse on the inner aspect of the upper arm by lightly pressing your fingers towards the bone on the inside of the upper arm and hold them there for five seconds.

Remember: try to use your second and third fingers when taking a pulse. This is because both your first finger and your thumb have a pulse that can be confused with the casualty's pulse.

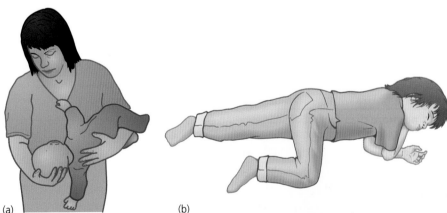

(a)   (b)

◀ Figure 15.7 (a) The recovery position for an infant (b) The recovery position for a child

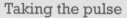

Think about ideas

Taking the pulse

In pairs, practise taking each other's pulse – both the *radial* pulse (at the wrist) and the *carotid* pulse (in the neck).

First aid for an infant and a child who is unresponsive and not breathing normally

An infant or child who is unresponsive and not breathing normally will need to be given CPR. CPR is a combination of rescue breaths and chest compressions. This keeps the vital organs alive until the ambulance service arrives and starts advanced life support.

Send for help: if you have carried out the checks above and the child is not breathing normally, if you have someone with you, send them to **dial 999** for an ambulance immediately. If you are alone, give one minute of CPR - *then* call an ambulance. If the casualty is under one year, take the infant with you to call an ambulance.

CPR: Resuscitation for a infant who is not breathing (from birth to one year)

1 **Open the airway** by gently tilting the infant's head back and lifting the chin

2 Give FIVE **rescue breaths** by placing your mouth over their **mouth and nose,** and blow gently for about one second, until you see the chest rise.

3 Place two fingers on the centre of the infant's chest, and give 30 **chest compressions** by pressing down about a third of the depth.

4 Then give TWO rescue breaths, followed by 30 chest compressions.

5 Continue this cycle of breaths and compressions for one minute.

If not already done, **call for an ambulance** now and continue the above cycle until help arrives or the infant starts to breathe.

CPR: Resuscitation for a child who is not breathing (from one year onwards)

1 **Open the airway** by gently tilting the child's head back and lifting the chin

2 Pinch the child's nose. Give FIVE **rescue breaths** by placing your mouth over their mouth and blow steadily until you see the chest rise.

3 Place one hand on the centre of the child's chest and lean over the child. Give 30 **chest compressions** by pressing down about a third of the depth of the chest.

4 Then give TWO rescue breaths, followed by 30 chest compressions.

5 Continue this cycle of breaths and compressions for one minute.

If not already done, **call for an ambulance** now and continue the above cycle until help arrives or the child starts to breathe.

When to administer CPR

CPR should only be carried out when an infant or child is unresponsive and not breathing normally.

If the infant or child has any signs of normal breathing, or coughing, or movement, **DO NOT** begin to do chest compressions. Doing so may cause the heart to stop beating.

How to administer CPR using an infant and a child manikin

The techniques of giving CPR should never be practised on a child. Infant and child manikins are designed to give a very close experience to the 'real thing' and should always be used to practise on.

How to deal with an infant and a child who is experiencing a seizure

A seizure is caused by a sudden burst of excess electrical activity in the brain, causing a temporary disruption in the normal message passing between brain cells. This results in the brain's messages becoming temporarily halted or mixed up. Seizures can happen at any time and generally last a matter of seconds or minutes, after which the brain usually returns to normal. Seizures are also called **convulsions** or **fits**.

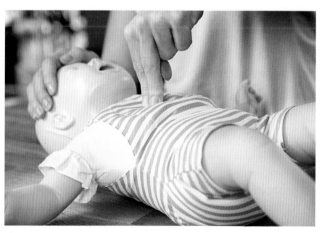

▲ **Figure 15.8** An infant resuscitation manikin

The most common causes of seizures in young children are high fever (known as a **febrile convulsion** or seizure), epilepsy, head injury and poisoning.

What happens during an epileptic seizure

The child:

- suddenly falls unconscious, often with a cry (caused by a tightening of the voice muscles)
- becomes stiff, often arching the back
- may stop breathing and the lips go blue
- begins convulsive movements: the limbs make rhythmic jerks, the jaw may be clenched and the breathing noisy
- may show saliva (frothing) at the mouth
- may lose bladder or bowel control.

Then the muscles relax and breathing becomes normal. Usually, in just a few minutes the child regains consciousness and may fall into a deep sleep or appear dazed. The child will not remember anything about the seizure when they come round and will need time to recover. Recovery time varies from minutes for some children to hours for others.

What to do if a child has a seizure

- Protect the child from injury by moving any furniture or other solid objects out of the way during a seizure.
- Make space around the child and keep other children away.
- Loosen the clothing around the child's neck and chest and cushion their head.
- Stay with the child until recovery is complete.
- Be calmly reassuring.

DO NOT:

- Restrain the child in any way.
- Try to put anything in their mouth.
- Try to move them unless they are in danger.
- Give the child anything to eat or drink until they are fully recovered.
- Attempt to bring them round.

Call an ambulance only if:

- It is the child's first seizure and you do not know why it happened.
- It follows a blow to the head.
- The child is injured during the seizure.
- The seizure is continuous and shows no sign of stopping – this could be a very rare condition called status epilepticus, where epileptic fits follow one another without recovery of consciousness between them.

Choking: first aid for a child who has a foreign body airway obstruction

What is choking?

Choking is when a child struggles to breathe because of a blockage in the airway.

Children under three years are particularly vulnerable to choking because their airways are small and they have not yet developed full control of the muscles of their mouth and throat.

What causes it?

Usually, choking in small children is caused when a small foreign object is blocking one of the major airways. This may be a small toy they have put in their mouth and inadvertently 'swallowed', or a small piece of food they have not chewed properly.

Symptoms

Choking often begins with small coughs or gasps as the child tries to draw in breath around the obstruction or clear it out. This may be followed by a struggling sound or squeaking whispers as the child tries to communicate their distress. The child may thrash around and drool and their eyes may water. They may flush red and then turn blue. However, if a small item gets stuck in a infant or toddler's throat, you may not even *hear* them choking – they could be silently suffocating as the object fills their airway and prevents them from coughing or breathing.

The difference between a mild and a severe airway obstruction

If the blockage of the area airway is mild, the child should be able to clear it; if it is severe they will be unable to speak, cough, or breathe, and will eventually lose consciousness. You need to act promptly if there is any difficulty with breathing.

If a child is choking, ACT QUICKLY!

1 First check inside the child's mouth: if the obstruction is visible, try to hook it out with your finger, but do not risk pushing it further down. *If this does not work ...*
   - *For a baby:* lay the baby face down along your forearm, supporting her head and neck with your hand. The baby's head should be lower than her bottom.
   - *For an older baby or toddler:* sit down and put the child face down across your knees with head and arms hanging down. Keep the child's head lower than the chest.

KEY TERM

Febrile convulsions – are seizures (fits or convulsions) occurring in children aged 6 months to 5 years, associated with fever without another underlying cause.

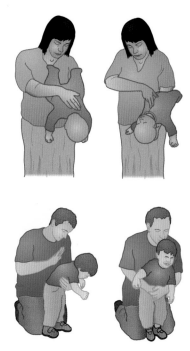

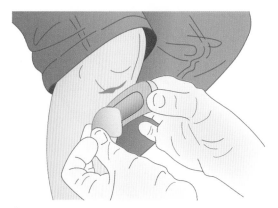

◀ **Figure 15.9** How to treat an infant or child who is choking

2 Give five back blows between the shoulder blades with the heel of your hand.

3 Turn the child over, check the mouth again and remove any visible obstruction.

4 Check for breathing.

5 If the child is not breathing, give five 'rescue breaths' (see ABC of resuscitation).

6 If the airway is still obstructed, give five chest compressions.

7 If the child is still not breathing, repeat the cycle of back slaps, mouth-to-mouth breathing and chest compressions.

8 After two cycles, if the child is not breathing, dial 999 for an ambulance.

(*Never* hold a baby upside down by the ankles and slap its back – you could break the baby's neck.)

The procedure to be followed after administering the treatment for choking

The child may experience difficulties after having treatment for choking – for example, a persistent cough or difficulties with swallowing or breathing. It is important to monitor and assess the child's condition and to seek medical help if the problem persists.

First aid for bleeding and wounds

In most cases bleeding stops quickly. However, if it is severe, you may need to control it to prevent **shock**.

The types and severity of bleeding and its effect

Even tiny amounts of blood can seem like a lot to a child. Any bleeding may frighten children because they are too young to realise that the blood loss will stop when clotting occurs. When a child loses a large amount of blood, he or she may suffer shock or even become unconscious.

Bleeding: cuts, grazes and nosebleeds

Even tiny amounts of blood can seem like a lot to a child. Any bleeding may frighten children because they are too young to realise that the blood loss will stop when clotting occurs. When a child loses a large amount of blood, he or she may suffer shock or even become unconscious.

Minor cuts and grazes:

1 Sit or lie the child down and reassure them.

2 Clean the injured area with cold water, using cotton wool or gauze.

▲ **Figure 15.10** Treating a graze

3   Apply a dressing if necessary.

4   Do not attempt to pick out pieces of gravel or grit from a graze. Just clean gently and cover with a light dressing.

5   Record the injury and treatment in the accident report book and make sure the parents/carers of the child are informed.

Nosebleeds

Bleeding from the nose usually occurs when tiny blood vessels inside the nostrils are ruptured, either by a blow to the nose, or as a result of sneezing, picking or blowing the nose.

1   Sit the child down with her head well forward.

2   Ask her to breathe through her mouth.

3   Pinch the fleshy part of her nose, just below the bridge.

4   Reassure her and tell her not to try to speak, cough or sniff as this may disturb blood clots.

5   After 10 minutes, release the pressure. If the nose is still bleeding, reapply the pressure for further periods of 10 minutes.

6   If the nosebleed persists beyond 30 minutes, seek medical aid.

Severe bleeding

When a child is bleeding severely, your main aim is to stem the flow of blood. If you have disposable gloves available, use them. It is important to reduce the risk of cross-infection.

1   **Summon medical help** - Dial 999 or call a doctor.

2   **Try to stop the bleeding**:
   ● **Apply direct pressure to the wound**: wear gloves and use a dressing or a non-fluffy material, such as a clean tea towel.

▲ **Figure 15.11** Treating a nosebleed

▲ **Figure 15.12** Treating severe bleeding

   ● **Elevate the affected part if possible**: if the wound is on an arm or leg raise the injured limb above the level of the heart.

3   **Apply a dressing**: If the blood soaks through, **DO NOT** remove the dressing, apply another on top and so on.

4   Keep the child warm and reassure them.

5   **DO NOT** give anything to eat or drink.

6   Contact the child's parents or carers.

If the child loses consciousness, follow the ABC procedure for resuscitation.

Always record the incident and the treatment given in the accident report book. Always wear disposable gloves if in an early years setting to prevent cross-infection.

Objects in wounds

Where possible, swab or wash small objects out of the wound with clean water.

If there is a large object embedded:

● Leave it in place.

● Apply firm pressure on either side of the object.

● Raise and support the wounded limb or part.

● Lay the casualty down to treat for shock.

● Gently cover the wound and object with a sterile dressing.

● Build up padding around the object until the padding is higher than the object, then bandage over the object without pressing on it.

If you suspect there may be something embedded in the wound, make sure you do not press on the object. Instead press firmly on either side of the object and build up padding around it before bandaging to avoid putting pressure on the object itself.

▲ **Figure 15.13** Treating a minor burn or scald

Minor burns and scalds

Burns occur when the skin is exposed to direct heat or to chemicals; for example, fire sunburn, friction, acid, bleach or garden chemicals. **Scalds** occur when the skin is exposed to hot fluids, for example boiling water, steam or hot fat.

1 **Cool down the area** by running it under cool water for at least ten minutes or until the pain eases – or soak in cold water for ten minutes. This will prevent the burn from getting worse.

2 Gently remove any constricting articles from the injured area before it begins to swell.

3 **Lightly cover the burned area** with a sterile dressing – or you can use cling film, a clean plastic bag or cold, wet cloth (but not wrapping). This will help to protect the sore skin from further irritation and infection.

4 Stay calm and watch for any **signs of shock**. If the child loses consciousness, open the airway, check her breathing and be prepared to begin rescue breaths.

DO NOT:

● use adhesive dressings

● apply lotions, ointments or grease to burn or scald

● break blisters or otherwise interfere.

Head injuries

Bruised or bumped heads are quite common in children. The recommended first aid for any head injury is to apply an ice pack to the affected area for ten minutes. First-aiders should be watchful for any deterioration in symptoms, such as mild headache, feeling sick and mild dizziness, and should seek medical help urgently if any of these symptoms occur. Children often bump their heads without further

consequences but parents should always be informed about head bumps so that they can look out for signs that the injury could be more serious. Most settings have a special 'head bump' letter that is sent out to parents following a head injury, however minor it seems. This letter advises parents how to observe the child for 48 hours following the injury, and what action to take if the child's condition deteriorates. Some settings also put a 'head bump sticker' on the child to alert other members of staff to the problem.

Sprains and strains

Follow the **RICE** procedure:

● **R** – **rest** the injured part

● **I** – apply **ice** or a cold compress

● **C** – **compress** the injury

● **E** – **elevate** the injured part.

1 Rest, steady and support the injured part in the most comfortable position for the child.

2 Cool the area by applying an ice pack or a cold compress. (This could be a pack of frozen peas wrapped in cloth.)

3 Apply gentle, even pressure by surrounding the area with a thick layer of foam or cotton wool, secured with a bandage.

4 Raise and support the injured limb, to reduce blood flow to the injury and to minimise bruising.

First aid for an infant and a child who is suffering from shock

Shock is a life-threatening condition that occurs when vital organs do not get enough oxygen due to reduced blood circulation. The most common cause of shock is severe blood loss, but it can also be caused by loss of other body fluids as in the case of severe

▲ **Figure 15.14** Elevate and apply a cold compress

burns or dehydration caused by prolonged vomiting and diarrhoea. When treating someone for shock it is important to remember that there could be internal bleeding following an injury.

Early signs and symptoms of shock in an infant and a child

After an initial adrenaline rush, the body withdraws blood from the skin in order to maintain the vital organs – and the oxygen supply to the brain drops. The infant and child will have:

- pale, cold, clammy skin that is often grey-blue in colour, especially around the lips
- a rapid pulse, becoming weaker
- shallow, fast breathing.

Symptoms as shock progresses

In an infant:

The anterior fontanelle is drawn in (depressed).

Both an infant and a child may show:

- unusual restlessness, yawning and gasping for air
- thirst
- loss of consciousness.

Treating shock

For both an infant and a child:

- If possible, ask someone else to **call an ambulance** while you stay with the child. Lay the child down, keeping her head low to improve the blood supply to the brain. Treat any obvious cause, such as severe bleeding.
- **Raise the child's legs** and support them with pillows or on a cushion rested on a pile of books, for example.
- **Loosen any tight clothing** at the neck, chest and waist to help with the child's breathing. For an infant: hold the infant on your lap while you loosen her clothing and offer comfort and reassurance.
- **Cover the child with a blanket or coat to keep her warm**. Never use a hot-water bottle or any other direct source of heat.
- **Reassure the child**: keep talking to her and monitoring her condition while you wait for the ambulance. If the infant or child loses consciousness, open her airway, check her breathing and be prepared to give rescue breaths.

- **Do not give the child anything to eat or drink**: if she complains of thirst, just moisten her lips with water.

How to recognise and manage an infant and a child who is suffering from anaphylactic shock

Anaphylactic shock is a severe and life-threatening allergic reaction that may occur following an insect sting or after eating certain foods, such as peanuts. The reaction can be rapid, developing within seconds or minutes of contact with the 'trigger'. Triggers include:

- nuts, peanuts
- shellfish
- eggs
- wasp and bee stings
- certain medications.

During an anaphylactic reaction, chemicals are released into the blood that widen (dilate) blood vessels and cause blood pressure to fall. Air passages then narrow (constrict), resulting in breathing difficulties. In addition, the tongue and throat can swell, obstructing the airway. An infant or child with anaphylactic shock will need urgent medical help as this can be fatal.

The following **signs and symptoms** may come all at once and the child may rapidly lose consciousness:

- high-pitched wheezing sound
- blotchy, itchy, raised rash
- swollen eyelids, lips and tongue
- difficulty speaking, then difficulty breathing
- abdominal pain, vomiting and diarrhoea.

If you suspect an infant or child is suffering from anaphylactic shock follow the steps below:

1 **Call an ambulance**. If the child has had a reaction previously, she will have medication to take in case of more attacks. This should be given as soon as the attack starts, following the instructions closely.

2 **Help the child into a comfortable sitting position** to relieve any breathing problems and loosen any tight clothing at her neck and waist. Comfort and reassure her while you wait for the ambulance.

3 **If the child loses consciousness**, open her airway, check her breathing and be prepared to start rescue breaths.

Recording and reporting accidents, incidents and illness

The accident report book

Every workplace is, by law, required to have an accident report book and to maintain a record of accidents. The accident report book must be:

- kept safely and accessibly
- accessible to all staff and volunteers, who know how to complete it
- reviewed at least half termly to identify any potential or actual hazards.

Information recorded includes:

- name of person injured
- date and time of injury
- where the accident happened (for example, in the garden)
- what exactly happened (for example, Kara fell on the path and grazed her left knee)
- what injuries occurred (for example, a graze)
- what treatment was given (for example, graze was bathed and an adhesive dressing applied)
- name and signature of person dealing with the accident
- signature of witness to the report
- signature of parent or carer.

One copy of the duplicated report form is given to the child's parent or carer; the other copy is kept in the accident report book at the early years setting.

Reporting accidents and incidents

Under the EYFS Safeguarding and Welfare Requirements: Safeguarding and Promoting Children's Welfare, Ofsted must be notified of:

- any food poisoning affecting two or more children looked after on the premises, and
- any injury requiring treatment by a general practitioner or hospital doctor, or
- the death of a child or adult as soon as possible or at least within 14 days of the incident occurring.

Local child protection agencies are informed of any serious accident or injury to, or the death of, any child while in the setting's care and they must act on any advice given by those agencies.

When there is any injury requiring general practitioner or hospital treatment to a child, parent, volunteer or visitor or where there is a death of a child or adult on the premises, a report is made to the Health and Safety Executive using the format for the Reporting of Injuries, Diseases and Dangerous Occurrences.

Reporting to the Health and Safety Executive

In compliance with RIDDOR, a report must be made to the HSE in the following circumstances:

- any accident to a member of staff requiring treatment by a general practitioner or hospital; and
- any dangerous occurrences. This may be an event that causes injury or fatalities or an event that does not cause an accident but could have done, such as a gas leak.

Any dangerous occurrence is recorded in the setting's incident book.

Reportable incident record

Incidents to be recorded include:

- break in, burglary, theft of personal or the setting's property
- an intruder gaining unauthorised access to the premises
- fire, flood, gas leak or electrical failure
- attack on member of staff or parent on the premises or nearby
- any racist incident involving staff or family on the centre's premises
- death of a child
- a terrorist attack, or threat of one.

In the incident book the following data is recorded:

- the date and time of the incident
- nature of the event
- who was affected
- what was done about it or if it was reported to the police, and if so a crime number.

Any follow up, or insurance claim made, is also recorded.

Forms relating to health and safety in early years settings

The following forms are required to be kept for each child in all early years settings. They are to be completed when necessary and kept in the child's confidential file. It is your responsibility to find out where the forms are kept and to record relevant information.

- **Accident form**: a form to record any accident or injury to a child while in the care of the setting – whether on the premises on an outing. When completed a copy is given to parents and the original stored in the child's confidential file.

- **Treatment record form**: a short form to record details of any long-term treatment a child needs, e.g. asthma inhaler. Once completed a copy is given to parents and the original stored in the first aid box for reference. When no longer required, this is stored in the child's confidential file.

- **Medication record form**: a short form to record details of any short-term medicine a child needs, e.g. prescription or over-the-counter cough medicines. Once completed this is stored with the medicine for reference. When treatment has been completed this is stored in the child's confidential file.

- **Parent administered medication form**: a short form to record details of medicine administered prior to the child's arrival and whether they have had this medicine before (i.e. to ascertain the risk of allergic reaction).

- **Existing injury form**: a short form in which parents can record a recent injury sustained by their child for the setting information and for the setting to record similar information provided by school/pre-school with a copy being given to parents, e.g. a graze or bruise.

- **Register of attendance**: a file should be used to record arrival and departure times to the nearest five minutes (rather than the time the parents arrive and depart) and to be completed by a parent/carer or childminder.

Reporting to parents

All accidents, injuries or illnesses that occur to children in a group setting must be reported to the child's parents or primary carers. If the injury is minor (such as a bruise or a small graze to the knee), the nursery or school staff will inform parents when the child is collected at the end of the session; or they may send a notification slip home if someone else collects the child. The parents are notified about:

- the nature of the injury or illness
- any treatment or action taken
- the name of the person who carried out the treatment.

In the case of a major accident, illness or injury, the child's parents or primary carers must be notified as soon as possible. Parents need to know that staff members are dealing with the incident in a caring and professional manner, and they will need to be involved in any decisions regarding treatment.

Recording illness

Records of a child's illness should be kept so that the child's parents and doctor can be informed. As with the accident report book, these records should include:

- when the child first showed signs of illness
- the signs and symptoms
- any action taken – for example, taking the child's temperature
- progress of the illness since first noticing it – for example, are there any further symptoms?

Helping a child who becomes unwell

- Staff in schools and nurseries should offer support and reassurance to a child who may have to wait a while to be taken home.

- Any incident of vomiting or diarrhoea should be dealt with swiftly and sympathetically, to minimise the child's distress and to preserve his or her dignity.

- A member of staff should remain with the child at all times and keep him or her as comfortable as possible.

- All early years settings should have a written policy on when to exclude children for childhood infections.

Giving medicines in an early years setting

Children may have a condition that requires medication, yet still be well enough to attend nursery or school; examples include asthma, eczema and glue ear. Prescribed medicines and paracetamol may be given to these children only after the parent or carer's written consent is obtained. The consent should be on a form that includes the following details:

- the child's name
- the name of the medicine to be given
- the precise dose to be given
- the timing of each dose, or, if given irregularly, parents must detail the precise circumstances or symptoms that would mean the medicine should be given
- how it should be given – for example, oral medicine, eye drops, inhaler
- parent's name and signature.

Keeping medicines in an early years setting

- Keep medicines in a locked cupboard, except for inhalers, which must be easily available at all times.

- Make sure that each medicine is labelled for a particular child; always check the label for the child's name before giving it.
- Keep a written record of medicines given, including the child's name, the date and time, the medicine and dose, and any problems with giving it.

Preparing a child for a stay in hospital

Every year one in four children under five years old goes into hospital, and over two million children are seen in accident and emergency units. How a child reacts to a hospital visit depends on:

- their age
- the reason for hospitalisation
- the tests and treatment needed
- the ambience of the ward
- their personality
- their previous experience of hospitals
- the attitude and manner of the doctors, nurses and other staff
- the carer's own anxieties and perceived ability to cope with what is often a very stressful situation.

When a child has to be admitted to hospital, either for medical treatment or for a surgical operation, it is best, if possible, to prepare them in advance. Often, the experience is stressful for parents, particularly if they have their own negative childhood memories of hospitalisation. In the event, the majority of children do enjoy their hospital stay, but adverse reactions can be avoided in younger children by careful preparation and complete honesty in all information given.

How you can help

For many children the idea of going to hospital for the first time can be very frightening. They are likely to be worried about having to stay away from home, and may be very afraid of what will happen to them in hospital. Parents and carers can help children to avoid much of this distress, by:

- helping the child cope with the change in routine
- helping the child feel less frightened
- helping the child understand why they are going to hospital
- correcting any wrong ideas the child may have about hospital.

Many hospitals now have pre-admission units where children can go a few days before admission to be examined and to become familiar with the

---

Guidelines for good practice

Preparing a child for hospitalisation

- ✔ The best way to prepare a child is by giving them information – but not to overload them.
- ✔ If possible, arrange to visit the ward a few days before admission – most wards welcome such visits and are happy to talk with carers. (This helps to overcome fear of the unknown.)
- ✔ Encourage the child to talk about his or her feelings, so that you know how to help him or her.
- ✔ Always be honest – never say that something will not hurt if it might, and only tell the child that you will be there all the time if that is your plan.
- ✔ Keep explanations simple – reading a book about a child going to hospital may help allay fears.
- ✔ If the child is going to have an operation, explain that he or she will have a 'special hospital sleep' that will stop him or her from feeling any pain.
- ✔ Do not let the child see your own worry, as this will make him or her feel frightened.
- ✔ Play hospital games using toys, to help the child act out any fears.
- ✔ Try to be involved in the child's care as fully as possible.
- ✔ Take the child's favourite toy or 'comforter' as a link with home – the child could even help to pack his or her case.
- ✔ Tell the ward staff about the child's eating and sleeping patterns, for example, and about particular preferences or special words that may be used for the toilet.
- ✔ If the child is of school age, the hospital school will provide educational activities. Health play specialists, nursery nurses or teachers will provide play activities for younger children.

---

hospital environment. Common questions children in hospital ask are:

- Will I get better?
- What will the doctors and nurses do to me?
- Will I be blamed – or laughed at?
- Can I go home?

Activities that may help a child

There are many ways in which you can help a child prepare for a hospital stay. These include:

- drawing and painting: this can help the child to express feelings
- playing hospital games using teddies and toys help a child to act out feelings

- reading a book about going to hospital with the child and encouraging questions
- encouraging role-play – perhaps set up a children's ward play area. Children can take on the roles of nurse, doctor and patient and practise 'giving injections' and putting on bandages etc.
- listening to the child and be alert for any wrong ideas about hospital he or she may have.

If possible, arrange for children to visit a hospital. Some hospitals arrange visiting days for children, where they get a special guided tour and are allowed to touch some of the instruments. Children often feel safer and more in control if they have been to a place before.

The day before admission

Depending on the age of the child, you can involve them in packing the things they need to take with them:

- comfort blanket or special cuddly toy, if used – plus a spare if possible
- some toys and books. Children usually regress when they are feeling ill, so choose books and toys that are on the young side
- pyjamas or nightie; dressing gown and slippers; wash bag with their own toiletries
- photo of family
- favourite fruit drink.

What the hospital needs to know

Apart from general information – such as name, age and date of birth, on admission the nurse will also find out about any allergies and medication the child is taking. They also need to know about the child's normal routine and preferences:

- **Communication**: what is the child's level of understanding and language development? Does the child need a hearing aid or glasses?
- **Hygiene**: what is the child's usual routine for bathing, washing and cleaning teeth?
- **Rest and sleep**: what is the usual pattern of naps and bedtime sleep?
- **Food and drink**: if a baby, is the baby bottle-fed, breastfed or weaned? Are there any dietary restrictions? Can an older child feed him/herself?
- **Play**: does the child have any favourite toys or games? What sort of play does the child enjoy?
- **Comfort**: does the child have any comfort habits, e.g. thumb-sucking or holding a comfort object or teddy?
- **Toilet habits**: does the child wear nappies? How independent is the child in going to the toilet? What are the normal bowel movements?

The care plan

The nurse will work with the parents to write an individual care plan for their child, which will cover all the categories of need mentioned above. The role of the parents will be discussed and arrangement made for them to stay with their child, if possible. If the child is going to have an operation, a health play specialist will prepare them for the event and parents are encouraged to accompany them to the anaesthetic room and stay until they are asleep. When the operation is over, the parent is invited to collect their child from theatre with the ward nurse.

Isolation

Some conditions – for example, leukaemia – result in damage to the child's immune system, and hospital care in such cases may involve reverse barrier nursing. This technique provides the child with protection from infection that could be introduced by those people who have regular contact.

- A separate cubicle is used.
- Gowns and masks must be worn by any person who is in contact with the child.
- Gloves and theatre caps may be worn during certain procedures.
- Items such as toys and clothes cannot be freely taken in or out.

Children in isolation need a parent or carer to stay with them to an even greater extent than those on an open ward, because of the strain of loneliness or boredom. Parents, in turn, need support from friends and relatives, as they are having to cope with many stressful events: the anxiety over their child's illness and treatment; the unnaturalness of being confined with their child; and the lack of privacy because of the need for continuous observation by nursing staff. Some hospitals provide a parents' room where they can go to have a cup of tea and share problems with others in similar situations.

Think about ideas

Learning about hospital play

Invite a health play specialist or nursery nurse working in hospital to come and talk about their job.

Prepare a list of questions beforehand and collect as much information as you can about the needs of the child in hospital.

Chronic illness

A chronic illness tends to last a long time (in contrast to acute illness – that is, illness of sudden onset and of short duration). A child with a chronic illness shows little change in symptoms from day to day and may still be able – though possibly with some difficulty – to carry out normal daily activities. The disease process is continuous, with progressive deterioration, sometimes in spite of treatment. The child may experience an acute exacerbation (flare-up) of symptoms from time to time.

Some examples of chronic illness in children are:

- juvenile rheumatoid arthritis
- psoriasis – a skin disorder
- diabetes mellitus (Type 1)
- thalassaemia major – an inherited blood disorder
- chronic renal failure
- atopic eczema
- sickle-cell disorders (sickle-cell-anaemia).

Long-term illness may mean that the child's ability to exercise freedom of choice in daily activities is curtailed. Frequent periods of hospitalisation disrupt family and social life, and impose a strain on all members of the family; siblings may resent the extra attention given to the sick child, and the parents themselves may also need financial support. Social workers based at hospitals will give advice on any financial help or benefits they may be able to claim and can provide a counselling service. They may also be able to put parents in touch with a voluntary organisation for the parents of children with similar conditions. Most children's units in hospitals have a separate playroom, with trained staff who provide the sick child with an opportunity for a choice of play activities.

Cystic fibrosis

Cystic fibrosis (CF) is caused by a faulty recessive gene that must be inherited from both parents – the parents are carriers if they do not display any symptoms. In people with CF, the abnormal gene causes unusually sticky secretions of mucus that clog the airways, leading to chest infections. The gene also affects food digestion, leading to an inability to absorb nutrients from the intestines. Although CF is present from birth, the condition may not become apparent for many months or years. By the time it is detected, damage to the lungs may have begun already. Among West Europeans and white Americans, 1 child in 2,000 is born with CF and 1 person in 25 is a carrier of the faulty gene.

Features of CF

- failure to grow normally, due to malabsorption of nutrients (failure to thrive)
- a cough that gradually gets worse
- recurrent chest infections
- severe diarrhoea, with pale, foul-smelling faeces.

Children with CF have a higher concentration of salt in their sweat; therefore, for diagnosis, a sample of the child's sweat can be taken and analysed. Genetic tests will also be carried out. Recent research has succeeded in locating the gene that causes CF. This means that it is now possible to detect the carrier state, and also to test for CF before birth. Once CF is suspected in the young baby, simple laboratory tests will confirm or disprove the diagnosis. Early treatment can limit lung damage and can help to ensure that failure to thrive is averted.

Treatment and care

- Vitamin supplements and pancreatin (a replacement enzyme) will be prescribed for the child to take with meals – this helps in the proper digestion of food.
- A high-energy diet (a diet high in calories) will be recommended.
- Parents and carers will be shown how to give physiotherapy (postural drainage), to clear mucus or phlegm from the lungs.

Guidelines for good practice

Working with children who have CF

✔ Children with CF can join in with whatever other children are doing, but they have to remember to carry out their physiotherapy, enzymes and exercise programmes.

✔ The lungs of a child with CF must be kept clear to prevent infection. If appropriate, learn how to perform the necessary postural drainage and physiotherapy techniques. Always obtain permission from the child's parents or guardians before performing any of these techniques.

✔ Children with CF can eat a normal diet, but also need to take enzyme and vitamin supplements; they may also need salt tablets if they are undertaking strenuous exercise in hot weather.

✔ A child with CF may tire easily, but should be encouraged to take lots of exercise to keep healthy. Good exercises are running, swimming, cycling and skipping.

343

- Children with this condition are susceptible to lung infections, and antibiotic treatment is very important in protecting the lungs.
- There is no cure for CF, but due to earlier diagnosis and new methods of treatment, most people survive into adulthood.

Sickle-cell disorders

Sickle-cell disorder (SCD) is an inherited blood condition caused by abnormal **haemoglobin**. Under certain conditions, the red blood cells that contain the haemoglobin and are normally round become sickle- or crescent-shaped. They clump together and lodge in the smaller blood vessels, preventing normal blood flow and resulting in **anaemia** (a lack of haemoglobin).

In the UK, the disorder is most common in people of African or Caribbean descent, but may also occur in people from India, Pakistan, the Middle East and the East Mediterranean. It affects about 1 in 2,500 babies born each year.

Features

Children with a SCD can almost always attend a mainstream school, but are subject to crises that may involve the following:

- Pain – this is often severe, occurring in the arms, legs, back and stomach; it is due to the blockage of normal blood flow.
- Infection – these children are more susceptible to coughs, cold, sore throats, fever and other infectious diseases.
- Anaemia – most sufferers are anaemic; only if the anaemia is severe, however, will they also feel lethargic and ill.
- Jaundice – this may show as a yellow staining of the whites of the eyes.

Treatment and care

- Blood transfusions may be necessary.
- Infections should be treated promptly.
- Immunisation against all the normal childhood diseases is recommended.

KEY TERMS

Haemoglobin – A substance in red blood cells that combines with and carries oxygen around the body, and gives blood its red colour.
Anaemia – A condition in which the concentration of the oxygen – carrying pigment, haemoglobin in the blood is below normal.

Guidelines for good practice

Working with children who have an SCD

✔ Know how to recognise a crisis. If the child suddenly becomes unwell or complains of severe abdominal or chest pain, headache, neck stiffness or drowsiness, contact the parents without delay – the child needs urgent hospital treatment.

✔ Make sure the child is always warm and dry. Never let a child get chilled after PE or swimming.

✔ Make sure the child does not become dehydrated. Allow him or her to drink more often and much more than normal.

✔ Advise parents that the child should be fully immunised against infectious illnesses and ensure that any prescribed medicines – for example, vitamins and antibiotics – are given.

✔ Give support. The child may find it difficult to come to terms with his or her condition; make allowances when necessary.

✔ Talk to the parents to find out how the illness is affecting the child.

✔ Help with schoolwork. If badly anaemic, the child may find it difficult to concentrate, and regular visits to the GP or hospital may entail many days off school.

Diabetes mellitus

Diabetes mellitus is a condition in which the amount of glucose (sugar) in the blood is too high because the body is not able to use it properly. Normally, the amount of glucose in our blood is carefully controlled by the hormone insulin, which helps the glucose to enter the cells, where it is used as fuel by the body. Most children will have Type 1 diabetes, meaning they can no longer produce insulin because the cells in the pancreas that produce it have been destroyed – without insulin, the body cannot use glucose.

Signs and symptoms

- increased thirst
- breath smells of pear drops (acetone)
- frequent passing of urine – especially at night. Children who have previously been dry at night might start to wet the bed (enuresis); this is caused by the body trying to rid itself of excess glucose
- genital itching, sometimes leading to thrush – a yeast infection
- extreme tiredness and lack of energy
- loss of appetite

- blurred vision
- loss of weight: the amount of weight lost can be quite dramatic – up to 10 per cent of the child's total body weight can be lost in as little as two months. This is caused by the body breaking down protein and fat stores as an alternative source of energy.

Treatment and care

Diabetes cannot be cured, but it can be treated effectively. The aim of the treatment is to keep the blood glucose level close to the normal range, so it is neither too high (hyperglycaemia) nor too low (hypoglycaemia, also known as a hypo). Most children with diabetes will be treated by a combination of insulin and a balanced diet, with the recommendation of regular physical activity.

Insulin has to be injected – it is a protein that would be broken down in the stomach if it were swallowed like a medicine. The majority of children will take two injections of insulin each day – one before breakfast and one before the evening meal. They are unlikely to need to inject insulin at school, unless on a school trip. In most cases, the equipment will be an insulin 'pen' rather than a syringe. The child's parents or carers, or a diabetes specialist nurse can demonstrate the device used and discuss where the pen and insulin should be kept while the child is in school.

Hypoglycaemia

Hypoglycaemia is the most common complication in diabetes where there is not enough sugar in the blood – usually because of too much insulin. It must be treated promptly to avoid possible brain damage from prolonged low blood sugar levels. Hypoglycaemic attacks (or hypos) are especially likely to happen before meals. They can also happen as a result of:

- too much insulin
- not enough food to fuel an activity
- too little food at any stage of the day
- a missed meal or delayed meal or snack
- cold weather
- the child vomiting.

Recognising a hypo

Hypos happen quickly, but most children will have warning signs that will alert them, or people around them, to a hypo. Signs include:

- weakness or hunger
- confused or aggressive behaviour
- loss of concentration or coordination
- rapid, shallow breathing
- sweating

- dizziness
- glazed eyes and pallor (pale skin)
- headache
- trembling or shakiness.

How to manage a hypo

- Stay with the child – never leave the child alone or expect him to go and get his own food or drink.
- Sit the child down and reassure him or her.
- Give the child a sugary drink – for example, a fizzy, non-diet drink – or sweet food.
- If the child recovers quickly after a sweet drink or food, give some more and allow the child to rest.

Guidelines for good practice

Meeting the needs of a child with diabetes in an early years setting

✔ Children with diabetes should be treated in the same way as any other child. Diabetes is *not* an illness and children should be encouraged to take part in all the activities on offer and the daily routine.

✔ Make sure that all contact details are up-to-date including, for example, home contact numbers, GP, diabetic specialist nurse.

✔ Always contact the child's parents immediately if the child becomes unwell, and keep them informed of the child's progress.

✔ Ensure that there is always a supply of glucose tablets or sweet drinks in the setting.

✔ When on outings, take a supply of sweet drinks or glucose tablets with you.

✔ Allow the child to take glucose tablets or snacks when required – most children with diabetes carry glucose tablets with them.

✔ Make sure you and all other members of staff know how to recognise and deal promptly with a child who has a hypoglycaemic attack.

✔ Always stay with the child if he or she feels unwell, and allow privacy if blood glucose testing is necessary during the day.

✔ Observe the child carefully during any vigorous exercise, such as swimming or climbing.

✔ Be understanding if the child shows emotional or behaviour problems caused by the necessary restrictions to their routine.

✔ Inform the child's parents if you are planning an activity that might involve extra strains or excitement.

✔ Make sure that the child eats regularly and that cooks are consulted about the child's dietary needs.

- If the child does not recover quickly or becomes unconscious, call an ambulance immediately and place the child in the recovery position. Always inform the parents of any hypoglycaemic attack, so that adjustments can be made to the child's treatment.

Epilepsy

Epilepsy is a condition of the nervous system affecting 150,000 children in the UK. It is not a mental illness and cannot be 'caught'. A person with epilepsy experiences seizures or fits (see pp. 333-334).

The type of seizure a child has depends on which area of the brain is affected. Some seizures involve convulsions, or strange and confused behaviour; others, such as absences, may be harder to recognise. Some may be unnoticeable to everyone except the child experiencing the seizure.

Some very young children have convulsions when there is a sudden rise in their body temperature; this is called a febrile convulsion. This is not classified as epilepsy.

Causes

In most cases of epilepsy there is no known cause, but sometimes a structural abnormality of the brain

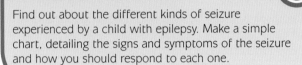

Think about ideas

Find out about the different kinds of seizure experienced by a child with epilepsy. Make a simple chart, detailing the signs and symptoms of the seizure and how you should respond to each one.

is found. In some children, individual attacks may be brought on by a trigger – for example, a flashing light; in others, the attacks have no trigger.

Treatment

The aim of medical treatment is to control the child's tendency to have seizures, so that he or she can get on with life with as little disruption as possible from epilepsy. Avoiding the things that may trigger seizures and taking anti-epileptic drugs are the main treatment methods. Different anti-epileptic drugs are best for different seizures, so each drug is selected according to the type of seizures that the child is experiencing. Although each drug has a slightly different way of acting, they all act on the brain to suppress seizures. They do not treat the underlying cause and do not 'cure' epilepsy.

See Chapter 14 for health and safety legislation which would also be useful to the study of this chapter.

Guidelines for good practice

Meeting the needs of a child with epilepsy in an early years setting

✔ Children with epilepsy should be treated in the same way as any other child. Epilepsy is *not* an illness and children should be encouraged to take part in all the activities on offer and the daily routine, unless otherwise advised by the child's parents or doctor.

✔ Teachers, early years practitioners and nursery managers should be aware of the child's individual needs and what is best for them should they have a seizure – for example:

  ✔ What kind of seizure does the child have?

  ✔ Are there any known triggers?

  ✔ How long does the seizure usually last?

  ✔ Does the child need to sleep after a seizure?

  ✔ Does the child need to go home?

  ✔ Is the child usually confused afterwards?

  ✔ Does the setting have a medical room where the child can recover before going back to class?

  ✔ Is there a school nurse to advise or help, if needed?

✔ Make sure that all contact details are up to date – for example, home contact numbers, and the number for GP.

✔ Record exactly what happened during a seizure; this will help in an initial diagnosis and also to build up a picture of the child's condition.

✔ Always contact the child's parents immediately if the child has a seizure, and keep them informed of the child's progress.

✔ Record any seizure in the appropriate record book.

✔ Make sure that you and all other members of staff know what to do when a child has a seizure.

✔ Try to minimise embarrassment for the child; if the child has been incontinent during the seizure, deal with it discreetly.

✔ Always stay with the child during a seizure and until he or she has recovered completely.

✔ Supervise activities such as swimming and climbing.

✔ Try to deal with seizures matter-of-factly. Your attitude will influence the attitude of other children towards the child with epilepsy.

Moving on

Play is an important part of recovery for a sick or convalescing (recovering) child. Children who are ill often regress and may want to play with toys that they have long since outgrown. While they are ill, children have a short attention span and tire quickly, so toys and materials should be changed frequently. You will need to be understanding and tolerant of these changes in behaviour. Never put pressure on a child to take part in an activity if they do not want to. If a child is ill for some time, you can achieve variation in toys and games by borrowing them from a local toy library.

Reflecting on practice

Activities which sick children might enjoy

Think about a child whom you have looked after while sick or recall a time as a child when you were sick, what kind of play activities might be attractive in this particular situation?

Select one or two play activities from the list below and plan in detail how you would present them to a child with a particular illness; say why you are presenting it in this way and how it meets the child's holistic needs.

Think about the practical details, for example; if the child wishes to draw or paint, or do some other messy activity, use protective sheets to protect the bed covers. Many activities are easier to manage if you supply a steady surface, such as a tray with legs or a special beanbag tray.

- Jigsaw puzzles: the child could start with simple puzzles and progress to more challenging ones, perhaps with family help.
- Board games, such as Lotto, Ludo and Halma.
- Card games, such as Uno, Snap and Happy Families.
- Making a scrapbook: provide magazines, photos, flowers, scissors and glue to make a personal record.
- Drawing and painting: provide poster paints, lining paper and a protective plastic apron; children also love to paint with water in 'magic' painting books.
- Play dough: either bought or homemade; playing with dough is creative and provides an outlet for feelings of frustration.
- Making models with Duplo® or Lego®.
- Playing with small world objects, such as toy farms, zoos and Playmobil®.
- French knitting or sewing cards can be used with older children.
- Crayons, felt tip pens and a pad of paper.
- Books to be read alone or with an adult.
- Audio CDs of songs, rhymes and favourite stories.
- Videos, cartoons, and computer games.
- Encourage other children and adults to visit once the child is over the infectious stage.

Further reading, weblinks and resources

Action for Sick Children

The UK's leading health charity, specially formed to ensure that sick children always receive the highest standard of care possible. Provides useful information for parents and professionals on all aspects of health care for children.
www.actionforsickchildren.org

Contact a Family

This website is for families who have a child who is disabled and those who work with children with disabilities or who are interested to find out more about their needs.
www.cafamily.org.uk

National Association of Health Play Staff

This organisation aims to promote the physical and mental well-being of children and young people who are patients in hospital, hospice or receiving medical care at home.
www.nahps.org.uk

Chapter 16

Diet, nutrition and food

This chapter describes the principles of a healthy diet for babies and young children. A balanced, healthy diet is particularly important for young children as early food experiences will influence their eating patterns and habits in their adult life. Young children need energy (in the form of calories from food) and nutrients such as protein, carbohydrate, vitamins and minerals to ensure healthy growth and development. Children have different nutritional needs from those of adults, and, as their bodies grow and develop, those needs change. Food and mealtimes can also provide valuable opportunities for learning, with activities such as cooking, shopping, helping to lay the table and eating out, or learning about different cultures.

The principles of a healthy diet

Good **nutrition** is important for young children because a healthy diet:

- ensures that they get enough energy (calories) and **nutrients** needed when they are growing rapidly, but not too much, which may lead to them becoming overweight or obese
- helps to improve their concentration, learning and behaviour, and builds up their strength
- promotes resistance to infection
- minimises future health risks such as iron-deficiency anaemia, obesity, Type 2 diabetes, heart disease, stroke, cancer and dental decay
- encourages them to eat a wide variety of foods and to develop good dietary habits to take with them into later childhood and adulthood.

A healthy diet for very young children should have:

- plenty of choice and balance
- lots of fruit and vegetables

- lots of starchy foods, bread, rice, potatoes, pasta
- calcium and iron-rich foods – milk and dairy, and other sources of protein, such as meat, fish, eggs, beans
- regular healthy meals and snacks
- low amounts of salt and added sugar.

Food and energy requirements

Food requirements vary according to age, gender, size, occupation or lifestyle, and climate. Different foods contain different amounts of energy per unit of weight; foods that contain a lot of fat and sugar have high-energy values. An excess of calories will result in weight gain, as the surplus 'energy' is stored as fat. An insufficient intake of calories will result in weight loss, as the body has to draw on fat reserves to meet energy requirements. Babies and young children have relatively high-energy requirements in relation to their size.

Food groups

Types of food can be arranged into five groups, based on the nutrients they provide. To ensure a balanced, healthy diet, some foods from each group should be included in a child's diet every day (see the Food groups table in the appendix). The easiest way to monitor our nutrition is to keep in mind the five food groups; eating a variety of foods from each of these food groups every day automatically balances our diet. The Eatwell plate (Figure 16.1) shows how much of what you eat should come from each food group.

KEY TERMS

Nutrition – The study of the food process in terms of the way that it is received and utilised by the body to promote healthy growth and development.
Nutrients – The essential components of food which provide the individual with the necessary requirements for bodily functions.

The eatwell plate

Use the eatwell plate to help you get the balance right. It shows how much of what you eat should come from each food group.

▲ **Figure 16.1** The Eatwell plate

The dangers of too much salt

Salt (sodium chloride) should be avoided as far as possible in the diets of young children, as their kidneys are not mature enough to cope with large amounts of salt. Be aware that many common foods, such as cheese, manufactured soups, packet meals and bread, are already quite high in added salt. Children will receive sufficient salt for their dietary needs from a normal balanced diet, without adding any salt to food as it is cooked or at the table.

On average children are eating twice the recommended amount of salt. The Recommended Nutrient Intake (RNI) for infants aged between one and three years is not more than 1.25 g of salt each day; children aged four to six years should consume no more than 1.75 g. A lot of manufactured foods are marketed at children, and some of these can exceed their daily salt requirement in a single serving, a bag of crisps for example. A small can (200 g) of pasta shapes in tomato sauce contains twice the daily RNI of salt for a child aged one to three years and a third more than the daily RNI for a child aged four to six years.

Dietary fibre

Dietary fibre – or roughage – is found in cereals, fruits and vegetables. Fibre is made up of the indigestible parts or compounds of plants, which pass relatively unchanged through the stomach and intestines. Fibre is needed to provide roughage to help keep the food moving through the gut. A small amount of fibre is important for health in pre-school children, but too much can cause problems, as their digestive system is still immature. It could also reduce energy intake by 'bulking up' the diet. Providing a mixture of white bread and refined cereals, white rice and pasta, as well as a few wholegrain varieties occasionally, helps to maintain a healthy balance between fibre and nutrient intakes.

Foods that contain fat and sugar

Young children under two years old need more energy from fat than older children and adults. The amount of saturated or 'bad' fat should be limited and some unsaturated fats – from vegetable oils and fish – should be provided. Cheap burgers, crisps, chips, biscuits, cakes and fried foods are all high in saturated fat. Meanwhile sugary food and drinks will lead to tooth decay. Sweet foods such as cakes,

Guidelines for good practice

Reducing salt in children's diets

✔ Cut down gradually on the amount of salt used in cooking, so that children become used to less salty foods.

✔ If preparing baby food at home, do not add salt, even if it tastes bland. Manufactured baby food is tightly regulated to limit the salt content to a trace.

✔ Try using a low-salt substitute, such as LoSalt, Solo or a supermarket's own brand low-sodium salt, in cooking or at the table. These products substitute up to 70 per cent of the sodium chloride with potassium chloride.

biscuits and sweets should be avoided wherever possible. Dried fruit can be provided but only during mealtimes.

Providing drinks for children

An adequate fluid intake will prevent dehydration and reduce the risk of constipation. The best drinks for young children are water and milk, and they are also the best drinks to give between meals and snacks, as they do not harm teeth when taken from a cup or beaker. You should offer children something to drink several times during the day.

Water is a very underrated drink for the whole family. It quenches thirst without spoiling the appetite; if bottled water is preferred, it should be still, not carbonated (fizzy), as this is acidic. More water should be given in hot weather in order to prevent dehydration. Many early years settings now make water available for children to help themselves.

Milk is an excellent nourishing drink which provides valuable nutrients. Cows' milk should not be given to children under the age of one, as it does not contain enough nutrients for them – they should have infant formula and/or breast milk. All toddlers should drink whole (full-fat milk) until they are two years old. Children above this age who are eating well can change to semi-skimmed milk. However, skimmed milk should not be given to children under the age of five.

Other drinks

All drinks that contain sugar can be harmful to teeth and can also affect children's appetites. Examples are:

- flavoured milks
- fruit squashes
- flavoured fizzy drinks
- fruit juices (containing natural sugar).

Unsweetened, diluted fruit juice is a reasonable option – but not as good as water or milk – for children, but ideally should only be offered at mealtimes. Low-sugar and diet fruit drinks contain artificial sweeteners and are best avoided. Tea and coffee should not be given to children under five years, as these prevent the absorption of iron from foods. They also tend to fill children up without providing any nourishment.

Providing drinks for children aged one to three

The normal fluid requirement for children aged one to three years is 95 ml per kg of body weight per day. The Guidelines for early years settings state that:

- Children must have access to drinking water throughout the day and be encouraged to help themselves to water.

- Children need six to eight drinks (each of 100–150 ml) a day to make sure they get enough fluid.
- Children may need extra drinks in hot weather or after physical activity as they can dehydrate quite quickly.
- Sweetened drinks, including diluted fruit juice, should only be consumed *with*, rather than between, meals to lessen the risk of dental decay, and should be avoided. Consumption of sugar-free fizzy or fruit-based drinks, again should be avoided and although not recommended, should also be confined to mealtimes because the high acidity level of these drinks can cause dental decay.

Providing drinks for children aged four to seven years

- The normal fluid requirement for children aged four to seven years is 85 ml per kg of body weight per day.
- The following drinks are recommended: still water, milk, plain or flavoured, diluted pure fruit juice, fruit and milk/yoghurt smoothies, vegetable juices, and no-added-sugar (sugar-free) squashes – well diluted.
- In-between meals and snacks, water and plain milk are still the best drinks as they will not damage teeth as acidic and sugary drinks do.

Recent research showed that some parents never offer children water to drink as they do not drink water themselves; some parents even consider it cruel to offer water in place of flavoured drinks. It is therefore important that children get into the habit of drinking water in the setting.

How much food should children be given?

Children's appetites vary enormously, so common sense is a good guide on how big a portion should be. Always be guided by the individual child:

- Do not force a child to eat when he or she no longer wishes to.
- Do not refuse to give the child more if he or she is really hungry.
- Some children always feel hungry at one particular mealtime. Others require food little and often. You should always offer food that is nourishing, as well as satisfying the child's hunger.

Providing nutritious snacks

Some children really do need to eat between meals. Their stomachs are relatively small, so they fill up and empty faster than adult stomachs. Sugary foods should not be given as a snack, because sugar may spoil the child's appetite for the main meal to follow. Healthy snack foods include:

- breakfast cereal and milk
- pieces of fruit – banana, orange, pear, kiwi fruit, apple or satsuma
- fruit smoothies
- fruit bread or wholemeal bread, with a slice of cheese
- milk or home-made milkshake
- low-fat yoghurt or fromage frais with crunchy muesli
- nuts or seeds (but see below)
- sticks of carrot, celery, parsnip, red pepper, cauliflower
- any type of bread including fruit bread, crumpets, teacakes, muffins, fruit buns, malt loaf, bagels, pitta bread or sandwiches. Suitable fillings for sandwiches might be cheese, yeast extract, banana, salad or combinations of these.

Never give a young child whole nuts to eat – particularly peanuts. Children can very easily choke on a small piece of the nut or even inhale it, which can cause a severe type of pneumonia. Rarely, a child may have a serious allergic reaction to nuts.

▲ **Figure 16.2** Enjoying a healthy snack

The Children's Food Trust do not recommend giving dried fruit such as raisins or dried apricots or diluted fruit juices in-between meals, because they are high in sugar and can cause tooth decay. The table below includes diluted fruit juice as suggestions, but you should ideally avoid giving these to children between meals.

- If they do eat them, dentists advise parents to ensure that children clean their teeth after eating dried fruit as the natural sugars stick to the teeth.

Breakfast	<ul><li>Orange juice</li><li>Weetabix® + milk, 1 slice of buttered toast</li></ul>	<ul><li>Milk</li><li>Cereal, e.g. corn or wheat flakes, toast and jam</li></ul>	<ul><li>Diluted apple juice</li><li>1 slice of toast with butter or jam</li></ul>	<ul><li>Milk</li><li>Cereal with slice of banana, or scrambled egg on toast</li></ul>	<ul><li>Yoghurt</li><li>Porridge, slices of apple</li></ul>
Morning snack	<ul><li>Diluted apple juice</li><li>1 packet raisins</li></ul>	<ul><li>Blackcurrant and apple drink</li><li>Cheese straws</li></ul>	<ul><li>1 glass fruit squash</li><li>1 biscuit</li></ul>	<ul><li>Peeled apple slices</li><li>Wholemeal toast fingers with cheese spread</li></ul>	<ul><li>Diluted apple juice</li><li>Chapatti or pitta bread fingers</li></ul>
Lunch	<ul><li>Chicken nuggets or macaroni cheese</li><li>Broccoli</li><li>Fruit yoghurt</li><li>Water</li></ul>	<ul><li>Thick bean soup or chicken salad sandwich</li><li>Green beans</li><li>Fresh fruit salad</li><li>Water</li></ul>	<ul><li>Vegetable soup or fish fingers/cakes</li><li>Sticks of raw carrot</li><li>Kiwi fruit</li><li>Water</li></ul>	<ul><li>Sweet potato casserole</li><li>Sweet corn</li><li>Spinach leaves</li><li>Chocolate mousse</li><li>Water</li></ul>	<ul><li>Bean casserole (or chicken drumstick) with noodles</li><li>Peas or broad beans</li><li>Fruit yoghurt</li><li>Water</li></ul>
Afternoon snack	<ul><li>Cubes of cheese with savoury biscuit</li></ul>	<ul><li>Milk shake</li><li>Fruit cake or chocolate or biscuit</li></ul>	<ul><li>Diluted fruit juice</li><li>Thin-cut sandwiches cut into small pieces</li></ul>	<ul><li>Hot or cold chocolate drink</li><li>1 small packet dried fruit mix,</li></ul>	<ul><li>Lassi (yoghurt drink)</li><li>1 banana</li><li>1 small biscuit</li></ul>
Tea or supper	<ul><li>Baked beans on toast or ham and cheese pasta</li><li>Lemon pancakes</li><li>Milk or yoghurt</li></ul>	<ul><li>Fish stew or fish fingers</li><li>Mashed potato</li><li>Fruit mousse or fromage frais</li><li>Milk or yoghurt</li></ul>	<ul><li>Baked potatoes with a choice of fillings</li><li>Steamed broccoli</li><li>Ice cream</li></ul>	<ul><li>Home-made beef burger or pizza</li><li>Green salad</li><li>Pancakes</li><li>Milk</li></ul>	<ul><li>Lentil and rice soup</li><li>Pitta or whole grain bread</li><li>Rice salad</li><li>Milk</li></ul>

▲ **Table 16.1** Providing a balanced diet

Vitamins and minerals in children's diets

Iron

Iron is essential for children's health. Lack of iron leads to **anaemia**, which can hold back both physical and cognitive development. Children who are poor eaters or who are on restricted diets are most at risk.

Iron comes in two forms:

1 in foods from animal sources (especially meat) – this form is easily absorbed by the body

2 in plant foods – this is not quite so easy for the body to absorb.

If possible, children should be given a portion of meat or fish every day, and kidney or liver once a week. Even a small portion of meat or fish is useful, because it also helps the body to absorb iron from other food sources.

If children do not eat meat or fish, they must be offered plenty of iron-rich alternatives, such as egg yolks, dried fruit, beans and lentils, and green, leafy vegetables. It is also a good idea to give foods or drinks that are high in vitamin C at mealtimes, as this helps the absorption of iron from non-meat sources.

Calcium and vitamin D

Children need calcium for maintaining and repairing bones and teeth. Calcium is:

- found in milk, cheese, yoghurt and other dairy products
- only absorbed by the body if it is taken with vitamin D.

The skin can make all the vitamin D that a body needs, when it is exposed to gentle sunlight. People with darker skin are at greater risk of vitamin D deficiencies, such as rickets, because increased pigmentation reduces the capacity of the skin to manufacture the vitamin from sunlight. Additional sources of vitamin D include:

- milk
- oily fish
- fortified margarine

Think about ideas

The balanced daily diet

Look at the following daily diet:

- **Breakfast** – A boiled egg, toast; a glass of milk.
- **Mid-morning** – A packet of crisps; a glass of orange squash.
- **Lunch** – A cheese and egg flan, chips, baked beans; apple fritters and ice cream; a glass of apple juice.
- **Snack** – Chocolate mini roll; a glass of orange squash.
- **Tea** – Fish fingers, mashed potatoes, peas; a glass of strawberry milkshake.

Arrange the servings in five columns – that is, one each for the four food groups and one extra column for extra fat and sugar. Count the number of servings from each food group and assess the nutritional adequacy of the diet.
How could you improve the menu to ensure a healthy balanced diet?

- tahini paste (this is made from sesame seeds, which may cause an allergic reaction in a small number of children)
- fortified breakfast cereals
- meat
- soya mince and soya drinks
- tofu.

Vitamins A and C

Vitamin A keeps skin and bones healthy, helps prevent nose and throat infections, and is necessary for vision in dim light. It is found in carrots, fish liver oils and green vegetables.

Vitamin C is important for the immune system and growth. It also helps in the absorption of iron, especially iron from non-meat sources. Vitamin C intakes are often low in children who eat little fruit and vegetables.

Young children can be given extra A, C and D vitamins in tablet or drop form. These can be obtained from local health centres and should be given as instructed on the bottle.

The nutritional needs of babies

The way babies are fed involves more than simply providing enough food to meet nutritional requirements; for the newborn baby, sucking milk is a great source of pleasure and is also rewarding and

KEY TERM

Anaemia – A condition in which the concentration of the oxygen carrying pigment, haemoglobin, in the blood is below normal.

enjoyable for the mother. The ideal food for babies to start life with is breast milk, and breastfeeding should always be encouraged as the first choice in infant feeding; however, mothers should not be made to feel guilty or inadequate if they choose not to breastfeed their babies. The health visitor and National Childbirth Trust can support mothers who are breastfeeding but it is important to remember that the decision to breastfeed will depend on the choice of the mother and their individual circumstances.

Breastfeeding

During pregnancy, the breasts produce colostrum, a creamy, yellowish fluid, low in fat and sugar, which is uniquely designed to feed the newborn baby. Colostrum also has higher levels of antibodies than mature milk and plays an important part in protecting the baby from infection. Mature milk is present in the breasts from around the third day after birth. Hormonal changes in the mother's bloodstream cause the milk to be produced, and the sucking of the baby stimulates a steady supply.

Management of breastfeeding

The most difficult part of breastfeeding is usually the beginning, and it may take two to three weeks to establish a supply and to settle into some sort of pattern. Even if the mother does not intend to breastfeed her baby, she should be encouraged to try for the first few days, so that the baby can benefit from the unique properties of **colostrum** (see page 355 for definition). Many of the problems that cause women to give up breastfeeding can be overcome with the right advice and support.

Breast milk may be expressed by hand or by breast pump, for use when the mother is unavailable. Expressed breast milk can be stored in a sterilised container in a freezer for up to three months.

Advantages of breastfeeding

- Human breast milk provides food constituents in the correct balance for human growth. There is no trial and error to find the right formula to suit the baby.
- The milk is sterile and at the correct temperature; there is no need for bottles and sterilising equipment.
- Breast milk initially provides the infant with maternal antibodies and helps protect the child from infection – for example, against illnesses such as diarrhoea, vomiting, chest, ear and urine infections, eczema and nappy rash.
- The child is less likely to become overweight, as overfeeding by concentrating the formula is not

possible, and the infant has more freedom of choice as to how much milk he or she will suckle.

- Generally, breast milk is considered cheaper, despite the extra calorific requirement of the mother.
- Sometimes it is easier to promote mother–infant bonding by breastfeeding, although this is certainly not always the case.
- Some babies have an intolerance to the protein in cows' milk (which is the basis of formula milk).

The UNICEF UK Baby Friendly Initiative offers a range of assessment, training and information services to help the health services to promote and support breastfeeding. The initiative was started after research found that:

- breastfed babies are less likely to suffer many serious illnesses – gastroenteritis, respiratory and ear infections are much less common in breastfed babies
- breastfed babies are less likely to suffer from eczema, wheezing and asthma as children, particularly if there is a family history of these conditions

Guidelines for good practice

The successful management of breastfeeding

✓ The mother should take a well-balanced diet; her diet will affect the composition of the breast milk and some foods may cause colic (see p. 356 for definition). Vegetarian mothers who drink cows' milk, eat a varied vegetarian diet and take vitamin supplements produce breast milk that is similar in nutrient value to non-vegetarian mothers; vegan mothers may need to take calcium and vitamin B12 supplements while breastfeeding.

✓ Put the baby to the breast straight after the birth – this has been shown to be a key factor in successful breastfeeding.

✓ Feed on demand – that is, when the baby is hungry – rather than routinely every four hours. Arrange extra help in the home if possible, at least until breastfeeding is established.

✓ Find the most comfortable position for feeding. If the mother has a sore perineum or caesarean scar, the midwife or health adviser will be able to advise. (See pp. 236 and 230 for definitions).

✓ Try not to give extra (complementary) milk feeds by bottle.

✓ Let the baby decide when he or she has had enough milk and allow him or her to finish sucking at one breast before offering the other.

- adults who were breastfed as babies are less likely to have risk factors for heart disease, such as obesity, high blood pressure and high cholesterol levels.

Disadvantages of breastfeeding

- In rare cases (about 2 per cent), the mother may not be able to produce enough breast milk to feed her baby.
- She may feel uncomfortable about breastfeeding her baby in public.
- If employed, the mother may need to arrange to breastfeed the baby during working hours, or may need to extend her maternity leave, which could have financial implications.
- The mother can become very tired, as breastfeeding tends to be more frequent than bottle-feeding.
- The mother may suffer from sore or cracked nipples, which makes breastfeeding painful.

Bottle-feeding

Commercially modified baby milks (formula milks) must be used for bottle-feeding. Any other type of milk, such as cows' milk or goats' milk, will not satisfy a baby's nutritional needs, and should not be given to babies under one year. A young baby's digestive system is unable to cope with the high protein and salt content of cows' milk, and it is likely to cause an adverse reaction. Soya-based milks can be used if the baby develops an intolerance to modified cows' milks (this happens very rarely). For the first four to six months, the baby will be given infant formula milk as a substitute for breast milk; he or she may then progress to follow-on milk, which should be offered until the age of one year.

Government Guidelines state that as each baby will have his or her own individual requirements, it is best to let them feed on demand. Newborn babies may take quite small volumes of infant formula milk to start with, but by the end of the first week of life most babies will ask for approximately 150–200 ml per kg per day (although this will vary from baby to baby) until they are six months old.

Advantages of bottle-feeding

- The mother knows exactly how much milk the baby has taken.
- The milk is in no way affected by the mother's state of health, while anxiety, tiredness, illness or menstruation may reduce the quantity of breast milk produced.
- The infant is unaffected by such factors as maternal medication; laxatives, antibiotics, alcohol and drugs affecting the central nervous system can affect the quality of breast milk.

- Other members of the family can feed the infant. In this way, the father can feel equally involved with the child's care, and during the night could take over one of the feeds so that the mother can get more sleep.
- There is no fear of embarrassment while feeding.
- The mother is physically unaffected by feeding the infant, avoiding such problems as sore nipples.
- It is useful for mothers who want to return to work before the baby is weaned.

Disadvantages of bottle-feeding

- Babies who are bottle-fed using formula milk do not have the same protection against allergies and infections as breastfed babies.
- When making formula milk, it is possible to get the mixture wrong and make it too strong, too weak or too hot.
- Babies tend to swallow more air when bottle-fed and need to be 'winded' more often.
- Babies may bring up feeds more often – this is known as possetting.

▲ **Figure 16.3** Bottle-feeding

- Babies who are bottle-fed tend to suffer more from constipation.
- There is a lot of work involved in thoroughly washing and sterilising all the equipment that is needed for bottle-feeding.
- Studies indicate that bottle-fed babies were found to have an increased risk of obesity until at least six years of age.
- Using formula milk can be expensive. It has been estimated that it costs at least £450 a year to feed a baby using formula milk.
- There is a greater risk of the baby developing gastroenteritis (see p. 272 for definition) – usually when equipment is not sterilised properly, or when the milk is incorrectly stored or becomes contaminated.

Making the choice between breastfeeding and bottle-feeding

A range of factors influences the mother's decision on how to feed her newborn baby:

- Breastfeeding is harder for some mothers than others – for example, if a new mother does not receive the support she needs to establish breastfeeding, it is more difficult to stimulate the 'let-down' reflex (when milk flows from the ducts towards the nipple). Some babies may have medical conditions that make breastfeeding difficult – for example, they may be tongue-tied or may have been born prematurely.
- The mother may have to return to work and find that bottle-feeding is more convenient when leaving her baby in the care of others.
- Many new mothers feel that there is a bottle-feeding culture in the UK. Breastfeeding is viewed by some as an embarrassing activity when carried out in front of others.
- The important thing is that a mother makes her own choice and is happy that her baby is feeding properly.

The National Children's Bureau states that:

Babies who are bottle-fed should be held and have warm physical contact with an attentive adult while being fed. It is strongly recommended that a baby in an early years setting be fed by the same staff member at each feed. Babies should never be left propped up with bottles, as it is dangerous and inappropriate to babies' emotional needs.

Guidelines for good practice

Bottle-feeding a baby

✔ Collect all the necessary equipment before picking up the baby. The bottle may be warmed in a jug of hot water. Have a muslin square or bib and tissues to hand.

✔ Check the temperature and flow of the milk by dripping it on to the inside of your wrist (it should feel warm – not hot or cold).

✔ Make yourself comfortable with the baby. Do not rush the feed – babies always sense if you are not relaxed and it can make them edgy too.

✔ Try to hold the baby in a similar position to that for breastfeeding and maintain eye contact – this is a time for cuddling and talking to the baby.

✔ Stimulate the rooting reflex by placing the teat at the corner of the baby's mouth; then put the teat fully into his or her mouth and feed by tilting the bottle so that the hole in the teat is always covered with milk.

✔ After about 10 minutes, the baby may need to be helped to bring up wind; this can be done by leaning him or her forwards on your lap and gently rubbing his or her back or holding him or her against your shoulder. Unless the baby is showing discomfort, do not insist on trying to produce a 'burp' – the baby may pass the wind out in the nappy.

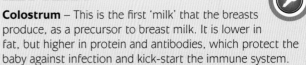

KEY TERM

Colostrum – This is the first 'milk' that the breasts produce, as a precursor to breast milk. It is lower in fat, but higher in protein and antibodies, which protect the baby against infection and kick-start the immune system.

Feeding problems in babies

Possetting

The baby regularly vomits small amounts of his or her feed, but is generally healthy and has no signs of illness. The cause is a weakness of the muscle at the opening of the stomach and eventually the baby will grow out of it – although the condition is messy, there is no cause for alarm! (See pp. 251 and 252 for more information on possetting).

Pyloric stenosis

This is a condition, more common in boys than in girls, in which the muscle surrounding the channel at the end of the stomach (the pylorus) thickens, narrowing the outlet. Symptoms usually appear about three weeks after birth:

- The baby becomes constipated.
- The baby will vomit quite violently – this is called projectile vomiting. The regurgitated food often shoots several feet away.
- Dehydration may occur and weight gain stops.
- Medical advice should be sought; pyloric stenosis is easily diagnosed and is usually cured by a simple operation.

Colic

Colic is an attack of abdominal pain caused by spasms in the intestines as food is being digested. It is sometimes called 'three-month colic', as it usually disappears by the age of three months. The condition causes the baby to draw up his or her arms and legs and cry inconsolably. Attacks of colic can last anything from 15 minutes to several hours; some babies only suffer in the evening. There is no known cause and no effective cure. The obvious distress of the baby and the helplessness of the carer makes caring for a baby with colic difficult. Parents need a lot of support and reassurance that the baby will grow out of it and that there is no lasting damage.

Constipation

This occurs when stools are hard or infrequent. Constipation can be caused by underfeeding and/or dehydration. The baby's fluid intake should be increased. If weaned, more fruit and vegetables should be included in the diet.

Diarrhoea

Diarrhoea is caused by food passing through the intestines too quickly, not leaving enough time for it to be digested. The baby will pass frequent, loose, watery stools. It may be caused by poor food hygiene or by viral infection. It should always be taken seriously in a young baby, especially if accompanied by vomiting. Seek medical advice and give cooled, boiled water; bottle-feeding should be stopped completely, but breastfeeding may continue if the baby wants it.

Weaning

The principles of weaning and its importance to the baby's development

Weaning is the gradual introduction of solid food to the baby's diet. The reasons for weaning are to:

- meet the baby's nutritional needs – from about six months of age, milk alone will not satisfy the baby's increased nutritional requirements, especially for iron
- satisfy increasing appetite
- develop new skills – for example, use of feeding beaker, cup and cutlery
- develop the chewing mechanism – the muscular movement of the mouth and jaw also aids the development of speech
- introduce new tastes and textures – this enables the baby to join in family meals, thus promoting cognitive and social development.

When to start weaning

Department of Health Guidelines advise parents to wait until their baby is around six months before starting him on solid food. When the following three key signs are present together, it means that the baby is ready for solid food:

- The baby can stay in a sitting position while holding his head steady.
- The baby can coordinate his eyes, hands and mouth – that is, look at food, grab it and put it in his mouth himself.
- The baby can swallow his food – if the baby is not ready, most of it will be pushed back out.

Babies who are born prematurely should not be introduced to solid foods just because they have reached a certain age or weight. They will need individual assessment before weaning.

Giving solids too early – often in the mistaken belief that the baby might sleep through the night – places a strain on the baby's immature digestive system. It may also make the baby overweight and increases the likelihood of allergy.

If parents do choose to introduce solid foods before 26 weeks, they should consult their health visitor or GP first. There are also some foods they should avoid giving their baby. These include:

- foods containing **gluten**, which is in wheat, rye, barley, oats
- eggs

> **KEY TERMS**
>
> **Clostridium botulinum** – A bacteria that grows on food and produces toxins that, when ingested, cause paralysis.
>
> **Gluten** – A mix of proteins found in wheat and other related grains such as rye and barley.

- fish and shellfish
- liver
- citrus fruit juices
- nuts and seeds.

Babies under one year old should not be given honey, because it is not pasteurised and can cause infant **botulism** – a rare, but very serious illness, which occurs when **Clostridium botulinum** or related bacteria produce toxins in the intestines of babies under one year old.

Stages of weaning

Every baby is different. Some enjoy trying new tastes and textures, moving through weaning quickly and easily, while others need a little more time to get used to new foods.

Stage 1 (around six months)

Give puréed vegetables, puréed fruit, baby rice and finely puréed dhal or lentils. Milk continues to be the most important food.

Stage 2 (about six to eight months)

Increase variety; introduce puréed or minced meat, chicken, liver, fish, lentils and beans. Raw eggs should not be used, but cooked egg yolk can be introduced from six months, along with wheat-based foods – for example, mashed Weetabix and pieces of bread. Milk feeds decrease as more solids rich in protein are offered.

Stage 3 (about nine to twelve months)

Cows' milk can safely be used at about 12 months, along with lumpier foods, such as pasta, pieces of cooked meat, soft cooked beans, pieces of cheese and a variety of breads. Additional fluids can be given – for example, diluted unsweetened fruit juice or water. Three regular meals should be taken, as well as drinks.

Methods of weaning

Some babies take to solid food very quickly; others appear not to be interested at all. The baby's demands are a good guide for weaning – mealtimes should never become a battleground. Even very young children have definite food preferences and should never be forced to eat a particular food, however much thought and effort has gone into the preparation. Table 16.2 offers guidelines.

The best baby food is home-made from simple ingredients, with no sugar, salt or spices. Any leftovers can be frozen in ice cube trays. Puréed, cooked vegetables, fruit and ground cereals such as rice are ideal to start weaning. Chewing usually starts at around the age of six months, whether the baby has teeth or not, and slightly coarser textures can then be offered. The baby should be fed in a bouncing cradle

Guidelines for good practice

Weaning

- ✔ Try to encourage a liking for savoury foods.
- ✔ Only introduce one new food at a time.
- ✔ Be patient if the baby does not take the food – feed at the baby's pace, not yours. Do not add salt or sugar to feeds.
- ✔ Make sure that food is the right temperature. Avoid giving sweet foods or drinks between meals. Never leave a baby alone when he or she is eating.
- ✔ Limit the use of commercially prepared foods – they are of poorer quality and will not allow the baby to become used to home cooking.
- ✔ Select foods approved by the baby's parents or primary carers.

or high chair – not in the usual feeding position in the carer's arms.

Food can be puréed by:

- rubbing it through a sieve using a large spoon
- mashing it with a fork (for soft foods such as banana or cooked potato)
- using a mouli-sieve or hand-blender
- using an electric blender (useful for larger amounts).

Finger foods

Finger foods are any foods that can be given to a baby to manage by him or herself. After weaning, encourage the baby to chew – even if there are no teeth – by giving finger foods or foods that have a few lumps. Examples of finger foods include:

- wholemeal toast
- pitta bread
- banana or peeled apple slices
- cubes of hard cheese – for example, Cheddar
- chapatti
- breadsticks
- cooked carrots or green beans.

Always stay near to the baby during feeding to make sure she does not choke and to offer encouragement.

Baby-led weaning

Some parents use a technique for weaning their babies called baby-led weaning. This involves letting the baby select those items of food that can be held or grasped by the baby and taken to her mouth. Starter foods

	4–6 months	6–8 months	9–12 months
You can give or add	<ul><li>Puréed fruit</li><li>Puréed vegetables</li><li>Thin porridge made from oat or rice flakes or cornmeal</li><li>Finely puréed dhal or lentils</li></ul>	<ul><li>A wider range of puréed fruits and vegetables</li><li>Purées which include chicken, fish and liver</li><li>Wheat-based foods, e.g. mashed Weetabix®</li><li>Egg yolk, well cooked</li><li>Small-sized beans such as aduki beans, cooked soft</li><li>Pieces of ripe banana</li><li>Cooked rice</li><li>Citrus fruits</li><li>Soft summer fruits</li><li>Pieces of bread</li></ul>	<ul><li>An increasingly wide range of foods with a variety of textures and flavours</li><li>Cow's milk</li><li>Pieces of cheese</li><li>Fromage frais or yoghurt</li><li>Pieces of fish</li><li>Soft cooked beans</li><li>Pasta</li><li>A variety of breads</li><li>Pieces of meat from a casserole</li><li>Well-cooked egg white</li><li>Almost anything that is wholesome and that the child can swallow</li></ul>
How	<ul><li>Offer the food on the tip of a clean finger or on the tip of a clean (plastic or horn) teaspoon</li></ul>	<ul><li>On a teaspoon</li></ul>	<ul><li>On a spoon or as finger food</li></ul>
When	<ul><li>A very tiny amount at first, during or after a milk feed</li></ul>	<ul><li>At the end of a milk feed</li></ul>	<ul><li>At established mealtimes</li></ul>
Why	<ul><li>The start of transition from milk to solids</li></ul>	<ul><li>To introduce other foods when the child is hungry</li></ul>	<ul><li>To encourage full independence</li></ul>
Not yet	<ul><li>Cow's milk – or any except breast or formula milk</li><li>Citrus fruit</li><li>Soft summer fruits</li><li>Wheat (cereals, flour, bread, etc.)</li><li>Spices</li><li>Spinach, swede, turnip, beetroot</li><li>Eggs</li><li>Nuts</li><li>Salt</li><li>Sugar</li><li>Fatty food</li></ul>	<ul><li>Cow's milk, except in small quantities mixed with other food</li><li>Chillies or chilli powder</li><li>Egg whites</li><li>Nuts</li><li>Salt</li><li>Sugar</li><li>Fatty food</li></ul>	<ul><li>Whole nuts</li><li>Salt</li><li>Sugar</li><li>Fatty food</li></ul>

Table 16.2 Introducing new solids to babies

may include pieces of broccoli, carrot or fruit cut into 'chip' shapes and offered to the baby on a tray. The use of bowls and weaning spoons is discouraged. The principles behind this way of feeding babies are that baby-led weaning:

- offers the baby the opportunity to discover what other foods have to offer, as part of finding out about the world around her
- utilises the baby's desire to explore and experiment, and to mimic the activities of others
- enables the transition to solid foods to take place as naturally as possible – by allowing the baby to set the pace of each meal, and maintaining an emphasis on play and exploration rather than on eating.

For more information, visit www.babyledweaning.com

Reflecting on practice

Weaning

Think about the ways in which your setting accommodates the needs and preferences of parents whose babies are being weaned onto solid food. For example, some settings arrange workshops for parents to discuss the different methods, including baby-led weaning.

What do you think might be the advantages of baby-led weaning to the baby's development?

Arrange to observe a baby who is being weaned. Is the feeding time relaxed and enjoyable? How does the baby react to a new taste or texture?

Preparing food for older babies and toddlers

A baby's immune system becomes more resistant to germs after the age of one year. Parents who are bottle-feeding their baby must continue to sterilise the bottles and teats for at least a year. This is because even if a tiny amount of milk gets trapped inside the bottle or teat, bacteria can start to grow and challenge the baby's immune system.

The baby's cups and mugs need only be sterilised for six months, and after this time they just require careful cleaning. See Chapter 12 for more information on sterilisation.

Foods to avoid giving to children

- **Salt** – There is no need to add salt to children's food. From the age of one to three years, children should be having no more than 2 g of salt per day. Even when buying processed food made specifically for children, remember to check the information given on the labels in order to choose those that contain less salt.
- **Nuts** – Do not give whole or chopped nuts to children under five years old because of the risk of choking.
- **Raw eggs** – Avoid food that contains raw or partially cooked eggs because of the risk of salmonella, which causes food poisoning. Make sure that eggs are always cooked until both the white and yolk are solid.
- **Undiluted fruit juice** – These contain natural sugars that are known to cause tooth decay; they are best only given at mealtimes and should be diluted when given to young children.
- **High-fibre foods** like brown rice and wholemeal pasta are too bulky for children under five years; too much fibre can also make it more difficult for the body to absorb some essential nutrients, like calcium and iron.
- **Shark, swordfish and marlin** should not be given because these fish contain relatively high levels of mercury, which might affect a child's developing nervous system.
- **Raw shellfish** – To reduce the risk of the child getting food poisoning.

Promoting healthy eating

Our eating habits, tastes and preferences are shaped very early on – in part, by the example set to us by our parents and other carers, and by the food offered in infancy. These early influences often mould our attitude towards food and eating throughout school and adult life. Families which lead such busy lives that each member prepares his or her own meal and eats it while watching television will have a very different perspective on the role of food and mealtimes to families who regularly sit together at the table for their evening meal. Some children can be choosy about the food they eat. This can be a source of anxiety for parents and for those who work with the children. However, as long as children eat some food from each of the five food groups – even if they are same old favourites – there is no cause for worry.

Children of school age and their diets

Once children reach primary school age, they have an increasing amount of freedom over food choice, and foods are often eaten outside the home – at friends' houses and at school. Also, outside pressures – such as peer pressure and advertising – start to influence food choice. Although growth is slower than in infancy or early childhood, school-aged children still have high nutrient needs, but fairly small appetites. It is therefore important that all meals and snacks provide lots of nutrients, even in a small volume of food.

Packed lunches

Many children take packed lunches to school. There are lots of different types of bread that can be used to add variety. You could offer pitta bread, chapattis, crusty rolls, muffins or bagels, with one of these healthy fillings:

- peanut butter and banana
- cheese and pickle
- tuna and tomato
- hummus and salad
- chicken with a low-fat dressing and salad
- bacon, lettuce and tomato
- salmon and cucumber
- egg with low-fat mayonnaise.
- Ideas for items to supplement a lunchtime sandwich include:
- fresh or dried fruit
- sticks of raw vegetables
- cherry tomatoes
- hard-boiled egg
- cheese cubes
- small pot of potato salad
- fruit juice
- pot of yoghurt or a yoghurt drink
- coleslaw
- soup in a flask.

Guidelines for good practice

Making mealtimes healthy and fun

- Offer a wide variety of different foods – give babies and toddlers a chance to try a new food more than once; any refusal on first tasting may be due to dislike of the new rather than of the food itself.

- Set an example – children will imitate both what you eat and how you eat it. It will be easier to encourage a child to eat a stick of raw celery if you eat one too! If you show disgust at certain foods, young children will notice and copy you.

- Be prepared for messy mealtimes! Present the food in a form that is fairly easy for children to manage by themselves – for example, not difficult to chew.

- Do not use food as a punishment, reward, bribe or threat – for example, do not give sweets or chocolates as a reward for finishing savoury foods. To a child, this is like saying, 'Here's something nice after eating those nasty greens.' Give healthy foods as treats – for example, raisins and raw carrots – rather than sweets or cakes.

- Encourage children to feed themselves – either using a spoon or by offering suitable finger foods.

- Introduce new foods in stages – for example, if switching to wholemeal bread, try a soft-grain white bread first. Always involve the children in making choices as far as possible.

- Teach children to eat mainly at mealtimes and avoid giving them high-calorie snacks – for example, biscuits and sugary drinks – which might affect their appetite for more nutritious food. Most young children need three small meals and three snacks a day.

- Offer regular meals and snacks rather than allowing a child to 'pick'.

- Ensure that children sit down at a table to eat their snacks, that they are supervised during these times, and are monitored to ensure they eat an appropriate amount of food safely to reduce the risk of choking.

- Presentation is important – make mealtimes fun. Use brightly coloured plates and present the food in an attractive way by using colours, shapes, themes and characters for example.

- Allow children to follow their own individual appetites when deciding how much they want to eat. If a child rejects food, do not ever force-feed him or her. Simply remove the food without comment. Give smaller portions next time and praise the child for eating even a little.

- Never give a young child whole nuts to eat – particularly peanuts. Children can very easily choke on a small piece of the nut or even inhale it, which can cause a severe type of pneumonia. Rarely, a child may have a serious allergic reaction to nuts. Always check with the parent or carer whether a child has any known allergies.

Savoury snacks, chocolate or a muesli bar can be added as an occasional treat. See p. 351 for a list of healthy snacks.

The Early Years Foundation Stage (EYFS) says that:

- Where Early Years settings give children meals, snacks and drinks, these must be healthy balanced and nutritious.

- Before a child is admitted to the setting the provider must also obtain information about any special dietary requirements, preferences and food allergies that the child has, and any special health requirements.

- Fresh drinking water must be available and accessible at all times.

- Providers must record and act on information from parents and carers about a child's dietary needs.

- There must be an area which is adequately equipped to provide healthy meals, snacks and drinks for children as necessary.

- There must be suitable facilities for the hygienic preparation of food for children, if necessary including suitable sterilisation equipment for babies' food.

- Providers must be confident that those responsible for preparing and handling food are competent to do so. In group provision, all staff involved in preparing and handling food must receive training in food hygiene.

- Food requirements vary according to age, gender, size, occupation or lifestyle, and climate. Different foods contain different amounts of energy per unit of weight; foods that contain a lot of fat and sugar have high-energy values.

Reflecting on practice

Menu planning

Write up or obtain a copy of an actual weekly menu of a nursery or primary school that you know, then answer the following questions:

- Does the menu provide a healthy balance of nutrients?
- Is there anything that you would change to promote healthy eating? Give reasons for any new foods you might wish to include.

- Food energy is traditionally measured in calories (kcal) or kilojoules (kJ).
  - 1 kcal = 4.2 kJ
  - 1000 kJ = 1 MJ (mega joule) = 239 kcal
- An excess of calories will result in weight gain, as the surplus 'energy' is stored as fat; an insufficient intake of calories will result in weight loss, as the body has to draw on fat reserves to meet energy requirements. Babies and young children have relatively high-energy requirements in relation to their size.

Government initiatives to promote healthy eating

The Eat Better, Start Better programme

This programme is run by The Children's Food Trust and aims to help early years providers meet children's nutritional needs more consistently, and to help families with young children to develop the cooking skills and confidence they need to cook and eat more healthily. Their practical guide includes the government-backed *Voluntary Food and Drink Guidelines for Early Years Settings in England*, as well as advice on encouraging children to eat well, including managing fussy eating and special dietary requirements.

The Schools Fruit and Vegetable Scheme (SFV)

It is recommended that children – like adults – eat at least five portions of fruit and vegetables every day. Children aged between four and six who attend a fully

Figure 16.4 'Just eat more' portion poster for the NHS 5 A DAY programme

state-funded infant, primary or special school, are entitled to receive a free piece of fruit or vegetable each school day.

Feeding young imaginations

The Pre-School Learning Alliance's campaign, Feeding Young Imaginations, supports parents and early years groups by providing information to promote a balanced diet for under-fives.

The Children's Food Campaign

Sustain (the alliance for better food and farming) launched the Children's Food Campaign. It wants to improve young people's health and well-being through:

- good food and real food education in every school
- protecting children from junk food marketing
- clear food labelling that everyone, including children, can understand.

Cool Milk

Cool Milk works in partnership with local authorities and early years groups to supply free and subsidised school milk to children in pre-schools, nurseries and primary schools. Cool Milk aims to make the provision of milk easier for schools, nurseries, local authorities and parents, while promoting the important health benefits and learning opportunities that school milk offers.

Change4life

The School Food Trust supports the NHS Change4life programme by ensuring that as many children as possible are eating healthy school food. All school lunches must now meet *nutrient-based standards* to ensure that they provide children with the fuel they need to lead a healthy, active lifestyle. Change4life also provides guidance and resources on the following:

- healthier breakfast clubs
- healthier tuck shops
- water provision
- healthier vending machines
- healthier lunchboxes
- dining room environment
- healthier cookery clubs

There are similar schemes in Scotland, Wales and Northern Ireland – see Resources section on p. 373.

The Nursery Milk Scheme

The Nursery Milk Scheme enables:

- Children under five to receive free of charge 189 ml (one-third of a pint) of milk for every day they attend approved day care facilities for two hours or more.

- Babies aged less than 12 months to receive instead dried baby milk made up to 189 ml (one-third of a pint).
- Day care providers who have been approved to supply milk under the scheme to be reimbursed for the cost of the milk they supply.

Eat Smart, Play Smart

Eat Smart, Play Smart is a Food Standards Agency teaching resource developed for primary school teachers throughout the UK to use with children aged five to seven years. Eat Smart, Play Smart materials have been developed to:

- help children to understand the need for healthy diets and to choose appropriately from different food groups for their meals
- encourage children to be more active in their everyday lives and to understand the benefits of being active. Ways of increasing activity in the home and at school are suggested in fun, energetic and easy-to-follow ways

Scotland: The Scottish Government has set a national target to reduce the rate of increase in the proportion of children outside the healthy weight range by 2018. This is underpinned by an NHS HEAT target for the provision of child health weight programmes incorporating diet, physical activity and behaviour change components and with an emphasis on involving parents/carers as well as children themselves.

Wales: The Healthy Eating in Schools (Nutritional Standards & Requirements) (Wales) Regulations 2013 states the type of food which can and can't be provided by schools.

- The legislation outlines what schools must do ensure they are serving nutritious food to learners, including:
    - not allowing schools to serve confectionery (such as chocolate and sweets) and savoury snacks (such as crisps)
    - increasing the availability of fruit and vegetables served by schools
    - limiting the number of times that meat products and potatoes cooked in fats and oils can be served each week
    - serving only healthy drinks, such as water and milk.
- The legislation also states what food can be served as part of our Free Breakfast in Primary Schools scheme.

Northern Ireland has launched a range of healthy eating programmes which promote healthy eating in early years settings and schools.

Food additives and behaviour

A food additive is any substance intentionally added to food for a specific function – for example, to preserve or colour it. It is not normally eaten as a food or used as a characteristic ingredient in food. When additives are used in food, they must be declared in the list of ingredients, either by name or **E number**. All food additives must comply with European Union legislation. They are only allowed to be used if experts decide that they are necessary and safe. However, some people can react to certain additives, just as some people react to certain foods that most people can eat without any reaction. People who react to additives normally have asthma or other allergies already. Reactions to additives usually bring on an asthma attack or cause nettle rash (also known as urticarial, composed of reddish itchy weals or swellings in the skin similar to ones resulting from contact with stinging nettle).

Some manufacturers and supermarket chains are now selling additive-free foods, which help parents and carers to avoid additives, should they wish to.

Research commissioned by the Food Standards Agency (2007) found that a combination of additives can cause hyperactivity in children. These additives include several food colours and a preservative, all of which are often found in children's soft drinks, sweets and ice cream.

KEY TERM

E number – The code which identifies food additives; food colourings are the additives most often linked to behaviour problems in children.

Reflecting on practice

Food labels

1. Visit a supermarket and look at the food labels on branded products.
2. What information is provided relating to its nutritional content (e.g. fats – saturated and polyunsaturated – energy values, protein, vitamins)?
3. How would the information given help in planning a balanced diet for young children?

Guidelines for good practice

Reducing children's intake of additives

To reduce additives in the diet, parents and carers should:

- ✓ always look at the labels on food containers and be wary of a long list of E numbers
- ✓ use fresh rather than highly processed foods
- ✓ cook their own pies, soups, cakes, for example.

Thinking about ideas

A healthy eating activity for young children

You will need: paper and felt-tip pens; food magazines; scissors; a chart or poster showing the healthy eating food circle (the Eatwell Plate, see Figure 16.1); paper plates – one for each child, and paper glue.

- Ask the children to sit in a circle on the floor and close their eyes.
- Ask them to imagine that it is lunchtime and they are quite hungry.
- Ask the children what they would like to eat. What are their favourite foods? Then ask them to open their eyes.
- Write their favourite foods down on a chart. Ask them to describe what their favourite foods look like.

- Draw a picture of their favourite foods. (Some young children may choose junk food as their favourites, depending on their previous nutrition experiences).
- Next, show the children a picture of the food circle (the Eatwell Plate). Ask them to find their favourite foods on this food pyramid. Point out the different foods recommended on the food pyramid.
- Pass out one paper plate to each child. Instruct them to cut out pictures of their favourite foods from the magazines. Then ask them to glue these pictures onto their paper plate to make a food collage. Encourage the children to pick nutritious food choices as well as their not-so-nutritious favourites.

Multicultural provision

The UK is a multicultural society. Dietary customs of different culture are wide and varied but some may be related to the beliefs of religious groups, including Muslims, Hindus and Sikhs.

Food and festivals from different cultures

There are particular foods that are associated with certain religious festivals – for example, in the Christian tradition, mince pies at Christmas and pancakes on Shrove Tuesday. Providing foods from different cultures within an early years setting is a very good way of celebrating these festivals. Parents of children from ethnic minority groups are usually very pleased to be asked for advice on how to celebrate festivals with food, and may even be prepared to contribute some samples.

Table 16.3 provides basic general guidance and you should consult a religious advisor or parents/carers for more information.

Children on vegetarian diets

Children who are on a **vegetarian** diet need an alternative to meat, fish and chicken as the main sources of protein. Alternatives might include:

- milk
- cheese and eggs
- pulses (lentils and beans).

They also need enough iron. As iron is more difficult to absorb from vegetable sources than from meat, a young child needs to obtain iron from sources such as:

- leafy green vegetables – for example, spinach and watercress
- pulses (beans, lentils and chickpeas)
- dried fruit – for example, apricots, raisins and sultanas (although some dentists believe that dried fruit contributes to dental decay, and so it should be given sparingly and only at mealtimes)
- some breakfast cereals.

Thinking about ideas

Different traditions

Find out about the dietary requirements and restrictions in one cultural or religious group different from your own. Choose from:
- Jewish
- Christian
- Muslim
- Hindu
- Sikhism
- Rastafarian.

Reflecting on practice

Cultural needs

The nursery school where you are working has 22 white British children and one child from Turkey. The nursery teacher says, 'We only offer English food here because we do not have any children from ethnic minorities.' Discuss this statement and decide what your approach would be if you were in charge of the nursery.

Muslim diets	Hindu diets	Sikh diets
Muslims practice the Islamic religion, and their holy book, The Quran, provides them with their laws regarding food. Fish (with and without scales) and seafood generally (with exceptions like crocodile and frogs) is considered halal by the majority of Muslim scholars. Unlawful foods (called haram) are: pork, all meat which has not been rendered lawful (halal), alcohol. Fasting: during the lunar month of Ramadan Muslims fast between dawn and sunset; fasting involves abstinence from all food and drink, so many Muslims rise early to eat before dawn in order to maintain their energy levels. Pre-pubescent children and the elderly are exempt from fasting.	Orthodox Hindus are strict vegetarians as they believe in Ahimsa – non-violence towards all living beings – and a minority practice veganism. Some will eat dairy products and eggs, while others will refuse eggs on the grounds that they are a potential source of life. Even non-vegetarians do not eat beef as the cow is considered a sacred animal, and it is unusual for pork to be eaten as the pig is considered unclean. Ghee (clarified butter) and vegetable oil are used in cooking. Fasting: common for certain festivals, such as Mahshivrati (the birthday of Lord Shiva).	Most orthodox Sikhs do not eat meat that has been ritually-slaughtered e.g. halal or kosher. Although some Sikhs are vegetarian, this is a personal choice and not a requirement of the faith. Fasting is forbidden in Sikhism.
Rastafarian diets	**Afro-Caribbean diets**	**Jewish diets**
Dietary practices are based on laws laid down by Moses in the Book of Genesis in the Bible. These laws state that certain types of meat should be avoided. The majority of followers will only eat Ital foods, which are foods considered to be in a whole or natural state. Most Rastafarians are vegetarians and will not consume processed, chemically altered, artificial or preserved foods. Therefore foods such as salt or drinks such as tea and coffee are rarely, if ever, consumed by strict Rastafarians.	The Afro-Caribbean community is the second largest ethnic minority group in the UK. Dietary practices within the community vary widely. Many people include a wide variety of European foods in their diet alongside the traditional foods of cornmeal, coconut, green banana, plantain, okra and yam.	Jewish people observe dietary laws which state that animals and birds must be slaughtered by the Jewish method to render them kosher (acceptable). Milk and meat must never be cooked or eaten together, and pork in any form is forbidden. Shellfish are not allowed as they are thought to harbour disease. Only fish with fins and scales may be eaten. Fasting: The most holy day of the Jewish calendar is Yom Kippur (the Day of Atonement), when Jewish people fast for 25 hours.

Festivals from different cultures	
Shichi-go-san (Japanese festival for young children)	November 15
Chinese New Year	Late January/ early February
Shrove Tuesday (Mardi Gras)	40 days before Easter
Rosh Hoshanah (Jewish New Year)	Usually September
Holi (Hindu Spring festival)	February or March
Eid Al Fitir (Muslim festival)	At end of Ramadan
Eid al Adha	At the end of the Hajj pilgrimage
Diwali (Hindu New Year)	October or November
Rastafarian New Year	January 7

▲ **Table 16.3** Multicultural provision and dietary implications

The vegan diet

A **vegan** diet completely excludes all foods of animal origin – that is, animal flesh, milk and milk products, eggs, honey and all additives that may be of animal origin. A vegan diet is based on cereals and cereal products, pulses, fruits, vegetables, nuts and seeds. Human breast milk is acceptable for vegan babies.

KEY TERMS

Vegetarian – There are two types of vegetarianism. Both types exclude red meat, poultry and fish: lacto-ovo vegetarians, who eat both dairy products and eggs, and lacto-vegetarians, who eat dairy products but avoid eggs.

Vegan – A vegan is a person who avoids using or consuming animal products. Vegans do not eat dairy products, eggs, or any other products that are of animal origin. They also avoid using fur, leather, wool and cosmetics or chemical products tested on animals.

The importance of healthy eating and diet-related illnesses

Good nutrition – or healthy eating – during childhood makes it easier to maintain a healthy weight and has been shown to improve children's concentration and behaviour. It can also help to reduce the risk of developing many common diseases including heart disease, cancer, diabetes, obesity, osteoporosis and dental decay.

Malnutrition and under-nutrition

In recent years there has been increasing public concern about the quality of children's diets, rapidly increasing rates of child obesity, diet-related disorders and low consumption of fruit and vegetables by children. There are various conditions that may occur in childhood that are directly related to a poor or unbalanced diet. These are a result of either **malnutrition** or **under-nutrition**, and include:

- **Failure to thrive (or faltering growth**) – poor growth and physical development. (This can also result from child abuse – physical abuse, emotional abuse, neglect and sexual abuse. This complex subject is discussed in Chapter 4.)
- **Dental caries or tooth decay** – this is associated with high consumption of sugar in snacks and fizzy drinks.
- **Obesity** – children who are overweight are more likely to become obese adults.
- **Nutritional anaemia** – this is due to an insufficient intake of iron, folic acid and vitamin B12.
- **Increased susceptibility to infections** – particularly upper respiratory infections, such as colds and bronchitis.

Childhood obesity

Obesity (grossly fat or overweight) results from taking in more energy from the diet than is used up by the body. Some children appear to inherit a tendency to put on weight very easily, and some parents and carers offer more high-calorie food than children need.

KEY TERMS

Malnutrition – When a person's diet is lacking the necessary amounts of certain elements which are essential to growth, such as vitamins, salts and proteins.
Under-nutrition – When people do not get enough to eat.

Obesity can lead to emotional and social problems as well as the physical problem of being more prone to infections. An obese child can become the target for bullying, and if severely obese, the child will be unable to participate in the same vigorous play as their peers. Some associated dietary problems are:

- **Changing lifestyles** – fast food is overtaking traditionally prepared meals. Many convenience meals involve coating the food with fatty sauces or batters.
- **Foods high in sugar and fat** – children eat more sweets and crisps and drink more fizzy drinks. This is partly because of advertising, but also because such foods are more widely available.
- **Poor fruit and vegetable consumption** – despite it being more readily available, many children do not eat enough fresh fruit or vegetables, preferring processed varieties that often contain added sugar and fat.

A child who is diagnosed as being overweight will usually be prescribed a diet low in fat and sugar; high-fibre carbohydrates are encouraged – for example, wholemeal bread and other cereals. The child who always has to go without crisps, chips and snacks between meals will need a lot of support and encouragement from parents and carers.

Food intolerances and food allergies

Food intolerances

Food intolerance is an adverse reaction to some sort of food or ingredient that occurs every time the food is eaten, but particularly if larger quantities are consumed. Food intolerance is not the same as:

- a food **allergy**, because the immune system is not activated
- food poisoning, which is caused by toxic substances that would cause symptoms in anyone who ate the food.

Food intolerance does not include psychological reactions to food. It is also much more common than food allergy.

Some babies develop an intolerance to cows' milk protein. The most common symptoms are vomiting, diarrhoea and failure to thrive. After weaning, foods most likely to cause an adverse reaction in babies are:

- hen's eggs
- fish

- citrus fruits
- wheat and other cereals
- pork.

Sometimes an adverse reaction will be temporary, perhaps following an illness, but the offending food should always be removed from the baby's diet. Dietetic advice should be sought before any changes to a balanced diet are made.

Food allergies

A food allergy is an abnormal response (an allergic reaction) of the immune system to otherwise harmless foods. Up to 5 per cent of children have food allergies. Most children outgrow their allergy, although an allergy to peanuts and some other tree nuts is considered lifelong.

There are eight foods that cause 90 per cent of all food-allergic reactions:

- peanuts
- soy
- tree nuts – such as almonds, walnuts, pecans, etc.
- wheat
- milk
- shellfish
- eggs
- fish.

Milk is the most common cause of food allergies in children, but peanuts, nuts, fish and shellfish commonly cause the most severe reactions.

What are the symptoms of an allergic reaction?

Symptoms of an allergic response can include:

- vomiting
- hives (or urticaria) – an itchy, raised rash, usually found on the trunk or limbs
- itching or tightness in the throat
- diarrhoea
- eczema
- difficulty breathing
- cramps
- itching or swelling of the lips, tongue or mouth
- wheezing.

Allergic symptoms can begin from within minutes to up to one hour after ingesting the food.

Anaphylaxis

In rare cases of food allergy, just *one bite* of food can bring on **anaphylaxis**. This is a severe reaction that

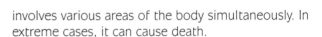

involves various areas of the body simultaneously. In extreme cases, it can cause death.

Anaphylaxis is a sudden and severe, potentially life-threatening allergic reaction. It can be caused by insect stings or medications, as well as by a food allergy. Although potentially any food can cause anaphylaxis, peanuts, nuts, shellfish, fish and eggs are the foods that most commonly cause this reaction.

Symptoms of anaphylaxis may include all those listed above for an allergic reaction. In addition, the child's breathing is seriously impaired and the pulse rate becomes rapid. Anaphylaxis is fortunately very rare, but it is also very dangerous:

- Symptoms can occur in as little as 5 to 15 minutes.
- As little as half a peanut can cause a fatal reaction in severely allergic individuals.
- Some severely allergic children can have a reaction if milk is splashed on their skin.
- Being kissed by somebody who has eaten peanuts, for example, can cause a reaction in severely allergic individuals.

See Chapter 15, p. 338 for more information on treating anaphylaxis and its symptoms.

How can food allergies be managed?

The only way to manage food allergies is strictly to avoid the foods to which the child is allergic. It is important to learn how to interpret ingredients on food labels and how to spot high-risk foods. Many children outgrow earlier food-allergic symptoms as they get older, but parents will need professional support and advice to ensure that their child is receiving a safe, balanced diet.

Keeping and sharing coherent records with regard to children's special dietary requirements

Information about special dietary needs and allergies should be recorded on each child's registration document – and should be regularly checked to ensure that the information is kept up to date. Most settings display this information clearly in the food preparation area, thus ensuring that the

Reflecting on practice

Food allergies and intolerances

In your setting:

- Find out how many (if any) children have food allergies or intolerances.
- How is information displayed about children's allergies?
- Is there a policy document relating to reporting and recording allergies and intolerances?

Think about ideas

Children and their diets

- What is an E number? What effects may foods with E numbers have on children?
- Why has there been an increase in childhood obesity? Give four possible reasons.
- What is food intolerance?
- What is anaphylaxis?
- Name six foods that commonly cause allergic reactions.

Guidelines for good practice

Coping with food refusal

- ✔ Never force-feed a child, either by pushing food into his or her mouth or by threatening punishment or withdrawal of a treat.
- ✔ Keep calm and try not to make a fuss of whether their child is eating or not. Instead, try to make mealtimes pleasant, social occasions, because if children associate mealtimes with an enjoyable event, they will want to repeat it.
- ✔ Encourage self-feeding and exploration of food from an early age, without worrying about the mess.
- ✔ Offer alternative foods from every food group – for example, if a child dislikes cheese, they may eat yoghurt.
- ✔ Provide healthy, nutritious snacks between meals as these play an important part in the energy intake of young children. Ideas include fresh fruit, yoghurt, crackers with cheese or peanut butter.
- ✔ Do not give sweets and crisps between meals to children who refuse food at mealtimes.

information is accessible to all staff involved in food provision. Each practitioner should take responsibility to report and record any new information they receive regarding children's special dietary requirements, and parents and carers should be involved in the recording process.

Other diet-related issues

Food refusal

Many children go through phases of refusing to eat certain foods or not wanting to eat anything much at all. This is particularly common in children up to the age of five years and is a normal part of growing up and asserting their independence. Eating can quickly become a focus for conflict and tension at home, with parents feeling anxious and out of control. Food refusal often starts because it is one of the few ways in which children can exert influence over their parents. Reasons for food refusal in young children include the following:

- **Slower growth and small appetites** – growth slows down in the second year. This means that toddlers often have small appetites and need less food. Children eat according to their appetite, and this can vary from day to day. Some children eat in spurts; they may eat a lot one day and very little the next. It also depends on how active they have been during the day.

- **Distraction** – young children have no concept of time. Their world has become an exciting place to explore and food can seem less important when there are so many other things to do.

- **Grazing and snacking** – toddlers rarely follow a traditional meal pattern. They tend to need small and regular snacks. Parents may offer sweets or crisps throughout the day so that children 'will not go hungry'. Children then become even less inclined to eat their meals when they know that they can fill up on their favourite snacks. Large quantities of milk or other drinks throughout the day also affect a child's appetite.

- **Fussy eating and food fads** – showing independence is part of normal child development and this often includes refusing to eat foods 'to see what will happen'. It is quite normal for children to have certain times when their food choices become very limited – for example, they will only eat food prepared and presented in a certain way. Some decide they do not like mixed-up food or different foods touching each other on the plate, and they develop strong likes and dislikes that frequently change.

- **New textures and tastes** – children are experimenting with, or being asked to try, new textures and tastes. Rejecting a food does not always mean the child does not like it – he or she may well eat it when it is offered the very next day.

- **Seeking attention** – Children may seek to gain attention in different ways: They may test their parents' reactions and learn the effects of their uncooperative behaviour. They may have learnt to say 'no' and may welcome all the attention they get by, for example, refusing to eat (or taking a long time to eat) a meal.

How to cope with food refusal

Research shows that one-third of all parents worry that their child is not eating enough, but unless they are ill, young children will never voluntarily starve themselves. If a child seems to be healthy and energetic, they are almost certainly eating enough. There is plenty of advice for parents and carers from health experts and child dieticians on how to cope with their child's refusal of food.

Economic and social factors affecting diet and nutrition

See Moving on section for economic and social factors affecting diet and nutrition.

The effects of illness on a child's appetite

Most children with a fever do not want to eat. While you should offer food, you should never force a child to eat. (See Chapter 15 for guidelines for encouraging a sick child to eat).

Special (or therapeutic) diets

Most children on special diets are not ill. Often they require a therapeutic diet that replaces or eliminates some particular nutrient to prevent illness.

The diet for diabetes mellitus

Diabetes mellitus occurs in 1 in every 500 children under the age of about 16 years, and results in difficulty in converting carbohydrate into energy, due to under-production of insulin. Insulin is a hormone that lowers the level of glucose (a type of sugar in the blood), and is usually given by daily injection. A diet sheet will be devised by the hospital dietician. It is important that mealtimes are regular and that some carbohydrate is included at every meal. Children with diabetes should be advised to carry glucose sweets whenever they are away from home, in case of hypoglycaemia (low blood sugar).

The diet for cystic fibrosis

The majority of children with cystic fibrosis (see p. 343) have difficulty absorbing fats. They need to eat 20 per cent more protein and more calories than children without the disease, so require a diet high in fats and carbohydrates. They are also given daily vitamin supplements and pancreatic enzymes.

The diet for coeliac disease

Coeliac disease is a condition in which the lining of the small intestine is damaged by gluten, a protein found in wheat and rye. In babies, it is usually diagnosed about three months after weaning onto solids containing gluten, but some children do not show any symptoms until they are older. Treatment for coeliac disease is by gluten-free diet, which has to be for the rest of the person's life. All formula milks available in the UK are gluten-free, and many manufactured baby foods are also gluten-free. Any cakes, bread and biscuits should be made from gluten-free flour, and labels on processed foods should be read carefully to ensure that there is no 'hidden' wheat product in the ingredients list.

Commercially available play dough is made from 40 per cent ordinary flour, as is the home-made variety used in nurseries and playgroups. Extra vigilance is needed by staff to stop children with coeliac disease putting it in their mouth, or – safer still – dough can always be made using gluten-free flour.

The diet for galactosaemia

Galactosaemia is a very rare genetic disorder leading to liver disease, eye cataracts and mental disability. It is caused by an inability to absorb galactose (a nutrient found in milk). The child with galactosaemia cannot digest or use galactose, which, together with glucose, forms lactose, the natural sugar of milk. A list of 'safe foods' with a low galactose content will be issued by the dietician, and food labels should be checked for the presence of milk solids and powdered lactose, which contain large amounts of this sugar.

The diet for children with difficulties chewing and swallowing

Children with cerebral palsy can experience difficulties with either or both of these aspects of eating. Food has to be liquidised, but this should be done in separate batches so that the end result is not a pool of greyish sludge. Presentation should be imaginative. Try to follow the general principle of making the difference in the meal as unobtrusive as possible.

Meeting children's individual dietary needs

Children with food allergies: all staff in early years settings should be aware of the identities of children who have food allergies, and should have clear instructions on how to deal with each case. In particular, lunchtime supervisors need to be kept informed. Most settings display a photograph of any child with a special dietary requirement or allergy in the food preparation area to ensure that permanent

▲ **Figure 16.5** An EpiPen

and supply staff are aware of each individual child's needs.

When a child has been diagnosed as having a **severe allergy** to a particular food, staff *may* decide to minimise the risk of exposure by avoiding having the food or ingredient in the setting. In severe cases it is essential that there is regular access to up-to-date advice from a registered dietician because ingredients in processed foods change frequently. Everybody involved in the care of children with known allergies should know:

- how to recognise the symptoms of a food allergy or intolerance
- how to avoid the foods he or she is sensitive to
- what to do if they have an allergic reaction
- how to use their adrenaline injector or EpiPen, if they have one
- when and how to record and report any suspicion of food allergy or intolerance.

Guidelines for good practice

Managing allergies and intolerances

✓ All staff should be aware of which children suffer from an allergy and to which food, and of the policy regarding first aid and administering medication.

✓ All staff involved in the care of that child must be aware of the foods and ingredients being offered to the child.

✓ Care must be taken in the preparation and serving of food not to cross-contaminate food being served to a child with an allergy.

✓ If you ever notice swelling of a child's mouth or face or breathing difficulties when eating, seek medical advice immediately. Symptoms such as a rash or vomiting after eating may also suggest that there has been a reaction to a food. Always inform the parent or carer.

✓ To lessen the risk of peanut allergies, peanut-containing foods should not be given to children under three years of age if the child has a parent or sibling with a diagnosed allergy. Whole nuts should not be given to any child under the age of five years because of the risk of choking.

Reflecting on practice

Special dietary requirements

Find out about the policy in your work setting covering special dietary requirements. In particular, find out about:

- special diets (which have been medically advised)
- preference diets (where there is no degree of risk attached)
- food allergies.

How does your setting ensure that any special dietary requirements are identified, and that every child is offered the appropriate food and drink?

The social and educational role of food and mealtimes

Eating patterns or habits may be influenced by various factors:

- religious beliefs or strong ethical principles
- cultural background and ethnic origin
- the availability of different foods
- time and money constraints
- preferences and tastes that are shaped during early infancy.

Food is part of every child's culture, and eating rituals vary with different cultures. Mealtimes can provide a valuable opportunity to further the child's **social development** by promoting:

- listening and other conversation skills
- independence, in eating and serving food, and in taking responsibility
- courtesy towards others and turn-taking
- a shared experience, which provides a social focus in the child's day
- self-esteem – the child's family and cultural background are valued through their mealtime traditions
- self-confidence – through learning social skills, taking turns and saying 'please' and 'thank you', the child gains confidence as a valued and unique member of their social situation.

Cognitive development is furthered during mealtimes by:

- promoting hand–eye coordination through the use of cutlery and other tools
- stimulating the senses of taste, touch, sight and smell
- enjoyment of interesting conversations
- promoting language development and increasing vocabulary

- developing the mathematical concepts of shape and size, using foods as examples
- creating opportunities for learning through linked activities – for example, stories about food, origins of food, preparation and cookery
- experiencing cultural variation in foods and mealtime traditions.

As an early years practitioner, you are ideally placed to ensure that *stereotyping* in relation to eating habits is not practised. Mealtimes and the choice of food can be used in a positive sense to affirm a feeling of cultural identity.

Raising awareness of healthy eating

Almost all children have some experience of cooking, or at the very least food preparation, in their own homes. This experience can range from watching tins being opened and the contents heated, seeing fruit being peeled and cut, or bread being put in a toaster and then spread, to a full meal being cooked.

Food preparation and cooking activities are also useful in raising children's awareness of healthy and nutritious foods, educating them about diet and choice. For example, by discussing the need for an ingredient to sweeten food, children can be introduced to the variety available and be made aware of healthy options.

Children learn through active involvement so any cooking activity must be chosen carefully to ensure that children can participate. There is very limited value in them watching an adult carry out the instructions and occasionally letting them have a stir!

Other learning outcomes include:

- development of **physical skills** through using the equipment – pouring, beating, whisking, stirring etc.

- **aspects of counting, sorting, measuring** – size and quantity – sharing, fractions, ordinal number (i.e. first, second), sequencing and memory through following and recalling the recipe instructions
- **independence skills** through preparation, controlling their own food and equipment, tidying up
- **expressing their ideas**, opinions, likes and dislikes
- understanding **how to present food** attractively through arrangement and decoration.

Planning a cooking activity with young children

When selecting a cooking activity, remember:

- that parental wishes must be respected
- to check that all children can eat the food to be cooked
- to check that there are no problems regarding allergies or religious dietary restrictions
- to follow the basic food safety and hygiene guidelines for preparation of food.

Ideas for planning and implementing a cooking activity include:

- cutting and preparing fruit, vegetables, salad items or cheese
- spreading breads, crackers or crispbreads with a variety of foods – butter, jam, cream cheese, yeast extract etc.
- making biscuits or cakes, although as these are never part of a healthy diet this activity should be an occasional treat.

Benefits of working in partnership with parents/carers in relation to special dietary requirements

See Moving on section for information on benefits of working in partnership with parents/carers in relation to special dietary requirements.

▲ **Figure 16.6** Cooking activities can support different areas of learning

Look, listen and note

Observe children carrying out a cooking activity

Plan the activity, using the ideas outlined above. Allow plenty of time for preparation, and follow the guidelines below.
After the activity, evaluate your activity and your observation:

- How successful were you in achieving your aims?
- Were all the children involved?
- What do you think the children learned about healthy eating?

Guidelines for good practice

Implementing a cooking activity with children

✓ Always prepare surfaces with anti-bacterial spray and clean cloths.

✓ Always ensure children have washed their hands and scrubbed their fingernails.

✓ Always provide protective clothing and, if necessary, roll up long sleeves.

✓ Always tie back long hair.

✓ Always check equipment for damage.

✓ Always follow the safety procedures and policies of the work setting.

✓ Always ensure adequate supervision.

✓ Always remind children not to cough over food or put their fingers or utensils in their mouths when handling food.

✓ Always check the use-by dates of food items and store them correctly.

✓ Always check for 'E' numbers and artificial ingredients in bought food items.

Always check any allergies and dietary requirements of the children involved. Remember that a child can have an allergic reaction just by touching something they are allergic to.

Reflecting on practice

Supporting healthy eating

Consider your own role when supporting healthy eating in your setting. Try to answer the following questions to help you reflect on your own experiences:

● Am I a good role model for the children?

● Do I actively seek to promote healthy eating through a thorough understanding of what constitutes a healthy diet?

● Are mealtimes and snack times enjoyable for all the children?

● Do I encourage children to help themselves to water throughout the day?

● Do I observe children to ensure they are eating a healthy diet?

● Am I aware of the food preferences of individual children or of their needs for a particular diet?

● Do I consult with parents or carers about their child's dietary needs?

● Do I try to involve both children and their families when planning food-related activities?

Moving on

Economic and social factors affecting diet and nutrition

Many families in the UK are on a reduced income – for example, as a result of sickness or unemployment. Surveys have identified four main problems for the many people who receive Income Support:

● Healthy food is relatively highly priced. Lean meat costs more than fattier cuts, and wholemeal bread can cost 25 per cent more than white bread.

● Fuel costs (gas or electricity) mean that it can be cheaper to cook chips than jacket potatoes.

● The siting of superstores on the outskirts of towns has meant that shops in inner-city areas are smaller and more expensive, so healthy foods become less available.

● Certain facilities and skills are required to prepare healthier foods. If a family is living in bed and breakfast accommodation, for example, cooking may be impractical.

Ideas for increasing the nutritional quality of the diet that may also save money are to:

● use less meat, adding pulses and lentils to stews and casseroles instead

● use as little oil or fat in cooking as possible

● cut down on meat and fill up on potatoes, rice and starchy vegetables.

Think about ideas

Budgeting for a healthy diet

Plan a menu for one week, for a family of two adults and three children, aged eight, four and two years. The menu should provide a varied and nutritionally balanced diet for the whole family. Cost the items needed and explain why you have included them.

Try to add some practical tips to the ones given above for improving diets with only a limited budget.

Benefits of working in partnership with parents/carers in relation to special dietary requirements

Many early years settings have written procedures for children with special dietary needs. This helps practitioners to work in partnership with parents to find out more about their child's requirements and to reassure them that their child's needs will be met. A procedure may include the following points:

- Before a child starts the nursery the child's parents will be asked by the key person to outline the child's dietary needs.
- If the child has a food allergy or requires a special diet the parents will be asked to identify in detail any food allergies or special dietary needs that their child has. They may be asked to complete a 'Special Dietary Needs' form, for example, depending on how the setting records this information.
- The key person will ensure that the Nursery Manager and all members of staff who may come into contact with the child know about the child's individual needs and any actions required.
- The Nursery Manager will ensure that a suitable individual menu is drawn up for the child (expert advice will be sought if necessary).
- Parents should advise the setting manager which foods can be given as alternatives, ones to be avoided and any triggers. They should also provide confirmation in writing.
- The child's parents will be given a copy of the individual menus and asked to sign an agreement that their child may have all the foods and drinks listed.
- The cook will be given a copy of the child's signed menu and will inform all other staff who may be involved in preparing the child's food about the child's individual needs and any actions required.
- The child's parents will be asked to give permission for their child's individual allergies or individual dietary needs to be displayed discreetly in the nursery to ensure that all staff members are aware of what the child may and may not be given to eat and drink.

- If a child is provided with particular products on prescription, for example gluten-free bread, it may be possible for parents to provide a quantity of these to the setting for cooks to use when preparing a meal.

It is well known that a diet of 'junk food' – too much sugar, additives in processed food, the wrong sorts of fats etc. – can damage children's physical development, causing problems such as obesity and diabetes. Now there is a growing public awareness of the damage that these harmful foods can also do to the child's developing brain.

Research the possible effects of a junk food diet on the developing brain. The following resources will be of use to you:

Palmer, S., 2007, *Detoxing Childhood*, London: Orion Books.

Jamie Oliver's 2015 campaigns (a) to make learning about growing and cooking food compulsory in all UK schools, and (b) to introduce a tax on drinks containing high levels of sugar.

Northstone, K., Joinson, C., Emmett P. et al., 'Are Dietary Patterns in Childhood Associated with IQ at 8 years of age? A Population-based Cohort Study', *Epidemiology Community Health*, 7 February 2011.

Food Standards Agency Food colours and hyperactivity:

https://www.food.gov.uk/science/additives/foodcolours

British Nutrition Foundation

www.nutrition.org.uk/healthyliving/lifestages/feeding-your-toddlerpre-school-child

Caroline Walker Trust

www.cwt.org.uk

Infant and Toddler Forum

www.infantandtoddlerforum.org

NHS Choices

www.nhs.uk

Further reading, weblinks and resources

British Nutrition Foundation

For information on healthy eating and the Balance of Health pictorial guide.
www.nutrition.org.uk

Food Standards Agency: Food colours and hyperactivity

https://www.food.gov.uk/science/additives/foodcolours

The Caroline Walker Trust

www.cwt.org.uk

Infant and Toddler Forum

www.infantandtoddlerforum.org

England – Change4Life

www.nhs.uk/change4life

Scotland - Take life on, one step at a time

www.takelifeon.co.uk

Wales - Change4Life Wales

www.change4lifewales.org.uk

Northern Ireland - Get a life, get active

www.getalifegetactive.com

Childrens Food Trust – Eat Better Do Better

The Children's Food Trust has a mission to get every child eating well at home, in childcare, at school and beyond. *Voluntary Food and Drink Guidelines for Early Years Settings in England – A Practical Guide can be found here.*
www.childrensfoodtrust.org.uk/childrens-food-trust/early-years

Vegetarian Society

www.vegsoc.org

Vegan Society

www.vegansociety.com

References

Palmer, S., 2007, *Detoxing Childhood*, London: Orion Books.

Northstone, K., Joinson, C., Emmett P. et al., 'Are Dietary Patterns in Childhood Associated with IQ at 8 years of age? A Population-based Cohort Study', *Epidemiology Community Health*, 7 February 2011.

17 Play, imagination and creativity

This chapter introduces key issues in relation to play in the early years of childhood. It looks at historical ideas of play and how they impact on our views of play today and also emphasises the importance of considering the cultural contexts of play. The play of babies, toddlers and young children is looked at, along with the role of the early years practitioner in supporting play and the principles that should underpin the provision of resources for play. The link between play, imagination and creativity and the early years curriculum is also discussed.

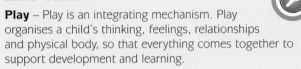

KEY TERM

Play – Play is an integrating mechanism. Play organises a child's thinking, feelings, relationships and physical body, so that everything comes together to support development and learning.

What is play?

Play is probably one of the most important elements of childhood and so understanding what play is, is fundamental to the professional knowledge of early years practitioners. Yet it is a word that is used in many different ways and so can be difficult to define. To explore our understanding of play we look at the ideas of historical figures who have championed play and how those ideas affect our approach to play today.

Pioneers of play

Jan Amos Comenius (1592–1670)

This Moravian (now the Czech Republic) educator and bishop anticipated some of the ideas of Friedrich Froebel by a century. He believed that children learn through the senses and through real, first-hand experiences. He thought that teachers should try to make learning interesting and enjoyable and that learning by doing and helping children to play was part of this. He thought play was important because children would use what they learnt through play later in life. In his book, *The Great Didactic*, published in Amsterdam in 1649 (the year Charles I was executed in England), Comenius emphasised movement and exercise; he believed that giving children interesting, real and play experiences was the key to education, and that children should understand the reasons for rules.

Friedrich Froebel (1782–1852)

Before theories about play were established, Froebel pioneered the view that play acts as a way of bringing together and organising learning; sometimes called an integrating mechanism. Play helps children to use what they know, to apply their knowledge and understanding as they think, have ideas and feelings, relate to people

and have confidence in their physical bodies. He thought that play helps children to show their deepest possible levels of learning. Play helps children to understand themselves, others and the universe.

Karl Groos (1861–1946)

Groos wrote a book called *The Play of Animals* in 1898. He believed that play is a way for children to run off excess energy, but, more importantly, that play is preparation for later life, as it gives children opportunities to practise skills they will need later; for example, playing with dolls may develop the nurturing skills needed for parenting.

Johan Huizinga (1872–1945)

The Dutch cultural historian saw play within an evolutionary framework. As animals inhabited the earth before humans did, and animals play, Huizinga proposed that play is therefore older than human culture. In 1938, Huizinga wrote a book called *Homo Ludens*, which translates as *Man the Player*. In it, he argues that play gives children freedom and experiences that are more than their ordinary, real lives, beyond their local space and time. He said that play gives children a sense of order and that no financial profit is gained from play.

Psychoanalytic perspectives on play

From a psychoanalytic perspective, play has a role in enabling children to explore their inner troubles and concerns, and to express or work through anxieties.

Melanie Klein (1882–1960) saw play as being a child's talk. She observed, listened to and took seriously the anxieties of very young children, being the first to recognise that children express their unconscious worries, wishes and actual experiences in a symbolic way through play and games.

Anna Freud (1895–1982) thought it was important to observe children at play, and to see how they use play to move in and out of reality, experimenting in this way with their feelings.

Donald Winnicott (1896–1971) argued that it is only in play that children and adults are able to be creative, through exploring who we are. When a baby receives the care it needs it can develop a creative and playful self (Winnicott 2005). Winnicott also identified that when a baby uses a transitional object (such as a blanket) as a substitute for the absence of their carer, it is an early creation of a symbol.

 ## Cognitive theories of play

Jean Piaget (1896–1980): For Piaget, play is about keeping balanced. He thought this had two aspects:

- accommodation – adapting to a situation
- assimilation – confirming what you already know through your experiences.

Play is mainly to do with assimilation, using what is known, familiar and understood. It is about applying what has already been learnt. There is a saying that you can only learn what you already know. That is what play does for you. It helps you to strengthen what you know in deep and far-reaching ways.

Piaget thought there were two aspects to play, in a developmental sequence:

- sensory and movement play
- imagination, pretend and symbolic play.

He thought that these increasingly turn into games with rules in middle childhood (at approximately 7–12 years old).

Lev Vygotsky (1896–1934): Vygotsky saw play as a 'leading factor in development' (Vygotsky 1978: 101). He thought that play creates a 'zone of potential development', in which children are able to function at their highest level of learning. He suggested that it is as if children become a 'head taller than they really are' in play. He valued imaginative play, so did not focus so much on play before the toddler age when that emerges. In his view, play creates a way of freeing children from the constraints of everyday life.

Jerome Bruner (1915–): Bruner suggests that children need a long childhood because there is so much for them to learn in preparation for their lives as adults. They learn about the technical aspects of life and about their culture. Play in the early years is the main way in which they experiment freely and learn to do this, and through which they are initiated into their culture. Children play with objects provided and chosen by adults, and by 'doing' (Bruner calls this enactive learning). They learn the rules of games from people who teach them as they play together (see Chapter 6 for more information) and they become

familiar with the rules of the culture through their play. See Bruce 1996, 2004 for more information.

Views of play

Play as recreation

Play is not the same as recreation or relaxation. This idea may come from notions of how adults 'play'. Usually this is through a form of recreational activity such as sport or a handicraft. For adults, such recreation is often defined by being different to 'work'; recreation is about relaxing and not thinking very hard.

Sometimes, in early years, play is discussed as children's work, which aims to make play sound important, as 'work' is associated with serious, purposeful, adult activity (Grieshaber and McArdle 2010).

The difficulty with this idea (as with play and learning) is that practitioners may only see play as important where they can understand the purpose of it. Play *is* purposeful; it is about the highest levels of development and learning and it is serious; sometimes play is difficult and challenging. But play is also fun and apparently frivolous, just as work can also be.

Play as a means through which children burn off excess energy

The idea of children needing to 'let off steam' through physical play can still be seen in practice when there is a differentiation between being inside and 'working' or 'learning' (usually while sitting down) and 'play' usually outside and running around. Here, play is used as some kind of reward or as a necessary process to enable better learning or concentration (school 'playtimes' for example). This view can lead to seeing physical play as unimportant and disregarding the learning that happens in all situations through active hands-on experiences.

Play as a rehearsal for later life

In this perspective, play enables children to practise the physical, intellectual and social skills they will need in adulthood. In practice this can be seen in the provision of 'home corners' and play equipment that includes miniature replicas of real life items such as drills, telephones and dolls, for example. It is important to consider that as well as exploring the adult roles that children see and experience around them, they are also reproducing or re-enacting cultural expectations in their play (James et al. 1998). So a difficulty with this might be that such equipment (or the way it is offered by adults) might lead to stereotyped play. This view may also lead practitioners and parents to inhibit certain types of play (boys dressing up in dresses is a classic example) as they think it may lead to undesirable character formation. The practitioner may also see their role as instructing the children in skills necessary for later on in life.

Play as therapy

Babies and young children express both their joys and worries in their play and they are learning about feelings and emotions as much as the properties of objects and materials. Hyder (2005) argues that play offers an important vehicle for children to play out their fears and anxieties. This view of play is apparent in early years practice when we provide an angry child with clay to pummel, or dolls for a child with a new sibling. Practitioners today understand the power of books and stories in facilitating young children's emotional understanding. Books such as 'Owl Babies' (Waddell 1994) can help young children to start to understand and manage their feelings.

Children who are in emotional pain can use play to find out more about how they feel, to understand their feelings and to deal with them, so that they gain a feeling of control over their lives. Sometime this might be in a more formal play therapy session, where the child's play is self-directed and takes place within a protected, uninterrupted time and space, with a play therapist who does not direct the play but gives the child their full attention and, in their comments, reflects back to the child what they think the child might be communicating in their play (Manning-Morton 2011).

Play as learning

This view has come to dominate our view of play in early years. So much so that the two words 'play' and 'learning' are sometimes used to almost mean the same thing. In the EYFS English curriculum guidance document (DfE 2014) they are always used together. This approach developed originally as a means to assert the importance of children's play and to move away from the 'play as recreation' view. However, the danger of this view now is that play may only be seen as valuable when the practitioner can perceive the learning taking place and measure it in terms of outcomes. This can result in practitioners taking over children's play and adult-led activities dominating practice, and certain forms of play (particularly lively, noisy or messy play) being discouraged.

Children learn through their play but in the widest sense of the word 'learning' (finding out, exploring, experimenting, problem-solving, practising): they learn about themselves, about others and about the world around them. Play opens up possibilities to reflect on, think about and apply ideas and imagination, to explore relationships and feelings, to be physically coordinated, to be capable of flexible thinking, to think about right and wrong, fairness and meanness etc. and to experience a sense of awe and wonder.

But it would be inaccurate to say that play is the only way in which children learn. Play is part of a network of ways in which children develop and learn. These include the importance of real, first-hand experiences in which children actively participate. Taking children to the shops, or for a walk in the park or by the river; encouraging them to help to prepare meals, wash up, wash clothes

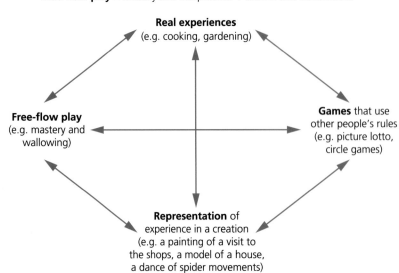

Free-flow play = mastery and competence + wallow and involvement

Real experiences
(e.g. cooking, gardening)

Free-flow play
(e.g. mastery and wallowing)

Games that use other people's rules
(e.g. picture lotto, circle games)

Representation of experience in a creation
(e.g. a painting of a visit to the shops, a model of a house, a dance of spider movements)

▲ **Figure 17.1** A network of play and learning

and learn how to dry them; going out in the rain with boots and umbrellas and raincoats – all these contribute to children's development and learning too.

The 12 features of play (Bruce 1996, 2004, 2011b) emphasise the important contribution that play makes to children's mastery in their learning, and the way in which it helps them to concentrate deeply and to reflect on their learning.

Theory and theorists: the 12 features of free-flow play – Tina Bruce

Bruce identifies that free-flow play is when children achieve mastery and competence and can wallow in ideas, experiences, feelings and relationships (Bruce 1991). Quite often, practitioners will observe children at play, and have a sense that this is a rich play scenario, but this does not help the adult to say why this might be. Bruce suggests 12 features of play that can be used to help practitioners to consider how children are playing and to share the importance of their children's play with parents and with other practitioners.

The 12 features of play:

1 Children use real, first-hand experiences in their play, such as going to the shops or preparing food.

2 Children have a sense of control when they play and they begin to make up rules – for example, 'the dog must be fed and his plate must be here, on the floor, because I say so'. Children feel powerful when they play.

3 Children find, use and make play props when they play. This is creative, as they use things in flexible and new ways. It is imaginative, as they rearrange their experiences to suit the play, themselves and the characters.

4 Children choose to play. No one can make a child play.

5 When children play, they sometimes rehearse the future – for example, in their role play, when they pretend to be adults.

6 Children might pretend when they play – for example, that they are the 'goodies' chasing the 'baddies'. They organise their thinking, transforming it as they do so.

7 Children might choose to play alone, needing some personal space and time to reflect and try out an idea they have – for example, with their small-world garage.

8 They might play with other children, in parallel (doing something similar alongside another child), associatively or cooperatively.

Look, listen and note

Observe children at play and afterwards analyse your observation in relation to the 12 features of play.

If 7 or more of the 12 features are present, then it is probably a rich play scenario. If only a few of the features are present, it does not necessarily mean the child is not doing something worthwhile, but it may not be play.

If you have observed a baby or toddler, you may notice fewer of the 12 features. Does this mean the child or children are not playing? If not, what do you think they are doing?

9 When children play they have a personal play agenda. They might want to put pretend jam on all the pretend cakes, or bath the dog. They will find a way to carry this out. Practitioners are welcome to play with children, providing that everyone respects each other's personal play agenda.

10 Children involved in rich play become deeply involved and are difficult to distract. Children wallow in their play.

11 Children show us their latest learning when they play. They might have just mastered riding a bicycle, so in their play they keep riding their bike to post a letter, to go to the shops, to take their child to school – anything, as long as they are on their bike!

12 Play brings together children's learning. It organises the learning, so that it becomes connected and an integrated whole.

Types of play

A traditional way of talking about play has been to break it up into types of play. This can help to make play more tangible or real– that is, less abstract (see Chapter 8, p. 152 for a definition) to understand. However, there is much to be said for looking at play as a whole, because it is so central to childhood. The huge variety of types of play shows that play creeps into most areas of a child's life.

The problem with breaking play up into different types is that people seem to add more and more types to the list and the number grows all the time, which makes analysing play less and less manageable as many of them overlap or use different words for similar types of play.

Theory and theorists: ludic and epistemic play – Corinne Hutt

Hutt et al. (1989) defined play in three categories: epistemic, ludic and games with rules. Epistemic play

▲ **Figure 17.2** Exploratory play is supported by providing children with a wide range of resources made from materials with different properties

relates to children gaining knowledge through exploring and problem-solving, seeing what things do and how they work; ludic play relates to the kind of fantasy and pleasurable play of children once learning has

been achieved. In this perspective, although all three categories are seen as important, 'epistemic play' is valued as being more likely to aid cognitive development, whereas ludic play, although it brings mastery of skills, is seen as being for sheer entertainment.

Epistemic and ludic play relate strongly to Piaget's theory of accommodation and assimilation. Accommodation is linked to the idea of epistemic play as it involves encountering and learning something new, while assimilation is linked to the idea of ludic play and the practice and enjoyment of repeating a learnt behaviour or skill.

Think about ideas

Review the types of play listed in Table 17.1. Which of them relates more to 'ludic play' and which to 'epistemic' play?

Symbolic play
When something stands for something else, it is symbolic of the real thing – for example, a leaf can symbolise a plate; a pebble can symbolise a potato on the plate. Symbolic play involves children making one thing stand for another.

Pretend play
When children pretend, they transform reality and rearrange it – for example, a clothes peg is not really a door key, but they pretend it is.

Imaginative play
The imagination is fed by the real experiences children have. The way they play shops will be richer if they have visited supermarkets, corner shops, markets and car boot sales. When children play imaginatively, they use their experiences, rearranging and transforming them – for example, a group of children who went regularly to the swimming pool later made a swimming pool using large hollow blocks.

Role play
Children imitate the roles of adults. They pretend to be a doctor, nurse, vet, parent, postman or postwoman, builder, cook, and so on. At first, they tend to be very literal, imitating what they see adults do. Gradually, they are able to become a character, such as the grumpy cook, the parent in a rush, and so on.

Domestic play
We see children preparing food, washing up crockery, washing clothes, ironing, shopping, putting dolls to bed and taking them for walks in prams, and so on. The first signs of role play in toddlers are often about their immediate experiences, such as feeding and changing babies. The play is very literal at first, imitating what they see people do. Later, they assume different characters, such as the Auntie.

Fantasy play
Fantasy play is more about roles the children do not know about, but might themselves take on one day – for example, going to the moon in a space rocket or diving in the sea with dolphins. Superhero play is a popular theme.

Dramatic (or narrative) play
Drama involves characters and a story. This kind of play prepares children in deep and important ways for later creative writing. It involves creative, imaginative and pretend play. It is more than simply retelling a story, because the children adapt the story and characters to meet the needs of the play scenario.

Socio-dramatic play
Dramatic play could take place alone. We often see this when children talk to themselves, assuming the different voices of their characters. Socio-dramatic play, on the other hand, involves several children, playing out characters and developing a story together.

Creative play

This description is often used in relation to play with sand, dough, clay, paints, sensory materials, and so on. It tends to emphasise the artistic aspect of play. In fact, creative play is about the scientific and humanities aspects of play as much as the artistic. Children certainly create ideas and play with paint, but they also play with scientific ideas and create using these. Sometimes children play creatively in ways that some practitioners discourage; making up silly words, for example. Rather than discourage this, practitioners could usefully turn it into a rhyming game, for example.

Play using props

Children sometimes use props that are very realistic in appearance, but often they prefer to make their own or to use 'found' objects. These usually have just a suggestion of what they are – for example, they might use a wooden block and pretend it is the iron; a stone might become a cake; they might make mud pies and pretend to cook them in a cardboard box which 'is' the oven.

Physical play: gross-motor play and developmental movement play

This occurs when children celebrate their physical ability – for example, by riding a two-wheeled bicycle or climbing to the top of the climbing frame. Some settings have developed 'developmental movement play' sessions based on the work of Bette Lamont (1991) to facilitate and encourage children's physical development and sensory integration.

Rough-and-tumble play

Rough-and-tumble play requires great sensitivity to others in order not to hurt them physically; for example, not using all your strength or weight. This form of play often occurs before going to sleep, and it bonds those playing emotionally and socially.

Dizzy play

This kind of play is rarely described in books about play in the UK. Marjatta Kalliala, who is Finnish, writes in detail about Callois's theory of dizzy play in her book, *Play Culture in a Changing World* (2006). Children sometimes just love to stand on the spot and spin round and round, making themselves dizzy on purpose. They tip and tilt and spin. Research is showing that this kind of play is important for brain development. Babies often lean sideways out of prams, or lean back to view the world upside down.

Manipulative play: fine motor play

Children use their hands, playing with small-world animals, the dolls' house or with construction kits such as Brio. In the 1900s there was great emphasis on exercises to develop the hands, but it is now realised that a rich play environment encourages this without the need for uninteresting exercises.

Daring and adventure play

From an early age, children love to test their physical skills as they play and to perform feats of daring – for example, they walk on narrow walls, jump off the stairs, and so on. Rather than placing too much emphasis on safety, it is now becoming better understood that children need environments that are only as safe as necessary. This requires that practitioners carry out risk assessments (see Chapter 14 for more information on risk assessments). Helen Tovey writes about this in her book, *Playing Outdoors: Spaces and Places, Risk and Challenge* (2008). It is the children who never engage in adventure play who are most likely to have accidents.

Heuristic play

Treasure basket play and heuristic play with objects (Goldschmied and Jackson 2004) encourage babies and toddlers to explore natural objects, such as shells, stones and wooden objects.

Water play, sand play, small-world play, messy play, natural-materials play, den play, outdoor play, music play, dance play

The list of types of play that are linked to an area of material provision could go on forever. It shows that the environment practitioners create for children is of great importance, in order for a rich variety of play scenarios to emerge.

Games with rules

Games involve rules. Whereas play is about the way that children experiment with what happens if they break, make or change rules, games teach children the rules themselves. In Piaget and Hutt's theories, games with rules are associated with older children. However games such as peek-a-boo played with babies have rules. There are different kinds of rules in different sorts of games:

- Social and cultural games – the rules of greetings and partings, thank-you games and taking-turns games. In different cultures, the rules will be different.
- Mathematical games – matching games, such as snap or games involving counting such as snakes and ladders.
- Ring games and songs – for example, 'The Farmer's in her Den' or 'Ring a ring a roses', and choosing partners, taking turns and joining in the chorus.

▲ **Table 17.1** Types of play

Look, listen and note

Types of play

Observe a group of children at play. How many of the different types of play set out in Table 17.1 can you see in one play scenario? Evaluate your findings.

Theory and Theorists: Mildred Parten's stages of play

In the 1930s, Mildred Parten (1932) identified the following different kinds of play:

- **Solitary play:** playing alone, babies playing with objects or their hands/feet or vocalisations.

- **Parallel play:** playing alongside, gradually the child begins to watch others in their play and perhaps imitate what they do, but does not interact with them yet.

- **Associative play:** by end of the children's third year there may be more interaction between them but each has their own agenda.

- **Cooperative play:** this develops as the child grows older, especially when they experience help and positive treatment from practitioners. Gradually, children begin to share and engage in shared projects – for example, deciding together to make a road from a set of wooden building blocks. They negotiate and exchange ideas.

This theory still has a lot of influence on adults' expectations of play, particularly of babies and toddlers.

It is useful to think about these approaches to play but not tie them to a particular age group or see them as a developmental hierarchy. For example:

- **Solitary play:** children sometimes want to have personal space and do things alone. Solitary play can be very rich. Children often play in very deep ways when they are alone. It used to be thought that small babies always played in a solitary way, but because of the work of researchers such as

Colwyn Trevarthen, it has become clear that babies enjoy playing with their close adults or practitioners from the beginning (and they need to do this). The idea that this is an early level of play is misleading.

- **Spectator play:** a child may choose to watch what others do, and not want to join in.

- **Parallel (or companionship) play:** there are times when children want companionship but not much interaction – for example, two children may sit side by side and draw together, but not look at each other or talk very much about what they are doing. From an early age, children enjoy the company of someone who plays alongside them, but they do not necessarily directly interact. When one child reaches for a wooden spoon, the other might do the same. They might appear to not take any notice of each other but this type of play helps children to be sensitive to and aware of others as they play.

- **Associative play:** two children might both choose to be the chef in a cafe but they do not develop a narrative, storyline or dramatic story together; they are each busy with their own play agenda. This type of play is a rehearsal for full-blown cooperative play. If each child has a separate idea that is not shared by the other, there will be conflict. This is partly why young children need help and support in their social play or when sharing materials together. It is not appropriate, however, to force sharing. Instead, early years practitioners will need to bring in another saucepan for the extra chef. Separate ideas are separate, and if an idea is not shared, materials cannot be either! Helping children at moments like this is an important role for the early years practitioner.

- **Cooperative play:** in this type of play, children relate to each other in their characters. They agree what their play props symbolise and they develop a story together and cooperate. If the cooperation breaks down, adults can help by stating each child's ideas – for example, 'Sean, you want to build a bridge. Meg, you want to build a row of shops. You both want to use the same blocks. What can we do about this?' Children often find solutions and then return to work together again. This play can become rich when it is sustained over a long period of time.

Cultural perspectives on play

It is important, when thinking about play, to always consider the sociocultural context in which it is taking place. Play takes different forms in different families and in different cultures. Parents shape their children's play from the day they are born, through their interactions, responses and expectations of their child (Sayeed and Guerin 2000), and the cultures children

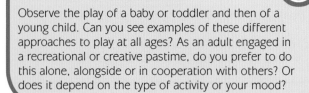

Think about ideas

Observe the play of a baby or toddler and then of a young child. Can you see examples of these different approaches to play at all ages? As an adult engaged in a recreational or creative pastime, do you prefer to do this alone, alongside or in cooperation with others? Or does it depend on the type of activity or your mood?

are born into will impact on how play is valued and how children play. For example:

• Some children in the world play mainly with bought toys.
• Some children are born into cultures where there are few commercially available toys; children play with home-made toys.
• Some children play mainly in their homes, often just in their bedrooms (Mitchell and Reid-Walsh 2002).
• Some children play mainly outside with natural resources from the environment (Oke et al. 1999).
• Some cultures see play as fundamental to children's learning so think it requires adult involvement.
• Other cultures do not see play as part of learning so adult intervention is not necessary.
• Some cultures emphasise the parent's role in play with their young children.
• Other cultures see play as children's business and older children oversee the play of the younger ones.

Culture also influences play through children's popular culture, which, in the industrialised parts of the world, is promoted through children's television programmes and related marketed toys and other items. Many practitioners are concerned about how this both exploits and influences children but there are also some positive aspects.

For example, sharing knowledge and understanding of characters and catchphrases can give children a useful starting point for conversations and playing together, creating already familiar play scenarios (particularly useful for children new to learning English). Having these familiar characters in a setting can also make children feel more at home.

Why play is seen as important

The UN convention on the rights of the child (Unicef 1989) states that every child in the world has the right to play, which gives a good indication of how important play is seen to be in the western world. The rationale for this is based on the following ideas:

• Play, communication and movement are thought to be overarching mechanisms in the brain that influence a child's development, and consequently in the way they learn.
• Play helps children to become imaginative and to develop symbols. These are important aspects of human development; we live in societies that are based on the use of symbols.
• Play involving symbolic and imaginative processes uses a very powerful mechanism in the brain that allows children to begin to transform experiences and to make sense of them. This enables children's minds to be flexible enough to think through alternatives, imagine how things could be or might have been, and to work out important ways of relating to self and others. This kind of problem-solving is an essential element of human creativity.
• Play helps children to apply their learning. Play is not so much about the new things that children learn. It is about how children begin to try things out and make sense of what they have been learning and put it to use.
• Play lifts learning to a higher level and shows children's deepest ideas, feelings and relationships and their physical possibilities. They begin to see the bigger picture, the wider world, and perhaps to think about the universe.

Play helps children to:

• reflect on life
• bring together and organise what they have been learning
• have opportunities to apply what they have been learning and to experiment safely, away from the dangers of the real world
• think flexibly
• transform what they know from the literal and real to the imagined and created
• create things they have imagined from real objects.

Play and imagination

At first, the brain forms separate images. Piaget thought that the period from three to four years was the most difficult to study, because images are internal, so it is not possible to know what is imagined. Gradually, children develop connected images. It is a bit like the difference between still photographs and a film. The technical way of saying this is that imagery becomes more mobile. Once imagery is mobile, the imagination can develop.

The imagination is important because it is the way that the human brain puts together and rearranges past experiences in new ways. The imagination transforms experience and supports creativity.

The role of the early years practitioner in supporting children's imaginative development

Even though we cannot see the images in a child's brain, we can help the imagination to develop.

- The practitioner models imaginative thoughts – for example, pretending to eat a biscuit, by picking up a piece of card and pretending to munch it.
- When looking at a conker in its spiky case, the practitioner might say, 'It looks like a hedgehog.'
- If a child says, 'Monkey', when looking through the bars of a staircase, after a visit to the zoo, he or she has an image of the cage and has used the experience of the staircase to imagine him or herself as a monkey in the cage. As a practitioner, you could say something like, 'Yes, you are like the monkey in the cage, aren't you?' to encourage their imagination.

Creativity

Creativity is about seeing things in a new way and putting ideas together differently, so that a new idea emerges. Creativity depends on the imagination. Imagination is about the images inside your head. Creativity is about bringing those ideas out of your head and making them more tangible.

The creative process

Creativity has two parts:

1 Incubation – during this part of the creative process, children gather ideas, simmer them and become aware that they have an idea they want to do something with. They do not always take form sufficiently to become a creation, because many creative ideas are abandoned along the way, as the child who is incubating them becomes distracted, loses focus, is constrained or stopped from carrying the creative process through.

2 Hatching the idea – it emerges and takes form, with a surge of energy, which sometimes makes the creator feel rather uncomfortable and restless. This means it is easy to lose the moment.
  - Sometimes creative ideas take a long time to develop. They incubate for different lengths of time, depending on the child or practitioner incubating them.

- There comes a point when the creative process of incubating results in an act of creation – the idea takes form and is hatched.
- The first creations of children are usually based on variations on a theme, doing the same thing over and over, in different places and with different materials.

Creativity in the curriculum

Creative development is discussed as a separate area of learning in the English and Welsh curriculum guidance document, which can lead to creativity as being seen as related to a narrow range of activities when in fact creativity of thought is a disposition to be nurtured across all aspects of the curriculum. In Scotland creativity is identified as one of the desired 'Approaches to Learning' and in the 'Aistear' of the Republic of Ireland, it is threaded through the 'themes of learning and development'. See the resources section on p. 392 for weblinks.

Creativity and the sciences

It is often thought that creativity is about the arts. But it is also possible to be creative in scientific ways, and in ways that are important for the humanities (human relationships and communities). When we talk about creative scientific ideas, we tend to describe these as problem-solving, or developing a theory or having a hypothesis (that is, testing an idea we have to see if it works, and if it is true); children do all these things in their play

Creativity and personal, social and emotional development

People who are creative are more likely to be fulfilled. This is because creativity takes the ordinariness out of life and makes it more satisfying and fulfilling. The psychologist Winnicott (2005) suggests that creativity relates to the feeling of 'being alive'.

In order to be creative, children need to feel emotionally safe enough to make new connections, new directions and new insights. Daring to do something different, or in a new way, is at the heart of creativity. This means that children need positive experiences of having personal space to be alone with themselves, while at the same time feeling connected to other people, especially those who are important to them emotionally.

Children who are creative are able to develop their own ideas, and are not over-dependent on the ideas of others. They develop a strong sense of self.

Children who enjoy their own company value having time for personal space; they mull over ideas and this leads to creative thinking. It is impossible to know quite how creative ideas arise, but having time for ideas to drift and simmer seems to help the creative process.

Supporting creativity

Most children do not become famous artists, music composers, dance choreographers, scientists or leaders who are known throughout the world for their creative ideas. Creativity of this kind is exceptional, but every child (including children with disabilities, SEN and learning difficulties) can be creative if they are given support and encouragement.

Children who are always being required to follow adult instructions and tasks cannot develop the control they need in order to be creative. Creativity is about doing things in new ways, not like other people. Therefore, it is impossible to know in advance how a model or painting, dance or wooden block play construction will look in the end.

▲ **Figure 17.3** Imagination and creativity is supported by providing open-ended play materials

Creativity means that adults need to give children opportunities to explore material and to free-flow in their play, and not to over-control and contain the ideas children have when they have them. On the other hand, practitioners are very important as people who can support and encourage creativity. This is further explored in the book *Cultivating Creativity: Babies, Toddlers and Young Children* (Bruce 2004).

Difficulties and challenges in play

Some children do not play

There are various reasons why children might not play:

- Sick children may not play.
- Unhappy children find it hard to play.
- The child's culture or family might not encourage play.
- Children might be expected to sit still for large parts of the day.
- Some children live over-occupied lives, with no personal space for play or time for themselves, as they are always following adult-led tasks and activities at home and in the setting.
- Lack of play during childhood, with too much sitting still, is becoming linked by some researchers with attention deficit hyperactivity disorder (ADHD). See Chapter 2 for more information on ADHD.
- Children who depend on adults directing them most of the time, when given opportunities to play will often say things like, 'I don't know what to do', 'I'm bored' or 'I need you to help me'. These children are not developing their inner resources, so they are unable to harness the energy they need in order to initiate play.

Guidelines for good practice

The role of the early years practitioner in supporting children's creativity

✔ Be there or join the child as an interested person, showing sensitive awareness.

✔ Tune into the child's thinking and do not impose your ideas.

✔ Make the child feel secure enough to let their creative ideas begin to flow.

✔ Help the child through the tricky moments when it looks as if they might give up.

✔ Help a child to develop their idea by protecting their personal space and giving them time there and then, before the creative idea evaporates and is gone.

✔ Help the child to be creative using a range of materials and techniques (dancing, making music, using clay, paint, wooden blocks, mark making and so on).

✔ Recognise that part of the creative process is letting the child's ideas ramble, meander and drift; the other part is helping the child as they try to bring all of this together as a creation.

✔ Remember that the child needs the right help at the right time in the right way.

✔ Help the child to develop the skills they need in order to carry out their creative ideas.

✔ Value the child's creation, if one emerges.

✔ Respect the child's creative thinking as a process that does not have to have a product, outcome or creation. The process is as important as any product or creation that emerges where a young child is concerned.

- Children who do not play have fewer opportunities to learn to see how others might feel or what the consequence of their actions would be for other people.
- Children are inclined to play, but they need people (including other children, practitioners and other adults) who encourage and help them to develop their play fully.

The importance of play in the development of children with learning difficulties, disabilities and complex needs

Not all children play in the same way. Some children with complex needs play using the senses and movement, rather than developing pretend play, involving the imagination and use of symbols. But it is important not to underestimate children with complex needs who are challenged in their movements and ways of engaging in play. Children with SEN and disabilities often 'dance' the developmental ladder. They may do some things at the same time as most children their age, or they may have a different timescale for different aspects of their development. The important thing is to observe what the child enjoys. This gives a very positive approach and encourages the development of play.

Children with English as an additional language

One of the powerful things about play is that it does not depend on language; it does, however, provide a relaxed context, with no pressure, and that is the ideal situation in which to learn a new language. Play gives children 'comprehensible input' (see Chapter 8)

Reflecting on practice

Dancing the developmental ladder

Joe is 4 years old, has autism and is fascinated by strips of material, which he loves to wave in front of his face and brush across his nose. The practitioner does not label this an obsession, but instead builds on his interest. She provides a variety of ribbon-like strips, and over several weeks he begins to experiment with a wider range. After a few months he is interested in eye contact with her, provided the ribbons are swaying in front of his face. One day, he parts the ribbons and looks her directly in the eye. He says, 'Boo.'

Observe a child with additional needs and identify their play interests. Plan how you might build on their play, remembering to keep your plans closely matched to the child's abilities.

Reflecting on practice

Comprehensible input through play

Noor (aged three years) has only just arrived in England. She has been separated from most of her family, but her mother is reunited with three of her children after fleeing from a war zone. Noor is in the home corner. She finds a sheet from the doll's bed and wraps it round her body. She puts the doll into the sling she has made. She finds the broom and sweeps the floor. She finds the saucepan and puts it on the stove, pretending to prepare the meal. The practitioner smiles when she catches her eye, and sits near her, but does not invade her focused play.

Noor is adjusting to her new surroundings. She does so by playing out familiar, everyday things, such as caring for the baby and preparing a meal. Learning to speak English can come later. Now what she needs is the sensitive encouragement of the practitioner.

Observe a child who is new to learning English playing with other children (who may or may not also be learning English as their second language). How does the play help them to communicate? How does the practitioner support this play? Are there any play props that might support their play interactions?

because children make props, they mime and gesture as part of their play, and they create shared meaning as they play.

Play for babies

Babies need safe opportunities to play in a way that allows them to do so through their senses and through their movements. In this context, 'safe' means physically safe and emotionally safe. Babies need the company of their practitioners in their play, to give them reassurance but mostly because, for babies, the play object is the practitioner and the environment is the psychological ambience they create (Manning-Morton and Thorp 2003, 2006).

The sensory-motor play (see Chapter 6) of babies includes:

- playing with their own hands and feet
- moving in whatever way they can
- playing with sounds, vocalising
- climbing on the adult, patting and prodding their eyes, hair, mouth
- watching interesting objects that move, particularly people and animals
- listening to interesting sounds, particularly familiar voices, music of all kinds, songs and lullabies

- mouthing interesting objects
- manipulating interesting objects with hands and feet
- feeling different textures with their whole bodies.

Babies' growth and development changes rapidly, so frequent observations must be made in order to ensure that play opportunities and materials remain safe and closely matched to their development.

For example, the principle of providing objects that are made from a range of materials to support sensory learning experiences must be carried out in a way that matches the baby's physical development. For babies lying on their backs, you might create a 'washing line' on which you can attach the object securely for the babies to bat with their hands and feet. This will usually hold more interest for the baby than most mobiles.

When the baby is able to sit up, these objects can then become part of their treasure basket, and when they become mobile, some of the objects may become part of their heuristic play materials (Goldschmied and Jackson 2004). However, not all of them may be used as part of their heuristic play because some objects that are safe in the hands of a non-mobile baby may not be safe for a mobile toddler.

Theories and theorists: the treasure basket – Elinor Goldschmied

Elinor Goldschmied (Goldschmied and Sachson 2004) pioneered treasure baskets for sitting babies who are not yet mobile. At this point in development, the sitting baby's view of the world changes as they can scan across the environment and can see interesting things but cannot get to them. By gathering interesting objects together in the treasure basket, the practitioner brings the world to the baby for them to explore, which the baby can do now from a sitting position, using their hands, feet and mouths. The objects are made from a range of materials and have different properties of weight, length, texture, temperature etc. They are not plastic because this material does not offer much to the range of senses through which babies learn. The way Goldschmied

Guidelines for good practice

The treasure basket

See useful resources on p. 000 for resources focusing on detailed discussions on the use of treasure baskets.

✔ Make sure the basket is the correct shape, height and size.

✔ The baby needs the companionship of a practitioner who sits near them but who does not join in.

✔ The treasure basket experience should take place in a quiet area, set aside for sitting babies to focus undisturbed.

✔ The objects should not be made of plastic, but of a range of natural materials that can be washed.

✔ As objects become shabby they should be removed, and there should be new objects to keep the interest of the baby who has regular use of the basket.

✔ Perishable objects, such as a lemon, should be replaced each time the basket is used.

✔ Babies need sufficient objects to be able to select from, so the basket should be full enough to encourage this.

✔ Never put an object in the treasure basket that makes you anxious about its safety for a baby or you will transfer your anxiety to the baby and put them off exploring.

✔ Remember that some babies have allergies so ensure that the objects you choose take this into account.

✔ You will need to share your understanding of this play with parents and discuss any concerns they have about the objects.

✔ Babies have different styles of approach to the basket; you need to allow for this.

✔ Observe each baby's interests and approach and think about how you can build on that during other times and play opportunities.

recommends that a treasure basket is presented is finely tuned to the needs and interests of a baby at this stage, so it is very important that they are presented to babies in the correct way or the baby will not get the full benefit of the learning the treasure basket offers.

Think about ideas

Revise your understanding of the development of babies and note down all the ways in which the treasure basket matches their development.

Research the principle of treasure baskets in Goldschmied and Jackson (2004) and Manning-Morton and Thorp (2006).

Play for toddlers and two-year-olds

Most toddlers are becoming increasingly mobile, and this becomes a key feature of their play. Because of this they are also moving from asking 'what is it?' in their play with objects to 'what does it do?' and gradually as their use of symbols increases, 'what could it be?' (Manning-Morton and Thorp 2003).

Toddlers and young children still need to explore objects using their senses and feedback from their movements, so materials, resources and environment need to match this need. All of the safety issues considered for babies still apply, including the emotional safety that the mobile toddler and two-year-old need from the 'secure-base' (Bowlby 1988) that the practitioner provides by being anchored and involved in their play.

Usually, toddlers are also beginning to talk and pretend in their play at this time. Their early symbolic play is based on imitation, whereby they are re-enacting and recreating their everyday experiences (Manning-Morton and Thorp 2015) so their play is very literal: they imitate drinking from a cup, stirring their tea, washing up, covering dolls with bedclothes and tucking them in to go to sleep. Because of this, resources need to be real objects as far as possible.

Toddlers and two-year-olds are interested in playing with other children but do not have the social skills or language for this to always be successful, so the support of the practitioner is essential in social play. But these children will share interests and will follow and imitate each other in their play.

They are also very interested in cause and effect and will test out how things work by taking them apart before they have the ability to put them back together again.

Schematic interests become apparent at this age; transporting, rotation, enclosure and envelopment are common concepts they are exploring in their play.

Theories and theorists: heuristic play – Elinor Goldschmied

Elinor Goldschmied developed heuristic play to closely match the development of the mobile toddler between 12 and 20 months old. The term 'heuristic' comes from the Greek word for 'to find' or 'to discover'. The same principles of using natural objects with a range of properties apply to this form of play as it does to the treasure basket. However, because it takes place in a group and because of the physical and social development of this age group, there are collections of objects so there is no need to share, and the space is set out to enable free movement for transporting the objects as the children choose.

KEY TERM

Schematic interests – Observable patterns of behaviour or themes of thought (see Chapter 7 for more information).

Think about ideas

Revise your understanding of the development of toddlers aged 12–20 months old and note down all the ways in which heuristic play matches their development.

Research the principles of heuristic play in Goldschmied and Jackson (2004), Manning-Morton and Thorp (2006), and Goldschmied and Hughes (1992).

Guidelines for good practice

Heuristic play

See p. 392 for useful resources focusing on detailed discussions on heuristic play.

✔ The area should have a warm, inviting floor space without lots of clutter that may distract children's attention.

✔ The space needs to be prepared in advance so that children come upon the carefully spaced piles of objects when they enter the area.

✔ All the collected objects are everyday items, such as cotton reels, cardboard tubes, keys, pine cones.

✔ The collections are each stored in their own bag.

✔ There are a collection of large tins (with safe smooth edges) for transporting items.

✔ The practitioner sits quietly and provides a calm atmosphere that supports the child's explorations without intervening, except to say something like, 'Yes, you have a lovely tin' if the child brings it to them. Otherwise, a warm smile is sufficient.

✔ Heuristic play sessions are of a particular length of time; they are not open-ended.

✔ The session ends with time built in for children to take an active part in putting the objects away in their allocated bag. This happens with positive encouragement and valuing their efforts.

Play for young children (aged between two and five years)

As play develops, children become increasingly able to engage in a world of pretend. They can imagine things beyond the literal and real imitation of things. They can move from the present into the past and the future, and as they do so they transform things. In real life, they are not a mother or a driver of a car, but once they can go beyond simply imitating what they see people do and can actually imagine what it is like to be someone else, they 'become the person'.

This is why we begin to see children experiment with ideas of feelings, relationships and social rules, such as: 'You be unkind to me and I will cry'; 'You be the baddy and I will be the policeman'. They want to explore what it is like to be good, bad, kind, unkind, and so on. Play gives them a safe 'space' to do this. They can decide not to play anymore if it becomes too much to explore evil and baddies, and they can escape from this imagined world of pretend back into the real world again. Play gives them opportunities to see how other people react when they have (pretend) temper tantrums, (pretend) refuse to eat their lunch, or (pretend) will not go to sleep. Children need to reassure themselves and those they are with that this is a world of pretend, and is not real; they often make remarks while they play such as, 'I'm pretending'.

Although the development of this possibility to transform the real world through the ability to pretend, imagine and symbolise is a key part of the development of play (typically from about 18 months/2 years until about 5/6 years), during this time children are also becoming increasingly coordinated physically and in their movements. This is why we begin to see pretend fights, in which they are learning not to really hurt one another. It is almost like a carefully choreographed dance as the drama unfolds. It is the reason why we see pirates climbing the rigging of the 'ship', children jumping off things and chasing each other without bumping into each other. They will often misjudge their movements at first, but the skills develop with practice over time. The play in the garden or at rural or urban forest school is of great importance in the development of this aspect of play (see Chapters 9 and 18 for more information on forest schools).

Play in primary schools (Key Stage 1)

One of the problems of children leaving early years settings at the age of four years and moving to primary school (reception classes in England) is that often the space is cramped, too formal and with a lack of outdoor educational opportunities. Children need to experience a curriculum that supports and extends their play until they are seven years of age. Many children are just beginning to grow in their play development at the ages of four to seven years. It is important that the sequence of play development is not stopped in its tracks or constrained because of transfer to primary school and inappropriate or unsuitable provision there.

Remember that play:

- helps children to move away from the here and now and to transform real life (pretend, imagine and symbolise), so that they make sense of their learning, reflect on what they have been learning, and apply what they know effectively and appropriately in relation to feelings, ideas, thoughts and relationships

- gives children opportunities to develop strong and well-coordinated physical bodies, which are 'thinking bodies'

- helps children to be flexible thinkers.

Play resources

It is impossible to list all the resources and materials that you might provide for children to play with, but there are some overarching principles that should be considered.

Play resources should match the development and interests of the children

Resources need to offer the right amount of challenge so that there is a balance of success and manageable failure for children. This should be assessed through close observation, which might reveal that a toy purchased for a particular age range of children is not helpful. For example, practitioners in a baby room had a selection of 'sorting boxes'. On close observation they saw that two of the boxes were far too complicated for the manipulative skills and cognitive understanding of the children. This resulted in the babies (who were very interested in the concept of 'in' and 'out') either getting frustrated and then abandoning their play or the adult getting drawn in to showing the babies the 'right' way of playing with the box. They passed those boxes to the older children's group and made their own 'posting boxes' instead, using tins with lids with holes for ping pong balls and corks, and cardboard boxes with slits for laminated slips of card.

Play resources should reflect the children's family cultural backgrounds and the wider world

Play resources need to be meaningful to all children in order to promote a sense of belonging. Toys, books, posters etc. should project positive images in order to promote a positive self-concept in all children. This includes those with SEN and disabilities and those without; it includes boys and girls, children from all backgrounds and cultures and those who speak different languages. This is important in monocultural settings, where children all share broadly the same cultural background, as well as multicultural settings.

Play resources should be open-ended

Open-ended materials and resources do not dictate what a child is expected to do with them. For example, a length of cloth can be a Batman cape, a wedding dress, a headscarf or a blanket, whereas a fire-fighter's uniform suggests that it is to be used to pretend to be a fire-fighter.

These kinds of resources encourage children to think, feel, imagine, socialise and concentrate deeply.

Play materials made from natural materials are open-ended and encourage children's creativity and scientific thinking. Children will tend to use a range of fine motor skills with these materials, such as working at the woodwork bench or making a clay coil pot.

Examples of open-ended materials are:

- found materials, such as boxes, jar lids, straws, etc. used in modelling
- dressing-up clothes and cookery items in the home area; lengths of fabric, wooden and metal bowls, conkers and pine cones
- wooden blocks; unit blocks and hollow blocks
- transforming raw materials, like clay and dough, soil and 'gloop' (cornflour and water mixture), sand and water.

In the outside area, provide resources and space for digging and planting, for exploring sand/water/mud and for plenty of movement through tunnels and tyres and on wheeled toys, on grass, soft surfacing and concrete. Bikes need to be three-wheeled and two-wheeled, some with trailers or platforms on the back so that two or three children can play with them cooperatively. Two-wheeler bikes with no pedals are excellent for children, as they can scoot them with their feet and tilt and balance without having to perform a complex combination of actions. Scooters and carts to push and pull are also important, as are prams and pushchairs.

There should be sufficient resources

This does not always mean having a lot of different items if it means that each set is too small to extend the play or to be used by several children at once. It is better to have a large amount of bricks or train track with plenty of figures, wheeled items etc. This will help to avoid competition and conflict in younger children.

A large set of wooden unit blocks has more potential for creative and imaginative play than several small sets of a plastic construction kit. It is best to keep adding to the wooden blocks, and to choose one construction kit that is as open-ended as possible, so that many different things can be constructed with it, and then to keep adding to that.

Stories and songs, books and music

These resources are fundamentally important to provision. Develop a large supply of books, including duplicate copies, kept in baskets/ boxes and in different locations to reduce competition. Develop a well-resourced music area with instruments and CD/ MP3 players from a wide range of musical styles and traditions.

Choose commercial toys and equipment carefully

It is important to note that toys are often expensive and of doubtful quality in terms of educational experience. Make sure bought toys are safe, sturdy and offer children opportunities for a range of experiences closely matched to their development and interests.

The early years practitioner's role in children's play

There are different ways of supporting children's play. All of these have a place, but it is the practitioner's professional skill to know where and when to apply an approach and the impact it may have. The practitioner's level of involvement will be determined by the age of the child/children, any particular needs the child has, the type of play and where it is, and the mood and social relationships of children in the group.

Being a facilitator

Practitioners facilitate play by providing a suitably safe and interesting environment and resources. In this way practitioners are always, to some extent, shaping the play of children in early years settings. So careful thought needs to be given to how this is done.

However, if practitioners adopt only this role, it can lead to what is called a 'laissez-faire' approach, where children are left to play without any support. Sometimes this is called 'free play'. In environments (usually not group settings) where children play across the age range, this can work because the younger children enjoy participating under the leadership of the older children. But in some settings, particularly

▲ **Figure 17.4** The practitioner might be a play facilitator, partner and observer all in the same moment

where children are divided into narrow age bands, lack of involvement from the practitioner can lead to low-level play.

Practitioners also facilitate play by making themselves available at the children's level, ready to become involved at the children's invitation or to support communications and negotiations between children. By being nearby, even if not directly involved, practitioners are providing a 'secure-base' for children's explorations.

Maintaining the environment

Being a facilitator includes the important role of maintaining order: reordering the environment so that it can continue to be played in by other children (without destroying a carefully made structure or interrupting a game). Pathways need to be kept clear and items replaced on shelves so that children can find what they need. Older children will be involved in this process when they want to move on from one activity to another.

One of the enormous advantages of open-ended continuous provision is that it is there all the time, so does not have to be set up every day. But it does need to be beautifully maintained, so that it does not look shabby or become dirty and unhygienic.

- Tabletops should be carefully wiped at the end of each day, so that they are hygienic.
- Floors should be clean, so that children can play safely on them.
- The garden should be checked each morning for rubbish.
- If there are puddles, these might be good for play in wellies and waterproof clothing.

- Equipment should be put away with care, with each item put in its proper place in the outdoor shed. (Children should not be in the shed unless a practitioner is with them.)
- Indoors, the shelves should be wiped regularly and storage boxes should be cleaned out and the contents washed.
- Storage boxes should be hygienically labelled, i.e. with pictures that are laminated so they can be wiped.
- Faults with outdoor and indoor equipment should be reported immediately, and they should be removed from use until mended.
- There should be regular checking and updating of policies, so that the indoor and outdoor play environments are as safe as is needed. Helen Tovey writes about this in her popular book, *Playing Outdoors: Spaces and Places, Risk and Challenge* (2008).

Being a role model

Being involved in children's play can help to model ways of interacting and communicating, offering words and phrases that will stimulate and extend children's spoken language.

Sometimes you might need to model how to use a particular piece of equipment, such as scissors, a hole-punch, a screwdriver or a potter's wheel.

Being a 'play tutor'

The practitioner might take a group of children to the shops, and on their return set up a shop for play. The practitioner will show the children how to play shops. It is important to remember that this is not play, because the adult is in complete control and leads all the time. But it is often an important way of helping children to learn how to play.

Being a play partner

When playing alongside children, it is important to be flexible and take your lead from the child, even though it may be different to your planned activity. You can then use opportune or suitable moments to sensitively expand the children's play by suggesting new ideas or adding new props to their play areas. A balance always needs to be kept between encouraging children to explore and experiment with materials in their own ways and making suggestions. Do not overwhelm the children's play with your own activity.

When being a play partner, it is important to be authentic. Babies and young children are very perceptive and will lose trust in you if they sense that your interest or enthusiasm is false. Share in children's pleasure and show your appreciation of specific efforts and actions rather than using indiscriminate praise. Saying, 'You have spent such a long time building that tall tower! You didn't give up even when it got knocked down,' encourages dispositions of concentration and persistence (Manning-Morton and Thorp 2006).

Avoid interrupting children's play; when a child is playing independently, do not hover or smother them with attention, just remain available if you are needed.

Being an observer

Providing well for children's play is based on regular observation of individual children, of particular groups of children and of how the environment and resources are used.

Guidelines for good practice

Narrative observation of play

When observing children at play, follow the four steps of narrative observation. (You might want to reread Chapter 5 first).

✔ The observer writes briefly about the context of the observation. (For example, where is the child?)

✔ The observer writes down as exact a description as possible of what the child says and does, and enough description of the conversations and actions of other children playing with the child, to give a clear picture of the child being observed.

✔ The observation can then be analysed and interpreted.

✔ The observation can be shared with the parents and other practitioners to further support and extend the development of play. See Figure 17.5.

Child's name: ....

Date of observation: ....

Time observation begins: .... ends: ....

Give a short description of the context in which the play is taking place: ....

....

....

Describe what is happening and any communication/language (both non-verbal and spoken): ....

....

....

....

Analysis of the play:

Which features of play are present?

- Using first-hand experience? How?
- Using rules, making rules, changing rules? In control?
- Finding, making or miming play props?
- Choosing to play? In what way?
- Rehearsing the future? How?
- Pretending? Example?
- Playing alone? Talking to themselves?
- Children and practitioners playing together? How?
- What is the child's personal play agenda?
- Deeply involved? What makes you think so?
- Showing latest skills and learning in the play? What are these?
- Sustained, integrated ideas, feelings, relationships in free-flow play?

▲ **Figure 17.5** Narrative observation of play (based on Bartholomew and Bruce 1994; Bruce 1991, 1996, 2004, 2011b)

Theory and theorists: the practitioner's role in play

Janet Moyles's play spiral (2010)

This approach to play argues that children need play materials first (Moyles gives the example of a plastic construction kit) in order that they can explore freely. Then the adult demonstrates how to make a box with the materials, and discusses this with the children, who also make boxes. Children are then left free to use the kit without the practitioner; in Moyles's observations, they will use the practitioner's teaching in their free play. The practitioner is either directly teaching and showing, or leaving children without adult presence, to use materials in their own way.

Tina Bruce's 12 features of play (1996, 2004, 2011b)

In this approach, the practitioner takes a partnership role, rather than a directing role. The practitioner tunes in to the child and builds the play with the child, more like a conversation (sometimes called co-construction). The practitioner can initiate play, or the child can. The important thing is that the practitioner is not taking control and doing all the leading, but instead is supporting what the child initiates or takes up. The supporting might be through a conversation during the play, or it might be that the practitioner sees some prop that might be useful for the child to take their play agenda and ideas forward, so adds this to the play provision for the child to take up if they choose to do so. This can be summarised as follows: the adult observes the play, and supports it by joining in, watching out for possibilities to extend and sustain the play through conversations and materials. Tuning in to children's play through observations and playing with children, and adding to what they need in their play in an informed way, deepens the quality of children's play.

Think about ideas

The practitioner's role in play

Compare the two approaches above and note down their strengths and limitations. How do you think they support children's creativity? Which age group of children are they appropriate for? How does your own practice relate to the approaches discussed in this section?

See Chapter 18 for more information on types of play, and other useful information and relevant legislation.

 # Moving on

Choose an aspect of play from this chapter that you are not familiar with. Read and research it further and then discuss with colleagues or fellow students about how you could introduce these ideas into your practice and provision.

You might choose:

Developmental movement play

Lamont, B., 2009, *Moving, Learning, Growing.* Available at http://vimeo.com/65216866.

Lamont, B., 1991, *Babies, Naturally.* Available at www.developmentalmovement.org.

LeVoguer, M. and Pasch, J., 2014, 'Physical Well-being: Autonomy and Risk Taking', in Manning-Morton, J. (ed.), *Exploring Well-being in the Early Years.* Maidenhead: Open University Press, McGraw-Hill Education.

'Dizzy' play

Kalliala, M., 2006, *Play Culture in a Changing World*, Maidenhead: Open University Press, McGraw-Hill Education.

Treasure basket and/or heuristic play

Forbes, R., 2004, *Beginning to Play: Young Children from Birth to Three*, Maidenhead: Open University Press, McGraw-Hill Education.

Goldschmied, E. and Jackson, S., 2004, *People Under Three, Young Children in Day Care* (2nd edn), London: Routledge.

Socio-dramatic or fantasy play

Albon, D., 2010, 'Reflecting on Children "Playing for Real" and "Really Playing" in the Early Years', in J. Moyles (ed.), *Thinking about Play: Developing a Reflective Approach*, Maidenhead: Open University Press, McGraw-Hill Education.

War, weapon and superhero play

Holland, P., 2003, *We Don't Play with Guns Here*, Maidenhead: Open University Press, McGraw-Hill Education.

Further reading, weblinks and resources

Play England

Based at the National Children's Bureau, Play England promotes free play opportunities for all children and young people, and works to ensure that the importance of play for children's development is recognised.
www.playengland.org.uk

Developmental movement play

Lamont, B., 2009, *Moving, Learning, Growing*. Available at http://vimeo.com/65216866

Scotland

Information on creativity in the curriculum can be found at this link.
www.educationscotland.gov.uk/learningandteaching/approaches/index.asp

Northern Ireland

Information on creativity in the curriculum can be found at this link.
www.ncca.ie

References

Albon, D., 2010, 'Reflecting on Children "Playing for Real" and "Really Playing" in the Early Years', in J. Moyles (ed.), *Thinking about Play: Developing a Reflective Approach*, Maidenhead: Open University Press, McGraw-Hill Education.

Bowlby, J., 1988, *A Secure Base: Clinical Applications of Attachment Theory*, London: Routledge.

Bartholomew, L. and Bruce, T., 1994, *Getting to Know You: A Guide to Record Keeping in Early Childhood Education and Care*, London: Hodder and Stoughton.

Bruce, T., 1991, *Time to Play in Early Childhood Education*, London: Hodder and Stoughton.

Bruce, T., 1996, *Helping Young Children to Play*, London: Hodder and Stoughton.

Bruce, T., 2004, *Developing Learning in Early Childhood*, London: Paul Chapman Publishing.

Bruce, T., 2011a, *Cultivating Creativity in Babies, Toddlers and Young Children* (2nd edn), London: Hodder Education.

Bruce, T., 2011b, *Learning through Play: Babies, Toddlers and Young Children* (2nd edn), London: Hodder Education.

Department for Education, 2014, *Statutory Framework for the Early Years Foundation Stage Setting the standards for learning, development and care for children from birth to five*, London: HMSO. Available from: https://www.gov.uk/government/publications/early-years-foundation-stage-framework-2.

Forbes, R., 2004, *Beginning to Play: Young Children from Birth to Three*, Maidenhead: Open University Press.

Goldschmied, E., 1987, *Infants at Work* (training video), London: National Children's Bureau.

Goldschmied, E. and Hughes, A., 1992, *Heuristic Play with Objects* (training video), London: National Children's Bureau.

Goldschmied, E. and Jackson, S., 2004, *People Under Three, Young Children in Day Care* (2nd edn), London: Routledge.

Grieshaber, S. and McArdle, F., 2010, *The Trouble with Play*, Maidenhead: Open University Press.

Holland, P., 2003, *We Don't Play with Guns Here*, Maidenhead: Open University Press.

Hutt, J. F., Tyler, S., Hutt, C., Christopherson, H., 1989, *Play, Exploration and Learning: A Natural History of Pre-School*, London: Routledge.

Hyder, T., 2005, *War, Conflict and Play*, Maidenhead: Open University Press.

James, A., Jenks, C., Prout, A., 1998, *Theorizing Childhood*, Cambridge: Polity.

Kalliala, M., 2006, *Play Culture in a Changing World*, Maidenhead: Open University Press and McGraw-Hill Education.

Lamont, B., 1991, *Babies, Naturally*. Available at: www.developmentalmovement.org.

LeVoguer, M. and Pasch, J., 2014, 'Physical Well-being: Autonomy and Risk Taking', in Manning-Morton, J. (ed.), *Exploring Well-being in the Early Years*. Maidenhead: Open University Press, McGraw-Hill Education.

Manning-Morton, J., 2011, 'Not Just the Tip of the Iceberg: Psychoanalytic ideas and early years practice', in Miller, L. and Pound, L., *Theories and Approaches to Learning in the Early Years*, London: Sage.

Manning-Morton, J. and Thorp, M., 2003, *Key Times for Play, The First Three Years*, Maidenhead: Open University Press.

Manning-Morton, J. and Thorp, M., 2006, *Key Times: A Framework for Developing High Quality Provision for Children from Birth to Three years*, Maidenhead: Open University Press.

Manning-Morton, J. and Thorp, M., 2015, *Two Year Olds in Early Years Settings; Journeys of Discovery*, Maidenhead: Open University Press.

Mitchell, C. and Reid-Walsh, J., 2002, *Researching Children's Popular Culture: The Cultural Spaces of Childhood*, London: Routledge.

Moyles, J. (ed.), 2010, *The Excellence of Play* (2nd edn), Maidenhead: Open University Press.

Oke, M., Khattar, A., Pant, P., Saraswathi, T., 1999, 'A Profile of Children's Play in Urban India', *Childhood*, 6: 2, 207–19.

Parten, M., 1932, 'Social Participation among Pre-School Children', *Journal of Abnormal and Social Psychology*, 27, 243–69.

Sayeed, Z. and Guerin, E., 2000, *Early Years Play: A Happy Medium for Assessment and Intervention*, London: David Fulton.

Tovey, H., 2008, *Playing Outdoors: Spaces and Places, Risk and Challenge*, Maidenhead: Open University Press.

United Nations, 1989, *Convention on the Rights of the Child*. Available at: http://www.unicef.org/crc/.

Vygotsky, L. S., 1978, *Mind in Society*, Cambridge, Mass: Harvard University Press.

Waddell, M., 1994, *Owl Babies*, London: Walker Books.

Winnicott, D. W., 2005,) *Playing and Reality* (2nd edn), Oxon: Routledge.

This chapter looks at a wide range of issues related to curriculum and learning in the early years. The question of how we define curriculum is explored, and it is suggested that a holistic view should be taken. Different approaches to constructing curricula frameworks in the UK and elsewhere are compared and some difficult issues in their approach discussed.

The chapter explores ideas for developing effective learning environments, inside and outside, and elements of the psychological environment such as adult–child interactions and care routines are raised as important aspects. Finally, the chapter examines how children's learning is planned for as part of a cycle of good practice, and how specific learning experiences are supported.

 Theory and theorists: Bruce's three 'C's

Tina Bruce (1997) sets out three aspects of the curriculum:

- **Child** – the child's development and learning, including movement, communication, play, symbolic behaviour, emotional development and relationships (with self and others).
- **Context** – the access which practitioners create so that every child is helped to develop and learn, and how learning builds on the child's social relationships, family and cultural experiences.
- **Content** – what the child already knows and understands, together with what the child wants to know more about (the child's interests), and what society and community decide the child needs to know in order to participate and contribute to the community and the wider world. The content of the curriculum is different in every country.

What do we mean by 'curriculum'?

Curriculum is often thought about as the programme which children follow to learn the concepts, knowledge, understanding, attitudes and skills that a society decides its young people need. This means that thinking about the curriculum might be confined to thinking about *what* is done in an early years setting, or just as the particular framework document that directs what is done.

However, babies and young children (and older children too) do not only learn from what is done, they also learn from *how* things are done. They learn that some activities are valued more than others because of the time and attention practitioners pay to them. They learn that some topics and ways of speaking are approved of and others not, and that some children are listened to more than others. They do not only learn from the planned play opportunities; they are learning all the time from the way adults speak to each other, the way they are held or fed and the way the environment is laid out.

During the learning process, beliefs and attitudes are transmitted and encouraged implicitly or discreetly through the **hidden curriculum**. So curriculum needs to be thought about in terms of everything a child experiences in a setting: all the activities provided by practitioners and all the activities children do for themselves; all the interactions between practitioners and children and everything a child sees and hears in their environment.

Holistic curriculum and structure

Addressing the implicit as well as the explicit aspects of the curriculum means taking a holistic approach and addressing the whole of children's experience in settings.

This includes considering how a group setting is structured, as this says something about how you believe children develop and learn. For example, having narrow age bands in groups of children may reflect a view that children develop and learn in stages in line with Piagetian theory; or having mixed-age groups might reflect the Vygotskian emphasis on children learning from their more experienced peers as well as from practitioners and adults.

In the UK it is usual that babies are in a separate room from older children but this has not always been the case; in the 1970s and 80s, some nurseries had 'family' groups with two practitioners working with a small group of children aged from a few months to five years.

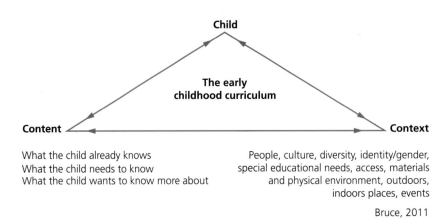

Child

The early
childhood curriculum

Content

Context

What the child already knows
What the child needs to know
What the child wants to know more about

People, culture, diversity, identity/gender,
special educational needs, access, materials
and physical environment, outdoors,
indoors places, events

Bruce, 2011

▲ **Figure 18.1** Framework for the early years curriculum

Think about ideas

The three 'C's

Review your curriculum:

- If you drew a triangle to represent the focus of your curriculum, would the sides be equal or would one side be longer than the others?
- How do you address each side of this triangle of the curriculum?

A main difference between settings now is whether two-year-olds are in a group of their own, with children from birth to three years, or with children aged two to five years. Greenman and Stonehouse (1996) set out the advantages and disadvantages of these arrangements from both the child's and the practitioner's point of view. What is clear is that whatever the arrangement, there are principles that always need to be maintained. One of these is that young children should not be expected to be in large groups for long periods of time. Children from birth to three years enjoy and benefit from the companionship and stimulation of being with older children, but they also become exhausted if they do not have a safe base/haven/nest to return to, where they can be quiet and calm. This, of course, is also true for older children.

Different approaches to curriculum

Curriculum frameworks or guidance documents vary across time and place. They are developed according to the knowledge and values of early years experts and politicians within their particular sociocultural, historical and political/economic context. Every culture decides what the children should learn, and there are variations across the world. For example, spirituality is emphasised in India, while in Laos and Hong Kong, literacy and numeracy are the focus.

Curricula can be centralised, contextualised or localised (Arthur et al. 1996):

- **Centralised**: a framework or guidance can be devised, monitored and assessed by central government or a government body, such as the EYFS and Ofsted in England. Sometimes a centralised curriculum will be **statutory** or it might be recommended practice. This seems to be linked with the level of professional qualification of practitioners in a country; the lower the level of qualification, the more directive the guidance.

- **Contextualised**: a framework can be developed for a particular sociocultural context to reflect particular local beliefs and traditions. The framework allows educators to develop further for their particular context. For example, Te Whāriki in New Zealand is a bicultural curriculum developed by the Maori people and the Pakeha (Caucasian or white people). It is based on four principles: empowerment (Whakamana), holistic development (Kotahitanga), family and community (Whanau Tangata) and relationships (Ngā Hononga). These principles are interwoven with five strands: Well-being (Mana Atua), Belonging (Mana Whenua), Contribution (Mana Tangat), Communication (Mana Reo) and Exploration (Mana Aoturoa) The Swedish curriculum is also contextualised. You can find out more about it here: http://teachfind.com/teachers-tv/sweden-early-years.

- **Localised**: a few settings develop their own approach such as the settings in Reggio Emilia

KEY TERM

Statutory schooling – The age at which children are legally required to attend full-time education, unless they have the agreement of the local authority that they will be home-educated.

▲ **Figure 18.2** The settings in Reggio Emilia emphasise all the different ways in which children express themselves

Reflecting on practice

Principles influencing early years curriculum frameworks in the UK

It is important to be a reflective practitioner and to be clear about the values and principles that underpin and guide your work. You should use official documents; you should not let documents use you! Frameworks and guidance documents should be used as something to help you reflect on your practice rather than a blueprint to be followed unquestioningly.

The principles set out below have a long tradition and have influenced and informed the early years curriculum frameworks of countries around the world (Bruce 1997, 2009b; Bruce and Spratt, 2010).

Review your practice, setting principles and/or the framework you use: How do they reflect the principles set out below?

in Northern Italy, which emphasise the creative communications of children. Malaguzzi (Edwards et al. 1998) coined the phrase 'the hundred languages of the child', to refer to all the different ways in which children express themselves – talking, singing, dancing, painting, making models, role play, and so on. He considered each of these to be a language.

Principles influencing early years curriculum frameworks in the UK

1   The best way to prepare children for their adult life is to give them a good childhood that meets their needs and builds on their interests.

2   Children are whole people, who have feelings, ideas, relationships involving a sense of self and others, and a sense of awe and wonder; they need to be emotionally, physically and morally healthy.

3   Children do not learn in neat and tidy compartments. Everything new that they learn links with everything they have already learnt.

4   Children learn best when they are respected and helped to be autonomous or independent, active learners.

5   Self-discipline is emphasised as the only kind of discipline worth having. Children need their efforts to be valued in their own right.

6   There are times when children are especially able to learn particular things.

7   What children can do (rather than what children cannot do) is the starting point for a child's learning.

8   There are many different kinds of symbolic behaviour. These show the inner thoughts, feelings and ideas of the child, through the way they draw,

paint, make things, dance, sing, talk/sign, enjoy making stories, make marks or pretend-play. The Italian educator Malaguzzi called this the 'hundred languages' of children.

9   Relationships with other people are central to a child's emotional and social well-being, and for opening up their possibilities for an intellectual life and a sense of fulfilment.

10 A good education is about the child, the context in which development and learning takes place, and the knowledge and understanding that evolves as part of the child's learning journey.

Frameworks across the UK

Because of the contexts in which they develop, frameworks cover different age ranges, emphasise different pedagogical approaches and are structured differently. Some use areas of development and/ or learning, while others emphasise a child's rights or entitlements. Some focus on future outcomes in readiness for the next stage of education, while others focus on life-long learning and outcomes for life and the wider community.

The Cambridge Review of Primary Education in England (Alexander et al. 2010) recommended 12 aims, some of which are reflected in the frameworks discussed below, while others are not:

Aims for the individual:

● well-being

● engagement

● empowerment

● autonomy.

Aims for self, others and the wider world:

- encouraging respect and reciprocity or 'give and take'
- promoting interdependence and sustainability; how we all rely on each other and the planet
- empowering local, national and global citizenship
- fostering skill.

Learning, knowing and doing:

- exploring, knowing, understanding and making sense
- exciting imagination
- celebrating culture
- enacting dialogue.

One effect this review had on curriculum development was the inclusion of 'the characteristics of effective learning' recommended by Dame Clare Tickell in her review of the EYFS (2011) and consequently included in the revised 2014 framework. Tickell emphasised that the framework needed to describe *how* children learnt not just *what* they learnt. The characteristics she identified are:

Playing and exploring

- finding out and exploring
- using what they know in their play
- being willing to have a go

Active learning

- being involved and concentrating
- to keep on trying
- enjoying achieving what they set out to do

Creating and thinking critically

- having their own ideas
- using what they already know to learn new things
- choosing ways to do things and finding new ways.

Stepping stones and outcomes

In Chapter 6 you will have read about normative development and Maturational perspective. This influence can be seen in frameworks that use milestones or 'stepping stones' to guide practitioners' thinking and practice. For example, the 'Development matters' (Early Education/BAECE 2012) guidance in England and the Developmentally Appropriate Practice approach in the USA (Copple and Bredekamp 2009).

Frameworks and guidance also often focus on the desired outcomes for children's early learning, such as the early learning goals in England where there is an aspiration that by the end of the academic year during which a child reaches the age of five, a child will have attained a prescribed range of skills, knowledge and abilities. This is a very contentious area which

---

Reflecting on practice

Use Table 18.1 to review the similarities and differences between frameworks across the UK.

You will note many similarities; for example, they all emphasise active learning, although the emphasis on play is variable. Some of the differences will only be noticeable by comparing the actual documents; for example, the English EYFS has a major focus on the expected outcomes for children at the end of the Foundation stage, whereas the Northern Irish guidance does not focus on outcomes at all.

You can access each of the documents on these websites:

England: The Early Years Foundation Stage document

https://www.gov.uk/early-years-foundation-stage

Scotland: Birth to three: supporting our youngest children and Curriculum for Excellence

http://www.educationscotland.gov.uk/learningandteaching/earlylearningandchildcare/prebirthtothree/index.asp

http://www.educationscotland.gov.uk/learningandteaching/thecurriculum/whatiscurriculumforexcellence/

Wales: Foundation Phase Framework

http://gov.wales/topics/educationandskills/earlyyearshome/foundation-phase

Northern Ireland: Curricular Guidance for Pre-School Education

http://ccea.org.uk/curriculum/foundation_stage

Think about ideas

1. Which country has a curriculum framework that includes children from birth? Discuss this with your colleagues.
2. Reflect on the advantages and disadvantages of curriculum frameworks with common themes throughout the different age phases. Discuss this with your colleagues.
3. How does the framework you use relate to the Cambridge review aims?
4. How do you address the 'characteristics of effective learning'?
5. If you were a child, what would you find helpful in the different curriculum frameworks? As a practitioner, reflect on what is helpful in the different curriculum frameworks.

KEY TERM

Active learning – Learning through hands-on direct experience and involvement.

	England	Scotland		Wales	N. Ireland	
Age range	0–6 statutory	0–3 non statutory	3–18 non statutory	3–7 statutory	2–4 non statutory	4–6 statutory
Themes	<ul><li>A unique child</li><li>Positive relationships</li><li>Enabling environments</li><li>Learning and development</li></ul>	<ul><li>Relationships responsive care</li><li>Respect</li></ul>	<ul><li>Wisdom</li><li>Justice</li><li>Compassion</li><li>Integrity</li></ul>			
Values / principles	<ul><li>Every child is a competent learner from birth, who can be resilient, capable, confident and self-assured.</li><li>Every interaction is based on caring professional relationships and respectful acknowledgement of the feelings of children and their families.</li><li>The environment plays a key role in supporting and extending children's development and learning.</li><li>Children develop and learn in different ways and at different rates, and *all* areas of development and learning are equally important and are interconnected.</li></ul>		<ul><li>Challenge and enjoyment</li><li>Breadth</li><li>Progression</li><li>Depth</li><li>Personalisation and choice</li><li>Coherence</li><li>Relevance</li></ul>	<ul><li>Learning by doing</li><li>The importance of first-hand experience</li><li>Learning though play</li><li>Active involvement in learning</li><li>Time to develop speaking and listening</li><li>Time to develop confident readers and writers</li><li>Practical mathematical experiences through everyday problem-solving experiences</li><li>Emphasis on understanding how things work and finding different ways to solve problems</li></ul>	Young children require a curriculum which: <ul><li>meets their physical, social, emotional and cognitive needs at their particular stage of development</li><li>motivates, challenges and stimulates them</li><li>is broad and balanced, allowing children to make choices and providing them with opportunities, through play and other experiences.</li></ul>	

▲ **Table 18.1** Curriculum frameworks across the UK

Aims			• A successful learner • A confident individual • A responsible citizen • An effective contributor	• Skills and understanding • The whole child – personal, social, emotional, physical and intellectual well-being • Positive attitudes to learning • Giving children high self-esteem and confidence encouraging children's development as individuals through creative, expressive and observational skills, and recognising that different children have different ways of responding to experiences • Learning about conservation and sustainability through outdoor, first-hand experiences involving real-life problems		Cross-curricular areas (which continue through the education stages) are: • communication • using mathematics • using ICT. Thinking skills are: • think critically and creatively • develop personal and interpersonal skills and dispositions • effectively function in a changing world. • Personal capabilities are: • lifelong learning • contributing effectively to society.
Areas	Personal, social and emotional development Communication, language and literacy Problem-solving, reasoning and numeracy Knowledge and understanding of the world Physical development Creative development		Expressive arts Health and well-being Languages Mathematics Religious and moral education Sciences Social studies Technologies	Personal and social development, well-being and cultural diversity Knowledge and understanding of the world Mathematical development Language, literacy and communication skills Welsh language development Physical development Creative development	The arts Language development Early mathematical experiences Personal, social and emotional development Physical development and movement The world around us	Language and literacy Mathematics and numeracy The arts The world around us Physical development and movement Personal development and mutual understanding Religious education

▲ **Table 18.1** (*Concluded*)

continues to cause much debate, since few children reach several of the literacy goals; for example, children with additional needs, with disabilities or who are learning English as an additional language may be unable to meet these goals at the identified age. Many early years experts have formed the view that these goals are not appropriate for such young children. Others identify that by focusing our attention only on children's futures, we are in danger of ignoring their present needs and that this may impact negatively on their well-being (Layard and Dunn 2009, Manning-Morton 2014)

A curriculum that includes all children

Most children learn in a rather uneven way: they have bursts of learning and then they have plateaux, when their learning does not seem to move forward (but really they are consolidating their learning during this time). This is why careful observation and assessment for learning of individual children, plus a general knowledge of child development are very important.

Catching the right point for a particular bit of learning during development is a skill, as is recognising the child's pace of learning. Children have their own personalities and moods. They are affected by the weather, the time of day, whether they need food, sleep or the toilet, the experiences they have, their sense of well-being, and their social relationships with children practitioners, and adults generally.

Some of the richest learning comes from experiences of everyday living. Examples would be getting dressed, choosing what to do, going shopping, using what you have bought for cooking, using a recipe book, washing up, sharing a story or photographs of shared events (visiting the park), laying the table, eating together, sorting the washing and washing clothes. It is a challenge to find ways of making this manageable for children to take part in with independence, but careful planning makes this both possible and enjoyable, and the learning goes deep.

Gifted and talented children

People who are gifted and talented in music, dance or mathematics, for example, tend to show promise early in their lives. The most important thing is that practitioners provide a rich and stimulating learning environment, indoors and outdoors, which encourages children to develop and extend their thinking, understand and talk about their feelings, and understand themselves and others. It is frustrating for gifted children when they are constrained and held back in their learning.

It is also important to remember that however gifted a child may be in a particular respect, she is still a child who needs all the things that any child needs, and should not be put under pressure to behave and learn in advance of her general development.

Children with SEN and disabilities

Some children will be challenged in their learning, and those working with children with SEN and disabilities will need to be particularly resourceful, imaginative and determined in helping them to learn. Many children with SEN and disabilities are underestimated by the practitioners working with them. For example, most six-year-old children can run confidently across a field. In general, children with visual impairments in mainstream settings are not expected to try to do this, so they do not try. No one suggests it to them or offers them help to do it. With the right help, the child might manage it, becoming physically more confident and mobile as a result. The experience of running across a field depends on the child's development, personality and mood. Walking hand-in-hand first might be important. Talking as you go helps. The child may need tips about picking up their feet, and eventually perhaps running towards your voice. If the child tumbles, he will need reassurance, and not an anxious practitioner. Saying, 'Can I help you up?' is more helpful than rushing over and asking, 'Are you hurt?'

Valuing and respecting the child's culture and family background

Every child needs to be included and have full access to the curriculum, regardless of her ethnic background, culture, language, gender or economic background. No child should be held back in their learning because of restricted access to learning opportunities.

When planning the curriculum, it is important to work closely in partnership with the child's parents/carers. Only then can you really provide resources and play opportunities that are meaningful for the child; that includes each child's context. With a genuine exchange of information and knowledge, the child gains and so do the parents and staff.

Boys and girls

A good curriculum benefits all children. There is a lot of discussion about the different learning needs of boys and girls, with boys being seen to favour learning with plenty of movement and outdoor learning, while girls are thought to favour language-based play, such as in the role-play area. But it is dangerous to stereotype children by gender. It is better to think about 'some boys' or 'this boy' for example to avoid stereotyping. It is important to think about how resources and play opportunities are presented that might give implicit or hidden messages about who they are for. Providing rich learning experiences that cater for all children's needs should be the starting point and within that, observing how different children access learning in different ways and making adaptations accordingly; for example, making a garage role-play area so that drawing and writing might be brought into bike play or bringing woodwork into the mark-making area.

Planning for the child's learning journey

Practitioners should remember that planning is a tool to help them think about how they are providing a broad and balanced curriculum, and facilitating the learning and development of each child. It is not a rigid timetable.

Planning is part of a cycle of practice which begins with the observation of the child as a unique, valued and respected individual, with their own interests and needs. This ensures that the learning environment not only helps all children in general but also caters for individual children. These observations are most usefully shared and discussed with parents, children and colleagues, who feed in information for developing plans. Observations are also used to evaluate play opportunities, areas and resources, which also feeds into the planning.

In this way the curriculum is:

- differentiated for individual children
- inclusive and embraces diversity
- offers experiences and activities that are appropriate for most children of the group because it considers the social and cultural context of the children developing in a community of learning.

▲ **Figure 18.3** A cycle of effective practice

The most effective approaches to planning are flexible, responding to what children are doing and are interested in. This is called planning for an '**emergent curriculum**'; where practitioners pay close attention to where children are taking their play and adapt their plans accordingly. Rigid plans, based only on practitioners' identified learning intentions, hold back learning. They do not meet the learning needs or develop the interests of individual children. They lead to an activity-based curriculum which does not help the group or individual children to develop and learn.

Planning the curriculum
Long-term planning

This focuses on:

- what is known about the general development and learning needs of most children between birth and five years of age
- the principles, values and philosophy that support the curriculum
- how general provision indoors and outdoors is planned according to the philosophy (approach) of the setting.

Medium-term planning

This is the way in which the principles and general framework set by the long-term planning are applied. Medium-term plans will most usefully engage practitioners in reviewing their provision and practice in the context of the time of year, changes in groups of children, local events, for example. This will include reviewing the physical environment, materials and resources. This will be under constant review according to practitioners' observations. For children from birth to three years, it needs to also include reviews of care routines, key worker relationships and the way the day is organised (Manning-Morton and Thorp 2006). As a result of the review, there may be a particular emphasis for a period of time (perhaps for several months) – for example, supporting and providing for musical experiences; how to get the most from the outdoor environment or the settling-in of children new to the group.

Short-term planning

Short-term plans are usually weekly. They are based on observation sheets of individual children's interests and needs, and are flexible enough to be changed as the week progresses. If short-term plans are useful, they may extend over several weeks and become medium-term plans, which are adjusted slightly each day. This is especially so if the curriculum offers continuous open-ended materials, equipment and resources, indoors and outdoors. Medium-term reviews are still useful.

Look, listen and note

Tuning in to children, and responding to what you have observed

Sometimes, practitioners think that children are stuck in their play because they stay doing something for ages. Sometimes they think they do not concentrate on anything but just flit from one thing to another. By carefully observing and tuning in to children, practitioners can understand a child's play and learning style better and why they do what they do.

Read the case studies; make notes about how you understand this child's play and how you would create a rich learning environment to cater for their interests.

Nadia (two years old) is exploring glue. She stays in the workshop area for a long time, dripping glue from a glue stick onto paper, and covering the paper until it is soggy. She watches the way the glue falls off the glue stick and makes a soggy mound of glue on the paper. She does not seem to be interested in the function of glue – to join things together. After a while, she dips her finger in the glue and pulls it across the paper then puts her finger in her mouth; her face shows disgust. She then pats the mound of glue with the palm of her hand. Looking at her now sticky hand, she looks concerned and tries to rub the glue off with her other hand; the glue stretches between her palms, she repeats pressing them together and pulling apart twice more. Then she notices that some of the glue has dried and is peeling off. She sits down and spends a few minutes just peeling the glue off but gets frustrated that some stays on. She looks around, sees her key person sitting nearby and holds out her hand, showing the glue and moaning, 'off, off'.

You might consider the following points:

- Nadia is learning about the properties of glue using all her senses.
- Always have different kinds of glue available in the workshop. You could offer Nadia flour and water glue in an attractive pot, showing her how she can use it by demonstrating this to her.
- When the paper is very soggy, and Nadia wants to continue but it is beginning to flow off the table, you might replace the paper with newspaper.
- Chat as you do so, saying you think the newspaper might help Nadia to carry out her idea of dripping the glue on the paper. Chatting is important in developing communication – not too much, not too little. Give Nadia key words, but in sentences, such as, 'Let's try it out, shall we?'

Hayley (three years old) comes into the garden. She goes to the two-wheeler bikes with no pedals and rides one to the end of the garden. Then she runs to the watering can and picks it up. She walks around with it, drops it on the path and runs to the practitioner who is putting up the sun umbrella. She looks up at its spokes, standing underneath it. Then she goes to the outdoor sandpit, and chooses to play with the wheel, tipping dry sand in and flicking it with her hand as the sand spins round in it. She takes the sand-wheel to the water pump and puts it under the spout, pumping water into it and watching it turn.

You might consider the following points:

- Everything Hayley has chosen to do has the same pattern in it: everything has a core and radials coming out of it – the spokes on the bicycle wheels, the spout on the watering can, the spokes on the umbrella, the sand-wheel, which becomes the waterwheel. The researcher Chris Athey would say that she is 'fitting', not 'flitting'.
- Perhaps Hayley would like to be offered similar objects with a core and radials, to broaden her experience.
- The practitioner could have a chat with her as she moves from one thing to another, helping her to build her vocabulary about core and radial objects and what they do, i.e. 'spin', 'rotate', 'centre', 'spokes', 'rim'.
- The practitioner could take photos of all the objects and make a book of these, calling it 'Hayley's interesting objects'.

The two case studies above indicate how important it is that planning focuses on process and the efforts children make, rather than just a product. An example would be finger-painting rather than hand-prints, so that children can freely make their own patterns in the paint. At the end, the paint is cleared away, with no pressure on children to produce a product. However, staff might photograph the processes involved in finger-painting and display these on the wall, to remind children of what they did. Children love to share process books later with practitioners and interested adults, other children and their parents/carers.

One type of plan that is widely used is called PLOD (possible lines of direction). This was first developed with staff at Redford House Workplace Nursery at Froebel College in Roehampton, and later developed with staff at Pen Green Children's Centre. These can be used for one child (as in Figure 18.4) or for several children with similar interests.

Planning the play environment

When planning the play environment, it is important to remember that you are not planning the way children play in it. Children need to be able to initiate their own ideas in their play and to be spontaneous. This is only possible if the environment is set up to encourage play.

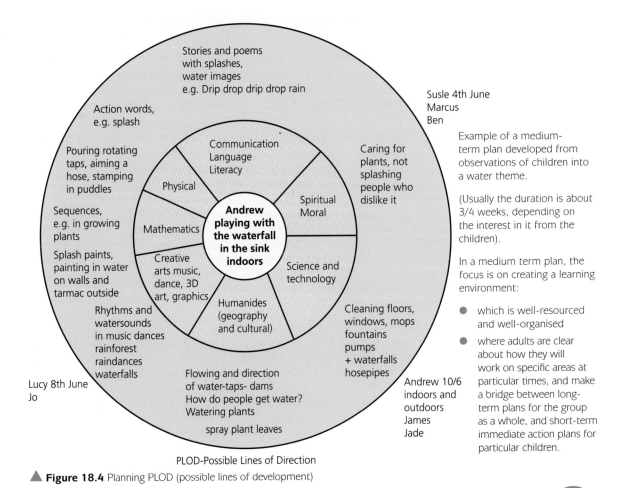

Susle 4th June
Marcus
Ben

Example of a medium-term plan developed from observations of children into a water theme.

(Usually the duration is about 3/4 weeks, depending on the interest in it from the children).

In a medium term plan, the focus is on creating a learning environment:

- which is well-resourced and well-organised
- where adults are clear about how they will work on specific areas at particular times, and make a bridge between long-term plans for the group as a whole, and short-term immediate action plans for particular children.

Lucy 8th June
Jo

Andrew 10/6
indoors and
outdoors
James
Jade

PLOD-Possible Lines of Direction

▲ **Figure 18.4** Planning PLOD (possible lines of development)

Look, listen and note

Linking observation and planning

Observations of Andrew, over a week, showed that a 'waterfall' consisting of three beakers of graded sizes was greatly used. Andrew lined them up next to the tap so that the water fell exactly as he wanted it to. He had a bowl of corks under the waterfall; he aimed the water at them one by one to make them bob about.

When the tap was turned on, a waterfall was created, which led to much glee and discussion.

The key person feeds back the observations of Andrew, to a group of staff. They decide to put the waterfall out again. In addition, they will provide a bigger version in the outside area, using buckets and old water trays. They plan who will be in which area and they hope that Andrew will learn that water:

- flows
- splashes
- cascades in the outdoor waterfall more than the indoor waterfall
- flows downwards if it can
- makes a trajectory (a moving line)
- has the force to move things that are in its way.

To extend Andrew's interest, the staff plan a visit to the local shopping centre where there is a fountain. They

also link the short-term plans made for Andrew with the medium-term plan and the long-term plan, which has a focus on knowledge and understanding of the world (science).

Review the steps you take in planning for individual children and note how you do the following:

1 Observe the child at different times, in different places, indoors and outdoors, at mealtimes, home time, with different people. What does the child choose to do? What interests the child?

2 Support the learning. Are there plenty of opportunities to repeat the experiences the child has chosen? Is there open and continuous material provision, rather than closed and prescribed activities? Do children have plenty of choice about how they spend their time? What kind of help do the children need? Do practitioners recognise when help is needed, and do they join children as companions and sensitively engage them in conversations? Do practitioners know not to interfere when the children are deeply involved?

Try using the PLOD planning format for an individual child or small group of children who share the same interest.

Quality learning takes place when you are able to match what is offered in the curriculum to the interests and needs of individual children. Good teaching means helping children to learn, so that they make connections with what they already know, and at times are helped to extend this.

Creating a rich learning environment indoors and outdoors

If not thought about and planned carefully, the environment can become part of the hidden curriculum, whereas in fact, it plays a major part in how you support children's learning through core experiences and open-ended, continuous material provision, equipment and resources, indoors and outdoors. In the approach used by the Reggio Emilia settings in Italy, the environment is called 'the third teacher' (Edwards et al. 1998). They remind practitioners in the UK of the importance of:

- an attractive and welcoming entrance area, where children and families are greeted and can find and share information, and feel part of a community
- natural light
- the feeling of space without clutter
- making spaces beautiful using natural materials.

Thinking about how children learn from the environment means thinking about the physical space, furniture and resources and what and how children learn from these. But we also need to think about the psychological environment, the atmosphere that children learn from too. This is created by the interactions and approach of the practitioners; how practitioners and parents communicate with each other; how practitioners

interact with children both verbally and non-verbally; and how the day is structured and flows.

The physical environment

The outdoor learning environment

Children should be able to learn outside for most of the day if they choose to do so. If children are allowed to move about freely between the indoor and outdoor areas, their play is calmer and of deeper quality. They need appropriate clothes (as do practitioners), so that everyone can be outside in all weathers. The idea that learning can only take place indoors is extraordinary. Settings that do not value the importance of the outdoor learning environment are only offering children half a curriculum.

The outdoor learning environment should echo and mirror the indoor area, but both will offer different experiences. Indoors, children will use felt-tip pens and pencils, while outdoors they might use chalk on the ground and make marks on a larger scale. Indoors, they might use paint and brushes on paper, but outdoors they may have buckets of water and large brushes, and paint on walls and the ground. They will make dens, play in tents and may wear dressing-up clothes indoors or outdoors.

The garden and outdoor areas offer children learning opportunities that they cannot have indoors. They help children to learn about nature: children need to feel rain, sun and wind, to explore plants, trees, flowers and vegetables, to learn about how they grow and to encounter small animals, bird and insect life. Ideally, children are taken to forests, or to parks with groups of trees, so that they experience being in woodland and in open green spaces. To play in these situations strengthens the play and encourages creativity.

Play outdoors allows for exploration on a larger scale: making bigger dens, throwing and kicking harder and farther, running and climbing faster and higher. Equipment such as guttering, water hoses and a water pump outside, give children opportunities for learning about how water works differently to the small scale of the water tray, for example.

Play outdoors gives children opportunities to try out, practise and consolidate their physical skills, becoming competent, adventurous and confident in their physical bodies. There should be different surfaces – smooth safe surfaces, grass, and hills to move on for babies and toddlers as well as older children.

Outside, children need:

- designated spaces (but children should be allowed to rearrange them and use them in a different way)
- connected spaces, which encourage children to join in (sand and water areas)
- elevated spaces (mounds, trees, ramps, steps, climbing frames)
- wild spaces, so that children experience the smell and texture of mud and long grass and encounter butterflies, ants for example
- spaces for exploring and investigating (e.g. sand pits, mud kitchens)
- spaces for mystery and enchantment (dens, winding pathways)

- natural spaces (digging patches and opportunities to grow flowers and vegetables)
- space for the imagination (providing children with open-ended props, logs, and so on)
- spaces for movement (climbing, dragging, swinging on bars, jumping, balancing, running, skipping and riding)
- spaces for stillness (sitting or lying in secluded, tucked-away places in peace and calm)
- social spaces (outdoor seats for chatting together)
- fluid places (flexible resources that can be moved about when needed).

(Tovey 2007)

Space to move

Free movement is central to early years; children need to move as much as they need to eat and sleep. Susan Isaacs thought that children cannot learn if they are made to sit still.

Children learn through action and need to be skilled in a range of movements, using both fine and gross motor skills. Movement needs to be appropriate – for example, stroking a dog gently, but throwing hard to make a splash with a pebble in a puddle. To achieve this, babies and young children need to be able to repeat and practise these skills. Being able to be still is the pinnacle of muscular control; you have to develop the muscles through movement before you can attain this ability.

Movement is important for all aspects of learning. Through rolling, crawling, spinning and tilting, pushing and pulling, children are integrating their senses, muscular and nervous systems and making crucial neural connections (Lamont 1991). They are also developing their kinaesthetic sense (see Chapter 7 p. 123 for definition); these are fundamental to understanding abstract concepts such as 'far' and 'near', then to be able to follow print with their eyes when reading, and to manipulate tools such as a pen for writing!

Provision for movement

Settings need to provide adequately for movement inside as well as outside.

Babies need plenty of opportunities to be on the floor so that they can feel their arms, legs and tummies against the ground. Experts in physical movement development, such as JABADAO, the National Centre for Movement, Learning and Health in Leeds, are finding that children often do not spend enough time on the floor. Babies need to be given opportunities to lie, belly crawl, roll and crawl on hands and knees as well as to sit (Greenland in Bruce 2009a). Layback or bouncy chairs, although they prop babies up to be able to see what is going on, prevent babies from developing their muscles and kinaesthetic sense adequately, so should be used sparingly. Baby walkers do not allow babies to develop the ability to use physical feedback to judge space and distance, and can be dangerous so should not be used in settings.

Providing interesting natural objects placed in front of young babies will encourage them to reach and move. The attentive adult can place things so that there is interest and challenge but not too much frustration, especially for new crawlers who often find themselves going backwards at first instead of forwards. Having something to push against can be just the right help at the right time!

This kind of play provision for movement is important for babies, toddlers and children up to at least five years old. Older children who have missed out on such opportunities can benefit from later opportunities. They also need an interested person, sensitively supporting and mirroring their movement play; practitioners need to get on the floor and move too!

For older children, floor work enables them to explore:

● transfer weight from one part of the body to another
● travel from one spot to another
● flight through jumping.

Making a movement corner is as important as making a book corner for brain development, learning and well-being. The floor needs to be clean and carpets should not be scratchy. The amount of large and small apparatus you use will depend on the space you have available, but developmental play opportunities can be created in whatever space you have.

The following examples of large equipment can be adapted for different ages and abilities of children:

● climbing frame (that can be added to and adapted with planks or lengths of fabric, for example, so it does not become boring)
● ropes to swing on
● planks to walk on
● things to jump off.

Small apparatus includes bats, balls, hoops, beanbags, ropes and pushcarts.

Safety, risk and challenge

Children are usually very good at knowing their own physical limits and will approach new or riskier activities with caution. But this is even more true for children who have been allowed to take risks, and encouraged and helped to use their bodies in all kinds of ways, by an adult sensitive and helpful to their needs. For example, toddlers can be encouraged to come down the stairs sliding on their tummies, feet first. Children who are not supported to take risks are more likely to have accidents because they do not have a chance to find out their own physical limitations.

In early years settings it is important that the environment is safe enough, but also offers challenge. The younger the children, the more attention to safety there must be. For example, babies put everything in their mouths so floors need to be clean, as a baby will stop to examine every piece of fluff, dropped crumb or spillage. They also need to be able to heave themselves up on furniture in ways that are safe; furniture needs to be sturdy and stable so it does not topple on them or slide away, making them fall unnecessarily. Toddlers will climb up on things as soon as they are able, so the room needs to be made safe enough for them to do this, with windows carefully fastened and bookcases firmly on the wall. Cupboards need to be fastened shut, or perhaps some will be allowed to be opened and explored safely. What is put in low cupboards will need to be carefully monitored for safety.

All practitioners need to be trained and rigorous about undertaking risk assessments while still providing environments in which children can find physical challenge. Young children are beginning to be able to take increasing responsibility for their own risk-assessing (at the woodwork bench, when cooking and gardening), but they need the support of a practitioner to learn to do this. Children benefit from discussions about safety, and taking care of themselves, others and equipment. See Chapter 14 for more information on risk assessments.

Space to create, and find out, to imagine and make, to think and understand

Given that children from birth to six years old learn through their senses, the environment and resources need to support and extend this kind of learning. The environment also needs to support and actively encourage and extend the symbolic /imaginative life of the child and the way that they understand cause-and-effect relationships.

Continuous provision

The resources that early years practitioners provide have a direct impact on play. If practitioners create an enabling environment that cultivates play, the quality of children's play will be deeper. This is best created through developing core, open-ended provision that is continuously offered. Other experiences can then be added or the provision can be adapted to be offered differently according to the children's play interests, for example.

This continuous provision ensures that each child learns in their own way. When young children are mostly given adult-led activities with tasks to perform, they cannot develop their own ideas and thinking, and their play and creativity are seriously constrained. This can lead to behaviour problems. By developing continuous provision, there is also the advantage that practitioners have more time and opportunity to support children's play and choices, rather than organising and directing adult-led 'activities' for most of the day.

The following are considered to be open-ended continuous provision because they allow children to develop their ideas in their own way:

- malleable (soft or flexible) natural materials (clay, mud, dough)
- home corner for domestic play or other role play
- workshop area, with found and recycled material for model making and mark-making, and including masking tape and scissors that cut (for left and right-handed children)
- small-world play (dolls house, farm, prehistoric animals, roads, trains)
- sand (wet and dry)
- water
- unit blocks and hollow blocks.

Double provision

Children need to be able to experience materials at different levels of complexity, since at times they are operating at their highest levels of possibility, while at other time they need to practise with familiar and less demanding activities. For example, sometimes it is good to have the simplicity of finger-painting, other times the challenge of a fine paintbrush. Providing both possibilities in a workshop area means that children can work at their own level.

Increasingly, children are integrating across the Foundation years for parts of the day, which can give a more natural and family-group feeling as long as children also have the secure-base of their key person nearby. Children with SEN and disabilities are also included in settings. All of this means that the traditions of wide provision are of central importance.

Through double provision, the different needs and interests of children from birth to five years can be

attended to. For example, having a water tray on the floor as well as on a stand caters for the younger children as well as the older ones.

This sample environment shows good practice:

- There might be a workshop area, with carefully selected and presented found (rather than bought) materials, such as boxes, tubes, dried flowers, moss, twigs, wool, along with string, masking tape, glue, scissors and card. Here, older children could become involved in making models and constructions, and practitioners can help them to carry out their ideas without losing track of them on the way or becoming frustrated. Children can be helped as they try to join things, and make decisions about whether a string knot would be better than masking tape or glue.
- Nearby, on the floor, there might be a beautiful basket full of balls of wool and string, which younger and less experienced children can enjoy unravelling and finding out about how these behave. Other children might like to return to this earlier way of using string too.

It is a good idea to try to offer everything at different levels of difficulty, so that there is something for everyone to find absorbing. Open-ended materials and resources, such as playdough and blocks, lend themselves better to being used differently by different children than commercially made toys.

Displays and interest tables indoors

Issues of gender, culture and disability need to be thought through when it comes to setting up displays. Positive images and multicultural objects need to be discussed and planned to avoid meaningless cultural tourism. Photos, models and objects from seasonal and cultural festivals and visits can be displayed to enable children to remember, reflect and discuss their experiences.

Wall displays for crawling babies, such as photographs of their families and pets, should be at their eye height, and laminated so they can be patted by the children as they look at them (Manning-Morton and Thorp 2003). Wall displays for older children should also be at their eye height. Remember not to clutter the walls; leave some walls blank and perhaps only put a display on one wall. Having too much on the walls can be overwhelming, especially for children whose sense are very acute, such as children with autism; children become calmer when the walls are calmer, in natural shades.

The work in Reggio Emilia (see Chapter 5) reminds us that practitioners need to consider the following

Guidelines for good practice

Displays and interest tables

✔ Displays should respect children's work – do not cut up children's paintings to make an adult's collage.

✔ The paintings children do should be mounted and displayed as they are.

✔ Practitioners should not draw or write on children's work without their permission.

✔ Any writing or notes about a painting should be mounted separately underneath the child's painting or drawing. The label should be discussed with the child, who should agree to the wording.

✔ Any lettering should be done carefully on ruled lines so that it looks attractive. Your writing must project a good role model for children.

✔ Writing should not be at 'jaunty angles' on a display, as children are developing their understanding of which direction the print goes when reading. Imagine going to a train station and trying to read the words on the display of arrivals and departures if they were all at jaunty angles! It would be very confusing.

✔ When writing labels in different languages remember that in English, for example, writing goes from left to right, in Urdu it goes from right to left and in Chinese it goes up and down.

✔ Use a piece of material that takes the eye to important parts of the display.

✔ Display the essential objects of the experience (e.g. autumn leaves, conkers and tree bark).

✔ Include a non-fiction book on the subject (about autumn for example).

✔ Include a book of literature, for example, a poem or a story about autumn.

✔ Include photos/audio of sights/sounds of the garden in autumn and the children raking up leaves, to help children to link into the experience and reflect.

in setting up displays, which are seen as part of what they describe as the 'microclimate'. Consider:

- how different parts of the display relate to each other in the way they are presented
- how light shines and is part of the display
- the way colours create different experiences
- the way materials create different experiences
- that the display can smell as well as be touched
- that sounds are an aspect to be built in to the display.

Space to feel safe and be quiet

Babies, toddlers and young children love to be busy and share the excitement of other people and interesting, novel experiences, but this can also quickly become overwhelming and exhausting, particularly for the very young ones. None of us, practitioners or children, are at our best all day and every day, and even practitioners who enjoy the hustle and bustle of the January sales or the street market need also to retreat to a quiet cafe for a coffee. Young children's senses are much more sensitive than adults and continuous sensory stimulation can lead to overload and breakdown, so they need ample opportunities and suitable space to be quiet and to relax in.

Comfortable book areas, canopied corners with cushions, relaxing music and leafy dens to curl up in, are all necessary parts of provision.

For very young children, large open spaces indoors can be very distracting, so using low dividers can make a play area feel safer and their play more focused.

The attentive presence of their key person is a central feature of space that feels safe, as we will discuss next.

Space to eat, sleep and get clean

Most of us put a lot of effort into making our kitchens, bathrooms and bedrooms relaxing and pleasant places to be, as well as being functional and convenient. Unfortunately, this is often not the case in early years group settings, where the spaces used for eating, sleeping and cleaning up may not be designed with the children in mind; they may either be cramped or overwhelmingly large and noisy, and inconvenient for children or staff, with toilets and basins that are too high or positioned too far away, and through several sets of doors.

Very young children spend a lot of time in these areas; they need to be pleasant, fit for purpose and designed to support children's growing autonomy and self-help skills.

The psychological environment

Helping children to learn

Although it can seem a daunting task to provide a quality learning environment for children from birth to seven years, remember that the thing that matters most is your relationship and communication with children, their families and the team of staff – that is, people.

Babies, toddlers and young children need:

- people who give them interesting and engaging experiences
- people who are tuned in to their interests and styles of learning
- to be greeted and made to feel welcome with their parent/carer as they arrive
- to be connected with their key person when they part from their parent/carer
- to feel physically, socially and emotionally safe, so that their intellectual lives open up as they relax and enjoy learning.

Babies, toddlers and young children learn better if they are not anxious. Anxiety closes the brain off to the possibility of learning. Children need practitioners who create a warm, affectionate atmosphere and have fun; laughing releases chemicals into the brain which open it up to learning. The key person in the setting is of great importance in this.

Children develop and learn with practitioners who are interested in what they do, and who support and extend their learning. It is very difficult for children when practitioners flit about and do not stay in one place for long enough for children to engage with them in focused ways. Children usually like to feel that an adult is nearby; it makes them feel safe and secure, especially when they are trying something new and unfamiliar. The first time glue is used or paint is mixed are good examples of this. It is important not to crowd, overwhelm or invade a child's thinking space, but it is vital to support a child's learning by being there for them, smiling and looking interested, and commenting on what they do from time to time – for example, 'You like red best, I think, because I've noticed that you have used it three times in your painting so far.'

It is a good idea, as part of planning the learning environments indoors and outdoors, to see where there might need to be practitioners anchored in an area, working in depth with children. The following points are important:

- The anchored practitioner needs to sit at the child's height or on the floor, so as to give full attention to a child or children in one area, while retaining an overview of the rest of the room.
- The practitioner must be free to focus on what the children in a particular area are doing (e.g. playing with wooden blocks or in the movement corner) and be able to have engaging conversations, listening to what children say and being sensitive to what they do, allowing them plenty of time (e.g. cooking together or planting bulbs in the garden).
- Another practitioner must be free to help children generally – for example, to deal with children's toilet needs, to hang up a painting or comfort a tearful child, or simply to respond to children who ask for help.
- If each adult has a clear understanding of their role in the team, it helps each practitioner to focus on the children and reduces the temptation to chat with other practitioners instead of engaging with the children.

Children need a safe and predictable environment. It is important for staff to work as a team so that different messages are not given by different people.

Children need to know where people are and why. If their key person is absent, children need to know who is looking after them. Children miss their friends when they are away or ill, and find it more difficult to get involved. A supportive practitioner is important at these times, offering companionship as the child chooses activities and experiences.

Children need to feel valued, appreciated and respected. When they feel their efforts are appreciated and celebrated, they learn more effectively. If practitioners only praise and recognise results or finished products, children are more likely to lose heart and become less motivated to learn. When children feel their efforts are appreciated and valued, they develop a positive self-image and a good sense of well-being. This, more than anything else, helps them to learn.

Look, listen and note

Adult–child interactions

The key person sat on the floor, facing Rebecca (two years old), and sang 'Row, row, row the boat' with her. She sang the song and did the actions twice through and then stopped. Rebecca touched her on the thigh and the key person responded, 'Again? You want to sing again?' The singing and moving were repeated, and Rebecca smiled with pleasure.

How is this practitioner fulfilling the adult's role in supporting learning as outlined in this chapter?

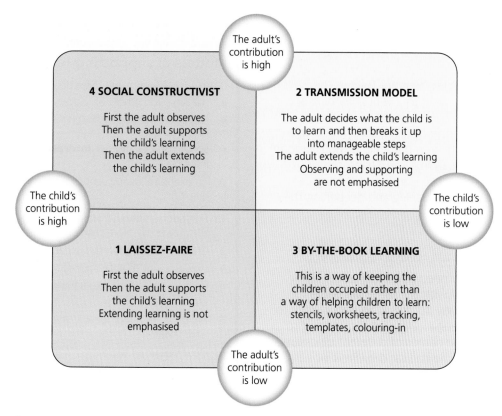

The adult's contribution is high

4 SOCIAL CONSTRUCTIVIST

First the adult observes
Then the adult supports
the child's learning
Then the adult extends
the child's learning

2 TRANSMISSION MODEL

The adult decides what the child is
to learn and then breaks it up
into manageable steps
The adult extends the child's learning
Observing and supporting
are not emphasised

The child's contribution is high

The child's contribution is low

1 LAISSEZ-FAIRE

First the adult observes
Then the adult supports
the child's learning
Extending learning is not
emphasised

3 BY-THE-BOOK LEARNING

This is a way of keeping the
children occupied rather than
a way of helping children to learn:
stencils, worksheets, tracking,
templates, colouring-in

The adult's contribution is low

▲ **Figure 18.5** Four different approaches to supporting children's learning

 Theory and theorists: models of supporting learning

In the **'laissez-faire' approach**, children make a very high contribution but practitioners hold back and take a very small part in leading their learning. They will prepare the environment and provide the resources according to what they have observed and then allow free exploration. See Table 6.1 on p. 110 for a list of advantages and disadvantages of this approach.

For example:

The children had been observed to enjoy drawing and painting, so the rooms in a nursery school were set up to support this. Great care was taken in the way that a variety of colours were put out in pots, with a choice of thick and thin paintbrushes. Children could choose paper of different sizes. A drying rack was close to the area and children could choose to paint at a table or on an easel. The practitioners would be on hand to help if needed, but would be careful not to talk to children while they were painting, in case they interrupt the children's thinking. Practitioners would not 'make' children paint, because not all children would be ready to do so. Readiness is important in this approach.

This is very different from the **transmission model**. In this approach, the adult practitioner has a very high input into the child's learning, taking control over the child's learning. The child's contribution is quite low.

The **'by the book' approach** to learning is not valuable and has not been covered in this book. Here, both the practitioners and the children have a very low level of participation. It is not really an approach to learning; it is just a way of keeping children occupied. Worksheets, colouring in, tracing, templates, filling in gaps and joining the dots all fall under this heading.

KEY TERMS

Laissez-faire model – An approach to children's learning where the practitioner mostly follows the child's lead.
Transmission model – An approach to children's learning where the practitioner defines and leads the learning.
Interactionist model – An approach to children's learning where the practitioner sensitively builds on the child's interests and capabilities.

The **social constructivist approach** is what is advocated generally in early years settings and in curriculum frameworks such as the EYFS. Here the practitioner sensitively engages with the child to support and extend learning but follows the child's lead and builds on their existing learning and interests. In the social constructivist (sometimes called interactionist) approach to learning, both the practitioner and the children put an enormous amount of energy into active learning (see Chapter 6 for more information on active learning). Learning can be extended both by broadening and deepening the learning.

For example:

- It is important not to automatically think that children constantly need new experiences. They might need to play with the same dinosaurs for several weeks. If they do, this is an opportunity to develop their understanding of dinosaurs and to help them learn the names of different dinosaurs, what they ate and the habitat they lived in. Dinosaur scenarios could be built with sand and water and plants in seed trays, so that children create their own small worlds about dinosaurs. This is often the best way to extend learning.

- It is important not to rush children into new learning when what they really need is to consolidate what they know. For example, a child might have enjoyed cooking roti or bread rolls at home. You may want to make a carrot cake in the setting with the children, for example. Making a carrot cake is a bit like making a roti, but it involves adding eggs and the mixture is stirred and beaten rather than pummelled. These differences could be talked about, but children will need to make both the roti and the carrot cakes so that the conversation will be possible. A book of recipes with pictures is helpful – you could make these and laminate them.

The structure of the day and physical care routines

Children are beginning to get a sense of the rhythms of the day and time passing as they become familiar with routines at home and the structure of the day in the early years setting. You can help them to

Think about ideas

Models of supporting learning

Draw a table with these three headings:

- transmission model of learning
- laissez-faire or 'leave it to nature' model of learning
- social constructivist or **interactionist model** of learning.

Which of the following sentences go under which heading?

1 Practitioners should mould children's learning. After all, they know more than children.
2 Children know what they need in order to learn.
3 Do you want to have a story first, or tidy up first?
4 We need to tidy up; we'll have the story afterwards.
5 Children are full of ideas if they are encouraged to have them.
6 Do it because I say so.
7 That child has been off-task all morning.
8 Children are born with everything they need in order to learn.
9 Children enjoy conversations with adults.
10 Children must be free to try things out.
11 Children will learn when they are ready and not before.
12 That child performed the task successfully today.

understand time if the shape of the day is predictable. This does not mean rigid or inflexible routines; it is hard for children to develop their play if the day is timetabled into rigid slots, with routines that break up the day. But it does mean having a consistent shape to the day, so that children can begin to participate fully in preparations, having experiences and a sense of closure as they join in clearing things up at certain times each day. This means that practitioners need to work together as a team to create consistent ways of doing things, so that children feel safe and secure and are able to contribute to the group.

See Chapter 13 for information on routines.

▲ **Figure 18.6** Meal times in early years settings need to also be a relaxed, enjoyable time where children feel part of the process and can chat with friends and enjoy their food

Sleep is important for learning

It is important to keep to the sleep-time rituals and patterns that are familiar to the baby at home. Some babies need to have a cuddle, being lowered into their cot as they fall asleep. Others might never go to sleep on a lap but need to be in a cot with their teddy, in order to fall asleep. Babies should never be left to sleep unsupervised.

Eating together

In all societies, eating together is an important social experience. Meal times in early years settings need to also be a relaxed, enjoyable time where children feel part of the process and can chat with their friends and enjoy their food. This cannot happen in large noisy environments, where children have little choice or autonomy and are hurried to finish either so the next 'sitting' can come in or the kitchen staff can finish their shift.

Manning-Morton and Thorp (2006, 2015) suggest the following:

- small groups of children sitting with their friends and/or key person
- attractively set tables (by the children) with table cloths and maybe flowers

- unhurried time
- support staff to bring and clear away the food and dishes
- small dishes and serving spoons and jugs of water for children to serve themselves at the table.

Belonging and contribution

Developing a sense of belonging and contribution are central aspects of the Te Whariki curriculum in New Zealand (New Zealand Ministry of Education 1996). 'Belonging' is brought about by providing an environment in which links between setting, family and community are strong and children feel comfortable and 'know they have a place'. This means creating an inclusive setting environment that embraces diversity in the layout and presentation of material provision and resources, and developing strong partnerships with parents who are involved in their children's learning and the life of the setting.

In Te Whariki 'contribution' is seen as 'playing a part in a common effort' (New Zealand Ministry of Education 1996, p. 99). Children can contribute to the group from a young age; caring for others, thinking of others, looking after the material provision and equipment, and making decisions and choices during the day are all part of this. Children do not respond well to being judged and chided

Reflecting on practice

Using everyday events for learning

At lunchtime, a group of sitting babies and toddlers were encouraged to choose their pudding. A plate of freshly prepared fruit was placed on the table. A tiny portion was given to the children to try out. Several showed they wanted more through their movements. The key worker passed the plate to the babies, who were allowed to take more for themselves.

This everyday event encouraged:

- learning about the taste of different fruits
- physical coordination
- a feeling of control over what happens
- decision-making.

When Joey (10 months) is changed, he dislikes the plastic changing mat – he tries to move off it. His key worker respects his feelings and puts a towel on the mat. She talks about what she is doing and why, and she sings 'Ten little toes' to help him relax. He giggles in anticipation of each toe being gently touched.

This everyday event has helped Joey to learn about:

- himself and his body
- affectionate and sensitive communication between people
- making sense of what someone says
- music, with its melody (tune) and pitch (how loud it is)
- eye contact when people talk to each other
- facial expressions
- having fun together.

by practitioners or adults generally; they do respond well to being helped to take responsible decisions.

Keeping the environment attractive, clean and tidy

If an area is dirty, shabby or disorganised, it is less attractive to children. Often a well-used area becomes cluttered and untidy halfway through a morning or afternoon. It is important that adults do not neglect abandoned areas and role-model reordering the environment and resources throughout the day. Children, who are not otherwise involved in play, can be encouraged to help with this. At the end of the session, all the older children can be involved in tidying up, unless there are good reasons for them not to, such as being upset or unsettled. Children should never be nagged or made to feel bad, but they should be encouraged and given specific but appropriate tasks as members of the learning community. Toddlers also enjoy collecting items and putting them in containers or putting rubbish in the bin, with support from practitioners. It is a question of finding something suitable for each particular child. The important thing is not to overdo the requests for help in tidying, and to remember that it is discriminatory to expect only a few children to do all the tidying. It is very important that great care is taken of equipment both inside and outside, so that jigsaw pieces do not end up on a flowerbed, for example. Sets of puzzles, crockery from the home corner or wooden blocks should be returned to the area they belong. This helps children to learn to care for equipment.

Guidelines for good practice

Developing the learning environment

- ✔ There is continuous and open-ended material provision, equipment and resources.
- ✔ The role of the practitioner in supporting children's development and learning through developmentally appropriate materials provision, equipment and resources is central.
- ✔ The environment (people and provision) needs to support all children, including those with SEN, disabilities, boys and girls, children from diverse backgrounds and different cultures, or with English as an additional language.
- ✔ Clutter confuses children. There should be nothing in a learning environment, indoors or outdoors, that has not been carefully thought through and well organised. The environment needs to signal to children how it should be used and kept.

- ✔ Children need to know what they are allowed to do, and what they are not allowed to do. When children feel insecure, they test boundaries to find out if there are any and what they are.
- ✔ The space indoors and outdoors is flexible, so that it can be set up and transformed for different uses in a variety of ways.
- ✔ Attention should be given to light, because the way that it shines into a building changes the atmosphere. If the sun is shining onto a child's face during story time, it will be difficult for the child to become engaged.
- ✔ The temperature is important. Being too hot or too cold makes it difficult to learn. Outdoors, children need suitable clothing, for all weathers (and so do the practitioners!), and indoors, the rooms should have good air circulation, so that the spread of infection is reduced.

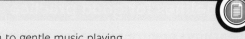

Guidelines for good practice

Learning environments for non-mobile babies (from birth to eight months)

✔ Babies depend on practitioners to bring interesting experiences to them because they cannot move about enough to reach for things when sitting. Treasure baskets are ideal for this (Goldschmied and Jackson 2004; see Chapter 17, p. 385 for more information).

✔ Sometimes babies need to be quiet, but they still need to feel that people are near.

✔ When outside it is important that the sun is not in their eyes, and that they are comfortable in temperature and wearing a clean nappy.

Babies need:

✔ interesting things to look at, swipe at, grab and hold, chew and suck, mouth, smell and shake

✔ to watch what is going on from the lap of their key person or from a baby sling

✔ to watch other children

✔ to listen to gentle music playing

✔ to listen to interesting sounds such as the birds singing

✔ to follow voices of people they know because they spend time with them

✔ to be cuddled and receive warmth and affection

✔ to be talked to and sung to, and bounced in time with music

✔ to share books with their key person

✔ opportunities to crawl on comfortable surfaces – a mixture of carpets and other surfaces to explore, including grass

✔ suitable places to sleep – some babies sleep best in a cot, others in a basket on a floor away from draughts, some tightly tucked in, others with loose bedclothes

✔ routines that follow their individual needs

✔ stable furniture so that they can pull themselves up and cruise in between. See p. 405 on safety of furniture.

Guidelines for good practice

Learning environments for mobile babies and toddlers (9–23 months)

Becoming mobile changes the life of a baby – they can reach things and their curiosity is further stimulated by their widening experiences.

Toddlers need:

✔ to be able to explore the learning environment indoors and outdoors, using all their senses and moving their whole bodies

✔ a range of surfaces to walk on, and to try to run

✔ large, bouncy balls to kick and throw, hoops and beanbags

✔ climbing opportunities (always carefully supervised); a small climbing frame or steps

✔ wheeled trucks to push and pull, pull-along toys, pushchairs for dolls and teddies and other soft toys

✔ a growing area and watering cans

✔ a well-drained sandpit

✔ heuristic play opportunities (see Chapter 17 for more information)

✔ a designated space for vigorous movement, with cushions to leap on and roll about on

✔ small wooden blocks

✔ finger/foot-painting

✔ non-toxic crayons, felt-tip pens, large paper and surfaces to draw/paint on

✔ wet and dry silver sand (not builder's sand)

✔ play dough – find some good recipes for play dough (some involve cooking, which makes the dough last longer); check the dough is safe to put in the mouth and even to eat, as some children might do this

✔ opportunities for water play, carefully supervised, at bath time, in paddling pools or with bowls of water – remember, children can drown in very shallow water, so always supervise these activities

✔ real objects such as bowls, cups etc. for emerging imaginative play

✔ objects to transport things with such as trucks, bags, and so on

✔ large and small boxes to put things into and take things out of

✔ blankets to cover teddies and dolls for example

✔ picture books and books with simple texts, and stories and rhymes, such as *Spot the Dog*

✔ simple dressing-up clothes – mainly hats, shoes and bags for toddlers

✔ action songs and finger rhymes.

Guidelines for good practice

Learning environments for young children (two to six years)

Just as babies and toddlers need plenty of time to be in the garden/outdoors, so too do older children. They also enjoy the toddler experiences outlined in the guidelines for learning environments for mobile babies and toddlers. They do not leave their sensory motor learning behind; they still learn through their senses and actions, but add their ability to symbolise and represent in their play.

Young children need access to the following every day:

- ✔ wet sand and dry sand (these are two entirely different learning experiences), with equipment nearby in boxes labelled with words and pictures for children to select

- ✔ clean water in a water tray or baby bath, with buckets, guttering, waterwheels, and so on, to make waterfalls, and boxes of equipment labelled with pictures and words

- ✔ found and recycled materials in a workshop area such as boxes, with glue, scissors, and masking tape for example

- ✔ book-making area, next to the workshop

- ✔ small-world – dolls' house, train set, garage, cars, farms, zoos, dinosaurs

- ✔ paint/graphics materials in a mark-making area, with a variety of paper and different kinds of pencils, pens and chalks (this might be next to the workshop area)

- ✔ malleable of flexible material such as clay or dough

- ✔ wooden set of free-standing blocks (not plastic, and not bits and pieces from different sets) – unit blocks, hollow blocks and mini hollow blocks (e.g. Community Playthings)

- ✔ construction kit (one or two carefully selected types, such as Duplo or Brio)

- ✔ book (reading) area, which is warm, light and cosy

- ✔ domestic play area

- ✔ dressing-up clothes (mainly hats and shoes)

- ✔ cooking activities with baking materials and equipment

- ✔ ICT, digital camera, computer – it is preferable to use computer programs that encourage children to use their imaginations, rather than responding to computer-led tasks

- ✔ nature table, with magnifiers, growing and living things, such as mustard and cress, hyacinths (flowers), wormery, fish tank

- ✔ woodwork bench, with glue to join things and tape to bind things together, saws, hammers, vice and safety equipment such as goggles and gloves

- ✔ a range of dolls and soft toys

- ✔ music and sounds area, with home-made and commercially produced instruments

- ✔ movement area (perhaps next to the music area)

- ✔ story props, poetry and song cards

- ✔ sewing table.

Key learning experiences

Stories, books and reading

Listening to stories

Children need practitioners to tell and read them stories. In one-to-one stories the child can interact with the reader and get deeply involved. The practitioner and child can pause, chat, go back and revisit, and read at their own pace. All children need these opportunities but for babies, toddlers and two-year-olds, this should be the main way in which they experience books.

Small-group stories are more difficult for children because the practitioner needs to keep the story going, so cannot allow constant interruptions. Skilled practitioners are able to welcome many of the children's contributions, but the larger the group, the more you will need to ensure that children are able to listen to what you have to say. Therefore this arrangement only works with older children. Large groups, with four to eight children, are less sensitive to the individual needs of children, so these need to be more of a theatre show or performance by the adult, in order to maintain the attention of the children; they cannot be so interactive. Small groups of two to four younger children need to be very interactive, with a lot of opportunities for movement and for handling objects.

It is important to remember that stories are not always in written form:

- stories can be told (the Gallic, Celtic and Maori traditions use storytelling powerfully)
- stories can be told in pictures, which are subtle.

Stories have a special way of using language called book language, such as 'Once upon a time …' Children need a wealth of experience of book language before they can read well and become enthusiastic readers.

Children need many different kinds of stories.

Guidelines for good practice

Selecting appropriate books

- Think about issues of gender, ethnicity, culture and disability, and be sure that all children see positive images of themselves in the stories you tell and in the books that you offer.

- Everyday events – these help children to recognise common events and feelings. They help children to heighten their awareness of words that describe everyday situations.

- Poems – these help rhyming and rhythm, and the chorus often gives a predictable element; the repetition helps children. This is also true of many stories, but poems are an enjoyable experience for young children, who may not be able to concentrate on a whole story in the early stages.

- Folk stories – these introduce children to different cultures. However, avoid stories in which animals behave as if they were humans or in which animals behave in a way that is out of character (e.g. a spider who saves the life of a fly in an act of bravery). These are called anthropomorphic stories. They can confuse young children, who are trying to sort out what is and is not true.

- True stories – these lead to an understanding of non-fiction books, which are full of information on different topics and subjects.

- Make-believe stories – these lead to an understanding of fiction. Avoid stories of witches and fairies for very young children (under four years); children need to be clear about the distinction between reality and imagination, otherwise they may be fearful and have nightmares, for example. Bear in mind that it is one thing for a four-year-old to make up their own stories about monsters, witches or ghosts (the child has control), but if a practitioner introduces these characters, the child may be scared.

- Action rhymes and finger rhymes – these help children to predict what is in a text. Predicting is a very large part of learning to read; knowing what comes next is important.

- Repeating stories – knowing a story well helps children begin to read. Sometimes practitioners say, 'Oh, but he is not reading, he just knows it off by heart' which you should not say to children. Knowing what comes next is probably one of the most important parts of learning to read.

- Decide as a team which books you will introduce as core texts, to help children become familiar with them. Note which books are favourites of particular children, and use these with the child in the same way.

Helping children to read

The aim of helping children to read is to produce children who are bookworms, who want to read for pleasure and understanding, information and knowledge, and not children who only look at books when directed to do so, or who are just dutiful readers.

You can help children to read by enjoying a book or poetry card together, without any pressure. Children can see how a book is used, where to begin, how to turn a page and the direction of print, using pictures as clues, finding familiar words and guessing. Being able to guess and predict what the print says is important. Children are usually fascinated by guesses that go wrong, realising this as they learn to link what they read with meaning, and to work out the words using their increasing ability to segment and blend the **graphemes** and **phonemes.** It is important to say, 'What do you think he says next?' Show the child any patterns – for example, a phrase that is repeated – and talk about the letters, words and sentences as you go. Picture cues are very important when learning to read, so talk about these and the clues they give.

Alphabet books and displays are important as they help children to focus on the initial grapheme and phoneme in a word, while offering a meaningful picture to help the child along. Regularly singing the alphabet is helpful too. Pointing out children with the same letter at the beginning of their names helps, and there can be fascinating discussions about why George is pronounced with a 'J' sound, while Gary is with a 'G' sound. English-speakers need to learn early to spot exceptions such as this with detective joy! Remember that the child's own name is the best starting point for learning letters, because children are emotionally attached to their name.

KEY TERMS

Grapheme – A letter or letters that spell a sound in a word.

Phoneme – The smallest unit of sound in a word such as, c / a / t (three sounds and three letters) or c / a / tch (three sounds and five letters).

Regular language – A language such as Spanish or Italian, where one letter usually has just one sound and verbs are structured in a regular way.

Irregular language – A language such as English, where a letter may have several different sounds ('a' sounds different in apple, want, any) and a sound may be spelled using different letters (i.e. the sound 'k' can be spelled c, k or ck) and where many verbs are irregular.

Phonics and English-speakers

English is an **irregular language**, which makes it particularly hard to learn to read and write in English. Most early years experts take the view that the human brain needs to be sufficiently mature to tackle the fine detail of discriminating the sounds and look of English print. Even in countries where the language is very regular, such as Finland and Sweden, this is the approach.

However, the brains of young children are particularly open to learning through communication (non-verbal and spoken/signed language) and music, gesture and movement. This means that singing, dancing, talking with and listening to children all have a huge contribution to make in helping children towards reading and writing at six or seven years of age. This age is generally regarded, throughout the world, as the best time to learn to read and write, because the structures in the brain for using more of the complex symbols needed for reading and writing are usually more developed at this age.

There is great opposition by early years experts in the UK to the suggestion that young children should be taught **synthetic phonics** through daily instruction in large groups. This approach teaches letters and sounds in isolation from the context of the whole language and meaning of a story or narrative. This can make learning to read and write more difficult for many children, particularly children with disabilities or SEN, such as visual or hearing impairments, or children with English as an additional language. Learning about rhyming through poems, songs, action rhymes, poetry cards and books are more powerful ways of helping young children to read in English than teaching isolated sounds, using flashcards as the main strategy. The more strategies we have to offer children as they learn to read, the more we can find the ones that suit each child best. One size does not fit all children.

Daily group time (remember, large groups are four to eight children), with song, dance and rhyme, and encouragement, helps children become:

- phonologically aware (aware of the sounds in the language)

KEY TERMS

Phonics – A method of teaching reading by matching sounds with symbols in the alphabet.
Synthetic phonics – A method of teaching reading (in English) which first teaches the letter sounds and then builds up to blending these sounds together to achive full pronunciation of whole words.
Flash cards – A card containing a small amount of information, held up for children to see, as an aid to learning.

Reflecting on practice

Different paths to reading

Tom and Hannah, both from the same family, needed completely different help. At six years of age, Tom, the second child in the family, liked his parents and older sister to read stories to him at bedtime. He enjoyed quite different stories from his sister, especially *The Tales of Narnia* by C. S. Lewis. He showed no interest in looking at the book. He preferred to lie down and listen before he settled down to sleep. Tom did enjoy looking at non-fiction books about beetles and bugs. He would willingly look up pictures of spiders, ladybirds and ants, to identify the creatures he found in the garden. He would read the short sentences describing them – this was his way into reading, rather than being read to.

When Hannah was six years of age, she liked to find books that she could read easily. She would read these aloud to her parents at bedtime. She also liked to read them to her younger brother Tom, who was then four years old. She read books like *Spot the Dog*. Then she wanted her parents to take a turn at reading, asking them to read books that were too difficult for her to read on her own. She liked to sit and follow the text as a parent read to her. In this way, Hannah began to fill in bits of reading and even to take over from the adult when she could manage it. She felt in control when tackling more difficult texts and did not lose the flow of the story because the adult took over as soon as she stopped reading.

- able to discriminate sounds with increasing ease
- able to link these with the print in the rhymes using poetry cards (a poem written on a single card).

Singing helps children because many of the words rhyme, and this makes the text predictable; it is also more manageable because the poetry is in a verse or small chunk.

If you sing, 'Dinner-time, it's dinner-time' to children – especially children with special needs, complex needs or who are learning English as an additional language – you will probably find they understand more easily what you are saying. It helps children to segment the sounds, and to identify and pronounce them.

Mark-making and writing

It is important to understand the ability to write as part of continuing development. Babies and toddlers begin to notice the different marks made by different actions, and use their whole bodies to explore materials and make marks. As their dexterity or skill develops, tools to make marks are increasingly used, though a *hands-on* approach continues to be preferred with many, but not all, children. At first tools that are effective with whole arm movements are more appropriate, until physical control has developed further down into the wrists and fingers. Babies and toddlers use all sorts of materials to explore making marks; for example, food, drink, sticks, stones and water, as well as paint and chalks. Two-year-olds often describe their pictures in relation to the nature of the actions they used to create it; for example they may describe something as 'round and round' rather than 'a circle' (Manning-Morton and Thorp 2003, 2006).

Babies, toddlers and young children need:

- a variety of such tools that can be easily grasped, such as thick stubby chalks, wax crayons, felt tips, pencils, charcoal, sticks, sponges, house paint brushes and rollers, as well as art paint brushes
- opportunities to practise, so materials need to be frequently available
- to see practitioners interested and engaged in the mark-making area
- different textured surfaces and surfaces at different angles; for example on brick walls, fabric, corrugated card, glass and mirrors so that they can discover the different effects and learn about the different materials and the fine motor skills they need to use for each
- freedom to experiment without the pressure to produce an end product.

Older children (approx. three to six years) need:

- to manipulate and try out different ways of 'writing', using their own personal code – tracing or copying letters undermines this because of their own movement patterns
- to explore what writing is
- practitioners who point out print in books and in the environment – for example, on notices and street signs.

It is important to value writing from different cultures – for example Urdu, Arabic (which is read from right to left) and Chinese (which is read up and down on the page) (DCSF 2008).

Supporting children to write

Writing has two aspects:

- what it says – the construction of meaning
- the look of it – the handwriting and letter shapes (transcription).

Writing develops when children begin to use symbols. Often they begin by putting letter-type shapes into their drawings. These gradually get pushed out to the edges of the drawing, to look more like words and sentences. Practitioners need to observe the

Guidelines for good practice

Creative writing for older children (approx. four to seven years)

✔ Learning about different roles, characters and themes is essential if children are going to learn to write stories.

✔ Having dressing-up clothes to act out stories helps children to create narratives – a skill needed for later writing.

✔ If children are encouraged to play in the early years, they will be better at creative writing at seven years of age.

shapes, sizes and numbers that children experiment with. Children need to be free to experiment, without criticism or pressure. Left-handed children must never be encouraged to write with the right hand. It is important to talk with children about environmental print, and to pick out their favourite letters (often those in their name).

Young children find capital letters, which are more linear, easier to write than lower-case letters, which have more curves, so they tend to experiment with capitals first. It is when children begin to experiment with curves that they are indicating they have more pencil control, so can begin to form letters more easily. It is important that children enjoy and see the point of reading and writing for the rest of their lives. A child's own name is important to them, and they often write the names of people they love, plus the words 'love from'.

▲ **Figure 18.7** Children's writing

Finding out and understanding: reasoning and problem-solving

Through their play and everyday experiences, children are exploring and finding out about how the world, and the objects and materials in it, work. They are developing scientific and mathematical understanding.

Learning about the world requires the ability to reason; to ask why things happen or work in certain ways and to come up with reasoned ideas based on your evidence and understanding. Finding out about how things work also involves problem-solving. These abilities depend on children being supported to develop positive dispositions (general approach to life) of curiosity and confidence in their learning (Dowling 2010). To support children's curiosity, practitioners may need to expand their own knowledge and understanding first to make sure that they do not mislead them with false information or close down children's interests through not knowing. The best response to a child's question when you do not know the answer is: 'Ooh, that's interesting, let's find out more about it. Here is a book that might tell us.'

In their play and daily experiences, children can come to understand the processes of how materials and objects behave in different conditions.

For example, you could use mixtures to demonstrate how materials can be changed and recovered (salt and water, sugar and water, earth and water, flour and water, mud pies, and mud and straw to make bricks). All these mixtures have properties that children can explore:

- Salt dissolves in water. So does sugar. When the water evaporates, the salt or sugar can be seen again.
- Flour and mud do not dissolve. They become suspended in water.
- You can look at transformations using water, ice and steam. You can reverse these, and turn steam into water again.
- Study what happens when you cook an egg. You cannot reverse this transformation.

Finding out about and understanding concepts in the physical sciences

Science is everywhere. Children can be helped to find out about and understand the physical sciences from an early age, but the learning opportunity must be matched to their understanding and ability.

The following are interesting concepts to explore with children:

- **Electricity**: electrical circuits are easy to make with children and can be used to make a light for the doll's house or the train tracks.
- **Heat**: remember, heat is not just about temperature. Heat is energy; temperature is a measure of how much energy. Cookery is the best way to help children understand about temperature. Making jelly or ice cream is a good way of looking at coldness. Making something that needs to be cooked in the oven helps children to learn about high temperatures. Play with ice cubes in the water tray. Talk about relative heat. Is this hotter than that? Describe what is happening; think about the cause and effect, why things happen as they do. Metal feels colder than wood, but why?
- **Sound**: listen to the sounds around you. Help children to be aware of them. Children love to record sounds and find ways to imitate sounds they hear. You could explore why some sounds are quieter and some are noisier than others.
- **Light**: use torches and lanterns. Make rainbows with prisms. Put on puppet shows and have lighting effects. Use cellophane to make different colours of light. Children in Key Stage 1 will enthusiastically make lighting effects for stories they have made up or enjoyed from books. Experiment with shadows and shadow puppets.
- **Gravity**: use parachutes or drop objects from heights.
- **Floating and sinking**: this is a difficult concept. Young children benefit from using solid and hollow objects such as corks and rubber ducks to experiment with in water, but true understanding takes time.

Finding out about and understanding technology

Low technology can be explored by looking at activities such as weaving. If you have a frame with string going up and down and from side to side, near the entrance to your setting, then children and families will enjoy the in-and-out movement of threading pieces of material, wool, ribbon and so on. These weavings often become attractive wall hangings in the office or entrance hall of the setting.

It is important to use technology that is easy for children to understand. Examples would be a tin opener, an egg whisk or scissors. Encourage children to use wooden blocks and construction kits.

High technology includes digital cameras, recording equipment for music and stories, computers, word processors and printers, and telephones for conversations.

Children benefit from using a word processor and printer, as well as using digital cameras. They enjoy picking out letters and punctuation marks, and through this kind of play they learn about important aspects of reading, writing and numbers, which will be used in a more elaborate way later.

The most appropriate computer programs invite children to be interactive.

Finding out about and understanding mathematical concepts

Mathematics involves problem-solving and reasoning in particular ways.

- **Space**: children learn about topological space (on/off, over/under, in/out, surrounding, across, near/far) before they learn about Euclidian space (circles, squares and so on). They need to physically explore and experience these concepts to help them understand them in the abstract (see Chapter 8, p. 152 for a definition).

- **Shape and size**: children need practitioners to describe things that are 'bigger than' and 'smaller than' in order to learn that these things are relative, not absolute sizes. Something is 'big' only in relation to something else. Always use relative terms with children.

  Introduce words like 'cylinder' and 'sphere' before 'oblong' and 'circle' because children can handle the three dimensional object. Use everyday things, like tins of food or a football, to explain what a cylinder and a sphere look like.

- **Length**: use words such as 'longer than' or 'shorter than'. Children need to be surrounded by rulers and tapes so that they become aware that things can be measured. Which is the tallest plant? Who has the longest foot? Gradually, they develop an understanding of the exactness of absolute measurements.

- **Volume and capacity**: 'This glass is full.' 'This bucket is nearly empty.' Listen to yourself speak and you will be surprised at how often you use mathematical language in everyday situations.

- **Area**: this is about ideas such as the blanket that covers the mattress on the bed. Children often explore area in their block play.

- **Weight**: introduce the concept of weight using relative ideas. 'This tin of soup is heavier than that apple.' Rather than using a weighing machine, use a balance, so that children see this. Remember that young children need to experience weight physically. They love to carry heavy things. They love to lift each other up, and often carry bags around.

- **Time**: time has different aspects. For example, personal time: 'it feels like a long time before a car journey ends'; and universal time, which includes succession: Monday, Tuesday, Wednesday, ... and duration: day, night, an hour, a minute, ...

Number

Number has several different aspects:

- matching – this looks like this (two identical cups in the home corner)

- sorting – this looks different from this (the cup and the saucer)

- one-to-one correspondence – one biscuit for you, one biscuit for me

- cardinal numbers – counting numbers that show quantity: the two cups remain two cups, however they are arranged (this means that the child understands the number, e.g. two)

- ordinal numbers – this is first, second, third (e.g. the sequence in cooking: first, I wash my hands; second, I put on my apron ...).

Children learn about number in the following ways:

- reciting – number songs

- nominal understanding – they pick out numbers, for example on house doors, buses, in shops, on shoe sizes

- subitising – remembering number patterns to recognise how many; for example, four dots, one on each corner of a square, or on a domino

- counting backwards – 5, 4, 3, 2, 1, lift-off!

Guidelines for good practice

Number

✔ Do not do exercises or tasks with young children that are isolated from their experience.

✔ Remember that children learn mathematics through cooking, tidy-up time, playing in the home area, painting and being in the garden. Mathematics is everywhere.

✔ Numbers are found on rulers, calibrated cooking jugs (i.e. ones that have measurements on them), the doors of houses, and so on.

✔ Counting is only one part of exploring numbers. It is one thing for children to be curious about numbers on calibrated jugs, weights and measures, but they need to be free to experiment and explore. This is very different from formally teaching them numbers through adult-led tasks, unrelated to real life.

▲ **Figure 18.8** Making the song `Ten green bottles' real in this activity makes learning about number a concrete fun experience

There are three counting principles:

1 A number word is needed for every object that is counted. This is the one-to-one correspondence principle.

2 The numbers always have the same order: 1, 2, 3 (not 1, 3, 2). This is called the stable-order principle.

3 When children count, they have grasped the cardinal number principle if they show they understand that a number is an outcome by counting 1, 2, 3, in the correct order, and know that the answer is 3.

Finding out about and understanding the natural sciences

Children are very interested in how bodies work; digestion and blood circulation, for example. It is important to be able to discuss and explore ideas about the body factually and scientifically without embarrassment or disgust – particularly when children are interested in genital body parts or how faeces are made.

Equally, it is important that practitioners can share children's interest in small creatures without transmitting any fears or squeamishness they feel.

Finding out and understanding about the human, cultural world

Young children are interested in people, families and homes. They like to learn about what people in the community do. Through role play and visits to offices, shops, clinics, the vet, the station so on, they learn about different communities. They develop a sense of geography.

Guidelines for good practice

Looking at animals

There are reasons why animals, birds and insects have developed as they have. The following points will give children an introduction to the evolution of the animal world in ways they can understand.

✔ Where do animals live? You can find ants, spiders and birds and look at their habitats.

✔ Remember, never kill animals, and always return them to their habitat; make a point of explaining this to the children. There are now pots available with magnifying glasses in them, which makes it easier to look at these creatures without squashing them accidentally.

✔ What do animals eat? Study cats, birds and fish, and talk about their diets.

✔ How do animals eat? Talk about claws, type of feet, mouths, beaks, types of teeth, jaws that chew and jaws that gnash.

✔ How do animals protect themselves? Look at camouflage, claws, tusks, fur for warmth, oil on ducks' feathers to make them waterproof.

Guidelines for good practice

Looking at plants

How can you help the children you work with to engage with plants and enjoy looking at them? Consider the following points:

✔ Why do plants have leaves? Do all plants have leaves?

✔ Why is a tree trunk like it is? Do all trees have exactly the same sort of trunk? Make some bark rubbings. Hug trees to see if you can reach all the way round them with your arms.

✔ Why do flowers have colours? Insects are important for plant life.

✔ Why do some flowers have scent and nectar?

They are also interested in old objects, in what things were like when they were babies or when their parents were babies, and what sort of childhood their grandparents had. Collecting artefacts of bygone days and inviting older people to share and talk about their lives, often with the help of photographs, helps children to develop a sense of history. Having a timeline helps too – again, using photos to show the order and sequence of events.

Creating and imagining

Creativity is integral to learning in all areas. Being able to think creatively and imagine possible outcomes to personal, social and emotional dilemmas, being able to problem-solve physical, scientific or mathematical problems are as much part of creative development as art, music, dance and drama (Bruce 2004a).

Creativity in the sciences and technologies

Creative scientists and technicians see new connections and new ways of doing things. They look at the same old things in a new way, which changes things forever. Seeing the barbs on a teasel plant when walking the dog by the river led one scientist to invent Velcro. This means that any of the materials indoors and outdoors can be used for artistic or scientific creativity.

Creativity in the humanities

Thinking in new ways about what has gone before can have a huge impact on history, geography and culture. For example, Nelson Mandela changed the world when, instead of following tradition and having trials to condemn the violence that had taken place during the period of apartheid in South Africa, he developed a council of reconciliation, so that people admitted and publicly faced the full horror of their actions, but without fear of reprisal or punishment in doing so. This showed great creative thinking in terms of his emotional and personal intelligence which has influenced the culture and history of his country.

Creativity in the arts and crafts

Children need a wide range of opportunities and materials to make their representations. Representing a dog is quite different when using clay, wood at the woodwork bench, paint or pretending to be a dog in the home corner (Matthews 2003).

Children make models with clay, wet sand, wax, soap-carving, wood, dough, junk and recycled materials. This will involve them in using sticky tape, scissors, rolling pins, string, wire and other materials.

Children draw and paint using a wide range of tools and materials on different surfaces; vertical and horizontal. Materials should be stored carefully so that children can take and access what they need when they need it and should also be able to mix paints as they need to.

All materials should enable children to represent a range of skin tones.

Guidelines for good practice

Supporting children's creativity in arts and crafts

Remember, these play opportunities are for the children, not for the adult practitioner. Do not:

✔ draw for children

✔ use templates for children to fill in to make a display

✔ ask children to trace

✔ ask children to colour in an outline

✔ ask children to copy your model step by step.

Do:

✔ give children real, first-hand experiences, such as looking at plants or mini beasts in a pond

✔ give children opportunities to represent things, and to keep hold of their experiences – for example, by making a model of the plant out of clay

✔ encourage lots of different ideas – it is best when every child in a group has made a different model; this means that children are doing their own thinking and are not dependent on practitioners for ideas.

Creativity in music, dance and drama

Music

Babies are tuned in to music from birth, and young children's brains are particularly tuned in to music, particularly the singing voices of their close adults. Everyday sounds have rhythm, such as the tick-tock of an alarm clock, tearing paper, shaking a salt cellar, jangling a bunch of keys, fire engines, and so on. Children love to go on listening walks, and to make the sounds they have heard using home-made musical instruments you help them to make. The importance of singing and listening to a wide range of music from different cultures cannot be overemphasised.

Music is about hearing and making sounds by:

- singing
- making a melody
- clapping rhythms
- making loud and soft sounds (the dynamic)
- making sounds going up and down (the pitch)
- using instruments, to pluck, blow, bow, bang
- singing and dancing action songs and ring games.

Drama

Some people argue that drama began in ancient times, when people tried to explore the forces of good versus evil. Similarly, in their play, children experiment with goodies and baddies, friendship and foes, kindness and unkindness. Penny Holland's work shows how practitioners can help children to explore these major themes of what it is to be human (Holland 2003). Encourage children to act out stories you have told or that they have made up and which you have written down for them. Vivian Gussin-Paley, in her school in Chicago, did this as a daily part of the curriculum (1991).

Young children should not be expected to perform stories in school assemblies or in situations with audiences full of strangers. They need to be able to make their own stories and to share these with friends and practitioners whom they know well before they perform. To perform becomes appropriate only in primary school. Any earlier, and some children begin overacting and playing to the audience rather than becoming involved in the story; other children are put off for ever because of the stress of being made to perform. The exercise is a failure in terms of involving a child in a story.

Dance

Children love to move their bodies in response to music and will absorb styles of dancing from their cultural context at an early age.

You can use what children do naturally – spinning, running, jumping, stamping – to make up a dance.

- Use an action phrase – for example, 'shiver and freeze'. Ask the children to move like the words in the phrase.

- Show different objects, perhaps something spiky like a thistle. Ask the children to move in a spiky way and make a dance.

- Take an idea from nature or everyday life: rush and roar like the wind; be a machine or a clock; dance like shadows moving or fish in an aquarium.

- For inspiration, use experiences that the children have had very recently.

The book by Mollie Davies (2003), *Movement and Dance in Early Childhood*, offers more ideas on how to help young children dance.

Moving on

Think about ideas

Research an approach to curriculum that is unfamiliar to you. This might be:

- Te Whāriki
- Reggio Emilia
- High/scope
- Forest schools

1 Can you see any of this approach reflected in your setting?

2 Are there any aspects of this approach that you think are particularly beneficial to children? Why?

3 How might you introduce some of the ideas from this approach into your setting?

Think about ideas

A setting's practice and provision should be regularly reviewed and evaluated, as discussed in Chapter 5.

One approach to evaluation, developed in Belgium by Prof. Ferre Laevers, is called the **Leuven involvement and well-being scales**. Although this approach uses observation to discover how children are deeply involved in what they are doing and what their level of well-being is, the purpose is not to assess the children but to evaluate how effective the provision is. Practitioners then look at what they are providing for children and make appropriate changes.

This approach also uses an **adult–child engagement scale** to help practitioners to see if they are being sensitive to the needs of children, helping them to be autonomous (self-motivated), independent and self-disciplined in what they are doing.

Find out more about this approach and use the scales to review the provision in your setting.

Further reading, weblinks and resources

Bruce, T., 2004b, *Developing Learning in Early Childhood*, London: Paul Chapman Publishing.

Drury, R., 2007, *Young Bilingual Learners at Home and School: Researching Multilingual Voices*, Stoke-on-Trent: Trentham Books.

Worthington, M. and Carruthers, E., 2003, *Children's Mathematics: Making Marks, Making Meaning*, London: Paul Chapman Publishing.

5x5x5=creativity

This organisation has been influenced by the work in Reggio Emilia in Italy.
www.5x5x5creativity.org.uk

Book Trust Children's Books

This organisation encourages children and parents to enjoy reading for pleasure and information; and for young children it supports adults in reading to children, recommending a wide range of books, rhymes and stories.
www.booktrustchildrensbooks.org.uk

Books for Keeps

It is important to use diverse texts about different cultures, disabilities, gender and age.
www.booksforkeeps.co.uk

Centre for Literacy in Primary Education

This organisation has undertaken pioneering work in supporting and training practitioners to enjoy helping children to love stories and books. It offers excellent training for those working with children in reception and Key Stage 1.
www.clpe.co.uk

Early Education

The booklet on *Core Experiences for the Early Years Foundation Stage* from Kate Greenaway Nursery School and Children's Centre can be ordered from this website.
www.early-education.org.uk

Forest schools

Through this link, information can be obtained about forest schools in urban settings, and also those in rural settings.
www.forestschools.com/history-of-forest-schools.php

Block play – Community Playthings

Foundations: CD-ROM illustrating the value of block play.
www.communityplaythings.co.uk/resources/ request-literature.html

Environments – Community Playthings

Spaces; Creating places; I made a Unicorn! Educational booklets.
www.communityplaythings.co.uk/ resources/request-literature.html

References

Alexander, R., Armstrong, M., Flutter, J., Hargreaves, L., Harrison, D., Harlen, W., Hartley-Brewer, E., Kershner, R., MacBeath, J., Mayall, B., Northen, S., Pugh, G., Richards, C. and Utting, D., 2010, *Children, their World, their Education: Final Report and Recommendations of the Cambridge Primary Review*, London: Routledge.

Arthur, L., Beecher, B., Death, E., Dockett, S. and Farmer, S., 1996, *Programming and Planning in Early Childhood Settings* (2nd edn), Sydney: Harcourt Brace.

Bruce, T., 2015, *Early Childhood Education,* London: Hodder Education.

Bruce, T., 2004a, *Cultivating Creativity: Babies, Toddlers and Young Children,* London: Hodder Arnold.

Bruce, T. (ed.), 2009a, *Early Childhood: A Guide for Students* (2nd edn), London: Sage.

Bruce, T., 2009b, 'Learning through Play: Froebelian Principles and their Practice Today', *Early Childhood Practice: The Journal for Multi-professional Partnerships* 10(2): 58–73.

Bruce, T. and Spratt, J., 2010, *The Essentials of Communication, Language and Literacy* (2nd edn), London: Sage.

Copple, C. and Bredekamp, S. (eds), 2009, *Developmentally Appropriate Practice in Early Childhood Programs Serving Children from Birth through Age 8* (3rd edn), Washington DC: National Association for the Education of Young Children (NAEYC).

Davies, M., 2003, *Movement and Dance in Early Childhood*, London: Paul Chapman Publishing.

Department for Children, Schools and Families, 2008, *Mark Making Matters: Young Children Making Meaning in All Areas of Learning and Development*, Nottingham: DCSF Publications.

Dowling, M., 2010, *Young Children's Personal, Social and Emotional Development*, London: Paul Chapman Publishing.

Early Education/BAECE, 2012, *Development Matters in the Early Years Foundation Stage*. Available at: http://www.foundationyears.org.uk/files/2012/03/Development-Matters-FINAL-PRINT-AMENDED.pdf.

Edwards, C., Gandini, L. and Forman, G., 1998, *The Hundred Languages of Children*, Westport, CT and London: Ablex Publishing.

Goldschmied, E. and Jackson, S., 2004, *People Under Three: Young Children in Day Care* (2nd edn), London: Routledge.

Greenman, J. and Stonehouse, A., 1996, *Prime Times. A Handbook for Excellence in Infant Toddler Programs*, St. Paul, USA: Redleaf Press.

Holland, P., 2003, *We Don't Play With Guns Here: War, Weapon and Superhero Play in the Early Years*, Maidenhead: Open University Press.

Katz, L., 1993, *Five Perspectives on Quality in Early Childhood Programs*, Urbana, IL: ERIC Clearinghouse on Elementary and Early Childhood Education.

Lamont, B., 1991, *Babies, Naturally*. Available from: www.developmentalmovement.org.

Layard, R. and Dunn, J., 2009, *A Good Childhood: Searching for Values in a Competitive Age. The Landmark Report for The Children's Society*, London: Penguin Books.

Manning-Morton, J. (ed.), 2014, *Exploring Well-being in the Early Years*, Maidenhead: Open University Press.

Manning-Morton, J. and Thorp, M., 2003, *Key Times for Play*, The First Three Years, Maidenhead: Open University Press.

Manning-Morton, J. and Thorp, M., 2006, *Key Times: A Framework for Developing High Quality Provision for Children from Birth to Three years*, Maidenhead: Open University Press.

Manning-Morton, J. and Thorp, M., 2015, *Two Year Olds in Early Years Settings*; Journeys of Discovery, Maidenhead: Open University Press.

Matthews, J., 2003, *Drawing and Painting*: Children and Visual Representation (2nd edn), London: Paul Chapman Publishing.

New Zealand Ministry of Education, 1996, *Te Whàriki Early Childhood Curriculum/He Whàriki Màtauranga mò ngà Mokopuna o Aotearoa*, New Zealand: Ministry of Education/ Learning Media Ltd.

Paley, V. P., 1991, *The Boy Who Would be a Helicopter: Uses of Storytelling in the Classroom*, Cambridge, MA: Harvard University Press.

Tickell, C., 2011, *The Early Years: Foundations For Life, Health And Learning*, London: Department for Education.

Tovey, H., 2007, *Playing Outdoors: Spaces and Places, Risk and Challenge, Maidenhead: Open University Press.*

This chapter gives an overview of how early years services are provided in England, the UK and some areas of the wider world. It explains how services are funded and regulated in the independent and maintained sectors. The historical, economic and political contexts of the development of early years services are explored and their impact on how services are delivered at the current time. This includes an overview of the 'pioneers' of early years services and the influences they still have on pedagogical practice today.

How services for children and families are provided

Statutory services

A **statutory service** is one that is provided by the state. Some statutory services are provided by central government and funded from central taxation – the National Health Service (NHS) is one example. Other statutory services are provided by local government and funded by a combination of local and central taxation – for example, education and social service departments.

The statutory sector is made up of central government departments in which policy is devised by a Secretary of State (who is an MP), helped by Ministers of State (also MPs) and managed by the Permanent Secretary (a civil servant); departments include:

- the Health Department
- the Department for Education.

There are also non-ministerial departments such as Ofsted (the Office for Standards in Education), which are led by an appointed person rather than an elected member of parliament.

Government departments all have executive agencies attached to them, contracted to deliver services; for example, the National College for Teaching and Leadership, which oversees early years qualifications as well as others.

Local authority councils also deliver statutory services. They are made up of locally elected councillors; some councils have an elected mayor. You may have a county, district, borough or city council, depending on where you live. Different councils have varying levels of responsibility for services in their area.

Local government department committees are chaired by an elected member of the local council and administered by a paid officer, who is director of a department – they may, for example, be a director of the:

- housing department
- local education authority
- children and young people's services.

Local provision for children

Most local authorities have a special department to coordinate all the services for children within their locality. These departments are often called Children's Services and deal exclusively with the needs of children and their families. The range of services provided varies greatly from one local authority to another, but typically will include the following services:

- housing for children and their families in need
- care and education for all children aged three to five years
- care and education for disadvantaged two-year-olds
- education and out-of-school care for children over five years
- social care for families where children are assessed as being *in need*, including adoption and foster care
- advice, information and counselling for families.

Health services for children

The government's Department of Health is responsible for providing health care through the NHS, which was set up in 1948 to provide free health care to the entire population. Since then there have been many changes and some services are no longer free in England – for example, dental care, prescriptions and ophthalmic services (prescriptions are free in Scotland, Wales and Northen Ireland). There are exemptions to these charges (people who do not have to pay these changes), so that certain groups of people are not disadvantaged by being on low incomes. Groups who are exempt from charges include:

- children under 16 or in full-time education
- pregnant women or with a baby under one year
- families receiving certain benefits.

The National Service Framework for Children, Young People and Maternity Services was set up by the Department of Health in 2004 and has the following aims:

- To help parents find and stay in learning or work, including having high-quality, affordable child care (for preschool and school-aged children) and child-friendly working practices.
- To ensure that families are made aware of the Healthy Start Scheme and encouraged to apply for it if they qualify. Healthy Start provides pregnant women and young families on a low-income with advice on diet and nutrition, local support to eat healthily, and vouchers to buy healthy food.
- To ensure families with low incomes are supported to claim all benefits to which they are entitled.
- To provide support for groups especially likely to be living in poverty – for example, teenage parents, families with children who are disabled and those who are homeless.
- To ensure as far as possible that local authority accommodation for families with children is not damp or cold (in line with the cross-government fuel poverty strategy), has adequate space for play and privacy, and at least one working smoke alarm and a carbon monoxide detector, where appropriate.
- To minimise environmental pollution in residential areas and around nurseries and schools.

(DoH 2004)

Social services for children

Since 2006, education and social care services for children have been brought together under a director of children's services in each local authority. But within them there are different roles and responsibilities undertaken by education and social care professionals.

Social care staff provide a range of care and support for children and families, including:

- families where children are assessed as being in need (including children with disabilities)
- children who may be suffering 'significant harm' – for example, from violence in the home or from some form of child abuse (this aspect of social work is known as child protection or safeguarding)
- children who require looking after by the local authority (through fostering or residential care)
- children who are placed for adoption.

Social workers with responsibilities for children and families may work in the following areas:

- **Safeguarding and promoting the welfare of children** – in the great majority of cases, children are safeguarded while remaining at home, by social workers working with their parents, family members and other significant adults in the child's life to make the child safe, and to promote his or her development within the family setting. (See Chapter 4 for more detail on safeguarding children.)
- **Supporting children with disabilities** – social care departments must provide a range of services to families who have children with disabilities to minimise the impact of any disabilities and enable them to live as normal a life as possible. Typically, they provide short-term breaks in foster families or residential care homes, support services in the home and, increasingly, assistance for children with disabilities to participate in out-of-school and leisure activities in the community alongside their non-disabled peers.
- **Supporting looked-after children** – where the local authority looks after a child following the issuing of a care order, or accommodates a child with the agreement of the child's parents, it is the role of the social worker to ensure that suitable arrangements are made for the child's care and that a plan is put in place, in partnership with the child, his or her parents and other agencies, so that the child's future is secure. Children are generally looked after in foster care. A minority will be cared for in children's homes, and some by prospective adoptive parents. *All* looked-after children will have a social worker and carers – for example, foster carers, residential care staff – responsible for their day-to-day care, who should be involved in making plans or decisions about the young person.

Education services for children

The Department for Education is headed by the Secretary of State for Education and is responsible for deciding on policies and funding to the local education authorities.

Local authorities provide and oversee schools in their area, although government policy has allowed maintained schools to govern themselves (self-governing) and only answerable directly to central government.

Local education authorities provide stand-alone nursery schools, nursery classes attached to primary schools and children's centres. They also provide advisory and support services for independent early years providers such as preschools in the voluntary sector, privately run nurseries and childminders. Although previously also regulated by local authorities, since 2000 all early years settings have been registered and inspected by Ofsted.

Leisure activities and recreation services

These services provide children and their families with activities and opportunities for recreation and sport. Some of these are provided by the local authority or by voluntary organisations and are either free or available at a subsidised (or lower/funded) cost; others are privately owned and charge higher fees. They include:

- sports centres, children's gyms
- music groups
- parks
- swimming pools
- adventure playgrounds and soft play areas
- holiday schemes and activities
- lessons – for example, dance and drama
- clubs – for example, Beavers, Cubs and Scouts; Rainbow Brownies and Guides; Woodcraft Folk
- libraries.

Voluntary services and self-help agencies for children and families

These are health, education and social care services that are set up by charities to provide services which

Think about ideas

What kind of provision?

Research the early years provision made by your local authority.

1 What proportion of four-year-olds are in reception classes?

2 What kind of provision are most three-year-olds and their families offered?

3 What kind of provision are most two-year-olds and their families offered?

4 What kind of provision are babies, toddlers and their families offered?

local authorities can buy in from them, benefiting from their expertise. Voluntary organisations are:

- not for profit (i.e. they are not set up in order to make money/a profit)
- non-statutory (i.e. not required by law)
- dependent on donations, fund-raising and government grants.

They range from very large national organisations, such as Barnardo's, to small, locally-based charities. Children England is an umbrella organisation that supports registered charities that work with children, young people and their families.

Voluntary organisations are often formed because:

- there is a gap in services – this is how playgroups started in the 1960s
- there is a need for a campaign, both to alert the public to an issue and to push for action to be taken – for example, Shelter was started in 1966 to help raise awareness of homelessness.

Within any local authority in the UK, there are childcare and education settings which come into the category of voluntary or self-help provision. Two examples are community nurseries and the Pre-school Learning Alliance community preschools. Voluntary organisations work closely with local authorities and sometimes also provide some of the statutory services – for example, after-school clubs or the day-care element of a Children's Centre – and will receive payment from the local authority or government so they can provide these services at reduced cost to the service user.

Integrated care and education for children

Young children need both education and care. Children are not made up of separate parts; a child is a whole person. It is inappropriate to talk about either educating or caring for young children. Instead, the term 'integrated early years settings' is used to describe places that provide education and care for young children. Children need good physical, emotional and health care as much as they need new, interesting and stimulating experiences.

From the late 1990s on, legislation led to a number of reforms in the delivery of care and education to children (Baldock et al. 2009).

While the school system remains largely unchanged, the statutory services for children from birth to five years have become increasingly integrated, with care, education and family support coordinated within the same department. This involved a new structure for the delivery of integrated services, including:

- Children's Trusts
- Sure Start programmes
- children's centres.

Children's Trusts

Children's Trusts are organisations which bring together health, education and social services for children, young people and families. Some take on responsibility for *all* children's services, from child protection to speech therapy, while others will focus on particularly vulnerable children, such as those with disabilities. The trusts employ a range of professionals, such as:

- social workers
- family support workers
- health visitors
- school nurses
- educational psychologists
- speech and language therapists
- child and adolescent mental health professionals.

Children's Trusts are underpinned by the Children Act 2004 duty to cooperate and to focus on improving outcomes for all children and young people. Trusts can also include Sure Start local programmes. Other local partners may include: housing, leisure services, the police, youth justice, independent sector organisations such as voluntary organisations, and community sector organisations such as churches.

Integrated early years services must include:

- early years provision (integrated childcare and early education)
- social care services
- relevant health services – for example, health visitors, antenatal, post-natal care
- services to assist parents to obtain work
- information services.

Sure Start

Sure Start was an extensive government programme launched in the late 1990s as a cornerstone of the government's drive to eradicate or remove child poverty in 20 years, and to halve it within a decade. The first Sure Start local programmes were established in 1999, with the aim of improving the health and well-being of families and children from before birth to four years, so that they can flourish at home and when they begin school. They started in the most disadvantaged areas in the UK. Sure Start local

programmes are delivered by local partnerships and are now called Sure Start Children's Centres (Baldock et al. 2009).

Sure Start Children's Centres have the following four key objectives:

- **To improve social and emotional development**, in particular by supporting early bonding between parents and their children, helping families to function and enabling early identification and support of children with emotional and behavioural difficulties.
- **To improve health**, in particular by supporting parents in caring for their children to promote healthy development before and after birth.
- **To improve children's ability to learn**, in particular by providing high-quality environments and child care that promote early learning and provide stimulating and enjoyable play, improve language skills and ensure early identification of children with special needs.
- **Strengthening families and communities**, in particular by involving families in building the community's capacity to sustain the programme and create pathways out of **social exclusion**.

The emphasis is on prevention in order to reduce social exclusion later on, and to improve the life chances of younger children through early access to education, health services, family support and advice on nurturing. These projects include support for:

- special educational needs
- outreach services and home visiting
- families and parents
- good-quality play, learning and child care

KEY TERM

Social exclusion – When individuals or whole communities of people are denied full access to various rights, opportunities and resources that are normally available to members of a society.

Look, listen and note

Think about a child and family you work with and list all the different ways that your setting provides for

- their care
- their learning
- the family's support needs.

If you removed one aspect of the provision, what would be the effect on the child and family?
If you find one list is short, identify what is not being provided and why.

- primary and community health care
- advice about child health and development
- advice about parent health, parenting and employment.

 # The pioneers of early years provision

Throughout history, there have always been people who have been prepared to stand up and fight for what young children need. They are the pioneers who still help everyone working with young children to move forward. Not all of us can be a pioneer, but each early years practitioner has a responsibility to develop their knowledge and practice so they can continue to move things forward and provide well for the children in their care.

The pioneers in this chapter are often called educational pioneers, but each one of them cared for children as much as they educated them; they all believed in **integrated early years provision**. This has a long and respected heritage, and the greatest influence in the UK in the nineteenth century has been that of Friedrich Froebel. Other pioneers include Maria Montessori, Rudolf Steiner, Margaret McMillan and Susan Isaacs (Bruce 2005).

Friedrich Froebel (1782–1852)

Froebel, who founded the first kindergarten (nursery school or centre) in 1840, studied for a time with Pestalozzi in his school in Switzerland. Through his observations of children, Froebel learned how important it was for them to have real experiences that involved them in being physically active. Froebel's ideas are now very much part of everyday thinking about early years practice but most people have never heard of the man himself – only his ideas remain.

Froebel believed that everything links and connects with everything else: he called this the principle of unity. He also believed in what he called the principle of opposition, so thought it was important for children to understand about the different, contrasting properties of objects such as hard and soft. For this reason the first 'Gift' (play material) is a soft ball, but the second 'Gift' is a hard, wooden ball.

A summary of Froebel's ideas

- Froebel thought that schools should be communities in which the parents are welcome to join their children.
- He believed that parents are the first educators of their child.
- Froebel thought that children learn outdoors in the garden, as well as indoors. He encouraged movement, games and the study of natural science in the garden.

- He invented finger play, songs and rhymes in the educational context.
- He encouraged the arts and crafts and a love of literature, as well as mathematical understanding.
- He thought that children should have freedom of movement, clothes that are easy to move about in, and sensible food that is not too rich.
- Froebel valued symbolic behaviour deeply, and he encouraged this even in very young children. He realised how important it is for children to understand that they can make one thing stand for another – for example, a daisy can stand for a fried egg, a twig can stand for a knife, a leaf can stand for a plate, a written word can stand for a name.
- He thought that the best way for children to try out symbolic behaviour is in their play. He thought that as they pretend and imagine things, children show their highest levels of learning. He thought that children's best thinking is done when they are playing.
- He also designed various items and activities to help symbolic behaviour. He encouraged children to draw, make collages and model with clay.
- He encouraged play with special-shaped wooden blocks, which he called the 'Gifts'.
- He made up songs, movements and dancing, and the crafts that he called his 'Occupations' (or activities).
- He allowed children to use the Gifts and Occupations as they wished, without having to do set tasks of the kind that adults usually asked of them. Thus he introduced what is now called free-flow play.
- He emphasised the importance of expressive arts, mathematics, literature, the natural sciences, creativity and aesthetic (beautiful) things. He believed that each brought important but different kinds of knowledge and understanding.
- He also placed great emphasis on ideas, feelings and relationships. Relationships with other children, he believed, were as important as relationships with adults.

Maria Montessori (1870–1952)

Maria Montessori began her work as a doctor in the poorest areas of Rome, Italy, at the beginning of the 1900s. She worked with children with learning difficulties. She spent many hours observing children

▲ **Figure 19.1** Froebel thought that children learn outdoors in the garden

and this is one of the great strengths of her work. She came to the conclusion, now supported by modern research, that children pass through sensitive periods of development when they are particularly receptive or open to particular areas of learning. Like Piaget (and others), she saw children as active learners.

A summary of Montessori's ideas

- Montessori devised a structured teaching programme, which she based on her observations of children with learning difficulties; she believed she was making Froebel's work more scientifically rigorous in doing this.

- She also used the work of an educator called Seguin, who had given manual dexterity exercises to children with physical disabilities. He did this because he believed that if they could learn to use their hands, they would be able to find work later.

- Montessori designed a set of what she called didactic materials. These are materials which are designed to teach the child a particular concept and encouraged children to use their hands. Her approach moved children from simple to complex exercises.

- Whereas Froebel stressed the importance of relationships, feelings and being part of a community, Montessori stressed that children should work alone. She thought that this helped children to become independent learners.

- For Montessori, the highest moment in a child's learning is what she called the polarisation of the attention. This means that the child is completely silent and absorbed in what he or she is doing.

- Unlike Froebel, Montessori did not see the point in play. She did not encourage children to have their own ideas until they had worked through all her

graded learning sequence; she did not believe that they were able to do free drawing or creative work of any kind until they had done this. Montessori has had more influence on private schools than on the maintained sector of education.

Rudolf Steiner (1861–1925)

Steiner believed in three phases of childhood. These involved:

- The will, birth to seven years: he believed that the spirit fuses with the body at this stage.

- The heart, 7 to 14 years: he believed that the rhythmic system of the beating heart, the chest and the respiratory system meant that feelings were especially important during this time.

- The head, 14 years onwards: this is the period of thinking.

There are a few schools in the UK that use Steiner's methods. Called Waldorf schools, these are all in the private sector. Like Montessori, Steiner has had less influence on the statutory public sector than on the private sector.

A summary of Steiner's ideas

- Steiner believed in reincarnation (that after death we are reborn in another body). To him, this meant that during the first seven years of life, the child is like a newcomer finding his or her way, and the child's reincarnated (or born again) soul needs protection.

- The child needs a carefully planned environment in order to develop in a rounded way.

- What the child eats is very important (Steiner was a vegetarian and advocated this). The child also needs proper rest (rest and activity need to be balanced).

- The child's temperament is also considered to be very important. A child might be calm (sanguine), easily angered (choleric), sluggish (phlegmatic) or peevish (melancholic). Often children are a combination of types.

- The golden rule for the practitioner is never to go against the temperament of the child, but always to go with it.

- Steiner was like Froebel in that he believed in the importance of the community. He believed that maintaining relationships with other people is very important, and for this reason children would keep the same teacher for a number of years.

- When children are about to sing and act out a circle game, everyone waits for the last child to join the group. The song is sung many times, so that children who learn quickly learn to help and support children who learn more slowly.

- Steiner's curriculum is very powerful for children with special educational needs who can integrate, because other children are actively helped to care about them.

- Steiner thought the symbolic behaviour of the child was important, but in a different way from Froebel. In the first seven years of life, he told special Steinerian fairy tales. He believed that children 'drink' these in and absorb them. He gave them dolls without faces, wooden blocks with irregular shapes, and silk scarves as dressing-up clothes, so that the children were free to use their imaginations and particular colour schemes in rooms that are believed to relate to the stage of development of the children (pink at first as it is seen to be gentle and nurturing). Baking, gardening, modelling, painting and singing would all take place in a carefully designed community.

Margaret McMillan (1860–1931)

Margaret McMillan, like Montessori, began her work using the influence of Seguin. This meant that she emphasised manual dexterity exercises, i.e. activities where children use their hands such as threading beads, long before Montessori's ideas reached the UK. However, as time went on, she used Froebel's ideas more and more and she became a member of the Froebel Society in 1903. McMillan pioneered nursery schools, which she saw as an extension of, not a substitute for, home. The British nursery school, as envisaged by McMillan, has been admired and emulated across the world. Nursery schools have gardens, and are communities that welcome both parents and children. Such nursery schools stood out as beacons of light in the poverty-stricken areas of inner cities like Deptford and Bradford in the 1920s.

A summary of McMillan's ideas

- McMillan believed first-hand experience and active learning to be important. In her book, *The Nursery School* (published in 1930), she wrote:

> *most of the best opportunities for achievement lie in the domain of free play, with access to various materials'. She said that in a nursery school, families could experience 'fresh air, trees, rock gardens, herbs, vegetables, fruit trees, bushes, opportunities to climb on walls, sandpits, lawns, flowers and flowerbeds and wildernesses.*

- She emphasised relationships, feelings and ideas as much as the physical aspects of moving and learning.

▲ **Figure 19.2** Margaret McMillan emphasised the importance of nursery schools having gardens

- She believed that children become whole people through play. She thought that play helps them to apply what they know and understand.

- She believed in very close partnership with parents; she encouraged parents to develop alongside their children, with adult classes in hobbies and languages made available to them.

- Perhaps her most important achievement of all is to have been described as the 'godmother' of school meals and school medical services. She believed that children cannot learn if they are undernourished, poorly clothed, sick or ill, with poor teeth, poor eyesight, ear infections, rickets, for example. Recent reports emphasise that poor health and poverty are challenges still facing those who work with families in the UK today.

- McMillan placed enormous importance on the training of adults or practitioners working with children, and on the need for them to be inventive and imaginative in their work.

Susan Isaacs (1885–1948)

Susan Isaacs, like Margaret McMillan, was influenced by Froebel. She was also influenced by the theories of Melanie Klein, the psychoanalyst. Isaacs made detailed observations of children at her Malting House School in Cambridge during the 1930s.

A summary of Isaacs's ideas

- Isaacs valued play because she believed that it gave children freedom to think, feel and relate to others.

- She looked at children's fears, their aggression and their anger. She believed that through their play, children can move in and out of reality. This enables them to balance their ideas, feelings and relationships.

- She said that young children cannot learn in classrooms where they have to sit at tables and write, because they need to move just as they need to eat and sleep. In her book, *The Nursery Years* (1929), she wrote:

  If the child had ample opportunity for free play and bodily exercise, if this love of making and doing with his hands is met, if his interest in the world around him is encouraged by sympathy and understanding, if he is left free to make believe or think as his impulses take him, then his advances in skill and interest are but the welcome signs of mental health and vigour.

- Isaacs valued parents as the most important educators in a child's life. She spoke to them on the radio, and she wrote for parents in magazines.

- She supported both Froebel's and McMillan's view that nurseries are an extension of the home and not a substitute for it, and she believed that children should remain in nursery-type education until the age of seven years.

- Isaacs encouraged people to look at the inner feelings of children. She encouraged children to express their feelings. She thought it would be very damaging to bottle up feelings inside.

- She kept careful records of children, both for the period they spent in her nursery and after they had left. She found that when they left her nursery and went on to formal primary schools, many of them regressed. Some modern researchers have found the same.

Reflecting on practice

Review the practice and provision in your setting.

- In what ways do you think they reflect the ideas of the pioneers?
- Do you have a set of wooden hollow blocks and wooden unit blocks?
- Do you use finger rhymes? Circle singing? Dance?
- How do you use your outside space? Can children garden, grow things and dig in the mud?
- Do you have any Montessori-type materials?
- How do you observe children? Do your observations include thinking about feelings? Do you discuss them with your colleagues?
- Are children free to choose their activities and play resources?

Early years provision in the UK

Families make decisions about childcare and early education based on personal issues and their particular sociocultural context (see Chapter 6, p. 102 for definition). But these decisions will be highly influenced by the prevailing sociocultural norms and attitudes of the day and are also defined by the economic climate and related government policy (Baldock et al. 2009, Moss 2003), as they can only choose what has been made available and how accessible it is to them.

Historical contexts

In nineteenth-century Britain, well-off upper and middle class families had nurse-maids, nannies and

▲ **Figure 19.3** Susan Isaacs said children need to move just as they need to eat and sleep

tutors to care for and educate their young children, while poorer mothers had to care for several children plus any work they were doing, such as laundry work in their own home or domestic or factory work outside. Consequently, the care of the youngest children would fall to older siblings or members of the elder generation (Hardyment 2007); such arrangements are familiar to many families in the UK and around the world today.

Baldock et al. (2009) note how at this time specialist services for young children of working mothers were limited to 'baby farmers' (unofficial childminders) in industrial areas, who, because they were unofficial, were often cheap, poor quality and unsuccessful. But in the late nineteenth century, workplace crèches or kindergartens were also being set up (such as those established by Robert Owen), and children as young as two years old would also attend the newly established infant primary schools with their older siblings. The pattern of individual benefactors (sponsors) responding to the need for childcare in this way can be seen to set the direction for the fragmented development of early years services in the twentieth century (Baldock et al. 2009), whereby education was provided by the state while care was provided by private individuals or organisations.

Sociocultural contexts

The historical development of provision has also been highly influenced by prevailing culture and attitudes – particularly in relation to concepts of 'family' and the roles of women in society. Cultural attitudes influence national policies, which in turn determine levels of provision and the extent to which it is publicly funded. For example, in the UK children are seen as primarily the private responsibility of their parents. Social policy and legislation underpinning policy has assumed that the family should be exclusively responsible for the care of young children. Up until very recently it has been only where the family has broken down or has been assessed to be in need of additional support that financial resources have been made available for day care (Moss and Penn 1996; Hennessey et al. 1992). This is in contrast to other countries, such as the Nordic countries, where the care as well as the education of young children is seen to be the responsibility of the whole society, so provision is widespread and publicly funded.

Economic contexts

Economic needs have a huge impact on the level of childcare services available. For example, during the Second World War the UK Government set up day nurseries as women were needed in the workforce. Immediately after the war when jobs were required

for the returning soldiers, there was a great stress on the importance of the mother staying at home to be with their children (Riley 1983), and funding for the day nurseries was cut by 50 per cent. The Ministry of Health therefore combined cultural values with economic need by stating that:

> *under normal peace-time conditions the right policy to pursue would be positively to discourage mothers of children under two from going out to work, to make provision for children of between two and five by way of nursery schools and nursery classes; and to regard day nurseries and day guardians as supplements to meet special needs.*
>
> **(Circular 221/45 HMSO 1945)**

This policy statement reflects the belief at the time that children should be cared for by their mothers until school age unless the child was seen to be in need. In so doing it produced the split between care and education in early years provision.

The Plowden Report (DES 1967) led to the expansion of nursery education but still emphasised that part-time places were preferable in order to discourage women from working. Baldock et al. (2009) cite this policy as having continued the care/education split as it continued to ignore the needs of working parents and of children from birth to three years. Moss (2003) identifies how these policy directions in the UK led to split government departmental responsibility between education and social services, and thereby not only to split services and structures but also to split principles and purposes.

As a consequence, a whole range of provision came into being to meet the different needs of families which remain in place today, coupled with new integrated services that have been established as a result of policy since the late 1990s (Baldock et al. 2009). These are covered below on p. 000.

Children's centres

Children's centres in England developed from Sure Start local programmes, neighbourhood nurseries and Early Excellence Centres (HMT 2004). This policy development aimed to heal the historical split between 'care' and 'education' by providing integrated services for children and families; Peter Moss (2003) suggests that the development of children's centres reflects a changing, more holistic understanding of early years services.

Sure Start Children's Centres are places where children under five years old and their families can receive seamless (or all-in-one), holistic, integrated services and information, and where they can access help from multidisciplinary teams of professionals such as health visitors or play therapists. Children's centres serve children and their families from the antenatal period until children start in reception (which is the final part of the EYFS) or Year 1 at primary school. They also offer a base within the community, linking to other providers of day care, such as childminder networks and out-of-school clubs.

Centres offer a range of services both on and off-site, including:

- day care and early education with extended hours for children from birth to five years
- family support services
- a base for a childminder network
- child and family health services, including antenatal services
- support for children and parents with special needs
- links with Jobcentre Plus, local training providers and further and higher education institutions
- training for parents – for example, parenting classes, basic skills, English as an additional language with a crèche service
- benefits advice and information
- toy libraries
- Stay and Play sessions.

Maintained nursery schools, nursery classes and nursery units

Maintained nursery schools, nursery classes and nursery units offer either full-time (school day) or part-time early education places for children aged three to five years. They are part of the provision made by local education authorities. A nursery school is a stand-alone-provision with its own head teacher with specialist training in the early years. Nursery classes are attached to primary schools and the headteacher of the primary school may or may not be an expert in early years education. Nursery units are usually in a separate building, with a separate coordinator. Maintained nursery schools, nursery classes and nursery units are now expected to become part of the Sure Start Children's Centres programme and offer extended services.

Extended services

In June 2005, the government launched the prospectus, *Extended schools: Access to Opportunities and Services For All*, outlining the vision of extended schools. This vision was for all children to be able to access the following, through schools, by 2010:

- high-quality 'wraparound' childcare, provided by

the school site or other local providers, available 8 am to 6 pm all year round

- a varied menu of activities – for example, homework clubs and study support, sport, music tuition, special-interest clubs and volunteering
- parenting support, including information sessions for parents at key transition points such as parenting programmes and family learning sessions
- swift and easy referral to a wide range of specialist support services – for example, speech and language therapy, family support services and behaviour support
- providing wider community access to ICT, sports and arts facilities, including adult learning.

Although much of this was achieved, the austerity measure implemented by the Government since 2010 has resulted in many cuts in funding and reduced services.

Voluntary-aided community nurseries and preschools

Community nurseries offer care and education to local children and their families. They are run by local community organisations – often with financial assistance from the local authority – or by charities. The age range of children they cater for varies as do the opening hours; although most are open long enough to suit working parents or those at college. Many centres also provide, or act as a venue for other services, including:

- parent and toddler groups
- drop-in crèches
- toy libraries
- after-school clubs.

Pre-school Learning Alliance community preschools (playgroups) offer children aged between three and five years an opportunity to learn through play. They usually operate on a part-time sessional basis; sessions are normally two-and-a-half hours each, morning or afternoon, although all-day playgroups also exist. At many preschool playgroups, parents and carers are encouraged to be involved, and there are often parent and toddler groups meeting at the same sites.

Private day nurseries, private nursery schools, preparatory schools and kindergartens

Private nursery schools offer early education for children whose parents who pay fees. The age range of children catered for varies but is usually between two-and-a-half and five years. The opening hours also varies. Independent/private schools often also have nursery units or kindergartens.

An increase in the number of working mothers has led to the setting up of more private day nurseries and workplace crèches, which offer care and education for babies and preschool children during the normal working week. Some offer further extended hours to cater for parents on shift work.

Childminders

Childminders are independent childcare providers who work either alone or with an assistant in their own home. They can care for children between birth and eight years old and offer flexible and extended hours. They are registered and inspected by Ofsted and can offer places under the free entitlement scheme if they meet the local authority's criteria.

Many parents find childminding an excellent choice of childcare, for the following reasons:

- Childminders can pay particular attention to individual needs.
- They may be well set up to look after babies.
- They can form a stable, ongoing relationship with the child, from when he or she is a baby through to when the child needs care around schooling.
- They may be able to look after siblings together.
- They can be flexible over the hours of care provided, and can pick up or deliver children to and from other forms of care.
- They can adapt readily to circumstances and the individual child's needs.
- They provide care in a home that can include involvement in activities such as cooking, shopping, gardening and family mealtimes.

To summarise:

Maintained provision is funded by the Government/ local authority through taxation. Voluntary aided provision is funded partially from grants from the local authority and charitable institutions. Private provision is funded wholly through fees paid by parents.

Consistency and differences

Policy development since the late 1990s has focused a lot on ensuring that quality across the different types of provision is consistent. All the providers listed here must be registered and comply with legal requirements. They are regulated by the following agencies:

- Ofsted in England
- Care and Social Services Inspectorate Wales (CSSIW) in Wales
- Commission for the Regulation of Care (Care Commission) in Scotland

- Local Health and Social Services Trust in Northern Ireland.

As well as statutory standards all early years settings or providers have to follow the EYFS (2014) unless they have been given an exemption (such as Waldorf Steiner schools).

The following providers do not have to follow the EYFS:

- mother and toddler groups
- nannies
- short-term, occasional care such as crèches.

The main differences then are between the age range of children catered for, the opening hours and the costs. The government is concerned that childcare should be affordable for families so has introduced the following strategies:

- childcare tax credit for working parents
- free places for all three- and four-year-olds, initially for 15 hours per week for 38 weeks of the year, increasing to 30 hours per week in September 2016.
- free places for two-year-olds who are identified as disadvantaged, of 15 hours per week.

This means, however, that outside of these hours, working parents pay fees so still make the major financial contribution to the costs of services, with 60 per cent of provision being in the privately run-for-profit sector (Pugh and Duffy 2014).

International perspectives on early years provision

The different sociocultural, political and economic contexts of countries across the world mean that there are different levels of provision and different approaches to practice. The Thomas Coram Research Unit (TCRU) researched differences between four 'English-language' countries: Australia, New Zealand, United Kingdom and United States; four Nordic countries: Denmark, Finland, Norway and Sweden; and seven other European countries: Belgium, France, Germany, Italy, the Netherlands, Portugal and Spain. They discuss differences of levels of provision, pedagogical approach, staffing levels and qualifications, and funding levels, among other issues (Moss et al. 2003).

A key difference between countries is the age at which children start compulsory schooling. In this survey it ranged from four years in Northern Ireland to seven years in Sweden; this policy thereby defines what early years provision is in different countries.

TCRU note that among the English-language speaking countries they studied, there are no entitlements to early years provision, except for nursery education in the UK. In the other European countries there is entitlement to education for children from three years but provision for children under three varies and is relatively low. They identified that levels of preschool provision are highest in the Nordic countries, particularly in Denmark and Sweden, where there is an entitlement to provision from at least 12 months old (Mooney et al. 2003). There is also an expectation that this provision integrates care and education.

In Sweden, 'Parents now expect a holistic **pedagogy** that includes health care, nurturing and education for their pre-schoolers' (see Chapter 6, p. 100 for definition of holistic), and:

> *Enrolling children from age 1 in full-day preschools has become generally acceptable. What was once viewed as either a privilege of the wealthy for a few hours a day or an institution for needy children has become, after 70 years of political vision and policy making, an unquestionable right of children and families.*

(Lenz et al. 2003 cited in Moss et al. 2003, p. 39)

This research also looked at pedagogical approaches and curriculum, and noted that although most countries have some kind of agreed curriculum framework, how specific or open to local interpretation it is varies, as does how closely provision is regulated. This seems to be linked to levels of professional qualification. For example, in the Nordic countries where practitioners are generally qualified to degree level, the interpretation and implementation of the curriculum is left more to their professional judgement (Mooney et al. 2003); the curriculum framework is usually broader and more open to professional interpretation and implementation than when practitioners are less highly qualified.

The researchers also make the point that cross-country research needs careful interpretation because of the different sociocultural contexts of the information, even where there is regular and standardised collection of information as in the **OECD countries**. This is particularly important when considering provision and practice in the wider '**majority world**' because there are differences in how and when data is collected. Many majority world countries do not have well-established data collection systems; after all, they often have more pressing issues to deal with such as war and poverty (Moss et al. 2003). Because of this, and because more is written and discussed about

KEY TERMS

Pedagogy – The approach taken to teaching children.
OECD countries – Organisation for Economic Co-operation and Development, an international economic organisation of 34, mainly European 'developed', countries.
Majority world – The remaining countries of the world which account for most of the world's population and area.
Minority world – Those countries which are sometimes referred to as developed or of the Northern hemisphere.
UNESCO – The United Nations Educational, Scientific, and Cultural Organization is an agency of the United Nations that sponsors programmes to promote education, communication and the arts.
UNICEF – An organisation concerned with improving the health and nutrition of children and mothers throughout the world, which provides long-term humanitarian aid to children and mothers in developing countries.

provision in the developed /'**minority world**', there is less information about practice and provision in other countries.

However, countries such as China, India and Mexico all have growing levels of provision, particularly in the larger industrialised cities. Often, provision reflects approaches that would be familiar to practitioners in the UK, such as private Montessori and Steiner schools in Beijing and Delhi. Such provision is often funded by international organisations such as **UNESCO** and **UNICEF** or by large religious charities or corporations. In Africa, early years provision is almost solely funded through foreign donors (Nsamenang 2007, Myers 2000).

A concern here is that this gives funders control over the curriculum, which can result in education or pedagogical approaches and curricula that have been developed in a European/American cultural context being imposed on a different culture. For example, the World Bank funds a lot of provision and advocates Developmentally Appropriate Practice (DAP) (Myers 2000). In DAP, independence is emphasised (as does the EYFS in England (DfE 2012)), whereas in many majority world cultures interdependence (depending on one another) and community rather than the individual is valued. An example of this perspective can be seen in the New Zealand early years curriculum Te Whariki (NZ Ministry of Education 1996), which reflects Maori traditions by emphasising the interdependence of child, family, practitioner, community and culture.

Ideas about what quality provision is, what appropriate practice is and how we understand children and childhood, depend on cultural values and perspectives. Rosenthal (cited in David 2006: 37) puts forward the idea that provision in the early years is dependent upon the 'role assigned to early years by a particular society'. In turn this will contribute to the types of provision a society provides for its children. What happens within that provision is dependent upon the outcomes that a particular society wants to see for its children. For example, whether a society emphasises individual educational achievement or social responsibility will be reflected in the focus of the curriculum its early years provision is expected to deliver.

In accordance with this idea, Woodhead (1999) developed the idea of contextually appropriate practice. He believes that developmental psychology should take account of variations of a child's experience, growth and change and that early years practice should be relevant to the local culture that the child is growing up in; it should be consistent with the learning experiences of the home and community, and it should recognise the many different ways in which children learn.

Further reading, weblinks and resources

Directgov

For information on statutory provision.
www.direct.gov.uk

National Children's Bureau

This charity works to advance the well-being of all children and young people across every aspect of their lives.
www.ncb.org.uk

Community Care

A professional journal for practitioners in the social care field.
www.communitycare.co.uk/children/

 # Moving on

Think about ideas

Choose to research either one of the 'pioneers', or a type of provision such as independent schools or children's centres that are discussed in this chapter.

For the 'pioneer' you are researching:

1   Research the different activities they would advocate to use with young children. Which age group would this be recommended for? What is the aim and purpose of the activity?

2   Implement the activity with a group of children and observe their responses.

3   Evaluate your observations, noting how your role as a practitioner reflected the approach you used.

4   Research their approach to environments for young children; how could you develop your provision to reflect this?

For the type of provision you are researching:

1   Find out how accessible this provision is for all children and families. You will need to think about:
    ● children with disabilities and additional needs
    ● the level of provision of this type in your local area – how far is it for families to get there?
    ● what the costs are to families
    ● the age range it caters for.

2   Find out about the pedagogical approaches used in this type of provision. How does it reflect the approach of any of the pioneers discussed in this chapter?

See Chapter 18, p. 399 for more information on provision for children with SEN, and gifted and talented children.

References

Baldock, P., Fitzgerald, D., Kay, J., 2009, *Understanding Early Years Policy* (2nd edn), London: Sage.

Bruce, T., 2005, *Early Childhood Education*, London: Hodder Arnold.

David, T., *The World Picture*, in Pugh, G. and Duffy, B. (eds), 2006, *Contemporary Issues in the Early Years* (4th edn), London: Sage.

Department for Education, 2012, *Statutory Framework for the Early Years Foundation Stage Setting the Standards for Learning, Development and Care for Children from Birth to Five*, London: DfE/HMSO.

Department for Education and Skills (2005) Extended schools: Access to Opportunities and Services For All. Dfes TSO. (The Stationary Office).

Department of Health, 2004, *The National Service Framework for Children, Young People and Maternity Services*. Available at: https://www.gov.uk/government/publications/national-service-framework-children-young-people-and-maternity-services.

H M Treasury (2004) Choice for Parents, the Best Start for Children: A Ten Year childcare strategy, London: The Stationary Office.

Hardyment, C., 2007, *Dream Babies: Childcare advice from John Locke to Gina Ford*, London: Frances Lincoln Ltd.

Hennessey, E., Martin, S., Moss, P. and Melhuish, E., 1992, *Children and Day Care: Lessons from Research*, London: Paul Chapman Publishing.

Ministry of Health, 1945, *Circular 221/54*, London: HMSO.

Moss, P., 2003, 'Getting Beyond Childcare: Reflections on Recent Policy and Future Possibilities', in Brannen, J. and Moss, P. (eds), *Rethinking Children's Care*, Maidenhead: Open University Press.

Moss, P. and Penn, H., 1996, *Transforming Nursery Education*, London: Paul Chapman Publishing.

Moss, P., Cameron, C., Candappa, M., McQuai, S., and Mooney, A., Petrie, P., 2003, *Early Years and Childcare International Evidence Project: Introduction*, London: Thomas Coram Research Unit.

Moss, P., (2006) Structures, Understandings and Discourses: Possibilities for re-visioning re-envisioning the early childhood worker, *Contemporary Issues in Early Childhood*, 7(1), PP. 30–41.

Myers, R., 2000, *Thematic Studies: Early Childhood Care and Development*, Paris: UNESCO.

New Zealand Ministry of Education, 1996, *Te Whàriki Early Childhood Curriculum / He Whàriki Màtauranga mò ngà Mokopuna o Aotearoa*, New Zealand: Ministry of Education/ Learning Media Limited.

Nsamenang, A., 2007, 'A Critical Peek at Early Childhood Care and Education in Africa', *Child Health and Education*, 1:1, 1–12.

Plowden Report, 1967, Central Advisory Council for Education, *Children and their Primary Schools*, London: HMSO.

Pugh, G. and Duffy, B. (eds), 2014, *Contemporary Issues in the Early Years* (6th edn), London: Sage.

Riley, D., 1983, *War in the Nursery*, London: Virago.

Woodhead, M., 1999, '"Quality" in Early Childhood Programmes – A Contextually Appropriate Approach', *International Journal of Early Childhood*, 6:1, 5–18.

This chapter focuses on you as an early years practitioner. It considers the skills and attributes required of practitioners and the roles, responsibilities and challenges faced in the workplace. We discuss the importance of working as part of a team and also explore the skills and attributes of those practitioners wanting to take on leadership roles. This includes supervision, reflective practice, appraisal and professional development and training. This chapter also outlines the different employment roles and opportunities available to qualified early years practitioners and gives useful information on workplace issues that practitioners may come across, such as contracts and trades union membership.

An effective early years practitioner

Being an effective early years practitioner requires good levels of knowledge and understanding about children's development, play and learning. The roles practitioners fulfil in their work are complex and demanding, so also require other skills such as being able to work in a team and attributes such as being approachable, nurturing and respectful.

The Children's Workforce Development Council (2010) identifies a broad range of understanding, skills, knowledge and attributes required by those working with children and families including:

- the ability to communicate and engage effectively
- knowledge and understanding of children's development
- the knowledge and skills to safeguard and promote the welfare of children
- the ability to support transitions
- multi-agency and integrated working
- information sharing.

Being a professional early years practitioner means working in relationship to others the whole time. So practitioners need to have good communication and **interpersonal skills**, and also bring a high level of maturity and self-awareness to their job. They need to be able to look at their own motivations, values and experiences that will enable them to better understand and adjust their responses to

children (Manning-Morton 2006). Above all else, an early years practitioner needs to be genuinely interested in how children develop and learn, and enjoy being with them on their learning journey.

The attributes of an effective early years practitioner

- **Listening** – active and attentive listening is a vital part of the caring relationship. Sometimes a child's real needs are communicated more by what is left unsaid than what is actually spoken. Facial expressions, posture and other forms of body language all give clues to a child's feelings. A good carer will be aware of these forms of non-verbal communication.
- **Comforting** – this has a physical side and an emotional side. Physical comfort may be provided in the form of a cuddle at a time of anxiety, or by providing a distressed child with a reassuring, safe environment. Touching, listening and talking can all provide emotional comfort as well.
- **Empathy** – this means understanding how a child might be feeling. Some people find it easy to appreciate how someone else is feeling by imagining themselves in that person's position. A good way of imagining how a strange environment appears to a young child is to kneel on the floor and try to view it from the child's perspective.
- **Sensitivity** – this is the ability to be aware of and responsive to the feelings and needs of another person. Being sensitive to others' needs requires the carer to anticipate their feelings – for example, the feelings of a child whose mother has been admitted to hospital, or whose pet dog has just died.
- **Patience** – this involves being understanding and being tolerant of other people's methods of dealing with things, even when you feel that your own way is better. It means waiting for children to speak and do things for themselves.

> **KEY TERM**
>
> **Interpersonal skills** – These are the skills you use when you interact with other people, including your capacity to listen carefully, to show empathy and understanding, and to communicate effectively.

- **Respect** – a carer should have an awareness of a child's personal rights, dignity and privacy, and must show this at all times. Every child is unique, so your approach will need to be tailored to each individual's needs.
- **Interpersonal skills** – this means understanding others and clearly expressing yourself through spoken and sign languages, and through non-verbal body language.
- **Acceptance** – a caring relationship is a two-way process. Warmth and friendliness help to create a positive atmosphere and to break down barriers. Acceptance is important: you should always look beyond any disability or disruptive behaviour to recognise and accept the person.
- **Self-awareness** – a practitioner or carer is generally more effective if she or he is able to perceive what effect his behaviour has on other people. Being part of a team enables us to discover how others perceive us, and to modify our behaviour in the caring relationship accordingly.
- **Coping with stress** – caring for others effectively in a full-time capacity requires energy, and it is important to be aware of the possibility of professional 'burnout' or exhaustion. In order to help others, we must first help ourselves: the carer who never relaxes or develops any outside interests is more likely to suffer from exhaustion than the carer who finds her own time and space to partake in activities that they enjoy.

Values and principles

Effective early years practice is based on practitioners' knowledge of children's development and their understanding of each child's development, interests and sociocultural contexts.

It is also based on teams of practitioners working towards a shared vision of what they want for children and families. This vision, though, can only be realised if practitioners are clear about their personal and professional values, and therefore the principles that guide their practice.

A value is something that you believe to be important in life, which arises from personal experience and often has a strong influence on our professional values and practice. For example, a practitioner who has fond memories of bedtime stories and visits to the library may strongly believe that books are important in children's lives and place a lot of emphasis on the provision of books and story-telling in their practice. Or a female practitioner, who longed to play with her brother's toys but was not allowed, may believe strongly in gender equality in resources.

Reflecting on practice

- Do you think some people are naturally good early years practitioners or are training and qualifications always necessary?
- Do you think there are any other qualities and skills that are necessary to work in an early years setting?
- How about working with different age groups or particular groups of children – are the skills the same or different?

Share your thoughts in a small group or with another learner.

Where values are explicit and shared, a team will be clear not just about what they do but why they do it.

Where values conflict and are not discussed, contradictory practices can occur and decisions to implement an approach to practice, such as free access to outdoor play for example, may be undermined. If individual and teams of practitioners are not clear about why they do things in a particular way, practice can decline to a low common level and improvements to practice will not be maintained or upheld.

The roles and responsibilities of a professional early years practitioner

An early years practitioner must:

1 Put the child first by:
   - ensuring the child's welfare and safety
   - showing compassion and sensitivity
   - respecting the child as an individual
   - upholding the child's rights and dignity
   - enabling the child to achieve his or her full learning potential.

2 Never use physical punishment.

3 Respect the parent as the primary carer and educator of the child.

4 Respect the contribution and expertise of staff in the childcare and education field, and other professionals with whom they may be involved.

5 Respect the customs, values and spiritual beliefs of the child and his or her family.

6 Uphold the equality of opportunity policies.

7 Honour the confidentiality of information relating to the child and his or her family, unless its disclosure is required by law or is in the best interests of the child.

Commitment to putting the needs of the children first

The needs and rights of all children should be paramount, and the early years practitioner must seek to meet these needs within the boundaries of the work role. Knowledge of children's needs in all developmental areas will enable you to fulfil the responsibilities within your role.

Central to putting the child first is the ability to form trusting key person relationships with the children in your care, to develop positive working relationships with parents and to observe each child closely in order to understand them well.

Never use physical punishment

This aspect includes treating children with respect as people in their own right. Physical punishment should never be used, neither should shouting, which can be as damaging as smacking. Ridiculing or shaming children in front of others, belittling them and being harshly critical are also harmful and are not professional behaviours. If you witness such behaviours in a practitioner working with young children, you should discuss your concerns with a manager.

Respect for parents and other adults

The training you have received will have emphasised the richness and variety of child-rearing practices in the UK. It is an important part of your professional role that you pay due regard to the wishes and views of parents and other carers. Where there is disagreement, this should be negotiated with respect and always with the welfare of the child as the paramount concern. You should also recognise that parents are usually the people who know their children best. In all your dealings with parents and other adults, you must show that you respect their cultural values and religious beliefs.

Respect the contribution and expertise of staff in the childcare and education field, and other professionals with whom they may be involved

Being responsible and accountable

Your supervisor or line manager will have certain expectations about your role, and your responsibilities should be detailed in a job description As a professional, you need to carry out all your duties willingly and be accountable to others for your work. It is vital that you know who your manager is, and how you would raise any concerns or seek guidance or support. All staff need to know how to obtain clarification of their own role and responsibilities, and to know how well they are carrying out that role. If you do not feel confident in carrying out a particular task, either because you do not fully understand it or because you have not been adequately trained, you have a responsibility to state your concerns and ask for guidance. If you have a difficulty or disagreement with another member of staff, you must handle this in a professional manner. This means raising your concern directly with that person, or with an appropriate manager. You should not complain about colleagues in the staff room, in front of parents or outside work with friends or family.

Communicate effectively with team members

The training you have received will have emphasised the importance of effective communication in the workplace. Good practice as a team member will depend on liaising and communicating with others, and reporting on and reviewing your activities. Conflicts between team members often arise from poor communication – for example, an early years practitioner who fails to report, verbally or in writing, that a parent will be late collecting his or her child on a particular day may cause conflict if a colleague challenges the parent's conduct.

Work effectively with professionals from other agencies

Working in the early years is increasingly about coordinating services for the benefit of children and their families. This places new demands on early years practitioners. It is very important that you are confident about your own training and expertise when working alongside other professionals. For example, if you are a child's key person, you will know a great deal about the child's development, learning and emotional well-being. You will need to communicate what you know in a clear and concise way. If an assessment of the child's development is needed, you will be able to offer records in the form of observations and assessments for your setting. It will also be important that you are able to listen carefully and take note of what other professionals have to say – for example, a paediatric dietician may need you to keep an accurate record of what a child is eating in nursery, and may ask you to follow a particular approach to encourage a child to eat more healthily. It is important that families do not get conflicting advice from different professionals, so you will need to follow the dietician's advice and avoid putting across your own personal views. If you feel there is a conflict between what you are being asked to do and what you see as good early years practice, it is important that you discuss this with your manager, head teacher or SENCO.

Respect the customs, values and spiritual beliefs of the child and his or her family and uphold the LEA's equality of opportunity policy

All children, parents and colleagues should be treated with respect and dignity, irrespective of their ethnic origin, socioeconomic group, religion, language, sexual orientation or disability. See Chapter 1 for more information on equality, diversity and rights.

Respect the principles of confidentiality

Confidentiality is the preservation or protection of privileged or private information concerning children and their families that is disclosed in the professional relationship. It is a complex issue, which has at its core the principle of trust. The giving or receiving of sensitive information should be subject to a careful consideration of the needs of the children and their families – for example, a child who is in need of protection has overriding needs which require that all relevant information be given to all the appropriate agencies, such as social workers or doctors. Within the childcare and education setting, it might be appropriate to discuss sensitive issues, but such information must never be disclosed to anyone outside the setting, unless you have concerns regarding safeguarding. Practitioners should never promise parents or children that they will not share what they are told as they may not be able to keep that promise should the information relate to a safeguarding concern. See Chapter 4, p.68 for more information on confidentiality.

The challenges of being an early years practitioner

Working with young children and their families is demanding. It is work which draws on your personal qualities and demands emotional engagement. This means that the work can be very satisfying, and can lead to feelings of great personal achievement and pleasure in helping others. Equally, during a full-on day, you may start to feel stress due to the demands of the children and parents. Teamwork can offer support, but tensions can quickly build and disputes can flare up between staff members.

While at work, you can expect to feel anxious, especially when faced with new and difficult tasks. Practitioners report that constant changes to policy and demands of new ways of working also put them under pressure and undermine their well-being (Manning-Morton 2014). Pressure can be motivating, and can help you to learn new things and perform

Look, listen and note

Keep a learning journal for a week, noting down how you feel at different times during the day or during particular activities. Note also any significant events that happen that make you feel either negative or positive. At the end of the week, review your notes to see if there are any particular things that make you feel stressed. Do you know why this is? Can you talk to your manager or mentor about this?

better at work. But when the pressure becomes too much, you may feel under stress.

It is not possible to avoid feelings of stress and anxiety at times when you are at work. What matters is how you manage and cope with these feelings; whether you feel supported when things are difficult or feel that you are merely left to manage on your own.

Some signs of stress include:

- finding it difficult to sleep
- withdrawing from friends and family
- eating or drinking too much
- feeling unusually tired, low in energy and unmotivated
- headaches and problems with digestion
- finding it hard to concentrate
- becoming short-tempered and anxious.

If you notice these signs in yourself, you should take action sooner rather than later. Speak to a trusted colleague or your college tutor. Ask for time to talk in confidence with your manager and explain the difficulties you are experiencing. Equally, your colleagues and your manager may notice that you seem a bit 'out of sorts' or are behaving out of character. It is useful to be open, honest and cooperative if someone approaches you for this reason – try not to be defensive or feel that you have to hide the difficulties you are having.

You can find out more about identifying and managing stress at www.hse.gov.uk/stress, or search online for 'work-related stress'.

Working in a team

All work in an early years setting involves team working of some kind. If you are a childminder or a nanny, you will be part of a team with the child's parents and family; while in an early years group setting you could be working with one or two other people or large teams of 20 people or more. But a team is not just a collection of people working in the same place; becoming a team can be a lengthy and complex process (Jones and Pound 2008). Teams go through recognisable processes of forming, storming, norming and performing (Tuckman 1965), not just when they first come together but also when the team changes in any way.

The principles of good teamwork

Effective ways of communicating

This will include on-the-spot communications such as a childminder having an informal discussion at the start of the day with a parent to find out about the child's weekend, or a practitioner in a group setting passing a quick message that they are going to be outdoors for an extra five minutes because a child is very focused on his play with the water. Such communications are important – for example, your colleagues know they have to cover your other tasks for a short while. It is important that such messages and discussions are clear and focused on key information; for example, finding out that the child had a late night, or was fascinated to see dinosaurs in the museum, so will want to talk and play around that theme in the day. Sometimes diaries, notebooks, post-it notes, texts and emails are good ways to share information. In a setting, all staff will need to be clear about what is happening, when, and what their roles are. Using whiteboards, post-its and other quick ways of leaving notes for each other are useful.

In addition, effective communication requires regular planned opportunities to discuss your work and children's progress with colleagues and parents.

Shared approaches and values

It is very important for staff in teams to feel that they have been part of developing a clear, shared sense of direction and principles that underpin their work. In this way, each person can align what they do with larger goals and aims, and feel a sense of pride and achievement when these are achieved. Teams also need leaders who can remind everyone of the core purpose of the work and point out shortcomings where they occur (Stacey 2009).

Constructive ways of making decisions and managing disagreements

Decisions are sometimes made in meetings and a significant amount of time is given to their discussion; equally, many decisions have to be made quickly and on the spur of the moment. It is important that staff in a team can make a

▲ **Figure 20.1** Being able to work as part of a team is essential for all early years practitioners

quick decision and stick with it. Problems and disagreements will certainly arise as you work; what matters is being able to talk about them, resolve difficulties and, if necessary, live with a decision that you do not agree with personally. Many disagreements can be healthy, leading to greater creativity and innovation. If they can be managed so everyone is encouraged to express their views openly and everyone is listened to, then a way forward can be agreed (Smith and Langston 1999).

The capacity to learn from mistakes

The best team leaders and team members will be open about mistakes they have made, and will use them as an opportunity to learn from the experience. If people are fearful of mistakes, or if leaders feel they must get everything right, the potential for learning and development will be minimal.

Respect for people's different contributions

One of the advantages of being in a team is that there may be others who can do things well which you find difficult, and you may be able to support others too. All practitioners need a core set of skills and abilities but some individuals may excel in some areas, such as music or displays: teams that work well together include people with different strengths.

An acknowledgement that everyone has a leadership role

A large team in a children's centre, nursery or school will have an overall leader or coordinator, but throughout the day different people could – and should – take on leadership roles. A member of staff on reception might notice a parent struggling to get their child through the door; the staff member might take the initiative and offer to help, by taking parent and child to the key person, for example. A lunchtime assistant might notice that a child is finding it difficult to manage the period after dinner, and might involve the child in helping to tidy up, to make him or her feel secure, rather than expecting the child to go out to play with all the others.

A clear focus on purpose

The principal purpose of an early years team is to provide high-quality care and early education for the children. The team needs to have ways of evaluating how well it is achieving its main purpose. These methods could include structured observations of children, monitoring by senior staff and feedback from parents. The team could look at how well the children transfer to the next room, and consider whether any of the difficulties the children have could be minimised by making changes. If necessary, the team's leader might have to take action if a member of staff's work falls short of the required standards, or goes against the best interests of the children. A good early years team is not just a friendly, supportive group of people: it concentrates on making sure the children are well cared for and are given a high-quality early education.

Attending and contributing to team meetings

In most work settings, being part of the staff team means participating in meetings, to discuss and make decisions about a wide range of issues. You are expected to attend and you must make your apologies to the person holding the meeting if you are unable to attend.

At any formal meeting, there is usually a set format:

- An agenda (or programme) – this is a list of items that will be discussed, with some items appearing at every meeting. Apologies for absence are usually received and recorded at the start of any meeting.
- A written record, called the minutes – most meetings begin by looking at the minutes of the last meeting, to remind everyone what was decided and to find out what has happened since. Someone will be given responsibility for taking the minutes.
- Any other business – most meetings allow time for issues not included in the formal agenda to be brought up and discussed; for example, a problem with children's behaviour that has arisen, or equipment that has been damaged since the meeting was arranged.
- Date for the next meeting – this is set and agreed by those attending the meeting.

Some meetings are informal – perhaps arranged to talk about planning next month's topic or theme, or to finalise arrangements for an outing. Others may be more formal – perhaps covering policy matters. There is one person who leads (or chairs) the meeting and makes sure the items on the agenda are being dealt with – it is very easy for people to begin their own conversations or stray from the subject in hand!

Remember that you are there to contribute your ideas and thoughts, and to listen to those of others. At a meeting, you should try to:

- listen carefully to information being given
- check that you know what is expected of you, at the meeting and afterwards
- take a pen and paper, and any other things that will be needed – for example, an observation of a child who is being discussed
- understand that you may not share the views of others or agree with all decisions made
- contribute your ideas and opinions clearly and at the appropriate time – not when everyone has started talking about the next item
- ask questions about anything you do not understand.

In most group settings, team meetings are held regularly and conducted according to an agreed agenda. Ideally, the written agenda should be given to all team members and should include a space for anyone to add their own item for discussion.

Certain factors may detract from the value of team meetings:

- Distractions – constant interruptions, from either telephone calls or visitors, will prevent progress being made.
- Irrelevant topics – some meetings become a forum for gossip or other topics that are irrelevant to the task in hand.
- A dominating member – one person may be aggressive and outspoken, blocking other people's contributions.

Assertiveness makes communication at team meetings more effective; this should not be confused with loudness or aggressive behaviour. Assertiveness

KEY TERM

Assertiveness – Behaviour which enables you to express your needs, wants, feelings, opinions and values in a way that does not affect the human rights of others.

may be defined, in this context, as standing up for your own rights and beliefs, without denying those of others, and making your behaviour 'match' your feelings.

If you are assertive in your behaviour, you:

- can express your feelings, without being unpleasant
- are able to state your views and wishes directly, spontaneously and honestly
- respect the feelings and rights of other people
- feel good about yourself and about others
- can evaluate a situation, decide how to act and then act without reservation
- are true to yourself
- value self-expression and the freedom to choose
- may not always achieve your goals, but feel that this is not as important as the actual process of asserting yourself
- are able to say what you have to say, whether it is positive or negative, while also leaving the other person's dignity intact.

Non-verbal forms of assertiveness include:

- good eye contact
- a confident posture – standing or sitting comfortably
- talking in a strong, steady voice
- not clenching your fist or pointing with a finger.

Verbal forms of assertiveness include:

- avoiding qualifying words – for example, 'maybe', 'only' or 'just'
- avoiding disqualifying phrases – for example, 'I'm sure this is not important, but …'.
- avoiding attacking phrases – for example, those that begin with 'you'; instead, use assertive phrases, such as 'I feel'.

(Dickson 1982)

Thinking about ideas

Research ideas about assertiveness. You can find out more by searching online for assertiveness skills where you will find many websites including video tutorials. Or you could look for a book in the library.

How might assertive behaviour help you in your work?

Becoming a leader and moving into management

Leadership and management may be thought of as two separate functions, or as tasks and behaviours that interlink. Many early years practitioners may not be in a formal management role but are responsible for managing their work with the children and often lead practice in many different ways. This might be a project to improve the outdoor play provision or leading a group meeting to discuss the mealtime routine, for example. Practitioners' first steps into explicitly leading a project or a team can be daunting, but with support from mentors, managers and training courses, they can find taking on leadership roles exciting and satisfying. It can help to think of the leadership of adults as using similar strategies to those you use with children. For example, effective leaders are present and notice the behaviours and communications of team members to understand their needs in the same way that practitioners notice and understand children's behaviours and respond sensitively (Jones and Pound 2008).

Many practitioners already have some of the characteristics, skills and attitudes seen as important for leaders and managers. They:

- have knowledge and experience of the complex and demanding nature of the work
- have highly developed communication skills
- are accessible and approachable
- appreciate other people's skills and contributions
- encourage and celebrate other people's achievements
- are motivated to develop their own and their colleagues' practice and provision
- have clear ideas about what they want for children and families and why
- are self-aware and know their own strengths and limitations, so can ask for help
- can cooperate and work as part of a team as well as lead
- can make decisions with consideration of how they impact on others.

With such skills and attributes already in place, a practitioner new to management and leadership can go on to learn and develop these and other skills further. This will include:

- knowledge of relevant legislation, procedures and protocols
- skills and confidence in liaising with a wide range of other professionals

- refining interpersonal skills to be able to handle difficult situations with teams and with families
- skills in delegating, mentoring, directing and supervising others
- understanding the dynamics and processes of groups.

Supervision and reflective practice

Reflective practice is a process through which changes in professional work are brought about in order to improve the experiences offered to children. Moon (2005) suggests that reflective practice is about learning through and from experience, which means not only being self-aware but also challenging assumptions about everyday practice.

This can be developed by keeping a reflective journal, which can help your thinking about why a particular event happened, how you felt about it, what you think the people involved thought and felt and how you want to respond. Bolton (2005) suggests that keeping a journal can really help practitioners and managers to slow down and think about their emotional reaction before responding to someone or something, and also to identify common themes that may keep coming up. She also suggests that discussion with colleagues about significant incidents, or simply pausing and thinking through the day or the week, are also

valuable. Reflecting in this way may not always offer a solution but can help to clarify one's thinking about a situation and thereby lead to a change in perspective or to a different course of action next time (Page-Smith and Craft 2008).

Professional reflection can also be facilitated or helped by regular support and supervision sessions, in which managers and leaders create a working culture that values time for practitioners to think about their work. In order to facilitate useful supervision discussions, leaders and managers need to develop their own interpersonal and **intrapersonal skills** (see page 448 for definition). This includes asking open ended questions and engaging in active listening to voice tone and body language as well as words; hearing exactly what the practitioner has said – not what you think they have said (Whitaker 1995).

The Tickell Review (2011) suggests that

> *supervision should be expressed in such a way that encourages reflective practice and moves away from the perception that it is merely a tick-box approach to check what practitioners are, or are not, doing.*

(Tickell 2011: 5.17)

Guidelines for good practice

Performance management or appraisal meetings

✓ Prepare for the meeting. Spend some time thinking about what you think is going well and what you are finding difficult. If you need help or support with something in particular, think ahead about how you will raise this topic. Look back at your targets from the previous year: did you meet them, or even exceed them? Did anything arise that prevented you from achieving them?

✓ The meeting provides an opportunity for both you and your employer or manager to identify any aspects of the job that you are doing really well and any that need to be improved. It is on these occasions that you can raise any problems you have – about dealing with particular situations, children, parents or staff.

✓ The meeting is also an opportunity for you to make sure that you understand the current priorities and aims of the nursery, setting or school where you are working, and how your work contributes to these.

✓ If you can show that you are carrying out all your duties well, you may be given more responsibility or you may be moved to work in a different area, to develop your experience with other age ranges or activities.

✓ Appraisal should be viewed by staff as a positive action which helps to promote good practice within the setting. This holds true even when there are criticisms of your performance. If you are starting to feel upset or nervous during the meeting, or if you feel that unfair criticisms are being made, ask for the meeting to pause for a few minutes so you can collect your thoughts. If appropriate, ask whether a colleague could accompany you for the rest of the meeting.

✓ Usually, there is an annual cycle of performance management, including observation of your work and review meetings.

✓ Appraisals are also useful in identifying staff development needs – for example, an early year's practitioner who is lacking in assertiveness may be sent on an assertiveness training course. All early years settings and schools are required to identify the training needs of staff and how they plan to meet them.

Intrapersonal skills – This is having a good awareness of your own feelings, motivations and the way you affect others.

Appraisal – The formal system used to evaluate how well you are doing in your job and to set targets for further improvement over the year ahead.

▲ **Figure 20.2** Developing professional practice can continue through training, reading and reflective supervision

This is useful because although the Statutory Framework for the EYFS states that: 'Providers must put appropriate arrangements in place for the supervision of staff who have contact with children and families' (DfE 2014: 3.21), the term 'supervision' often means different things to different people.

Sometimes supervision in settings is mistaken for, or combined with, **appraisal**. Appraisal is about judging your performance; it has an evaluative rather than reflective focus so is not suitable for considering the emotional aspects of practice.

Performance management and appraisal

Employers look for a range of personal and professional qualities in their staff. A system of performance management, or appraisal, helps you and your manager or employer to assess how you are performing in your job and whether you are happy. Usually, goals will be set and your performance will be measured in relation to these targets.

Professional development

Working in the field of early years care and education can be physically and emotionally exhausting, and professionals will need to consolidate or combine their skills, and develop the ability to be reflective in their practice. Professional development in the workplace through mentoring or supervision sessions is very important.

Professional development can also happen through professional discussions in meetings and through keeping abreast of all the changes in childcare practices by reading relevant magazines, such as *Nursery World* and *Early Years Educator*.

Attending post-qualification or continuing professional development training courses is essential for all practitioners throughout their career; we can all continue to learn and it is important to remain open to new ideas and to be knowledgeable about new policies and approaches in order to maintain effectiveness, no matter how experienced you are.

Qualification training

The need for qualified early years practitioners is increasing, and more courses are being developed all the time. The National College for Teaching and Leadership (NCTL) is responsible for defining the full and relevant qualifications that staff must hold. They define the criteria for courses that qualify practitioners as what is now called an 'early years educator' at Level 3, and provide a searchable list of all early years qualifications.

The qualification criteria lay out the minimum requirements for what an early years educator should know, understand and be able to do, to be considered qualified to support young children age birth to five in the EYFS as of 2014. This does not invalidate existing Level 3 qualifications. However, some practitioners will need to update some areas of their qualification.

Increasingly, qualifications are offered in a modular way. This would mean that a practitioner with a Level 3 qualification in early years education and childcare could take some additional modules to be qualified to work as a Level 3 teaching assistant in a primary school, or to work with children aged under two years in a nursery setting. It would not be necessary to start a whole new course.

There are greater opportunities than ever before for practitioners to enhance their qualifications up to and beyond degree level. It is clear that the future in early years education and care will favour those who are the best qualified.

Degrees for early years practitioners include foundation and full honours degrees in early childhood or early years care and education. Foundation degrees are studied part-time and build on the student's practical, workplace experience. They are offered by colleges of higher education and universities.

Think about ideas

There are different routes into gaining EYT status. Information on these can be found at:

- https://getintoteaching.education.gov.uk/explore-my-options/become-an-early-years-teacher
- *Nursery World* have produced guidance in partnership with the Department of Education available at: www.nurseryworld.co.uk.

Honours degrees can be studied full-time or part-time, usually at a university. Many early years practitioners study part-time for degrees with a modular design, which enable the candidate to fit studying around work.

Early years teacher (EYT) status is the new, specialist postgraduate qualification for practitioners working with children in the EYFS. Early years professional (EYP) status is replaced by this qualification but remains valid. Practitioners with EYP or EYT status are qualified to lead provision for children aged up to five years.

Different roles and employment opportunities in the early years field

Having satisfactorily completed a recognised course in childcare and education, a professional early years practitioner will be qualified to work in a variety of settings, in either the maintained, private or voluntary-aided sectors and in home-based or out-of-home settings.

There are lots of different early years settings, and each one offers its own mix of benefits and drawbacks. Although the different sectors may offer some different opportunities and have different emphases, there are good and not so good settings in all sectors so it is advisable to spend time in a setting that you may work within, watching the children play, talking to staff and reading information provided for parents and staff. This will give you a 'flavour' of the setting's approach and ethos (Bruce, 2010).

Home-based settings

Babysitting and childsitting

Although babysitting may often be undertaken by inexperienced and unqualified young people, for example a neighbours' teenage child, it is a big

responsibility and should be taken seriously. When parents trust you to babysit, they are placing their child's safety in your hands. For this reason many parents like to use agencies for babysitting so they have some assurances from checks and references. For the practitioner too, it is wise to take some precautions when accepting a new babysitting job:

- Know your employer – only accept jobs from people you already know or for whom you have reliable, personal references.
- Make sure that your parent (or someone you live with) knows where you are babysitting – leave them the name, address and telephone number of the people you are sitting for, and let them know what time to expect you home. Keep your mobile phone with you.
- Find out what time the parents expect to be home – let them know if you have a curfew. Ask them to call if they are running late.

Working as a nanny

A nanny is a qualified early years practitioner who makes a career out of caring for children in the child's own home. Most jobs involve the nanny having full responsibility for all aspects of childcare, although some nannies are employed as maternity support alongside the mother, especially if it is a multiple birth (the mother has twins for example). As a nanny, you would be responsible for:

- the children's health and welfare while they are under your supervision
- their social, emotional and educational development
- ensuring that the children always play in a safe environment, one that is free from danger and minor hazards
- some light domestic tasks, closely related to the care of the children.

Responsibilities vary widely from post to post but for most qualified nannies, domestic tasks such as cooking or washing up are usually only undertaken as they relate to the care of the child. This is different to an au pair, who is usually unqualified in child care, is usually from abroad and in the UK to learn English; in return for accommodation, the au pair may undertake domestic tasks which may include babysitting.

Some employers place greater emphasis on experience and personality than on professional qualifications. Other parents will only employ someone with a recognised childcare qualification. Nanny-sharing is popular as it reduces the costs for parents. In this

Guidelines for good practice

Caring for children in the child's home

Babysitters and nannies need to consider the same range of care issues as other early years practitioners and some different ones too. You need to know:

- the full address of the house
- phone number at the house and parents' mobile phone number(s)
- name and phone number of GP
- nearest hospital and number
- where the parents will be
- phone number where the parents can be reached
- what time the parents are expected home
- name and phone number of neighbours
- other contacts – for example, grandparents
- any allergies or special medical information for children.

Safety issues for nannies and babysitters:

- If the house has an electronic security system, learn how to use it.
- Do not open the door to strangers. Do not let anyone at the door or on the phone know that you are there alone. If asked, respond by saying that you are visiting, the children's parents cannot come to the door and you will deliver a message.
- If you plan to take the children out, make sure that you have a key to lock and unlock doors; do not forget window locks.
- When you get back to the house, do not go inside if anything seems unusual – for example, a broken window, an open door. Go to a neighbour and call the police.
- Make sure that you have an escort home if you are babysitting at night.

In an emergency:

- Try not to panic. Not only will it prevent you from thinking clearly, it will also frighten the children.
- If there is a fire, get the children and yourself out! Go to a neighbour and call the fire service – dial 999. If you can, call the parents and let them know where you and the children are, and what is happening.
- If you suspect that a child has swallowed a poisonous substance, call 999 immediately. Be able to identify the poison and the amount taken.
- If you suspect a child is having an allergic reaction because they start having difficulties breathing, call 999 immediately.

See Chapter 14 for more information on dealing with emergencies.

---

situation the nanny will care for the children from more than one family in one of the families' homes.

There are many nanny employment agencies, which usually offer qualified nannies the following:

- contact with a wide range of suitable employers within your chosen area of work
- advice on matters of pay, tax and contractual obligations, such as hours of work, rates of pay and specific duties
- a formal contract between a nanny and the employer
- a free follow-up service after the start of employment, with the aim of sorting out any teething problems that may arise.

Childminding

Registered childminders are early years practitioners who work in their own homes to provide care and learning opportunities for other people's children in a family setting.

Childminders are registered, and their practice and provision regulated by Ofsted. As a childminder you may look after up to six children under eight years old depending on your registration restrictions.

Childminders are self-employed so fix their own charges and working hours. Many early years practitioners choose this career option when they have children of their own, and for some parents it can be a first step on the road to a career in the early years field. Childminders can be part of a network, supported by their local children's centres, and some childminders work together to care for a small group of children. PACEY (Professional Association for Childcare and Early Years) also runs accredited networks. To be part of an accredited network, a childminder has to undertake further training and development, and meet the quality requirements of the scheme. Childminding offers flexibility, close relationships with a small number of children and families, and all the benefits of being your own boss. But it is also very demanding; there are no breaks during the day, and all record-keeping, planning and financial records must be completed in the evening or at weekends.

For more information visit www.pacey.org.uk.

▲ **Figure 20.3** Attending a childminding setting may give children more opportunities for being out in the local community

Caring for children outside the family home

Employment in out-of-home settings can be in the maintained sector, which is funded completely by the government and local authorities from taxes, where you are employed by the local or education authority or health trust. Settings in the maintained sector are nursery and primary schools, children's centres, family centres and hospitals.

- **Maintained nursery schools** have high levels of qualified staff, including specialist teachers and a headteacher who takes a leading role in the planning, implementation and evaluation of the curriculum.
- **Nursery and reception classes** in primary schools are comparatively well resourced and have a high proportion of trained teachers and staff with Level 3 qualifications. There may be opportunities to develop your work across different age ranges and areas, and training opportunities will generally be good. Sometimes, early years staff can feel rather like a 'poor relation' to the staff in the rest of the school, and might suffer when headteachers without early years experience introduce initiatives and changes that may be unsuitable for young children.
- **Children's centres** are often large and well-funded organisations. Staff will generally benefit from higher rates of pay, better facilities and better resourcing. There will be opportunities to work in a multi-agency team with a range of different professionals, which can widen horizons and open up new opportunities. Training and development is often given a high priority. Staff will usually be led by a qualified, specialist early years teacher, or early years professional.

The roles that early years practitioners have in the maintained sector are diverse. This can include the following:

- The care and education of children from birth to six years as an early years practitioner/educator or an early years teacher in a nursery, children's centre or school, sometimes in small groups, sometimes in large classrooms. In schools the early years practitioner usually works alongside an early years/primary teacher.
- Working with individual or small groups of children with additional needs either in mainstream schools, nurseries or specialist units, either as a nursery nurse or a teaching assistant.
- Working with older children in after-school clubs and breakfast clubs in extended schools.
- Roles in children's centres can include care and education for children from birth to five years (although in some children's centres this facility is provided by an independent organisation), or working with parents and their children in crèche or stay-and-play sessions. Roles can also include working with children and their families as an outreach or family worker in the centre and the family's home.

Working in children's hospitals in the UK can include working with children with health needs in a maternity or children's unit or as play specialists, play leaders and nursery nurses in the hospital play departments. In general hospitals, small teams of play staff work in different areas of the hospital, such as outpatient clinics, children's wards and adolescent units.

Hospital play specialists work as part of a multidisciplinary team; their role is to:

- organise daily play and art activities in the playroom or at the bedside
- provide play to achieve developmental goals
- help children to cope with anxieties and feelings
- use play to prepare children for hospital procedures
- support families and siblings
- contribute to clinical judgements and diagnoses through their play-based observations
- act as the child's advocate
- teach the value of play for the sick child
- encourage peer group friendships to develop
- organise parties and special events.

In the independent private sector you might either be employed by a business that runs a chain of nurseries, an independent school or a small single private nursery.

- A **large nursery chain** will have a clear and formal hierarchy, with the most senior staff working centrally for the company and making decisions on a company-wide basis. Senior staff will then work below this layer of management, for the day-to-day management of each setting. This structure depends on good communication in both directions: the senior management must set clear goals and staffing structures, and provide the necessary resources – for maintenance, buying equipment, food, and for staff training and development. Big organisations can also offer good training and development opportunities and career prospects. On the other hand, in some large private nursery chains, an individual member of staff can feel rather like a small cog in a big machine, and feel that the primary purpose of the enterprise is to make money.

- A **smaller private day nursery** will have fewer layers of management, and the owner may be very hands-on. This can create a supportive, family-like atmosphere, where staff feel individually looked after and known as individuals. Commitment and loyalty can be noticed and appreciated. However, it is not easy to run a nursery business, and owners can feel under great pressure to balance the finances. Sometimes, expectations of staff in terms of their time and flexibility might be unreasonable.

Many early years practitioners go on to start their own nurseries later in their career or start them as parents due to a lack of provision in their area, then go on to qualify as early years practitioners.

In the independent private sector, the role of the early years practitioner is usually in the care and education of children from birth to five years in a private day nursery, workplace crèche or nursery school, or five to seven years in independent schools. There are, however, also jobs within the holiday and leisure industry – for example, as a ski or summer resort nanny, or as a nanny in a special children's hotel.

The independent voluntary-aided sector includes early years provisions that are usually charities and which receive grants from the local authority and are self-managed by parents' committees. In this sector, early years practitioners are usually employed in care and education of children from birth to six years in nurseries, crèches and playgroups.

- **Community nurseries, playgroups or preschools** are usually quite small. There will generally be a culture of volunteering to support the work of paid staff, and parents and others from the local community may help out with projects such as decorating or developing the outdoor space. Community support and involvement will be strong, and this can give the organisation a vibrant sense of purpose. But it is also the case that voluntary management boards can be difficult employers if

too much is expected and pay or conditions are poor. If there is a lot of dependence on grant-funding, there can be periods of great pressure to economise in all areas, including staffing.

Preparing a curriculum vitae

Your **curriculum vitae** (CV) is a summary of your education, training, qualifications and experience that you provide for a prospective employer. It is always useful to compile a CV and to keep it up to date.

The purposes of a CV are to:

- provide a brief outline of your education and work history
- set out basic factual information in a concise manner
- help in filling out application forms.

Microsoft Word and OpenOffice both have templates for a CV or résumé. The main headings to include are:

- First name and family name.
- Personal details – full postal address, telephone number and email.
- Education and qualifications – include names of schools and colleges attended, with dates and qualifications obtained.
- Employment history – if you have not worked before, include babysitting experience, college work experience and Saturday and holiday jobs.
- Other experience – include any voluntary work, involvement in local organisations or groups, sport and leisure interests.
- Referees – give the names, positions and addresses of two people who are willing to provide references for you. Always ask them first.

CVs should be well presented and free of any mistakes. Use your spellchecker, and also get a friend to check it through for you. In general, if you are applying for a post in a school or local authority children's centre or day nursery, CVs will not be accepted because they supply their own application forms and only use the information on these. Read the guidance on job applications very carefully before you complete the forms to apply for a post.

KEY TERM

Curriculum vitae – 'Curriculum vitae' is Latin for 'course of life'. It sets out an account of your education and work history, your qualifications and interests. A CV helps an employer to decide whether an applicant might be suitable for the job.

Guidelines for good practice

Preparing for an interview

✔ Dress: dress smartly – first impressions are very important.

✔ Details: check the address and that you know how to get there. If possible, make the journey beforehand so that you can judge how long it will take.

✔ Timing: ensure you arrive in plenty of time.

✔ Facial expression: you may be very nervous, but make an effort to smile and to appear cheerful and relaxed.

✔ Eye contact: try to maintain eye contact when the interviewer is speaking to you and when you reply.

✔ Handshake: shake hands firmly with the interviewer and try not to fidget; clasp your hands loosely in your lap; never sit with your arms folded.

✔ Experiences: refer to your own experiences, giving examples (whenever they are relevant) to demonstrate your understanding.

✔ Documents: take any relevant material with you – for example, certificates, portfolio of work with children.

✔ Sustenance: eat before the interview, so that your stomach does not rumble.

✔ Be realistic: there may be many other applicants for the post; if you are not successful, it does not necessarily reflect on you personally.

Conditions of employment

The law in the UK requires that any employee who works for more than 16 hours a week should have a contract of employment. This document must contain the following information:

- the name of the employer and employee
- the title of the job
- the date when employment commenced
- the scale of pay
- the hours of work
- entitlement to holidays
- the length of notice required from employer and employee
- the procedures for disciplinary action or grievances
- sick-pay provision
- pensions and pension schemes
- provision for parental leave.

Responsibility for paying income tax and National Insurance contributions will need to be decided; such payments are usually deducted from your gross pay. Those applying for jobs within the private sector may

want to consider using a reputable nanny agency; such agencies are used to negotiating contracts designed to suit both employer and employee.

The trades union VOICE has comprehensive advice for its members about contracts, terms and conditions and all other matters relating to the employment of early years practitioners. If you are a member, go to www.voicetheunion.org.uk and select 'Downloads', or search online for 'voice the union information packs'.

Grievance and complaints procedures

If a dispute arises in the workplace, either among employees or between employees and employers, it must be settled. Usually this is achieved at an early stage through discussion between colleagues, or between the aggrieved person and his or her immediate superior. If the grievance (or complaint) is not easily settled, however, an official procedure is needed.

- All employees have a right to seek redress or compensation for grievances relating to their employment, and every employee must be told how to proceed in this matter.
- Except in very small establishments, there must be a formal procedure for settling grievances.
- The procedure should be in writing, and should be simple and rapid in operation.
- The grievance should normally be discussed first between the employee and his or her immediate supervisor.
- The employee should be accompanied, at the next stage of the discussion with management, by his or her employee representative, if he or she so wishes.
- There should be a right of appeal.

Managers should always try to settle the grievance 'as near as possible to the point of origin', in the words of the Industrial Relations Code of Practice. In other words, they should discuss the issues with the people directly involved a soon as possible.

Trades unions and professional organisations

Trades unions (see page 454 for definition) and professional organisations exist to represent and protect their own members' interests. Their main functions are to:

- negotiate for better pay and conditions of service
- provide legal protection and support
- represent members at grievance and disciplinary hearings.

KEY TERM

Trades union – An organisation of workers who join together in order to improve their pay and working conditions.

In early years education and care, trades unions campaign for higher pay and better job and career opportunities. They also support members if they are in danger of being made redundant, or if they are experiencing difficulties at work (such as being bullied).

Two such organisations which early years practitioners can join are:

- UNISON – Britain's largest union for public sector workers
- VOICE – the union for education professionals (formerly known as the Professional Association of Nursery Nurses, PANN).

In addition to representing their members' interests, most trades unions and professional organisations publish newsletters and hold regular local meetings to discuss workplace issues.

Moving on

Reflecting on practice

Review your professional journey and plan your goals

Take some time to reflect on and review your professional journey so far:

- What led you into the early years field?
- Why did you want to work with young children?
- What do you enjoy most about your work?
- What do you find most challenging?

Look at your CV (or compile one):

- What have been your biggest achievements?
- What were the missed opportunities?
- What are the gaps? Which aspects of practice or provision would you like to find out more about/ have training on?
- Where do you want to go in your career?
- Where do you see yourself in five years' time? – What first steps do you need to take towards your goals?

Further reading, weblinks and resources

Council for Awards in Children's Care and Education (CACHE)

CACHE is the specialist awarding organisation for qualifications in children's care and education.
www.cache.org.uk

The Family and Childcare Trust

This is a national childcare charity that provides information for parents, childcare providers, employers, trades unions, local authorities and policymakers.
www.familyandchildcaretrust.org

Health and Safety Executive (HSE)

The HSE is a government-funded organisation that works to protect people against risks to health or safety arising from work activities.
www.hse.gov.uk

The National College for Teaching and Leadership (NCTL)

This government organisation is responsible for overseeing early years qualifications.
https://www.gov.uk/government/organisations/ national-college-for-teaching-and-leadership

Nursery World

This is the leading magazine for everyone working in early years education and care. It includes job adverts, news and in-depth articles on good practice.
www.nursery-world.co.uk

Child Care

This is a monthly magazine for all childminders, nannies and child carers.
www.professionalchildcare.co.uk

References

Bolton, G., 2005, *Reflective Practice*, London: Sage.

Bruce, T. (ed.), 2010, *Early Childhood: A Guide for Students*, London: Sage.

Children's Workforce Development Council, 2010, *The Common Core of Skills and Knowledge.* Available at: www.cwdcouncil.org.uk

Department for Education, 2014, *Statutory Framework for the Early Years Foundation Stage. Setting the Standards for Learning, Development and Care for Children from Birth to Five.* Available at: https://www.gov.uk/government/

Dickson, A., 1982, *A Woman in Your Own Right: Assertiveness and You*, London: Quartet Books.

Jones, C. and Pound, L., 2008, *Leadership and Management in the Early Years*, Maidenhead: Open University Press, McGraw Hill Education.

Manning-Morton, J., 2006, 'The Personal is Professional: Professionalism and the Birth to Threes Practitioner', *Contemporary Issues in Early Childhood*, 7:1, 42–52.

Manning-Morton, J. (ed.), 2014, *Exploring Well-being in the Early Years*, Maidenhead: Open University Press.

Moon, J., 2005, *Reflection in Learning and Professional Development*, Oxford: Routledge Falmer.

Page-Smith, A. and Craft, A., 2008, *Developing Reflective Practice in the Early Years*, Maidenhead: Open University Press.

Smith, A and Langston, A., 1999, *Managing Staff in Early Years Settings*, London: Routledge.

Stacey, M., 2009, *Teamwork and Collaboration in Early Years Settings*, Exeter: Learning Matters.

Tickell, C., 2011, *The Early Years: Foundations For Life, Health And Learning*, London: Department for Education.

Tuckman, B., 1965, 'Developmental Sequence in Small Groups', *Psychological Bulletin*, 63, 384–99. The article was reprinted in *Group Facilitation: A Research and Applications Journal*, 3, Spring 2001. Available at: http://psycnet.apa.org/journals/bul/63/6/384

Whitaker, P., 1995, *Managing To Learn*, London: Cassell.

Appendix: Tables of Normative Development

The following tables summarise normative developmental sequences. When using them practitioners should always remember 3 key ideas:

1 Children's development may have general patterns but is also unique to each child and is greatly influenced by children's socio-cultural contexts as well as their biological, genetic inheritance. Students and practitioners should also remember that these ideas of the sequences of development reflect the western European context in which they have been developed.

2 Children's development does not follow a neat straight line; it loops and spirals in its progression. Sometimes development progresses rapidly for a time then pauses, sometimes in one aspect, sometimes in several aspects.

3 Development does not happen in separate areas, all aspects of development are linked and each influences the others. Also, development, growth and learning are all linked together: Development is holistic.

Young infants: Approximately 0–3 months

Physical development: Touch and movement give babies feedback about the world and their bodies.	
Gross Motor skills	Lies supine (on the back) with the head in a central position
	When placed on their front (the prone position), the baby lies with head turned to one side but by 1 month can lift the head
	If pulled to sitting position, the head will lag, the back curves over and the head falls forward
	Arm and leg movements are jerky and uncontrolled.
	Begins to lift their head briefly from the prone position.
	Begins to turn from side to back
	Begins to lift head and chest off the bed in prone position, supported on forearms.
	There begins to be less head lag in sitting position
	The legs can usually kick vigorously, both separately and together
	Begins to move the head to follow adult movements.
Fine motor skills	Hands are usually tightly closed in the beginning
	Then the baby will use their hand to grasp the carer's finger, cannot loosen their grasp at first
	Later, the baby will wave their arms and bring hands together over their body
	Watches their hands and plays with their fingers.
	Holds a rattle for a brief time before dropping it.
Social development, Communication and language: Babies need to share language experiences and interact with others from birth onwards. From the start, babies are interested in and need other people.	
	The baby is fascinated by human faces, making eye contact and gazing attentively at carer's face when fed or held
	Responds to familiar voices and quietens when picked up
	Cries to indicate needs
	The baby shows interest and excitement at facial expressions and may imitate them. For example, they may put out their tongue if you do.
	A baby's first smile in definite response to their carer is usually around 5 to 6 weeks.

	Begins to recognizes their primary carer and familiar objects
	Begins to make non-crying noises, such as cooing and gurgling. Hearing-impaired babies babble and cry too
	The baby listens to people's voices, is comforted by the voices of those who are close to them and will especially turn to the voices of their family.
	The baby 'calls out' for company
	When adults close to the baby use 'infant directed speech', the baby moves, listens, and replies with babbling and cooing.
	The baby begins to recognise differing speech sounds.
	By 3 months, the baby may imitate low or high-pitched sounds

Personal and emotional development

	The baby enjoys feeding and cuddling and uses total body movements to express pleasure at bath time or when being fed.
	In the first month, the baby is learning where they begin and end – for example, their hand is part of them, but mother's hand is not.
	The baby will begin to smile in response to adults
	The baby may stop crying when they hear, see or feel their carer
	The baby responds with obvious pleasure to loving attention and cuddles.
	The baby's cries become more expressive of different needs: Distress and anger to show tiredness, hunger, pain or discomfort. Sadness to show loneliness.
	The baby stays awake for longer periods of time.

Perceptual and cognitive development: Concepts (ideas) are beginning to develop already. Concepts are based on the senses and in what is perceived (i.e. the baby is aware of a sensation). The baby explores through their senses and through their own activity and movement.

Sight / Vision	Can usually focus on objects 20 cm away
	Is sensitive to light.
	Can usually track the movements of people and objects.
	Will usually scan the edges of objects.
	Turns their head towards the light and stares at bright or shiny objects
Touch and movement (kinaesthetic)	The face, abdomen, hands and the soles of their feet are very sensitive to touch. From the beginning, the baby feels pain
	The baby perceives their own movements and the way that other people move them about, through their senses.
	The baby gives a 'startle' response if they are moved suddenly. This is called the Moro or startle reflex.
Sound / hearing	Even a newborn baby will turn to a sound. The baby might become still and listen to a low sound, or quicken their movements when they hear a high sound.
	Reacts to loud sounds, but by 1 month may be soothed by particular music or constant sounds such as the washing machine
	A baby often stops crying and listens to a human voice by 2 weeks of age.
	The baby begins to look for sounds, showing excitement at the sound of approaching footsteps or voices.
	By 4 months, the baby links objects they know with the sound, for example, mother's voice and her face.

Taste	The baby likes sweet tastes such as breast milk.
Smell	The baby turns to the smell of the breast
	The baby knows the difference between the smell of their mother from that of other mothers.
	The baby begins to suck or lick their lips when they hear the sound of, see or smell food preparation.

Young infants: Approximately 3–6 months

Physical development: Babies are very interested in all movement and activity	
Gross Motor skills	The baby moves their head around to follow people and objects.
	They develop more head control and begin to sit with support.
	They roll over from back to side and begin to reach for objects
	When supine, the baby plays with their own feet.
	The baby holds their head up when pulled to sitting position.
Fine motor skills	The baby is beginning to use a palmar grasp and to transfer objects from hand to hand.
	Everything is taken to the mouth
	The baby can coordinate more – for example, they can see a rattle, grasp the rattle, put the rattle in their mouth (the baby coordinates tracking, reaching, grasping and sucking).
Communication and language development: As babies become more aware of others, they communicate more and more.	
	As the baby listens, they imitate sounds they can hear, and react to the tone of someone's voice – for example, the baby might become upset by an angry tone or cheered by a happy tone.
	Begins to use vowels, consonants and syllable sounds – for example, 'ah', 'ee aw'.
	Begins to laugh and squeal with pleasure.
Personal, social and emotional development: Being able to tell the difference between people supports the development of attachment relationships.	
	The baby shows trust and security with their familiar adults.
	The baby often has recognisable sleep patterns but these change when there is a growth spurt or disruption to routine.
	By 5 months, the baby has learned that they only have one mother and is disturbed when shown several images of their mother at the same time.
Perceptual and cognitive development: Babies use their sensory experiences to make sense of and understand people, objects and the world around them	
	By 4 months, the baby reaches for objects, which suggests that they recognize and judge the distance in relation to the size of the object. This is called depth perception.
	The baby prefers complicated things to look at from 5 to 6 months. The baby enjoys bright colours and contrasts.
	The baby realises that people are permanent before they realise that objects are.
Taste	The baby may develop favourite tastes in food and recognise differences by 5 months

Infants: Approximately 6–9 months

Physical development: Opportunities to lie, roll and stretch strengthen babies' muscles	
Gross Motor skills	The baby can usually roll from front to back.
	The baby may attempt to crawl, but will often end up sliding backwards.
	The baby may grasp feet and place them in their mouth.
	The baby can usually sit without support for longer periods of time.
	The baby may 'cruise' around furniture and may even stand or walk alone.
Fine motor skills	The baby is beginning to use pincer grasp, with thumb and index finger.
	The baby transfers toys from one hand to the other and looks for fallen objects.
	The baby explores everything by putting it in their mouth.

Communication and language development: As babies become more aware of others, they communicate more and more.	
	Babble becomes tuneful, like the lilt of the language the baby can hear (except in hearing-impaired babies).
	The baby begins to understand words like 'up' and 'down', raising their arms to be lifted up, using appropriate gestures.
	The baby repeats sounds

Personal, social and emotional development: Babies are very alert to people and objects.	
	The baby can usually manage to feed themselves using their fingers.
	The baby is now more wary of unfamiliar people, sometimes showing stranger anxiety.
	The baby might offer toys to others.
	The baby might show distress when their mother leaves.
	The baby typically begins to crawl, and this means they have a keener sense of themselves as separate individuals.
	The baby is now more aware of other people's feelings and cries if another cries, for example. They love an audience to laugh with them and cry and laugh with others. This is called recognition of an emotion.

Perceptual and cognitive development: Babies use their sensory experiences to make sense of and understand people, objects and the world around them.	
	The baby understands signs – for example, the bib means that food is coming. Soon this understanding of signs will lead into symbolic behaviour.
	From 8 to 9 months, the baby shows that they know that objects exist when they have gone out of sight, even under test conditions. This is called the concept of object constancy, or object permanence.
	The baby is fascinated by the way objects move.
	The baby typically begins to crawl, and this means they can reach objects and get to places and people, this stimulates interest and curiosity.

Infants: Approximately 9–12 months

Physical development: Becoming mobile means the baby has a greater sense of themselves as a separate person. This often leads to clinginess and stranger anxiety.	
Gross Motor skills	The baby may sit up on their own and lean forward to pick things up.
	They are now usually mobile: Crawling, bear-crawling, bottom-shuffling, cruising while holding on and sometimes walking.
	The baby may bounce in rhythm to music.
Fine motor skills	The pincer grasp is usually now well developed, and the baby can pick things up and pull them towards themselves.
	The baby will poke with one finger and point to desired objects.
	May clasp hands and imitate adults' actions.
	May manage a spoon and finger foods

Communication and language development: Babies are already experienced and capable communicators by this time. In the short space of a year, babies know about facial expressions, combined sounds, gestures, shared meanings, persuading, negotiating, cooperating, turn-taking, interest in others, their ideas, their feelings and what they do.	
Neuroscientists are finding that the baby's brain develops the ability to think better if they are spoken to in a warm tone of voice, rather than in a sharp, shouting one. Intonation is important.	
	Word approximations appear such as mumma, dadda and bye-bye in English-speaking contexts.
	Their babble is very expressive.
	Tuneful babble develops into 'jargon', and the baby makes their voice go up and down just as people do when they talk to each other. 'Really? Do you? No!'
	The baby uses emergent language or proto-language.
	The baby knows that words stand for people, objects, what they do and what happens. The baby is taking part in the language of their culture.

Personal, social and emotional development: Cooperation develops further from the early proto-conversations. For example, when adults wave bye-bye or say 'show me your shoes', the baby enjoys waving and pointing.	
	Enjoys shared songs and action rhymes.
	Likes to be near to a familiar adult.
	May drink from a cup with help.
	The baby has and shows definite likes and dislikes at mealtimes and bedtimes.
	Enjoys social games such as peek-a-boo.
	Likes to look at themselves in a mirror
	May imitate other people, for example, clapping hands but there is often a time lapse after the actual event
	May cooperate when being dressed.
	The baby 'catches' the moods and feeling of other people such as sadness, joy or anger. This emotional contagion is the beginning of sympathy for others.

Perceptual and cognitive development: Mouthing, holding and manipulating objects enables the baby to form a mental representation of it in their mind.	
	The baby is beginning to develop images and conscious memory develops further allowing them to be able to remember the past.

	The baby begins to be able to anticipate the future. This is facilitated by predictable routine daily sequences which give them a very early understanding of time sequence– for example, a feed, then changing and then a sleep with teddy. This thinking is very linked to people and objects.
	The baby imitates actions, sounds, gestures and moods after an event is finished – for example, waving bye-bye when remembering Grandma has gone to the shops.

Young toddlers: Approximately 12–18 months

Physical development: Toddlers are usually 'on the go' exploring movement in whatever way they can.	
Gross Motor skills	Probably walks alone, with feet wide apart and arms raised to maintain balance. They are likely to fall over and sit down suddenly a lot.
	Can usually get to standing without help from furniture or people, and kneels without support.
	May climb up stairs and onto low items of furniture but will need supervision.
Fine motor skills	May build with a few bricks and arrange toys on the floor.
	May hold a crayon in palmar grasp and turn several pages of a book at once
	Points to desired objects.
	Shows a preference for one hand, but uses either.

Communication and language development: Children understand more language than they can express. They understand a lot through non-verbal communications; facial expression and gestures and so on. Their use of gestures develops alongside words. Gestures are used in some cultures more than in others.	
	Talk with words or sign language emerges
	Enjoys action songs and tries to sing as well as listen to songs and rhymes.
	Uses gestures to communicate. For example, waving arms up and down to mean 'start again', or 'I like it', or 'more'.
	Understands things have names and points to ask what things are called.
	Often has own words for things

Personal, social and emotional development: Toddlers tend to focus on one aspect of a situation. It is difficult for them to see things from different points of view. The way people react to what they do help them to work out the impact they have on other people.	
	Is developing a sense of identity
	The child is aware when others are fearful or anxious for them.
	May be wary of new situations
	Will explore when supported by familiar trusted adult
	Uses trusted adults as a secure base

Spiritual development: Spirituality is about the developing sense of relationship with self, relating to others ethically, morally and humanely, and a relationship with the universe. Babies experience a sense of awe and wonder as they experience the world: For example, a daisy on the grass grasped and looked at and mouthed, may be a spiritual experience for the baby. They also experience love and self-worth through their close loving relationships.

Perceptual and cognitive development: The child learns about things through exploration, experimentation and trial and error.

	Looks for things that are out of sight, often remembering where things are
	Recognizes differences in shape, size and amount
	May be interested in combining objects together and holding an object in each hand
	Often responds enthusiastically to music, moving the whole body

Older toddlers: Approximately 18–24 months

Physical development: Toddlers are usually 'on the go' exploring movement in whatever way they can.	
Gross Motor skills	May walk confidently and is able to stop without falling
	May kneel, squat, climb and carry things around
	May be able to climb onto an adult chair forwards and then turn round to sit.
	May walk upstairs holding on
	Begins to be able to come downstairs, usually by creeping backwards on their tummies.
	May communicate that they have a wet nappy and may show awareness of bowel or bladder urges
Fine motor skills	As dexterity develops, the child uses their pincer grasp to pick up small objects and manipulate tools and objects such as threading large beads, building a tower of several cubes or scribbling with a chunky marker to and fro on paper.
	Can usually use a throwing action.
Communication and language development: Children understand more language than they can express. They understand a lot through non-verbal communications; facial expression and gestures and so on. Their use of gestures develops alongside words. Gestures are used in some cultures more than in others.	
	The child expresses their needs in words and gestures.
	Uses one word or sign to stand for several things (holophrases). For example, 'Cat' may mean all animals, not just cats. This is sometimes called extension.
	Echoes the last part of what others say (echolalia) and copies familiar phrases.
	May start putting two words together
	The child often 'talks' to themselves while they are playing.
	Understands the names of objects and may follow simple instructions.
Personal, social and emotional development: Emotional changeability is usual as the toddler explores who they are and how they relate to other people.	
	Is eager to try out independence but often retreats into dependence
	Plays co-operatively with a familiar adult
	Is interested in other children and may watch them as they play
	Often likes to look at pictures of themselves and their families and pets
Cognitive development: The child learns about things through exploration, experimentation and trial and error.	
	Uses toys or objects to represent things in real life as long as they have something in common. For example, using a doll as a baby, or a block as a phone.
	Begins to have a longer memory.
	May show interest in making marks through movement

	May like to organize objects into groups and to fit shapes into spaces
	Explores schemas dynamically, typically; containing, transporting, enveloping and trajectory
	Often shows interest in animals and moving objects such as vehicles
	Understands that things are used in different ways

Young child: Approximately 2–3 years old

Physical development: 2 year olds need many opportunities to move in a wide range of ways to refine their still rapidly expanding physical skills	
Gross Motor skills	The child is usually very mobile and can usually run safely.
	The child may try to kick a ball with some success
	May climb at any opportunity
	Usually enjoys scooters and trikes or ride-astride bikes
	May walk upstairs and downstairs, usually two feet to a step.
Fine motor skills	May draw circles, lines and dots, using preferred hand.
	Usually picks up tiny objects using a fine pincer grasp.
	May build a tower of six or more blocks (bricks), or similar, with longer concentration span.
	Usually enjoys picture books and turns pages singly.
Communication and language development: Vocabulary and expressive language, spoken or signed, usually expands rapidly during the 3rd year of life; becoming a competent speaker of the languages they experience.	
	The child uses short phrases (telegraphic speech), for example, 'doggie gone'
	Usually knows their own name and will name themselves
	May spend a great deal of energy naming things and what they do. The child also names movements – for example, 'up', 'gone'. For example, as they go up a step, they might say 'up'.
	The child may follow a simple instruction or request. For example, 'Could you bring me the spoon?'
	Increasingly wants to share songs, dance, conversations, finger rhymes, and so on.
Personal, social and emotional development: Typically 2 year olds begin to understand that other people might think differently from them. This is called developing theory of mind. It leads to having empathy for others.	
	The child begins to be able to say how they are feeling, but often feel frustrated when unable to express themselves.
	May dress self with easily managed items of clothing.
	Is usually able to control their bowels and bladder more and to use the potty or toilet more independently
	May play more with other children but finds sharing very difficult.
Cognitive development: The child is impulsive and curious about their environment.	
	Pretend play develops rapidly when adults foster it.
	The child has improved memory skills, which help their understanding of concepts, for example, naming and matching two or three colours (usually yellow and red).
	May hold a crayon and other tools and move them deliberately and with intention

	Usually understands cause and effect. For example, if something is dropped, they understand it might break.
	The child may talk about an absent object when reminded of it – for example, seeing an empty plate, they say 'biscuit'.

Young child: Approximately 3–5 years old

Physical development: Children's dexterity, sense of balance and spatial awareness is developing and physical skills are being refined	
Gross Motor skills	A sense of balance is shown through: • jumping and landing on two feet • walking backwards and sideways • standing and walking on tiptoe • standing on one foot • walking along a line • bending at the waist to pick up objects from the floor
	The child usually enjoys climbing trees and frames.
	The child usually rides a tricycle, using pedals.
	The child can usually climb stairs with one foot on each step, and come down stairs with two feet per step at first. Later they can run upstairs and downstairs, one foot per step.
Fine motor skills	Increasing spatial awareness is shown through: • Catching and throwing • Maneuvering and placing themselves in relation to people and things
	Increasing dexterity is shown through: • Building taller and more complex constructions • controlling mark making tools using thumb and first two fingers – a dynamic tripod grasp • Using scissors to cut • Copying shapes • Threading small beads or similar
Communication and language development: During this period, language and the ability to communicate develop so rapidly that it is almost like an explosion.	
	The child may begin to use plurals, pronouns, adjectives, possessives, time words, tenses and sentences.
	The child makes what are called virtuous errors in the way they pronounce (articulate) things. It is also true of the way the child uses grammar (syntax). They might say 'two times' instead of 'twice', or 'I goed there' instead of 'I went there'.
	They usually love to chat and ask questions (what, where and who). They ask why, when and how questions, as they become more and more fascinated with the reasons for things and how things work
	The child usually enjoys much more complicated stories and asks for their favourite ones again and again.
	It is not unusual for the child to stutter because they are trying so hard to tell adults things. Their thinking goes faster than the pace at which they can say what they want to. They can quickly become frustrated.
	Past, present and future tenses are used more often.
	The child can be taught to say their name, address and age.

	As the child becomes more accurate in the way they pronounce words, and begin to use grammar, they delight in nonsense words that they make up and jokes using words. This is called metalinguistics.
	The child's talk reflects their socio-cultural context: Using the style and inflection of the language (s), dialects and accents familiar to them. This may include swearing if they hear it.

Personal, social and emotional development: Pretend play helps the child to decentre and develop theory of mind. (This means the child begins to be able to understand how someone else might feel and think.)

	The child usually begins to explore gender roles as they become aware of being male or female.
	The child usually makes friends and is interested in having friends.
	The child learns to negotiate, to give and take, through experimenting with feeling powerful, having a sense of control, and through quarrels with other children.
	The child can usually think about things from somebody else's point of view, but only fleetingly.
	As they begin to use their imaginations more, they may become easily afraid, as they imagine all sorts of things.
	The child likes to be independent and may be strongly self-willed.
	May show a sense of humour
	Can usually undress and dress themselves; except for laces and back buttons.
	Can usually toilet, wash and dry their hands and brush their teeth.

Moral and spiritual development: During this period children are beginning to develop a moral sense. They know what hurts and upsets their family and friends and they know what delights them and brings about pleased responses. Through pretend play, and conversations about how people behave, hurt and help each other, children learn about how other people feel and to think beyond themselves.

Cognitive development: Children are fascinated by cause and effect and are continually trying to explain what goes on in the world.

	The child can usually think back and forward much more easily than before.
	They wonder what will happen if. . . (problem-solving and hypothesis-making).
	The child develops symbolic behaviour. This means that: • they use language • they pretend, often talking themselves while playing • they take part in simple, non-competitive games • they represent events in drawings, models, and movement.
	Personal images dominate, rather than conventions used in the culture – for example, writing is 'pretend' writing.
	They can usually identify common colours, such as red, yellow, blue and green.
	At about age 4, the child usually knows how to count
	They usually understand ideas such as 'more' and 'fewer', and 'big' and 'small'.
	They may enjoy music and playing sturdy instruments, and joins in groups singing and dancing.

Young child: Approximately 5–8 years old

Physical development: Children have increased agility, muscle coordination and balance.	
Gross Motor skills	The child can usually use a variety of play equipment such as slides, swings and climbing frames; climbing and jumping off
	May play ball games and skip
	The child can usually hop and run lightly on toes and can move rhythmically to music.
	May develop competence in riding a two- wheeled bicycle.
Fine motor skills	The child may be able to thread a large-eyed needle and sew large stitches.
	The child has good control over pencils and paintbrushes. They may copy shapes and draw a person with head, trunk, legs, nose, mouth and eyes; and later with detail such as clothes and eyebrows
	The child may build complex and precise constructions.
	They may write the letters of the alphabet at school, with a similar writing grip to an adult.
	The child may catch a ball thrown from 1 metre with one hand.
Communication and language development: A young child does not learn well in isolation from other children and adults. The child begins to share as they learn. Sharing sharpens and broadens the child's thinking.	
	The child tries to understand the meaning of words.
	The child usually talks confidently, and with more and more fluency, using adverbs and prepositions and adding vocabulary all the time.
	As the child becomes part of their culture, they become aware of the roles of the language(s) they speak
	The child may use language creatively.
	The child's articulation becomes more conventional.
	The child usually begins to realise that different situations require different ways of talking; establishing a sense of audience (who they are talking to).
Personal, social and emotional development: Being able to sympathise and empathise and a greater ability to think about abstract things makes this a time for beginning to understand right and wrong, fairness and justice.	
	The child has usually developed a stable self-concept, including gender identity
	The child has usually internalised the rules of their culture.
	They may hide their feelings once they can begin to control their feelings.
	The child can usually think of the feelings of others.
	The child may take responsibility, for example, helping younger children.
	The child may be interested in their own development, from babyhood to now
	The child begins to try to work out right and wrong. For example, hurting people physically or their feelings

Moral and spiritual development: With the help and support of their family, early years workers and the wider community, the child develops further concepts, like being helpful and forgiving, and having a sense of fairness. As children get older, these concepts become more abstract – for example, justice, right, wrong, good versus evil, beauty and nature, the arts and scientific achievements.

Cognitive development: Cultural conventions in writing, drawing, and so on, begin to influence the child increasingly. Where there is a balance in the way the child uses personal and conventional symbols, they are described as creative. Lack of creativity is linked with a lack of personal symbols. Colouring in templates and tracing discourages the child from developing personal symbols.

	The child begins to move into deeper and deeper layers of symbolic behaviour. Communication through body language, facial gestures and language is well established, and opens the way into literacy (talking, listening, writing and reading). Personal symbols still dominate until 6 or 7 years of age.
	They may include more detail in their drawing, for example, a house may have not only windows and a roof, but also curtains and a chimney
	They usually begin to understand book language, and that stories have characters and a plot (the narrative) and they may use their voice in different ways to play different characters in pretend play. They develops play narratives
	The child may recognise their own name when it is written down and can usually write the first letter or the whole name themselves.
	Thinking becomes increasingly coordinated, as the child is able to hold in mind more than one point of view at a time. Concepts – of matter, length, measurement, distance, area, time, volume, capacity and weight – develop steadily.
	They may enjoy chanting and counting as they begin to understand numbers
	The child may begin to be able to define objects by their function – for example, 'What is a ball?' 'You bounce it.'
	The child is usually beginning to establish differences between what is real and unreal/fantasy. This is not yet always stable, so they may be easily frightened by supernatural characters.

Appendix: Food groups

Food groups	Examples of food included	Main nutrients provided	Recommended servings
Starchy foods	Bread, potatoes, sweet potatoes, starchy root vegetables, pasta, noodles, rice and other grains, breakfast cereals	Carbohydrate, fibre, B vitamins and iron	Four portions each day Provide a portion as part of each meal (breakfast, lunch and tea) and provide as part of at least one snack each day
Fruit and vegetables	Fresh, frozen, canned, dried and juiced fruit and vegetables, and pulses	Carotenes (a form of vitamin A), vitamin C, zinc, iron, and fibre	Five portions each day Provide a portion as part of each main meal (breakfast, lunch and tea) with some snacks
Meat, fish, eggs, beans and non-dairy sources of protein	Meat, poultry, fish, shellfish, eggs, meat alternatives, pulses, nuts*	Protein, iron, zinc, omega 3 fatty acids, vitamins A and D	Two portions each day Provide a portion as part of lunch and tea (Two to three portions for vegetarian children)
Milk and dairy foods	Milk, cheese, yoghurt, fromagefrais, custard, puddings made from milk	Protein, calcium, and vitamin A	Three portions each day provided as part of meals, snacks and drinks

***Nuts**: children under five should not be offered whole nuts as they may cause choking. Nut butters and ground or chopped nuts in recipes are fine. However it is important to check if a child has a nut allergy before offering nuts. See p 366, Food allergies

Glossary

ABC approach The ABC model of behaviour analysis can be very useful in identifying the causes of negative behaviour and ways in which the issue can be addressed. In the approach, A represents the antecedent, which means the conditions or stimulus that are present before a behaviour occurs; B is for the behaviour or response to the stimulus; and C represents the result of the behaviour.

Ablism Discrimination in favour of able-bodied people.

Abstract A thought or idea that does not have a physical or concrete existence, such as beauty or fairness.

Accommodation How the brain changes a schema to take account of new experiences.

Active learning Learning through hands-on direct experience and involvement.

Ageism Prejudice or discrimination on the grounds of a person's age.

Allegation This is when a child alleges (or discloses) information that causes an adult to be concerned about the child's safety and well-being. This can happen through children talking, acting things out in their play, or drawing and painting. It is essential that early years practitioners listen and watch very carefully, but do not question the child or put words into the child's mouth.

Allergy Abnormal sensitivity reaction of the body to substances that are usually harmless.

Alpha-fetoprotein (AFP) A protein, produced by the foetus's liver, which can be detected in the mother's blood most accurately between the 16th and 18th weeks of pregnancy. High levels of AFP may be associated with spina bifida; low levels may be associated with **Down's syndrome.**

Amnesia Partial or total loss of memory.

Amniotic sac Often called 'membranes' or the 'bag of waters', the amniotic sac is the bag of amniotic fluid that surrounds and cushions the foetus.

Amygdale A structure in the brain that is linked to emotions. It deals with emergency fear responses and the formation of emotional memories

Anaemia A condition in which the concentration of the oxygen-carrying pigment, haemoglobin, in the blood is below normal.

Anaphylaxis An immediate and severe allergic response; a shock reaction to a substance.

Anterior fontanelle A diamond-shaped soft area at the front of the head, just above the brow. It is covered by a tough membrane and you can often see the baby's pulse beating there under the skin. The fontanelle closes between 12 and 18 months of age.

Anti-bias practice Actively working against bias, prejudice and discrimination in early years practice.

Antibodies Antibodies are proteins made by the body's immune system to kill bacteria and viruses.

Anti-discriminatory practice This is an approach to working with young children that promotes diversity and the valuing of difference and that actively challenges prejudice and discrimination. Anti-discriminatory practice means understanding the connections between all aspects of our social identity such as our gender, ethnicity, class, ability, our sexuality, religion and language/s, and so operates in all aspects of early years practice.

Apartheid This is when groups of people are segregated from others, in education, housing and employment. This almost inevitably means that groups of people become ignorant about each other. The practice of apartheid was taken to an extreme in South Africa before 1990, when black South African people were segregated by law from white South Africans. This situation was repeated in the southern states of North America and in Australia.

Appraisal The formal system used to evaluate how well you are doing in your job and to set targets for further improvement over the year ahead.

Asperger's syndrome People with Aperger's syndrome have difficulties with social communication, social interaction and social imagination. There are diagnostic differences between conditions on the autism spectrum. Sometimes people may receive a diagnosis of autism or ASD, high-functioning autism (HFA) or atypical autism instead of Asperger syndrome.

Asphyxia Lack of oxygen in the blood.

Assertive/assertiveness Expressing thoughts, feelings and beliefs in direct, honest and appropriate ways and also respecting the thoughts, feelings and beliefs of other people.

Glossary

Assertiveness Behaviour which enables you to express your needs, wants, feelings, opinions and values in a way that does not affect the human rights of others.

Asset-based community development An approach to community development which aims to discover and use the strengths already available in a local community. This is understood as a way of giving choice and power to local communities. It is in contrast to the usual model of trying to establish what is wrong in a community, and send people in (more social workers, more police) to fix it.

Assimilation This is the process by which new information is interpreted through existing schemas.

Attachment A warm, affectionate and supportive bond between child and carer that enables the child to develop secure relationships.

Autonomic nervous system The part of the nervous system that is responsible for control of the bodily functions which are not consciously directed. This includes breathing, the heartbeat and digestive processes.

Autonomy Being able to do things for yourself, without needing help or waiting for permission.

Balanced bilingualism This is when a child speaks more than one language, each with equal fluency. In fact, the child's home language is usually more fluent than English. Very few children are completely balanced across two languages. For most, one language is more developed than the other.

Behaviour modification This is an approach to working with children who have BESD which draws on the theory of behaviourism. In order to change the child's behaviour, the adult focuses on what is observable and tries to change it using rewards such as praise or stickers.

Behavioural, emotional and social difficulties (BESD) Signs that a child may have BESD include withdrawn or isolated behaviour, highly disruptive or disturbing behaviour, hyperactivity and significant difficulties with social interactions. It is difficult to assess whether a young child has BESD, and an educational psychologist or clinical child psychologist should always be involved.

Behaviourism A perspective on child development which understands human behaviour only through the objective analysis of behaviours and reactions and does not consider people's internal mental states and emotions.

Behaviourist Practices that are influenced by the observation and understanding of external behaviours only, rather than their underlying causes.

Bias An inclination or prejudice for or against a person or group, especially in a way considered to be unfair.

Bilingual Having the ability to speak two languages.

Bisexuality Emotional and sexual relationships with members of both sexes.

Blastocyst The rapidly dividing fertilised egg when it enters the woman's uterus.

Blueprint A design or plan which determines how something is built.

Brain plasticity The ability of the brain to organise and reorganise itself according to life events so that different areas can take over the function of damaged or unused areas of the brain.

Caesarean section A Caesarean or C-section is when the baby is delivered through an incision in the mother's abdomen and uterus. It is used when a woman cannot give birth vaginally or if the baby is in distress or danger.

Cartilage This is a connective tissue which can be found in areas of the body such as joints including those between the elbows and knees. It is a firm but softer and more flexible tissue than bone.

Centile charts Also known as percentile charts or growth charts, these are used to monitor a child's growth regularly and are contained in the child's PCHR.

Central nervous system (CNS) This is comprised of the brain and spinal chord. It is the network of nerve tissues that controls the activities of the body.

Centration The child cannot hold in mind several ideas at once, so focuses on one aspect.

Cerebral cortex The outer layer of grey matter of the brain, largely responsible for higher brain functions, including sensation, voluntary muscle movement, thought, reasoning, and memory.

Cerebral Palsy The general term for a number of neurological conditions that affect movement and coordination.

Glossary

Chemical inhibitors The brain produces chemicals that either allows an impulse from one nerve cell to pass to another nerve cell or inhibits or stops it.

Child in need Any child who has been assessed as needing extra services from the local authority in order to attain good health or good development is a 'child in need'. This includes children with a disability.

Child poverty There is no single agreed definition for 'child poverty' in the UK. But it is generally understood to describe a child living in a family that lacks the resources that would enable the child to participate in activities and have housing and material goods that are customary in the UK. Child poverty does not necessarily have to mean lacking physical necessities, like food and clothing.

Chromosomal abnormality An abnormality in the number or structure of chromosomes. Chromosomes are the structures that hold our genes.

Chromosome A structure in all living cells that consists of a single molecule of DNA.

Cilia The fine hair-like projections from certain cells such as those in the respiratory tract that help to sweep away fluids and particles.

Clostridium botulinum A bacteria that grows on food and produces toxins that, when ingested, cause paralysis.

Cognition The process of making sense and thinking about the world and experiences to develop ideas and form concepts.

Cognitive development The development of the mind: the processes in the brain that enable us to recognise, reason, know and understand. It involves: what a person knows and the ability to reason, understand and solve problems; memory, concentration, attention and perception; imagination and creativity.

Cognitive development The processing of information in the mind to understand and make sense of the world.

Colostrum This is the first 'milk' that the breasts produce, as a precursor to breast milk. It is rich in fats, protein and antibodies, which protect the baby against infection and kick-start the immune system.

Comfort object Often a soft toy or blanket to which a child becomes attached, a comfort (or transitional) object is used by a child to provide comfort and security while he or she is away from a secure base, such as parents or home.

Communication The transmission of thoughts, feelings or information via body language, signals, speech or writing.

Concepts Ideas that can be shared, such as fairness, weight and time.

Congenital A trait, habit or physical abnormality present from birth.

Constipation Not able to pass stools.

Constructivism Regarding children as actively involved in constructing their knowledge.

Containment This refers to an adult or practitioner's state of mind in relation to a baby or young child. Through containment, the adult can receive the baby's communications of anxiety, pain, distress or pleasure.

Context This can refer to the child's sociocultural context of family and community or it can also refer to what is going on in the environment at a particular time that an observation is made.

Cortex The outer part of the brain, the grey matter, that is responsible for higher brain functions, including sensation, voluntary muscle movement, thought, reasoning, and memory.

Curriculum vitae 'Curriculum vitae' is Latin for 'course of life'. It sets out an account of your education and work history, your qualifications and interests. A CV helps an employer to decide whether an applicant might be suitable for the job.

Cystic fibrosis A condition that affects certain organs in the body, especially the lungs and pancreas, by clogging them with thick sticky mucus. New treatments mean people with cystic fibrosis can live relatively healthy lives.

Depth perception The visual ability to perceive the world in three dimensions and the distance of an object.

Developed country A country that has a highly developed economy and advanced technological infrastructure.

Developmental niche A particular sociocultural context that influences children's development.

Glossary

Disability Under the Equality Act 2010, a person has a disability if they have a physical or mental impairment, and if the impairment has a substantial and long-term negative effect on their ability to perform normal day-to-day activities.

Disablism Discriminating or prejudiced against people who are disabled.

Disclosure This is when a child or individual tells you something that is secret or private to them.

Down's syndrome A genetic disorder resulting from the presence of an extra chromosome; children usually, but not always, have learning difficulties.

Dynamic systems Seeing development progressing as a result of the interactions that take place within the body and the mind.

Dysphasia A language disorder marked by deficiency in being able to speak, and sometimes also in understanding speech, due to brain disease or damage.

E number The code which identifies food additives; food colourings are the additives most often linked to behaviour problems in children.

Early intervention This approach seeks to offer extra help and support to a family before the child starts to lag behind in development or experience neglect or abuse. Early intervention is about working cooperatively with parents and carers, giving them a chance to make choices about which services they need.

Echolalia The repetition or imitation of other people's vocal sounds.

Effortful control This is children's capacity to override their immediate wants, desires and responses with a more socially acceptable and effective response. Children who can see that there are cakes on the table but wait for the practitioner to say that they can have one, are showing high levels of effortful control.

Embryo The unborn child during the first eight weeks after conception

Emergent curriculum A way of planning the curriculum that follows and builds on children's interests. This requires close observation, documentation and flexibility by practitioners.

Empathy Awareness of another person's emotional state, and the ability to share the experience with that person. To see the world from someone else's point of view.

Empiricism Theories that stress the environmental influences on development.

Enactive learning This is about learning by doing, through first-hand experiences.

Encopresis Incontinence of faeces (soiling) not due to any physical defect or illness.

Endometrium The lining of the womb that grows and sheds during a normal menstrual cycle and which supports a foetus if a pregnancy occurs.

Enuresis The medical term for bedwetting.

Episiotomy A small surgical cut in the perineum.

Equifinal Different developmental pathways can lead to the same or similar outcome.

Equilibrium This is the state of cognitive or mental balance that the mind tries to maintain. When a child's existing schemas are capable of explaining what they can perceive, they are in a state of equilibrium. New information upsets the balance until existing schemas change to accommodate the information and regain balance.

Febrile convulsion seizures (fits or convulsions) occurring in children aged 6 months to 5 years, associated with fever without another underlying cause.

Fertilisation is the moment when sperm and egg meet, join and form a single cell. It usually takes place in the Fallopian tubes. The fertilised egg then travels into the uterus, where it implants in the lining before developing into an embryo and then a foetus.

Fight or flight response Physical changes in the body (such as increased heart rate) in response to stress, such as fear.

Fine motor skills These use the smaller muscles and depend on muscle coordination, such as drawing, writing and doing up buttons.

Flash cards A card containing a small amount of information, held up for children to see as an aid to learning.

Foetal alcohol sydrome (FASD) This is a group of conditions that can occur in a person whose mother drank alcohol excessively during pregnancy. Problems may include an abnormal appearance, short height, low body weight, small head, poor coordination, low intelligence, behaviour problems, and problems with hearing or seeing.

Foetus The unborn child from the end of the eighth week after conception until birth.

Free-flow play Tina Bruce identifies that free-flow play is when children achieve mastery and competence and can wallow in ideas, experiences, feelings and relationships (Bruce, 1991).

Gastroenteritis Inflammation of the stomach and intestines, often causing sudden and violent upsets diarrhoea, cramps, nausea and vomiting are common symptoms.

Genes The individual instructions that tell our bodies how to develop and function. They govern our physical and medical characteristics, such as hair colour, blood, type and sustainability to disease.

Gluten A mix of proteins found in wheat and other related grains such as rye and barley.

Grapheme A letter or letters that spell a sound in a word.

Gross motor skills These use the large muscles in the body (the arms and legs) and include walking, running and climbing.

Haemoglobin A substance in red blood cells that combines with and carries oxygen around the body, and gives blood its red colour.

Hazard A source of potential harm or damage, or a situation with potential for harm or damage.

Head lice Head lice are tiny grey/brown insects that live on the scalp and neck. Although they may be embarrassing and sometimes itchy and uncomfortable, head lice do not usually cause illness.

Hidden curriculum The information practitioners want children to learn that is not written down. The hidden curriculum is concerned with indirect messages children receive about themselves and others, for example, social and gender roles can be learnt this way. They often reproduce power relations from society.

Holistic Seeing a child as a whole person and how all aspects of development link together.

Holistic approach Adopting an holistic approach means thinking about children and their experiences in an integrated way rather than dividing the focus into different areas. This kind of integrated thinking is effectively developed through undertaking holistic, narrative observations.

Holophrases Using a single word to convey a more complicated meaning.

Homophobia This literally means having a fear of homosexuals, which, of course is nonsense. It is sometimes mistakenly used instead of the correct term which is heterosexism.

Homosexuality Emotional and sexual relationships between members of the same sex.

Hypothalamus This functions to regulate body temperature, certain metabolic processes, and other autonomic activities.

Hypothesis A hypothesis makes a prediction that something will happen and tests it out in a scientific way to see if it is true or not.

Iconic thinking When an image stands for a person, experience or object, perhaps through a photograph.

Immunisation Immunisation protects children (and adults) against harmful infections before they come into contact with them in the community. This is usually done through administering a vaccine.

Immunity A condition of being able to resist a particular infectious disease.

Impetigo A contagious bacterial skin disease which causes pustules that develop yellow crusty sores.

Independent services These are provided independently of the state and do not receive government funding; they include independent schools.

Inhaler (or puffer) is a medical device used for delivering medication into the body via the lungs.

Insecure attachments Children form insecure attachments to carers who are insensitive to or reject their needs, or are unpredictable in the care they offer. These children may either be very clingy or unhealthily independent.

Glossary

Integrated early years provision The bringing together of care, education and family support within a department or setting.

Interactionism Theories that stress both the biological and sociocultural influences on development.

Interactionist model An approach to children's learning where the practitioner sensitively builds on the child's interests and capabilities.

Inter-agency protection plan If a child's health or development has been significantly impaired as a result of physical, emotional or sexual abuse or neglect, an inter-agency protection plan may be drawn up. The plan will identify the steps that the family needs to take to safeguard the child, with the support of Children's Services and other agencies. The child's safety, health, development and well-being will be regularly monitored throughout the plan.

Interpersonal skills These are the skills you use when you interact with other people, including your capacity to listen carefully, to show empathy and understanding, and to communicate effectively.

Intrapersonal skills This is having a good awareness of your own feelings, motivations and the way you affect others.

Involuntary Controlled by the autonomic nervous system, without conscious control.

Irregular language A language such as English, where a letter may have several different sounds ('a' sounds different in apple, want, any) and a sound may be spelled using different letters (i.e. the sound 'k' can be spelled c, k or ck) and where many verbs are irregular.

Jaundice caused by immaturity of the liver function.

Key group The group of children allocated to the same key person.

Key person system A system within a nursery setting in which care of each child is assigned to a particular adult, known as a key person; The role of the key person is to develop a special relationship with the child, in order to help the child feel safe and secure in the nursery. The key person will also liaise closely with each child's parents.

Kinaesthetic sense Sense of movement; how to move your body for standing, sitting, running, crawling, jumping, dancing etc.

Label To attach a descriptive word or phrase to someone to control and identify them with stereotypical behaviour.

Laissez-faire model An approach to children's learning where the practitioner mostly follows the child's lead.

Language A recognised system of gestures, signs and symbols used to communicate.

Lanugo Downy, fine hair on a foetus. Lanugo can appear as early as 15 weeks of gestation, and typically begins to disappear sometime before birth.

Lead professional The lead professional takes the lead to coordinate provision, and acts as a single point of contact for a child and their family when a TAC (Team around the Child) is required.

Limbic cortex A group of interconnected structures deep in the brain that deal with emotions (such as anger, happiness and fear) as well as memories.

Locomotion Movement or the ability to move from one place to another.

Majority world The remaining countries of the world which account for most of the world's population and area.

Malnutrition When a person's diet is lacking the necessary amounts of certain elements which are essential to growth, such as vitamins, salts and proteins.

Maternal serum screening (MSS) A blood test offered to pregnant women if they want to find out if they have a greater risk of having a baby with downs syndrome, neural tube defects (such as spina bifida) or Trisomy 18 (which is a chromosomal abnormality).

Maturation The genetic or biologically determined process of growth that unfolds over a period of time.

Mentalisation –The ability to understand another person's mental state through observing their behaviour; for example, a child saying, 'I think Sophie wants to be my friend; she is trying to hold my hand.'

Metacognition Being aware of your own thinking and being able to analyse this.

Metalinguistics Being aware of the structure of the language you use, such as something rhyming; for example, four-year-olds love to make nonsense words and to play with language rhymes of their own making.

Milia Small whitish-yellow spots which may be present on the face at birth.

Mindsight the ability to understand your own mind and the minds of others.

Minority world Those countries which are sometimes referred to as developed or of the Northern hemisphere.

Mosaic approach A method of gathering information, involving children in using a range of different tools, including observation, photography, drawing, play and story-telling to ensure that children's voices are heard in the organisation of the setting.

Multi-disciplinary approach This is where professionals from different professional specialisations work together or where a topic is looked at from different academic disciplines.

Multifinal Similar or the same early experiences do not necessarily lead to the same outcome.

Multilingual Having the ability to speak a number of languages.

Nativism Theories that stress the biological influences on development.

Naturalistic observation A research method that involves observing subjects in their natural environment.

Nebuliser is a machine that changes liquid medicine into a fine mist. This can then be inhaled through a mask or mouthpiece.

Neonatal Relating to the first few weeks of a baby's life.

Neural tube defects This term includes anencephaly, encephalocoele and spina bifida. These conditions occur if the brain and/or spinal cord, together with its protecting skull and spinal column, fail to develop properly during the first month of embryonic life.

Norm The usual or standard thing.

Nutrients The essential components of food which provide the individual with the necessary requirements for bodily functions.

Nutrition The study of the food process in terms of the way that it is received and utilised by the body to promote healthy growth and development.

Object constancy Shape, size and colour of objects remaining the same

Object permanency The idea that an object still exists even when it cannot be seen.

Object relations A perspective in psychoanalytic theory that emphasises relationships and babies and young children's actual experiences in their relationships and interactions with others, such as feeding, being held and being cleaned up.

OECD countries Organisation for Economic Co-operation and Development, an international economic organisation of 34, mainly European 'developed', countries.

Open body language When your body language is 'open', you are turned towards the other person with your arms in a relaxed open position, showing interest and attentiveness. Your body language is closed when you have your arms and legs crossed, turn away and look away from the other person.

Optimal period A time that might be the best time possible for learning a particular skill

Orthoptist A professional who investigates, diagnoses and treats defects of vision and abnormalities of eye movement.

Parental responsibility The legal conferment of responsibilities for a child on an adult.

Pathogen A microorganism, such as a bacteria or virus, which causes disease. The lay term is 'germ'.

Patois A form of a language that is spoken only in a particular area and that is different from the main form of the same language.

Pedagogy The approach taken to teaching children.

Perceptual skills The ability to take in and use sensory information.

Perineum The skin between the vagina and the rectum.

Glossary

Phoneme The smallest unit of sound in a word such as, c / a / t (three sounds and three letters) or c / a / tch (three sounds and five letters).

Phonics A method of teaching reading by matching sounds with symbols in the alphabet.

Physical play Play that involves movements of all the major muscle groups, e.g., legs. It can range from activities with small intermittent movements, e.g., clapping hands, to large movements involving the whole body, e.g., climbing and running. It tends to be used to describe young children's physical activity.

Physiologist Someone who studies biological activity.

Plaque Plaque is a soft, sticky, and colourless deposit that is continually forming on our teeth and gums. Often undetected, plaque attacks the teeth and gums with the acid it produces from bacteria in your mouth. This acid attack breaks down the tooth's enamel, causing tooth sensitivity and ending with varying degrees of tooth decay.

Plaque Plaque is a soft, sticky, and colourless deposit that is continually forming on our teeth and gums. Often undetected, plaque attacks the teeth and gums with the acid it produces from bacteria in your mouth. This acid attack breaks down the tooth's enamel, causing tooth sensitivity and ending with varying degrees of tooth decay.

Play Play is an integrating mechanism. Play organises a child's thinking, feelings, relationships and physical body, so that everything comes together to support development and learning.

Play therapy A form of counselling that uses play to communicate with and help children, to resolve emotional difficulties and traumatic experiences.

Possetting The regurgitation (or bringing back) of a small amount of milk by babies after they have been fed.

Pre-frontal lobes The part of each hemisphere of the brain located behind the forehead that processes complex cognitive, emotional, and behavioural functions. Limbic system The inner part of the brain which is responsible for emotions and memories.

Pre-intellectual speech The early vocalisations (vocal sounds) babies make to engage with others. Vygotsky called this 'primitive' speech and suggested that it did not involve any intellectual thought.

Prejudice A preconceived opinion that is not based on reason or actual experience.

Pre-linguistic thought Thought can take place without language, but for Vygotsky this was provided by and dependent on the interactions of the carer, whose responses provide the thinking about the experience.

Premature (or preterm) baby A premature baby is one who is born before 37 weeks of gestation.

Prion A protein that can fold in multiple, structurally distinct ways, at least one of which is transmissible to other prion proteins. It is this form of replication that leads to disease that is similar to viral infection.

Private services Profit-making services offered by private providers, including private nurseries and independent preparatory schools. They are inspected to ensure that the health and safety of the children are maintained and the EYFS is being delivered.

Proprioception The ability to recognise and use the physical sensations from the body that give feedback on balance and the position of our limbs.

Psychodynamic Theories in psychology that explain personality in terms of conscious and unconscious processes.

Psychologist Someone who studies mental processes and behaviour.

Psychosocial Psychological development in interaction with the social environment.

Puerperium The period of about six weeks which follows immediately after the birth of a child.

Qualitative Changes in the characteristics of an object. For example, Piaget proposed that a child's thinking in the sensory-motor stage of development was qualitatively different to their way of thinking in the pre-operational stage.

Quantitative Changes in the size or amount of an object.

Racism Prejudice, discrimination, or antagonism directed against someone of a different race based on the belief that one's own race is superior.

Reflex An involuntary action or response, such as a sneeze, blink, or hiccup.

Regress To go back to an earlier point of development.

Regular language A language such as Spanish or Italian, where one letter usually has just one sound and verbs are structured in a regular way.

Representational ability The ability to form mental representations in the mind.

Responsive care Building close relationships with babies and children, being observant of them and meaningfully involved with them. Adults need to demonstrate a sensitive and caring approach through words and facial expressions.

Retinopathy of prematurity An abnormal growth of blood vessels in the retina at the back of a premature baby's eye; when severe it can cause loss of vision.

Reverie The adult can process the baby's communications and hand them back to the baby, either sharing the pleasure in a loving and intimate interaction, or handing back distressing thoughts in a way that the baby can manage.

Reye's syndrome A very rare condition that causes serious liver and brain damage. Many children who develop Reye's syndrome have previously taken the painkiller aspirin to treat their symptoms. It is recommended that no child under 16 years should be given aspirin.

Risk The possibility of suffering harm, loss or danger.

Risk assessment The assessments that must be carried out in order to identify hazards and find out the safest way to carry out certain tasks and procedures.

Routine The usual way in which tasks or activities are arranged.

Rubella Also called German measles or three-day measles, this is a contagious viral infection best known by its distinctive red rash.

Safeguarding In the context of child protection, this refers to aspects of keeping children safe and preventing harm. In an early years setting, this means that staff will need to ensure that children are kept safe and that staff are aware of hazards in the learning environment.

Safeguarding policy A safeguarding policy is a statement that makes it clear to staff, parents and children what the organisation or group thinks about safeguarding, and what it will do to keep children safe.

Scabies Scabies is an itchy rash caused by the human scabies mite. It is spread easily through close physical contact.

Schemas Patterns of linked behaviours, which the child can generalise and use in a whole variety of different situations (Bruce 1997).

Schematic interests Observable patterns of behaviour or themes of thought (see Chapter 7 for more information).

Secure base The feeling of safety and security that close caring adults provide for children through being physically and emotionally available. This allows the child to go off and explore.

Self-regulation In terms of behaviour, self-regulation is the ability to act in your long-term best interest, consistent with your values. Emotionally, self-regulation is the ability to calm yourself down when you are upset and cheer yourself up when you are down.

Semantics The sense and meaning of language.

Sensitive period A time when the mind may be particularly open to certain kinds of learning.

Sensory experiences Experiences that offer a range of sensory information, such as texture, temperature, weight, taste, sound, colour, movement, odours etc.

Sensory function The extent to which an individual correctly senses skin stimulation, sounds, proprioception, taste and smell, and visual images.

Sensory stimuli/input Information such as texture, temperature, weight, taste, sound, colour, movement, odours etc. that are taken in through the ears, nose, mouth, eyes and skin.

Separation anxiety A normal part of development in babies and young children that arises at times when the child perceives itself as separated from the mother/carer and is unable to do anything that will bring them back into proximity.

Seven areas of learning and development The Revised EYFS uses the term 'learning and development' to describe seven areas of learning. They are divided into prime and specific areas. Prime areas are personal, social and emotional development, communication and language, physical development. Specific areas are literacy, mathematics, understanding the world, expressive arts and design.

Sexism Prejudice, stereotyping, or discrimination, typically against women, on the basis of sex.

Signs of illness These can be directly observed, for example, a change in skin colour, a rash or a swelling.

Social competence A child's ability to get along with other people and communicate with other children and with adults.

Social constructivism Regarding children as actively involved in constructing their knowledge, but within a social context.

Social exclusion When individuals or whole communities of people are denied full access to various rights, opportunities and resources that are normally available to members of a society.

Social referencing This is when a baby or young child checks an adult's emotional response before taking action. An example would be a baby who sees something on the grass in a park and looks back at her mother before deciding whether to crawl confidently forward to grab it, or to stay away and watch warily.

Socially constructed A perception of an individual, group, or idea that is shaped through cultural or social practices.

Sociocultural The combination of social and cultural factors that influence personality and behaviour.

Special dietary needs When considering special dietary needs, you will need to think about things like allergies, intolerances, medical conditions, religious requirements, and social and cultural requirements.

Speech Verbal communication; the act of speaking; the articulation of words to express thoughts, feelings or ideas.

Spina bifida This occurs when the spinal canal in the vertebral columns is not closed (although it may be covered with skin). Individuals with spina bifida can have a wide range of physical disabilities. In the more severe forms the spinal cord bulges out of the back, the legs and bladder may be paralysed, and obstruction to the fluid surrounding the brain causes hydrocephalus (which is an abnormal amount of cerebrospinal fluid in the brain, often called 'water on the brain').

Statutory schooling The age at which children are legally required to attend full-time education, unless they have the agreement of the local authority that they will be home-educated.

Statutory service These are provided by the government (or state). The services that are provided are set by laws passed in Parliament.

Stereotype A set idea that people have about what someone or something is like, especially an idea that is wrong. These ideas are usually based on certain characteristics.

Stimulus Something that causes a response.

Symbolic representation When children make something stand for something else.

Symptoms of illness These are experienced by the child, for example, pain or discomfort or generally feeling unwell.

Synthetic phonics A method of teaching reading (in English) which first teaches the letter sounds and then builds up to blending these sounds together to achieve full pronunciation of whole words.

Telegraphic speech Speech in which only the most important words are used.

Theory of mind The ability to understand that you have beliefs, desires and knowledge, and that others have beliefs, desires, intentions and perspectives that are different from your own.

Tracking The smooth movements made by the eyes in following the track of a moving object. These are sometimes called 'smooth pursuit'.

Trades union A trades union is an organisation of workers who join together in order to improve their pay and working conditions.

Transition Times of change; they are part of everyday life and take place from the earliest years. Children make transitions from home to setting, within settings and from early years setting to school.

Transmission model An approach to children's learning where the practitioner defines and leads the learning.

Umbilical cord The cord connecting the foetus to the maternal placenta. It contains blood vessels that carry nutrients to the placenta and remove waste substances from the placenta.

Under-nutrition When people do not get enough to eat.

UNESCO The United Nations Educational, Scientific, and Cultural Organization is an agency of the United Nations that sponsors programmes to promote education, communication and the arts.

UNICEF An organisation concerned with improving the health and nutrition of children and mothers throughout the world, which provides long-term humanitarian aid to children and mothers in developing countries.

Vaccine A substance that stimulates the body's immune system in order to prevent or control a particular infection.

Vegan A vegan is a person who avoids using or consuming animal products. Vegans do not eat dairy products, eggs, or any other products that are of animal origin. They also avoid using fur, leather, wool and cosmetics or chemical products tested on animals.

Vegetarian There are two types of vegetarianism. Both types exclude red meat, poultry and fish: lacto-ovo vegetarians, who eat both dairy products and eggs, and lacto-vegetarians, who eat dairy products but avoid eggs.

Vernix A protective white greasy substance that often covers the skin of the newborn baby.

Viable Able to maintain an independent existence to live after birth.

Voluntary Intentional or controlled by individual will.

Voluntary services These are provided by organisations such as charities. Volunteers and paid staff provide services in the same way as in the statutory sector. Some or all of their funding comes from donations, and some are paid for by the state.

Whistleblowing This means reporting concerns, for example, about abuse or unsafe practices to management and/or other authorities.

Index